KU-788-907

THE
CAMBRIDGE HISTORY OF
ENGLISH LITERATURE

EDITED

BY

SIR A. W. WARD

AND

A. R. WALLER

VOLUME VI

THE DRAMA TO 1642

PART TWO

CAMBRIDGE
AT THE UNIVERSITY PRESS
1950

PUBLISHED BY
THE SYNDICS OF THE CAMBRIDGE UNIVERSITY PRESS

London Office: Bentley House, N.W.1
American Branch: New York

Agents for Canada, India, and Pakistan: Macmillan

First edition	1910
Reprinted	1919
Cheap edition (*text only*)	1932
Reprinted	1934
,,	1949
,,	1950

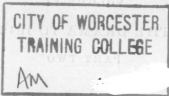

CITY OF WORCESTER
TRAINING COLLEGE

AM

UNIVERSITY COLLEGE WORCESTER LIBRARY

$5-7738

820.9
cAm

P. 820.0

820.9
CAM

Printed in Great Britain at the University Press, Cambridge
(Brooke Crutchley, University Printer)

PREFATORY NOTE

The Cambridge History of English Literature was first published between the years 1907 and 1916. The General Index Volume was issued in 1927.

In the preface to Volume I the general editors explained their intentions. They proposed to give a connected account of the successive movements of English literature, to describe the work of writers both of primary and of secondary importance, and to discuss the interaction between English and foreign literatures. They included certain allied subjects such as oratory, scholarship, journalism and typography, and they did not neglect the literature of America and the British Dominions. The History was to unfold itself, "unfettered by any preconceived notions of artificial eras or controlling dates," and its judgments were not to be regarded as final.

This reprint of the text and general index of the *History* is issued in the hope that its low price may make it easily available to a wider circle of students and other readers who wish to have on their shelves the full story of English literature.

CAMBRIDGE
1932

CONTENTS

Contents

CHAPTER I

BEN JONSON

BEN JONSON the man is better known to us than any of his literary contemporaries. Drummond's record of his conversations has preserved an unkindly but vivid picture of his manners and opinions; and, indeed, his egoism made everything that he wrote partly a portrait of himself. Almost every contemporary reference to him has added something personal and characteristic. We hear of his quarrels, his drinking-bouts, his maladies and his imprisonments, as well as of his learning and his theories of literary art. We know him as the huge galleon of Fuller's account, 'built far higher for learning, solid but slow in his performances,' engaging in those memorable wit combats at the Mermaid tavern with that 'English man-of-war,' Shakespeare, who 'took advantage of all winds by the quickness of his wit and invention'; and, again, as the autocrat of those later lyric feasts of Herrick's reminiscence, where each verse of his 'outdid the meat, outdid the frolic wine.' His humours, his dissipations, his prejudices make distinct and human for us the main interests of his life. Huge of body, bibulous and brawling, he yet loved Latin as heartily as canary, and could write the tenderest epitaph as well as the grossest epigram. Laborious and pertinacious, he rode his hobbies hard, confusing his scholarship with pedantry and his verse with theory; but few have ever served learning and poetry with so whole-hearted a devotion.

Since the days of Fuller, Jonson's personality and work have rarely been discussed or even mentioned without reference to his 'beloved master' Shakespeare. The myth of his devouring jealousy of Shakespeare, supported by Chalmers and Malone, was demolished by Gifford nearly a century ago. But the facts about which the dispute was waged may be again recalled, because of the light that they throw on Jonson's character and friendships. That he criticised Shakespeare is known from the remark to

Drummond that Shakespeare wanted art and from the well known passage in *Discoveries*. It also seems likely, from a reference in *The Returne from Pernassus*[1], that, in the famous 'war of the theatres,' Shakespeare and Jonson were on opposite sides. In addition, there are scattered about the works of Jonson various remarks directed against Shakespeare's plays—especially, the ridicule of chronicle history plays, like *Henry V*, in the prologue to *Every Man in His Humour*, the remark on 'tales, tempests, and such like drolleries' in *Bartholomew Fayre* and the petulant gird at *Pericles* in the *Ode to Himself*. In each of these instances, Jonson is defending one of his own plays and censuring a dramatic fashion contrary to his own practice and hostile, in his opinion, to the best interests of the drama. While it would be absurd to regard Jonson as representative of a dramatic theory and practice at all points opposed to Shakespeare, we shall find his plays representative of carefully considered views which imply a close criticism of much in Shakespeare and the contemporary drama[2]. His criticism of Shakespeare was based on a definite literary creed and methods, and not on jealousy or personal feeling. On the contrary, we have abundant tradition of his close friendship with Shakespeare, and we have the appreciative as well as discriminating passage in *Discoveries*, together with the generous eulogy prefixed to the folio, to testify to Jonson's admiration of his friend's plays, as 'not of an age, but for all time.' No other of Shakespeare's contemporaries has left so splendid and so enthusiastic an eulogy of the master.

Of Sidney, Spenser, Drayton, Beaumont and Donne, Jonson has likewise left us words of sharp censure and of ardent praise. With regard to Beaumont, Donne, Fletcher, Chapman, Bacon and others, as in the case of Shakespeare, he has mingled praise of their work with protestations of personal affection. With Marston, to whom, for a time, he was most bitterly hostile, he came to a full reconciliation. In all his relations with his literary rivals, we see a man, vain, assertive, arrogant, quick to censure, strong in his loves and hates and always ready for a fight, but also one whose quarrels often ended in friendships, and who was loved and admired by the worthiest of his time. His boasting and carping could not conceal his sturdy honesty of intellect and heart, and his generous admiration for high merit in either art or conduct.

[1] Part II, act IV, sc. 3.

[2] Cf. Jusserand, J. J., 'Ben Jonson's Views of Shakespeare's Art,' in *Works of Shakespeare*, 1907, vol. x, pp. 297—321.

The events of his life[1], apart from his writings, can here be traced only in meagre outline. He was born in Westminster in 1572 or 1573, and 'poorly brought-up,' working, probably, at the trade of his step-father, a bricklayer. In spite of poverty, however, he was sent to Westminster school, where Camden, his life-long friend, was master. He did not enter either university[2], although, later, he received honorary degrees from both; and the details of his life for a decade after he left school are unknown. He married, possibly in 1592, a wife 'curst but honest'; had several children, none of whom survived him; enlisted and served a time in Flanders; and, in 1597, is found employed as both actor and playwright by Henslowe. He must have already won considerable reputation as a dramatist, for, in 1598, Meres, in his *Palladis Tamia*, mentions him as one of the six most excellent in tragedy. On 22 September 1598, he killed a fellow actor, Gabriel Spencer, in a duel. His goods were confiscated and he was branded with a T; but he escaped capital punishment by pleading benefit of clergy. While in prison, he became a Roman Catholic; but, twelve years later, he returned to the church of England.

In the same year, 1598, and according to a letter of Sir Toby Matthew to Dudley Carleton, just before the duel with Spencer, Jonson's *Every Man in His Humour* was acted with great success by the Chamberlain's men, Shakespeare's company. The tradition, preserved by Rowe, that the play was accepted through Shakespeare's efforts, may be founded on truth, but, manifestly, is erroneous in particulars. The play marks the beginning of a revolutionary movement in dramatic methods and the institution of a new species, the comedy of 'humours.' It is an important turning point in the course of the Elizabethan drama, and furnishes an announcement of Jonson's programme for the rest of his dramatic career. In the half-dozen years, however, which immediately followed its production, Jonson failed to write any comedy of comparable merit or of equal popular success. He seems to have been a sort of free lance, writing now for one

[1] The chief recent authorities for the life of Jonson are Fleay, F. G., *English Drama*, 1559—1642, 2 vols. 1891; *Ward, A. W.*, vol. II, pp. 298 ff.; Herford, C. H., art. in *Dict. of Nat. Biogr.*; Castelain, M., *Ben Jonson, l'Homme et l'Œuvre*, 1907. See, also, Small, R. A., *The Stage Quarrel between Ben Jonson and the so-called Poetasters*, 1899. A life by Gregory Smith is promised in the English Men of Letters Series.

[2] Certain indications—they cannot be called evidence—in favour of the supposition that Jonson, about 1590, was resident for a short time at St John's college, Cambridge, are discussed by J. Bass Mullinger in *The Eagle*, vol. xxv (1904).

company and now for another[1]; and the carrying out of his programme for reforming the drama was hindered both by the necessity of suiting the immediate stage demand, and by quarrels with his fellow dramatists, Munday, Marston, Dekker and, possibly, Shakespeare. *Every Man out of His Humour*, acted 1599 by the Chamberlain's men, carries on the comedy of humours without dramatic success; *Cynthia's Revels* and *Poetaster*, acted, respectively, in 1600 and 1601 by the children of the chapel, are interesting as satires rather than as dramas. They were concerned with the famous stage quarrel between Jonson and his foes[2]. Probably, there was some personal satire in the earlier of these plays, and its successor attacked Marston and Dekker, calling forth Dekker's rejoinder, *Satiro-mastix*. Jonson seems to have replied to Dekker only in his *Apologetical Dialogue*, withdrawn after it had been once on the stage, and appended to the first edition of *Poetaster*. In this, Jonson refused to carry the quarrel further, and promised to forsake comedy for tragedy. In 1598—9, he was also writing for Henslowe's companies, both in collaboration and alone, on plays not now extant, and, in 1600—1, he prepared for Henslowe additions to *The Spanish Tragedie*, presumably those of the edition of 1602. Two other plays, *The Case is Altered* and *A Tale of a Tub* (in an early form), belong to this period.

In *Sejanus*, acted by Shakespeare's company in 1603, Jonson carried his theories of dramatic art into tragedy. The 'war of the theatres' was now over, and his reconciliations were made with his enemies; furthermore, the accession of James I brought him acceptable employment—for an entertainment at Althorp, and, in collaboration with Dekker, for the royal progress in London. Jonson seems to have been living at this time with lord d'Aubigny and to have won the patronage of several men of prominence; but, apparently, he had made enemies as well as friends at court. In connection with *Sejanus*, he was accused by the earl of Northampton of papacy and treason; and, in connection with *Eastward Hoe*, 1604/5, he was imprisoned with his collaborators, Marston and Chapman. Letters by Jonson and Chapman, recently discovered

---

[1] The attempt to trace him back and forth from one company to another has led Fleay and his followers into many errors.

[2] The most satisfactory account of this conflict is given by Small, R. A., *op. cit.* An interpretation opposed to Small's is held by Fleay, Penniman, J. H., *War of the Theaters*, 1897, and Schelling, F. E. They are in general agreement; especially in giving Jonson's enmity for Daniel a large importance. Penniman and Schelling identify Matthew in *Every Man in His Humour* with Daniel. (See also below as to *Bartholomew Fayre*.)

by Bertram Dobell[1], probably refer to this later imprisonment[2]. Jonson, though fearing the loss of his ears, apparently escaped without punishment.

The year 1605, moreover, marked not only the escape from these difficulties but the beginning of Jonson's happiest days. His *Masque of Blacknesse* was the first of the long series with which he delighted the court of James; and his comedy *Volpone* achieved a triumph both in London theatres and upon its presentation at the two universities. The ensuing decade was Jonson's prime. He produced his four masterly comedies: *Volpone* in 1605 or 1606[3], *The Silent Women (Epicoene)* in 1609, *The Alchemist* in 1610 and *Bartholomew Fayre* in 1614; and his tragedy *Catiline* in 1611; he wrote nearly all the important masques for the court, and won increasing favour with his patrons and the king; and, at the Mermaid tavern, which beheld his wit-combats with Shakespeare and the meetings vividly described by Beaumont, he gained recognition as a leader among London poets and wits. Of his occupations outside literature, we know little, except that he was employed in connection with the discovery of the gunpowder treason, and, in 1613, was tutor to Ralegh's son in France.

In 1616, there appeared a folio edition of his works, carefully edited[4], including his entertainments, masques and plays (except *The Case is Altered*) already produced, with collections of poems entitled *Epigrams* and *The Forest*. This edition set an example for the recognition of the drama as literature. In the same year, his play *The Divell is an Asse* was acted; and, in 1618, he made a pedestrian expedition to Scotland, where he was entertained by the *literati* of Edinburgh, and was a guest of the poet Drummond of Hawthornden, who proved an unadmiring Boswell. On his return, he spent some time at Oxford, where he met with the welcome due to him as a scholar and a poet. In 1616, he had been granted a pension of a hundred marks, and, later, he received the reversion to the mastership of the revels; but he did not live to enjoy the benefits of that lucrative office. This was an era of great prosperity for Jonson. James considered the question of making him a knight; his masques continued to be received with great favour at

---

[1] *The Athenæum*, March-April, 1901; reprinted in F. E. Schelling's ed. *Eastward Hoe.*

[2] For a different opinion and a summary of all the evidence, see Castelain, *Ben Jonson*, appendix C, p. 901.

[3] Fleay and Holt, L. H., Jr., *Mod. Lang. Notes*, 1905, find evidence for dating the play early in 1606, probably in March.

[4] Probably edited by Jonson 1611—12. The later masques are edited less carefully. See Fleay, vol. I, p. 349; Castelain, p. 46.

court; and he was able to withdraw entirely from the public stage. At the Apollo room in the Devil tavern he had established a new court of wits, whither young poets thronged to hail him as oracle. Outside literary circles as within, his friends included the greatest and worthiest of the time—Camden, Selden, Clarendon, Falkland, d'Aubigny, the Pembrokes and the Cecils[1]. Clarendon tells us that 'his conversation was very good and with men of most note.'

The later years of Jonson's life brought many misfortunes. All his books and several manuscripts of unpublished works were burnt in 1623[2], the year in which the Shakespeare folio appeared, introduced by Jonson's fine tribute. Within a few years, he was suffering from paralysis and dropsy, and had become much bed-ridden. After an interval of nine years he now again essayed the public stage; but his comedies, *The Staple of Newes*, acted in 1625, *The New Inne*, in 1629, *The Magnetick Lady*, in 1632, and the revised *Tale of a Tub*, in 1633, were either failures or only partial successes. With the accession of Charles I, Jonson seems, for a time, to have lost favour at court; and, later, a quarrel with the architect Inigo Jones led to loss of employment as a writer of masques. Jonson's appeals to the king, however, brought a gift of one hundred pounds in 1629, and, later, the increase of his pension from a hundred marks to a hundred pounds, together with the grant of an annual butt of canary. He succeeded Middleton in the office of city chronologer in 1628, and, when he was deprived of this because of neglecting his duties, the king obtained his restoration in 1635. In 1631, after an interval of six years, he wrote two court masques; and, in 1633 and 1634, he prepared two entertainments for the king at the earl of Newcastle's. On 6 August 1637, Jonson died. He was buried in Westminster Abbey; the troublesome times that ensued prevented the erection of a monument in his memory; but the inscription of a chance admirer upon his grave has proved unforgettable: 'O rare Ben Jonson!'

Among his unpublished manuscripts were a collection of miscellaneous poems entitled *Underwoods, Timber: or, Discoveries: made upon men and matter*, a translation of *Ars Poetica*, a frag-

---

[1] See lists of persons mentioned in his work, Fleay, *Biog. Chron.* vol. I, pp. 335—340.

[2] See his *Execration upon Vulcan* for a list of lost works: a translation of *Ars Poetica*, with a commentary from Aristotle, an English grammar, a poetical narrative of his journey to Scotland, a poem in three books on the rape of Proserpine, a history of Henry V, philological collections of twenty-four years and 'humbler gleanings in divinity.'

ment of a tragedy *The Fall of Mortimer*[1], the *English Grammar* and an unfinished pastoral *The Sad Shepherd*[2]. These were included in the second folio edition of his works, published in 1640. A collection of memorial verses, edited by Bryan Duppa, bishop of Winchester, appeared in 1637/8, under the title *Jonsonus Virbius*, and contained eulogies from the most famous men of the time.

Even a brief summary of Jonson's life indicates its importance in the history of literature. The forty years of his literary career were marked by varied and influential activity in both prose and verse, in other forms as well as the drama, and as a critic no less than as a creator. Four or five of his plays won immediate recognition as masterpieces of realistic comedy; his tragedies, also, were regarded as models; and his masques were not the least important source of his contemporary reputation. As a scholar, he was highly regarded; as a writer of occasional verse, he was the laureate of James and Charles and the leader of the younger poets of the early seventeenth century; as a critic, seeking the reform of abuses and the definition and maintenance of standards of literary art, he exercised an influence comparable to that of Dryden or Samuel Johnson on later generations. During the major part of his career, he was a sort of literary dictator, encouraging or restraining the literary endeavours of his fellow craftsmen, by means of his conversation as much as of his published writings. Though Jonson was often opposed to prevailing fashions, no other writer so comprehensively represents the course of English literature from the end of the sixteenth century to the outbreak of the civil war.

Of the significance of his criticism, we can now form an idea only through a study of the fragmentary comments in his *Discoveries, Conversations with Drummond*, prologues and prefaces, taken in connection with his actual poetic and dramatic practices. A reconstruction of that criticism, therefore, can be only hypothetical and partial, and must be concerned, mainly, with his own work in the drama. But it should be observed that, in the main, his career was a consistent application of certain fundamental views of literary art. These comprised a high estimation of the dignity and value of literature, a complete acceptance

---

[1] *The Fall of Mortimer* was completed by William Mountfort and published in 1731. Later, in 1763, it was revived, acted and published with a satirical dedication by Wilkes to Bute. Schelling, *Eliz. Drama*, vol. I, p. 306, apparently connects Jonson's fragment with the non-extant play mentioned by Henslowe.

[2] Published as completed by Waldron, F. G., 1783. See Greg's reprint in Bang's *Materialien*, vol. XI, 1905.

of classical authors as the great models and, also, a clear recognition of the high opportunity and great achievement of English
poetry and drama. Further, Jonson believed in a painstaking,
laborious and self-conscious art, dictated, in some measure, by
standards and rules as well as by individual genius or caprice.
He worked with the precepts and definitions of *Poetics* and
Ars Poetica for guides, and he desired judgment and approval
only from those acquainted with these standards. Hence, at times,
he was rigid in adhering to rules, given overmuch to imitation
of the classics and slow to accept modern achievement when it
seemed foreign to ancient law and precedent. He demanded a
workmanship that laboured over details, and he was suspicious of
eccentricity, incongruity, or fantasy, whether in figure and rhythm,
or in structure and treatment. In an age of romanticism, he was,
in some degree, a classicist and a realist—the former, in his reverence for the masterpieces of Greece and Rome, in his view of art as
imitating nature by means of fixed forms and regularised methods
and in his insistence on restraints and proprieties; the latter, in his
fidelity to details, and in his preference, whether in theme or expression, for the actual rather than the splendid, the usual rather
than the adventurous and the general rather than the fantastic.

Jonson's non-dramatic writings include two unfinished works
in prose, both in the nature of compilations. His *English
Grammar*[1] has little interest for anyone today; *Timber, or
Discoveries*, however, contains miscellaneous observations of
striking pith and eloquence and the matter for an essay on style or
literary art. Swinburne, in a successful effort to recall *Discoveries*
to general appreciation, devoted the major part of his *Ben Jonson*
(1889) to praise of this production, declaring, with characteristic
extravagance, that it outweighs in value all the dramatic works,
and is, in comparison with Bacon's *Essays*, superior 'in truth of
insight, in breadth of view, in vigour of reflection and in concision
of eloquence.' When the attention of scholars was directed to the
book, the extent of its indebtedness to Latin writers became
gradually apparent. Jonson's sub-title, 'made upon men and
matter: as they have flow'd out of his daily Readings; or had
their refluxe to his peculiar Notion of the Times,' had always
been accepted as describing a sort of commonplace book, in
which citations from his reading and original observations were
mingled; but investigation has reduced the original element to
a minimum. Schelling was the first to trace a large number

[1] Ed. Waite, Alice W., New York, 1909

of borrowings; Spingarn and others added to the list; which, recently, Maurice Castelain has so extended that it seems to include nearly everything in the book[1]. A few observations on contemporaries remain wholly Jonson's, and the impress of his individuality is apparent even in direct translation. The book also shows the opinions that he selected and shared, and the wide range of his reading, especially in later classical writers, such as Seneca, Pliny and Quintilian, and in renascence scholars, Erasmus, the Scaligers, Lipsius and Heinsius.

In his non-dramatic poetry, Jonson rarely attains high excellence. A large portion belongs to the class headed 'miscellaneous' in collected editions, and is of interest rather for the information which it supplies as to his friends and patrons, and for its satirical pictures of contemporary life, than for any charm of verse. Few of the odes, epistles and epigrams show aught but careful writing, but there are also few that can be praised unreservedly or read with delight. The *Epigrams* (1616) are characteristically coarse; and some of the satirical sort recall the persons of his comedies; as those on alchemists, Lieutenant Shift, Court Worm, Sir Voluptuous Beast, or Lady Would Be. Others are laudatory in praise of Camden, Donne or Sylvester, or the poet's noble patrons, or the king. Perhaps the best of these is that on Lucy countess of Bedford[2]. But the only epigram that has been widely remembered is the beautiful epitaph on the child actor, Salathiel Pavy. The fifteen poems that compose *The Forest*, taken as a whole, are of a higher order than the *Epigrams*; but, except the immortal 'Drink to me only with thine eyes'[3], none, today, has much interest beyond what is historical. In spite of occasional fine lines, their style is fatally marred by that stiffness with which Swinburne justly charges Jonson's verse. *To Penshurst*, written in heroic couplets, is one of the best—sober, dignified, adequate. The lyric note is absolutely wanting in most. A vocabulary that seems purposely prosaic and realistic, an absence of figures, correctness and sanity of expression—these are the qualities of Dryden's verse; but Jonson's has neither Dryden's animation nor his melody.

This description, in general, also applies to *Underwoods*[4], a much larger collection, not published until after Jonson's death.

---

[1] Cf. *ante*, vol. iv, pp. 348—9, and see *ibid.* p. 524, for a list of writings in which the sources of *Discoveries* have been investigated. To these should be added Briggs, W. D., *Mod. Lang. Notes*, Feb. 1908.

[2] Fleay attempts to date the individual epigrams, vol. i, pp. 316—322.

[3] Richard Cumberland, in *The Observer*, No. 74, was the first to point out that this lyric is a free translation from Philostratus.

[4] The famous epitaph on the countess of Pembroke, now usually included in

Two groups begin the collection—the first of devotional pieces, and the second of love poems forming *A Celebration of Charis*. The miscellaneous poems that follow include the charming *A Nymphs Passion*, the graceful *Dreame*, a long series of eulogistic verses— the best and most famous of which is the poem to Shakespeare, a sonnet to lady Mary Wroth and several epistles, of which that entitled *An Epistle to a Friend, to perswade him to the Warres (Master Colby)* (xxxii)[1], in terse, vigorous couplets, may be instanced as representative of Jonson's satirical verse at its best. A series of four elegies (lvii—lx) in regard to a lover's quarrel is quite different from the rest of the poems, and quite in the manner of Donne. The second of these (lviii), indeed, appeared in the 1633 edition of Donne's poems, and, doubtless, should be assigned to him. But if this be given to him, why not the other three[2]? It is true that reminiscences of Donne are found elsewhere in *Underwoods*, and that Jonson may have been writing in direct imitation; but the four poems deal with the same subject and, apparently, express the feelings of the same lover. The remaining poems in *Underwoods* include *An Execration upon Vulcan*, one of the best of the occasional poems; the elaborate and regular Pindaric ode on the death of Sir H. Morison, which contains the beautiful strophe beginning

> It is not growing like a tree
> In bulke, doth make men better bee...

and the curious *Eupheme; or, the faire fame...of...Lady Venetia Digby*, which begins with 'the dedication of her cradle' and rises to its height in 'the picture of the mind':

> Thou entertaining in thy brest
> But such a Mind, mak'st God thy Guest.

The impression made by Jonson's non-dramatic poetry, as a whole, falls far short of that produced by the half-dozen short lyrics which, alone, have survived in men's memories. These have a unique and happy grace, a sure touch of immortality. And the two songs, *To Celia* ('Drink to me only with thine eyes') and 'Goddess excellently bright[3],' have the allurement of Elizabethan

---

Underwoods, was first printed as Jonson's in the edition of Peter Whalley (1756). Weighty, though by no means decisive, evidence that it was written by William Browne is given by Bullen, A. H., in his article on Browne in *Dict. of Nat. Biogr.* (Cf. *ante*, vol. IV, p. 124, where it is assigned to Browne.)

[1] The numbering follows Cunningham's edition.

[2] Castelain, pp. 801—4, would give these to Donne. See, also, Swinburne, p. 106; Fleay, *Biog. Chron.* vol. I, pp. 326, 328; and E. K. Chambers's edition of Donne, vol. I, p. 241 and vol. II, p. 307. Cf., on this subject, *ante*, vol. IV, p. 209.

[3] The refrain of Hesperus's song in *Cynthia's Revels*, act V, sc. 3.

poetry at its best. On the other hand, the great majority of his poems are lacking in melody, charm, or distinction. They are the work of a forerunner of classicism, of one who departs from Spenser, and looks forward to Dryden. The frequent choice of occasional subjects, the restriction to definite forms, the prevalence of satire —all tend toward pseudo-classicism. Moreover, as Schelling has shown, the character of the versification, the use of the rimed couplet, the prosaic vocabulary, the avoidance of *enjambement,* the fixed caesura, point the same way. That Jonson's verse was very influential in advancing the change in poetic taste, can, however, hardly be maintained. Doubtless, his preaching and precepts had something to do with promoting a tendency toward classicism; but the tribe of Ben—Carew, Cartwright, Suckling, Herrick and others —did not profit largely from their master's practice. Herrick, who most imitated him, greatly excelled him; and his general influence was not comparable to Spenser's or to Donne's[1].

His plays fall into well defined classes: masques, comedies and tragedies, with the addition of the unfinished pastoral, *The Sad Shepherd.* As the pastoral and the masque are treated elsewhere in this work[2], Jonson's contributions to these two dramatic types must be very briefly noticed here. *The Sad Shepherd*[3], probably, represents an attempt of his last years to revise and complete for the stage (then addicted to pastorals) a play written, in part, many years before. Whenever his little excursion to Arcadia was first planned, it has since succeeded in carrying many readers thither. It is another of those delightful surprises in Jonson's work, not unlike the *trouvaille* of the 'Queen and huntress' hidden in the impenetrable jungle of *Cynthia's Revels.* Among later comedies, *The Sad Shepherd* is like a breeze in a drowsy lecture-room. Its Arcadia is called Sherwood and is inhabited by Robin Hood and his merry men, but it has visitors from the fantastic Arcadia of the pastorals, and others from fairyland; and it most resembles the rural England of Jonson's observation. The plan of bringing together Robin Goodfellow and Robin Hood, Maudlin the witch of Paplewick and Aeglamour the sad, was ingenious. And Jonson managed to write about little fishes without making

---

[1] More will be said concerning Jonson's lyric verse in the chapter on Caroline lyrics in vol. vii. [2] See *post,* chap. xiii.

[3] Probably it is not identical with the lost *May Lord,* but was written, in part, before Jonson's visit to Drummond. See Fleay, vol. i, pp. 379—381; Greg, *The Sad Shepherd,* in Bang's *Materialien,* 1905, vol. xi, p. xviii; Schelling, *Eliz. Drama,* vol. ii, pp. 166—8. For discussion of the play, see, also, Greg, W. W., *Pastoral Poetry and Pastoral Drama,* 1906.

them talk like whales. He evidently had collected a formidable array of data in regard to fairies, folklore, rustic terms and habits; but, as he wrote, sweet fancy, for once, shared with realism in guiding his pen. No other of his plays can be read from beginning to end with such genuine refreshment.

Less refreshing are the masques[1], with which Jonson delighted both the pleasure-loving court and the pedantic king. The *libretti* of these splendid entertainments are rather flavourless, without the music, dancing and spectacle. To the elaboration of these compositions, however, Jonson devoted his ingenuity and learning, his dramatic and lyrical gifts, in prodigal effort. Moral allegory, classical myth, English folklore, with realistic and satirical pictures of contemporary life, were all summoned to provide novelty, grandeur, or amusement as might be desired. For the masque, as for other forms, Jonson conceived definite rules and restrictions; but he was bound, of course, to respond to the desires of his royal patrons. Remembering the limitations and conditions, we must allow that his work in these masques displays in full all the remarkable talents which he exhibited elsewhere. The anti-masques gave opportunity for comic scenes, in which persons similar to those of his comedies find a place. The spectacular elements called for the play of fantastical invention, such as Jonson denied to his regular dramas. And the songs gave a free chance for lyrical verse. It must be said, however, that neither in dramatic nor lyric effects is there supreme excellence. No lyric in all the forty masques is unforgettable, and few rise above a mediocre level of adequacy. But Jonson virtually invented and perfected the court masque in its Jacobean form. Its history is mainly the record of his contributions.

We turn now to by far the most important division of Jonson's writings, the comedies and tragedies which he wrote for the popular theatres. At the beginning of Jonson's dramatic career, however, we are confronted by a lack of data. What were the plays that, by 1598, had gained him praise as one of the best writers of tragedy? None survives; but there are some hints that his early work did not differentiate itself from that of his fellow dramatists. From 1597 to 1602, he wrote at least one play a year for Henslowe, none of which could have been a comedy of humours. These include an unnamed play of which he made the plot; *Hot Anger Soon Cold*, which he wrote with Porter and Chettle; *Page of Plymouth*, a domestic tragedy on the story of a murder of 1581, in

---

[1] See under Soergel, Brotanek and Evans in the bibliography.

collaboration with Dekker; a tragedy, *Robert II King of Scots*, with Dekker and Chettle; and another tragedy, *Richard Crookback*. At the time when he was writing this last play, he was also engaged on additions to *The Spanish Tragedie*. In spite of definite external evidence, these have sometimes been denied to Jonson because of their theme and style[1]. The style is not, indeed, like that of his later plays; but we may fairly assume that it is not unlike that which he was employing on domestic and historical tragedies[2]. Splendidly imaginative in phrasing and conception, rehabilitating the old Hieronimo, giving his madness and irony new truth and new impressiveness, the 'additions' far surpass in imaginative power most of the contemporary attempts at tragedy which they rivalled. But they imply an unhesitating acceptance of the whole scheme of the old revenge play at which Jonson was wont to scoff. Further evidence that his early work was romantic rather than realistic may be found in the romantic elements of *The Case is Altered*, and in the Italian scene and names with which *Every Man in His Humour* was first decked. Of plays still earlier than those named, we may surmise that, whether realistic or romantic, tragic or comic, they conformed to the fashions of the time. Jonson was serving his dramatic apprenticeship and writing the kind of plays demanded; but he early showed that imaginative power which gave him high rank among his fellows, at least in tragedy.

The presentation of *Every Man in His Humour* apparently marked a change of plan on his part and his devotion to a new propaganda. By 1598, the drama was long out of its swaddling clothes. Since the union of poetry and the theatre on the advent of Marlowe, ten years earlier, the importance of theatres in the life of London had been rapidly increasing, and the drama had been gaining recognition as a form of literature. Marlowe, Kyd, Peele, Greene, Lyly and others, as well as Shakespeare, had played important parts in creating a drama at once national, popular and poetical. On the whole, this dramatic development, while breaking away from classical models and rules, had established no theory or criticism of its own. It had resulted from the individual innovations of poets and playwrights, who strove to meet the demand of the popular stage through the dramatisation of story. The main divisions of tragedy and comedy were recognised,

---

[1] Castelain, Appendix B, pp. 886—901. Cf., as to these additions, *ante*, vol. v, chap. VII *ad fin*.

[2] See Symonds, J. A., *Ben Jonson*, English Worthies Series, and *Shakespeare's Predecessors*, on the 'romantic tone' in Jonson's early work.

and a third, the chronicle history, created; and there were various species corresponding to the initiative of individuals, as a Marlowe type of tragedy or a Lyly type of comedy; but there were no accepted laws for any species, and hardly any restrictions or principles guiding the presentation of narratives on the stage.

To those acquainted with classical drama, these tragedies, comedies and histories offered much that was absurd and lawless. Frequent change of place, long duration of time represented, absence of a unified plan or coherent structure, mingling of farce and tragedy, of clowns and kings, lack of definite aesthetic or ethical aims, seemed errors that could find little palliation. The matter was as objectionable as the form, for it was similarly unrestricted. As Sidney asserted, dramatists did not always distinguish a dramatic fable from a narrative, and they brought any matter whatsoever into their plays. They did not mirror nature or imitate life, they merely told impossible stories. The impulses that had found freest expression in the popular drama were, indeed, romantic. Marlowe, Greene, Shakespeare and the rest had been inspired to give the thrills and glory, the wonder and sentiment of life. They had dealt with remote places, idealised persons, marvellous adventures, conquests and vicissitudes; they had not attempted an orderly analysis of history or a rationalised imitation of the life of their own day. The drama was romantic, in the sense that it ran counter to the theory and practice of the Greeks and Latins, and, also, in the sense that it departed from a veracious representation of actuality. Inevitably, criticism cried for classical form and a realistic presentation of life.

While the main tendency was toward romanticism, neither classicism nor realism had, by any means, been lacking in the earlier drama, particularly in comedy. In tragedy, classicism had been driven from the stage to the closet; but, in comedy, Plautus and Terence were still largely followed as models. The Plautian model, early anglicised in *Ralph Roister Doister*, had notable copies in Lyly's *Mother Bombie* and Shakespeare's *Comedy of Errors*. Moreover, not only its stock characters, its clever servants, parasites, misers, braggart soldiers and so on, but, also, its general scheme of a series of tricks brought about through disguises, had come to be widely adopted in the English drama. This scheme lent itself readily to realism and formed the basis for most comedies of intrigue or manners, and of some romantic plays. Another species of comedy, the satirical, may be traced back to moralities, and found an important early representative in the plays of Wilson[1]. Again, sheer farce, often Plautian in scheme, naturally took realistic themes, and plays of English domestic manners were not uncommon. In addition to these incompletely defined species, there was a good deal of realistic comedy mingled with the various types of romantic drama. Tragedy, however gruesome, usually admitted some realistic farce; romantic comedy had its servants, drunkards, constables and clowns; and chronicle history delighted in the elbowing of its monarchs by humorous persons from low life. Falstaff and his crew were already on the stage, and they certainly betokened the keenest scrutiny of London manners. In fact, the Elizabethan drama had always devoted itself to the representation of contemporary manners as well as to romantic story. It had delighted not only in the heroisms, villainies and aspirations of romantic vision, but, also, in the absurdity, frivolity and grossness of daily actuality.

What Jonson intended was to recall comedy from its romantic entanglements and to restore it to its ancient province. In 1598, he was a playwright seeking success on the public stage, and trained in its conventions and practices. Neither at that time nor at any other did he plan plays that should break from the popular theatres and become academic or closet affairs. His purpose was to alter his own practices, and to reform the stage; and he represented the critical tendencies already existing: first, a reaction from the absurdities of current forms; secondly, a recourse to classical standards as a cure for lawlessness; and, lastly, the establishment of a realistic and satirical comedy on a rational plan. The first two positions were those of Sidney's *Apologie*, which must have potently influenced Jonson; the third was being promoted by contemporary dramatists, especially by the comedies of his friend Chapman. Chapman's earliest romantic comedy, *The Blinde begger of Alexandria*, 1598, acted about 1596, was immediately followed by *An Humerous dayes Myrth*, realistic in matter and, apparently, preceding *Every Man in His Humour*, and then by his *Al Fooles* (acted about 1599), a play both Terentian and Jonsonian. Similarly, Middleton's early romantic comedies, *The Old Law* and *Blurt Master-Constable*, were soon followed by a series of realistic comedies of manners; and the romance of Marston's *Antonio and Mellida* (acted 1598 or 1599) was followed by the satire of his *Malcontent* (acted 1601). Moreover, a series of formal satires by Marston, Donne and Hall had vogue in the years 1597—9. But, to whatever extent Jonson was

---

[1] As to Robert Wilson, see vol. v, chap. XIII.

anticipated by Chapman, and to whatever extent his attitude was due to the same immediate influences that acted on his fellows, there is no doubt that he was leader in a movement which gave to realistic and satirical comedy a new importance, or that, of the early representative plays of this class, *Every Man in His Humour* was the masterpiece. Its famous prologue[1] sets forth a definite programme. It protests especially against chronicle history plays, discards tragedy and romance, implies an observance of the proprieties and promises

> deeds, and language, such as men do use:
> And persons, such as comedy would choose,
> When she would show an image of the times,
> And sport with human follies, not with crimes.

The play, happily, is free from the laboriousness that often results from devotion to a theory. The plot, of Jonson's own invention, deals with tricks played upon the elder Knowell and the jealous Kitely, involving the exposure of various humours and ending happily with the marriage of young Knowell and Kitely's sister. The term 'humour,' then applied to any oddity of manner, is used to designate the prevailing traits of a number of distinctly defined characters, illustrative of London manners[2]. The braggart soldier, the clever servant, the avaricious and jealous husband, the gay young men and even the gulls, are all, obviously, suggested by the common types in Plautus; to whom, also, are due the plot of tricks and the device of disguises. Nevertheless, both plot and persons are developed with abundant originality and represent Jonson at his best. Bobadill, indeed, is almost the very greatest of Jonson's creations, and is distinct from the other representatives of *miles gloriosus* which preceded and followed him in the Elizabethan drama. Whenever he appears, there is more than mere satire or farce—an amazing and sustained *vis comica* that reaches its culmination in the great scene[3] in which he meets with discomfiture. The play is written mainly in terse and pointed prose, only the two old men and the ladies using blank verse. One superb purple patch, the defence of poetry, Jonson ruthlessly cut out in the revised edition.

In comparison with *Every Man in His Humour*, Jonson's comedies for the next few years do not exhibit any advance. A

---

[1] Not printed until the folio of 1616, but probably connected with an early presentation of the play. At all events, it represents opinions similar to those set forth in *Every Man out of His Humour*.

[2] Cf., as to the origin and application of the term, *ante*, vol. IV, chap. XVI.

[3] Act IV, sc. 5.

large portion of his work, including the additions to *The Spanish Tragedie* and other plays for Henslowe, shows a return to old ways. The comedy entitled *The Case is Altered* hardly belongs to the class of humoristic comedies. Never admitted by Jonson among his collected works, it may be a revision of an earlier play; at least, it was not approved by his later standards. Though Plautian in plot and introducing personal satire on Munday, it is romantic in tone, with its scene in Milan and its element of averted tragedy.

The comedy of humours was carried on in *Every Man out of His Humour*. A vainglorious knight, a public jester[1], an affected courtier, a doting husband and others exhibit their humours and are finally forced out of their affectations through the agency of Macilente, who, also, is cured of his besetting envy. In the induction, Asper, representing Jonson himself, presents the play in a long conversation with two friends, who remain on the stage to serve as an expository chorus. Jonson announces a highly satirical and moral purpose, akin to that of *Vetus Comoedia*:

> I will scourge those apes
> And to these courteous eyes oppose a mirror,
> As large as is the stage whereon we act;
> Where they shall see the time's deformity
> Anatomised in every nerve and sinew,
> With constant courage, and contempt of fear.

Jonson's induction and comments show how conscious was his art, and how carefully considered his aims. He exhibits his knowledge of the history and rules of classical comedy; but, at the same time, he declares,

> I see not then but we should enjoy the same license, or free power to illustrate and heighten our invention, as they did; and not be tied to those strict and regular forms which the niceness of a few, who are nothing but form, would thrust upon us.

To this extent, he declares for the national tradition; but he rejects the conventions of romantic comedy,

> of a duke to be in love with a countess, and that countess to be in love with the duke's son, and the son to love the lady's waiting maid; some such cross-wooing with a clown to their servingman.

He succeeds in removing all elements of romance from his plot; but what remains, while 'familiarly allied to the time,' has little dramatic merit. The comedy is long-winded, and didactic, rarely

---

[1] Fleay (*Chronicle History*, vol. I, p. 97), Herford, Penniman and Schelling identify Carlo Buffone with Marston; but see Small's discussion, *op. cit.*

either rapid or amusing. The faults that beset all Jonson's subsequent comedies, even the best, are manifest: an over-elaboration of uninteresting characters, and a too detailed exposure of folly.

Cynthia's Revels resembles *Every Man out of His Humour* in its general plan of a group of would-be gallants and ladies whose follies are exposed to ridicule and shame through the efforts of a censor representing the author's attitude. The devices of gods, a masque, an echo dialogue, the fountain of self-love and—to some extent—the gallants and pages, remind one of the plays of Lyly, which had recently been revived. Apparently, it was with these suggestions from Lyly and his Aristophanic scheme that Jonson set at work on his court entertainment. He also introduced personal satire (perhaps already used in *Every Man out of His Humour*), though the only part that can with much confidence be identified is that of Anaides, which Dekker promptly took to himself. In spite of the evident care taken in construction and phrasing, the play is inordinately tedious, with the exception of the lively induction. All the persons bathe in the fountain of self-love, but, in the end, find restoration in the well of knowledge. In the epilogue, Jonson forestalls the obvious taunt that he has mistaken the fountain, and proclaims of the play:

> By God 'tis good, and if you like 't, you may.

Jonson's arrogance had occasioned enmities with his fellow dramatists. In *Poetaster*[1], he undertook their castigation. The scene is placed in Rome; the story of Ovid's love for Julia is introduced; and the satirical scheme is not unlike that in the preceding comedies—a voluble captain, an actor, a beggar poet and an affected gallant come in for exposure, and Vergil and Horace (Jonson) are the censors. In the end, Demetrius (Dekker) and Crispinus (Marston) are tried for calumniating Horace, and to Crispinus is administered a purge which causes him to vomit up a prodigious vocabulary. Probably, other personal references were intended in addition to those indicated, but they are not discernible now. Jonson seems to have been attempting a further extension of comedy on Aristophanic lines, satirical allegory, praise of himself and direct personal satire.

Jonson now deserted comedy for a time. His additions to *The Spanish Tragedie* and the non-extant *Richard Crookback* were

---

[1] Act III, sc. 1 is based on Horace's ninth satire of book I; and there are other imitations of Horace, Lucian and Homer. See Koeppel, E., *Quellenstudien*, 1895; Small, *The Stage Quarrel*, pp. 25—27, and Mallory's ed. of the play, Yale Studies, 1905.

acted within the next two years. In connection with *Sejanus* (acted 1603)[1], we may consider *Catiline* (acted 1611) as representing Jonson's contribution to tragedy ; *The Fall of Mortimer* is only a fragment, and, apparently, was intended to be even more classical than *Catiline*.

In these two plays, Jonson attempted in tragedy a reform similar to that which he had striven for in comedy. He sought to treat Roman history with scholarly accuracy and to exemplify upon the public stage what he regarded as the essential rules of tragic art. Such representations of Roman history as Lodge's *The Wounds of Civill War*, or the still more incongruous medley of Heywood's *Lucrece*, must have excited in him even greater condemnation than did the English chronicle plays. We know that Shakespeare's *Julius Caesar* provoked a sneer or two from Jonson[2], though its dramatisation of Plutarch's portraits apparently excited his emulation and suggested much in his treatment of Sejanus and Catiline. Mere spectacle and farce disappear, and events are treated in accord with a well thought-out theory of historical tragedy. But Jonson's theory proved hampering; while his effort to secure fidelity to the historical authorities led him to encumber *Sejanus* with an absurd paraphernalia of notes, and to transcribe large portions of Cicero's orations into *Catiline*. And, as he was forced to confess, the historical material and the style of action demanded by the audiences of the day did not readily lend themselves to the restrictions of classical rules.

His plays, it must be remembered, were intended for the public stage, and are not to be classed with closet dramas like those of Fulke Greville and William Alexander. Jonson had already contributed to current popular forms of tragedy, and he started with these as a basis, attempting to rebuild them into something more like classical models. His cardinal error was his acceptance of the belief of the classicists that the essential difference between epic and dramatic fable lay in the observance of the three unities and similar proprieties. In *Sejanus*, he gave up unity of time, but kept that of place ; he retained the comic scenes of the courtesan, but avoided any grotesque mixture of the comic and the tragic. He omitted battles, jigs and

---

[1] In the address prefixed to the 1605 quarto of *Sejanus*, Jonson acknowledges the share of 'a second pen' in the play as first written and acted, for which he had substituted his own work in the published play. This 'so happy a genius' has been identified as Chapman among other dramatists; but there is no evidence to support these conjectures.

[2] *Bartholomew Fayre*, act II, sc. 1.

spectacles, and secured a coherent and carefully integrated development of the main action. In *Catiline*, which he boldly proclaimed a 'dramatic poem,' he adopted the Senecan technique of an introductory ghost and a segregated chorus. In both plays, he was following both humanistic and popular practice in choosing for his themes the evil effects of ambition resulting in conspiracy and civil war.

When we consider the self-imposed restrictions by which he was bound, his achievement must seem remarkable. His interest lay largely in characterisation, and in this resides the chief merit of the plays. Jonson, to be sure, never learned Shakespeare's art of transforming incidents and events into terms of a spiritual conflict. His method is rather that of exposition, each scene illustrating and emphasising some trait without securing much illusion of life. Yet the chief persons, Sejanus and Tiberius, Catiline and Cicero, are thoughtfully conceived and faithfully represented. Moreover, the minor characters are depicted with care and even with vivacity, so that the picture of Roman life carries a strong impression of truthfulness, due to the whole-hearted concentration of Jonson's imagination upon his task as well as to his painstaking study of authorities. In their interpretation of historical characters, his tragedies resemble those of his friend Chapman; but he lacks Chapman's extraordinary eloquence. Jonson's style, especially in long speeches, is too often rhetorical, and rarely displays great beauty or dramatic power. Yet it is masterly in its way, competent to its purposes and free from obscurity or over-ornamentation. The two tragedies, however, in spite of their excellences, must be regarded as representing another failure to turn popular English tragedy back into the classical mould.

Jonson's return to comedy after *Sejanus* was made in 1604/5, in collaboration with Chapman and Marston, in *Eastward Hoe*. No success has attended any endeavour to disentangle the contributions of the three authors, and their cooperation was probably very intimate[1]. It seems likely that Jonson aided largely in plan and suggestion, and that comparatively little of the prose text was by him.

The four comedies which followed rank with *Every Man in His Humour* as his masterpieces. They are all comedies of humours; but each is a peculiar development of the type. In

---

[1] Cf. *post*, chap. II, and see the edition of this play by Schelling, F. E. (Belles Lettres Series), 1903.

Volpone, the Plautian model appears only in the use of the clever servant as the mainspring of the action, and of entanglements based on the trickster-tricked type of plot. The subject and persons, however, are different from those usual in either Latin or English comedy[1]. Volpone, a miser and sensualist, works on the greed of his acquaintances, and, by false reports of his sickness and death, excites their hopes of inheriting his fortune, and lures them into all kinds of abominable knavery. A shameless lawyer, a father who disinherits his son in order to satisfy his own greed and a wittol who offers his wife in return for an inheritance, are the chief dupes; while Sir Politick Would Be, a foolish English traveller, and his affected wife, who quotes Plato and knows of *Pastor Fido* and 'Montaignié,' play lesser parts. The play has little mirth; but it is a vigorous exposure of greed and iniquity. Its purpose is not amusement but satire, its subject not folly but vice, its protagonist not the managing servant but his master, a monster of villainy. Utterly bad men are common in Elizabethan tragedy, and are found, occasionally, in comedy. But nowhere else, unless in Iago, has vice been drawn with such fulness of detail and yet with such consistency as in Volpone. No tragic elevation lends majesty to the theme. The play depicts human meanness, unrelieved by any greatness of purpose or unselfishness of passion. It presents men as beasts, with the greed of swine, the craft of foxes and the rapacity of wolves.

Plot, characters and blank verse, unusually vigorous and flowing, all show Jonson at his best; and he was justly proud, as he boasted in the prologue, of having written in five weeks a comedy that observed the laws of time, place and persons, and swerved from no needful rule. In the dedication to both universities, he excuses the punishment of the vicious in comedy, defending himself by the example of the ancients, and still more because 'it is the office of a comic poet to imitate justice, and instruct to life.' This is interesting as an adumbration of Rymer's 'poetic justice,' and as an expression of the purpose of Jonson's satiric comedy. Other passages in this same dedication give noble expression to the aims at which his art had now arrived,

to reduce not only the ancient forms, but manners of the scene, the easiness, the propriety, the innocence, and last, the doctrine, which is the principal end of poesie, to inform men in the best reason of living.

[1] As to the actual source, Lucian's *Dialogues of the Dead,* v—ix, see Adams, J. Q., *Modern Philology,* vol. ii, p. 289 (1905), and Browne, W. H., *Modern Language Notes,* vol. xxi, p. 113 (1906).

It must be confessed, however, that Jonson's vainglorious proclamation of reform exhibits an insolent disregard of his great
predecessors and contemporaries. He promises

the maturing of some worthier fruits; wherein, if my muses be true to me,
I shall raise the despised head of poetry again, and stripping her out of
those rotten and base rags wherewith the times have adulterated her form,
restore her to her primitive habit, feature, and majesty, and render her
worthy to be embraced and kist of all the great and master-spirits of our
world.

The Silent Woman[1] is much less intent on moral castigation
than is *Volpone*, and, also, much merrier. Its plot is farcical,
dealing with the entrapping of Morose, who hates noise, into
marriage with Epicoene, who turns out to be a noisy tartar,
and, after Morose has forgiven his nephew, proves to be a boy.
Sir Dauphine, the nephew, and his friends, are the wits; Daw,
La Foole and the Ladies Collegiates, the butts of their jests.
There is abundant satire of the manners and affectations of the
day; but the skilfully complicated action depends on numerous
disguises, and does not rise above the level of admirable farce.
In *The Alchemist*[2], Jonson essays another large canvas of
tricksters and gulls. Subtle, the alchemist, Dol Common and Face,
a housekeeper, have set up their snares in the house of Face's
master. Hither come an extraordinary procession of gulls, whose
very names are enough to recall the lifelike characters—Dapper, a
lawyer's clerk; Abel Drugger, a credulous tobacco man; Sir Epicure
Mammon, a voluptuary with a Micawber-like gift of eloquent
anticipation; Pertinax Surly, a doubting Thomas; Tribulation
Wholesome and Ananias, two brethren of Amsterdam, who make
an effort to serve both God and Mammon, without forgetting the
weaker brethren; Kastrill, a foolish heir and Dame Pliant, his sister,
a widow. One after another, they expose their folly and greed, and
add to the fun and entanglement, until the master of the house
returns and joins with Face to keep the spoils, including the
widow, and to lock the doors on dupers and duped. Perhaps
in no other play has Jonson so completely succeeded in accomplishing what he intended as he has in this. There are no tiresome
excursuses, as in *Volpone* and *Bartholomew Fayre*; in everything,
he uses 'election and a mean.' The entire play is in blank verse,

[1] The edition of the play by Aurelia Henry, Yale Studies, 1906, discusses
suggestions for this play in Libanius and Plautus.

[2] On the relation of *The Alchemist* to *Il Candelaio* of Giordano Bruno, see a note by
Child, C. G., in *The Nation*, 28 July 1904. See, also, Schelling, *Eliz. Drama*,
vol. I, pp. 540, 541.

which is most skilfully adapted to the rapid dialogue or to the orations of Tribulation and Sir Epicure. The language is varied, idiomatic and precise ; the style, finished and animated. The ingenuity of the plot, which Coleridge ranked among the three most perfect in literature, the liveliness of the action and the delineation of manners, harmonise in a work which, of its kind, could hardly be bettered. The satire on alchemy, which was not without daring in the days of Simon Forman, flavours the fun without destroying it ; and the picture of Elizabethan London is without an equal, unless it be in *Bartholomew Fayre.*

In the presentation of manners and character, *Bartholomew Fayre* may, indeed, be held to outrank even *The Alchemist.* In many respects, however, its inferiority is palpable. It is unwieldy in structure ; its fun is often gross and farcical ; and it is over-crowded with persons and incidents. There are thirty speaking parts and many supernumeraries. Nowhere else, perhaps, in literature, have so many people been so vividly presented in a three hour entertainment as here. The usual pair of witty friends, a pompous judge bent on reform, a proctor who has written a puppet show[1], a foolish widow, a puritan zealot, Cokes, a booby, and his man Waspe, mingle in the fair with a cutpurse, a ballad singer, a tapster, a bawd, a bully and that Falstaffia of the stews, Ursula the pig woman. The trouble here, as in other plays by Jonson, is that every character is worked out with elaborate detail. If some of the subordinate parts were removed, and others reduced in proportion, the play, doubtless, would be improved. Certainly, much of Littlewit's puppet play could be spared. But all the personages mentioned, and as many more, are drawn not only with painstaking exactness, but, also, with unflagging animation. A play which unites such masterpieces of comic characterisation as justice Overdo, Cokes and Zeal-of-the-land Busy, together with much uproarious fun, must, surely, be accounted an amazing achievement of comic invention.

In the amusing induction, Jonson protests against the attribution of personal satire to the play, and against the tendency of the public to judge everything by their old favourites, such as *Jeronimo* and *Andronicus.* His protests, in fact, are directed at the whole field of romantic drama, and include scoffs at *The Winter's Tale* and *The Tempest.*

If there be never a servant-monster in the fair, who can help it, he [the author of *Bartholomew Fayre*] says, nor a nest of antiques? he is loth

---

[1] Littlewit is identified by Fleay, Penniman and Schelling with the poet Daniel.

to make nature afraid in his plays, like those that beget tales, tempests, and such like drolleries, to mix his head with other men's heels; let the concupiscence of jigs and dances reign as strong as it will amongst you; yet if the puppets please any body, they shall be intreated to come in.

'The concupiscence of jigs and dances,' to which he also alludes in the address 'To the Reader' prefixed to *The Alchemist,* seems to refer to the introduction of dances and other elements from court masques into comedy, as in *The Winter's Tale, The Tempest* and other contemporary plays. Jonson, always a precisian, preferred to keep his masques and comedies separate. It seems clear that he intended to make *Bartholomew Fayre* an example of pure realism. Perhaps for this reason he wrote it, like *Epicoene,* wholly in prose, remarkable for its clearness and flexibility, admirably suited to the different speakers and imitative of the manners of the time. Characters and incidents, also, are freer from imitation of Plautus or Aristophanes than are those of any other of his comedies, though the usual scheme of gulls and knaves is preserved and amplified. Further removed from classical models than his other comedies, nevertheless, it is Aristophanic in the breadth and liveliness of its mirth and in its unhesitating realism. Original in its scheme and subject, daring in its invention, it marks the highest development of the comedy of humours as a national type. The kind of comedy which it presents has continued in prose fiction, in Fielding, Smollett and Dickens ; but, since the Elizabethan period, our theatre has never permitted such robust fun and so unvarnished a presentation of the absurdities of human nature.

The Divell is an Asse betrays a flagging invention, as was to be expected after the prodigal expenditure of the four preceding comedies. The machinery of the devils is not very happy. Pug, a lesser devil, is despatched by Satan to do some mischief; but his stupidity renders his expedition unsuccessful, and, indeed, leaves it without effect on the action of the play. Jonson, apparently, planned to enlarge his collection of gulls by proving the devil one ; but the result of this humorous conception is merely to add another stupid and uninteresting person to the *dramatis personae.* The other characters are more or less repetitions of those in earlier plays, though the chief gull, Fitzdottrel, who aims to become 'Duke of Brownlands' through taking part in a project for draining the waste lands of the kingdom, gives rise to plenty of humour. The satire is lively, especially that on the exorcism of supposed evil spirits, and that on projectors and projects—among which is one for 'serving the whole state with toothpicks.' Mrs Fitzdottrel is drawn with more sympathy than is common in the case of Jonson's female characters, and all the characters are, as usual, carefully differentiated. But the comic entanglements are cumbersome, and the play moves heavily.

Nine years intervened before the appearance of Jonson's next comedy, *The Staple of Newes.* Though his prologue is as boastful as ever, yet, in the induction and the intercalary scenes, there are indications that he felt the uncertainty of his powers and was driven back to the stage by want. He went to Aristophanes for a model, composing an allegorical satire based on *Plutus*, from which and from *The Wasps* he borrowed certain passages. The main allegory of Pecunia, Pennyboy, Mortgage and the rest, is tiresome; but the secondary plot, dealing with the Staple-of-News office, has excellent satire and fun. So, too, has the scheme of the Canters' college. But the details of the plan are not fused into a dramatic whole. More than any play since *Cynthia's Revels*, this production lacks the movement and verisimilitude indispensable in comedy.

The remaining comedies come near to deserving Dryden's harsh criticism: 'mere dotages.' *The New Inne* was incontinently damned at its first representation, and published two years later (1631) by Jonson with an angry address to the reader. The improbable plot, dependent on the disguises of Lord Frampul as an inn-keeper, his wife as a vulgar Irish beggar and their second daughter as a boy, deals, mainly, with the winning of the elder daughter by Lord Lovel, thanks to two elaborate orations on love and valour before a mock court of love. The play aims at taking advantage of the current interest in 'platonism' fostered at court by the queen[1]; and both the platonic Lady Frampul and her suitor are treated sympathetically. But the platonic addresses are dull ; and so, indeed, is the low comedy supplied by Fly, Bat Burst, Sir Glorious Tipto and others. The failure of the play called forth Jonson's ode 'Come, leave the loathèd stage'; but one's sympathies incline to remain with the audience. Four years later, *The Magnetick Lady: Or Humors Reconcil'd* attempted a continuation and conclusion of the series of comedies of humours begun thirty-five years before. A marriageable young niece of the magnetic lady is constituted the 'centre attractive, to draw thither a diversity of guests, all persons of different humours, to make up his (the author's) perimeter.' This plan is carried out in a half-hearted way, though with the usual elaborate attention to details,

---

[1] On this topic, see Fletcher, J. B., 'Précieuses at the Court of Charles I,' in *The Journal of Comparative Literature*, vol. I, p. 125.

and explanatory intermezzos. But, while the acts conform to the laws of *protasis, epitasis* and *catastasis*[1], there is no life or wit. *A Tale of a Tub* was acted in the same year. Various references to the queen make it likely that the play was first written about 1597; but the satire on Inigo Jones as In and In Medley must have been incorporated in the 1633 revision. The separation of the early crudities and the later dotages is now impossible. The action, of the trickster-tricked variety, deals entirely with rustics, and presents considerable ingenuity and possibility of fun. The characters, however, are all beneath interest, and the whole treatment reveals neither fresh nor worthy impulse.

Two additional plays, which, on some seventeenth century authority, have been ascribed in part to Jonson, probably owe little or nothing to his pen. *The Widdow*, published (1652) as by Jonson, Fletcher and Middleton, was, probably, wholly by Middleton[2]. *The Bloody Brother* (entered in the Stationers' register, 1639, as by 'B. J.', and printed in 1640 as by 'B. J. F.') is, undoubtedly, in part by Fletcher[3]. Jonson's share can hardly have extended beyond the second scene of act IV.

Jonson's qualities as a dramatist, with regard to which there is general critical agreement, have, perhaps, been sufficiently indicated. His wide and penetrating observation of manners, whether of city or of court, and his ingenious and systematic construction of plots, are obvious merits. But the great excellence of both his tragedies and his comedies is their delineation of character. This is conditioned less than in other Elizabethan dramatists by the story, but more by classical models and rules, as in his observance of the unities, or his fidelity to historical authorities, or his copying of the Plautian plan and types. It is also conditioned by his method of making each person the illustration of one trait or humour, and by his disposition to substitute description for drama, and satire for fact, and to exaggerate his satire into farce. Thus, in *Every Man in His Humour*, only Bobadill represents the complete transformation of a type into an individual; and, in *Bartholomew Fayre*, the individualisation follows the broad lines of caricature. Again, each person is set forth with such distinctness of detail that, while it aids visualisation, it often distracts from the interest of situation. Only in *The Alchemist* is there an entire absence of this impeding

---

[1] Cf. act I, *ad fin.*   [2] See *post*, chap. III.

[3] See chap. v, and cf. Fleay, F. G., *The English Drama*, vol. I, pp. 203—5, and Oliphant, E. F., *Eng. Studien*, vol. xv, pp. 353—5. Concerning the anonymous Latin comedy *Querolus* as the source of the scene (IV, 2) attributed to Jonson, see Garnett, R., *Mod. Phil.* vol. II, p. 491.

garrulity. Akin to this defect are Jonson's over-use of the long
monologue after the fashion of classical models, the heaviness and
coarseness which his realism often gives to his vocabulary and his
thoroughness, which refuses to let go person, speech, or situation
until it is absolutely exhausted. Yet, in spite of all these limitations, Jonson's comic characterisation remains among the greatest
achievements of the English drama, because of its clearness and
certainty, its richness of humour and its dramatic veracity. A. W.
Ward is justified in giving him pre-eminence in the highest species
of comedy, that 'in which everything else is subordinated to the
dramatic unfolding of character.'

What most discourages the reader of Jonson is the absence
of charm. Jonson was certainly not incapable of depicting noble
passions or of writing winsome verse; but in his plays he resolutely
refused to attempt either. This refusal, in marked contrast with
the practice of his fellow Elizabethans, is precisely the negative
side of his most positive characteristics. He did not write of
passions, but of follies—not of fairyland, but of London ; he often
deliberately preferred prose to poetry, and he always restrained
poetry to his subject. If poetry must, at times, have freedom, it
must, at times, have restraint ; if, at times, it may soar on fancy's
wing or evoke glorious or appalling habitants for our reflection,
at other times it may well cling to the actualities of daily existence.
Comedy, of all forms of literature, has its duties in the street or
tavern as well as in Arden or on the sea-coast of Bohemia. Jonson
found neither charm nor heroism in London streets, though
both were unquestionably there. He found neither the truth
and passion that lay at the heart of puritanism, nor the joy and
fancy that stirred the light-hearted moods of Fletcher, Shirley, or
Herrick. But he mirrored what he saw of men and manners with
an untiring fidelity, heightened and coloured his picture with a
hearty and virile humour and interpreted it by a sound and
censorious morality. Imaginative idealism, characteristic of the
Elizabethan age and its literature, had another and a greater master;
but interest in the depiction and criticism of the actual life of the
day—an interest essential to vitality in the literature of any age,
and manifest in the golden days of the Armada as well as in
degenerate Jacobean times—had its chief exponent in Jonson.

His influence, commanding in his own day, has continued down
to the present. His comedies were imitated so soon as they
appeared ; witness *Everie Woman in her Humor* (1609, acted
by 1600). Beaumont and Fletcher studied in his school, as *The*

Woman Hater, written by the former[1], testifies; and Marston, Middleton and Chapman profited from his example. Of later dramatists, Field, Randolph, Cartwright, Nabbes and May—to name no others—employed Jonson's methods and wrote plays in his manner. The comedy of humours became, in fact, an established model, which few later writers altogether disregarded. All realistic comedy owned its influence, and reminiscences of its most effective scenes and types of character found their way into every kind of drama. There were other leaders in realistic comedy, Middleton in particular, who may be said to have set an example of a less satirical, less moral, but hardly less Plautian, representation of London manners. But Jonson continued through his life time the chief advocate and exemplar of serious realism.

After the Restoration, Jonson's reputation, for a time, increased. Dryden's praise was echoed by Dennis and others, especially by those who were most eager to see neo-classical rules and models prevail in the theatres. Both his tragedies and his comedies were held in high esteem. The former were revived, but did not long hold the stage. The latter found a warm welcome on the stage and maintained themselves there during the long period when Shakespeare's romantic comedies failed to please. *Bartholomew Fayre* disappeared (1731), even before *As You Like It* returned to the stage (1740), and, of *Volpone, The Silent Woman* and *The Alchemist*[2] not one has outlasted the eighteenth century on the public boards. The last three were revived by Garrick, who also brought out a revision of *Every Man in his Humour*. That play continued on the stage well into the nineteenth century.

Jonson's influence, moreover, has been felt in the novel as well as in the drama. His plays have been constantly read and have always encouraged a study of the absurdities of character and the incongruities of manners. Fielding and Smollett were conscious of their incentive, and Dickens, who knew them well and himself acted Bobadill, must, to no inconsiderable extent, have been indebted to their suggestion. Not only are there specific resemblances, as between Zeal-of-the-land Busy and Stiggins, but Dickens's comic invention and characterisation are often strikingly Jonsonian in method and effect. Whether Jonson's comedies are ever again revived on the stage or not, they are likely to continue long to encourage in fiction a frank and searching presentation of foible and folly.

---

[1] See below, chap. v.

[2] A droll, *The Empiric* (1676), and a farce, *The Tobacconist* (1771) were based on *The Alchemist*. A satirical tragedy, *The Favourite*, based on *Sejanus*, appeared in 1770.

CHAPTER II

CHAPMAN, MARSTON, DEKKER

AMBITIONS are naturally fired in an age of unusual achievement in any field of human activity, and men of every variety of genius or talent, however unfitted to command success in it, are drawn to the glittering arena. Many men were dramatists in 1600 whose gifts were not conspicuously dramatic, and whose instincts in another epoch would hardly have driven them to the service of the stage. Of these, George Chapman was an example. He was a poet ; but his muse did not point him towards the theatre, and, had she designed him for drama, she would have delayed his birth. For, in 1600, when Jonson was about twenty-seven and Dekker thirty, Chapman was already forty years old. He was twenty-eight when Marlowe's *Tamburlaine* was produced, and thus did not in early youth, nor until his mind had already taken its mould, come under the dramatic influences or inspiration which formed Shakespeare and the greater playwrights. Nor is it even certain that he was greatly interested in drama till within five years of the close of the century. He did not serve a youthful apprenticeship to the theatrical art, and he never learnt to think in any character but his own.

We gather from one of his early poems (*Euthymiae Raptus*) that Chapman was born in or near Hitchin in Hertfordshire, and, from the title-page of his *Homer*, that his birth year was 1559. It is frequently said that he studied at both universities, but there is no certain evidence that he was at either. Wood asserts that he spent some time at Oxford, in 1574 or thereabouts, 'where he was most excellent in the Latin and Greek tongues, but not in logic or philosophy,' and that he left without taking a degree. Of his personal affairs for the next twenty years, we know nothing. It is not improbable that he travelled, and a passage in one of his poems suggests that, like Jonson, he may have served in the Netherlands. As a man of letters, his first appearance, apparently, was made in a volume of poetry, *The Shadow of Night*, when he was thirty-five. From this time, he was busy as poet and dramatist until 1614, and seems to have achieved reputation and gained distinguished friends, though he gathered little wealth. Meres speaks of him in 1598 as a renowned scholar, tragedian and comedian. We know that he found a patron in the earl of Essex, and that, after the earl's execution in 1601, he was befriended by prince Henry, to whom he was appointed 'server in ordinary.' The prince encouraged him in his work of translating Homer, and appears to have promised him a pension; but he died in 1612, and Chapman received no further royal favours.

> To all times future this time's mark extend,
> Homer no patron found, nor Chapman friend.

In 1605, he had shared with Marston and Jonson the displeasure of the authorities for the satire in *Eastward Hoe* on the Scottish king's needy followers, and had suffered imprisonment. Again, in 1608, he narrowly escaped punishment for an unhappy reference to the French queen in *The Conspiracie, And Tragedie of Charles Duke of Byron,* which roused the indignation of the French ambassador. From 1614, Chapman appeared less frequently as an author, and he died in no very prosperous circumstances in 1634. He was buried in St Giles's in the Fields (Habington, in his *Castara,* speaks of his tomb as without the church), and a monument by his friend Inigo Jones, to whom he had dedicated his translation of Musaeus, was then erected to his memory, as 'a Christian Philosopher and Homericall Poett.'

It is difficult to escape the conviction that Minto was correct in his identification of Chapman with the 'rival poet' of Shakespeare's *Sonnets*; and it has been argued with great force and ingenuity[1] that the rivalry here indicated may be traced elsewhere in the work of both authors, and that the note of anger in the strain of invective which frequently appears in Chapman's poems and prefaces, hitherto interpreted in his favour as the natural scorn of a great artist for inferior work, was the outcome of bitter personal resentment at the success of the unlettered Shakespeare and was directly aimed at him. According to this view, *The Amorous Zodiac,* in the 1595 volume of poems, is the poem indicated by Shakespeare in his twenty-first sonnet; Holofernes, in *Love's Labour's Lost,* is a satirical portrait of Chapman in reply to his malevolent attacks, and *Troilus and Cressida* an elaborate castigation of

---

[1] *Shakespeare and the Rival Poet,* by Arthur Acheson, 1903.

Chapman's extravagant laudation of Homer, his praise of Greek ideals and his contempt of all poets who were not his equals in scholarship. Though not proven, the thesis cannot be lightly dismissed.

We are told that Chapman was a student of the classics who made little progress in philosophy ; but his earliest works exhibit him rather as a metaphysician in verse than as a disciple of the canons of ancient art. Passages in *The Shadow of Night* (1594) and in *Ovid's Banquet of Sence*, containing *A coronet for his Mistress Philosophy*, *The amorous Zodiac* and other poems (1595), may be praised with justice; but they will never be widely read. In the dedication of the second volume, he disclaims all ambition to please the vulgar—'The profane multitude I hate, and only consecrate my strange poems to those searching spirits, whom learning hath made noble and nobility sacred.' Yet, even among 'searching spirits,' some reluctance to return to poems in the main so warped and obscure as these may well be found. Better work was to come. In his continuation of Marlowe's *Hero and Leander* (1598), Chapman not unworthily completed an incomparable fragment, and, in *The Tears of Peace* (1609), dedicated to his young patron, prince Henry, he reaches his happiest moods as an original poet. By *Andromache Liberata* (1614), he added nothing to his reputation. The subject was an unfortunate one—the marriage of the earl of Somerset and Frances Howard, the divorced lady Essex—and was treated in so enigmatic a manner as to make necessary a subsequent prose justification of its aims and intentions. Distinction of mind and intellectual vigour are apparent in all Chapman's work ; but, though he may occasionally soar, he never sings, and his finest verses possess gnomic and didactic, rather than lyric, quality. When it emerges from the entanglements amid which the current of his reflections is usually split, his poetry can be as limpid as it is stately. But not often do we hear such music as when he tells us that Fletcher's *Faithfull Shepheardesse*

> Renews the golden world and holds through all
> The holy laws of homely Pastoral,
> Where flowers and founts and nymphs and semi-gods
> And all the Graces find their old abodes.

Though Chapman was well known as a dramatist in 1598, only two plays by his hand are extant which were produced before that date—*The Blinde begger of Alexandria* (printed 1598) and *An Humerous dayes Myrth* (printed 1599), probably the play

mentioned by Henslowe as *The comodey of Umers* in 1597. Both
are comedies; but neither deserves any particular notice, though
the first appears to have been successful on the stage, and the
second contains one or two characters drawn with some cleverness
and spirit. *Al Fooles* (printed 1605), another comedy, was first
produced under the title *The World runs on Wheels*, and displays
a surprising advance in dramatic technique. The plot, partly
borrowed from Terence, is ingenious and excellent, and makes
a good framework for a satirical sketch of humours developed
through amusing situations in the manner of Jonson. As a writer
of comedy, here, and in *Eastward Hoe* (to be noticed later), where,
however, he had collaborators, Chapman appears to the greatest
advantage. When dealing with lighter themes, he condescended,
though with apologies, to write an uninflated style; and, however
he may himself have preferred the heightened and fantastic rhetoric
of his tragedies, they are indisputably inferior in construction
and far less natural in tone than the dramas he affected to
despise.

For four or five years after the opening of the seventeenth
century, Chapman, doubtless because he was occupied with the
continuation of his translation of Homer, contributed nothing to
dramatic literature. By 1605, he had, evidently, resumed his
connection with the theatre; for two plays were printed in the
following year—*The Gentleman Usher* and *Monsieur D'Olive*.
In the first of these, Chapman threw his chief strength into a
romantic love episode introduced into the comic scheme of the
play, and succeeded in imparting to it an intensity and sweetness
foreign to his character and talent. *Monsieur D'Olive* opens
strongly; but the main plot is subsequently obscured by the
shifting of the centre of interest to the character who gives his
name to the piece. This cleverly conceived and diverting town
gull, whose wit and coolness in a trying situation are pleasantly
rendered, at once spoils the play as a work of art and keeps it
alive as an entertainment. Later in his career, Chapman wrote
two more comedies—*May-Day* (printed 1611), shown by Stiefel
to be an adaptation of the *Allesandro* of Allesandro Piccolomini,
and *The Widdowes Teares* (printed 1612)—and took part with
Shirley in a third, *The Ball* (printed 1639). The last named owes
little to Chapman[1], and neither of the others rises to anything
approaching excellence. *The Widdowes Teares*, the idea of which
is borrowed from Petronius, is not altogether wanting in power and

[1] Cf. *post*, chap. VIII.

has some characteristic passages, but entirely fails to arouse interest in its characters or admiration for the contrivance of the action.

His translations apart, Chapman's fame rests upon his tragedies founded on French history, of which *Bussy D'Ambois* (printed 1607) and *The Revenge of Bussy D'Ambois* (printed 1613) have always and rightly received most attention. The subjects here chosen were singularly adapted to display the qualities of his genius, never impressive save on an elevated stage. *Bussy D'Ambois* was by far the most successful of his dramas, its popularity being due, in part, to its revival of recent history, in part to the character and career of the chief figure, formed by nature for an invincible hero of romance, and in part to the glowing rhetoric which certainly rises in places to pure and impassioned poetry. Some entries in Henslowe suggest that *Bussy D'Ambois*, and not Marlowe's *Massacre at Paris*, as Collier thought, may have been the play for which payments were made in 1598[1]; but, if we assign to it so early a date as this, we must allow a revision after the death of Elizabeth, who is spoken of as the 'old Queene.' The sources of this drama have not been precisely determined—De Thou's *Historiae sui temporis* and Rosset's *Histoires Tragiques*, from which it was supposed that the author derived his incidents, were not published in 1607—and Chapman, therefore, must have had recourse to contemporary accounts. The part of Bussy was acted by Nathaniel Field. A revised version of the play by Thomas D'Urfey was produced on the stage of the Theatre Royal in 1691. For *The Revenge of Bussy D'Ambois* and the tragedies *The Conspiracie, And Tragedie of Charles Duke of Byron* (printed 1608), he drew directly from a translation of Serres's *Inventaire Général de l'Histoire de France* by Edward Grimeston, published in 1607[2]. Grimeston supplemented Serres, whose narrative ends in 1598, from Matthieu's *Histoire de France* and other contemporary writers.

In his first tragedy, the court of Henry III is employed as a frame for the full length portrait of the brilliant adventurer, Bussy, whose love affair with Tamyra, countess of Montsorry, betrayal to her husband and last stand when encircled by his enemies, make an admirable drama of the heroic and melodramatic type. It is successful in a style thoroughly Elizabethan (the antithesis of the classic), in which violent scenes and extravagant rhetoric

---

[1] Cf. Greg's *Henslowe's Diary*, part II, pp. 198, 199, and *Henslowe Papers*, p. 120, note.

[2] *Bussy D'Ambois* and *The Revenge of Bussy D'Ambois*, ed. by Boas, F. S., 1905.

mingle with profound reflection and magnificent outbursts of poetry—a strange compound of the fantastic and forbidding with the noblest and most inspiring elements in art. Dryden, in his famous depreciation of this play, went too far:

I have sometimes wondered in the reading [he said] what has become of those glaring colours which amazed me in *Bussy D'Ambois* upon the theatre; but when I had taken up what I supposed a fallen star, I found I had been cozened with a jelly; nothing but a cold dull mass, which glittered no longer than it was shooting; a dwarfish thought, dressed up in gigantic words, repetition in abundance, looseness of expression, and gross hyperboles; the sense of one line expanded prodigiously into ten; and to sum up all, incorrect English, and a hideous mingle of false poetry and true nonsense; or, at best, a scantling of wit, which lay gasping for life, and groaning beneath a heap of rubbish. A famous modern poet used to sacrifice every year a Statius to Virgil's manes; and I have indignation enough to burn a *D'Ambois* annually to the memory of Jonson.

We have here a typical example of Restoration feeling and criticism. Chapman exhibits in excess precisely those Elizabethan qualities which a later age found Gothic and barbaric. The faults of the romantic school are all present in an exaggerated degree. But Dryden overlooked the fiery energy, the imaginative splendours and rich suggestiveness of phrase and imagery which were its glory, and beside which the undeniable excellences of his own age of literature seem the cold and lifeless offspring of uninspired labour. *The Revenge of Bussy D'Ambois* (printed 1613), written after an interval during which Chapman had produced his Byron tragedies, though inferior as a drama for the stage, is stronger in its reflective passages and contains by far the most interesting and profound of Chapman's character studies. This is Clermont d'Ambois, a brother of the dead Bussy invented by the dramatist, who is incited by Bussy's ghost, as Hamlet is by his father's spirit, to undertake the mission of revenge. Clermont, the 'senecal man,' who, like Hamlet, is of a speculative habit of mind and disinclined towards violence, only after delays accomplishes his task, and, in the end, dies by his own hand. *The Revenge* is suffused with memories of Shakespeare's play, to which, undoubtedly, it owes its plan and many of its episodes, while Clermont's philosophy is largely drawn from Epictetus. It is somewhat remarkable that this drama, the interest of which is centred in a true philosopher moving amid the intrigues and violences of a renascence court, makes him the faithful follower of the infamous duke of Guise, whose portrait, as given us here, is no less flattering than it is unhistorical—a piece of perversity certainly not calculated to commend the play to reformation England.

If high intellectual interest and authentic eloquence sufficed to constitute a dramatic masterpiece, *The Conspiracie, And Tragedie of Charles Duke of Byron, Marshall of France* might give Chapman rank among great playwrights. But we have here rather 'a small epic in ten books or acts' than a drama. The verse runs more smoothly, however, than in the Bussy plays, the poetry is less pestered with the cloudy turbulence of his 'full and heightened style,' and nowhere does Chapman win more completely upon his reader. In his next tragedy, *Caesar and Pompey* (printed 1631), he turned from contemporary to classical history, and, standing on scholar's ground, might have been expected to derive powerful inspiration from his theme, but the design is feebly handled, and he fails, as before, to communicate movement to the action or vitality to the *dramatis personae*. Only the oratorical passages, especially those placed in the mouth of Cato, can be read with much pleasure.

The remaining plays of Chapman were not published during his lifetime. In *Chabot Admirall of France* (printed 1639), for which materials were drawn from Pasquier's *Les Recherches de la France*, he had the assistance of Shirley, and it seems fruitless to attempt the task of partitioning their respective contributions. *Revenge for Honour* (printed 1654), an eastern tale of which the scene is laid in Arabia, may have been written by Chapman; but the play is by no means in his usual manner, and it is difficult to believe that, in his old age, he could have assimilated the style of the later dramatists. (A play printed for the same publisher and entitled *The Paraside, a Revenge for Honour* was entered in the register (1653) as by Henry Glapthorne.) Neither play possesses any great distinction, though some critics have found in the variety of incident and portraiture in the last named drama reason for assigning to it a high place among Chapman's works. It is certainly superior to *Alphonsus Emperour of Germany* (printed 1654), also ascribed to Chapman on more slender grounds. The intimate knowledge of the German language and German life displayed by the author has been variously explained. Either Chapman spent some time in Germany, or he was assisted by some unknown writer intimately acquainted with the language and customs of that country. There remains the possibility that he had no hand in it. Zeal for Chapman's reputation might easily be better expended than in the attempt to prove this play his. *Sir Gyles Goosecappe* (printed 1606), an anonymous play, has been ascribed to Chapman or a disciple by several critics, on internal evidence of method and manner. Two of his plays, never printed, were destroyed in manuscript by

Warburton's cook, *The Yorkshire Gentlewoman and her Son,* and *Fatal Love,* a French tragedy. Jonson told Drummond that 'next himself, only Fletcher and Chapman,' both of whom 'he loved,' 'could make a masque.' Only one such composition by Chapman is extant, *The memorable Masque of the two honourable Houses or Innes of Court; the Middle Temple, and Lyncolnes Inne,* performed at Whitehall in 1614. Probably he wrote others; the merits of this piece afford insufficient warrant for Jonson's compliment. While it would be absurd to deny the presence of masculine force and fervid poetry in Chapman's best tragedies, it would be mere irony to claim for him fine sensibility or delicate discrimination in the portrayal of character. He is not great either in invention or construction, and, though his work abounds in wise sayings, moral apophthegms and high pitched sentiments, and though the talent for observation is not absent, there is an invincible coarseness in his fibre. The comedies show all men either as deceivers or deceived; his tragic heroes are often little more than the embodiment of physical energy and tenacious will; pathos he never attains; and he seems to have been incapable or undesirous of painting the portrait of a lovable woman. Chapman's immense pretensions and determination to storm Parnassus hardly win our allegiance. Nor need we pay homage to his scholarship, though reputed as vast. He was overburdened not so much by the weight of his learning as by a mistaken sense of its importance and authority. Approach him first by way of his original poems and dramas, and it will not easily prove practicable to find the measure of the man. Like Milton writing in prose, he is using, as it were, his left hand. But approach him first under the spell of Homer, who was 'angel to him, star and fate,' when both genius and character are sublimated, and he will be known for what he is. In Chapman's view, Homer was not only emperor among the poets, he was the greatest of men and philosophers. 'Of all books extant in all kinds, Homer is the first and best ... out of him, according to our most grave and judicial Plutarch, are all Arts deduced, confirmed, or illustrated.' At this shrine, he burns continual incense, and he would seem to have conceived himself as directly inspired by the spirit of his great original. It was impossible, indeed, that, out of the Elizabethan age, should issue a version of Homer marked by the Homeric qualities of simplicity and directness, nor does Chapman so much translate Homer as reproduce his narrative with a certain divine ardour. He describes it as 'an absurd affectation in the interpretation of any author to turn him word for word,' and disclaimed in his own case any such intention. In Chapman, the bright equable stream, that reflected sun and stars and open heaven, dashes through the chasms and ravines of a mountain country. The stately breadth and sweeping curve and quiet eddy are lost, but speed and volume and majesty remain. The famous version deserves its fame[1].

'Our Homer-Lucan,' as Daniel styled him, did not appear as a translator till he was nearly forty years old. The first instalment of his labours, *Seaven Bookes of the Iliades of Homere* (I and II and VII to XI), was published in 1598, and dedicated to the earl of Essex. In 1609 were published the first twelve books, dedicated to prince Henry, and the completed *Iliad*, without date (books I and II having been re-written) about 1611. It appears from his own statement that he wrote the last twelve books in fifteen weeks. The metre, a fourteen-syllabled riming couplet, one of the oldest English measures, was a sixteenth century favourite, and had been employed in a translation of ten books of Homer, from a French version, in 1581, by Arthur Hall. Chapman's *Achilles Shield*, 'translated out of' the eighteenth book, in the heroic couplet, and prefaced by an epistle attacking Scaliger, was also published in 1598. The first twelve books of the *Odyssey* in the heroic couplet appeared in 1614, with a dedication to the earl of Somerset, and the second twelve within another year. The *Works and Days* of Hesiod were next undertaken and completed in 1618. In 1616, both the *Iliad* and the *Odyssey* were issued in a folio entitled *The Whole Workes of Homer, Prince of Poets*, and, with *Batrachomyomachia*, the *Hymns* and the *Epigrams* in 1624, the first complete translation of Homer into English was made, and the author could say, 'The work that I was born to do is done.'

Like the pyramid of Caius Cestius, it was planned as 'a refuge for his memory'; to Homer's keeping Chapman committed his name and fame. And to Homer he owes his reputation, as to his long companionship with Homer he owed his chief happiness in life. In the presence of that mighty shade, he forgot his quarrel with the world, the cloud of anger that sat upon his brow dispersed and his soul had peace.

John Marston, a man of good Shropshire family and son of John Marston, a member of the Middle Temple, was probably born, and certainly educated, in Coventry. Italian blood on his mother's side (she was the daughter of an Italian physician,

[1] See, for further remarks on Chapman's *Homer*, vol. IV, chap. I, pp. 21, 22.

Andrew Guarsi) helps us to understand some features of his genius and character which distinguished him among his fellows and made him at the same time a typical representative of his age. He was admitted to Brasenose college, Oxford, and graduated in 1593. Marston began his literary career as a satirist, changed his muse and entered the dramatic field in the last year of the sixteenth century, but deserted the theatre for the church in 1607. He was presented to the living of Christchurch in Hampshire, and married the daughter of a clergyman, William Wilkes, chaplain to James I. Ben Jonson sarcastically observed to Drummond that 'Marston wrote his father-in-law's preachings, and his father-in-law his comedies.' A collected but incomplete edition of his plays was published in his lifetime by William Sheares (1633), who speaks of him as 'now in his Autumn and declining age,' and 'far distant from this place,' but claims for him a position among the best poets of his time. He made no demands of his own upon the attention of posterity. When he died in 1634, he was buried beside his father in the Temple church, 'under the stone,' says Wood, 'which hath written on it *Oblivioni Sacrum.*' Marston was thus faithful to the sentiment which, in derision of the ambition of most poets, induced him, in his earlier life, to dedicate his works to forgetfulness.

> Let others pray
> For ever their faire poems flourish may;
> But as for mee, hungry Oblivion
> Devour me quick, accept my orizon.

In any estimate of Marston, it ought to be remembered that he suffered from no illusions—

> Farre worthier lines, in silence of thy state,
> Doe sleep securely, free from love or hate.

And, again, 'He that thinks worse of my rimes than myselfe, I scorn him, for hee cannot: he that thinks better is a foole.' As man of letters, Marston embarked at once upon 'a troubled sea of noises and hoarse disputes.' In 1598, he published two volumes, *The Metamorphosis of Pygmalion's Image, And Certain Satires,* and, later, *The Scourge of Villanie,* dedicated 'to his most esteemed and best beloved Selfe,' crossing blades with Hall, who, with some arrogance, had claimed the title of father of English satire:

> I first adventure: follow me who list,
> And be the second English satirist.

This unedifying duel has been dealt with in a previous chapter of the present work, and need not detain us here[1]. Marston had now achieved something of a reputation. He is mentioned by Meres, in his *Palladis Tamia* (1598), among the chief English satirists, and, in *The Returne from Pernassus* (acted in 1601), he is addressed by the title 'Kinsayder,' under which he had written a note in *The Scourge of Villanie*. Here, his portrait is boldly drawn as 'a ruffian in his style,' who 'backs a proper steed' and 'cuts, thrusts and foins at whomsoever he meets.' No sooner had he joined the ranks of the dramatists than he set about him in the same deliberately aggressive fashion, 'his shield hung ever in the lists.' In the famous 'war of the theatres,' a war in which most of the dramatists of the day were involved, Marston's name is unceasingly prominent. He aimed an occasional shaft at Shakespeare, as in the parody (in *The Scourge of Villanie*)

A man, a man, a Kingdom for a man,

or the line in *The Malcontent*

Illo, ho, ho, ho! arte there, old Truepenny?

but his chief violence was directed against Jonson. 'He had many quarrels with Marston,' said Jonson, of himself, to Drummond, 'beat him and took his pistol from him, wrote his *Poetaster* on him; the beginning of them were that Marston represented him on the stage.' Jonson represents himself as patiently sustaining the 'petulant styles' of his enemies 'on every stage' for three years, and, at last, unwillingly forced into rejoinder. It is sometimes argued—on slender evidence, however—that Marston's first attack on Jonson was made not in a play but in *The Scourge of Villanie*, under the name 'judicial Torquatus.' But Jonson, at least as early as 1598, had expressed some of his literary judgments upon the stage. Daniel, in his opinion, 'a good honest man, but no poet,' had been publicly ridiculed in *Every Man in His Humour*, and the noble parts which Jonson assigned to himself—Asper in *Every Man out of His Humour*, Crites in *Cynthia's Revels*, Horace in *Poetaster*—no less than his unflattering portraits of enemies, naturally provoked and suggested reprisals. We need not wonder that he was facetiously saluted by Dekker in his 'three or four suites of names,' 'Asper, Criticus, Quintus, Horatius, Flaccus.' Theatregoers familiar with the characteristics, literary and personal, of the popular dramatists were, probably, amused by these personal rivalries, assaults and counter assaults, and pleasure to the

---

[1] Cf. *ante*, vol. IV, chap. XVI, pp. 331, 332; and bibl. p. 517.

audience brought profit to the authors. So, at least, we gather
from Jonson's remarks in *Poetaster*:

> What they have done 'gainst me,
> I am not moved with: if it gave them meat,
> Or got them clothes, 'tis well: that was their end.
> Only amongst them, I am sorry for
> Some better natures, by the rest so drawn
> To run in that vile line.

In 1599, a play was performed at court, probably by the boys
of Paul's, which carried on the practice of staging contemporary
authors, and, in the personage of Chrisoganus, 'Master Pedant' and
'translating scholler,' who is advised, 'goe, get you clothes,' the
audience of the day probably recognised the most learned of the
dramatic circle, Jonson, who 'excelled in a translation,' and was
famous no less for his scholarship than for his shabby garments.
This play, *Histrio-Mastix*, based on an earlier drama, possibly
by Chapman, was directed against adult players, perhaps with
special reference to the Chamberlain's company, and authors
who wrote for it, of whom Jonson was one, and the evidence is
strongly in favour of Marston's responsibility for the greater share
in its production.   Jonson, when, for the first time, he attacks
Marston in *Every Man out of His Humour*, selects for derision
words used in this play as well as in Marston's *Scourge of Villanie*,
and, in the opinion of some critics, presented him as Carlo
Buffone, 'a most fiend like disposition,' 'a public scurrilous and
profane jester ... who will swill up more sack at a sitting than
would make all the guard a posset.' We are told that 'he will
sooner lose his soul than a jest, and profane even the most holy
things to excite laughter.'   The identification, however, is far from
certain, and Carlo may have been intended for a certain Charles
Chester, a familiar city character. Attempts have been made to
identify various other characters in the play with well known contemporaries of Jonson—Fastidious Brisk with Daniel, Fungoso
with Lodge and Sordido with Henslowe—but with more ingenuity
than success. So far, Dekker had not been in the battle. Before
this date, he and Jonson had been collaborators and may have
been friends. Some critics have thought Emulo a portrait of
Jonson; but nothing could be more inapplicable to that sturdy
shabby scholar than a description such as this—

My brisk spangled baby will come into a stationer's shop, call for a stool
and a cushion, and then asking for some Greek poet, to him he falls, and
then he grumbles God knows what, but I'll be sworn he knows not so much
as one character of the tongue.

In *Jacke Drums Entertainment*, an anonymous play performed in
1600 by the children of Paul's, in which Brabant Senior, 'the cen-
surer,' is probably a portrait of Jonson, and Sir Edward Fortune
may be intended for Edward Alleyn, there is again evidence of
Marston's hand, his rhodomontade and fustian vocabulary, and
these are ridiculed in *Poetaster*. 'The new poet Mellidus' was
probably a representation of the author himself. Jonson had
already returned to the charge in *Cynthia's Revels*, where Dekker
has been thought to be staged for the first time as Anaides, and
where, most probably, Marston is pilloried as Hedon:

> The one a light voluptuous reveller,
> The other a strange arrogating puff,
> Both impudent and arrogant enough.

Both are represented as engaged in a plot against Crites, who, they
agree to give out, is a plagiary, 'all he does is dictated from other
men,' and 'the time and place where he stole it' is known. Anaides
is described as one 'who will censure or discourse of anything, but
as absurdly as you would wish. His fashion is not to take knowledge of him that is beneath him in clothes. He never drinks
below the salt.' He has a voice like the opening of some justice's
gate or a postboy's horn, 'a great proficient in all the illiberal
sciences.' 'He will blaspheme in his shirt. The oaths which he
vomits at one supper would maintain a town of garrison in good
swearing a twelve month.' We hear from him that, in argument
with Crites, 'because I could not construe an author I quoted at
first sight, he went away and laughed at me.' Anaides revenges
himself by describing Crites as smelling of 'lamp-oil with studying
by candle-light.' The Amorphus of this play may be Anthony
Munday, who 'walks most commonly with a clove or pick-tooth in
his mouth,' and is 'more affected than a dozen waiting women.' He
will 'usurp all the talk, ten constables are not so tedious,' and he
has been 'fortunate in the amours of three hundred forty and five
ladies, all nobly, if not princely descended.' The epilogue to
Cynthia's Revels connects this play with Marston's *Antonio and
Mellida*. The actor who pronounced it had injunction from the
author

> I'll only speak what I have heard him say:
> By God, tis good, and if you lik't, you may.

The epilogue to *Antonio and Mellida* enters armed and remarks:
'I stand not as a peremptory challenger of desert, either for him
that composed the Comedy, or for us that acted it; but as a
most submissive suppliant for both.' To the armed epilogue of

Marston's play succeeded the armed prologue of *Poetaster* (1601), Jonson's most elaborate attack upon his detractors, where Marston is Crispinus, Dekker Demetrius. Hedon, in *Cynthia's Revels* is supposed, by some critics, to be Dekker; but it seems more probable that as 'a dresser of plays about the town here,' 'one of the most overflowing rank wits in Rome,' he appears for the first time upon the stage as Demetrius. *Poetaster* doubtless presents other portraits of contemporaries; Virgil, a complimentary picture, may have been intended either for Shakespeare or Chapman. The pill which Caesar permits Horace to administer to Crispinus forces him to disgorge a number of Marston's fustian words, which offended Jonson's taste; and both he and Demetrius are sworn never again 'to malign, traduce or detract the person or writings of Quintus Horatius Flaccus, or any other eminent man.' The reply to *Poetaster* was entrusted by the aggrieved fellowship to Dekker, and his *Satiro-mastix* was produced in 1601. It seems certain that Jonson knew of the intention to reply to *Poetaster*, and that Dekker was to share in it, for the part of Demetrius looks like an afterthought. He is introduced as a stranger in the third act 'hired to abuse Horace, and brings him in a play.' The controversy is carried on by the author of *Satiro-mastix* in a light, pleasant and facetious vein. Dekker cleverly introduces some of Jonson's own characters, and even improves that of the swaggerer Tucca, and, while this play falls far short of *Poetaster* in construction, its mockery is more genial, its humour more subtle and sparkling and the management of the whole is marked by a delightful air of irresponsibility. Jonson is charged with having 'arraigned two poets against all law and conscience.' There are a number of jocose references to his personal appearance, his scholar's pride, his slow methods of composition, his early trade as a bricklayer, his military service in the Netherlands, the duel in which he killed his adversary. The 'humourous poet' is 'untrussed,' and condemned to wear a crown of nettles. He is no longer to swear he will hang himself if he thinks any man could write as well as he, nor to enter the gallery when his comedies are performed, and there make vile and bad faces at every line to make men have an eye to him and make the players afraid.

Besides, you must forsweare to venter on the stage, when your play is ended, and to exchange curtezies, and complements with Gallants in the Lordes roomes, to make all the house rise up in Armes, and to cry that's Horace, that's he, that's he, that's he, that pennes and purges Humours and diseases.

And, again, 'when your plays are misse-likt at Court, you shall
not crye Mew like a Pusse-cat, and say you are glad you write out
of the Courtier's Element.' 'We come,' says Crispinus, 'like your
Phisitions, to purge

> Your sicke and daungerous minde of her disease.'

In yet another play was Jonson made the target of satirical
jest, Marston's *What You Will*, probably written (1601) before
Poetaster and revised later. But, while some investigators identify
Jonson with Lampatho and Marston with Quadratus, others reverse the portraits. The evidence is somewhat conflicting; yet,
if Marston intended anything but general satire, it would harmonise with all we know of him that he should here introduce his
old *nom de plume* of Kinsayder, and thus present himself as
Lampatho. He engages in a hectoring match with Quadratus,
who abuses him as 'a ragged satirist,' 'an envy-starved cur,'
'a libertine'; but Marston, who 'presented his poetry to Detraction,'
was indifferent to abuse, and prepared to invent and discharge it
against himself with the same zest that he hurled it at others.

> Then do but rail at me—
> No greater honour craves my poesy.

With this play the famous *poetomachia* comes to an end. In the
same year, we find Marston collaborating with Jonson in *Love's
Martyr*, and, with Chapman and Jonson, three years later, in
Eastward Hoe. He also dedicated to Jonson his *Malcontent—
Benjamino Jonsonio poetae elegantissimo, gravissimo, amico suo,
candido et cordato*—and, in an equally generous strain, praised
his *Sejanus* in 1605—

> For never English shall, or hath before
> Spoke fuller graced.

The chief interest today of this ancient literary logomachy,
waged on the boards of the Elizabethan theatre, lies in the
personalities which assist us to envisage men with whose works
we are familiar, and the attempt to identify in the plays the
authors represented finds its justification in our natural curiosity
to know these celebrities in their habits as they lived. Here, as
elsewhere, we are baffled by the elusive personality of Shakespeare,
for of the man in whom our interest is deepest no certain identification is possible, and the most plausible critical conjectures
lack convincing quality. Wellbred in *Every Man in His Humour*
may be Shakespeare, so may Posthast in *Histrio-Mastix*, Amorphus

in *Cynthia's Revels*, Planet in *Jacke Drums Entertainment*, Ovid or Virgil in *Poetaster*, William Rufus, 'learning's True Maecenas, poesy's king,' in *Satiro-mastix*. But for the passage in the anonymous *Returne from Pernassus* (1601) we might be spared all speculation with respect to the part played by him in the theatrical wars and conclude that he was never at any time found in either camp. Yet the speech of Kemp to Burbage in that play draws conjectures like a magnet and is encrusted with speculation.

Few of the university pen plaies well, they smell too much of that writer *Ovid* and that writer *Metamorphosis*, and talke too much of *Proserpina* and *Juppiter*. Why heres our fellow *Shakespeare* puts them all downe, I and *Ben Jonson* too. And that *Ben Jonson* is a pestilent fellow, he brought up *Horace* giving the Poets a pill, but our fellow *Shakespere* hath given him a purge that made him beray his credit.

The 'purge' has been held to be the play of *Troilus and Cressida*, which would make the characters Thersites and Ajax Marston and Jonson. But, until we understand *Troilus and Cressida* better, it is wise, perhaps, to regard the 'purge' as nothing more than Shakespeare's triumph as a popular dramatist over the ablest and most celebrated of his contemporaries. Yet, if Shakespeare eludes us, we learn some interesting particulars about others of the dramatic group. Marston's hair (he is Rufus) and thin legs are a subject of continual mirth; if he desire to be a poet, he is advised 'to change his hair'; 'he is proud of his gentle birth,' 'a gentleman parcel-poet,' 'your legs do sufficiently show you are a gentleman born, sir; for a man borne upon little legs is always a gentleman born.' Of Jonson we hear that, as Drummond also tells us, he was a great lover and praiser of himself—'Thou lovest none,' says Tucca, 'neither wisemen nor fools but thyself'; Demetrius speaks of his 'arrogancy and his impudence in commending his own things'; we hear of his shabby clothes—'that Judas yonder that walks in rug'; his 'rocky face,' 'a very bad face for a soldier,' a face 'puncht full of oylet-holes like the cover of a warming pan,'

the most ungodly face ... it looks for all the world like a rotten russet-apple, when 'tis bruised. It's better than a spoonful of cinnamon-water next my heart, for me to hear him speak; he sounds it so i' th' nose, and talks and rants ... like the poor fellow under Ludgate ... its cake and pudding to me to see his face make faces, when he reads his songs and sonnets,

his slowness in composition, 'Will he bee fifteene weekes about this Cockatrice's egge too?' Other identifications are very precarious. Of Daniel, if Fastidious Brisk and Hedon be Daniel, as some suppose, we are told that he will 'creep and wriggle into acquaintance with all the brave gallants about the town,' 'a light voluptuous reveller,' a 'rhyme-given' rascal who utters 'sonnets by the gross,' and will 'overflow you half a score or a dozen at a sitting,' 'a neat, spruce, affecting courtier, one that wears clothes well, and in fashion ; practiseth by his glass, how to salute,' who 'believes rich apparel hath strange virtues' and 'had three suits in one year made three great ladies in love' with him,

has a rich wrought waistcoat to entertain his visitants in, with a cap almost suitable. His curtain and bedding are thought to be his own; his bathing tub is not suspected. He loves to have a fencer, a pedant and a musician seen in his lodging a-mornings.

While some of the satire in these descriptions may have been ill natured, it is hard to believe that much of it was more than stage exaggeration of the good humoured banter which passed between rivals at their actual meetings in tavern or ordinary.

Marston's dramatic activity was confined to about eight years in a lifetime of fifty-eight.

We may take it that the reference in Henslowe's diary to a 'new poet' Maxton or Mastone, in 1599, referred to the author of *Antonio and Mellida*, his first play, acted in 1600. The first part deals with 'the comic crosses of true love,' the second, *Antonios Revenge*, with a world of vice and passion. Here, as elsewhere, Marston displays at moments a flash of tragic grandeur, but as often falls away into bombast and mere verbal gesticulation. It is impossible to deny to him in tragedy something of Marlowe's passion and Webster's solemn splendour, yet, whether through haste, or carelessness, or deficiency in taste, he is unable to maintain the heights to which he occasionally attains. Scenes and passages, such as Lamb selected, do not unfairly represent his power, but, when read as a whole, the dramas from which they are taken prove disappointing. Furious or monstrous characters, like duke Piero in the play under notice, or Isabella in *The Insatiate Countesse*, artificial rhetoric and the absence of reasonable construction, may not have alienated the sympathies of spectators who delighted in *The Spanish Tragedie*, but they distress and repel the modern reader. The source of *Antonio and Mellida*—probably an Italian story— is not known, but the drama belongs to the well known 'blood and thunder' species, and irresistibly reminds us of Kyd's famous play and, necessarily, also of *Hamlet*. In the second part, we have the familiar ghost who clamours for revenge, the device of the dumb-show and the horrors of mutilation as well as death, repeated from *The Spanish Tragedie*. It is clear that Marston was a student of Seneca and knew Shakespeare's work, for there are quotations from *Thyestes* and reminiscences of *Richard II* and *Richard III*. Marston's first play, which was produced when he was twenty-four, bears all the signs of youth and must be described as a patchwork of such violent scenes as delighted the groundlings, entirely destitute of unity or skill in characterisation.

A marked advance is apparent in *The Malcontent*. Of this comedy, there exist two editions of 1604, one of which ascribes the authorship of the play to Webster and the augmentations to Marston. That it is chiefly Marston's work is clear, however, from the preface, in which he expresses regret that scenes invented merely to be spoken should be printed for readers, but concludes that the least hurt he can receive is to do himself the wrong. Here, again, we have an Italian story, of which the source is unknown; but we are once more reminded of *Hamlet* in the person of the hero, and of *Richard III* in the villain Mendozo. The malcontent, a banished duke, returns in disguise to his former court. Like Hamlet's, 'his own soule is at variance within herselfe,' and, under the guise of a mad humour, he contrives to speak the bitterest home truths. The situation has great possibilities, of which, perhaps, the fullest advantage is hardly taken; but Marston had already learnt important lessons in stagecraft and the delineation of character. In the cynical hero, we find depicted a type of mind somewhat akin to that of the author, and the humour of the piece is of the satirical variety which he himself appears most to have affected.

The Dutch Courtezan, published in 1605, shows a further advance in the handling of plot and character. There are scenes both serious and comic which revive memories of Beatrice and her cousin, and of Dogberry and the watch, in *Much Ado about Nothing*; both the men and women are fairly drawn and contrasted; the secondary plot—in part borrowed from the last novel in *The Palace of Pleasure*—with the knavish tricks of Cockledemoy, makes excellent fooling. The prologue apologises for the 'slight hastie labours in this easie play' and declares that it was meant not for instruction but delight. It needs no apology, however, and, though charged by Antony Nixon (*The Black Year*, 1606) with 'corrupting English conditions,' only the sourest of moralists could feel resentment against the author of the comedy, one of the cleverest and most amusing of its time. It was revived late in the seventeenth century, with the alterations of Betterton, the actor, under the title *The Revenge, or The Match in Newgate.*

The Dutch Courtezan, though a capital play, is surpassed by *Eastward Hoe,* but, since the drama was written in conjunction with Chapman and Jonson, the entire credit for this brilliant and delightful performance cannot be claimed for Marston. While it might not be difficult to assign with some confidence certain scenes to each of these writers, the attempt exactly to apportion their respective contributions would lead to a succession of unverifiable conjectures. All must share in the praise due to it, as all were partakers in the misfortune to which it led. It was written shortly after the accession of James I to the throne of England, and contained sarcastic references to the multitude of needy Scottish adventurers who came south with their king, and many of whom successfully claimed place and fortune. Stage jesting at the expense of Scottish men and manners had been complained of to lord Burghley by the English agent at the Edinburgh court in 1598, and it had now become possible to deal with it. Attention was called by Sir James Graham, who may himself have been glanced at in the play, to a passage in the third act, in which captain Seagull remarks

> But as for them [the Scots] there are no greater friends to Englishmen and England, when they are out on't, in the world, than they are. And for my part, I would a hundred thousand of 'hem were there, for we are all one countrymen now, ye know, and we should find ten times more comfort of them there than we do here.

The consequences of the mild freedom of comment which the dramatists here allowed themselves was related by Ben Jonson to Drummond—

> He was dilated by Sir James Murray to the King, for writing something against the Scots, in a play *Eastward Hoe,* and voluntarily imprisoned himself with Chapman and Marston, who had written it amongst them. The report was, that they should then [have] had their ears cut and noses. After their delivery, he banqueted all his friends; there was Camden, Selden and others; at the midst of the feast his old mother dranke to him, and shew him a paper which she had (if the sentence had taken execution) to have mixed in the prisson among his drinke, which was full of lustie strong poison, and that she was no churle, she told, she minded first to have drunk of it herself.

Some copies of the play, of which several editions appeared in 1605, omit the matter complained of, and other slight variations are to be found in the extant copies. A version by Tate was acted in 1685 under the title *Cuckold's Haven, or An Alderman*

no Conjurer. As a picture of city life, *Eastward Hoe* has no
superior in our dramatic history. The old goldsmith Touchstone,
with his wife and daughters, and the idle and the industrious
apprentice, form an admirable and life-like group, which instantly
engages interest and attention. The reckless and extravagant
Sir Petronel Flush, burning to repair his fortunes and escape his
creditors by a treasure seeking voyage to Virginia, and ravished by
Seagull's account of its wealth, declares

> I tell thee, golde is more plentiful there than copper is with us ... all the
> chaines with which they chaine up their streets are massie gold; all the
> prisoners they take are feterd in gold; and for rubies and diamonds, they go
> forth on holydayes and gather 'hem by the sea-shore.

This adventurer, with his companions, gives the authors an
admirable opportunity for depicting the shifty society of the city
which lives by its wits, and a vivid contrast is thus furnished to the
household of the honest tradesman. The plot is complicated by
intrigue, and well managed, the action has a lively movement and
the conclusion contrives 'to reconcile us to ourselves and to human
nature.' Few Elizabethan comedies can be praised so unreservedly
as this.

'Comedies are writ to be spoken, not read; remember the
life of these things consists in action,' remarks the author in
the preface to his play entitled *Parasitaster, Or The Fawne*
(printed in two editions 1606), and certainly, though no doubt
fairly successful on the stage, this drama has no great literary
merit. The chief character, duke Hercules, appears in disguise at
the court of Urbino, whither he has sent his son as an ambassador
of love, and the situation reminds us of *The Malcontent.* The
heroine, Dulcimel, is of the type already portrayed in Crispinella
(*The Dutch Courtezan*) and Rossaline in *Antonio and Mellida*,
the gay, sparkling and vivacious damsel, who holds her own in the
company of men. In Beatrice, the sister of Crispinella, and in
Mildred (*Eastward Hoe*) we have another of Marston's favourite
types of feminine character, the good, simple girl, modest and
affectionate. Marston is not rich in female types, and if we add,
to those mentioned, the strong-willed passionate woman who
appears in some of his tragedies, we exhaust his range. The story
is taken from the third novel of the third day of *The Decameron*;
but the idea is an old one and had already been employed by
Terence in his *Adelphi.*

In *The Fawne*, Marston had promised shortly 'to present a
tragedy which should boldly abide the most curious perusal.' But

the tragedy, when it came, certainly belied the author's promise. *The Wonder of Women Or The Tragedie of Sophonisba* is the crudest of Marston's performances. The story, told by Livy and other historians, has been frequently dramatised—in English by Lee (1676) and Thomson (1730); in French by Corneille (1663), and in German by various hands. Sophonisba herself is rendered not without force and skill, but, for the rest, the play is a singularly feeble attempt to do justice to a powerful tragic theme. The witch Erichto and the scenes in which she appears are almost ludicrous in their failure to produce the intended impression of mystery and horror. It is difficult to understand how the author could have believed the piece to possess any literary quality; it is easy to see that he has overleaped the limits of his power.

Marston's last play, *The Insatiate Countesse* (printed 1613), does not appear in the 1633 edition of his works, and in an extant copy of 1631 its authorship is assigned to William Barkstead. It is generally, and, no doubt, correctly, assumed that this was the actor William Barkstead, author of two poems—*Mirrha, the Mother of Adonis* (1617) and *Hiren, or the Faire Greeke* (1611). Two of the best lines in the play are found in the first named poem—

> Night, like a masque, is entered heaven's great hall
> With thousand torches ushering the way.

Of tragedies assigned to Marston, this contains the most interesting work, but much of it, clearly, is by another hand. The text is corrupt, and it seems probable that Marston devised the plot (taken from the fourth and fifteenth novels of Bandello and reproduced in *The Palace of Pleasure*), that he wrote the first draft and that the play was then completed by Barkstead, and finally printed without revision from a stage copy. Marston, evidently, was attracted by Shakespeare, and Shakespeare reverberates through this play. It echoes *Hamlet, Julius Caesar, Macbeth, Richard II* and *Henry IV*; but some of these echoes may be due to the player Barkstead's unconscious memories. The subject of the drama—the unbridled passions of Isabella, countess of Swevia, and her dealings with her many lovers—is too remote from nature and modern life to command our sympathy; but there are scenes which it is impossible to read without a thrill of admiration. Webster alone has excelled them in their own kind, while passing through the same dark region of things violent and forbidding, lust, cruelty, madness and death. A Latin pageant for the visit of king Christian of Denmark to England in 1606 and an entertainment for a visit of the countess of Derby to her son-in-law, lord Huntingdon, complete the list of Marston's extant works, unless, with Collier, we attribute to him the amusing *Mountebank's Masque*, performed in 1616.

The texture of Marston's genius was singularly unequal, and he constantly promises more than he performs. In comedy only can it be truly said that he achieved success, yet in his more ambitious and less successful work there resides an arresting quality. When we are about to condemn unreservedly, he flashes into unexpected splendour; when we lay down the book, his characters refuse to be altogether dismissed into the *limbo* of forgotten things. Marston, as he himself tells us, was powerfully 'enticed with the delights of poetry,' and confesses that, 'above better desert,' he was 'fortunate in these stage pleasings.' As a young man, he essayed what all young men of talent were essaying, the highest reaches of a most difficult art. Nor was his measure of success inconsiderable, for we are told by Wood that he was 'in great renown for his wit and ingenuity in 1606.' Yet it was at this time, while still a young man and on the very threshold of fame, that he resolutely turned away to take up the unexciting routine of parish business. Too little notice has been taken of this remarkable renunciation, and Marston's character too much obscured by the unrelieved emphasis laid upon the heady violences of his satirical youth and his extravagances of diction and humour in the theatrical wars. He outgrew these affectations and absurdities; but, at the same time, he outgrew the passion for distinction. There seems no good reason to doubt the sincerity of his own statements,—'of men of my own addiction I love most, pitie some, hate none'; 'I have ever more endeavoured to know myself than be known of others'—and, without hesitation, we may ascribe his neglect of his 'unfenced reputation,' and his retirement from the pursuit of fame, to his having deliberately 'esteemed felicity a more solid contentment,' and readily responded to the summons, when life's current ran less turbulently, of 'his bosom friend, good Epictetus,' to the quiet meadows and sober pleasures of philosophy.

Thomas Dekker, in whose case, as in that of many of his contemporaries, we possess no certain record of the facts of his life, was born and bred in London—'thou beautifullest daughter of the two united Monarchies! from thy womb received I my being; from thy breasts my nourishment.' He spoke of himself as 'old' in 1628, of his 'three score years,' a vague phrase, in 1637; and we may take it he was born, or not long in the world, in the year 1570. The first mention of Dekker, as author of a book called *Phaeton*, appears in Henslowe's diary in 1597, and his name appears again in 1599, when he is associated with Chettle, an experienced playwright, in the production of a play entitled *Troilus and Cressida*. In the same year, he received various payments for other pieces of work. And, though the popular narrative poem *Canaan's Calamitie* (1598), signed T. D., is, probably, Deloney's and not Dekker's, it is evident that he was early involved in the multifarious literary activities to which his life appears to have been devoted without cessation. Of his parentage and education, we know nothing, but it is improbable that he was ever a student at either of the universities. Since the theatre of the time offered the only remunerative career to poetical talents, to the theatre Dekker betook himself; but his energies, stimulated by necessity, overflowed into other channels. Plays, pageants, pamphlets followed each other with amazing rapidity. Yet, despite all his labours, early in life he made acquaintance with the misfortunes which dog the steps of poverty. In 1598, Henslowe provided forty shillings to secure his release from the 'Counter in the Poultrey,' and we are told by Oldys that he was in prison from 1613 to 1616, and 'how much longer he could not tell.' It has been conjectured, not without probability, that his phrase 'the Bed in which seven years I lay Dreaming' (*Dekker his Dreame*, 1620) has reference to this unhappy period. Some letters to Alleyn which have been preserved prove that he was several times befriended by that open-handed actor. For the rest, we know that Dekker was married before 1594, and that his last book was printed in 1637. Here the story ends; but, if the details of his private life, like those of Shakespeare, are hidden in the cloud, his work, like Shakespeare's, offers an ample field for the study of the author's personality. Many of his writings of which the titles survive have been lost, and others, doubtless, have perished with them; yet so much remains that, even in the absence of personal knowledge of the man, it is possible to estimate his genius and character with unusual precision. To the mental energy and literary facility of Defoe, he added the unpractical temperament, the genial kindliness, the happy heart of Goldsmith. Of the Elizabethan playwrights, excluding Shakespeare, he is not the greatest, but he is the most lovable, not the most learned but the most sympathetic; he was not the most skilful craftsman among them, but he possessed the most natural vein of inspiration. Dekker 'was a rogue,' said Jonson;

but we are not prepared to believe it of so sweet and so good-humoured a disposition as his. There is no such mirror of con-temporary Elizabethan and Jacobean life and ways as is offered us in the works of Dekker[1]. In his natural sympathies and in his choice of subjects, he clings more closely to his own country than any dramatist of his age. No writer since Chaucer, with whom Dekker may fruitfully be compared, has painted so many essentially English pictures of men and manners in so natural and realistic a style. In his first extant play, the comedy entitled *The Sho-makers Holiday* (printed 1600), his admirable talent and charac-teristic interests are displayed. The rise in fortune of the jovial and honest shoemaker, Simon Eyre, gives the poet opportunity to depict the life of the London he knew—rich in shifting scenes of love, intrigue, commerce and domestic doings. The canvas is crowded with portraits of tradesmen, apprentices, alder-men, courtiers, their wives, daughters and sweethearts, a motley procession surging through the streets, each elbowing the other in shop and tavern. No dramatist of the day supplies so vivid and humorous a spectacle of the city world which lay around him—the world for which his plays were written—as Dekker. In the same year was printed *The Pleasant Comedie of Old Fortuna-tus*, a drama in which the poet in Dekker emerges rather than the observing humorist. As in the well known fifteenth century romance, Fortunatus meets lady Fortune, and, of her gifts—'wisdom, strength, health, beauty, long life and riches'—a choice among which is offered him, he selects riches, and receives a purse which is never empty however much may be withdrawn from it. His travels after his unwise choice, and his unhappy fate, with that of his sons, make up the story of the play. The theme is simple, the con-struction somewhat rambling; but much of the poetry is exquisite. It was, perhaps, revised for a performance at court. Dekker never surpassed these early dramas. His rapid, careless methods be-trayed him, and, though he preserved to the last something of the sweetness of fancy, the quickness of invention and the lightness of touch for which he is justly famed, he constantly offends against the stricter canons of art which require unity of design, coherence and precision in construction and character. In these and other plays, Dekker followed Shakespeare in the mingling of prose and verse. Where prose serves his purpose, as in the humorous scenes of ordinary life, he employs it freely, exchanging it for verse where

---

[1] See vol. IV, chap. XVI, pp. 351—7, where his contributions to pamphlet literature are discussed at length.

a deeper key of feeling, a higher pitch of passion or sentiment is reached, passing into rimed verse in tender or pathetic passages. The singing note is heard throughout his best work, and to the charming lyrical vein in his genius we owe such perfect songs as the familiar

Art thou poor, yet hast thou golden slumbers,

where the melody breaks into a child-like overflow of almost inarticulate joyful emotion. After *Satiro-mastix*, already referred to, in which he took up arms against Jonson, Dekker reverted to a more congenial sphere in *The Honest Whore*. Although he had been one of the 'screaming grasshoppers held by the wings' of Jonson's *Poetaster*, Dekker, in his reply, had exhibited no malevolence, nor did he return to the attack. In the first part of *The Honest Whore* (printed 1604), Middleton, as proved by an entry in Henslowe, had a share; the second and superior part is wholly Dekker's (printed 1630), and indisputably a masterpiece as well in execution as invention. The father of Bellafront (whose return to virtue makes the point of the action) is one of the most interesting characters in Elizabethan fiction, and the conception would have done honour to any dramatist. Orlando Friscobaldo, as Hazlitt wrote in his admirable appreciation, is one of the characters who 'raise, revive and give a new zest to our being.' Bellafront's husband, Matheo, is an equally life-like portrait of the unprincipled libertine whose vices are due as much to lack of brain as lack of heart. No single play by Dekker more worthily represents him, or better reflects the blend of humour, pathos and poetry which made the man. But he was never a sure artist. In *The Whore of Babylon* (printed 1607), we have a play without merit, whose only interest lies in some few passages descriptive of London manners and fashions, and in its exhibition of protestant and patriotic sentiment, displayed in references to queen Elizabeth, under the name of Titania, to the Armada and to the *Drake*,

Who from their rivers beat their water fowl,
Tore silver feathers from their fairest swans,
And plucked the Halcyon's wings that rove at sea.

If It Be Not Good, the Divel is in it (printed 1612) is a sufficiently extraordinary title for a worthless dramatic fantasy, based upon *The Pleasant History of Friar Rush* (1567), which presents a bewildering group of human and superhuman beings, from Ravaillac and Guy Faux to Pluto and Charon. If, to these last named works, we add *Match mee in London* (printed 1631) and *The*

Wonder of A Kingdome (printed 1636), neither of which add much
to Dekker's laurels, we exhaust the list of plays which can with any
confidence be assigned to his unassisted pen.   But there remain a
number of dramas to which he was a contributor and of some of
which, perhaps, he was the chief architect.   The habit of collaboration, 'the noble practice of the times,' in which Elizabethan playwrights freely indulged, left to criticism numerous problems not yet
solved—many, no doubt, never to be solved.   Dekker had partners,
good and bad, in various theatrical ventures.   We know that
Middleton had a share in the first part of *The Honest Whore*, and
a share, almost certainly the largest, in *The Roaring Girle* (1611),
whose heroine, Moll Cutpurse, masquerades as a London gallant;
we know that Webster took part in the composition of *West-Ward
Hoe* and *North-Ward Hoe*, comedies of intrigue, and *The Famous
History of Sir Thomas Wyat* (all printed 1607), possibly an
unfinished or unskilful attempt to recast an older historical play
on the subject of lady Jane Grey in two parts, both mentioned by
Henslowe.   We find Massinger's name associated with Dekker's in
connection with *The Virgin Martir* (printed 1622) and, though the
comic scenes and the characters of Dorothea and Angelo have been
claimed for Dekker, the conception and framework of the play may,
without injustice, be assigned to the younger dramatist[1].   *The
Pleasant Comodie of Patient Grissill*, printed anonymously in 1603;
but, in all probability (though Jonson may have had a hand in a
revision), rightly assigned, on the evidence of certain entries in
Henslowe, to Chettle, Haughton and Dekker, is generally believed
to owe its two beautiful lyrics and much of its merit to the most
celebrated of its three authors[2].   *The Witch of Edmonton* (printed
1658), a fine play, raises some very difficult questions.   The witch
scenes, in which an aching spirit of human sympathy appears, and
the tender character of Susan, have been very generally allotted
to Dekker, but Mother Sawyer is by some critics thought to have
been a creation of Rowley.   The first act, the plan and general
management of the piece, indisputably belong to Ford[3].   To Ford,
also, may, without hesitation, be assigned a large part, probably the
last two acts at least, in *The Sun's-Darling: A Moral Masque*
(1656), which, perhaps, is a hasty revision of Dekker's *Phaeton*.
Another masque by the same authors, entitled *The Fairy Knight*
(licensed in 1624), has not come down to us, and we know the names
of a number of other dramas in which Dekker assisted or was
assisted by Jonson (*Robert the Second*, and *Page of Plymouth*), by

[1] See *post*, chap. VI.   [2] See *ante*, vol. V, chap. XIII.   [3] See *post*, chap. VIII.

Drayton (*The Civil Wars in France*) and by Haughton and Day (*The Spanish Moor's Tragedy*, identified by some critics with *Lusts Dominion*, at one time ascribed to Marlowe, but not published till 1657). There are passages in *Lusts Dominion* which certainly suggest Dekker, and, whether we identify it or not with the last drama, we may grant it as possible that he had a hand in it. *The magnificent Entertainment: Given to King James* (1603), in which Jonson joined, and to which Middleton contributed a speech, and various civic pageants, are evidence of contemporary appreciation of Dekker's versatile talent, but possess no serious literary interest.

Quick, impulsive sympathies and a deep vein of humanity were the qualities beyond price in Dekker's dramatic equipment, and to these good gifts of nature the muses added their authentic inspiration. 'A priest in Apollo's temple many years,' as he said, his place and honours were acknowledged by his own age and remain unchallenged. The 'poetry enough for anything,' of which Lamb spoke, was joined in Dekker to an amazing and unflagging interest in life, without touch or trace of weariness or cynicism. It would be absurd to claim for him the intellectual range, the sure-footed judgment or unerring taste of the great masters, and perilous to assert that his faults became him; yet, from his very artlessness, there shines a charm denied to better considered and far more perfect work. By the way of unaffected simplicity, Dekker almost captured greatness, and, while some of his fellows have secured a larger share of the admiration of posterity, he has crept into its more affectionate remembrance. If we incline to criticise his haste and carelessness, we ought to remember that he wrote 'with the printer's devil and the bailiff always at his elbow,' and we may well be astonished not so much at the demerits as at the wealth and value of his performance. 'The right happy and copious industry' which, in Webster's estimate, placed 'Master Dekker' beside 'Master Shakespeare,' is a tribute from a critic who knew what excellence was, and against what mighty currents men must struggle to attain it. As a humorist, London was his province, a sufficient field. Sinful humanity did not lie beyond his pale, but the sunny breadth of mind which was his, while he retained reverence for the things that call for reverence, transforms and transfigures the world, and we are the more reluctant to dismiss it as merely common and unclean. Dekker's satire is without sting, for, while he laughs, he loves, and is honest without being angry. He only among the men of his time seems to have

recognised the whole hardness of the fate of the poor, and to
have ranged himself on the side of distressed persons, maltreated
animals, misjudged, lonely and eccentric members of society.

For the student of Elizabethan social life, Dekker's prose is
even more important than his plays. There are no surviving
documents so rich in material for the reconstruction of its manners
and fashions as these vivid and entertaining pamphlets. Of some
of these an account has been given in a previous volume of the
present work[1]. Both in *The Wonderfull Yeare* (1603) and in *A Rod
for Runawayes* (1625), which also deals with appalling incidents of
the plague and upbraids those who fled from the city in its need,
Dekker anticipates Defoe in the realism and force of his descriptions,
not unmingled in the former work with certain grimly humorous
narratives, designed, as he said, 'like a merry Epilogue to a dull
Play, to shorten the lives of long winter's nights, that lie watching
in the dark for us.' *Worke for Armorours, or the Peace is
broken* (1609), with its motto, 'God help the Poor, the rich can
shift,' allegorises the eternal conflict of classes in the war of the
rival queens, Money and Poverty, and the perplexed social
problems of our own no less than Dekker's day are poignantly
presented. Here, again, Dekker refers to 'the purple whip of
vengeance,' the plague, and its effects on the city life. Like many
others, the poets and players are in evil case, the playhouses are
closed, their flags and bushes taken down, the muses more sullen
than monkeys,

> no good doing in these dayes but amongst Lawyers, amongst Vintners, in
> Bawdy houses and at Pimlico. There is all the Musick (that is of any
> reckning), there all the meetings, there all the mirth, and there all the
> money.

Among incidental descriptions which give interesting glimpses
into the city's life is that of the bear pit, 'the Dogges, like so
many Divels inflicting torments upon it,' in which savage entertainment was included sport with a blind bear, not baited by
dogs, but whipped 'till the blood ran down his old shoulders'
by 'a company of creatures that had the shapes of men and faces
of christians.'

> Methought [says Dekker] this whipping of the blinde Beare, moved as
> much pittie in my breast towards him, as ye leading of poore starved wretches
> to the whipping posts in London (when they had more neede to be releeved
> with foode) ought to move the hearts of cittizens, though it be the fashion now
> to laugh at the punishment.

[1] See the passages in vol. IV, chap. XVI, and bibl., to which reference has already
been made.

Dekker's prose is not always faultless, but it is clear to any student of Shakespeare or of Elizabethan literature in general that what Arnold called 'the victory of the prose style, clear, plain and short' was already won by our dramatists before the advent of Dryden, the virtues of whose prose were derived from his studies in their school. At his best, Dekker is as simple and lucid and direct as any later writer. Take this, from the complaint of Paules steeple in *The Dead Tearme* (1608)—

> The Marriner there called mee his sea-marke, for to him I stood as a watch-tower to guide him safely to our English shore. No sooner did the traveller by land see me but his heart leaped for joy, and the wearisomnesse of his way seemed to go from him, because he knew he was in sight of the most goodly Cittie which he loved.

Dekker his Dreame (1620) (to which was prefixed a woodcut representing the poet asleep in bed) is a mixture of prose and verse, which opens with an apocalyptic vision of the end of all things and the last judgment, and describes the author's progress through the infernal regions. It reveals an intense and vivid consciousness of the guilt and peril of sin but is singularly devoid of the natural grace and distinction of another religious book, *Fowre Birds of Noahs Arke* (1609). This is a very remarkable collection of prayers, distinguished by a deep spirit of devotion, exquisite feeling and perfection of phrasing. There is probably no prayer book in the language from a single hand which can bear comparison with this for simplicity and beauty.

CHAPTER III

MIDDLETON AND ROWLEY

It is believed that Thomas Middleton was born in London about 1570; he died there, and was buried at Newington Butts on 4 July 1627. The known facts about his life are that he married a daughter of one of the six clerks in chancery, and had a son in 1604; that he was city chronologer from 1620 till the time of his death, when he was succeeded by Ben Jonson; that, in 1624, he was summoned before the privy council, with the actors who had played in his *Game at Chesse*, and, it appears, put in prison at the instigation of Gondomar, the Spanish ambassador; and that, in 1619, Ben Jonson spoke of him to Drummond of Hawthornden as 'a base fellow.' This hard saying may, after all, have been meant as no more than a literary criticism. The words are: 'that Markham (who added his English Arcadia) was not of the number of the Faithful, *i.e. Poets*, and but a base fellow. That such were Day and Middleton.' This might mean no more than that, to Jonson, Middleton's art or verse seemed 'base,' in the sense of pedestrian, or going on a low level. Nothing more was said about him by anyone of consequence, except a passing word from Scott, before the appearance, in 1808, of Lamb's *Specimens of English Dramatic Poets*. Lamb gave copious and carefully chosen extracts from his plays, and said almost all the essential things about him; Leigh Hunt followed, picking up the one grain left over by Lamb; and, in 1860, Dyce brought out a complete edition of the plays, which was re-edited and extended by Bullen in 1885.

Of William Rowley, there has never been any edition, and we know even less of him than of Middleton. It is conjectured that he was born about 1585 and died some time after 1637, the year of his marriage. He was an actor in various companies, and is supposed to have revised plays for new performances. For the most part, he collaborated with other playwrights, especially with Middleton; and the finest work of both Middleton and Rowley was done in this collaboration. Rowley's chief play, *Alls Lost by Lust,* has never been reprinted from the scarce original edition of 1633. Besides the plays, he published, in 1609, *A Search for Money; or, the Lamentable Complaint for the Loss of the Wandering Knight, Monsieur L'Argent,* a pamphlet in the manner of the time, full of crude realistic satire, written in his abrupt, lean and straightforward prose.

The earliest work attributed to Middleton is an endless composition in six-lined stanzas called *The Wisdom of Solomon Paraphrased,* published in 1597. The dedication to lord Devereux, and an address, wanting in some copies, 'To the Gentlemen-Readers,' are both signed Thomas Middleton, and we can but hope that it was someone else of the same name. Addressing critics as Momus and Zoilus, the writer regrets, not quite truthfully, 'I lack a scarecrow,' and bids them 'if you gape for stuffing, hie you to dead carrion carcases, and make them your ordinaries.' But no better fare is provided, and a sufficient scarecrow has been set up over this unploughed field by every subsequent editor. The task, if he really endured it, must have effectually cured Middleton of any further inclination for preaching. 'O weak capacity of strongest wit!' he laments, and with justice; yet, two years afterwards, he seems to have attempted satire with no less futility than sermonising. *Micro-cynicon. Sixe Snarling Satyres,* published in 1599, has been attributed to Middleton for no more certain reason than the signature 'T. M. Gent,' following the introductory *Defiance to Envy* with which the writer, in imitation of Hall, introduces his first and only book of satires. They are weakly imitated from Marston.

> My pen's two nebs shall turn into a fork,
> Chasing old Envy from so young a work,

the writer threatens; but the threat could not possibly have been needed. The 'snarling Muse' that 'now thundered rhyme' thus feebly must have been beyond the reach of envy, and has become too insignificant to need identification. But Middleton was an unequal writer, and it is impossible to regard even such bad work as this unlikely, because unworthy, to have been written by him.

His mark is much more distinctly to be traced in two pamphlets published in 1604, signed 'T. M.' in their epistles to the reader. The less interesting of these is *Father Hubburd's Tales,* which contains a good deal of indifferent verse, no better than Middleton's lyric verse usually is. Its main interest for us is in the very kindly and regretful praise of Nashe, whom he calls 'honest soul,' 'too slothful to thyself,' 'cut off in thy best blooming May':

> Drones eat thy honey: thou wast the true bee.

The tract is one of the allegorising satires of the time, written in a slow narrative style, with abundant detail of the manners and fashions censured, and a good deal of quite sober realism in the descriptions and incidents. *The Black Book* is more extravagant and more pungent, and is like a sample of the raw material, presented to us by the writer in his first self-conscious pose as moralist. He parades as one 'diving into the deep of this cunning age' and bringing to light 'the infectious bulks of craft, cozenage, and panderism, the three bloodhounds of a commonwealth.' He professes that his lively exposures are meant for the warning and confirming of the 'truly virtuous,' and commends himself for 'the modesty of my phrases, that even blush when they discover vices and unmask the world's shadowed villanies.' The tale is put into the mouth of Lucifer, who speaks his own prologue in a vigorous piece of blank verse and rime, by way of response to Nashe's dedication of *Pierce Penilesse* to 'the high and mightie Prince of darknesse, Donsell dell Lucifer, King of Acheron, Stix and Phlegeton, Duke of Tartary, Marquesse of Cocytus, and Lord high Regent of Lymbo.' The pamphlet is done in Nashe's manner, and shows a knowledge of its subject not inferior to Nashe's own. It describes what may possibly have been Nashe's actual deathbed, seen by 'the sullen blaze of a melancholy lamp that burnt very tragically upon the narrow desk of a half-bedstead, which descried all the pitiful ruins throughout the whole chamber.' It shows glimpses of 'your twelve tribes of villany,' engaged in much the same machinations as in the plays; and the devil, having gone to and fro in London, 'to gorge every vice full of poison,' sits down to make out his last will and testament, leaving legacies 'like ratsbane, to poison the realm,' in a catalogue of the more profitable of the vices. We see Middleton, for all his drawing of a moral, very interested and at home in the details of all that he denounces; preparing himself, deliberately or not, for his work as a writer of dramatic comedy.

It is quite possible that *The Mayor of Quinborough*, which was printed with Middleton's name in 1661, is the earliest play of his that we have; and quite possible that we have it only in a revised state. Such merit as there is in the play lies almost wholly in individual lines and passages, which stand out from a

confused and rather hideous mingling of tragic bombast and strained
farce. The dumb-show and choruses between the acts are not less
immature than the horrors in action by which we can imagine
Middleton to be trying to force himself to be tragic. No trace of
Rowley is to be seen anywhere in the play, least of all in the comic
scenes, which have distinct traces of the manner of Middleton.
The whole play seems to be the premature attempt of a man,
not naturally equipped for tragic or romantic writing, to do the
tragic comedy then in fashion; and this attempt was probably
continued in the plays, now lost, at which we know Middleton
was working in 1602: *Caesar's Fall*, with Munday, Drayton and
Webster; *The Two Harpies*, with the same and Dekker; and
The Chester Tragedy. In *Blurt Master-Constable*, which belongs
to the same year and is the first of his published plays, we see
him recovering himself after his false start, and setting off
spiritedly on the comedies of intrigue which were to form the
first division of his work. The prose has become alive, and swift
of foot; the dialogue slips easily from prose into verse and
back again; the action, and the unchastened tongues, gallop.
Middleton has found a theme and a technique; and to these he
will be almost wholly faithful for the long first half of his career,
the fifteen years of comedy.

That is, unless we are to believe, on the strength of a dubious
allusion, that Middleton, before writing *The Mayor of Quinborough*, wrote *The Old Law*, or part of it, and that Massinger
and Rowley, who would both have been too young to have collaborated with him at the time, added large portions later. Of
Massinger, though he may conceivably have revised it at a much
later date than that of its original production, there is no trace in
the play[1]; but of Rowley the traces are unmistakable, not so much
in the actual writing of the comic parts as in the whole conception
of the main scenes and characters. In a sense the play is the
preparation for *A Faire Quarrell* (1617), which both wrote
together; it seems to mark the beginning of the collaboration,
and of that new influence which came into Middleton's work with
Rowley. It is in these two plays that we find, for the first time,
that 'exquisiteness of moral sensibility' which Lamb divined in
the one, and that 'delicacy of perception in matters of right and
wrong' which he distinguished in the other.

From 1602, the date of *Blurt Master-Constable*, to 1617, the
date of *A Faire Quarrell*, almost the whole of Middleton's work

[1] Cf. *post*, chap. VI.

is in farcical comedy, at once realistic and satirical. It is to the
early part of this period that a play is generally attributed into
whose authorship no one would have troubled to enquire if it had
not been published as 'written by W. S.' *The Puritane* is still
printed among what are called the 'doubtful plays' of Shakespeare.
When Swinburne says that it is 'much more like Rowley's than
like Middleton's worst work' he is strictly correct; but he is not
to be taken to mean that Rowley wrote it. There is nothing
sufficiently individual in the play to give so much as a solid
starting-point for conjecture. Compare it with the worst of
Middleton's comedies, *The Famelie of Love*, and it will be found
that, in that tedious satire, there is at least some intention, though
it is now mainly lost to us; we have here the realist's attempt to
show up the dulness of dull people by making them speak and act
no more nimbly than was natural to them. The parody, apparently, is so close that we can mistake it for the original. But the
diction, though creeping, is not ignoble; it is like the fumbling of
a man on an instrument which he is on the way to master. The
fumbler of *The Puritane* will get no further[1].

In 1604, Middleton had some, but no very considerable, share
in *The Honest Whore* of Dekker, so far as his manner can be
traced there; and, seven years later, we find him collaborating
again with Dekker in *The Roaring Girle*, though here, also, what
is finest in the play seems to be Dekker's. Apart from these two
divergences, and an occasional masque or pageant, done to order,
Middleton's course is direct, and his main concern, as he defines it
later, in commending *The World tost at Tennis* to the reader and
understander, is to be 'neither too bitterly taxing, nor too soothingly
telling, the world's broad abuses.' In a prefatory address to the
'comic play-readers' of *The Roaring Girle*, he is still more
explicit.

'The fashion,' he says, 'of play-making I can properly compare to nothing so
naturally as the alteration in apparel; for in the time of the great crop-
doublet, your huge bombasted plays, quilted with mighty words to lean
purpose, was only then in fashion: and as the doublet fell, neater inventions
began to set up. Now, in the time of spruceness, our plays follow the
niceness of our garments; single plots, quaint conceits, lecherous jests, drest
up in hanging sleeves: and those are fit for the times and the termers.
Such a kind of light-colour summer stuff, mingled with divers colours,
you shall find this published comedy.'

The early comedy of Middleton is as light, rancid and entertaining as anything in Elizabethan drama. It is irresponsible

[1] As to *The Puritane*, cf. *ante*, vol. v, chap. x.

rather than immoral, and does not exactly recommend, or approve of, the trickeries and debaucheries which it represents in a life-like way, under improbable conditions. Yet the writer is no more careful of his ethical than of his other probabilities, and takes little trouble to keep up any consistency in the minds or morals of his agile puppets. His aim is at effect, and he rarely fails in his aim. Even when we do not believe in the persons, and do not care about the upshot of the action, we are almost constantly enlivened, and, willingly or unwillingly, carried along.

The main material of his comedy is in the acts and moods of the human animal. The idea of sex dominates the whole Eliza-bethan drama; here, however, it is not a terror, a fascination, or a sin, but an occupation. A passage in *The Phoenix* might be applied to almost any of these plays:

> What monstrous days are these!
> Not only to be vicious most men study,
> But in it to be ugly; strive to exceed
> Each other in the most deformed deed.

Is it a merit in Middleton that he shows us vice always as an ugly thing, even when he seems to take pleasure in it, and to forget to condemn it? The 'beggarly fools and swarming knaves,' to use a phrase of his own, who traffic in souls, bodies and possessions throughout the travesties, confusions and 'familiar accidents which happen in town,' are set agog by no moralist, but by so keen and unprejudiced an observer of the human comedy that, for the most part, they come out in their naked colours, almost against his intention. And, as he lets vice peep through all cloaks and stand self-condemned, so he shows us a certain hardly conscious 'soul of goodness in things evil.' There is true and good human feeling in some of the most shameless scenes of *Your five Gallants,* where a whole lost and despised world of 'strange devils and pretty damnable affections' is stirred up into plausible action. They take place where there is 'violet air, curious garden, quaint walks, fantastical arbours, three back-doors, and a coach-gate,' in a 'music-school' or Maison Tellier of the period, and the very names of the characters are hardly quotable. The humanity is accidental, and comes from absolute knowledge of a world where 'every part shoots up daily into new subtlety; the very spider weaves her cauls with more art and cunning to entrap the fly.' Middleton, though the spider preoccupies him, and lends him a web for spinning, puts the fly, too, into the pattern.

If we seek a reason for the almost universal choice of brothels and taverns as favourite scenes of Elizabethan comedy, we shall find it partly in a theory, taken over from Latin and Italian drama, that this was the proper province of the comic muse. The accidents of a player's or professional writer's life gave opportunities for knowledge of just that world into which he was naturally thrust. The Elizabethan audience was accustomed from the first to the two extremes of noble tragedy and brutal comedy. This violent contrast appealed to a taste always hungering and thirsting for strong meat and strong drink. Puritan limits had not yet fixed themselves; they were but divined as a thing one could be aware of and mock at. At the same time, the stage was not exactly respected; it had no character to keep up. Thus, the dramatist, being as free as a modern French caricaturist to make his appeal in the most direct way, to the animal through the animal, had no hesitation in using the gross material at hand grossly. In the more serious dramatists, we get no more than painful attempts to please a taste which Middleton must have found it easy to gratify. He was no dreamer; he was not a poet in the instinctive irrepressible sense in which Dekker, for instance, was a poet; and he shared a love which was common to Dekker and to others at that time, for mean adventures of loose people in cities, knaves who gulled and fools who were gulled, sharpers and, outside cities, highwaymen and gipsies. His eyes were open to every folly of fashion or freak of religion; he knew his law and his lawyers, and he saw their capabilities for entertainment; he had all the terms of astrological and other cant at his fingers' ends, and realised the savour of the oddities of popular speech. It was easy for him to set these people talking as they would really talk, or with just that heightening which his sense of pungent and appropriate words gave him; and he could set scene after scene galloping across the stage, without taking more trouble than his public demanded as to making his plots consistent or probable, so long as they went at full speed along familiar ways; not caring, most of the time, to create individual characters, but relying upon the effect of vividly realised moods, of people very much alive for a given moment. A character so ripely developed as Sir Bounteous Progress in *A Mad World, My Masters* is rare among these nimble types and instances of fixed follies or ascertained 'humours.'

We remember Middleton's comedies, not for their separate characters, but for their brace of gallants, their 'school' of wantons, their clash of cozener with cozener, their ingenuities of deceit, the 'heat of fury' of their entangled action. We remember single scenes, of a marvellous and sometimes cruelly comic reality, like the deathbed of Dampit the drunkard in *A Trick to catch the Old-one*, or that other death scene in *A Chast Mayd in Cheape-side*, where an old sinner makes his exit in grotesque and frightened repentance, while the man and woman whom he may be supposed to have most wronged remember the fact for the first time, as they foresee the stopping of their shameful revenue. Here, as often in Middleton, irony comes out of the mere faithfulness with which he sets before us exactly what would happen at such a moment. His plays are full of these paradoxes of event, which it is the custom to call unpleasant—and which, sometimes, certainly are unpleasant, when the playwright seems to be unaware that some hideous piece of villainy is being set to rights (so far as relative justice is concerned) by a trick of ' virtue ' hardly less pardonable.

If Bullen is right in his conjecture that *The Widdow* (a play published in 1652 as a 'lively piece, drawn by the art of Jonson, Fletcher, and Middleton') belongs to about this date, though revised later, it would seem to be curiously innocent, for a play by Middleton, notwithstanding all its vivid banter and thieves' foolery. In how many plays of this period could the characters say to one another at the close, without irony, 'Be good' and 'Be honest,' as two of the characters do in this? Jonson is for nothing in it, unless as a passing influence; but it is hard to see why Fletcher might not have been the reviser, as well as the writer of one or two of the songs. But the main part, unmistakably, is Middleton's, and it is, perhaps, in this play that the romantic element first shows itself among the incidents and actualities of knavery.

It took Middleton a long time to recognise, as a dramatist, that there was such a thing as honour, even in transactions which he felt it his business to watch from the knaves' point of view because that view was the one which would best entertain his audience. He chose stories, persons and surroundings for their immediate stage effect, making them as real and amusing as he could, scene by scene; and it was so rarely that it occurred to him to temper the trick-eries of his plots by some honest motive that we find him confusing moral values without due indication of his being aware of it. There is no doubt that he wrote hastily, and with ease, and a man who writes hastily and with ease for the stage will readily sacrifice a point of conscience to a theatrical solution. Once, in *The Roaring Girle*, some frank and convincing honesty comes into the bad company, and has the best of it there. But how much of what gives a pleasant quality to that play is Middleton's, though the play is not less astir than the others with his usual crew and company?

Though the work of each overlaps occasionally, there can be little doubt of the main shares of Middleton and Dekker in *The Roaring Girle*[1]. It was Dekker, undoubtedly, who created, and mainly set in action, the good honest hoyden who masquerades through the play in the name of Moll Cutpurse—a creature of another colour, if we can believe contemporary records. 'Worse things I must needs confess,' says Middleton in his preface 'To the Comic Play-Readers,' 'the world has taxed her for than has been written of her; but 'tis the excellency of a writer to leave things better than they are.' To paint a woman who asks justly,

> must you have
> A black ill name, because ill things you know?

and to show her talking thieves' slang among thieves with an easy familiarity, and yet going through this evil company like a knight-errant, helping honest lovers and putting down knaves, was a task more within the power of Dekker than of Middleton, whose metre and manner come and go with the gallipots and rattling roguish shopkeepers who cry their wares and carry on their complicated private doings through the whole underplot of the play. But little of the really significant speech of Moll can be attributed to Middleton, and, though much of the business and movement of the play is his, and much of the 'manners,' Dekker, too, is responsible for the fifth act with its almost too liberal local colour of 'canting.' The play is untidy, but very much alive; and Dekker seems to bring fresh air into musty rooms, not only by the presence of this vital woman, not to be paralleled elsewhere in his associate's comedies, but by a way of writing which is more a poet's way than Middleton's. The very sound of the lines has a lilt and spring in them, as in a casual image of this kind:

> my thoughts must run,
> As a horse runs that's blind round in a mill,
> Out every step, yet keeping one path still.

Middleton's verse, for all its sinews, could not have given just that turn to a line; and Dekker brings with him that beauty which was always a natural accident in his speech.

The prose of Middleton, as we see it in the comedies, where it is employed more largely than verse, but drops easily into and out of verse, is a pungent, fluent, very natural and speakable prose.

---

[1] For the view, according to which the larger part of this play was Middleton's, see *ante*, chap. II.

It has lightness and yet is not empty, is often witty without going unduly beyond the probabilities of talk ; only at times, as in *The Famelie of Love*, does it become pedantic ; and it rarely loses a certain deftness even when it drops into coarseness. Touches of the edged speech of the period, which shines and strikes, are not wanting. 'Bright Helena of this house, would thy Troy were a-fire, for I am a-cold,' says someone, on no particular occasion. The prose goes at a great rate, and carries you with it, while you travel slowly with Rowley, whenever he takes Middleton's place. And the verse is hardly less swift, galloping often on more feet than the measure demands, but rarely jarring the measure. In some of the plays, Middleton takes no care to modulate from prose into verse, but jumps forward and backward with little need, barely lifting the verse above the measure of the prose. Gradually, the quality and adaptability of the verse improve ; developing directly out of the prose, it becomes not less flexible. And we find him cultivating with increasing skill what had always been a homely colloquial tendency, dealing in culinary and haber-dashery similes, more at home with a dish or dress than with the moon, and able to set dumb things into gesture, thus :

> Troth, you speak wondrous well for your old house here;
> 'Twill shortly fall down at your feet to thank you,
> Or stoop, when you go to bed, like a good child,
> To ask your blessing.

Verse, to Middleton, is a native idiom ; he speaks in it naturally, bending it as he pleases, to any shade of meaning, filling it with stuff alien to poetry and yet keeping its good metre. He does not write for the sake of the verse, and only a native honesty of ear keeps him from dropping clean out of it, without knowing, into prose. Thus, he has few fine passages ; yet a few of them he has, where imagination has fastened upon him, and dictated his words. His lines run often, in his later work, to fourteen syllables, yet their feet slide easily within the measure. As he lets his lines grow longer, so he allows himself longer speeches, because he knows that he can keep the ear awake and following them. And, by the time of *The Changeling*, the versification has become graver, with a new thrill in it, through which passion, and not only the mind's energies, can now speak. Was it Rowley who first showed Middleton the possibility of that passionate note, by which drama becomes not only drama but poetry?

If, as has been conjectured, *The Old Law* leads the way from the farcical comedies to the tragic comedies like *A Faire Quarrell*, it is in that play that the influence of William Rowley may be first distinguished ; and it is impossible not to connect it with the change which came about in the work of Middleton, a change from work almost wholly comic, and of the city kind, to work partly tragic and partly comic in a higher and more romantic sense. We find Rowley's name beside Middleton's on the title-pages of *The Old Law, A Faire Quarrell, The World tost at Tennis, The Spanish Gipsie* and *The Changeling* : most, that is, of the finest of Middleton's later work, with only the two exceptions of *Women beware Women* and *A Game at Chesse*. The manner and measure of this collaboration is not so easy to discover as may at first sight appear. It is his faults that are most obvious in Rowley, his dissonant verse, his over-strained speech, his incapacity for construction, something jagged and uneven in his whole work ; and it is only gradually that critics are beginning to realise that these defects are not the essential part of him. His plays have had the not unnatural misfortune to be chaotically printed ; verse and prose never clearly distinguished from one another ; and some of them are only to be found in a few rare copies of the original editions. It is difficult to be certain of his exact share in many plays to which, rightly or wrongly, his name is appended. One thing is certain : that the plays written by Rowley and Middleton together are finer than any of the plays written by either separately. And it is almost equally certain that Rowley's share in the work was not confined to those scenes or passages in which his actual hand can be distinguished in the versification, but that there was a further and closer collaboration of a kind which no tests of style or versification can ever disentangle. We have seen Middleton working alone, and, to some extent, with Dekker; we shall see him, at the end of his career, again working alone. We have now to consider what is discoverable about Rowley, in such work as he did by himself or in company with others, before we can hope to arrive at any conclusion in regard to the work in which he is the companion of Middleton.

The plays published under Rowley's name or initials are : *A new Wonder, A Woman never vext*, 1632 ; *Alls Lost by Lust*, 1633 ; *A Match at Midnight*, 1633 ; and *A Shoo-maker a Gentleman*, 1638. Of these, *A Match at Midnight* has little resemblance to any of his known work, while it has a close resemblance to the early work of Middleton. It goes with something of the rapidity of the wild and whirling comedies of about the time of *Your five Gallants*, but would add more credit to an imitator than to Middleton. Here, as elsewhere, Rowley, in his capacity of actor, may have made slight changes for acting purposes, which would account for the use of his initials. There is no reason for supposing that he had even so much as that to do with *Fortune by Land and Sea*, published, in 1655, as by Heywood and Rowley, or with *The Thracian Wonder*, attributed to Webster and Rowley by Kirkman in 1661. There is little more probability in the same publisher's attribution to the same writers of *A Cure for a Cuckold*, which he brought out in the same year. Kirkman's word is valueless as evidence, and there is nothing in the play of which we can say with much probability that it is by either Webster or Rowley. Only the slow and thoughtful quality of some of the verse gives any real suggestion of Webster ; and verse of Webster's kind is quite possible to imitate. The drearily comic prose is done after the pattern of the time, and there is nothing in it distinguishable from similar hackwork, whether done by Rowley or by others for the day's wage[1].

In *The Travailes of The three English Brothers*, published in 1607, with a dedication signed 'John Day, William Rowley, George Wilkins,' it is easy, but not very profitable, to trace the share of Rowley. He probably put in Zaripha, the Shylock of the play, and wrote some of the more pompous blank verse and of the coarser verbal fooling. In *The Maid in the Mill*, licensed to Fletcher and Rowley on 29 August 1623, and played at the Globe with Rowley as one of the actors, his share and Fletcher's are quite distinct, and they are divided pretty equally. Rowley's verse, by the side of the winged verse of Fletcher, seems somewhat crabbed and abstract, and the prose (interspersed with Fletcher's songs) somewhat cold and laboured. In *The Witch of Edmonton*, published in 1658 as 'a Tragi-Comedy By divers well-esteemed Poets ; William Rowley, Thomas Dekker, John Ford, etc.,' where Dekker and Ford are both equally evident, in their direction of the two main currents, the share of Rowley is difficult to make out, and could hardly have been considerable. There remains *The Birth of Merlin*, which was published in 1662 as by Shakespeare and Rowley. Langbaine tells us that ' William Rowley was not only beloved by those great men, Shakespeare, Fletcher, and Jonson, but likewise writ, with the former, *The Birth of Merlin*.' The share of Shakespeare need not be discussed here; the play is crude and lumpish; it is stilted and monotonous in the verse, gross

---

[1] Cf., as to the indications of a cooperation by Webster in this play, *post*, chap. VII.

and tame in the prose. It would be pleasant to think that Rowley
had no more to do with it than Shakespeare; but it is difficult to
be positive in the matter after reading *A Shoo-maker a Gentleman*[1].

This incongruous and incoherent piece is a tragic farce, which
has never been reprinted from the execrable first edition of 1638[2],
where the printer, in his address to 'the honest and high-spirited
gentlemen of the never decaying art, called the gentle craft,'
admits with some candour: 'I know it may come short of that
accurateness both in plot and style that this witty age doth with
greater curiosity require'; yet excuses it, on the ground 'that as
plays were then, some twenty years ago, it was in the fashion.'
It is a sad jumble of cobblers, kings, 'a wise virgin in Wales' and
a Juliet's nurse; at one moment, 'an angel ascends out of the
well and after descends again,' at another, there is drinking of
blood, and we hear in detail of tortures endured in war; the
language varies from 'Moulting tyrant, stop thy scandalous
breath,' used by quarrelling kings, to 'Clapperdudgeon' and
'Knipperdolin,' flung as pet names by the cobbler at his wife.
The few good lines which we come across at rare intervals are
almost cruelly wasted; the farce which submerges them is a mere
desperate attempt at comic realism.

On the title-page of *A new Wonder*, Rowley is described as
'one of his Majesties Servants'; he is mentioned among the
principal actors in *The Maid in the Mill*; in *The Inner-Temple
Masque*, he played Plumporridge; and, in the list of persons in
Alls Lost by Lust, we are told that Jaques, 'a simple clownish
gentleman,' was 'personated by the poet.' In the plays which he
wrote in collaboration with Middleton, his hand has been most
generally traced in the comic underplots, and, sometimes, as a dis-
turbing element there, working for hardly more than the ears of
the groundlings. In the low peasants' humour, earthy and almost
animal, over which he takes much trouble in all these plays, sometimes making it really droll, always making it emphatic and
telling, there seems to have been something which he really cared
to do, perhaps because it was what he could represent best on the
stage. In the two chief plays which he wrote by himself, he
wove comic prose not ineffectively into more serious substance;
but in *A Shoo-maker a Gentleman*, and, indeed, in most of the
work done with Middleton, it stands out in sharp contrast. And

[1] As to *The Birth of Merlin* and its relation to Middleton's *The Mayor of Quinborough*, see *ante*, vol. v, chap. x.

[2] [An edition has been published since the above was written. See, *post*, p. 429,
under Stork, C. W.]

this is the more curious, as we shall find unmistakable signs of a very different kind of influence exercised by him upon precisely that serious substance.

For it is not as a comic poet that Rowley is most himself, or most admirable. Of his two remaining plays, one is a heroic tragedy and the other a pathetic domestic comedy; and we find in both, very differently exhibited, the same qualities of sincerity and nobility, often turning to uncouthness or exaggeration, but never, as in Middleton, losing the moral sense, the honesty of insight. The action in each is strained beyond probability, and in one becomes barbarous, in the other artificial; the verse follows the action, and halts not only through the treasons of a more than usually treacherous printer. Yet, as the verse is but an emphasis upon profoundly felt speech, so the action rests always on a strong human foundation.

In *Alls Lost by Lust* (which deals with a subject made more famous by Landor in *Count Julian*), Rowley shows himself a poet by his comprehension of great passions, his sympathy with high moods, and by a sheer and naked speech, which can grasp filth or heroism with equal strength. He has no measure, though sometimes constraint; no subtlety, though he will set consciences or clowns arguing in terms of strange pedantry; no sentiment, though he has all the violences of direct emotion; and he says what he wants to say and then stops. He has no ease or grace, and often labours to give point to his humour and weight to his serious utterances. The kind of verse that characterises him at his best is

> Thy soul is a hired lackey towards hell,

and he can sharpen it thus :

> Time's ancient bawd, opportunity,
> Attends us now, and yet our flaming blood
> Will scarce give leave to opportunity.

Often he will go beyond the bounds of natural speech, not on a carrying imagination, but under the dragging weight of an emphasis which eloquence can do better without. In some of Blake's drawings of naked men with prodigious muscles, sweeping beards and frantic eyes, the intense imitation of emotion has gone further than nature can support. Just so does some of the tragic speech in Rowley falter through defects of mere force. 'Rough Rowley, handling song with Esau's hand,' as Swinburne has called him in a significant line, sets himself to construct imagery, and does it, sometimes with splendour, but a splendour prolonged to extinction. Thus, he will develop a figure after this manner :

> We'll make so high to quench their silver moons
> And on their carcases an isthmus make
> To pass their straits again and forage them.

Both in fun and in earnest, he plays on words, and is capable of writing 'My heart's triangled,' as Donne might have done, and of distinguishing the number and position of the points. More often he does it in this wholly Elizabethan manner :

> My honoured friends,
> What we all thought to have borne home in triumph
> Must now be seen there in a funeral,
> Wrecked honour being chief mourner; here's the hearse
> Which we'll all follow.

Even his 'virgin martyrs,' like Jacinta, who act nobly, are sometimes set talking with horrible detail, as, like Jacinta, they spit at their tormentors and wish

> that my tongue
> Were pointed with a fiery Pyramis
> To strike thee through.

It is impossible for him to realise, even in his Dionysia, who dies with some of the ecstasy of Shakespeare's Cleopatra, that a woman can be lascivious without talking like a courtesan. His men can say memorable things, in which there is some of the passion of meditation; but, however well he knew 'what kind of thing a man's heart' is, he did not know how to give continuously adequate speech to those passions of whose habitation there he was aware.

In *A new Wonder*, of which the scene lies in London, and which shows us the strange vehement passions, both petty and ardent, of business men, their small prides and large resolutions, we have a speech more easily on the level of the occasion, whether in this heightened way :

> Then be not angry, gentle sir,
> If now a string be touch'd, which hath too long
> Sounded so harshly over all the city;
> I now would wind it to a musical height;

or whether the unrelenting father in prison repels his son with the direct cry :

> Ha! what art thou? Call for the keeper there,
> And thrust him out of doors, or lock me up.

Here, as elsewhere, the language is sometimes injured by emphasis, yet there is nothing of Middleton's aim at point and cleverness, but a speech vividly, and sometimes grossly, natural, which sticks close to the matter. Its comedy is a kind of literalness, and so is its pathos; both are crammed with fine substance, thoughtful humour and thoughtful pity, with that simple acceptance and rendering of things as they are which Lamb noted in the play with much satisfaction. It is of this play that he says: 'The old play-writers are distinguished by an honest boldness of exhibition, they show everything without being ashamed.' Here, there is coarseness and there is clumsiness, but there is no flaw in the essential truthfulness and reality of the contest in hearts, in which a natural human charity has its way with invincible softness.

Now, if we begin to look for the influence of Rowley upon Middleton, we shall find it not so much in the set scenes of low comedy which he inserted among Middleton's verse, as in a new capacity for the rendering of great passions and a loftiness in good and evil which is not to be recognised as an element in Middleton's brilliant and showy genius, and which hardly survives the end of his collaboration with Rowley. The whole range of subject suddenly lifts; a new, more real and more romantic world (more real and more romantic because imagination, rather than memory, is at work) is seen upon the stage; and, by some transformation which could hardly have been mere natural growth, Middleton finds himself to be a poet.

That Middleton learnt from Rowley, or did, with his help, more than either of them could do by himself, is evident for the first time clearly in *A Faire Quarrell*. The best part of the actual writing is not Rowley's. Middleton was a man of flexible mind, and we find in him everywhere a marvellous tact of matching his matter and manner. Never, in his wild comedies, does he bring in false heroics; he can keep on a due actual level beyond any dramatist of his time; and, when a great human moment comes to him, and has to be dealt with, he rises easily, and is no less adequate. He does not rise of himself—his material compels him, he is obedient to it, and, as it would seem, awake to a fiercer impulse like Rowley's. It is certain that Rowley could not have written the two great captain Ager scenes as they stand; but it is equally certain that, with all his promptness of response to an emotion, Middleton could not have begun to render, at such a moral height, such an 'absolute man,' without some spiritual aid or lift from Rowley. When there, when started, he drew his poetry, as he was wont to do, directly from his subject, and the natural emotion of it ; and made a great scene where a weak one would have been contemptible. Can nature and poetry go further together, poetry hardly distinguishable from the direct speech of nature, so warmed is it by human breath ? Captain Ager's last words to his mother shine like fire and cut like steel, and are mere plain words with no more rhetoric in them than in this line, which strikes straight :

> I never shall have need of honour more.

In the scene of the duel, when all this fire in the man's soul is out, the tamer verses are not less absolute in their disheartened speech :

> What shall be done in such a worthless business
> But to be sorry, and to be forgiven;
> You, sir, to bring repentance, and I pardon?

That the writing, in the two great scenes of captain Ager, is Middleton's, and owes nothing in form, whatever it may owe in substance, to Rowley, can be proved beyond doubt by a mere reading over together of two speeches, one in this play, one in a play so wholly and characteristically Middleton's as *A Chast Mayd in Cheape-side*—the speech of captain Ager, which begins

> Mine? think me not so miserable,

and ends

> Without which I'm ten fathoms under coward,
> That now am ten degrees above a man,
> Which is but one of virtue's easiest wonders[1];

and the speech of Sir Walter which begins

> O death! is this
> A place for you to weep?

and ends

> this shows like
> The fruitless sorrow of a careless mother,
> That brings her son with dalliance to the gallows,
> And then stands by and weeps to see him suffer[2].

The difference is all in the feeling ; there is none in the phrasing.

But the difference in the feeling ! There is no indication, in anything which Middleton has so far written by himself, that he was capable of conceiving a character like captain Ager, or of keeping such a character on a single level of high emotion. This Rowley could do, and it can scarcely be doubted that he was the 'only begetter' of what he left to Middleton to develop. It is Rowley who writes the dedication, and it is evident that he takes much of

[1] Act II, sc. 1.   [2] Act v, sc. 1.

the credit of the play to himself. 'You see, sir,' he says, 'I write as I speak, and I speak as I am, and that's excuse enough for me.' His share in the actual writing, indeed, is almost too evident; there is cold, pedantic, sour and crabbed prose, aping comedy, and, in the scene between Jane and the physician, a hard, reasoning kind of serious verse which jars singularly on the rich and copious verse of Middleton, in the finer parts of the play. Some of the worst of the mechanical fooling in prose was added in a second edition, and (the public being much the same in all ages) it was probably added because the original sample had given much satisfaction. Rowley worked for hire, and this is some of his hired work.

It was not long after the time of *A Faire Quarrell* that Middleton and Rowley collaborated together in the admirable and entertaining masque, *The World tost at Tennis.* For the most part, Middleton's masques are tame and tedious, without originality in the invention of lyrical quality in the songs. In one only, *The Inner-Temple Masque,* is there any natural gaiety, any real quaintness or humour; and, as we find Rowley's name among the actors, in the humorous peasant part of Plumporridge, may it not be conjectured that he had some share in the writing? His heavy tread is as distinctly heard through all the opening part of *The World tost at Tennis,* as Middleton's new voice is heard in the later part. Middleton rarely wrote a lovelier succession of cadences than in these lines spoken by Deceit to Simplicity :

> The world, sweetheart, is full of cares and troubles,
> No match for thee; thou art a tender thing,
> A harmless, quiet thing, a gentle fool,
> Fit for the fellowship of ewes and rams;
> Go, take thine ease and pipe; give me the burden,
> The clog, the torment, the heart-break, the world:
> Here's for thee, lamb, a dainty oaten pipe.

And there is suavity, swiftness and a quaint fantastic colouring in the verse chattered against hypocrites and puritans by the Five Starches.

It was probably about the time when he was engaged on his masques that Middleton wrote *The Witch*; and this may well have been his first attempt at a purely romantic play. The versification is done with astonishing ease, in long, loose, rapid lines ; and, in the witches' songs, there is not only a ghastly fancy awake, but something nearer to a fine lyric cadence than he ever caught before or since. It is through the interpolation, as it obviously was, of some of these lines in the very imperfect text of *Macbeth,* that a play in which the main action is almost a parody of the romantic drama has come to be looked upon as one of Middleton's chief works. The mere writing throughout is good; but the easy eloquent dialogue covers no more than the gaps and deformations of the main outline. The witches bring a new element into Middleton's work, a wild fancy, of which he had shown hardly a trace; in the rest of the play, he does but practise in the romantic manner. They stand in dim middle air, between the old vile pitiable crone of Dekker in *The Witch of Edmonton*, who is dreadfully human, and the 'crowned empress of the nether clefts of hell' in *Macbeth*, who bears no resemblance to the other Hecate but in her name, and who is more dreadful because she is not human. But Lamb has said finally all that need be said on these fundamental differences.

After the experiment of *The Witch*, Middleton seems to have returned to his collaboration with Rowley, and it is to this period that we must assign the play by which both are now chiefly remembered, the tragedy called *The Changeling*. It is Rowley who begins the play, and thus introduces and characterises both Beatrice and De Flores. The germ of both is there, and the rest of the play is but its growth. But, even in this opening, there are distinct, though slight, traces of Middleton, as if collaboration had begun already. Middleton takes up the thread in the second act, and has both hands upon it in the third, though, at the end of the great scene, Rowley seems to snatch the whole web out of his hands and to twist it into an abrupt end. In all this part, mainly written by Middleton, there is a restraint never paralleled elsewhere in his work; nowhere else are words used with such fruitful frugality, or so much said in so little. And this bareness, this fierce reticence, lead up, with a stealthy directness, to that outbreak of evil joy when De Flores cries

> O this act
> Has put me into spirit!

and the modest murderess answers in astonishment

> Why, tis impossible thou canst be so wicked,
> Or shelter such a cunning cruelty
> To make his death the murderer of my honour!

The whole scene is written in words of white heat; Middleton has distilled into it the essence of his own genius and of the genius of Rowley; in Leigh Hunt's famous and revealing words concerning De Flores, it is 'at once tragical, probable, and poetical' beyond almost any single scene in the Elizabethan drama—a scene unlike anything in Shakespeare, but comparable, not as poetry but as drama, with Shakespeare. And it is on the level of this great scene that the play ends, in a splendid horror, and it is Rowley who ends as he began the dreadful lives of De Flores and of Beatrice. Rowley's underplot and some of Middleton's intermediate action do what they can to deform a play which, but for them, would be a noble and complete masterpiece. Yet the single impression left upon our minds is scarcely affected by them. The play is De Flores, and De Flores seems to grow greater as he passes from one to the other of the two playwrights, as they collaborate visibly at his creation. This great creation is the final result and justification of Middleton and Rowley's work in common; for it is certain that De Flores as he is would never have been possible either to Rowley or to Middleton alone.

The Spanish Gipsie is generally put down almost as a whole to Middleton, and even Swinburne refuses to see the hand of Rowley in 'the more high-toned passages.' It seems possible that Rowley wrote a larger part of the play than Middleton, and not by any means only the gipsy scenes, with their jollity, dancing and crabbed ballad singing. The opening, no doubt, was actually written by Middleton; but it has a quality unusual in his work, and not unusual in the work of Rowley. It is as if Rowley stood behind Middleton, controlling him. Most of the prose, both when it goes creeping and tedious with Sancho and Soto, and when it overflows into doggerel and occasionally unsavoury snatches of song, has Rowley's manner and substance; but he is to be traced, also, in the slow and powerful verse which ends the third act, in lines like

> This is the triumph of a soul drowned deep
> In the unfathomed seas of matchless sorrow,

and in the whole attitude and speech of a father who speaks with the very accent of Julianus in *Alls Lost by Lust* :

> Teach me how I may now be just and cruel,
> For henceforth I am childless.

Rowley is heard, also, through much of the fourth act, though Middleton comes in unmistakably towards the end, and is the writer of the whole fifth act. The characters are distributed between them, and so charming a person as Constanza is decidedly at her best when she speaks through Middleton. The whole play is not made very probable, or meant to be so; it is a frank romance, with stage mysteries, some of them thrilling, like the wonderful opening scene, some, mere tricks of convenience; and there is a freshness and pleasantness about it which seem to show us Middleton in full and final acceptance of the romantic manner.

Yet it is difficult to assign to any other period the comedy of *Any Thing for a Quiet Life*, printed in 1662, and so badly printed that it is not easy to distinguish prose from verse, the more so as the one seems to be set to run in no very different measures from the other. It seems to be a late and only return to the earlier manner of the farcical comedies of city life, with shopkeeping scenes of the old random brilliance and the old domestic fooleries. Even more matter is crammed into it, and this even more hastily, and there is the old fierce vigour of talk. But, in two plays, published together in 1657, we see what seems to be almost the last mood of Middleton, after his collaboration with Rowley was at an end, and the influence, perhaps, not wholly evaporated. *More dissemblers besides Women*, which is characteristic of Middleton in its tangle of virtues and hypocrisies, its masquerade of serious meanings and humorous disguises, is written in verse of a lovely and eager quality, which bends with equal flexibility to the doings of ' those dear gipsies' and to the good cardinal's concerns of conscience ' in a creature that's so doubtful as a woman.' It is a particoloured thing, and has both beauty and oddity. But, in *Women beware Women*, we find much of Middleton's finest and ripest work, together with his most rancid ' comic relief'; a stern and pitiless ' criticism of life' is interrupted by foul and foolish clowning; and a tragedy of the finest comic savour ends in a mere heap of corpses, where

> vengeance met vengeance
> Like a set match, as if the plagues of sin
> Had been agreed to meet here all together.

' I've lost myself in this quite,' Middleton might say with the duke, and rarely has better material been more callously left to spoil. There is no finer comedy of its kind in the whole of Elizabethan drama than the scene between Livia, Bianca and the widow; and the kind is a rare, bitter and partly tragic one. The human casuistry is flawless; the irony is an illumination rather than a correction of reality. And these vile people are alive, and the vices in them work with a bewildering and convincing certainty. The technique of such scenes as that in which husband and wife flaunt their new finery at each other is not less than astonishing. All the meaner passions are seen in probable action, speaking without emphasis, in a language never too far from daily speech for the complete illusion of reality. There is not even the interruption of a mere splendour; no one speaks greatly or utters irrelevant poetry ; here, poetry is the very slave and confidant of drama, heroically obedient. But the heights of *The Changeling*, the nobility of even what was evil in the passions of that play, are no longer attained. Middleton, left to himself, has returned, with new experience and new capacity, to his own level.

With one more experiment, and this a masterpiece of a wholly new kind, 'the only work of English poetry,' says Swinburne, 'which may properly be called Aristophanic,' the career of Middleton comes, so far as we know, to an end. *A Game at Chesse* is a satire, taking the popular side against Spain, and it was the Spanish ambassador Gondomar, the 'Machiavel-politician' and Black Knight of its chess-board, who caused the suppression of the play, and the punishment of all concerned in it. It is the most perfect of Middleton's works, and it carries some of his most intimate qualities to a point they had not reached before. Banter turns into a quite serious and clear and bitter satire ; burlesque becomes a severe and elegant thing ; the verse, beginning formally and always kept well within bounds, is fitted with supreme technical skill to this new, outlandish matter ; there are straight confessions of sins and symbolic feasts of vices, in which a manner acquired by the city chronologer for numbering the feasts and fastings of the city is adapted by him to finer use. We learn now how

> fat cathedral bodies
> Have very often but lean little soul,

and the imagery, already expressive, takes on a new colour of solemn mockery.

> From this leviathan-scandal that lies rolling
> Upon the crystal waters of devotion,

is sometimes the language of the Black Knight, and sometimes

> In the most fortunate angle of the world
> The court hath held the city by the horns
> Whilst I have milked her.

Technique, in drama and verse alike, never flags ; and the play is a satire and criticism, no longer of city manners or of personal vices, but of the nation's policy ; and that it was accepted as such, by the public and by the government of the time, is proved by the fifteen hundred pounds taken by the actors in nine days, and by the arrest of Middleton for what was really a form of patriotism.

We have no record of anything written by Middleton during the three remaining years of his life. *A Game at Chesse* is the culmination of those qualities which seem to have been most natural and instinctive in him, in spite of the splendid work of another kind which he did with Rowley in *The Changeling.* His genius was varied and copious, and he showed his capacity to do almost every kind of dramatic work with immense vigour. Life is never long absent from the tangled scenes, in which a heterogeneous crowd hurries by, not stopping long enough to make us familiar with most of the persons in it, but giving us an unmistakable human savour. Few of the plays are quite satisfactory all through ; there is almost always some considerable flaw, in construction, in characterisation, or in aesthetic taste ; yet hardly one of them can be neglected in our consideration of the dramatist's work as a whole. In single scenes of tragedy and of comedy (romantic comedy, the comedy of manners, farce and satire) he can hold his own against any contemporary, and it is only in lyric verse that he is never successful. He became a remarkable dramatic poet; but he was not born to sing. Poetry came to him slowly, and he had to disentangle it from more active growths of comic energy. It came to him when he began to realise that there was something in the world besides cheating shopkeepers and cozening lawyers, and the bargains made between men and women for bodies, not souls. With the heightening of emotion his style heightens, and as his comedy refines itself his verse becomes subtler. In Middleton's work, the cry of De Flores

> Ha! what art thou that tak'st away the light
> Betwixt that star and me? I dread thee not:
> 'Twas but a mist of conscience ;

is almost unique in imagination. And it is drama even more than it is poetry. His style is the most plausible of all styles in poetry, and it has a probable beauty, giving an easy grace of form to whatever asks to be expressed. It rarely steps aside to pick up a jewel, nor do jewels drop naturally out of its mouth.

CHAPTER IV

THOMAS HEYWOOD

IT is in writers of the second rank—and of these, with his abundant merit and attractive idiosyncrasy, Thomas Heywood unmistakably was—that we find it easiest to study the progress and expansion of the form of art practised by them. In the brief but often interesting addresses prefixed by Heywood to his plays, he was fond of referring to the changes in public taste which playwrights had been called upon to consult in the course of his own long experience; but he seems to care little about indicating his own preference for either old style or new, being manifestly as ready to fall in with the latter as he had been to put forth his best endeavours in the former. When commending to favour a drama depending for its effect entirely on character, situations and dialogue, and introducing

> No Drum, nor Trumpet, nor Dumbe show,
> No Combate, Marriage, not so much Today
> As Song, Dance, Masque, to bumbaste out our Play—

he hastens to add:

> Yet these all good, and still in frequent use
> With our best Poets[1].

And, as with matter, so with form: recalling the time when rime was in fashion in plays and 'strong lines were not lookt after,' he takes occasion to observe that what is out of date now may come into fashion again 'and sute well'—and, for himself, he is clearly quite ready to stop or rime his lines with his fellows[2]. He has no wish to criticise or to theorise, or to set himself up as a representative of any special class or select sort of English drama. Had he not, at the beginning of his twoscore or more years of labours for the stage, dramatised both history and historical romance in plays to

---

[1] Prologue to *The English Traveller.*
[2] Epilogue (to the Reader) to *The Royall King, and The Loyall Subject.*

which no bold prentice could listen without breaking into rapturous applause and no citizen's wife without dropping a sympathetic tear ; and, as for 'song, dance and masque,' had not Homer and Ovid and Apuleius been alike laid under contribution by him for providing entertainments from which neither learned nor lewd would go home unsatisfied ? Even dramatic species to which he felt no personal attraction—such as that comedy of 'humours flash'd in wit' which satirised types of humanity neither heroic nor attractive—he declined to depreciate, merely urging those who cultivated them not to eschew the treatment of other and loftier subjects: the deeds of 'great Patriots, Dukes and Kings,' for the memorising of which the English drama (some plays of his own with the rest) had hitherto been notably distinguished[1].

But, while Heywood, cheerfully suiting himself and his art to a variety of dramatic genres, attained to virtuosity rather than to supreme excellence in the chronicle history and the romantic drama, and did as well as many others in the comedy of manners and the mythological play, he associated his name after a more intimate fashion with a species which had a character, and a future, of its own. This was the domestic drama, which, on the background of ordinary family life, presents an action of deep and commanding moral interest. Heywood was not the inventor of the domestic drama, which is as thoroughly English in its genesis and in a great part of its development as the national historical drama itself, justly held in high honour by him. Nor was it given to him, or to any of his contemporaries, to realise in the Elizabethan age the possibilities of this species with a fulness comparable to that reached by others—the comedy of manners, for instance. But he achieved memorable and enduring results in a field in which few of his fellow dramatists whose names are known to us made more than tentative efforts, and to which the greatest of them abstained from turning his attention except, as it were, in passing. The simplicity of these works cannot be held to detract from the honour due to the art which produced them, or to impair the recognition implied in the fact that, in the history of European literature, the name of Thomas Heywood is linked to those of great writers, to some of whom it was probably unknown—Steele and Richardson, Diderot and Lessing.

Thomas Heywood was born, somewhere about the year 1572, in Lincolnshire, where his family must have been of good standing

---

[1] See the interesting prologue to *A Challenge for Beautie*, where the superiority of English historical plays to the dramatic efforts of other nations is roundly asserted.

and repute. We have it on his own authority that he was at one time a resident member of the university of Cambridge, where he saw 'tragedyes, comedyes, historyes, pastorals and shewes, publicly acted,' and 'the graduates of good place and reputation specially parted' in these performances[1]. The time-honoured tradition, which unfortunately it is impossible to corroborate with the aid of either college or university records, that he was a fellow of Peterhouse, rests on an explicit statement made by the bookseller and actor William Cartwright not more than ten years after Heywood's death[2]. But it is practically certain that he never held a fellowship at Peterhouse, and, among the few incidental references to Cambridge scattered through his writings, there is but one which introduces the name of the college to which he is said to have belonged—and that, it must be confessed, in no very helpful way[3].

By 1596, Heywood is mentioned in Henslowe's diary as writing, or having written, a play; but as to the time and circumstances of his taking up the twofold vocation of actor and playwright we know nothing. No link of any sort can have existed between him and the 'university wits,' whose academical experiences and entrance into London life belong to the preceding decade, and from whose arrogance and affectations he was equally free. He became connected in turn with several companies of players—probably beginning with the Admiral's men at the Rose, and, in 1634, becoming a servant of the king (Charles I). While a sound patriot, Heywood seems to have had no love for courts[4]; though he celebrated the glories of the great queen in one of his early plays as well as in a history of the trials of her youth, indited the praises of Anne of Denmark five years after he had attended her funeral and hailed queen Henrietta Maria's hopes of motherhood in more than one loyal prologue. On the other hand, his attachment to the city of London, though not, so far as we know, due to any official or hereditary tie, was very strong and enduring, and comprehended both the town and its inhabitants[5]. He celebrated the erection of the Royal

---

[1] *Apology for Actors* (Shakespeare Society edition), p. 28.

[2] In the dedication prefixed to his edition of the *Apology*, published in 1658 under the title *The Actor's Vindication*.

[3] In *The Wise-woman Of Hogsdon*, act IV, Sencer, disguised as a pedant, caps the assertion of 'Sir Boniface' that he was 'student in Brazennose' by '*Petrus dormit securus*: I was Sir of Peeterhouse.' Fleay promptly concluded that Heywood acted Sencer.

[4] Compare with the general tone of *The Royall King, and The Loyall Subject*, Wendoll's words on making his exit in *A Woman Kilde with Kindnesse*.

[5] Fleay's suggestion that Heywood was one of the Master Stationers is hardly offered as more than a happy thought.

Exchange[1], whose interior is admirably described in a comedy generally attributed to him[2], and of 'Crosbie House[3]'; he wrote, as we shall see, a series of mayoralty pageants for divers city companies, and immortalised their coats of arms as blazoned on the shields borne at the siege of Jerusalem[4]; he commemorated the labours of the docks[5]. He held up to honour the name of a princely merchant like Sir Thomas Gresham[6], and, for the *flos juventutis*, the prentices of the city, he always kept a warm corner in his heart[7]. In short, he was a Londoner every inch of him; and, though few of our Elizabethan dramatists have better pictured the freshness of rural life, and the jollity of its sports and pastimes, he recognised the perennial superiority of the vicinity of St Paul's, and was capable of contrasting, in a daring paradox,

> the toil and travell of the country
> And quiet gaine of cities blessednesse[8].

It may be added that the moral code of the citizens of London was not one with which Heywood can have been naturally inclined to quarrel; though, of course, in his latter days, he was obliged by his 'quality' to retort upon 'that most horrible *Histriomastix* and the bitter juice of that *Coloquintida* and *Hemlocke*, which can neither relish the peace of the Church nor Common-weale[9].' There is little to be found in his plays against puritans or puritanism[10], and even in his *Apology* he abstains from those *Satirica Dictaeria* and *Comica Scommata*, which he declares to be contrary to his practice[11].

Heywood's industry as a playwright was, beyond all doubt, extraordinary, though far from unparalleled. His often quoted statement, made in 1633[12], that he had 'either an entire hand, or at the least a main finger' in two hundred and twenty plays, Fleay, rather perversely, has sought to interpret in the sense which

---

[1] *Part II of If you know not me*, etc.   [2] *The Fayre Mayde of the Exchange.*
[3] *Part I of Edward IV.*   [4] *The Foure Prentises.*
[5] His pamphlet on the royal ship *The Sovereign of the Seas* contains an account of ship-building from Noah's ark downwards.
[6] *Part II of If you know not me*, etc.
[7] *The Foure Prentises* and *Part I of Edward IV*; in *Loves Maistresse*, Vulcan has 'cyclops and prentices' in his smithy.
[8] *Part II of If you know not me*, etc.
[9] 'To the Reader,' prefixed to *A Mayden-Head well lost.*
[10] In *Part II of If you know not me*, etc., the dishonest factor Timothy Thinbeard is said by his principal to have been 'so pure of life that I would have trusted him with all I had.' In *A Woman Kilde with Kindnesse*, Mrs Frankford's seducer comments on her remorseful reflections: 'Fie! fie! you talk too much like a puritan.'
[11] 'To the Reader,' prefixed to *The Iron Age.*
[12] 'To the Reader,' prefixed to *The English Traveller.*

the words assuredly will not bear, that this total included all the plays in which Heywood had acted during the thirty years (or thereabouts) in question—inasmuch as in most of these plays he had, no doubt, inserted 'gag,' while many of them had been altered by him. This, in Fleay's opinion, would warrant the conclusion that only about two score plays were actually written by Heywood, who is not known to have been a frequent collaborator with other playwrights. In 1633, however, Heywood's connection with the theatre had extended over at least thirty-seven years, and an average of half-a-dozen plays *per annum*, in which he was concerned as sole or joint author, or as reviser, is not inconceivable, if, together with the general character of his dramatic writings, which will be considered immediately, the spirit in which he composed them and the little care which he took of them, after their appearance on the stage, be taken into account.

Nothing is more certain than that he gave little or no thought to the destiny of his plays as 'literature.' He wrote them, *inprimis*, no doubt, for a living, and, also, in obedience to that impulse towards dramatic production which was never more prevalent than in the period of his connection with the stage, but which is not necessarily the same thing as poetic inspiration. Manifestly, he loved the theatre, which was to him a world in itself[1], as it is to many actors and to not a few playwrights whose sense of their importance in the world outside is too great to allow them to confess it. But this did not make him anxious to find new ways and methods for compassing old ends. Like his fellow dramatists, he was constantly on the look-out for interesting dramatic subjects, and he took them where he found them, setting to work, we may rest assured, without loss of time and accomplishing his task 'all of a piece.' To have finished his play and brought it on the stage, was enough for him : he was careless about printing, and, on at least one occasion, had to submit as well as he could to the appearance of a corrupt copy, taken down by some enterprising expert in stenography and 'put in print (scarce one word trew)[2].' Such plays of his as he allowed to be published he sent forth 'with great modesty and small noise,' and, above all 'singly,' not 'exposed to the publike view of the world in numerous sheets, and a large volume'—like Ben Jonson's 'works,' or Shakespeare's[3].

---

[1]   He that denyes then theaters should be,
      He may as well deny a world to me.
                     'The Author to his Booke' (*An Apology for Actors*).

[2] See prologue to *If you know not me*, etc.

[3] See the address 'To the Reader' prefixed to *The Fair Maid Of The West* (printed 1631).

But, whether or not his rapidity of production was such as to expose him, as Fleay conjectures, to contemporary dramatic satire in the character of Posthaste[1]—whether or not we are to believe Kirkman's ingenious statement that he was in the habit of writing his plays on the back of tavern-bills (which, no doubt, would satisfactorily account for the loss of many of them)—whether or not, according to the same authority, he, for several years together, imposed on himself the rule of writing a minimum of a sheet a day—his rate of productivity cannot be said to be left unexplained. His pen was facile, because his mind was both fresh and ready, and because, to use a vigorous German colloquialism, he 'sang as his beak had grown.' Heywood's *naïveté* is, perhaps, the most delightful element in his genius, although the directness of expression to which it leads him frequently sins against refinement.

After Heywood had been an actor and a playwright for twelve years or more—possibly at an earlier date—he bethought himself of turning his proved ability as a writer, and the studies which he cannot have allowed to lie fallow since his Cambridge days, to what the age would deem a more strictly literary account. Beginning with a translation of Sallust (1608), he produced a long series of compositions, of which as complete as possible a list will be furnished elsewhere[2], but which in no instance, with the exception of the *Apology for Actors*, and, perhaps, the historical narrative entitled *England's Elizabeth* (to be noticed below in connection with the play which he based upon it), have any special interest for a generation not so much addicted to useless learning as was the author's own. We therefore leave aside his two long poetical productions, *Troicus Britannicus, or Great Britain's Troy*, which tells its tale *ab ovo* down to the pedigree of king James I, and the didactic *Hierarchy of the Blessed Angels*, equal at all events to the ornate promise of its title-page. On a similar encyclopaedic pattern he composed *Nine Books of Women*, reprinted after his death under the still more ambitious title *The General History of Women*. Posterity would probably consent to burn these compilations, if from their ashes could be produced the *Lives of all the Poets*, with which the author had made some progress and which began with 'the first before Homer'—and may have ended with Shakespeare[3]. *The Lives and Acts of Nine of the most Worthy Women* (three Jews, three Gentiles and three Christians) savours, it must be

[1] In Marston's *Histrio-Mastix*. [2] See bibliography.

[3] In *The Fayre Mayde of the Exchange*, generally attributed to Heywood, Bowdler, 'a humerous gallant,' says: 'I never read anything but Venus and Adonis.' 'Why,' replies the Cripple, 'that's the very quintessence of love.'

confessed, more entirely of the bookmaker. In addition, Heywood was an indefatigable translator and paraphraser, and one of his lengthiest publications, *Pleasant Dialogues and Drammas* (of which the date of publication is 1637), consists, mainly, of versions of Erasmus, Textor and Lucian in heroic verse, and of Ovid in blank, together with a long (and disagreeable) dialogue reproduced from the *Maechden-Pflicht* of Vader Cats (1618). To these pieces are added a series of prologues and epilogues, with as many epitaphs, elegies, epigrams, acrostics and anagrams thrown in as a last search of the author's cupboards can have produced. This piece of bookmaking has scant interest for the literary student except in so far as it helps to illustrate the extraordinary influence of the *Colloquies* of Erasmus, which continued for more than a century after their original appearance, and which, as has been pointed out by the editor of the *Pleasant Dialogues*, is distinctly noticeable in the English drama of the Elizabethan and Jacobean ages[1].

It cannot be said that the *Apology for Actors* (published in 1612) holds a very important place in the controversy between the stage and its adversaries, which is narrated in a later chapter of this volume, where Heywood's contribution to the contention is discussed with the rest[2]. Biographically, it interests us as giving proof not only of his learning, which is solid and firsthand, as well as varied and ready for use, but also of a natural moderation and courtesy which led him to abstain from all personalities. And, while we find him anxious for the good report of the profession to which he belonged, and which such men as himself and Alleyn— not to mention greater names—adorned, he at the same time shows a modesty harmonising with all that we know of him as a writer. In the double capacity of actor and playwright—for it is noticeable that he seems to have no wish to distinguish between the two functions—he describes himself as 'the youngest and weakest of the nest wherein he was hatcht,' and liable to the charge of presumptuousness for venturing to 'soare this pitch before others of the same brood, more fledge, and of better wing' than himself[3]. To his own plays he makes no reference or allusion

---

[1] See the introduction to W. Bang's edition, where Fleay's assumption that any of the pieces contained in the book had previously formed part of the *Five Plays in One* performed in 1597, is rightly rejected as hazardous.

[2] See *post*, chap. xiv.

[3] Heywood's admiration of his chief fellow dramatists, and the kindly way in which these men spoke of one another, are illustrated by the well known lines in the *Hierarchy of the Blessed Angels*, cited in Collier's introduction to his edition of the *Apology for Actors*.

in the course of his tract, except in the passage where he insists
on the moral purpose of the drama :

The unchaste are by us shewed in their errors in the persons of Phryne,
Lais, Thais, Flora ; and amongst us Rosamond and Mistresse Shore.

The most rigid of censors could not set up a more 'respectable'
standard of morality and regard for authority than that desired by
the author of the *Apology* ; though there is obviously a polemic
meaning in his protest against the practice of putting 'bitternesse'
and 'liberall invective' into the mouths of children—say of the
chapel—'supposing their juniority to be a priviledge for any
railing.'

It has been concluded—though it cannot be proved—that from
1634—5 onwards Heywood ceased to write for the stage. His
Pleasant Dialogues and Drammas, a miscellaneous collection
of essays such as many a modern author has indulged himself by
publishing towards the close of his career, was completed by 1637 ;
and the last of the seven pageants which he produced, from 1631
onwards, was for the year 1639. These compositions attest his
cordial appreciations of the glories of the city under the auspices
of haberdashers, ironmongers and drapers — 'the dignity of
Merchants,' he exclaims with conviction, 'who can tell[1]'? He
seems to have still been living in 1641, when a *Life of Ambrosius
Merlin*, compiled by him, appears to have been printed; indeed,
he is spoken of, as if alive, so late as 1648, in *The Satire against
Satirists*[2].

It seems to agree best with Heywood's method of production
to name his numerous dramatic works in their chronological
sequence, so far as this can be ascertained or, with more or less
probability, surmised, without, however, adhering to it with absolute rigidity. A classification of his plays could be attempted
without much difficulty, if it were worth while ; but he, at least,
would certainly not have thought it so.

Priority of mention may, accordingly, be given to *The Foure
Prentises of London. With the Conquest of Jerusalem*, though,
possibly, it was preceded on the stage by one or both parts of
Edward IV. In the earliest extant edition, which is dated 1615,
the preface states the play to have been in the fashion 'some

---

[1] See *Porta Pietatis*.

[2] Introduction to *Apology*, p. vi. The passage is quoted in Pearson's reprint,
vol. i, p. xxv:

So may you come to sleep in fur at last
. . . . . .
And Heywood sing your acts in lofty verse.

fifteene or sixteene yeares agoe'; but Fleay has shown that there
must have been an earlier edition in, or not long after, 1610, and
that Heywood's play, probably, was the *Godfrey of Bulloigne*
performed by the Admiral's men as early as July 1594[1]. And,
though Heywood certainly did not take the story of his play
direct from Tasso, it must be considered a curious coincidence
that, in 1594, Richard Carew's translation of five cantos of
Gerusalemme appeared in print[2]. Whatever its immediate source,
this play, which combines the crude compiling method of the
early chronicle history with the violently symmetrical improba-
bilities of the popular romance, is primitive to the last degree.
The four heroes of the piece, whom their sire, the 'olde Earl
of Bulloign' had, under stress of misfortune, apprenticed in
London city, after taking service for the holy wars pass through
divers strange adventures in divers lands till they meet at last
before the 'high wals of Hierusalem.' Their sister, whose spirit
equals theirs, follows her star to the same spot, disguised as a
page; and a French lady, in love with one of the brothers, ac-
companies him in similar gear. After the victory has been won
(to the cries of 'A Syon! A Jerusalem!'), each of the brothers
obtains a crown—Godfrey preferring one of thorns—and the story
ends in an accumulation of happiness. Presenter and dumb-show
have helped on the epic movement of the action, hardly any
attempt being made by the author to soar into poetry, though he
abounds in classical allusions. But the simplicity of Godfrey's
enthusiasm on beholding the

> sacred path our Saviour trod
> When he came riding to Hierusalem

is impressive; and the whole play must have told irresistibly upon
'the Honest and High-spirited Prentises' to whom it was afterwards dedicated, and to whom Godfrey's accurate description of his
own and his brother's military functions, which has a strong smack
of the Artillery Garden, must have specially appealed.

In the amusing farce, *The Knight of the Burning Pestle*[3], in
which Beaumont and Fletcher ridiculed those very civic tastes
which Heywood's play had sought to gratify, fun is incidentally
made of *The Foure Prentises*, as well as of the plays which will
be noted next, and of a drama entitled *The Bold Beachams*

---

[1] Cf. Fleay, *English Drama*, vol. i, p. 282. The difficulties in the way cannot,
however, be ignored; see Greg, W. W., *Henslowe's Diary*, vol. ii, pp. 166, 284. The
indication noted by Collier that this was the play in which, in 1602, Wentworth Smith
collaborated with Heywood is not convincing.

[2] Warton, vol. iv, p. 350.   [3] Cf. *post*, chap. v.

(Beauchamps), which, without good authority, has been attributed to Heywood[1].

In the two plays, each of them in two parts, which next come under consideration, Heywood worked on the model of the old chronicle history pure and simple. Though doubt has been thrown on Heywood's authorship of the earlier of these plays, *King Edward IV*, on the ground of its superiority to the rest of the dramatist's earlier work[2], it may confidently be accepted as his, in view of the general unevenness in the relative merits of his plays, and of the fact that, in its sentimental as well as its humorous scenes, the piece is in a vein thoroughly his own. *Edward IV*, which, after the full title[3] had been entered in the Stationers' register in 1599, was printed in the following year, makes no attempt at dramatic unity—for it can hardly be said to derive this from the personality of the city's favourite king, Edward of the 'gadding eye.' As has been pointed out by Schelling[4], the two parts of the play contain 'not less than five stories indifferently connected together by personages that fill *rôles* in two or more'—viz. the story of the bastard Falconbridge's siege of London, in which were possibly incorporated reminiscences of *The Siege of London*, a play revived by the Admiral's men in December 1594, and in which the gallant flat-caps are not forgotten, while we meet with an original humorous figure in the person of the well-meaning but unintelligible Maister Josselin; the diverting episode of Hobs the tanner of Tamworth, a figure borrowed from an old ballad, who accurately represents the indifference of the populace towards the question at issue in the wars of the Roses; the futile expedition of king Edward to France (in which Louis XI makes his first appearance on the English stage); the murder of the little princes in the Tower, a tragic tale told with homely pathos; and, lastly, the story of Jane Shore, which alone stretches from the first into the second part of the play. The long-lived popularity of this story, which, also, was taken from an old ballad, and which found its way again and again into English dramatic and epic literature[5], needs no

[1] See Fleay, *u. s.*, vol. I, p. 287.

[2] By Fleay, who, I think, is successfully controverted by Greg, *Henslowe's Diary*, vol. II, p. 173.

[3] See bibliography. [4] vol. I, pp. 282—3.

[5] As to Churchyard's *Shore's Wife* in *A Mirror for Magistrates*, cf. vol. III, pp. 182 and 198. It is open to question whether Chettle and Day's play of *Shore* ('wherein Shore's wife is written'), acted in 1602, was an independent piece of work; in Rowe's *Jane Shore* (1714), which, at a recent date, was still to be seen on the stage, no trace of a connection with Heywood's play is apparent.

explanation. Heywood's treatment of the figure of the erring wife, whose goodness of heart is attested by her openness to melting charity, and by her sorrow for her sin, as well as that of the high-minded and forgiving husband, is full of fine feeling; and it is to be regretted that, near its close, the episode should be marred by the unnecessary fool's play of Jockie and Jeffrey, with which the dramatist thought it his duty to gratify his patrons. The minor character of Mistress Blague, Jane Shore's sunshine friend, is admirably drawn. As for the death of husband and wife, it is sentimental drama of the purest water, but none the less in its place for that.

As it stands, Heywood's other chronicle play, *If you know not me, You know no bodie*[1]: *Or, The troubles of Queene Elizabeth*, surreptitiously printed from a stenographic copy in 1605, and revived in 1631, near the time of the publication of the author's *England's Elizabeth*, is, so far as *Part I* is concerned, little better than a jumble of misprinted fragments. It is clear, at the same time, that this portion of the work must, at best, have been a crude *ad captandum* treatment of Elizabeth's experiences before her accession, following its text-book, Heywood's own monograph *England's Elizabeth*[2], in depicting the martyr-like rectitude of the Protestant princess, who suffered *tanquam ovis* in adversity, and who, after her fortune had turned, received from the hands of the lord mayor her prize and palladium—an English Bible. What availed the doubledyed animosity of the ruthless Gardiner against a fortitude so innocent that even king Philip was loth to be unkind? Repeated dumb-shows and some very unsophisticated clownery helps on the action. *Part II*, which is much better preserved, was not better worth preserving. After a long and tedious treatment of the magnificence of Sir Thomas Gresham, and the reckless prodigality of his nephew Jack, we have, as a sudden episode, the attempt against the queen's life by William Parry (which was plotted in 1583—4)[3]; whereupon, a chorus, professing to bridge the interval between 1585 and 1588, brings us to

---

[1] The phrase, which the instincts of the publisher may be supposed to have suggested as a title, seems to have been used proverbially; in *Part I of Edward IV*, Hobs the tanner applies it to himself.

[2] Queen Elizabeth also figures as 'the last of the three Women Worthies among the Christians' in Heywood's *Nine Most Worthy Women of the World*. *England's Elizabeth* was not published till 1609, a date that may account for the freedom with which certain actions of Henry VIII are narrated, though not, perhaps, for the contrast drawn (*s.a.* 1547) between the 'sweet lady' Elizabeth's determination to remain unmarried, and what 'may be said of women in general.'

[3] This episode is also treated by Dekker in *The Whore of Babylon*.

the year of the Armada. But nothing follows except a rather bald account of this climax of Elizabethan glories, finishing with a succession of 'posts,' recalling with a difference, the ἄγγελοι of the *Persae*. No doubt the whole of this production was brought out hurriedly soon after the death of the great queen, having to serve its purpose *tant bien que mal*; and, though it is not without details of interest and contains at least one passage of real poetic feeling[1], it bears the fatal mark of haste.

A third dramatic composition of the same class which has been ascribed to Heywood is the play entitled *No-Body, and Some-Body. With the true Chronicle Historie of Elydure*, which was entered in the Stationers' register in 1606, and must have been performed before 1604. But, though Heywood's authorship seemed unquestionable to Fleay, stronger evidence than that which satisfied him[2] seems requisite before we burden the dramatist's reputation with this ascription. The main plot, taken from Geoffrey of Monmouth, of king Elidure's threefold accession to the British throne, is of the antique cast of *The True Chronicle History of King Leir*; the by-plot which gives its name to the play is an elaborate development of the grim old jest of Οὖτις, which savours of the personifications familiar to the moralities and, like them, has a satirico-didactic aim[3].

To the same early period in his career in which Heywood produced examples of a species soon to become all but obsolete belongs a series of plays from his hand which in subject seem to associate themselves with the tastes of more learned audiences than those for which he had thus early shown himself ready to cater. But, in the preface to *The Iron Age*—the last of *The Four Ages* in which he dramatised a long series of classical myths from Saturn and Jupiter down to Ulysses, who, alone among the Greek kings banded against Troy, survives to speak the epilogue—he expressly tells us that these plays were

often (and not with the least applause) Publickely Acted by two Companies uppon one Stage at once, and have at sundry times thronged three severall Theaters, with numerous and mighty Auditories.

There is every reason for believing that *Parts I and II of Hercules*,

---

[1] See Tawny-coat's apostrophe to the earth, out of which his spade is to procure his sustenance, beginning

　　　Hard world, when men dig living out of stones. (*Part II.*)

[2] Viz. the spelling *ey* for *ay* or *I*, which he had observed to be peculiar to Heywood. It may be added that the references to games of cards (ll. 1523 ff.) recall a scene in *A Woman Kilde with Kindnesse*, and that the author of *No-Body, and Some-Body* was evidently familiar with London.

[3] See the bibliography as to this play.

performed by the Admiral's men as new plays from May 1595, are, respectively, *The Silver Age* and *The Brazen Age* of Heywood's series[1]; but Fleay's daring identification of *Selio and Olimpio* (*Caelo et Olympo?*), performed by the same company in 1594, with *The Golden Age*, and his conjecture that *Troye*, performed by them in 1596, is *Part I*, or an earlier and shorter edition of both parts, of *The Iron Age*, must remain questionable. In any case, these plays are more invertebrate than the most loosely constructed of chronicle histories; and not only is the number of characters very great, but it might seem as if, to any audience far away from Cam or Isis, even the indefatigable exertions of 'old Homer' as presenter and chorus, aided by occasional dumb-shows, would have proved inadequate. There is, no doubt, a good deal of life and stir in the action—the amorous scenes, indeed, are often very highly coloured—quite apart from the stimulus of occasional unexpected parallels[2] and a large amount of clowning. But it is incontestable that these plays offer a significant measure of the imaginative powers on which an Elizabethan dramatist could reckon in his audience. Homer might safely venture, in Heywood's phrase, to unlock the casket of which the learned kept the key; and there is something contagious in the opening boast of the poet-magician, that he had 'raised out of the earth' the gods who served the playwright as his puppets.

Proceeding in chronological sequence, we now arrive, among Heywood's extant undoubted plays, at a group in which the earliest in date is his acknowledged masterpiece, *A Woman Kilde with Kindnesse*. It should, however, be noted that, on the strength of the occurrence of some Latin ribaldry, both in *The Wise-woman Of Hogsdon*, which is probably Heywood's, and in the popular *How a man may chuse a good Wife from a bad* (published anonymously in 1602), Fleay confidently asserts that the two plays must be by the same author. Some further indications of Heywood's authorship of the second of the pair might be sought in its general tendency and tone, and in at least one touch of true human kindness in his best manner[3], as well as in the humour of Pipkin, which

[1] See Greg's *Henslowe*, vol. II, p. 175, and cf. *ibid.* pp. 180 and 284.
[2] Not only do Tytan and Saturn, in *The Golden Age*, irresistibly recall Esau and Jacob; but, in *The Silver Age*, the audience is apprised that the prolongation of night, which favours Jupiter on his visit to Alcmena, also serves Joshua in his battle against the Canaanites. In *The Golden Age*, the clown informs Jupiter (when in search of a father) that 'the parish' ought not to be troubled with him.
[3] The courtesan's sense of shame in taking the wronged wife's place at table (act III, sc. 3). This play, which could not have been written without a knowledge of the tomb scene in *Romeo and Juliet*, is printed in vol. IX of Hazlitt's *Dodsley*.

is very like that of Heywood's clowns and especially like Roger's in
The English Traveller; but such resemblances, and perhaps one
or two others which might be pointed out, are not evidence, and
there is more tirade in this piece than is usual with Heywood;
for the rest, it is deftly constructed and contains a good deal of
humour.

In any case, when, in 1603 or earlier, Heywood produced *A
Woman Kilde with Kindnesse*, which was first printed in 1607, he
was not moving on untrodden ground[1]. The germs of the species
which we call domestic drama, and to whose growth in English
dramatic literature incidental reference has already been made in
this volume and in its predecessor, are discernible in the realistic
scenes introduced into the mysteries as novelties by way of
relief, and in those interludes in which, as in the case of Inge-
lend's *Disobedient Child*[2], a serious treatment of a realistic situation or plot was essayed. In due course, however, the choice of
actions localised in English everyday life fell more or less into
disuse, as the regular drama developed itself, and as themes
derived from national history, on the one hand, or from classical
and Italian sources, on the other, found favour with an age
filled with high aspirations and eager for the glittering contents of the newly opened treasurehouse. But a reaction was
not long in coming; as Heywood repeatedly hints, new subjects
were a necessity for the stage; and, soon after the beginning of
the last decade of the sixteenth century, and for several years in
the seventeenth, there was a constant flow of plays dealing with
actions taken from ordinary life, and coming home to men's
business and bosoms with a directness alien both to *tragoedia
cothurnata* and to half allegorical, half satirical comedy.

Nor was it a mere change of preference which accounts for
the impetus given to the dramatisation of experiences, sorrows and
consolations familiar to the country squires and town merchants
and their wives and children in contemporary England. In a
period of the national history when the middle classes were beginning to assert themselves in the social system of the country—
a movement which it would be a mistake to regard as altogether
identical with the striving of puritanism for ascendancy—it could

[1] On the subject of the domestic drama, compare the excellent chapter on the
subject, *passim*, in *Schelling*, vol. I, and *Creizenach*, vol. IV, part I, pp. 237 ff.
See, also, Greg's *Henslowe*, vol. II, pp. 204 ff., and Fleay, *passim*; and cf. a very striking
dissertation by Singer, H. W., *Das bürgerliche Trauerspiel in England*, Leipzig, 1891,
and the opening remarks in Eloesser, A., *Das bürgerliche Drama*, Berlin, 1898.

[2] Cf. vol. v, chap. v.

hardly be but that room should have been found in the drama for exposition of the middle class point of view, middle class morality and middle class humanity, as distinct from the historic pretensions of kings and nobles and prelates, from the easier social codes of palaces and castles and, again, from the violent impulses and freer ways of life habitual to an uninstructed populace. Shakespeare, whose muse was at home on the throne of kings, in the strife of battlefields, or in communion with nature in her moods of elemental agitation or of woodland calm, and who (save in so exceptional an excursion into a new field as *The Merry Wives*) looked upon civic life in a satirical humour, was not responsive to this movement, and, indeed, appears to have been very imperfectly aware of it. When domestic troubles are his dramatic theme, they are conflicts in heroic minds or tempests of romantic passion[1]. Jonson, and his school—including Middleton—on the other hand, treat such griefs and their agents or victims from the point of view of critical superiority. The large majority of Elizabethan plays which may be classed as domestic drama proper are anonymous; and, with the exception of Dekker, who produced powerful work of the kind in *The Honest Whore* (assuredly his in the main) and in many scenes ascribable to him in plays of joint authorship, Heywood, in many ways specially attracted and suited to this genre, is the only Elizabethan dramatist of note who attained to eminence in it.

The currents which united in the flow of Elizabethan domestic drama were of various origin: perhaps the largest in volume was that which set in earliest, and which cannot be more succinctly described than as that of the murder plays. The earliest of these and the most effective—inasmuch as in no other Elizabethan drama has realism of treatment so completely matched the terrors of incident and situation—was *Arden of Feversham*, published in 1592, but probably brought on the stage some six or seven years earlier[2]; one of the latest of the series was *A Yorkshire Tragedy*, acted and printed in 1608, and founded on a ballad commemorating a murder committed in 1604. This is also, in its way, a remarkably powerful piece; but, unlike *Arden*, it is tinged with the sentimentality which had become almost inseparable from domestic drama[3].

---

[1] The very accessories of the dramatic catastrophe, as Singer aptly remarks, are lifted into an uncommon atmosphere, and Desdemona's handkerchief has a mysterious history of its own—

> dyed in mummy which the skilful
> Conserved of maidens' hearts.

[2] See vol. v, chap. x.   [3] See *ibid.*

The intervening murder plays include, with *A warning for Faire Women* (printed in 1599)[1]—a notable play of its kind, in which Shakespeare has been confidently, but on no satisfactory grounds, held to have had 'at least a finger'—a number of pieces which have perished, and in which, among other dramatists, Chettle, Day, Haughton, Dekker, Jonson and Samuel Rowley were in various combinations concerned[2]. To these should be added, as rather later in date than the above-mentioned group, the extremely interesting *Witch of Edmonton* (printed in 1658, but probably acted in 1621 or soon afterwards), which was at first attributed to 'Dekker, Ford, Rowley, etc.,' and in which the hands of the first two of the authors named can almost certainly be recognised[3]. All these murder plays are, in their surroundings, confined to English middle class life; but this fact, of course, does not exclude the influence either of the Italian domestic tragedies of real life which have been described as 'more horrible than anything in Ford or Webster[4],' or of Italian and other foreign fiction.

In occasional combination with the realistic appeal to the sentiment of terror which gives much direct force to the murder plays, the Elizabethan and early Jacobean domestic drama also occupies itself with other motives, the operation of which powerfully affects the course of human life and is most clearly perceptible when its conditions are least complicated and unusual. The faithful observance of the marriage tie and the shameful neglect of it, parental love and the pangs inflicted by filial ingratitude—such are the themes which frequently recur in the dramatic literature of this period. The faithful wife appears in *How a man may chuse a good Wife from a bad*, mentioned above, from which *The Faire Maide of Bristow*, possibly by Day, printed in 1602, is imitated, though the story of the latter play is thrown back into

---

[1] Rptd in *The School of Shakspere*, ed. Simpson, R., vol. II, 1878.

[2] Chettle and Day wrote *Black Bateman of the North* (1598); Day and Haughton, *Cox of Collumpton* (for date, cf. Greg, *Henslowe's Diary*, vol. II, p. 207) and *Thomas Merry, or Beech's Tragedy* (1599?). This seems to have been combined with an Italian version of the story of the Babes in the Wood (which, apparently, had been dramatised by Chettle and Day as *The Italian Tragedy*, printed 1605, and thought by Greg (*u. s.* p. 210) to have possibly been identical with *The Orphans' Tragedy*) into a play printed in 1601 under the title of *Two Lamentable Tragedies*, as by an unknown, and possibly fictitious, Robert Yarington (rptd in *Old Plays*, ed. Bullen, A. H., vol. IV, 1882). Dekker and Jonson wrote *Page of Plymouth* (1599), as to the subject of which cf. 'Dramaticus' in *Shakespeare Society Papers*, vol. II (S. S. Publ. 1845); and Samuel Rowley *The Bristow Tragedy* (1602), the identification of which with the comedy *The Faire Maide of Bristow* is more than doubtful.

[3] See below, chap. VIII.

[4] Cf. Smith, P. L., *Life of Sir Henry Wotton* (1907), vol. I, p. 22.

the reign of Richard I[1].   *The Miseries of Inforst Mariage*, by
George Wilkins, printed in 1607, in a measure varies the theme;
but the pathos of the first two acts loses itself in a picture of
reckless despair which is neither probable nor pleasing, and, though
the sentimental element reappears, it is effectually submerged by
the most imbecile of 'happy endings[2].'   The graceless son plays
his part in *The London Prodigall*, noticed above among the plays
attributed to Shakespeare[3], where the figure of the faithful wife
also recurs in the person of Luce, one of the many reproductions
in the English drama of the Patient Grissel type, which Chettle,
Dekker and Haughton brought on the stage by their treatment of
the famous romantic theme[4].   It seems unnecessary to pursue
further in this place the development of English domestic drama,
though, among the abnormally conceived and artificially constructed plays of the early Stewart period, there are not a few in
which the directness distinctive of the entire species asserts itself
either in the main action of the play or in particular scenes, even
when overspread by some rank exotic intrigue or driven into the
corner by the intrusion of some supernatural fancy[5].

A Woman Kilde with Kindnesse, which deservedly holds a
foremost rank among the classics of domestic drama, derived its
title, like several other of its author's plays, from a proverb or
proverbial phrase.   The expression 'to kill a wife with kindness'
occurs in *The Taming of the Shrew*[6], which must have been produced on the stage some six or seven years before the performance,
by Worcester's men, early in 1603 (N. S.), of Heywood's play[7].   It
was first printed, without having been entered in the register,

---

[1] Edited by Quin, A. H. (?), Philadelphia, 1902.   See Brereton, J. Le Gay, in *The
Modern Language Review*, vol. III, p. 74 (cf.).

[2] Rptd in vol. IX of *Hazlitt's Dodsley* (1874).

[3] See vol. V, chap. X.

[4] Cf. *ante*, chap. II.   As to the '*Griseldis-Motiv*' in English drama, cf. Gothein, M.,
'Die Frau im engl. Drama vor Shakespeare,' in *Shakespeare Jahrbuch*, vol. XL (1904),
pp. 40 ff.

[5] Cf. Schelling, *u.s.* pp. 349 ff.   [6] Act IV, sc. 1, 192.

[7] See the entry in Henslowe's diary *ap.* Greg, vol. II, p. 234.   Later uses of the phrase
'to kill with kindness' are noted in the present writer's edition of Heywood's play in
the Temple Dramatists Series (1897).   Other proverbial titles of plays by Heywood
are, besides *If you know not me*, etc., those of the non-extant *The Blind eats many a
Fly; Christmas comes but once a year; Joan and my Lady*.   The following are some of
the proverbs or proverbial phrases to be found in the dialogue of his extant dramas:
in *A Woman Kilde*, etc. 'comparisons are odious'; in *The Royall King*, etc. 'thou canst
have no more of the cat but his skin'; in *The Fair Maid Of The West* 'Base is the
man that paies'; in *The Golden Age* 'cast your old cloak about ye'; in *The Wise-
woman Of Hogsdon* 'a cat may look at a king'; in *The English Traveller* 'January
and May.'

in 1607; the third edition of the play, 'as it hath been oftentimes
acted by the Queen's' men, appeared in 1617. This popularity
was due to no adventitious attractions; and the author was
perfectly conscious of the simplicity of the means by which the
desired dramatic effect had been achieved; in the words of his
prologue it was

a barren subject, a bare scene

which he presented—nothing more than a sad experience of
everyday life, redeemed from the dreariness of its melancholy
only, so far as the erring wife is concerned, by the pity of it, and
by the nobility of soul which, in the very depth of his grief, the
wronged husband proves capable of revealing. In the strength of
its sentiment and the directness of its appeal to a more than
fleeting sympathy lie the main causes of the effect which this
play produces; but the skill with which its action is constructed
and the chief situations are devised should not be overlooked.
While the seducer falters long on the threshold of his crime, but,
when he has once crossed it, drags on his victim relentlessly from
transgression to transgression, she is caught in the toils half un-
awares, and, with an 'O Master Wendoll O[1],' is lost—to awake to
bitter remorse even before the hour of discovery has come. The
nocturnal return of the betrayed husband to his closed door is
presented with admirable theatrical effect—it might, as has been
said, almost be described as a 'prose' reproduction of some of
the terrors of *Macbeth*. The magnanimity of the husband—pre-
figured by that of Master Shore in the chronicle play—might,
conceivably, have failed to come home to an Elizabethan audience,
but for the picture of the broken-hearted and penitent woman in
the last act, which wins over all hearts to an acknowledgment of
her husband's kindness, and of the Power which overrules both
human sorrow and human sin. The scene of the play is laid in
the midst of English country life, characteristic features of which
—fresh air and hawking in the morning, and a game at cards o'
nights[2]—are reproduced without an effort, but with a realistic
effect which materially helps to bring home the story of the
tragedy enacted thus amidst familiar surroundings.

---

[1] Compare with this electrical touch another, almost equal to it—Mistress Frankford to her lute: 'We both are out of tune, out of tune' (act IV, sc. 3).

[2] Heywood must be pardoned the allusive ingenuity of the card playing scene,
which probably pleased the taste of his patrons. Cf. the repeated allusions to the
game of Maw in Dekker's *Match mee in London*, which Fleay thought identifiable with
The Set at Maw, acted in 1594.

While a criticism of certain details in the main action of *A Woman Kilde with Kindnesse* seems unnecessary here, it cannot be ignored that, in this as in several other of his plays, Heywood should have felt himself obliged to contrive a by-plot which, instead of relieving tension, offends judgment. In the present instance, though we would not willingly lose the hawking scene out of which the subsidiary plot arises, we have to accept a pedestrian version of the story of *Measure for Measure*, with a solution such as might, possibly, have commended itself to the author of *Pamela*[1].

If Heywood wrote *The Wise-woman Of Hogsdon*, a comedy which, though not printed, with his name, till 1638, cannot have been produced at a date much later than 1604[2], no more striking instance is to be found of his versatility. It is true that this play opens with a gambling scene as true to life as the hawking scene in *A Woman Kilde with Kindnesse*, and that, later, it suddenly changes its manner into that of domestic drama—of the *comédie larmoyante* variety—so as to make the reckless young libertine who is the hero of the action exclaim :

Here's such wetting of Handkerchers, hee weepes to thinke of his Wife, shee weepes to see her Father cry. Peace foole, wee shall else have thee claime kindred of the Woman Kill'd with Kindnesse.

But Heywood is hardly likely to have introduced this half sarcastic allusion into a play of his own, and the general character of this comedy of manners is such as to make his authorship doubtful, notwithstanding the mention in it, noted above, of his Cambridge college. *The Wise-woman Of Hogsdon* is, at the same time, a play full of life and spirit, with a plot very well managed in spite of its complications, between the two Luces and a third young lady and the gay Young Chartley who flutters round the trio, depending on the services of the evil old intermediary, the avowed rival of Mother Bombie, Mother Phillips of Bankside, and half a dozen other wise women and procuresses. Much fuller of humorously grotesque characters than any known play of Heywood's, this play, at the same time, exaggerates all the blemishes which elsewhere he shows no similar eagerness to parade—a profusion of doggerel, of bad puns and equivoques and of unequivocal obscenity.

The case is different with *The Fayre Mayde of the Exchange*.

---

[1] As to Heywood's indebtedness to the queen of Navarre and Bandello for the double plot of this play, see *Creizenach*, vol. iv, part i, p. 264.

[2] See *Fleay*, vol. i, p. 291.

With The pleasaunt Humours of the Cripple of Fanchurch,
which, though printed anonymously in 1607 and later, has been
usually attributed to Heywood, and upon which, treating it as his,
Charles Lamb bestowed high praise. The present writer, without
accepting Fleay's conjecture that the play was written by Machin,
cannot persuade himself that Heywood was its author. Though
the comedy offers a very lively picture of the Royal Exchange
(from a shop front point of view), there is little else to convey
the sense of freshness and originality which few of Heywood's
dramatic productions fail, in some respect, to leave upon the
reader. The heroine Phillis fails to charm, and her repartees
exhibit her as a very secondrate Beatrice, while her passion for
the 'noble' Cripple, who is magnanimous enough to reject it, is
not so much unpleasing as unconvincing. Apart from the Cripple's
loyalty to the city and the virtue of its shopwomen (a touch of
characteristic directness) there is little to suggest Heywood; the
wittiness of some of the passages of the play, and the cleverly
symmetrical construction of its plot[1], are merits not common in
his dramas.

In *The Royall King, and The Loyall Subject,* which, though not
printed till 1637, was, undoubtedly, of a relatively early date[2], we
have an indisputable piece of Heywood's workmanship. His muse
took a lofty flight on this occasion, seeking renown in romantic
drama. Like Fletcher's similarly named play, from which it
altogether differs in treatment, Heywood's is founded on a novel by
Bandello[3]; but the dramatist is clearly anxious that his localisation
of the story in England should be express and explicit; so that it
is difficult—though useless—not to speculate on the possibility of
some personal application being intended. Yet the story of the
play is wildly improbable, and before the long-suffering fidelity of
the Marshal and his family even Patient Grissel's pales; in short,
an impression of artificiality mars the total effect. Moreover, the
action, as it were, begins over again, after it had seemed to have
reached its height. In a word, though the diction, in the case of

---

[1] In the actual close of the play, which leaves the arrest of Phillis's father for
felony without explanation or sequence, there must have been something wrong in
the stenography.

[2] See the references to versification and costume in the epilogue. *Fleay* (vol. I, p. 300)
insists that this play was an altered version of *Marshal Osric,* by Heywood and Wentworth Smith (performed by Worcester's men in 1602), brought out, in consequence
of the success of Fletcher's *Loyal Subject,* soon after that play, probably at Christmas
1633.

[3] Cf. Koeppel, E., *Quellenstudien zu den Dramen Ben Jonsons* (1895), appendix,
pp. 133—5.

the principal plot, maintains a level unusual with Heywood, the conception is superior to its execution, and the by-plot, which essays to illustrate the commonplace saying that clothes make the man, is, as not unfrequently with Heywood, extravagant and in part offensive. This play, which, very possibly, was earlier than *A Woman Kilde with Kindnesse*, cannot claim to be ranked beside it.

The Rape of Lucrece, printed in 1609, but first produced soon after the accession of James I[1], is, again, in a different style, if style of any sort can be ascribed to this odd medley of tragedy and vaudeville. As to the serious action, all that need be said is that the dramatist has contrived to provoke a strange thrill of mixed pity and terror by the picture of the house of Collatinus when the morning dawns on Tarquin's crime. It is here that he introduces the one exquisite lyric known to have come from his pen[2]. The other songs—a budget of what at the present day would be called music hall ditties interspersed in the action of this 'true Roman tragedy' by Valerius, 'the merry Lord among the Roman peers'— are, in part, of antiquarian interest (such as the list of London taverns, and that of the street cries of Rome); they reach the nadir of shameless inappropriateness in the catch with which the merry lord, Horatius Cocles and the clown 'follow on,' when the tragic action is suspended at its height.

In *The Fair Maid Of The West*, printed in 1631, which is undoubtedly and unmistakably Heywood's, we have another romantic comedy, but one in which the patriotic note sounds clearly and the salt breeze of the sea blows to and from our island shores. *Part I* of this dramatic Odyssey (which must have been founded on some popular tale unknown to us) begins with a delightfully vivid picture of English seaport life, localised at Plymouth and dated by a dumb-show as at the time of the expedition of Essex to the Azores. On the Hoe, the gallant Spencer parts from the lovely Besse Bridges, the pride of the Castle inn— he to sail for 'Fiall,' she to keep her faith and fortune for him at Foy. Soon afterwards, we are transported into the land of eastern romance, and, after divers marvellous adventures—all redounding to the honour and glory of Elizabethan England and her sailors— we leave the lovers reunited as the honoured guests of king Mullisheg of Fesse. *Part II* completes the story in three stirring acts, brimful of lust, courage, sensitive honour and royal magnanimity, enough in their combination to furnish forth an entire

---

[1] See *Fleay*, vol. I, p. 292.
[2] 'Packe cloudes away, and welcome day,' etc.

drama. But, as in *The Royall King,* the author cannot leave well alone, and, in acts IV—V, adds a further series of adventures in Italy, beginning with a shipwreck, which must have gone near to surfeit even an Elizabethan audience. But the English 'spirit and fire[1],' and the kindly clowning of Clem, Besse's faithful 'drawer' and constant follower in east and west, hold out to the end.

The English Traveller, printed in 1633, was probably acted in or about 1627; but the evidence on the subject is slight. The story of Geraldine is told by Heywood in his *History of Women*[2] as having 'lately happened within' his 'own knowledge'; but the attempts which have been made to identify the hero remain mere conjectures[3]. The main plot with which the young traveller is concerned turns on the idea which lies at the root of Heywood's finest dramatic designs—that, if to err is human, to forgive is what raises humanity beyond the earth. There is genius in the twofold capacity for thinking nobly and beyond the range of common minds, and for bringing home such thoughts to their comprehension and sympathy. The by-plot of this drama is derived from Plautus[4].

A few words will suffice as to the remaining extant plays of which Heywood was sole author. Among these, *The Captives, or The Lost Recovered,* which was not printed till 1883, when Mr Bullen found a copy of it in the British Museum, is, by external evidence as well as by that of style and manner, proved to be that entered as 'by Hayward' in Sir Henry Herbert's office book under the date 1634. This romantic comedy exhibits the writer's patriotic spirit, as well as his love of the sea and its ways. The main story is taken from the *Rudens* of Plautus, several passages in which are translated in the play, but it seems to have reached the author through the Italian hand of Masuccio Salernitano. The underplot, which is derived from an old French *fabliau,* translated into an English jest-book and retold by

[1]   These bold Englishmen
         I think are all compos'd of spirit and fire,
         The element of earth hath no part in them.
                                        Part II, act IV, *ad fin.*

[2] Book IV, *A Moderne History of an Adulteresse.*

[3] See *Fleay's* endeavour (vol. I, p. 297) to find the original of the young Levantine traveller in George Sandys; and cf. the suggestion hazarded by Bang (*Materialien,* etc., vol. III, p. 376) that Young Geraldine was meant for Sir Peter Pindar, whom in a distich (*ibid.* p. 266) Heywood couples with St Paul—'both travel'd.'

[4] The *Mostellaria.* This part of the play introduces the celebrated fancy of *Naufragium joculare,* to which Heywood recurs in less elaborate fashion in *The Captives,* and which comes from the *Deipnosophia* of Athenaeus.

Heywood in his *History of Women*[1], recalls the scenes with the friars in *The Jew of Malta*, a play which Heywood worked up for representation before he published it in 1632, possibly himself introducing into it these very scenes[2]. Another romantic drama, *A Mayden-Head well lost* (printed in 1634, but acted some time earlier—it contains dumb-shows, but little rime) has little or nothing in it to redeem the offensiveness of its plot, one of the numerous versions of the story of *All's Well that Ends Well*, relieved by drollery very inferior to that of Parolles. *A Challenge for Beautie* (printed in 1636, and probably produced on the stage only a year or two earlier) is, in some respects, more characteristic of Heywood, and is, in truth, written throughout in a vein of the most blatant national self-consciousness[3]. The main argument of the piece, the pride of the Spanish-born queen who arrogantly sends forth one of her courtiers to find her superior if he can—of course he finds her in England—resembles an Arabian night's tale, but the loss of the fair Hellena's ring in a washhand-basin is a trivial expedient. The by-plot of Ferars and Valladolid's rivalry, which ends in the discovery that the lady adored by both is the sister of the Englishman, is extremely theatrical but not the least satisfactory. Finally, the latest of Heywood's plays in date of production is, probably, *Loves Maistresse: Or, The Queens Masque*, performed in 1633, and again in the following year at Denmark house on the king's birthday, and printed in 1636. This dramatic entertainment, into which Fleay has read the signs of a theatrical quarrel between Apuleius (Heywood) and Midas (Christopher Beeston), cannot have given much pleasure even to the instructed except in some pretty passages[4], especially in the earlier scenes dealing with the story of Cupid and Psyche; to the uninstructed, it must have seemed a shapeless jumble of mythological learning. Heywood lacked the lyrical gift needed to animate an effort of this nature; and Midas, who repeatedly declines to see out the play, may be pardoned for finding consolation in the dances.

Thus, passing by Heywood's seven pageants (1631—9), to the

---

[1] Cf. Book v, *The Faire ladie of Norwich*.

[2] Cf. Kittredge, G. L., in *The Journal of Germanic Philology*, vol. ii, p. 13.

[3] 'Of all the Christians this arme e'er stay'd,' says the Turkish captain, 'you come the neerest men? What country?' 'England,' replies Ferars, as if he could have been mistaken for a 'Diego' or a mounseer.

[4] The fine lines

>   Oh griefe, that silver haires should crowne his head
>   By whom the Muses are dishonourèd

are, probably, a reminiscence of Spenser.

civic enthusiasm of which reference has already been made, we come, in conclusion, to two plays in which he collaborated with other writers. Of these, *Fortune by Land and Sea* was not printed till 1655, as the joint production of Thomas Heywood and William Rowley (both of whose names were mis-spelt on the title-page); but it belongs to a far earlier date—possibly 1607—9, when both dramatists were included in queen Anne's company[1]. The strong hand of William Rowley may be discernible in this piece, which has a firmer texture than is usual with his fellow playwright, and it may (or may not) have been that hand which gave dramatic form to the adventures and sentiments of the pirates Clinton and Walton (the purser), apparently long-lived favourites of the public—for pirates and patriots were not so very far apart in that spacious age. In substance, however, it is a domestic drama in Heywood's most characteristic manner, while it bears witness once more to his love of the sea. The admirable opening—a tavern brawl, the bloody ending of which forms the starting point of the action[2]—resembles that of Heywood's masterpiece; the troubles of Old Forrest are treated with gentle pathos; and the very humours of the clown are tinged with the kindliness which can relieve even tomfoolery.

The late Lancashire Witches was printed in 1634 as the joint work of Thomas Heywood and Richard Brome. But the story of the play was based, in part, upon an account, published by T. Potts in 1613, of the doings of certain Lancashire women, of whom twelve had suffered death as witches in the previous year; and it is possible that Heywood was the author of a play much earlier than that put on the stage in 1634. In this year, another 'discovery' of witches had attracted public attention, and the principal witness in this case (who appears in the play as the boy) had been brought up to London. This ingenuous creature afterwards confessed that his evidence before the Lancashire magistrates had been suborned, and the accused, unlike their unfortunate predecessors in 1612, were pardoned. But the authors of *The late Lancashire Witches* cannot be acquitted on the charge that they had, *pendente lite*, done their utmost to intensify public feeling against 'witches'— whether or not their play was furbished up from an earlier piece

[1] Cf. *Fleay*, vol. i, p. 294; where see, also, as to the verse account of the two pirates, first entered in the Stationers' register in 1586. The form of the play, in which there is a great deal of rime, favours the assumption of an early date.

[2] Barron Field, in his edition of the play, rightly points out that the degradation of the disinherited eldest son and his wife to the position of farm labourers may not have seemed unnatural to an Elizabethan audience.

written by one of them[1]. This makes it difficult to peruse with
patience the reproduction in this drama of the superstitious fictions
which did twelve unhappy women to death—the 'ridings' through
the air and the unholy assemblies, together with the mischievous
interference at a wedding feast and other rites. Yet, in this
farrago of half realistic nonsense, it is possible to discern the
elements of effective domestic drama, and the touching scene in
which Master Generous seeks to redeem his misguided wife from
her evil practices breathes a spirit akin to that which animates
some of the finest passages in Heywood's dramatic work.

The above, necessarily compendious, review of the extant
writings of this dramatist may have gone some way to make good
the conclusion that the flexibility of his talent as well as his
indefatigable industry enabled him to hold his own in dramatic
species so diverse as the chronicle history, the romantic drama
and the comedy of manners. In addition, he achieved at least one
masterpiece in domestic drama—a species in which his sincerity
and directness, together with a pathetic power springing from a
manly, candid and generous nature, found their most congenial
expression ; while several other of his plays may, at least in part,
be regarded as having contributed to this artistic growth. While
he possessed the gift of genuine pathos, he was incapable of
lending words to passion ; his satiric gift was small, and he rarely
sought to exercise it, his wit and humour moving more or less
within conventional bounds, though his clowns are by no means
invariably tedious. He was not strong in the art of construction,
and the total effect of several of his plays suffers from the by-plots
with which he thought it incumbent on him to eke out their
main action ; but he was singularly skilful both in devising
most effective dramatic situations, and in providing for his plays
a background—usually disclosed in an excellent opening—which
gave to them individuality and variety. He was devoid of any
lyric vein, though the popular sympathies by which he was stirred
might have seemed likely to move him to song—for patriotism,
both national and civic, was second nature to him. Few features
are more striking in him than the love of learning which he
had brought with him from Cambridge and which he nourished by
lifelong application. But from drying up into a pedant he was

[1] See the present writer's account of the play in *English Dramatic Literature*, vol. II,
p. 575; and cf. the late James Crossley's *Introduction* to Potts's *Discoverie of Witches*,
etc. (Chetham Society's Publications, vol. VI, 1845), where will be found much learning
on the subject.

preserved by the manysidedness of his intellectual interests, and by the freshness of spirit that was in him.

A 'prose Shakespeare' Heywood deserves to be called only in so far as he, too, could, on occasion, probe the depths of human nature, touching with the wand of poetic imagination what seemed to him of interest in the homely figures and everyday experiences of contemporary life. When he imitated Shakespeare, as in passages of his plays he did more or less unconsciously[1], this was only in the way of business. He was not the man to dream of donning the armour of Achilles, any more than to aspire to an enduring fame—though of such as is his due meed he is not likely to be deprived.

[1] One or two of these passages may be noted here:

A horse! a horse! (*Part II of If you know not me*, etc.)
What seek ye from the throne?
                   That in which Kings
Resemble most the Gods: Justice. (*A Challenge for Beautie*, act v.)
And hand to hand in single opposition. (*Fortune by Land and Sea*, act ii.)

CHAPTER V

BEAUMONT AND FLETCHER

THE collection of plays with which the names of Beaumont and Fletcher are traditionally associated constitutes the most important body of dramatic work which was produced by the successors of the Elizabethans, that is to say, by those dramatists whose activity belonged wholly to the Stewart period. With this new generation, a new fashion had come in. The genuinely national interest in the drama which especially characterised the last fifteen years of Elizabeth had, to a great extent, passed away, and the taste of the court had become gradually more and more the prevailing influence. This tendency had outwardly expressed itself, nearly at the beginning of the reign of James I, in the fact that all the companies of actors in London then came to be directly under the patronage of the royal family, while the production of plays was, at the same time, subjected to the control of the master of the revels; and, as the older generation of dramatists disappeared, the new fashion showed itself more and more in the character of the plays produced. Ben Jonson's inductions are full of protests against the taste of the day in drama, and especially against the growing tyranny in the matter of criticism exercised by gallants who occupied seats on the stage and assumed the right to damn a play at their pleasure; but he found himself helpless to modify the prevailing fashions. The court of James I had lost the chivalrous aspirations of the earlier time, and the moral corruption which had been held in check, at least to some extent, by noble ideals, had become alarmingly prominent in the life of the upper classes of society. Shallowness and frivolity characterised the manners of the court, even where these were not tinged with gross vices, and a certain superficial brilliancy had taken the place of more estimable qualities. Such a society was naturally disinclined to serious reflection upon the issues of human life, and Shakespearean tragedy was both too wide and too deep for its sympathies. It was, perhaps, a perception of this change of conditions, rather than any marked change in his own genius or temperament, that led Shakespeare to abandon tragedy during the latest years of his connection with the stage, and to entertain his public with dramatic romances. However this may be, a definite preference was manifested, in the period which was then beginning, for that hybrid form of drama which became specially characteristic of the English stage— tragicomedy; in which serious matters are dealt with, but a tragic solution is avoided. Closely connected with this want of moral earnestness was the demand for theatrical entertainments which did not make any serious appeal to the intellect; and, hence, on the one hand, the exaggerated love of pageantry, which was gratified by the magnificence of the masques presented at court, and, on the other, the growing preference, even of the better portion of the audiences at the playhouses, for plots full of interesting events and surprising turns of fortune, rather than such as were developed naturally from situations and characters : the result being a comparative neglect of character interest, and a disregard for the principle of artistic unity.

But, apart from the general relaxation of moral and intellectual fibre which was indicated in these tendencies, there were far more serious evidences of moral decadence. The manners of society had not yet sunk to the prosaic level of profligacy which characterised the period of the Restoration, and the feeling for poetry and romance had not altogether departed; but the court standard of morals with regard to the relations of men and women was decidedly low, and false notions of loyalty and honour, to a great extent, had established themselves in the higher classes of society. In these respects, there is no reason to doubt that the drama of the period reflected the prevailing fashions. Themes of love and honour are those in which an artificial society of this kind is chiefly interested, and it is these which it desires to see dealt with upon the stage. The moral standard of the drama is apt to be the same as that of the community for which it is composed; and where false ideals of conduct in regard to chastity and honour prevail in a society, we may reasonably expect to find them reflected in the drama which is patronised by it.

The tastes of the society which had its centre in the court of James I were, in fact, very faithfully provided for in the series of dramas which have come down to us under the names of

Beaumont and Fletcher; and that these should have been better liked upon the stage than those of Shakespeare ought not to be matter for surprise. In the former, poetry and romance were found in combination with the code of manners and the standard of morals which prevailed among gentlemen; the spectator was entertained by a lively succession of events, contrived with consummate stage-craft to produce the most interesting situations and the most pleasurable surprises, and by a considerable variety of characters, for the most part well sustained, though very deficient in depth and truth to nature when compared with Shakespeare's; while, at the same time, the language was a model of lucidity and purity, altogether free both from tasteless conceits and from the obscurity to which a style either highly figurative or overloaded with thought is liable. Moreover, in the comedies, the audience was interested and delighted by a new style of wit in conversation, which was recognised as just that kind of brilliancy which every courtier would wish to display, and beside which 'the old Elizabeth way' seemed clumsy and oldfashioned.

> Shakespeare to thee was dull, whose best wit lies
> I' the ladies' questions and the fools' replies,
> Old-fashion'd wit, which walk'd from town to town
> In trunk-hose, which our fathers call'd the clown.

So William Cartwright, a fellow poet and dramatist, addressed Fletcher; and Dryden was only repeating a commonplace when he said, comparing Beaumont and Fletcher with Shakespeare, that 'they understood and imitated the conversation of gentlemen much better, whose wild debaucheries and quickness of wit in repartees no poet can ever paint as they have done.' The morality of their plays, bad as it may seem to us in some cases, was by no means looked upon as a just ground of complaint by their contemporaries. On the contrary, the moral improvement to be gained from them is one of the points insisted upon by their panegyrists:

> Vices which were
> Manners abroad, did pass corrected there;
> They who possessed a box and half-crown spent
> To learn obsceneness, returned innocent.

We find here, fully developed for the first time, a species of stage entertainment which is rather an acted romance than a drama in the strict sense of the word; without the intensity of tragedy, but with more emotional interest and a more poetical style of expression than is proper to comedy. The poetical comedy of Shakespeare's middle period had been, to some extent, of this kind; and the species was exemplified further in the work of his latest period, in *Cymbeline, Pericles, The Tempest* and *The Winter's Tale*. Even by Shakespeare, the line between tragedy and comedy, in some instances, is doubtfully drawn, and reconciliations are huddled up when a tragic solution seems rather to be required—as, for example, in *Measure for Measure* and in *Cymbeline*; and still more is this the case with Beaumont and Fletcher. The name 'tragicomedy' is applied usually to about a third of the whole number of their plays, and is equally applicable to a good many more, which are commonly called tragedies or comedies. In fact, the great majority of the plays in this collection are of the intermediate class to which the term 'dramatic romance' is properly applicable, whether they have or have not a tragic catastrophe; and it was this kind of drama that was especially agreeable to the taste of the more aristocratic playgoer. In dramas of this type we may say that variety of incident was aimed at rather than unity of design, diffuseness took the place of concentration, amorous passion became almost the only dramatic motive and the conflict of emotions was of less importance than the romantic interest of situation. The impression made upon the mind of the reader of this large collection of plays is one of astonishment at the richness and variety of dramatic invention which they display; but it is seldom that he is able to commend one of these dramas without very serious reserves, either moral or artistic. The merit belongs usually to particular scenes in a drama rather than to the drama as a whole; and, in cases where there is no ground for criticising the conduct of the design, it is often found that the plot deals with morbid or doubtful situations.

In spite, however, of these general characteristics, it is not the case that the collection which passes under the names of Beaumont and Fletcher is strictly homogeneous, and it is certain that some of the differences which we observe between one portion of it and another arise from diversity of authorship. An attempt, therefore, must be made to distinguish the personalities of the principal contributors.

Of Beaumont and Fletcher as individuals, we know little, except what we can gather from their works. John Fletcher, the elder of the two, born in 1579, was the son of a clergyman, Richard Fletcher, then minister of Rye in Sussex, and afterwards successively dean of Peterborough, and bishop of Bristol, Worcester and London. This 'comely and courtly prelate,' who had the misfortune to fall out of favour with queen Elizabeth because of a second marriage,

died in 1596, leaving a large family very poorly provided for. The
poets Giles and Phineas Fletcher were sons of his younger brother,
first cousins of the dramatist. John Fletcher was educated at Bene't
(Corpus Christi) college, Cambridge, and probably began rather
early to write for the stage. At what time his literary association
with Beaumont began must remain uncertain. Dryden tells us that
Philaster was the first play that brought them into esteem, 'for
before that they had written two or three very unsuccessfully.' Each
may have written plays separately in this early period; but, when
their connection was formed, it was of a more intimate and permanent
character than any other of those partnerships which were frequent
in the history of the Jacobean drama—being based upon personal
friendship rather than upon any merely occasional purpose. They
lived together 'on the Bankside, not far from the Play-house,'
and are reported to have carried their friendship so far as to have
had all things in common. It is, perhaps, worthy of note that
there are several passages in Fletcher's later work which seem to
be reminiscences of such a friendship as this. After Beaumont
left off writing for the stage, Fletcher worked either by himself
or in conjunction with other dramatists, and particularly with
Massinger. He died, of the plague, in 1625, and was buried in
St Saviour's, his parish church. The testimony of Fletcher's
contemporaries is to the effect that he was very sparkling and
brilliant, as good as a comedy in himself, and that his attitude
towards the public was distinguished both by modesty and by
self-respect. Jonson loved him and 'was proud to call him son,'
distinguishing him as one of the few living writers 'besides himself' who could make a masque[1]. His ceaseless activity in the
production of plays, and his readiness to cooperate with various
dramatists in supplying the needs of the stage, suggest the
idea that he was dependent for his livelihood upon the theatre;
but both he and Beaumont were gentlemen by position, and had
probably seen more of fashionable society than most of their
fellow dramatists.

Francis Beaumont was the youngest son of Sir Francis Beaumont of Grace-dieu in Leicestershire, one of the justices of the
common pleas, and brother of John Beaumont, author of
Bosworth Field. He was born probably in 1585, was educated
at Broadgates hall (afterwards Pembroke college), Oxford, and

[1] There are no independent masques attributed to Fletcher, but several are to be
found in the plays to which he contributed, as *The Maides Tragedy* and *The
False One*.

was entered as a member of the Inner Temple in the year 1600. A long poem, after the model of Marlowe's *Hero and Leander*, entitled *Salmacis and Hermaphroditus*, which was published anonymously in 1602, was afterwards attributed to him; but the evidences of authorship are by no means conclusive. He became acquainted with Jonson very early, and wrote a copy of verses in 1605, 'To my dear friend Master Ben Jonson, upon his Fox' (that is, the comedy *Volpone*), in which he declared that to Jonson alone the English stage owed the rules of dramatic art. He paid a similar compliment to two subsequent plays, *The Silent Woman* and *Catiline*; and in all these pieces he expressed a contemptuous opinion of public taste. On one occasion, while staying in the country, he wrote to Jonson a poetical epistle, in which the doings at the Mermaid are alluded to in the well known lines,

> What things have we seen
> Done at the Mermaid, etc.

and Jonson replied in verses which testify respect as well as affection. A tradition reported by Dryden tells us that Beaumont was

> so accurate a judge of plays, that Ben Jonson, while he lived, submitted all his writings to his censure, and 'tis thought used his judgement in correcting, if not contriving, all his plots.

In the freedom of his conversations with Drummond, Jonson let fall the remark that 'Francis Beaumont loved too much himself and his own verses.' Fletcher also, as we have seen, was on terms of friendship with Jonson; and the two young dramatists may have become acquainted with one another through him. We shall see, however, that Beaumont produced at least one play, *The Woman Hater*, independently of his future partner, and in this the influence of Jonson is distinctly predominant. The verses of Beaumont on the stage failure of Fletcher's *Faithfull Shepheardesse*, probably in 1609, again express much contempt of popular judgment. On the marriage of the princess Elizabeth, early in 1613, the inns of court prepared masques, to be presented at Whitehall, and Beaumont supplied that which was provided by the Inner Temple and Gray's inn. This masque is dedicated to Sir Francis Bacon, solicitor general, as one who had 'spared no time or travel in the setting forth, ordering and furnishing' of it. Beaumont was himself married, apparently about two years before his death, to Ursula, daughter of Henry Isley, of Sundridge in Kent; and from this time his relations with Fletcher must have been less intimate, and he may then have given up writing for the stage. He

died in March 1616, a few weeks before Shakespeare, and was
buried in Westminster abbey, in a place not far from the tombs
of Chaucer and Spenser. He wrote several occasional poems,
besides those already mentioned, including elegies on lady Markham, lady Penelope Clifton (a daughter of Sidney's Stella) and the
countess of Rutland (Sidney's daughter); but none of them rise above
mediocrity, and they are disfigured by examples of false taste, from
which the author's dramatic work is free. Among his intimates
was Drayton, who speaks of the two Beaumonts and of Browne as
his dear companions,

> Such as have freely told to me their hearts,
> As I have mine to them.

A certain amount of interest was taken by the succeeding generation in apportioning the qualities of genius displayed in the
Beaumont and Fletcher dramas between these two leading authors
of them. Some, it is true, adopted the convenient, but wholly
uncritical, notion, that Beaumont and Fletcher were so absolutely
alike, that it was a matter of indifference whether they were
regarded as one author or as two, there being a complete 'con-
simility of fancy' between them; but, in general, we note the
acceptance of the conclusion which Pope has made familiar, namely,
that Fletcher contributed the wit and Beaumont the judgment,
and that Beaumont's function was to check the overflowings of
Fletcher's genius. It was natural that, as Fletcher ruled the stage
for a long period after his partner's death, the chief positive
merit should be attributed to him by the generation for whose
tastes he had successfully catered, and that to Beaumont, whose
separate personality was little known, and whose genius, in fact,
was more nearly allied than that of his friend to the spirit of the
former age, should be assigned the negative function of criticism.
So far as the claim to superior judgment may be taken to imply
a more truly artistic conception of dramatic art, it is probable
that it should be admitted in favour of Beaumont; but the idea
that his work consisted chiefly of criticism must be rejected.
It is noticeable that, in the only copy of commendatory verse
which claims to date from the time of Beaumont's death, we hear
nothing of his critical activity, but of

> those excellent things of thine,
> Such strength, such sweetness couch'd in every line,
> Such life of fancy, such high choice of brain.

Moreover, the writer of this, John Earle, does not think it necessary
even to mention the name of Fletcher, while attributing *Philaster*,

The Maides Tragedy and *A King and no King* to Beaumont alone. This, no doubt, is the result of a personal partiality; but we must remember that the verses written later, for the folio of 1647, were, for the most part, equally affected by partiality in the other direction, and, in general, these later compositions can only be relied upon as evidence of the vague impressions prevailing in the public mind in the age which succeeded the death of Fletcher.

The statements of publishers as to the individual or joint authorship of particular plays are scanty and untrustworthy. Four only were printed in Beaumont's lifetime—*The Woman Hater, The Faithfull Shepheardesse, The Knight of the Burning Pestle* and *Cupid's Revenge*—and, of these, two appeared anonymously, while two, *The Faithfull Shepheardesse* and *Cupid's Revenge*, were ascribed to Fletcher alone, the latter, no doubt, wrongly. Five more were printed during the lifetime of Fletcher, *The Scornful Ladie, A King and no King, The Maides Tragedy, Philaster* and *Thierry and Theodoret*. Of these, *The Scornful Ladie, A King and no King* and *Philaster* were ascribed to Beaumont and Fletcher, the other two being anonymous; but there is no probability that these publications were, in any instance, made with Fletcher's authority, and the publisher of *A King and no King* in 1619 was, apparently, unaware that one of the authors to whom it was ascribed was dead. Most of the above-mentioned dramas were reprinted, and a few more were added to the list of published plays, before the death of Massinger, who, as we shall see, contributed largely to the Beaumont and Fletcher collection; and it has been argued that the mention of Beaumont upon the title-page of any quarto published before 1639 proves, at least, that the play was originally produced before Beaumont's death. But it is evident that this kind of reasoning is very unsafe. In 1647, five years after the closing of the theatres, Humphrey Moseley, the bookseller, brought out a folio which professed to contain all the plays of Beaumont and Fletcher that had not hitherto been printed, with the exception of one, of which the copy had been mislaid. Moseley declared that it had been his intention to print Fletcher's works by themselves, but he had finally decided not to separate him from Beaumont. It is probable that he could not have done so if he had desired; but the publication of this folio produced a protest in verse (which might much better have been in prose) from Sir Aston Cokayne, against the general ascription to Beaumont of plays in which, for the most part, he had no share; and, since nearly all the dramas in the composition of which

Beaumont was concerned had already been printed and were, consequently, excluded from this edition, it cannot be denied that the complaint was well founded. He added that his old friend Massinger had contributed to some of the newly printed plays, but that, for the most part, they were 'sole issues of sweet Fletcher's brain.' The same complaint is contained in an epistle to his cousin Charles Cotton, who, as being 'Fletcher's chief bosom friend,' ought to have seen that justice was done to him by the printers. The main importance that these protests have for us consists in the incidental statement about Massinger, whose name had not hitherto been publicly mentioned in connection with the plays of Beaumont and Fletcher; and one of the most interesting and trustworthy results of modern criticism has been to establish, on metrical and other grounds, the extent to which this dramatist collaborated with Fletcher. With regard to Beaumont, our conclusions are, in detail, more uncertain; and possibly, in some cases, plays in which he had a share have been subsequently altered or rewritten, so as partly to obliterate the traces of his hand. A good deal of labour and ingenuity has been expended in the endeavour to solve, by critical methods, the very intricate problems of authorship which present themselves, and it has been found possible to arrive at a tolerably clear idea of the main characteristics of Beaumont's work as distinguished from that of his partner[1]. In certain particular cases, however, there remains much uncertainty, and opinions of very various kinds have been maintained with a confidence of assertion which is by no means justified by the available evidence. When a critic, with no external evidence of authorship before him, concludes that a certain play was originally written by Beaumont, afterwards revised by Fletcher and finally re-written by Middleton, he is evidently dealing in mere guesswork. On the other hand, these investigations have, undoubtedly, been accompanied by a more accurate and systematic study than had previously been made of the individual marks of style by which the dramatists of the period are distinguished, and have, doubtless, helped towards a clearer perception of the true value of metrical tests, as well as of the dangers of a too-mechanical application of them.

The general result of criticism seems to be as follows. It is probable that, of the fifty-two plays which have commonly passed

---

[1] The progress made in recent times may be estimated partly by the remark of Hallam in 1843, that no critic has perceived any difference of style between the two dramatists (*Literature of Europe*, vol. III, p. 98).

under the joint names, at least one belongs to Beaumont alone, and that in some eight or nine others he cooperated with Fletcher, taking, usually, the leading part in the combination; that Fletcher was the sole author of about fifteen plays, and that there are some two-and-twenty, formerly attributed to the pair conjointly, in which we find Fletcher's work combined with that of other authors than Beaumont, besides five or six in which, apparently, neither Fletcher nor Beaumont had any appreciable share. To the general total may be added *Henry VIII*, by Shakespeare and Fletcher, which is commonly regarded as Shakespeare's; *A Very Woman*, which passes under the name of Massinger, but in which Fletcher, probably, had a share; and *Sir John van Olden Barna- velt*, by Fletcher and Massinger, which remained unprinted till quite recently. Among the dramatists with whom Fletcher worked after the retirement of Beaumont, by far the most important place is taken by Massinger, who has a considerable share in at least sixteen plays, and who in justice ought to have been mentioned upon the title-page of the collection. There is evidence, also, of the occasional cooperation of Fletcher with Jonson, Field, Tourneur, W. Rowley and, perhaps, Daborne.

It is evident that any investigation which may be made of the separate styles of Beaumont and Fletcher must, in the first instance, be based upon those plays which may reasonably be attri- buted to Fletcher alone, and these, in fact, will be found to supply a tolerably satisfactory criterion. The metrical style of Fletcher is more unmistakably marked than that of any other dramatist of the period. Its most obvious characteristic is the use of redun- dant syllables in all parts of the line, but especially at the end. So much is this the practice with him that, out of every three of his lines, usually two, at least, have double or triple endings, and even this proportion is often far exceeded. No other writer has anything like this number of feminine endings: in a play of 2500 lines, while Massinger, who approaches Fletcher most nearly in this respect, might, possibly, have as many as 1200 double or triple endings, and Shakespeare, in his latest period, as many as 850, Fletcher would normally have at least 1700, and might not impossibly have as many as 2000; and his marked preference for this form of verse is emphasised by the fact that very often the feminine ending is produced by the addition of some quite unnecessary word, such as 'sir,' 'lady,' 'too,' 'now,' introduced, apparently, for this sole purpose. A characteristic feature, also, of Fletcher's double endings, though not peculiar to him, is that the redundant syllable is occasionally a word of some weight, which cannot be slurred over, *e.g.*

> As many plagues as the corrupted air breeds,

or

> Welcome to the court, sweet beauties! Now the court shines.

The use of redundant syllables elsewhere than at the end of the line is also very frequent, so that the number of syllables in Fletcher's verse ranges, in comedy at least, from ten to fifteen or more.

These peculiarities of rhythm were deliberately adopted for dramatic purposes. Fletcher was quite capable of writing blank verse of the usual type, and in his pastoral drama, *The Faithfull Shepheardesse*, we have nearly two hundred lines of blank verse with not more than ten double endings, and with hardly any superfluous syllables in other parts of the line. For his ordinary dramatic work, however, he chose a form which, in his opinion, was better suited for dramatic expression. The object aimed at was to make the line more loose and flexible and to gain an effect of ease and absence of premeditation. No mouthing is possible in this verse, no rounding off of a description or sentiment with a period; all is abrupt and almost spasmodic, apparently the out-come of the moment. The quick and lively action of the later English stage, with its easy assumption of the ordinary speech of gentlemen, thus developed a metre which could supply the place of prose in the lightest interchange of fashionable repartee.

With this freedom in the matter of syllabic measure, Fletcher combines a singular absence of free movement from verse to verse. His lines, for the most part, are 'end-stopped,' that is to say, they have usually a marked final pause, so that each verse tends to become an independent unit of expression, and the running-on of the sentence from line to line is comparatively rare. The free distribution of pauses in the verse, which is naturally connected with a periodic structure of sentence, is thus seriously restricted, and the intention of excluding, so far as possible, the more rhetori-cal form of expression, and of favouring the use of short sentences of simple structure, is evident. This, no doubt, conduces to clearness, and the effect of discontinuity, which is obtained by coincidence of pause with the end of the loosely constructed line, helps, perhaps, to suggest a spontaneous development of thoughts from the circumstances of the moment. But these advantages are dearly bought by the tiresome monotony which the system involves, a monotony which is only, to some extent, relieved by variation of the position of the internal pause and by the frequent use of the so-called 'lyric' caesura. It is by the combination of the double ending with the stopped line that Fletcher's verse is chiefly distinguished from that of Massinger. Jonson's later verse exhibits, to some extent, the same combination as Fletcher's, and must, to some extent, have been influenced by it. The informal character of Fletcher's verse structure enabled him to dispense entirely with prose in his later work; but it must not be assumed that he never used it at any period. He seems to have almost always avoided rime in his ordinary dramatic verse; employing it occasionally, however, at the end of a scene.

Fletcher's metrical style, generally, is intimately associated with his endeavour to achieve a more lively and dramatic presentation of thought. Shakespeare, in his later work, to a great extent discarded the periodic structure of the sentence, and adopted what we may call the disjointed style, as more dramatic; but his method was altogether different from that of Fletcher. Instead of strengthening the end pause, he, to a great extent, abolished it, and attained his object by methods which, in the hands of an inferior writer, would have altogether disorganised the verse. Indeed, a comparison of Fletcher with Shakespeare generally would tend chiefly to emphasise the difference of their styles. Shakespeare's unequalled rapidity of imagination makes him concise even to obscurity, especially in his later work; he more and more abounds in metaphor, finding no leisure to do more than indicate his comparisons; and this pregnant brevity carries with it extraordinary force. Fletcher, on the other hand, notwithstanding the rapidity of action in his dramas, is inclined to move slowly in the expression of thoughts and feelings. 'He lays line upon line, making up one after the other, adding image to image so deliberately that we see where they join. Shakespeare mingles everything, he runs line into line, embarrasses sentences and metaphors; before one idea has burst its shell, another is hatched and clamorous for disclosure[1].' But this very quality of Fletcher's style, this clear presentation of ideas and images in due succession, was likely to make him the more popular of the two poets upon the stage, and helps, in some measure, to account for the fact that, in the latter part of the seventeenth century, two of 'Beaumont and Fletcher's' plays were acted for one of Shakespeare's or Jonson's.

In the plays which there is good reason to attribute partly or entirely to Beaumont, characteristics of style appear that are quite different from those which we have noticed in Fletcher's work.

[1] Lamb, *Specimens of the Dramatists.*

We find here a type of verse which rather resembles that of Shakespeare's middle period, with a small proportion of double endings, few redundant syllables in other parts of the verse, no marked tendency to pause at the end of the line, but a measured eloquence, and a certain rounded fulness of rhythm, which lend themselves well to poetical narrative and description. With this, there are tolerably frequent instances of occasional rime at the end of speeches and, also, elsewhere, and a free use of prose as the language of ordinary conversation. In verse passages, instead of a succession of short sentences, we notice a tendency, rather, to complex structure, and to enlargement by repetition or parenthesis, though without any failure in lucidity, and usually with a faultless balance of clauses. Such sentence and verse structure as we have in the following passage is quite alien to Fletcher's style :

> It were a fitter hour for me to laugh,
> When at the altar the religious priest
> Were pacifying the offended powers
> With sacrifice, than now. This should have been
> My rite, and all your hands have been employ'd
> In giving me a spotless offering
> To young Amintor's bed, as we are now
> For you. Pardon, Evadne; 'would my worth
> Were great as yours, or that the king, or he,
> Or both, thought so! perhaps he found me worthless·
> But till he did so, in these ears of mine
> These credulous ears, he pour'd the sweetest words
> That art or love could frame[1].

In addition to the more external marks of style, we note in these plays a feature which is hardly to be found in any of Fletcher's admitted work, namely, the element of burlesque or mock-heroic. *The Woman Hater*, which abounds in this form of humour, is now generally assigned to Beaumont alone, and *The Knight of the Burning Pestle* is admitted to be either entirely, or almost entirely, his.

Apart from these, the dramas which, upon critical grounds, can, with confidence, be attributed to the joint authorship of Beaumont and Fletcher are the following: *The Scornful Ladie, Philaster, The Maides Tragedy, A King and no King, Cupid's Revenge, The Coxcombe* and *Four Plays in One.* A few others, as *Wit At severall Weapons, The Nice Valour, Loves Cure* and *The Little French Lawyer,* have been assigned partly to Beaumont, not so much on the evidence of style, as because it has been thought that, in their original form, they date from a time when Beaumont

---

[1] *The Maides Tragedy,* act II, sc. 1.

and Fletcher were working in partnership. But the assumption of an early date for these plays is extremely doubtful, and, even if this were admitted, it would not follow that the attribution of part authorship to Beaumont was correct.

From the above list, the superiority of Beaumont's genius in 'tragedy,' that is to say, drama upon the tragic level of seriousness, is apparent, for it includes the three most celebrated plays of this kind in the whole series. And, when we come to examine these plays more closely, we find reason to believe that the principal part in them was decisively taken by the younger writer. The plotting and construction of *Philaster, The Maides Tragedy* and *A King and no King*, in spite of obvious faults, show a firmer hand than is visible in any of Fletcher's later work, and it is significant that no source has been found for the plots of any one of these three plays, which, not improbably, are of the authors' own invention. In the essential feature of artistic unity, they suggest the work of the young dramatist who, according to tradition, was consulted by Jonson about his plots, and it seems probable that, in constructive faculty at least, Beaumont was markedly superior to his colleague. Beaumont shows much the same liking for romantic incidents which we find in Fletcher, and sometimes gives a happy solution of an otherwise tragic plot; but he has far more intensity of conception, and in some of his work this is combined with an effective use of tragic irony, such as we do not find in Fletcher's more loosely constructed drama. His characters, too, are more original and striking, and it seems probable that the remarkable creations of Evadne and Arbaces are to be attributed chiefly to Beaumont. Of the more ordinary characters, certain particular types seem to belong especially to him, the love-lorn maiden, for example, as exemplified by Euphrasia in *Philaster* and by Aspatia in *The Maides Tragedy*, and the poetical and romantic young man, as shown in the persons of Philaster and Amintor. Fletcher's heroines, however deep in love, are less poetical, more full of resource and less pureminded than Beaumont's maidens; while his young men have more of the fashionable gentleman and less of the idealist than these rather sentimental heroes. A peculiar vein of tenderness and delicacy marks some of Beaumont's delineations of lovers in the less exalted sphere, as the Gerrard and Violante of *The Triumph of Love*, and the Ricardo and Viola of *The Coxcombe*. Beaumont, as has been already observed, shows a more distinct affinity than Fletcher with the older Elizabethan school. In pure comedy, Jonson is his master; but, even here, the imitation of Shakespeare is frequent, and still more so in *Philaster*, which has many points of contact with *Hamlet* and with *Cymbeline*, the latter of which was produced, perhaps, in the same year[1]. Fletcher, also, has imitations of Shakespeare; but they are neither so numerous nor so close as those of his partner.

As regards the remaining plays, we have to take account of some other authors, and more especially of Massinger. Massinger is distinguished by a type of verse which has a large proportion of double endings (though far fewer than Fletcher's), combined with a free distribution of pauses and a free running-on from line to line; he uses a periodic structure of sentence in serious or poetical passages, and inserts parentheses frequently. He can also be traced by a habit of repeating certain favourite phrases and images, and the combination of these characteristic expressions with the metrical and other indications to which we have referred may generally be regarded as decisive evidence of his authorship. The features imported by Massinger into the work which he shares with Fletcher are a more oratorical style of expression, greater moral earnestness and, in particular, a tendency to throw scenes into such a form that they contain pleading both for and against a given thesis. He is stronger than Fletcher in plotting and construction, and it is observable that, in several of the plays in which these two are fellow workers, Massinger supplies a framework which is filled in by Fletcher, whose strength lies in the management of particular scenes rather than in the conduct of the drama as a whole. This seems to be the case, for example, with *The False One*, *The Beggars Bush* and *The Elder Brother*. On the whole, it may be said that considerable injustice has been done to Massinger by the popular ascription of much of his work to Fletcher: several of the best dramas of the collection owe their merit very largely to Massinger.

Fletcher excelled as a master of immediate stage effect, and none knew better how to compensate for the want of higher artistic aims by variety of characters, and by a lively succession of incidents and actions, which leave the spectator no time to reflect upon the effect of the whole. His aim was to keep his audience well entertained, and he was often content to produce a series

---

[1] See Leonhardt, B., in *Anglia*, vol. VIII, pp. 424 ff.; and Thorndike, A. H., *The Influence of Beaumont and Fletcher on Shakespeare*. The contention of the latter, that *Cymbeline* is an imitation of *Philaster*, and not *vice versa*, is rendered less probable by the fact that there are many undoubted imitations of Shakespeare in *Philaster*, as well as elsewhere in Beaumont and Fletcher.

of effective situations, with no true principle of unity. Langbaine says,

I have either read or been informed that it was generally Mr Fletcher's practice, after he had finished three acts of a play, to show them to the actors, and after they had agreed upon terms, he huddled up the two last without that proper care which was requisite.

The statement is either true or well invented; and, if true, it would account for the phenomena observed in such plays as *The Custome of the Countrey* and *The Pilgrim*. Fletcher's almost regular practice was to take two separate stories, so that the play might not be deficient in persons and incidents, and to work them out side by side, establishing such links between them as he conveniently could, but often leaving them without vital connection. The desire for immediate effect leads to the frequent use of surprises in the development of the plot, and the introduction of incidents for which no due preparation has been made. Hence, also, a too great fondness for violent situations, and for the representation of extreme physical agony, as in *Valentinian* and *A Wife for a Month*. Naturally, stage conventions were utilised by such a dramatist in every possible manner, and a considerable part is played by sudden change of feeling, including violent and irresistible love, and dramatically unjustifiable conversion of character[1].

Characterisation is naturally weakened by the excess of incident in the plot. As Dryden says, 'the manners can never be evident where the surprises of fortune take up all the business of the stage, and where the poet is more in pain to tell you what happened to such a man than what he was.' Fletcher's character drawing, in fact, is rather superficial, and his tendency is to follow certain well marked lines, so that types, rather than individuals, are produced. We have, to some extent, a recurrence of the types already presented in the Beaumont plays; the wicked and lustful monarch reappearing in Valentinian, Antigonus and Frederick, the impossibly loyal subject in Aecius and Archas, the blunt soldier in Memnon and Leontius. On the other hand, Fletcher seems especially responsible for the types of superhuman virtue and of incredible vice in women, which appear in his serious drama, Lucina, Ordella and Evanthe, on the one hand, and, on the other, Brunhalt, Lelia and Hippolyta. About all these there is a certain element of exaggeration: Fletcher's imagination is not fully to be trusted to present the simple and natural effects of true modesty and chastity in women, and this is an undeniable blot upon his

[1] See *John Fletcher* by Hatcher, O. L., pp. 60 ff., where this subject is well worked out in detail.

work in the higher drama. In the characters which properly
belong to comedy, he draws from the life and is often highly
successful. There is the young man of wit and gallantry, brilliant
and irresponsible, who may or may not be in love, but is entirely
free from romantic sensibility : Monsieur Thomas, for example, or
Don John, Mirabel or Valentine. These, we feel, are the men
whom Fletcher has actually known in living society : their profligacy is rather a matter of fashion than anything else ; they are
generous and good-hearted, as a rule, and the vice which colours
their conversation and behaviour is not of a very deep dye. Then,
we have the corresponding young woman, witty and resourceful,
well able to take care of herself for the most part, but wanting in
the poetical tenderness of a Viola or an Aspatia. There is a
certain charm about these girls ; but their chastity is too much of
the formal order, and, if we are to judge them by their speech,
we must condemn them as wanting in delicacy. Nevertheless,
Fletcher's Celia and Oriana, Mary and Alinda, are, to some extent,
akin to Shakespeare's Beatrice and Rosalind.

The stories which Fletcher uses for his plays are, perhaps, never
of his own invention. Occasionally, he draws from historical or
quasi-historical sources, as in *Thierry and Theodoret*, *Valentinian*,
Bonduca, *The False One*, *The Island Princesse* and *The Prophetesse*; but he deals with these as with romance. The only
example of a drama in which regard is paid to the truth of history
is afforded by *Barnavelt*, which is based upon contemporary
events in the Netherlands. He took stories from many various
authors, from Bandello (through Painter's *Palace of Pleasure*)
from the *Astrée* of Honoré d'Urfé and from d'Audiguier ; but the
material which suited his genius best was that which he derived
directly or indirectly from Spanish sources[1]. To these, he turned
comparatively late in his career ; but, from the year 1619 onwards,
he used them very freely. Among the Spanish stories of which
he is known to have made use are *Historia de Aurelio y de
Ysabela*, *El Español Gerardo*, no less than three of the *Novelas
Exemplares* of Cervantes, and also his romance of *Persiles y
Sigismunda*. Besides these, very probably, there were others which
have not been distinctly identified. The abundance of incident
and the lively style of narration in these stories exactly suited
Fletcher's purpose; but, even here, he usually follows his method of
combining two stories together, so as to increase the number of

---

[1] Cf. on this subject the chapter on the influence of Spanish upon English literature
in vol. VIII, *post*.

characters and the bustle of the action. For the most part, it is evident that French or English translations of these Spanish stories were used by Fletcher in the construction of his plots, and it has been questioned whether he was acquainted with the Spanish language. The contemporary Spanish stage might have supplied him with abundant materials, and its methods in comedy were not very unlike his own; but Spanish plays were not very accessible to English readers; and, though the assumption has frequently been made that the Beaumont and Fletcher plays are partly founded upon Spanish dramas, it is to be noted that this has in no instance been actually shown to be the case. A recent attempt to prove that *Loves Cure* is taken from a comedy by Guillén de Castro can hardly be regarded as successful[1].

Fletcher's rapidity of production, evidently, was very considerable, and a tolerably correct estimate may be formed of it from the work of some of his later years, which, owing to the existence of official records, may be dated with tolerable accuracy. In the four years 1619—22, he seems to have produced at least sixteen plays, six by himself alone and the remainder in combination with Massinger. The total reckoning of about forty plays for the last twelve years of his life, of which fourteen or fifteen were written by himself alone, and the remainder in combination with other authors, gives a result not very different from this, and implies a ceaseless activity in production which would leave little leisure for reflection. He was not a great literary artist, but a highly gifted craftsman, with much fertility of invention and a thorough mastery of the practical requirements of the stage; while, at the same time, his work bears witness to a true vein of poetical feeling, and has an easy grace of style which must attract even those who are most repelled by his want of high ideals. In this connection, it seems opportune to call attention to the exceptional excellence of the songs which appear throughout this collection of dramas. Massinger does not introduce songs into the plays of which he is sole author, and, though Beaumont was certainly a song-writer—there is an excellent song in *The Woman Hater*, for example, and some of those in *The Maides Tragedy* are probably his—yet it is evident that the songs which we find in the plays must be due, for the most part, to the lyrical genius of Fletcher. Altogether, there are upwards of seventy; and, of these, at least twenty are extremely good. Besides being of exquisite quality, the lyrics have a remarkable range of subject and treatment: ' Hence all you vain

---

[1] Stiefel, A. L., in Herrig's *Archiv*, xcix, pp. 271 ff.

delights,' the poet's celebration of melancholy, is followed, in the same play, after the lapse of a few scenes, by the spirited laughing-song 'O how my lungs do tickle'; in *Valentinian*, 'Care-charming Sleep' stands side by side with the drinking song, 'God Lyaeus, ever young.' 'All ye woods and trees and bowers' in *The Faithfull Shepheardesse*, 'Tell me, dearest, what is love' in *The Captaine* and 'Beauty clear and fair' in *The Elder Brother* are examples of the more gracefully poetical form of lyric; while a more popular and spirited kind is exemplified in the battle song 'Arm, Arm,' the convivial lyrics 'Sit, soldiers, sit and sing' and ''Tis late and cold,' the beggars' songs in *The Beggars Bush*, 'Cast our caps and cares away,' and the rest, the kitchen song, 'Three merry boys,' in *The Bloody Brother*, and the spirited ballad 'Let the bells ring' of *The Spanish Curate*. It may fairly be said that no dramatist of the age except Shakespeare has given such undeniable proof of lyrical inspiration as Fletcher.

The plays of Beaumont and Fletcher are traditionally classified as tragedies, tragicomedies and comedies, and, in the preface to *The Faithfull Shepheardesse*, Fletcher defines the second of these forms in a characteristically superficial manner, as follows:

A tragicomedy is not so called in respect of mirth and killing, but in respect it wants deaths, which is enough to make it no tragedy, yet brings some near it, which is enough to make it no comedy, which must be a representation of familiar people, with such kind of trouble as no life be questioned.

The happy ending of what Dryden calls 'serious plays' was, as we have seen, more in accordance with the taste of the public than the tragic catastrophe, and, like Beaumont and Fletcher, Shakespeare also accommodated himself to the popular demand. Of the whole collection which passes under the names of Beaumont and Fletcher, twelve dramas rank as tragedies, in the strict sense of the term, and about twenty may be called tragicomedies. There would, however, be no advantage in attaching importance to this distinction: the tragedies and tragicomedies belong essentially to the same class—plays in which the romantic interest predominates; while, at the same time, though there may be a difficulty, some-times, in drawing the line between tragicomedy and comedy, the latter, on the whole, is to be regarded as a distinct genus, and may properly be dealt with separately.

Apart, then, from comedy, the first production was probably *The Faithfull Shepheardesse*, a pastoral drama by Fletcher alone. Though superior in liveliness of dramatic action to the Italian

pastoral dramas which served as its models, it was unsuccessful on
the stage—a fact attributed by its author to the absence of that
peculiar combination of 'mirth and killing' intermixed with
'Whitsun ales and morris-dances' which the public expected from
a 'pastoral tragicomedy.' In respect of poetical beauty, *The
Faithfull Shepheardesse* ranks very high, and Milton paid it the
compliment of imitation in *Comus*[1]. The greater part is in rime;
but the opening scenes are mainly in blank verse, and it is noticeable
that here Fletcher does not display the metrical peculiarities which
are a marked feature of his style elsewhere, a fact which, perhaps,
should make us cautious in the application of metrical tests to
the earliest plays of the series, though in *The Maides Tragedy*
Fletcher's characteristics are already quite apparent.

Philaster is said by Dryden to have been the first play which
brought Beaumont and Fletcher into notice, and it certainly
enjoyed great popularity. Its merits, both dramatic and poetical,
are undeniable; but the plot has been justly criticised because of
the too ready credence given by Philaster to the charge against his
mistress. The character of Euphrasia-Bellario, who follows in the
disguise of a page the person to whom she is romantically attached,
is, to some extent, a reproduction of Shakespeare's Viola, and close
resemblances have been noted between this play and others of
Shakespeare; but the use which we have here of surprise as a
means of dramatic effect is highly characteristic of the authors.
The poetical merit of several passages in *Philaster* is well known,
and especially the description of the first finding of Bellario.

The leading place among the dramas of Beaumont and Fletcher
has always been held by *The Maides Tragedy*, and the justice of
this popular judgment cannot reasonably be questioned. The plot,
like those of *Philaster* and *A King and no King*, seems to be of
the authors' own invention. The tragic situation, unpleasing as it
may be, is admirably developed, and the two principal characters,
the brother and sister Melantius and Evadne, are powerfully presented and may fairly claim the merits of truth and consistency.
There is a certain weakness, however, in the character of Amintor,
whose reverence for the sacred name of king amounts to a disease;
and Aspatia, in spite of the pathos of her situation and the poetical
attractions with which she is invested, is lacking in reserve and
dignity and displays too much extravagance in seeking her own
death at the hands of Amintor. Little further fault is to be found

[1] As to the place of *The Faithfull Shepheardesse* in English pastoral drama, cf. *post*,
chap. XIII.

with *The Maides Tragedy,* of which the action is developed in a series of scenes of great dramatic effectiveness, culminating in that between Melantius and Evadne at the crisis of the plot. The dramatists exhibit a true knowledge of human nature in showing us how the profligate effrontery of Evadne, against which the pure-minded Amintor is powerless, breaks down when confronted with her brother's ruthless determination. Her sensuous nature is, at first, capable of being influenced only by physical terror, and it is through this motive that she is brought to realise the depth of infamy to which she has fallen. With equal truth, she is represented as readily accepting the idea of blotting out her guilt by a deed of violent revenge, and as imagining that she will pave the way to a reconciliation with Amintor by a deed which merely strikes him with new horror. Some of the minor characters are excellently drawn, and the scene in which Melantius urges Callianax in the very presence of the king to yield up to him the keys of the fort has true comic humour, while, at the same time, it is strictly appropriate to the plot and the characters. A good deal of imitation of Shakespeare is again apparent—especially in the cele-brated quarrel between Melantius and Amintor, which is partly suggested by that between Brutus and Cassius in *Julius Caesar.*

A King and no King, licensed for the stage in 1611, was hardly less celebrated than *The Maides Tragedy,* and undoubtedly it displays dramatic power of a very high order. The praise of this play must be qualified, however, by consideration of one capital fault. The supposed incestuous passion, with which the plot deals, instead of leading to a tragic catastrophe, is fully condoned on the strength of a merely accidental discovery. Apart from this, the drama is admirable. In the vainglorious and passionate character of Arbaces, we have an original creation of great merit, to which the blunt Mardonius, with his fearless plainspeaking, serves as an ad-mirable foil; while Bessus, imitated, to some extent, from Bobadill, is one of the most amusing specimens of his class. There is a concentrated power in the development of this drama which creates a strong impression as to the dramatic ability of the authors, though, for the reason which has been stated, the total result remains not altogether satisfactory.

Cupid's Revenge was, perhaps, acted in 1612. The plot has been found fault with as based upon mythology; but this does not seem to be a valid objection here. Whatever the machinery may be, we accept the actual results as the natural punishment of youthful arrogance, the brother and sister who have planned to put down the worship

of love being themselves involved in ruin through their passion for
unworthy objects. The real weakness of the drama lies in the want
of concentration: the death of Hidaspes occurs in the second act,
before the main complication has been fully developed, and the
death of her brother Leucippus at the end of the fifth act is, after
all, accidental and unnecessary. The characters of Leucippus and
of Bacha are well sustained, and the scenes between them are
effectively conducted. In the disguises of Urania and in the
rescue of Leucippus by the citizens, we have a repetition of devices
already used in *Philaster*.

Four Plays in One, of uncertain date, consists of an induction
and four '*Triumphs*'—'*of Honour*,' '*of Love*,' '*of Death*' and '*of
Time*[1]'—the former two, probably, by Beaumont and the latter two
by Fletcher. Beaumont's contributions are here distinctly the
more interesting and valuable.

The Captaine is an ill constructed drama (as the authors seem
to be aware), having two sets of characters with little connection
between them. It has no merits sufficient to compensate for the
odiousness of the character of Lelia, whose conversion is not rendered in the least credible. The play, however, contains two charming
songs, 'Tell me, dearest, what is love,' and 'Away delights.'

The Honest mans Fortune was played in 1613; but it contains
no apparent trace of Beaumont's style. Several authors—probably
Tourneur, Massinger and Field—were here concerned with Fletcher,
and, between them, they produced a piece of patchwork which is
far from satisfactory as a drama, though particular scenes and
speeches deserve praise. Fletcher's part, apparently, is confined to
the fifth act. To nearly the same date belongs the first production
of *King Henry VIII*, in which we find excellent work by Fletcher
in combination with that of Shakespeare[2].

Bonduca, for which Fletcher was mainly responsible, is one
of the most effective of the tragic romances. It is founded upon
ancient British history ; but the materials are very freely handled,
the stories of Boadicea and Caractacus being brought into combination. The play presents a spirited succession of camp and
battle scenes, made interesting, first, by the figures of Bonduca and
her daughters, and then by those of the heroic Caractacus and the
brave boy Hengo—the latter an original creation of the dramatist,
which strongly engages our sympathies.

[1] Cf. *ante*, chap. IV, as to *Five Plays in One* assigned on insufficient grounds to
Thomas Heywood.
[2] Cf. *ante*, vol. v, chap. VIII, p. 195.

Valentinian, by Fletcher alone, is, in some respects, the most typical example of his work in tragedy. The situation is admirably prepared in the first act, and the events are successfully conducted through the scenes of the second to a tragic climax in the third. From this point, however, the author's desire to rouse interest by new and surprising developments gets the better of his feeling for dramatic propriety. A new series of events is introduced, for which we are totally unprepared; and the revolting treachery of Maximus towards his friend, together with the revelation of his selfish designs, turns our sympathy away from the quarter to which it was at first directed, and leaves us finally puzzled and dissatisfied. Aecius, perfectly plainspoken to his sovereign on the subject of his vices, but steadily maintaining the principle of loyalty and discipline, is an excellent character, and by no means deserves the reproach of servility which was cast upon him by Coleridge and has been repeated by other critics. It may be added that this tragedy is exceptionally rich in beautiful lyrics.

The date of *The Bloody Brother, or Rollo, Duke of Normandy* is uncertain; but it was probably produced about the year 1616. It is an effective drama, and was reckoned by Rymer with *Philaster*, *The Maides Tragedy* and *A King and no King*, as among the most celebrated tragedies of its age. Four authors seem to have been concerned in this play, and it is probable that the remarkable political reflections in the first scene of the fourth act are to be ascribed to Jonson. A small part only is by Fletcher, to whom, however, are due the striking scenes between Rollo and Edith in the third and fifth acts. Of the former of these scenes, Coleridge remarks that it exhibits 'probably the grandest working of passion in all Beaumont and Fletcher's dramas'; the latter he criticises severely because of the momentary weakening of Edith's resolve, comparing her with lady Anne in *Richard III*. But it is one thing for a woman to hesitate in the execution of her purpose to kill, because of the apparent repentance of her victim, and quite another for her to yield to flattery and accept as a lover the murderer of her husband. Fletcher, Massinger and a third author, apparently, took part in the tragedy of *Thierry and Theodoret*, which probably belongs to the year 1617. Here, the purity and self-sacrifice of Ordella are well contrasted with the wantonness and cruelty of Brunhalt, and the scene in the fourth act between Thierry and Ordella has been justly admired. 'I have always considered this to be the finest scene in Fletcher,' is Lamb's remark, followed, nevertheless, by criticisms of the conduct of it, as slow and languid compared with Shakespeare's best.

The Queene of Corinth is a poor play. The sympathy which Merione at first excites is totally destroyed by her subsequent behaviour. *The Loyal Subject*, licensed in the autumn of 1618, exhibits, in the person of its hero Archas, a partial repetition of Aecius. Like many of Fletcher's plays, this is simply a dramatised romance, with no proper complication or resolution. The story is interesting enough; but the disguise of young Archas serves no such useful purpose as to compensate for its improbability, and the conversion of Boroskie can hardly be called natural.

The Knight of Malta has many of the elements of a fine drama, especially in the first and fifth acts, which are by an unknown author. The character of Oriana is exalted and yet human; while Mountferrat is a genuinely romantic villain. But the device of Miranda in fighting against Oriana's champion, in order to save her credit by voluntary defeat, has no merit except that of surprise.

The plot of *The Mad Lover* is hopelessly absurd, and very deficient in respect of unity; but the courtship of Memnon is certainly amusing, and the conclusion of the play is well managed. There is a poor attempt at a fool, the only character of the kind in Beaumont and Fletcher's plays. *Women pleas'd* is still more faulty in construction. It contains two very distinct plots, with two separate sets of characters, which have little or nothing to do with one another, a practice too often followed in the later plays. There are some interesting scenes, but the drama cannot be said to be of much value as a whole.

The tragedy of *Sir John van Olden Barnavelt*, by Fletcher and Massinger, has special interest as a dramatisation of contemporary history, and is remarkable as an indication of the readiness with which these authors were able to utilise such materials as presented themselves. It is a somewhat hasty piece of work, produced in August 1619, and dealing with events which had taken place in May of the same year. The trial scene is rhetorically effective; but the character of Barnavelt is not represented in a sufficiently consistent manner, and the necessity of reproducing the actual course of events was not favourable to a strictly dramatic development.

The Custome of the Countrey, by Fletcher and Massinger, founded on the *Persiles y Sigismunda* of Cervantes, is a drama of considerable merit, but unfortunately marred by grossness in some of the scenes. The scene in which Guiomar conceals the supposed slayer of her son is admirably managed, and the contrast of Zenocia and Hippolyta is effective; but the conversion of Hippolyta is one of those sudden turns to which Fletcher too frequently sacrifices consistency of character.

It is doubtful whether Fletcher had any hand in *The Lawes of Candy*, and certainly no scene can be attributed to him as a whole. Massinger probably was the principal author, and the judicial pleading between father and son is quite characteristic of him. *The double Marriage*, by Fletcher and Massinger, is a poor play, with a confused plot and no sufficient reason for the catastrophe. On the other hand, *The False One*, produced by the same authors at about the same time, is a drama of considerable interest, and contains much brilliant rhetoric, especially in the speeches of Caesar in the second act. At the same time, it cannot be said to have a genuinely dramatic structure, and, though the conclusion involves the death of several persons, the play, properly speaking, is not a tragedy.

In the plays which immediately follow, romantic interest decidedly predominates. *The Pilgrim*, usually classed as a comedy, is, in fact, as Coleridge calls it, a 'romantic entertainment,' and one of considerable merit, though the high promise of the opening scenes is not fully kept. We could very well dispense with the madhouse; but the public of that day evidently found such representations attractive. *The Prophetesse, The Island Princesse* and *The Sea Voyage* have little merit as dramas, and such interest as they possess is due partly to the remoteness from ordinary experience of the circumstances and localities represented. In *The Beggars Bush*, on the other hand, though the plot is romantic, the interest of the play depends not on this, but upon the attempt at a realistic representation of vagabond life. In this it has distinct originality, and the authors have gone direct to native English sources. The liveliness and truth to nature of these scenes are sufficient to account for the exceptional popularity of the play.

The Lovers Progress is an interesting drama, originally, perhaps, by Fletcher, but extensively revised and altered by Massinger. The play exhibits love and friendship in an exalted and poetical manner : the speech of Clarange near the beginning of the second act, describing his friendship with Lidius, reads like a personal reminiscence by Fletcher of his own relations with

Beaumont. The ghost scene at the inn, which was greatly admired by Scott, has some comic humour, but serves chiefly to show how incapable Fletcher was of dealing with the supernatural. The later appearance of the ghost, which is more impressive, occurs in a scene which, in its present form, is due to Massinger.

The Maid in the Mill, by Fletcher and William Rowley, is an ill constructed play, with some poetry, and some fairly good comic business[1].

A Wife for a Month, by Fletcher alone, has an ingeniously complicated plot, and is far superior in construction to most of the author's dramatic romances. The rather unpleasant situation is developed with considerable power and skill, and the play contains many poetical passages. The immodest speeches of the 'chaste wife' Evanthe, and the easy forgiveness of Frederick and his instruments of villainy, are characteristic of Fletcher.

The vexed question of authorship connected with *The Two Noble Kinsmen* cannot here be discussed. Fletcher's contribution to this fine heroic romance is, on the whole, of secondary importance; but one of his scenes, the last in the third act, is, dramatically, perhaps the most effective in the play[2]. *Loves Pilgrimage* is a romance from Cervantes, apparently rewritten by Shirley with insertions from Jonson's *New Inne*. It has some merit as a story, and the serious scenes are unusually thoughtful. *The Faire Maide of the Inne* was produced after Fletcher's death, and it is doubtful whether he had any hand in it, for his style is not clearly perceptible in any scene. The plot, derived from Spanish sources, is badly put together and extremely improbable. Another example of a drama wrongly ascribed to Beaumont and Fletcher in the seventeenth century is *The Coronation*, which is contained in the folio of 1679, but is known to be by Shirley. On the other hand, *A Very Woman, or The Prince of Tarent*, ascribed to Massinger, is, apparently, in part by Fletcher, to whom we may reasonably ascribe the whole of the third act, including the lively slavemarket scene, and a part of the fourth. *The Faithful Friends*, printed for the first time in 1812, has no sufficient claim to be included among Beaumont and Fletcher's works.

The list of comedies begins with *The Woman Hater*, which, apparently, is by a single author, and is now generally attributed

---

[1] As to the distinctness of the shares of Fletcher and Rowley in this play, see *ante*, chap. III.

[2] Compare *ante*, vol. v, chap. X.

to Beaumont alone. It exhibits strongly the influence of Jonson, and, though not a comedy of humours, in the full sense of the term, turns entirely upon the 'humorous' eccentricity of the principal character. This feature is still discernible, though much less obvious, in *The Scornful Ladie*, an excellent comedy of its kind, dealing with English domestic manners. This was one of the most popular plays of the series, and exercised a considerable influence on the later comedy, especially by virtue of the character of the steward Savile, and his relations with his masters. The conversion of Morecraft, which is criticised by Dryden as unnatural, is not really open to this objection. The usurer has become convinced by experience that what pays best is extravagance, and, therefore, he is following his natural instincts in becoming a prodigal. The mock heroic style, which is one of Beaumont's characteristics, appears, to some extent, in these comedies, and reaches full development in *The Knight of the Burning Pestle*, a masterpiece in its own kind. The idea suggested by *Don Quixote* was here ingeniously and brilliantly applied to the purpose of ridiculing the taste of the city in drama—a fact which probably accounts for its being coldly received by the popular audience before which it was first acted. Its comic merits are, undoubtedly, of a high order, especially in the characteristic figures of the citizen and his wife and in their criticisms of the performance.

In *The Coxcombe*, we have a romantic comedy with two distinct plots. For the Ricardo and Viola story, Beaumont is mainly responsible, and this little romance is treated in a charming manner. The tinker and his trull are represented, probably by Fletcher, with effective realism, and the scenes at the farmhouse are interesting and natural. Side by side with this, we have a comedy of intrigue, taken, perhaps, from the *Curioso Impertinente* of Cervantes. Some of Antonio's tricks recall those of Loveless in *The Scornful Ladie*.

It cannot be said with certainty that Beaumont had a part in any of the remaining comedies, and the genius of Fletcher is decisively dominant from this point onwards, though other writers sometimes worked with him. The faults of Fletcher as a dramatist—looseness of construction and superficiality in character—are less fatal in comedy than in serious drama, while his abundance of lively incident and his brilliant dialogue produce their full effect. Nevertheless, his comedies suffer too frequently from want of vital connection between the various intrigues utilised by the plot, and even the best of them succeed rather by clever stagecraft than by genuinely artistic merit.

Several of these plays may be classed together as exhibiting the Jonsonian principle of 'humour,' though hardly in the Jonsonian manner. These are, especially, *The Little French Lawyer*, *The Nice Valour* and *The Humorous Lieutenant*. In the first, by Fletcher and Massinger, the character of La Writ, who gives a title to the play, is genuinely comic, but not absolutely necessary to the plot. *The Nice Valour* is a poor play, notwithstanding a confident assertion to the contrary in the epilogue; but it contains several good lyrics, including the song, 'Hence all you vain delights.' *The Humorous Lieutenant*, by Fletcher alone, takes its name, like *The Little French Lawyer*, from a character which has no very essential connection with the principal plot. The part which concerns the lieutenant is pure farce, lively and amusing enough; while, in the main plot, we have the romance of an unusually attractive pair of lovers, though it must be remarked that their situation is a very improbable one.

This combination, or juxtaposition, of a romantic with a comic plot, which has been noted as a frequent feature of the so-called tragicomedies, is exemplified, also, in *The Spanish Curate*, which consists, in fact, of a romance and a comedy, combined under a title which belongs properly to the comedy. We have here two distinct stories with very small connection between them, though an attempt is made at the conclusion to unite them under a single moral lesson. Roughly speaking, it may be said that the romance is by Massinger and the comedy by Fletcher: each is excellent, but the comedy is the better of the two. The character of the curate and his relations with his parishioners are presented with the greatest comic vigour, and the intrigue of Leandro and Amaranta furnishes a good example of the manner in which Fletcher anticipated the comedy of the Restoration.

The cooperation of two or more dramatists was evidently favourable to the production of this class of drama. But there is to be found, chiefly among the plays which are ascribed to Fletcher alone, a type of pure comedy which is less liable to the charge of want of unity. Some of these plays, as *Wit At severall Weapons*, *Wit Without Money*, *The Womans Prize* and *The Night-Walker* have London for their locality and represent, more or less, the manners of contemporary English life. *Wit At severall Weapons* is a poor play, and the authorship is very uncertain. *Wit Without Money*, by Fletcher alone, is much better, having, at least, a tolerably well connected plot and lively dialogue. *The Womans Prize: or, The Tamer Tamed* is a supposed continuation of the marriage experiences of Petruchio, the tamer of the shrew. His Katharine being dead, he has been transplanted to English ground and is united in marriage to an English wife, who turns the tables upon him in an exhilarating manner. This comedy is a good example of Fletcher's more farcical style. *The Night-Walker, or the Little Theife* has more of London local colour than any of the rest, but this is probably to a great extent due to Shirley, who worked upon the play after Fletcher's death. It is a lively comedy, but the plot is a tissue of improbable incidents, with melodramatic scenes of coffins and graveyards.

Fletcher's best comedies, however, are to be found among those of which the scenes are laid abroad and the plots taken from foreign sources, while the manners are those of the society with which he is familiar. *Monsieur Thomas* can hardly be called a good play, though it has good scenes. The dilemma of the travelled young gentleman, who is obliged, at the same time, to convince his father that he is a rake and his mistress that he is a reformed character, has comic possibilities which are not quite effectively worked out. On the other hand, *The Chances* and *The Wild-Goose Chase* stand in the first rank among Fletcher's comedies, and in them we see, in full perfection, that lively and brilliant style of dialogue which gained him the reputation of understanding the conversation of gentlemen better than any other dramatist of his time. In *The Chances*, there is a series of highly improbable incidents, derived from a novel of Cervantes; but the very name of the comedy suggests the idea of fortuitous complications, and the treatment is in accordance with this idea. The two young gentlemen, Don John and Don Frederick, are presented in a very lively and natural manner, and their landlady is a decidedly happy creation, for which, however, hints had been given by Cervantes. *The Wild-Goose Chase*, again, has good characterisation and a well managed plot, though the tricks to catch Mirabel are rather too palpable, and his final yielding not quite natural. Of this play, the actors who first published it record that, notwithstanding his innate modesty, the author, when he saw it performed, could not forbear to join in the general applause. It is the original of Farquhar's comedy *The Inconstant*. Of all Fletcher's comedies, *Rule a Wife And have a Wife* is that which was most popular and kept the stage longest, and it is certainly a very good specimen of its kind. Its two plots are reasonably well connected, the characterisation is firm and good and several of the scenes, especially that in which Leon asserts himself, are, dramatically, very effective. The underplot is amusing, but less so than the novel of Cervantes from which it is taken.

Loves Cure, or The Martial Maid apparently contains little or nothing which can be ascribed to Fletcher. It is not without merit, if we concede the very improbable situation upon which its action depends; but the merit, perhaps, is chiefly due to a Spanish original, though it seems unlikely that this original was the comedy of Guillén de Castro which deals with the same story. *The Noble Gentleman* and *The Elder Brother* were both produced upon the stage after Fletcher's death. The former is a rather poor play, and has no apparent traces of his hand; the latter, one of the best comedies of the series, is by Fletcher and Massinger. The construction is good and the characterisation excellent.

It was said by Dryden in *An Essay of Dramatick Poesy* that in Beaumont and Fletcher's plays the English language perhaps arrived at its highest perfection; and certainly, for purity of phrase and vocabulary, for simplicity of expression and for absence of conceits and violent metaphors, they present an admirable model both of the more poetical and the more familiar style of dramatic expression. This merit of style was recognised by their contemporaries, especially with regard to Fletcher, as we see from the prologue to *The Chances* and in compliments such as are addressed to him in the next generation by Berkenhead,

> No savage metaphors (things rudely great)
> Thou dost display, nor butcher a conceit:
> Thy nerves have beauty which invades and charms,
> Looks like a princess harness'd in bright arms.

But the praise must also be shared by Massinger, whose poetical eloquence contributes much to the grace of style which characterises the later romantic plays mentioned in this chapter, and who may be said to have taken the place of Beaumont by Fletcher's side in this respect, though inferior to him in constructive skill and in power of dramatic presentation. It is probable that the popularity of Beaumont and Fletcher on the stage in the latter part of the century, together with the acceptance of their language by Dryden as a standard of pure English, had more influence than is commonly acknowledged upon the development of English style during that period in the direction of classical simplicity.

APPENDIX TO CHAPTER V

List of the plays which have been attributed to Beaumont and Fletcher, in approximately chronological order, with indications of the probable authorship of the plays and of the several portions of them, and also of the chief sources from which their plots are derived.

In cases where no source is mentioned, none is certainly known. Where no date of printing is given, it may be assumed that the play was first printed in the folio of 1647.

The Woman Hater, entered in Stationers' register, 20 May 1607; printed 1607. Beaumont. Plot, partly from Paulus Jovius, *De Romanis Piscibus*, cap. v.

The Faithfull Shepheardesse, printed before May 1610. Fletcher. Some traits suggested by Tasso's *Aminta* and Guarini's *Pastor Fido*.

The Knight of the Burning Pestle, perhaps acted at Whitefriars, 1609; printed 1613. Chiefly Beaumont. General idea suggested by *Don Quixote*, though this is denied by the publisher.

The Scornful Ladie, acted 1609 or 1610; printed 1616. Beaumont and Fletcher.

The Coxcombe, first acted probably 1610. Beaumont and Fletcher. For the story of Antonio, cf. Greene's *Philomela* and *El Curioso Impertinente* in *Don Quixote*.

Philaster, acted probably 1610 (but the supposed reference in *The Scourge of Folly* is doubtful); printed 1620. Mainly Beaumont; Fletcher, perhaps act v, sc. 3, 4 and detached passages elsewhere.

The Maides Tragedy, acted probably 1611; printed 1619. Beaumont, acts I, II, III, IV, sc. 2, act v, sc. 4; Fletcher, act IV, sc. 1, act v, sc. 1, 2, 3.

A King and no King, licensed 1611; printed 1619. Beaumont, acts I, II, III, IV, sc. 4, act v, sc. 2, 4; Fletcher, acts IV, sc. 1, 2, 3, act v, sc. 1, 3.

Cupid's Revenge, perhaps acted at court, Jan. 1612; printed 1615. Beaumont and Fletcher. From Sidney's *Arcadia*, bk. II.

Four Plays, or Morall Representations, in One; no indication of date. Beaumont probably wrote the induction and the first two *Triumphs*, Fletcher the rest. *The Triumph of Honour*, partly from Chaucer, *of Love*, Boccaccio, *Decameron*, day v, nov. 7, *of Death*, cf. *Palace of Pleasure*, bk I, nov. 42, *of Time*, probably suggested by Lucian's dialogue *Timon*.

The Captaine, acted at court early in 1613. Fletcher and another, perhaps Massinger.

The Maske of the Gentlemen of Grayes-Inne, and the Inner-Temple, performed Feb. 1613; printed probably 1613. Beaumont.

King Henry VIII, acted June 1613; printed in the Shakespeare folio, 1623. Shakespeare and Fletcher, perhaps revised by Massinger.

The Honest mans Fortune, acted 1613; licensed again, probably with alterations, 1624. Apparently by four authors, divided perhaps as follows: Tourneur, act I; Massinger, act III, sc. 1; Field, act IV; Fletcher, act v; the rest doubtful. The very distinctive metrical style of act I is like that of *The Atheist's Tragedie*, the only extant play published with Tourneur's name.

The style of Field resembles somewhat that of Beaumont. The same story is found in Heywood's *History of Women*, printed 1624.

Wit At severall Weapons, date unknown. Probably Middleton and Rowley.

Monsieur Thomas (also known as *Father's own Son*), date uncertain; printed 1639. Fletcher. Partly from the *Astrée* of d'Urfé, vol. II, published 1610.

The Tragedie of Valentinian, not later than 1614 (by list of actors). Fletcher. From the *Astrée*, vol. II, bk. XII.

The Tragedie of Bonduca, not later than 1614 (by list of actors). Fletcher and, perhaps, Field (*e.g.* act II, sc. 1 and act IV, sc. 4). Holinshed; some traits perhaps from *The Valiant Welshman*.

Wit Without Money, soon after Aug. 1614; printed 1639. Fletcher.

The Womans Prize: or, The Tamer Tamed, date unknown. Fletcher. A sequel to Shakespeare's *Taming of the Shrew*.

The Bloody Brother, or Rollo, Duke of Normandy, date uncertain; printed 1639 ('by B. J. F.') and 1640 ('by John Fletcher'). Probably four authors: Massinger, acts I, V, sc. 1; Fletcher, act II, sc. 3, act III, sc. 1 (part), 2, act V, sc. 2; Jonson, act II, sc. 1, 2, act IV, sc. 1, 2; Field, act III, sc. 1 (except scene of Rollo and Edith), act IV, sc. 3.

The Queene of Corinth, probably 1617 (allusion to Coryate's *Greeting* (1616), act III, sc. 1). Fletcher, Massinger and a third author. Based on a common story, cf. *Gesta Romanorum*, tale 4; not taken from *La Fuerza de la sangre* of Cervantes.

Thierry and Theodoret, probably after April 1617; printed 1621. Fletcher, act I, sc. 1, act II, sc. 2, act IV, sc. 1, act V, sc. 2; Massinger, act I, sc. 2, act II, sc. 1, act IV, sc. 2; a third author, acts III and V, sc. 1. Historical basis; immediate source, perhaps de Serres. The name de Vitry seems to indicate an allusion to the death of marshal d'Ancre, April 1617.

The Loyal Subject, licensed Nov. 1618. Fletcher. (The plot of Heywood's *Royall King and Loyall Subject*, from Painter, bk. II, nov. 4, has only a slight resemblance to this story.)

The Knight of Malta, 1618 or the beginning of 1619 (by list of actors). Fletcher, acts II, III, sc. 1, act IV, sc. 2, 3, 4; Massinger, act III, sc. 2, act IV, sc. 1(?); third author, acts I, V. The style of the third author is somewhat like that of Field, but better than his usual work.

The Mad Lover, before March 1619. Fletcher.

The Humorous Lieutenant, 1619 (by list of actors). Fletcher. Partly from Plutarch, lives of Pelopidas and Demetrius. A somewhat fuller text than that of the folios was printed by Dyce in 1830 from a MS in which the play is entitled *Demetrius and Enanthe*.

Sir John van Olden Barnavelt, acted 1619; printed 1883. Fletcher and Massinger. Founded on the events of May 1619.

Women pleas'd, 1619 or 1620 (by list of actors). Fletcher. From the *Historia de Aurelio y de Ysabela*, of Juan de Flores, of which several translations were current, combined with Chaucer's *Wife of Bath's Tale*. For various scenes of the underplot, cf. Boccaccio, *Decameron*, day VII, nov. 6, 8, and day VIII, nov. 8.

The Custome of the Countrey, 1619 or 1620. Fletcher, acts I, III, sc. 1, 2, 3, act IV, sc. 3, 4, act V, sc. 5 (part); Massinger, acts II, III, sc. 4, 5, act IV, sc. 1, 2, act V, sc. 1, 2, 3, 4, 5 (part). Two principal elements of the plot are from Cervantes, *Trabajos de Persiles y Sigismunda* (Eng. trans. Stationers' register, 22 Feb. 1619), bk. III, chap. 6, and bk. IV, chaps. 6–10, and most of the names are from this romance, but some applied differently.

The Little French Lawyer, 1619 or 1620. Fletcher, acts II, III, sc. 2, 3, acts IV, V, sc. 1 (*a*), 2, 3; Massinger, acts I, III, sc. 1, act V, sc. 1 (*b*). Partly from part II of *Guzman de Alfarache* (vol. I, chap. 4), or from a similar story elsewhere.

The Lawes of Candy, about 1620. Probably Massinger and another author (not Fletcher) Partly from Cinthio, *Hecatommithi*, dec. x, nov. 9.

The False One, about 1620. Fletcher, acts II, III, IV; Massinger, acts I, V.

The double Marriage, about 1620. Fletcher, acts II, III, sc. 2, 3, act IV, sc. 3, 4, act V, sc. 1; Massinger, acts I, III, sc. 1, act IV, sc. 1, 2, act V, sc. 2, 3. For the plot, cf. *Gesta Romanorum*, tale 5.

The Pilgrim, acted at court, Christmas 1621. Fletcher. Perhaps partly from d'Audiguier, *Les diverses fortunes de Pamphile et de Nise* (1614), which, again, is from Lope de Vega's romance *El Peregrino en su patria*; but the resemblance is only in trifling details, and there may be no connection.

The Wild-Goose Chase, acted at court, 1621; printed 1652. Fletcher.

The Island Princesse, acted at court, 1621. Fletcher. From *La Conquista de las Islas Malucas* by Bart. de Argensola, printed 1609; but Fletcher deviates from his source in acts IV and V.

The Beggars Bush, acted at court, 1622, but produced probably some time earlier. Fletcher, act II, sc. 1, 2, acts III, IV; Massinger, acts I, II, sc. 3, act V.

The Prophetesse, licensed 14 May 1622. Fletcher, acts I, III, V, sc. 3; Massinger, acts II, IV, V, sc. 1, 2. Partly historical: the story of Diocletian and the prophetess is told by Vopiscus.

The Sea Voyage, licensed 22 June 1622. Authors doubtful: considerable portions of acts I and IV are by Fletcher, but no scene, as we have it, can be attributed wholly to him; it is doubtful whether Massinger had any share: the metre, generally, is very defective.

The Spanish Curate, licensed 24 Oct. 1622. Fletcher, acts II, III, sc. 1, 2, 4, act IV, sc. 3, 5, 6, 7, act V, sc. 2; Massinger, acts I, III, sc. 3, act IV, sc. 1, 2, 4, act V, sc. 1, 3 (Massinger deals with the main plot, and Fletcher with the underplot). From *Gerardo the Unfortunate Spaniard*, a translation, published 1622, of the (prose) romance by Gonzalo de Cespedes y Meneses, entitled *Poema tragico del Español Gerardo*. The situation in the main plot, of Don Henrique, Don Jamie, etc., is from the conclusion of the first part of *Gerardo*, pp. 231 ff. (ed. 1622), but the final development is different: the plot of Leandro, Lopez, etc. follows closely the story told by Leandro in the second part, pp. 246–266, omitting the conclusion as supplied by Violante.

The Maid in the Mill, licensed Aug. 1623, as by Fletcher and W. Rowley. Fletcher, acts I, III, sc. 2, 3, act V, sc. 2 (*a*). From *Gerardo*, pp. 394–418, with change of conclusion, and Painter, bk. II, nov. 22.

The Lovers Progress, end of 1623 (by list of actors); the original play was, perhaps, *The Wandering Lovers*, licensed 6 Dec. 1623 as by Fletcher. In its present form it has been revised by Massinger (see prologue), and this being a case of revision and not cooperation, mixed work is to be expected and occurs frequently. Acts IV and V are almost entirely by Massinger. From d'Audiguier, *Histoire tragicomique de nostre temps sous les noms de Lysandre et de Caliste*, 1616.

A Wife for a Month, licensed 27 May 1624 (the name of Tooley among the actors is probably a mistake for Lowin). Fletcher.

Rule a Wife And have a Wife, licensed 19 Oct. 1624, printed 1640. Fletcher. The underplot is from Cervantes, *El Casamiento engañoso* (*Nov. Exempl.*).

The Two Noble Kinsmen, date uncertain; printed as by Fletcher and Shakespeare, 1634. Fletcher wrote act II, sc. 3, 4, 5, act III, sc. 3, 4, 5, 6, act IV, sc. 1, 2, act V, sc. 2, and parts of other scenes. From Chaucer's *Knight's Tale*.

The Nice Valour, or, The Passionate Mad-man, in its present form not earlier than 1624 (allusions in act v, sc. 3), but the play bears marks of revision, and was, perhaps, originally much earlier. Fletcher and another, perhaps Rowley, but Fletcher's part is much altered.

The Chances, acted 1625 or 1626 (after Fletcher's death, see prologue). Fletcher, but probably touched here and there by another hand, *e.g.* in act i, sc. 1, 9, act ii, sc. 4. From Cervantes, *La Señora Cornelia* (*Nov. Exempl.*).

The Elder Brother, acted after Fletcher's death (see prologue), printed 1637. Fletcher, acts ii, iii, iv; Massinger, acts i, v. Source connected with that of Calderon's later drama, *De una causa dos efectos*.

The Faire Maide of the Inne, licensed 22 Jan. 1626. Massinger and another (not Fletcher). The disowning of Cesario by his mother is probably taken from *La Cour Sainte* of Nicolas Caussin, published in 1624 (not 1632, as stated by Koeppel). The plot of the play does not at all resemble the story of *La ilustre Fregona* of Cervantes.

The Noble Gentleman, licensed 3 Feb. 1626 as by Fletcher. He may have planned the play and written some passages, but no complete scene can be attributed to him.

Loves Cure, or The Martial Maid, date uncertain but not earlier than 1622 in its present form. No scene can be attributed to Fletcher; Massinger probably wrote acts i, iv, v, sc. 1, 2. There is no real ground for the suggestion (by Stiefel, A. L.) that this play is taken from the Spanish comedy by Guillén de Castro, *La fuerza de la costumbre*. The two dramas are founded on the same story, but the treatment is entirely different.

The Night-Walker, or the Little Theife, licensed as corrected by Shirley, 11 May 1633; printed 1640; the original play was, perhaps, as early as 1614. As it stands, the first three acts are by Fletcher, with revision, and the last two by Shirley, who must have rewritten this part of the play.

Loves Pilgrimage, revived 1635, with alterations, perhaps by Shirley, including some matter from Jonson's *New Inne*. Fletcher appears most markedly in act i, sc. 2, acts ii and iii. From Cervantes, *Las dos Doncellas* (*Nov. Exempl.*).

A Very Woman, or The Prince of Tarent, licensed 1634; printed as Massinger's, 1655, and never included among Beaumont and Fletcher's plays. As we have it, it is revised from an earlier drama (see prologue): Fletcher was probably the author of acts iii and iv, sc. 1, 3. It is commonly identified with *A Woman's Plot*, acted at court 1621, because of the entry in Stationers' register, 9 Sept. 1653 of 'A Very Woman or The Woman's Plot,' but this second title has no justification in the play, and is, perhaps, a mistake.

The Coronation, printed in the folio of 1679, is by Shirley. *The Widow*, attributed in the quarto to Jonson, Fletcher and Middleton, is probably by Middleton.

The Faithful Friends was entered in Stationers' register, 29 June 1660 as by Beaumont and Fletcher, and first printed in Weber's edition, 1812; but it is not likely that they had any share in it.

The following appear to be lost: *The History of Cardenio*, entered in Stationers' register, 9 Sept. 1653 as by Fletcher and Shakespeare, and, perhaps, the same as the *Cardenes, Cardema* or *Cardano*, which was acted at court, 1613; *The Jeweller of Amsterdam*, entered Stationers' register, 8 April 1654 as by Fletcher, Field and Massinger, probably produced about 1616; *A Woman's Plot*, acted at court, 1621; *The Devil of Dowgate, or Usury put to Use*, 'written by Fletcher,' mentioned as a new play in Herbert's official register, 17 Oct. 1623; *A Right Woman*, entered in Stationers' register, 29 June 1660 as by Beaumont and Fletcher; *Mador, King of Great Britain*, attributed to Beaumont, Stationers' register, 29 June 1660. These two latter attributions must be regarded as very doubtful.

CHAPTER VI

PHILIP MASSINGER

EVERY biographer of Philip Massinger must echo the frequently repeated complaint that we know very little about the life of many of the chief dramatists of the times of Elizabeth and the first two Stewart kings. We may consider it an exceptional good fortune that we know at least the chief facts of Massinger's early days—that he was born at Salisbury in 1583, the son of Arthur Massinger, who, in some manner, was intimately connected with the 'noble family of the Herberts,' to use Philip's own expression, and who was evidently highly esteemed by his employers; that his baptism took place on 24 November 1583, and that he was entered on 14 May 1602 at St Alban hall in the university of Oxford. In 1606, he left the university for unexplained reasons without having taken his degree. From Oxford he came to London, where we lose sight of him for many years as totally as of the great immigrant from Stratford-on-Avon about twenty years before.

One fact, however, stands out clearly — that Massinger's London career was far from prosperous. When we hear of him again, in 1613 or 1614, we find him already immersed in those financial difficulties which remained the heavy burden of his life. He reappears as one of the three signatories of a petition for the loan of five pounds, addressed to that powerful personage to whom many needy dramatists used to look more or less hopefully—the theatrical manager and broker Philip Henslowe. In a few additional words, Massinger pathetically calls him his 'true loving friend,' and the joint request was granted. There was a similar pleading in 1615.

As in the case of this epistle to Henslowe, most of the first dramatic ventures of Massinger seem to have been joint productions. The first time we meet his name in print, on the title-page of an evidently successful drama, we find it coupled with the name of an older and very popular dramatist. In 1622 was published *The Virgin Martir, a Tragedy*, written by Philip Massinger and Thomas Dekker. But Dekker, whose poetical temper was different from Massinger's, was neither his first nor his most important fellow worker. A good many years before the composition of *The Virgin Martir*, he must have fallen under the sway of John Fletcher. It is a curious fact that no early edition of any one of those dramas which have been recognised as the joint labours of Fletcher and Massinger makes the slightest reference to the participation of the younger dramatist; all were printed as by Fletcher alone. Massinger seems to have been quite content to leave the risk and the glory to his teacher; so far as we know, he never protested against the omission of his name on the title-pages of the dramas printed during his lifetime. However, one of his most enthusiastic benefactors and friends, Sir Aston Cokayne, repeatedly insisted on the fact of Massinger's cooperation with Fletcher—an assertion which, in the case of a considerable number of Fletcherian plays, has received support from the philological researches of later times. And that he was buried in Fletcher's grave, probably by his own wish, may be taken as a striking proof that no coldness had arisen between Massinger and the man with whom he had associated in the early years of his dramatic writing.

We are not able to fix the time when Massinger ventured to present himself as an independent author to the public of the metropolis; but we may assume that this did not happen much before the end of the second decade of the seventeenth century. For the ensuing period of his life we possess a considerable number of direct utterances of his own, the authenticity of which is not to be questioned, but the biographical value of which is somewhat impaired by their official character and by the consideration necessarily shown in them for the position and feelings of the persons addressed. These utterances consist in the dedications prefixed by Massinger to the ten dramas published by himself. In these letters, Massinger's prose appears to the greatest advantage; it is, perhaps, a little pompous now and then, but it is clear and perfectly free from Euphuistic tricks of style.

Much less pleasing are the glimpses of the poet's private life afforded by these documents. Both the first dedication, preceding *The Duke of Millaine* (1623), and the last, composed for *The Unnaturall Combat* in 1639, about a year before his death, exhibit the poet as much dissatisfied with his vocation as a dramatic writer. He speaks of the misfortunes which cast him on this course and numbers himself among those whose 'necessitous fortunes' made them choose poetry as their profession. Complaints about the neglect which his age showed to the 'contemned sons of the Muses,' and about his own depressed circumstances, protestations that he could never have lived without the help of those kind patrons who endeavoured 'to rebuild the ruins of demolished poesy' and declarations of his gratitude and his devotion, are intermingled in these epistles with rarer outbursts of consciousness of his poetical powers, remarks about the intrinsic value of his works and hints that there were some eminent men who 'have not thought themselves disparaged, I dare not say honoured, to be celebrated the patrons of my humble studies.'

Two of the dedications show that the poet did his best to keep up that connection with the Pembroke family which he regarded as a paternal inheritance. In 1624, he dedicated his tragi-comedy *The Bond-Man* to the younger brother of the third earl of Pembroke—Philip Herbert, earl of Montgomery—with respectful allusions to the many happy years his father had spent in the service of that honourable house ; and, nine years later, in 1633, he recommended his famous comedy *A New Way to Pay Old Debts* to the favourable acceptance of Montgomery's son-in-law, Robert Dormer, earl of Carnarvon, in very humble and complimentary terms. Besides these dedications, two of his rare non-dramatic poems refer to members of the same family. One of these poems is a poetical supplication of uncertain date, addressed to the 'Earl of Pembroke, Lord Chamberlain.' The earl's Christian name is missing ; but the whole tenor of this petition leads to the conclusion that it was meant to reach the ear of the third earl of Pembroke, the William Herbert frequently mentioned in biographies of Shakespeare, who had been appointed lord chamberlain in 1615. It is to be feared, however, that this most persuasive poetical begging-letter, in which Massinger speaks of his 'trod-down poverty,' had not the desired effect ; for, had the earl proved kind, Massinger would assuredly have shown his gratitude by dedicating one of his later dramas to this powerful nobleman. There is an old tradition that William Herbert had been the protector of young Massinger during the years of his university life, but had withdrawn his helping hand later, for unknown reasons. This rumour is not verified by the epistle in question, the manuscript of which was rediscovered but a few years ago ; for it contains no reference to former benefits received by the poet.

The other poem, with the motto *Sero sed serio*, is an elegy on the death of Charles, lord Herbert, third son of Philip Herbert, who, after the death of his brother, in 1630, had become fourth earl of Pembroke. The poet blames himself for having remained silent on the occasion of the wedding of this unfortunate young nobleman, which had taken place at Christmas 1634, a few weeks only before his early death at Florence in January 1635; and he evidently tries to compensate for this sin of omission by courtly flattery in a funeral poem, the most undignified of all his compositions and a striking contrast to the above mentioned supplication, in which the poet declares that neither a pension nor a place could induce him 'to part with his own candour!' It is stated that this fourth earl of Pembroke granted him an annuity of £30 or £40 with reversion to his widow.

The dedications and poems make us acquainted with numerous members of the nobility to whom Massinger felt himself bound for benefits received, or whom he wished to number among his patrons. About his relations to his literary contemporaries we gain very little information from Massinger himself, and not much more from other sources. One of his shorter poems is addressed to James Smith, an obscure clerical poet, whom he praises as the author of a 'neat' poem, calling him, after the fashion of Ben Jonson, his 'son.' One of the many dramas of James Shirley, entitled *The Grateful Servant* (1630), Massinger ushered in by some commendatory verses, whose well weighed and carefully worded praise leaves a deeper impression than the customary hyperboles of similar compositions. Among the poets who did him a similar service at the publication of his own dramas, we find, together with Shirley, Massinger's other fellow dramatists John Ford, Thomas May, Thomas Goffe and his faithful friend and fervent admirer Sir Aston Cokayne.

Massinger is said to have been married: a Miss Massinger, who died in 1762, claimed a direct descent from him. But all the other circumstances of his life, which seems to have had its full share of cares besides ceaseless work, are hidden from us. He died in March 1640 and was buried on the 18th of that month in the churchyard of St Saviour's church in Southwark, where John Gower had also found his resting place.

Massinger's dramatic apprenticeship, the period of his collaboration with other dramatists, especially with Fletcher, has, of late, frequently attracted the attention of English scholars. Their investigations have resulted in a great increase of the number of plays for which this cooperation is to be assumed. At the time of the publication of the first collected edition of Beaumont and Fletcher's works, in 1647, Cokayne blamed the editor on account of the injustice towards Fletcher implied in the title, inasmuch as Beaumont had written but few of those dramas. As Massinger's friend, Cokayne availed himself of this opportunity to inform the world of another noteworthy fact about which the editor had been silent: he pointed out that Massinger also had to claim a partnership 'in other few,' adding that he got this information from 'Fletcher's chief bosom friend'—possibly from Massinger himself. Not content with Cokayne's few plays, modern enquirers have traced the hand of Massinger in about twenty pieces of the Fletcherian series. It cannot be denied that the modern method of settling questions of doubtful authorship is sometimes purely subjective, and many discrepancies have, accordingly, to be noted between the conclusions reached by different scholars. But, in Massinger's case, the task was facilitated by a striking peculiarity in the writer. Massinger is afflicted with the itch of iteration to an exceptional degree: his repetitions of the same phrases and similes are countless. Wherever such marks appear in great numbers, Massinger's cooperation may safely be held to be very likely. On the other hand, it is not to be doubted that, in all their joint compositions, the older and more experienced Fletcher was the leading spirit, the chief builder, to whose directions Massinger had to attend. That, no doubt, is the reason why he never himself thought of proclaiming his partnership to the world[1].

A second, much smaller, group of plays consists of those which, in the old prints, are assigned to Massinger and some other dramatist. The oldest of these pieces seems to be the amusing comedy called *The Old Law*. Though published very late, in 1656, as the work of Massinger, Middleton and William Rowley, the mention of the year 1599 in the dialogue of this piece seems to prove that it was composed several years before the beginning of Massinger's dramatic career. It is just possible that he revised the old play; but, if he did so, he carefully abstained from any material alterations. No trace of his individual style is to be discovered in the existing text.

Not the slightest doubt, on the contrary, can be entertained concerning Massinger's cooperation in two other plays attributed to him and Dekker and Field respectively on the title-pages of the

[1] As to the probable shares of Massinger and Fletcher respectively in the dramas in which they collaborated, see appendix to chap. v.

old prints. Both plays were published in the lifetime of the
three authors : the coarse, but by no means ineffective legendary
drama *The Virgin Martir*, in 1622, as the work of Massinger and
Dekker, and, in 1632, the impressive tragedy *The Fatall Dowry*,
assigned to him and Nathaniel Field, his old friend, the writer of the
letter to Henslowe signed also by Massinger and Daborne. Internal
evidence corroborates the statements of the printers. As to the
scenes of Massinger and those of Dekker, even a careless reader
must be struck by the difference of character between them[1]; but
it is a more delicate task to distinguish between the work of
Massinger and that of Field.

Massinger's name alone fronts the ten plays, published within
the period 1623 to 1639, for which he wrote his dedications, and
four other plays, posthumously printed in 1655 and 1658. One
of the three dramas which appeared together in 1655, entitled
A Very Woman, or The Prince of Tarent, is regarded, but without any certainty, as another joint effort of Fletcher and Massinger[2].
In the course of the nineteenth century, two more plays bearing
the unmistakable stamp of Massinger's authorship were discovered.
Besides these sixteen plays, on which our study of Massinger's
art must be based, we know the titles of twelve more, which seem
to be irretrievably lost.

Among Massinger's sixteen genuine dramas, only three tragedies are to be found. All his other plays end without blood-
shed, even a drama whose historical foundation might exact
the death of the hero—one of the new-found plays, bearing the
fanciful title *Believe as you List*, published for the first time in
1849. This drama is mentioned in all discussions of the question
whether Massinger frequently gave vent to political opinions
in his dramas. Generally speaking, the dramatists of his time
shrank from touching on the politics of the day, for excellent
reasons: they knew but too well that political dramas might
have unpleasant consequences for both actors and writers. George
Chapman's two sensational dramas, for instance, treating of the
story of the life and sudden fall of an ambitious French politician,
Charles, duke of Biron, marshal of France, who had been be-
headed in Paris but a few years previously, 31 July 1602, caused
a complaint by the French ambassador, in consequence of which
the representations of the plays were stopped and some of the
actors sent to prison. The author seems to have escaped scot-
free; but, in 1608, at the printing of his plays, he experienced

---

[1] Cf. *ante*, chap. ii.   [2] Cf. *ante*, chap. v.

the wrath of the censor, who mutilated his text in so ferocious a manner that, in his dedication, Chapman speaks of 'these poor dismembered poems.' Another playwright, Thomas Middleton, in 1624, in his allegorical drama *A Game at Chesse* made himself the interpreter of the intense dissatisfaction of the great majority of the English people with the policy of James I, who endeavoured to keep up friendly relations with Spain in opposition to a strong national feeling against any alliance with the arch-enemy. The incensed king threatened the players with heavy fines in case of another misbehaviour; but the poet himself was not to be found, and the king's resentment seems to have been of short duration[1].

That, notwithstanding those warning examples, Massinger could not resist the temptation of meddling with politics, we know on good authority. In January 1631, the master of the revels, Sir Henry Herbert, refused to license one of Massinger's plays, 'because it did contain dangerous matter, as the deposing of Sebastian, King of Portugal, by Philip II, and there being a peace sworn betwixt the Kings of England and Spain.' From the same 'Cato of the stage' we hear, besides, that, in 1638, king Charles himself, perusing a new play by Massinger, entitled *The King and the Subject*, marked one passage for alteration with the words: 'This is too insolent, and to be changed.' The play itself is lost; but the objectionable verses have been preserved for us by the censor himself. They are taken from an angry speech of Don Pedro, king of Spain, proclaiming despotically the absolute right of the king to raise new taxes. It was then the time of king Charles's exaction of ship-money, stoutly resisted by many of his subjects, and it is hardly to be doubted that the poet when composing, and the king when cancelling, this passage were both thinking, from a very different point of view, of the possible effect this manifestation might have on the audience.

Believe as you List, against which the censor had entered his veto in order to avoid giving offence to the Spanish government, was licensed a few months later, in May 1631, in a revised shape, the poet having made it acceptable by changing the costume of his *dramatis personae*. Instead of the Portuguese king deposed by Spain, Massinger introduced a fabulous Asiatic king Antiochus, deposed and pitilessly persecuted by Rome. After this change, the censor found nothing smacking of recent political changes in the play; and this proves that he did not think of the possibility of another political interpretation, since suggested by

[1] For an account of *A Game at Chesse*, cf. chap. III.

S. R. Gardiner[1]. According to this view, Massinger's play had a very real meaning indeed, being intended to mirror the fate of the unfortunate brother-in-law of Charles I, Frederick V, elector Palatine and titular king of Bohemia, who, at that time, was a landless fugitive persecuted by his powerful enemies, just as Massinger's dethroned Antiochus was by the Romans. Prusias king of Bithynia, who, against his own inclinations, is forced to give up his guest to his enemies, is said to represent Charles himself, who refrained from actively assisting his brother-in-law; Flaminius, the Roman ambassador, is the Spanish ambassador, intriguing against Frederick at the English court; Philoxenus, the king of Bithynia's counsellor, who made common cause with Rome, is the lord treasurer Weston, who used his influence with the king in the Spanish interest; and, finally, the kind queen of Bithynia, who tried in vain to save the hapless fugitive, is Henrietta Maria, queen of England, who cordially disliked Weston.

Some years after the publication of Gardiner's ingenious hypothesis, the main source of Massinger's plot was discovered in the French historian Pierre Victor Palma Cayet's account of the fate of the Portuguese pretender, known as the false Sebastian[2]. A detailed comparison led to the result that the dramatist found the prototypes of all his chief characters in Cayet's work, with the sole exception of the nameless wife of Prusias. It is quite possible, however, that her introduction was caused by the same need of the dramatist which made him add two amatory incidents to his plot: he wanted some female characters to brighten a political story which offered him only male personages. Gardiner's assumption that the dramatist, when he made his Antiochus a fugitive, must have been thinking of Frederick's wanderings, because there was nothing similar to be found in the Sebastian story, is refuted by an examination of Massinger's source. Cayet gives a detailed account of the wanderings of the Portuguese impostor, and tells how, flying before the persecutions of the Spaniards, he came first to Venice in the hope of being acknowledged and protected by the republic, and afterwards to the court of the grand duke of Florence, who, by the pressure of Spain, was finally obliged to deliver the pretender into the hands of his enemies. Also, the surprising fact already alluded to, that, at the end of the English drama, we hear only of the imprisonment, not of the death, of the hero, is ex-

---

[1] 'The Political Element in Massinger,' *Contemporary Review*, August, 1876; reprinted in the *Transactions of the New Shakespere Society* for the same year.

[2] Cayet died in 1610.

plained by the circumstance that Cayet, when penning his account, was not yet aware of the final execution of the pretender.

The decisive influence of the French chronicler on Massinger's plot is not to be questioned; nevertheless, it is possible that the dramatist was reminded by some of the circumstances of the Sebastian story of the sad fate of the German prince and the vacillations of the English king, and that, induced by his personal and political sympathies, he did his best to surround Antiochus and his friends with a poetical nimbus. His fugitive, certainly, is no impostor, but a man of kingly bearing. Gardiner observed that the two Herberts, the brothers William and Philip, were opposed to Weston, trying to counterbalance his influence by means of the queen: and the introduction into Massinger's play of the nameless queen of Bithynia and the part taken by her in its action remain the only substantial arguments in favour of the historian's political interpretation.

That Massinger was sincerely interested in the fate of the quondam elector is proved by certain passages in another play, *The Maid of Honour*, containing veiled but unmistakable allusions to his fate and to James I's tardiness in assisting his son-in-law, a slackness which had been blamed by many of his subjects and which was repeated by Charles. Some further passages, which, possibly, may refer to political personages and events of his days, have been pointed out in several other of Massinger's plays, particularly in the tragicomedy *The Bond-Man*, which seems to convey a severe criticism of the royal favourite, George Villiers, duke of Buckingham, and of the unsatisfactory state of the English fleet. All the utterances of Massinger which are supposed to be of a political character show him in opposition to the faction of the court.

The same intellectual courage which made Massinger utter his political opinions without deference to the sentiments of the influential court party was displayed in his dealings with another power whose favour was of the utmost importance to him: he dared to cross the current of one of the most violent prejudices of the public which filled the metropolitan theatres. The church of Rome was regarded by the mass of the English nation as the most dangerous and implacable enemy of their country, and was hated accordingly; the English members of the Roman church were watched suspiciously, being popularly regarded in the light of spies belonging to that hated outlandish power; all Roman Catholic priests had been banished from London by James I, in

1604. The anti-Romish propaganda had also invaded the stage. Thomas Dekker, in his allegorical play *The Whore of Babylon,* strained all his powers, with the exception of his charming poetical gift, to incense his countrymen against Rome and Spain; Barnabe Barnes, in his tragedy *The Devil's Charter,* which was played before the king, afforded Londoners an insight into all the abominations of the Roman curia, and, finally, the delightful spectacle of a vicious and murderous pope in the clutches of the devil; while, in Middleton's political play *A Game at Chesse,* Ignatius Loyola, founder of the society of Jesus, is made to speak the prologue and to proclaim his vices and his evil intentions concerning England in the most shameless manner. In view of this inveterate hostility, which formed an integral part of the religious and political persuasions of most Englishmen, it needed great strength and independence of mind to write and publish a drama like Massinger's *The Renegado.* In this play a priest of the church of Rome acts as the friend and leader of all the characters for whom the sympathy of the audience is engaged; in all their difficulties, they appeal to him with a confidence which is justified by his saving them from destruction. And this benefactor is not only a priest, but also a member of that brotherhood whom protestants thought they had especial reasons to fear and to hate— a Jesuit.

We do not know whether Massinger, who had been baptised according to the rite of the Anglican communion, ever publicly conformed to the church of Rome: the supposition that he became a Roman Catholic at Oxford and, in consequence of this step, lost the protection of the earl of Pembroke, is nothing more than a guess. But it cannot be doubted that he repeatedly showed a marked predilection for the religious observances of the papal church. One of his noblest women, the virgin Camiola, heroine of the fascinating drama *The Maid of Honour,* being afflicted by the discovery of the faithlessness of her lover, resolves to take the veil—a harmonious climax to her devoted life, in adopting which Massinger departed from his well known source, a novel in Painter's *Palace of Pleasure.* The saintly Dorothea, whose martyrdom is the subject of the tragedy *The Virgin Martir,* is, it is true, a daughter of the primitive church, to whose glorification even the anti-Popish Dekker did not object.

To the question whether the remarkable independence Massinger manifested in freely expressing his political and religious sympathies be also a distinctive quality of his dramatic art, an affirmative answer cannot be given without some restrictions. When Massinger entered the theatrical world of London, which was suffering already from an excess of competition and production, he found established in it a great tradition from whose influence it was impossible for him to escape. We may well suppose the sensitive soul of a young poet to have been impressed and overwhelmed by the magnificent multitude of Shakespeare's heroes and heroines! Not that the younger dramatists surrounding Fletcher always pronounced the name of Shakespeare with awe and veneration—we have proofs enough that the younger generation delighted in parodying famous passages of his works, and that many of them were ready to extol Ben Jonson or Fletcher in a more exalted strain than that in which they praised him—but they could not help succumbing to the influence of his creations, repeating and imitating him in thoughts, words, characters and situations in numberless scenes and passages of their own dramas. And, in Massinger's plays, we meet with many reminiscences of this kind, though he carefully avoids anything like plagiarism. Generally speaking, it cannot be said that he possessed an over-scrupulous conscience in literary matters. In this respect, he was no better and no worse than most of his contemporaries, who remorselessly appropriated the intellectual goods of their fellows : the general story of his successful comedy *A New Way to Pay Old Debts*, for instance, he borrowed from a play of the defunct Middleton, without deeming it necessary to allude to his model in his dedication. But, in dealing with Shakespeare, his sentiments seem to have been akin to the feeling tersely expressed later in the verse : 'Within that circle none durst walk but he.'

Not Shakespeare, who, searching the human soul, became conversant with all the great problems of life—not the dead master, whose eyes had penetrated to the core of things, became Massinger's teacher, but the living Fletcher, the creator of a partly realistic, and partly shadowy, world, who always aimed at stage effects and applause, and was prepared to risk probability in order to secure them. Undoubtedly, Massinger owed much of his own dramatic cunning to this apprenticeship to Fletcher's cleverness in all the technicalities of the stage—but this gain could not outweigh the heavy loss in power. In reading Massinger's plays, we often become aware of the contest between two very different forces, his own serious and earnest manner, as it were, wrestling with the injunctions of his master to lay hold of the attention of the audience by any means, however frivolous.

In view of the protracted joint authorship of the two dramatists, which must have covered many years, it is difficult to say whether Massinger transplanted Fletcherian motives and types into his own plays. It is true that the duchess Aurelia of Siena, whom he added to the plot of *The Maid of Honour*, greatly resembles her namesake, the sister of the emperor Carinus in *The Prophetesse*; that the warlike duke Lorenzo in *The Bashful Lover*, who is suddenly vanquished by Matilda's beauty, strongly reminds us of the rough old warrior Memnon in *The Mad Lover*, adoring on his knees the suddenly revealed charms of the princess Calis; and that intimate connections are noticeable between Massinger's *Parliament of Love* and Fletcher's *The Little French Lawyer*—but it is possible that, in these and some similar cases, we have to assume not a borrowing of Fletcherian motives, but only a readjustment of his own contributions. To repeat himself was perfectly admissible according to Massinger's artistic code.

As to his relations with either Shakespeare or Fletcher, Massinger himself leaves us in the dark. Shakespeare he never mentions, Fletcher but once, and then only to tell us that Fletcher never had

> Such reputation and credit won
> But by his honor'd patron, Huntingdon.

Furthermore, the name of Shakespeare's famous rival, whom many younger poets delighted to honour—the name of Ben Jonson—never appears in Massinger's writings. Perhaps he was not on the best of terms with that outspoken poet. A few ironical words by Massinger about the strange self-love of a writer who professed

> that when
> The critics laugh, he'll laugh at them agen

have been thought—not without some likelihood—to refer to the angry old man who tried to console himself for the failure of one of his last dramas, *The New Inne*, by bitterly inveighing against hostile critics. As to the possible influence of Jonson's dramatic method on the compositions of the younger poet, it is discoverable, perhaps, in his two domestic dramas *A New Way* and *The City-Madam*. The impressive but exaggerated personifications of the vices of avarice, hypocrisy and pride presented in these comedies are in the manner of Jonson's types, which were assiduously imitated by later dramatists. In Massinger's other plays, the traces of Jonsonian influence are very slight: the small group of patriotic Romans in *The Roman Actor* calls to mind a similar chorus in *Sejanus his Fall*, and the foolish wooer of *The Maid of Honour*, Signior Sylli, may claim kinship with Sir Amorous

La-Foole in *The Silent Woman,* by virtue of his name and some remarks about the family of the Syllis.

The most striking feature of Massinger's individual art, undoubtedly, is to be found in his great constructive power. The structure of his best plays is admirable in the severity of its lines and in the wise economy shown in the use of his materials. In most cases, he was content with working out a single action; the mixture of plots which many of his brother poets preferred, and of which Shakespeare's *King Lear* had been the great example, seems to have had no attraction for a dramatist whose intellect favoured clearness above all other poetical charms. Some of the dramas of his contemporaries resemble mazes in whose artfully interwoven paths both writers and spectators ran the risk of losing themselves—a danger which Richard Brome, for instance, perceived and tried to avoid by drawing attention to particularly difficult complications by an explicit remark of one of his *dramatis personae*; Massinger's best plays convey the impression of being well built and ample halls, in which we move with a feeling of perfect security. That he was a severe critic of his own labours is proved by the clear progress to be noted in the construction of his plots in the course of years. *The Unnaturall Combat,* which the author calls an old work in his dedication, and which appears to be a free rendering of the story of the crimes of the Cenci family, has, no doubt, a central figure in Malefort, the destroyer of his own children; yet it contains not one but two separate tragedies. First, the tragedy of young Malefort, the son, who revenges the death of his mother and is himself killed by her murderer, his father; and then, the tragedy of the daughter, hunted to death by the father's incestuous passion. In what probably is his second tragedy, *The Duke of Millaine,* we meet with a striking proof that the dramatist had not yet learned to economise his subject: the fate of his heroine reaches the tragic climax at the end of the fourth act, so that he was obliged to fill the fifth act with a new action, not clearly hinted at before, a brother's revenge for the injury done to his sister. It is true that, in the last tragedy composed by Massinger alone, *The Roman Actor,* Paris, the actor, falls a victim to the jealousy of the emperor also in the fourth act; nevertheless, the poet was entitled to speak of this drama as 'the most perfect birth of his Minerva,' because the fate of the player was not his chief object: he wished to present the tragedy of the bloodthirsty madness of the Roman Caesars, personified in Domitian, whose ruin is prepared and effected in the fifth act.

Our admiration of Massinger's power of dramatic construction is further heightened, if we come to look at the raw materials at his disposal. Nothing, for instance, could be more interesting than to observe how, in *The Roman Actor*, the process of blending the accounts of historians, of Suetonius and Dio Cassius principally, results in well arranged scenes in which no trace of patchwork is to be discovered. Not less cunningly the plot of *The Renegado* is pieced together out of different works of Cervantes. That Massinger's predilection for a single action is not to be explained by the inability to marshal and, finally, to unite a greater number of figures, is demonstrated by the lively scenes of his *Parliament of Love*, for the intrigues in which he availed himself of motives drawn from Martial d'Auvergne, Shakespeare, Marston and, probably, also from Middleton. It must be confessed, however, that, in this case, the fusion is not flawless, Leonora's senseless cruelty showing that the dramatist's wish to use a striking episode of a Marstonian drama was stronger than his respect for what the laws of psychology allow to be possible.

In obedience to the taste of his time, Massinger twice transplanted the action of his plays from the localities named in his sources to the favourite country of the Elizabethan dramatists, Italy, and, in both cases, with entire success. Without knowledge of his authorities, it would be impossible to find out that the duke of Milan and his wife Marcelia, killed by her husband's jealousy, have been substituted for Herod, king of the Jews, and his wife Mariamne; or that the story told in his charming comedy *The Great Duke of Florence*, with its variation of the motive of the treacherous friend, is a transformation of an old legend rooted in the soil of England.

Many of Massinger's independent additions to the stories in his sources are also well calculated to deepen the impression left by his works. For a few of his plays, no literary source has been so far traced; but it would be rash to assert that he entirely invented any of his plots. A far more striking sign of a certain weakness in inventive power is his tendency to repeat himself in his technical artifices and in the means used for eking out his plots. The necessary revelation of a hidden passion is frequently attained by the simple stratagem of letting a conversation between lovers be overheard by their enemies. The passionate attempt of Antoninus to waken the flame of an earthly love in Dorothea's bosom is overheard by his father and by the princess in love with the youth (*The Virgin Martir*); Cleora and Marullo are surprised

in prison (*The Bond-Man*); Donusa and Vitelli, Domitia and Paris
are watched by the Turkish princes and Domitian respectively (*The
Renegado* and *The Roman Actor*); the rivals of Hortensio listen
to his decisive talk with Matilda (*The Bashful Lover*). Also, in
other emergencies, the timehonoured artifice of the listener is
freely resorted to. Another of Massinger's favourite situations is
the introduction of one of his male characters with a book in his
hand, like Hamlet, indulging in some short philosophical speculation. By way of amplifying his plot, he repeatedly brings in a
brother revenging a wrong done to his sister. In the last act of
The Duke of Millaine, we are surprised by the statement that the
ultimate scope of Francisco's perfidies was to punish Sforza as the
seducer of his sister Eugenia; Marullo-Pisander acts the part of a
slave in Syracuse only to approach Leosthenes, the faithless lover
of his sister Statilia (*The Bond-Man*); Vitelli risks his life among
the Turks to liberate or to revenge his sister Paulina, robbed by
the Renegado (in the play of that name). The deserted woman
herself repeatedly appears as the servant of the new object of her
faithless lover's affection: Statilia serves Cleora (*The Bond-Man*),
Madame Beaupré the clever and resolute Bellisant (*The Parliament of Love*).

In view of this inclination of Massinger to repeat himself, we
are not surprised to find, also, that many of his *dramatis personae*
resemble each other in a pronounced manner; the theory of the
typical characters of a dramatist[1] stands confirmed by many of
his figures. The most typical of his heroines is the passionate
woman who falls violently in love at first sight and runs to the
embraces of her beloved without any reserve. This class of
women is most characteristically represented by the Turkish
princess Donusa, who offers herself to the unsuspicious Vitelli
and persists in her wooing until he becomes the victim of her
seductive charms, notwithstanding his Christian scruples about her
being an infidel. With the same self-abandonment, the empress
Domitia makes love to the handsome player Paris. Nor can
Aurelia, the duchess of Siena, in *The Maid of Honour*, who, at
the first sight of young Bertoldo, forgets all about her princely
dignity, and claims him for herself, to his intense surprise and to the
great dissatisfaction of her court, be rated higher than her heathen
sisters, though she retains at least an outward show of decency.
Less objectionable, but not less masterful, appears this form of the

---

[1] See, on the subject of 'typical characters,' Schröer, A., *Über Titus Andronicus*
(Marburg, 1891), *passim*.

passion of love in the character of another duchess, Fiorinda of Urbino, in *The Great Duke of Florence*, who abjectly endeavours to induce the unwilling Sanazarro to take herself and her duchy, though she knows that he loves another, the charming Lidia. Another copy of the same type is the inconstant Almira in *A Very Woman*, who obstinately refuses to listen favourably to the wooing of the prince of Tarent, but, later, when he crosses her way once more in the habit of a slave, is immediately charmed with him to such a degree that she, the daughter of the viceroy of Sicily, does not hesitate to offer a nocturnal meeting to him, a slave. Massinger himself so much affected scenes in which a woman acts the part of the wooer, that he introduced a similar situation in a play where there was no pressing need for it : queen Honoria in *The Picture* seeks to seduce the knight Mathias, only in order to be able to refuse him, and, in this manner, to punish him for having praised the beauty and the chastity of his wife.

A somewhat subtler art of character painting we observe in Massinger's delineation of the nature of those women who are not the powerless victims of a sudden passion. Nevertheless, it cannot be denied that the utterances and the behaviour of his virtuous women often reveal that, in drawing female characters, he could rarely escape from the region of the senses. But, though most of Massinger's women are of the earth, earthy, we must not forget that he was able to create at least two women in another mould : the chaste Camiola and the lovable Lidia. Camiola, the Maid of Honour, deserves this appellation, though, perhaps, the poet impaired the nobleness of her presence and of her actions by two superfluous additions: the violence of her refusal of an unwelcome, boisterous wooer—whose bodily defects she criticises in a strain approaching, though by no means equalling, the invectives which the passionate Donusa hurls at the head of the unfortunate basha of Aleppo when he comes to court her—and the cautious contract (taken from the source of the play) by which Bertoldo, to liberate whom Camiola spent a fortune, is placed under an obligation to marry her. Perfectly delightful is Lidia, the youthful heroine of *The Great Duke of Florence*. In her, everything is charming : the simplicity with which she talks of her love for prince Giovanni; her naïve conviction that the fiercest enemy 'would let fall his weapon' when looking on the sweetness of her lover ; her anxious pleading at the feet of the duke, who is righteously angry with his deceitful nephew, and her trembling readiness to sacrifice her own hopes to the happiness of the prince. Nothing could be more winning than the manner of her receiving the fatal letter of her boy lover: she kisses it, she scarcely dares to hurt it by breaking the seal fastened by the beloved hand—even Shakespeare's Julia did not prattle more tenderly when kissing and piecing together the fragments of the letter of her beloved Proteus.

With this exception, a comparative survey of the women of Shakespeare and Massinger is the surest means for convincing us how rapidly the moral character of the English stage had changed since the days of the greater poet. The effrontery of Donusa and Massinger's other women of the same stamp would suffice to indicate the rise of a taste demanding stronger stimulants; but he went far beyond the loss of dignity and of delicacy of feeling which they exhibit. He created the Syracusan Corsica, the lewd wife of old Creon, who tries to seduce her stepson (*The Bond-Man*); Iolante, who, in the absence of her husband, is ready to accept the first handsome stranger as lover (*The Guardian*)—not to speak of bawds like Calipso in the same play, or the drunken hag Borachia in *A Very Woman*. We are but rarely allowed to forget that Massinger is separated from Shakespeare by Fletcher, whose plays had accustomed the public to the open licence of women.

Massinger's male characters, as a rule, are more interesting than his women. If we except one short scene of the patriotic Cleora, his women think and talk of nothing but the dominating passion of love in its different gradations; while their lovers, though meeting their desires, are yet, at the same time, not rarely made the interpreters of the views of the author. The Venetian Vitelli, whose virtue is too weak to resist the temptations of the infidel Donusa, is, by the admonitions of his ghostly counsellor, the Jesuit Francisco, filled with a repentance which rises to religious ecstasy, so that, in the end, he even aspires to the glory of the death of a martyr, becoming the most eloquent exponent of Massinger's religious feelings. Still more distinctly, we hear the voice of the poet himself in one of the speeches of Paris, the Roman actor, in a splendid apology for the stage and its poets and players. Paris, the favourite of the Roman public, is cited before the senate, being accused of satirical attacks on persons of rank and of being a libeller 'against the state and Caesar.' The gist of the actor's defence is that he and his companions cannot help it, if the conscience of the spectators is shaken by what is done and said on the stage. The energetic flow of this *oratio pro domo*, one of Massinger's rhetorical masterpieces, and its superfluousness from the dramatic point of view—for it stands quite outside the action of the tragedy—show how willingly he availed himself of the opportunity offered by the part of the actor to speak against the detractors of his art in general, and against those 'Catos of the stage' of whose persecutions he bitterly complains in one of his rare prologues.

In several plays, the passion of Massinger's heroes takes the form of violent, though groundless, jealousy. The jealous whims of Leosthenes irritate the noble Cleora and, finally, estrange her from him; Mathias doubts the fidelity of his wife; the suspicions of Theodosius, the Emperor of the East, threaten the life of Athenais; Marcelia, the proud wife of Sforza, is murdered by the selfish passion of her husband. A far more imposing figure than these egoists, tormented by their own folly, is the hero of the tragedy *The Fatall Dowry*, the sombre Charolais, who kills his adulterous wife and her gallant, and himself falls a victim to his revenge.

Besides these men who, fighting the battle of life, are not entirely absorbed by the passion of love—for, even in the sketch of the murderous Sforza, much stress is laid by the poet on his warlike qualities and the astuteness of the Italian politician who, standing between the French king and the emperor, knows how to reconcile his loyalty with his advantage—we find among Massinger's lovers, also, the conventional types of the contemporary drama: the devoted lover who lives on the smile of his lady, such as Ladislaus, the humble husband of the proud Honoria, Caldoro and the over-bashful Hortensio, and young libertines like Adorio and Alonzo, whose conversion, usually, is as incredible as it is sudden. Massinger's most attractive boy lover, who really has no other hopes, as yet, than 'to stonden in his lady grace,' and who utters his feelings with charming freshness, is prince Giovanni, the 'north-star' to whom Lidia looks up adoringly.

Guilty women of the stamp of lady Macbeth and the two daughters of king Lear, in whose lives not the passion of love but a stormy, and, if need be, sanguinary, ambition is the dominant influence, are not to be found in Massinger's dramas; only his men appear capable of conceiving and executing criminal plans. His villains, generally, are monsters of the darkest dye; they resemble each other in being free of any redeeming quality. Even if they act as avengers, they display so much baseness of mind that the wrong suffered by them is forgotten in our indignation at their perfidiousness. Francisco, the treacherous favourite of the duke of Milan, is spurred on by his desire to punish Sforza for having dishonoured his sister, an impulse of which we are informed much too late, long after he has forfeited all our sympathy by the wickedness of the means he uses to gain his end. First of all, he tries to seduce Sforza's wife, and, as he is foiled in this attempt by the resistance of the duchess, he accuses her of having made love to him, and succeeds in instigating her jealous and credulous husband to kill her. Finally, after having been bitterly reviled by his sister for cautiously sparing the life of her seducer, he enters the ducal palace in the disguise of a Jewish doctor and covers the lips and hands of the corpse of Marcelia with poisonous paint, so that Sforza is killed by kissing her : from beginning to end he acts the part of a perfidious coward, carefully abstaining from any direct attack on his mighty adversary himself. A still more despicable villain is Montreville, who, pretending to be the friend of old Malefort, avenges himself on him for injuries borne in silence during many years by dishonouring his innocent daughter Theocrine. As to the murderous and incestuous Malefort himself, one would feel inclined to regard him as an impossible monster, an isolated creature of the poet's fantasy, did not this very isolation strengthen our belief that Massinger's freely treated model was a historical personage, an Italian villain—that Francesco Cenci who had been killed, by murderers hired by his own daughter, some twenty years before the composition of Massinger's tragedy. Through the enormity of his crimes, Malefort's dark shape assumes gigantic dimensions, and we are not astonished that the poet himself felt the need of annihilating his monstrous creation, not by mortal agents, but by the direct interference of Heaven itself.

Massinger's imperial malefactor, the bloodthirsty tyrant Domitian, does not stand so entirely beyond the limits of humanity as Malefort. He becomes vulnerable by his infatuation for the profligate Domitia, and this one human weakness proves fatal to him : he spares her life, forfeited by her adulterous passion for Paris, and when, later, infuriated by her imprecations at the murder of the player, he resolves to kill her, it is too late ; Domitia herself heads the crowd of his assassins. By a skilful arrangement of the historical background, the dramatist succeeds in making us believe in the life-likeness of his tyrant as the natural outcome of a cruel age.

These criminals, who are finally struck down by the nemesis of their evil deeds, are the central figures of tragedies whose action lies in the far past and in foreign lands. But, even in those two comedies whose *dramatis personae* are intended to represent countrymen and contemporaries of the poet, we meet with two great villains : with the heartless usurer Sir Giles Overreach in *A New Way to Pay Old Debts,* and with the hypocrite Luke Frugal in *The City-Madam.* Sir Giles Overreach, who tries to bring his spendthrift nephew, one of the victims of his extortions, to the gallows, who commands his amiable daughter to offer herself to the lord to whom he wishes to marry her, and who boasts of his cruelties towards his debtors, be they widows or orphans, becomes so tremendous a villain, that, in order to free humanity of the fiend, the conclusion of the comedy—as, indeed, the whole conception of this ruthless character—touches the borders of tragedy. Deluded in all his ambitious hopes, the infuriated usurer goes mad. In the case of Luke Frugal, who has not hesitated to cause the betrayal of the women entrusted to his care—the wife and two daughters of his brother—the poet contents himself with stripping him of all his splendour and with exposing him to the contempt of all around him. In these two domestic comedies, one of the most glaring defects of Massinger's dramatic world, its frequent want of truth, strikes us most forcibly. The usurer's bragging proclamation of his vices and his crimes, which reminds us of the equally impressive and equally unlikely self-accusation of Chaucer's pardoner, is quite as incredible as is the obtuseness of the insidious Luke, when confronted by the gross deception practised on him. The sober light of day is unfavourable to Massinger's characters ; they stand in need of the romantic twilight of the past, in order to gain a certain, but too often limited, likeness to life.

As to Massinger's comical scenes, in which the male element again preponderates, his tragedies indicate an evident tendency to re-establish the purity of the tragic style. In what probably was his earliest tragedy, *The Unnaturall Combat,* a comical character appears in the person of Belgarde, a needy and ever hungry soldier, who, at a sudden favourable turn of his fortunes, is overwhelmed by claims of paternity something like Molière's Monsieur de Pourceaugnac ; but his chief scene is in harmony with the serious tenor of the whole work. Finding himself excluded from a banquet in the governor's palace on account of his threadbare old suit, he comes to it in the habit which he had worn for the welfare of his country 'in the heat and fervour of a bloody fight'—in his armour, eloquently and bitterly blaming the ingratitude of the world which lets soldiers starve in times of peace. In *The Duke of Millaine*, the report of the jailor as to the effect of a whipping on some of his former prisoners is more satirical than comical; and in *The Roman Actor* the dignity of tragedy is never disturbed by an attempt to raise a laugh. In the comedies, on the other hand, the usual stock of servants and gulls, of pert pages and humorous old men is to be found. There appear Calandrino, the boorish servant, aping the manners of the court; Gazet, the ambitious servant, who aspires to the office of an eunuch; and many others. The slaves of Syracuse, who, in *The Bond-Man*, rebel against their oppressors, are represented as ridiculous and abject creatures, with that curious indifference to the sufferings and rights of the people frequently to be noted in the drama of the period. Two of Massinger's comical old men, the voracious and venal judge Greedy in *A New Way*, and the courtier Cuculo, who, in view of his frequent hints at his statesmanship, appears to be a weak reproduction of the Polonius type, are farcical, while the free-spoken Eubulus and the merry Durazzo sometimes speak very much to the purpose between their jokes: Eubulus, like Belgarde, in favour of the neglected soldiers for whom the poet, patriotically anxious about the defence of his country, puts in a good word on every occasion; Durazzo, chanting the praise of healthy country life and of the delights of the chase, especially of falconry, of which 'royal sport' he gives a very pleasing description.

One cannot help observing with what persistency the satire with which dramatists frequently combined the fun of their lighter scenes is by Massinger aimed at the inmates of the courts of princes. In two of his plays, depraved courtiers, who, persuaded of the force of their own fascinations, think the seduction of women an easy task, become the victims of practical jokes and are exposed to general contempt. The exaggerated importance attached to exterior appearance and to more or less worthless ceremonies, the frequent neglect of true merit, the ridiculous pride shown by noblemen 'of the last edition'—these and many other unpleasant peculiarities of court life are referred to by the poet repeatedly, and with a force of expression which might lead us to think that his bitterness was caused by disagreeable personal experiences. Other objects of Massinger's satire are the projector and the monopolist, the empiric and the astrologer. Now and then, he attacks his countrymen in general, dishing up once more the well worn complaints about their fondness for hard drinking and for aping in their dress and manners outlandish, particularly

French, fashions; and, once, he even permits a connoisseur of human wares, a slave merchant, the remark that all English people, men and women, are stark mad—remembering, very likely, one of the best known jokes of the grave digger in *Hamlet*. Notwithstanding such occasional humorous criticisms, we are made to feel that the poet himself was proud of being an Englishman. At the end of an uncomplimentary conversation of some Italian servants about the gross feeding and the correspondingly gross understanding of Englishmen stands the telling line: 'They can fight and that's their all,' and Bertoldo, the faithless lover of *The Maid of Honour*, utters a sincere panegyric on England, 'the empress of the European isles,' though it is true that we can discover a melancholy inflection in the poet's voice, the eulogy referring not to the present but to a past state of things. Concerning the political situation of his own days, Massinger shared the dissatisfaction felt by many patriotic contemporaries.

It is noteworthy that Massinger's satirical allusions avoid two themes frequently treated by other dramatists of his time: neither satirical remarks of a literary kind, parodies of passages of the works of older writers, nor violent invectives to the address of the irreconcilable enemies of the stage, the puritans, are to be found in his plays, the nearest approach to such an attack being the statement of the jailor in *The Duke of Millaine*, that a sectary who would not yield to any argument of reason was made a 'fine pulpit-man' by a trussing of his haunches. Probably, Massinger, who was himself prone to religious meditation, admired in secret the moral rectitude of the puritans and their energy of purpose; he may even have felt oppressed by the consciousness that he was helping to heighten the animosity of their adversaries by participating in the scurrility and viciousness then characteristic of the stage. As it is, his comic dialogue abounds in coarse innuendos. Massinger's comic characters, advisedly, perorate in blank verse; the quacksalver, however, and the star-gazer are allowed to announce their wisdom in prose, possibly because it would have been a difficult task to versify smoothly the strange, half-Latin terms of their pseudoscientific *galimatias*.

As to versification and poetic diction, Massinger's mastership is indisputable; his dramas contain many passages in which the beauty of the style equals the vigour of the thought. He is a great orator, excelling in speeches in which, after the fashion of lawyers, speakers have to defend some particular position and to put their case in the most favourable light. Belgarde, insisting on the merits of the soldier; Sforza, endeavouring to convince the emperor that he, too, might find him a faithful and useful ally, notwithstanding his loyalty towards the French king; Timoleon of Corinth, soundly rating the Syracusans for having shamefully neglected the means of defence of their country ; Paris, in his apology for the stage ; Lidia, in her pathetic pleading for her lover ; Athenais, appealing to the compassion of Pulcheria—these and many other heroes and heroines of Massinger's are never at a loss for powerful, convincing or moving words when in critical situations. The mechanical tricks of the Euphuistic style are, for Massinger, a thing of the past ; his use of alliteration is very discreet, in most cases undoubtedly unconscious, and the insertion of Latin words or quotations, in which the older dramatists delighted, is a great rarity with him—in these respects, he strikes us as a far more modern writer than his predecessors and many of his contemporaries. But, on the other hand, it cannot be denied that he also has his peculiar blemishes and tricks of style, and, among them, one which is very obtrusive and for which he has been frequently censured—a mania for repeating himself. He possesses a considerable store of set phrases, metaphors and similes, which he strews around on every occasion without troubling himself to vary and individualise his expressions. Especially numerous and monotonous are his classical illustrations : Aeson and Medea, Hippolytus, Diana and Phaedra, Pasiphaë and her bull, Alcides and his poisoned shirt, and a great many other figures and objects of classical mythology continually remind us of Massinger's having received a classical education, a fact which is also recalled to us by the frequent translations of famous passages of ancient authors noticeable in his verse.

On the other hand, many of Massinger's similes, however bookish, mirror genuinely English impressions, originally received from the contemplation of the sea, its coasts and the life of sailors. The foam-covered rock, the stream which loses its name in the ocean, the ship, returning or outward bound, the small boat wrecked by the weight of its own sails, and many other maritime incidents, are frequently mentioned. In certain situations, which repeat themselves in his dramas, stereotyped formulas are sure to be used: if a beautiful lady is to be won, Massinger's personages never forget to talk of her 'virgin fort'; the charms of his passionate ladies, when they take the wooing upon themselves, are so powerful that even an ascetic hermit would be at a loss how to resist them; Lidia and Camiola, both of them in love with men of a higher social position, talk of their north-star and of the impossibility of the wren's building near the eagle. Too often the tinsel of these colourless phrases reminds us of the haste of the dramatist, sacrificing one of the greatest charms of any poem, its freshness of expression, to the wish to have done with his work.

Massinger's fatal fondness for conventional repetitions, which has been pointed out in the situations, characters, thoughts and words of his plays, apprises us of the limits of his merits as a dramatic artist. Notwithstanding our readiness to admire the firmness of his construction and the splendour of his diction, we are too often offended by the monotony of his characters and by the narrow range of their ideas; and his treatment of them exhibits hardly any process of development. As a playwright, it is true, he seeks to perfect himself in the technical part of his art; as a psychologist, he is too much inclined to remain on the surface, from beginning to end. We feel that the dramatist does not sufficiently identify himself with his creations, that he does not live in them, that they are formed more from the outside than from the inside. In consequence of this coldness of their maker, we do not recognise in his figures living beings of our own flesh and blood; too many of them remain cleverly formed and ably managed theatrical puppets. It is a great pity that the straitened circumstances of his life, which obliged him to work rapidly, prevented him from devoting a greater measure of love and care to the delineation of his characters. That he would have been able to rouse them to an intenser, fuller life, is impressed upon us as we look on the thoroughly lovable Lidia, on the pure presence of Camiola and at some of his secondary characters, as, for instance, the faithful Adorni, whose love for Camiola is deeper than the selfish desire to win her for himself.

As to the reception of Massinger's plays by the public of his own days, we know very little. In his dedications, he repeatedly laments the neglect shown by his contemporaries to poetry in general, mentioning, with bitterness in one instance, his own 'despised studies'; and the cutting remark that he presumes his *Roman Actor* will, in consequence of 'the severity and height of the subject distaste such as are only affected with jigs and ribaldry,' indicates, perhaps, that this tragedy had not been successful on the stage. On the other hand, he alludes to the friendly reception of *The Bond-Man*; and, in the dedication of *The Picture*, one of his most entertaining dramas, he is able to mention the general approbation the play had found at its presentment. Of prologues expressive of his sentiments, we have but few, because, with characteristic, and, in this case, very justifiable, conservatism, he strongly objected to this innovation, not falling in with it before the performance of his tragicomedy *The Emperour of the East,* printed in 1631, the first prologue to which begins with a few angry words about the imperiousness of custom. Nevertheless, we are indebted to his poems of this kind for a few noteworthy biographical details. In the two prologues composed for *The Emperour of the East,* he complains of the censures of those

> who delight
> To misapply whatever he shall write,

and of

> the rage
> And envy of some Catos of the stage

by whom ' this poor work ' had suffered ; while, in the prologue of *The Guardian,* he informs us of the failure of two of his dramatic ventures, which was followed by a silence of two years. We are ignorant of the nature of those two unfortunate plays, because many of Massinger's dramas were never printed and the manuscripts were inadvertently destroyed by Warburton's cook.

The posthumous popular fame of Massinger is chiefly based on his comedy *A New Way to Pay Old Debts,* which has kept the stage till recently, the brilliant part of the bold usurer captivating many famous actors. In a more indirect way, the appreciation of the dramatic power of the tragedy *The Fatall Dowry,* printed as a joint production of Massinger and Field, but, undoubtedly, chiefly Massinger's work, has been proved by the adaptations of later poets : by Nicholas Rowe's tragedy *The Fair Penitent,* composed in 1703, which did more for the preservation of Rowe's name as a dramatist than all his independent plays ; and by the recent successful version of Beer-Hofmann, entitled *Der Graf von Charolais,* which revived the memory of Massinger all over Germany. The first traces of his influence on the German stage date back to his lifetime : in 1626, an imitation of his and Dekker's dramatisation of the legend of Dorothea was performed at Dresden, where his attractive *Great Duke of Florence* also appeared on the boards in 1661. Later, Massinger attracted the attention of the poets of the romantic school of Germany as one of the most fascinating of Shakespeare's successors : count Baudissin translated several of his plays, and, within the last decades, German translators have repeatedly had recourse to him.

CHAPTER VII

TOURNEUR AND WEBSTER

THE two dramatists who are to be considered in the present
chapter have certain points in common. Both, at their best,
display a peculiarly sombre genius. The tragedies of both belong
to the same school; and both are utterly unknown to us, except
by their writings. In point of date, Tourneur would seem slightly
to precede Webster. And, for this reason, as well as for others
which are more material, it will be convenient to take him first.

Of Cyril Tourneur's life, we know nothing beyond the dates at
which his various plays and poems were published. They are as
follows: *The Transformed Metamorphosis*, 1600; *A Funeral
Poem* on Sir Francis Vere, 1609; *A Griefe on the Death of
Prince Henry*, 1613; and his two dramas, *The Revengers Tragoedie*,
1607 and *The Atheist's Tragedie*, 1611[1]. It should be noted that
two of these, the poem on Vere and *The Revengers Tragoedie*, have
no name on the title-page, and that it is by these alone that
Tourneur survives. There is a tepid reference to the author,
'as not to be despised nor too much praised,' by an anonymous
contemporary; and that is all.

On his poems, it is not necessary to dwell. None of them has
any merit; and the most elaborate of them, *The Metamorphosis*,
is written in that uncouth jargon which had been brought into
fashion by Marston in his satires (1598), and which is assailed by
Jonson in *Poetaster*. It is, moreover, an involved allegory, the key
to which is lost, but which Churton Collins ingeniously interpreted
as a cryptic reference to the fortunes of Essex.

A question has been raised as to the relative priority of the
composition of the two dramas. The order of publication makes a
presumption in favour of *The Revengers Tragoedie*; but it is a
presumption which might easily yield to substantial arguments on
the other side. The only argument, however, which has been
brought forward is the inferiority, or, as it has been called, the

---

[1] A tragicomedy, *The Nobleman*, acted at court in 1613, is now lost.

'immaturity,' of *The Atheist's Tragedie*. Such an argument is manifestly perilous and, if applied to the works of other writers, would lead to curious results. On the other side must be set the fact that *The Revengers Tragoedie*, though it abounds in striking passages and scenes, is singularly lacking in originality of conception; that it belongs to a type of tragedy which had been in vogue for many years before its appearance; that, in fact, it is a rearrangement of the material already treated by Marston in *Antonios Revenge* (1602)[1]. *The Atheist's Tragedie*, on the other hand, though, doubtless, inferior in some respects, is strikingly original in its central conception. And it would seem improbable that, after following his own path with much boldness, the dramatist should, in a later play, have fallen back obediently into the well worn rut. The same conclusion is suggested by the metre, which, in *The Revengers Tragoedie*, is exceptionally regular, while, in *The Atheist's Tragedie*, it is marked by what can only be called an abuse of the light endings which abound in the later plays of Shakespeare. We have other grounds for saying that Tourneur was a zealous student of Shakespeare; and it is surely more natural to suppose that, after the example of his master, he passed from the stricter to the looser system, than from the looser to the stricter. The point is by no means certain. On the whole, however, it would appear likely that the order of publication is, also, the order of composition; in other words, that *The Revengers Tragoedie* was written in or before 1607, and that *The Atheist's Tragedie* falls some time between it and 1611[2].

Neither play can be said to show much trace of dramatic power. The plots are poor in themselves, and one of them is largely borrowed. The characters are, at best, little more than types; and, in one instance, at any rate, the revenger's mother, the type is hardly improved by an incredible conversion. The most original character in the whole gallery is that of D'Amville, the atheist. But even he has a fatal resemblance to the Machiavellian monster who, from the time of Kyd and Marlowe, had been a familiar figure to the Elizabethan playgoer. The other characters are either puppets or incarnate abstractions of the various virtues and vices. The wanton personages of *The Atheist's Tragedie* are frankly caricatures. It is as poet that Tourneur claims our attention: a poet whose imagination is poisoned by the sense of universal vanity and corruption, but who lights up this festering material with flashes of high genius, and who is capable, at rare moments, of rising to visions of true beauty, and even grace: 'To have her train borne up, and her soul Trail

[1] See *ante*, chap. II.   [2] [See addenda.]

in the dirt' is an instance of the one; the alleged discovery of Charlemont's body by Borachio, of the other. And, to the former, at any rate, many parallels could be brought. His imagination needed a dramatic matter to kindle it; but, when kindled, it followed its own path and paid little heed to any but the purely formal requirements of the drama. To him, a tragedy was an outlet for the expression of his bitter judgment on man and his essentially gloomy view of human life. To this, all personages, all incidents, are subordinated. Of this, all that is memorable in his dramas is the imaginative symbol. In these points, he presents a certain analogy to Webster, but an analogy which is, at the same time, a faint reflection and a caricature.

The outward life of John Webster is as much a blank to us as that of Tourneur. The years of his birth and death are, alike, unknown to us. It may be conjectured, from the known dates, that he was born in the decade 1570—80; and he must have survived at least until 1624, the year of the production of the *Monuments of Honor*. Further than that we cannot go. It would be unsafe to accept the statement—not made until 1698, and not confirmed by the parish registers—that he was clerk of St Andrew's, Holborn. And the one outward fact with which we are left—a fact recorded on the title-page of the *Monuments of Honor*—is that he was a member of the Merchant Taylors' company. With this, we must rest content.

His literary activity falls, naturally, into three periods: the first, that of collaboration and apprenticeship (1602—7); the second, that of the two great tragedies (1610 to 1614); the third, that of the tragicomedies and, probably, of *Appius and Virginia*, beginning about 1620, the probable date of *The Devils Law-case*, and ending at a time unknown. It will be well to take each of these periods singly, and then to consider the characteristics of his genius as a whole.

During the first period, Webster produced no independent work. He was engaged in collaboration with other dramatists, particularly Dekker; and, owing to a peculiarity of his genius, his individuality was entirely merged in that of his fellow workers. After joining with Middleton and others in two plays, *Caesar's Fall* and *The Two Harpies*[1], which have perished, he is found in partnership with Dekker, Heywood and Wentworth Smith over a play entered as *Lady Jane*[2], and immediately followed by a *Second Part* (27 October), apparently from the

[1] See Henslowe's diary, 22, 29 May 1602.   [2] *Ibid.* 15 October 1602.

hand of Dekker only.   It has been universally assumed that
these two plays are either wholly or in part identical with
that which has come down to us under the title *The Famous
History of Sir Thomas Wyat* (published 1607); and there is no
reason for questioning this assumption[1].   As to the exact relation
of the two parts of *Lady Jane* to the existing *Wyat*, there is
considerable doubt.   The most plausible conjecture is that of
Dyce, who held the published version to be rudely cobbled together, with many omissions, from the two parts as originally
composed.   And the shapeless build of the drama, together with
the entire absence of the 'coming in of King Philip' mentioned
on the title-page, is in favour of this explanation.   The only
names occurring on the title-page are those of Dekker and
Webster; and it would seem tolerably plain that the former was
the predominant partner.   He was already an old hand at historical
subjects.   French history, Scottish, Portuguese and, above all,
English, had all, during the last four years, been freely dramatised
by him.   Moreover, the treatment of character, the peculiarities
of versification, the general cast of sentiment—all these have
analogies in his unaided work.   And there are few things, if any,
which remind us of the unaided work of Webster.

We turn, therefore, to the next recorded work—the contributions of Webster to the second edition of Marston's *The Malcontent*
(published 1604)[2].   It would seem probable that Webster is
responsible for nothing more than the induction to that strange
and 'bitter' drama.   Such is the natural interpretation of the
words on the title-page, and in the heading to the induction itself.
It is confirmed by the manifest identification of 'additions'—and
this is the word which has caused much misunderstanding—
with 'induction' in the opening dialogue (ll. 87—91).   And no
argument, except such as rests upon a strained construction of
the title-page, has hitherto been brought to the contrary.   The
body of the play, which the induction describes as having been
'lost, found' and subsequently 'played by the King's Servants,'
is of earlier date.   There are strong reasons, as Stoll points
out, for fixing it as early as 1600, though this view is not
wholly free from difficulties.   But it was not printed until 1604,
and that year saw two distinct editions: the first without, the
second with, the induction.   The second edition also contains
the 'augmentations,' which, it may well be, are rather restora-
tions of the 'lost' text, as originally written by Marston.   The

[1] Cf. *ante*, chap. II.   [2] Cf. *ibid.*

induction—and it is that alone with which we are concerned—can hardly have been written much before the moment of publication. Its composition would naturally fall between the dates of the first and second editions. And this intrinsic probability is supported by internal evidence. The main object of the piece, seemingly, is to justify the king's company for performing a play in which a rival company, that of the Blackfriars, had certain rights. And that company, in its 'decimo-sexto' shape—the 'little eyases' of the second quarto of *Hamlet*—was not licensed until January, 1604[1]. Any allusion to it in its earlier form, before it passed into the hands of the 'children,' would be irrelevant. It may be added that, in the words of Sly, 'No, in good faith, for mine ease,' there is a manifest quotation from the Osric of the second quarto of *Hamlet* (1604). Altogether, then, we can hardly be wrong in dating the composition of the induction within the year 1604. And, on the evidence of the title-page, we are justified in saying that Webster was sole author. That he had much reason to be proud of it, no one will assert. The 'additions,' as Burbage modestly remarks, 'are not greatly needed'; and, save in so far as they serve to introduce a hit against the children of the queen's revels, they do little more than 'entertain time and abridge the not received custom of music.' The induction was a common device of the Elizabethan stage. It had been employed, for instance, in *The taming of a Shrew* (printed 1594), in *Every Man out of His Humour*, in *Cynthia's Revels* and in *Antonio and Mellida*. And it must be confessed that Webster's effort is both flatter in itself and stands in a looser relation to the play which follows than any of these.

We now pass to what have been called the citizen comedies, *West-Ward Hoe* and *North-Ward Hoe*, both written in partnership with Dekker[2]. Both were printed in 1607; but the former was entered at Stationers' hall as early as March, 1605; the latter not until August, 1607. The first three acts of *West-Ward Hoe* have been thought by some critics to belong to 1603, and their authorship assigned to Webster. But there is no valid reason for passing the hatchet between these acts and the last two. And, as the fourth act (sc. 2) contains an allusion to the fall of Ostend—an allusion which is probably, though not certainly, anticipated in the first act (sc. 1)—and as Ostend did not surrender until the autumn of 1604, it is likely that the composition of the whole falls into the last quarter of 1604, and that it was first acted at the beginning

of 1605.   In no case can *North-Ward Hoe* be dated earlier than
about the middle of 1605, seeing that it is plainly a reply to *Eastward Hoe* (by Jonson, Chapman and Marston), which was almost
certainly written, as a retort to *West-Ward Hoe,* in the earlier part
of that year.   And if, as seems probable, it contains a borrowing
from Marston's *Parasitaster, Or The Fawne*[1], which appears to
have been first acted, as well as registered, early in 1606, then the
composition of Dekker and Webster's second comedy must be
placed in 1606—7.   In any case, it is clear that, during the time of
partnership, long or short, the intercourse between Webster and
Dekker, begun (as we have seen) in 1602, must have been of the
most intimate kind.   And, once more, it was the younger and
deeper poet who sat at the feet of the elder and more facile.

The plays in question bring us into the thick of one of those
battles of the dramatists which give much liveliness to the history
of the Elizabethan stage.   It may be called an afterswell of the
storm which had raged between Jonson, on the one hand, and
Dekker and Marston, on the other, in 1601—2; the storm of which
Cynthia's Revels, Poetaster and *Satiro-mastix* are the abiding
record[2].   Times had changed since the first round of the contest.
Marston was now the partner of his terrible enemy ; and, on both
sides, the game was now played with the best temper, a compliment which could certainly not be paid to Jonson's share in the
earlier encounter.   The main plot of *West-Ward Hoe* is a tale of
three merry wives who, putting their husbands on a false scent,
jaunt off with three gallants to spend the night at Brentford, then
a familiar trysting-place.   They are pursued by their husbands and
run to earth at the inn, but, thanks to a sudden freak of respectability, are able to prove their innocence ; all ends in good temper
and reconciliation.   With this is ingeniously interwoven the story
of Mistress Justiniano, who is wooed by a rakish earl and yields to
his entreaties, but, at the critical moment, is seized with scruples
and joins with her husband to work a like repentance on her lover.
Having thus set his own house in order, Justiniano acts as managing
director to the comedy of the three citizens and their wives, which
forms the staple of the drama.   The reply of Jonson and his partners
in *Eastward Hoe* is notably respectful.   In the main, it is a piece
of friendly emulation rather than of satire.   And the picture of
citizen life is among the most pleasing, as well as vivid, which have
come down to us.   The theme is plainly suggested by the citizen
and prentice portraits in which Dekker was past master.   The

[1] See Bullen's *Marston*, vol. ii, p. 21; Stoll, p. 16.   [2] See *ante*, chap. ii.

spirit of Simon Eyre and Candido is caught with such skill that,
a few phrases and other touches apart, the play might easily have
been taken for the work of Dekker himself.   Yet, in the edifying
conversion of Master Francis Quicksilver, the idle apprentice, and
most engaging of scapegraces, there is, manifestly, a spice of
burlesque ; and it is hard not to believe that the shaft was aimed
at such scenes as the sudden conversion of Bellafront (1604), or of
Mistress Justiniano in *West-Ward Hoe* itself.   The satire, however,
is unexpectedly genial ; not comparable to that which had been
showered on Dekker and Marston in *Poetaster*, nor even to that
which was aimed at king James and his countrymen in this
very play, and which brought the authors within danger of the
law.   Equally good humoured is the satire of the rejoinder.
Jonson is let off without a scratch.   The banter—for it is nothing
more—falls entirely on Chapman.   There can be no doubt that
the 'little hoary poet' of *North-Ward Hoe* is intended for the
latter.   His *Caesar and Pompey*, his liking for French themes,
his 'full and heightened style,' his professional vanity—all come in
for gentle mockery.   But the banter consists in nothing worse
than placing the 'reverend' and moral poet in impossible situations ; in bringing him to the house of a courtesan who falls
violently in love with him and in causing him to be seized, if only
for a moment, as a fit subject for confinement in Bedlam.   And, on
the whole, the portrait of Bellamont is the most attractive thing
in the whole piece ; Chapman himself can hardly have taken it
amiss.   Apart from such quizzing, the plot of the comedy is uncommonly simple.   Mistress Mayberry, the wife of a rich citizen,
is persecuted by the attentions of two worthless gallants.   After
repeated rejections, one of them snatches the ring from her finger
and shows it to her husband, as a proof of her infidelity.   Guided
by Bellamont, Mayberry is soon able to convince himself of her
innocence, and bides his time for an appropriate revenge.   He
beguiles the two slanderers into a trip to Ware, in the course of
which he brings conclusive proof that one of them has corrupted
the wife of the other.   The injured husband is overwhelmed with
confusion, and Mayberry completes his vengeance by entrapping
the other rogue into marriage with the lady who has already
figured gaily in the satire on Chapman.   It can hardly be said that
either this comedy, or that which opened the series, is so vivid or
so full of sparkle as that of Jonson and his associates.   But the
merit of *Eastward Hoe* is so extraordinary that a play may
well fall short of it and yet be extremely good.   And that will

be the verdict of most readers both on *West-Ward Hoe* and *North-Ward Hoe.*

It remains to ask whether there is any means of determining the part played by Webster in the composition of these plays. The two are strictly of a piece. In both—whether we regard construction, situations, characters or phrases—we can trace reminiscences or anticipations of Dekker's acknowledged work[1] and there is little or nothing which can be said to bear the stamp of Webster. Whichever of the partners held the pen, it can hardly be doubted that the inspiration, alike in small things and in great, was Dekker's. If there be any one scene where the reader might be tempted to recognise the hand of Webster, it is that in which the earl, expecting to find his mistress, is confronted by her husband in disguise, while a curtain is drawn aside so as to reveal the apparently lifeless body of the woman he had expected to see at his mercy. But even this scene, as Swinburne and others have pointed out, is, so far as the central situation goes, to be closely paralleled from the *Satiro-mastix* and *The Honest Whore* of Dekker. And, though the disguise of Justiniano and some touches both before and after his entry are well in accordance with what we know of Webster, the style of the whole passage, in the main, is rather that of Dekker ; and where so much is his, it is hazardous to assume that anything of moment was contributed by his partner. Of the citizen comedies then, as of *Wyat,* it may be said that the conception is Dekker's and that the execution—whether as regards characters, incidents, or style—is, on the whole, entirely in his spirit. That they contain a good deal of Webster's work, need not be doubted. But such work is executive rather than original, derived rather than creative.

So ends the period of Webster's apprenticeship and collaboration. We now pass to the earlier of the two periods which contain his original and unaided work (1610—18). This is the period of *The White Divel* (afterwards known as *Vittoria Corombona*) and *The Dutchesse Of Malfy.* Some three or four years separate their period from the preceding. For *The White Divel* was printed in 1612; and the repeated borrowings from Rich's *New Description of Ireland,* published in 1610, forbid us to place its composition earlier than that year; it may well have been written in 1611. The exact source of this great tragedy is a problem which still remains unsolved. That it is based on events connected with the life of Paolo Giordano, duke of Bracciano, and that these events took place in 1581—5, that is, within the lifetime of Webster himself, is certain. Beyond

---

[1] Cf. Stoll, pp. 64—79.

that, all is obscure. The case, so far as our present knowledge goes, is as follows. Many versions of the story, contemporary or nearly so, exist in Italian[1]; one, by François de Rosset[2], is known in French. All these are in substantial agreement with each other; and all differ, in many crucial points, from Webster's. The question at once arises : how are Webster's variations to be accounted for? Had he before him a written account differing from all those which have come down to us? Or had he heard an oral statement substantially agreeing with that given in his play and traceable in the last resort to one who had either travelled in Italy, or come, as visitor, from Italy to the north? Or had he read a version corresponding more or less closely with those accessible to us, and retained nothing more than a confused and indistinct memory of it? Or, finally, having, from written or oral sources, a tolerably accurate knowledge of the true facts, did he deliberately alter them for purposes of dramatic effect?

This is not the place to discuss the question in detail. So much, however, may be said. The first supposition, so far as it relates to any record professing to be historical, may be dismissed as highly improbable. The story, as we have seen, was well known and accurately recorded. The actors in it were among the most marked figures of their times: Francesco, grand duke of Florence, the typical Italian 'despot' of his day; Sixtus V, the soul of the League and the Armada, the last of the popes who can fairly be described as great. The heroine of the story was niece by marriage of the latter. The circumstances of her second marriage and her murder had formed the subject of trials—one at Rome, the other at Padua and Venice—familiar to all Italy. It is hardly to be conceived that any chronicler should have departed widely from facts thus generally known. Novels and dramas remain. And it is not impossible that, some day, either a novel or, less probably, a drama may be discovered which criticism will recognise as the source from which Webster drew. None such, however, has hitherto been found; though Tempesti, writing a century and a half later (1754), says that the 'story was known all over Europe' and had been told by 'hundreds of authors.' The only novel at present known is the 'tragic history' of de Rosset; and that, with the exception of the assumed names and minute additions of obviously romantic embroidery, is in complete accordance with the chronicles; so that, even if it can be proved to have appeared before *The White Divel*

---

[1] Cf. Gnoli, D., *Vittoria Accoramboni* (1870), pp. 2—6.

[2] *Histoires tragiques de nostre temps*, in or shortly before 1615.

was written, it will in no way account for Webster's departure from the historical facts. Of dramas, previous to Webster's, still less is to be said. Santorio, indeed, a contemporary chronicler (1562—1635) says: *Scio ego apud quosdam actitatum tragœdiœ argumentum, datumque spectantibus haud suppressis personis nominibusque.* But in what language this tragedy was written—whether, as we shall see in the analogous case of *The Dutchesse Of Malfy*, the reference may not even be to *The White Divel* itself—unfortunately does not appear.

The other alternatives are not mutually exclusive. It is perfectly possible that an oral statement, for which either an English traveller or an Italian visitor was ultimately responsible, may have reached Webster and that some, at least, of his inaccuracies may be due to the natural negligence of his informant. Intercourse with Italy had never been broken off. France was a common meeting ground of English and Italian. We know, for instance, that Vittoria's own stepson, Virginio Orsini, the Giovanni of the play, had been sent as envoy to England by his uncle Ferdinand, successor to Francesco, at the close of Elizabeth's reign. We know that the same Virginio was reputed lover to Marie de Medici, and that the attention of English dramatists was at this time keenly directed to the doings of the French court, and not least to the love affairs of the royal house[1]. All this would make it natural enough that rumours, more or less accurate, relating to the Orsini and Medici, should reach the ears of Webster. But, once again, there is no evidence. Some, indeed, of Webster's inaccuracies are almost certainly due to lapse of memory. For instance, he has given the official name of Sixtus V wrongly, and has inverted the parts of Flamineo and Marcello. Neither of these changes can plausibly be set down to deliberate intention.

There remains the final possibility that Webster had read an account not substantially different from that given by the chronicles, and that most of his variations are made of set purpose; that is, with a view either to suit his own conception of what the leading characters in such a tragedy should be, or to secure a more impressive effect. Among the changes made with the former object would be reckoned the transformation of the characters of Vittoria's husband and mother, the one for ill, the other for good; the strain of hypocrisy, not, however, very consistently worked out, in the character of Vittoria; the obvious

[1] See the circumstance connected with the performance of *The Conspiracie, And Tragedie of Charles Duke of Byron*, 1608, *ante*, chap. II.

adaptation of her circumstances to those of her kinswoman, Bianca Capello (the heroine of Middleton's undated drama, *Women beware Women*)[1]; above all, the change in the character of Lodovico who, in the play, is moved neither by avarice, nor by the desire to assert the honour of his family, but by the fixed resolve to exact vengeance for the murder of an adored mistress, Isabella. Among the alterations made for the sake of effect might be counted the appearance of the 'lieger ambassadors' at Vittoria's trial and the election of Sixtus (the presence of the English envoy is historically impossible), the murders of Marcello and Brachiano, the appearance of Francisco as a direct agent in the latter crime, the ghastly scene at Brachiano's deathbed and, very possibly, the transference of the riddling *Manet alta mente repostum* from Lodovico to Isabella. It would clearly have weakened the dramatic force of the tragedy to reserve the final act, or even a closing scene, for the nemesis of Lodovico. And it may well be for this reason that, in defiance of historical facts, Webster placed his death within a few moments of his victim's. That would at once bar out the situation in which the memorable phrase was actually uttered—the formal questioning of Lodovico by the magistrates of Padua. And Webster, impressed (as he well might be) by the phrase, was, on this assumption, at the pains to introduce it under circumstances entirely different, but hardly less dramatic.

If this be the true explanation—and many things point that way—it would follow that Webster's treatment of his subject is far more original than has sometimes been supposed. If we may believe him to have worked on a chronicle such as those embodied in Tempesti's *Vita di Sisto V*, or on a novel resembling that of de Rosset, he has, manifestly, made far more sweeping changes in his 'source' than seems to be implied by those who speak of his play as drawn from 'an Italian novel.' He would, in fact, have breathed a new spirit into the whole train of incidents. The figure of Vittoria, indeed, remains much as we might divine it to have been from the historical records; though the lines are deepened, the colours heightened and harmonised, by the hand of genius. The same applies, though in a less degree, to the defiant figure of Brachiano and the deep dissimulation of Francesco and Monticelso. The last, indeed, is the one case in which the dramatist has fallen short of the model supplied by history. In a drama where he could not be the central figure there was no room for the grand, yet sinister, figure of Sixtus. All

---

[1] See *ante*, chap. III.

else, however, would be the creation of Webster: the tragic
resignation of Isabella, the fatuity of Camillo, the pathos of
Cornelia, the profoundly interesting and subtle portrait of Lodovico.
The crucial change, alike for its own sake and for its bearing on
the whole structure of the tragedy, is that in the character and
motives of Lodovico. The attribution of his long cherished
schemes to outraged love and the thirst for vengeance alters the
whole nature of the action. It provides the atmosphere of doom
which hangs over the drama from beginning to end, and which is
deepened by the scenic effects, the sombre episodes, of which
Webster was master without rival.

But, whether the positive changes made by Webster in his
unknown authority be large or small, the advance of *The White
Divel* on any or all of his previous work is incalculable. To the
'prentice, seeing through the eyes and speaking with the voice of his
master, has succeeded the skilled craftsman, with an almost perfect
command of his material and instruments, with the keenest eye for
the hidden possibilities of his task and the utmost originality in
handling it. During the half dozen years or so which followed,
Webster was by far the most striking figure, Shakespeare excepted,
in the long roll of contemporary dramatists. With the men of his
own day, he had not the vogue of Beaumont and Fletcher or
the personal authority of Jonson. But modern criticism, with
one voice, has pronounced his genius to be of a higher and rarer
kind. And, though we can still trace a certain awkwardness in
his management of the plot—a defect from which he never shook
himself entirely free—his work, in other respects, is singularly
self-contained, as well as absolutely original. There is, perhaps, no
poet on record who leaped so suddenly into the full possession of
his powers. It is, of course, true that the influence of other writers
can be traced very plainly in this, as in his other, tragedy. His
debt to Shakespeare has often been pointed out. It appears in
many turns of thought and phrase; in the portrait of the boy,
Giovanni; in the haunting beauty of Cornelia's dirge; in the consummate art, bold yet unostentatious, with which the figure of
the heroine is painted: above all, in that union of imaginative
reflection, pure poetry and dramatic genius which brings him
nearer than any of his fellow dramatists to the author of *Hamlet*.
In his fusion of the two former of these qualities, again, we cannot
fail to recognise his relationship, perhaps his indebtedness, to the
greatest lyric poet of the period, Donne.

These, however, are matters which concern the individual

genius of the dramatist. Still more significant is his place in the general development of the Elizabethan drama ; and, in particular, his debt to the dramatists of revenge. Here, he falls into line with that long succession of writers, beginning with Kyd, who took up the tale of Seneca's *Thyestes* and *Agamemnon* and, during more than twenty years, rang the changes upon the theme of vengeance through every key and with every variety of accompaniment. To explain his position, a slight sketch of the history of this theme, as handled by Elizabethan dramatists, may be attempted.

In the older versions of the theme there are three essential features, all of which, in the last resort, are inherited from Seneca. These are, that a murder has been committed ; that revenge is a duty from which the next of kin cannot escape ; and that this duty is enforced by the ghost of the murdered man, which appears at intervals to drive home the demand for blood. So it is with *The Spanish Tragedie*; so with *Antonios Revenge*; so, allowing for certain modifications, with *The Revenge of Bussy d'Ambois* (published 1613) and *The Second Maiden's Tragedy* (licensed 1611)[1]; so, unless all indications are misleading, with the lost *Hamlet* (in or before 1596), which has been attributed, on probable, but not conclusive, grounds, to Kyd; so, finally, with the *Hamlet* of Shakespeare. The first change in the outward framework of the story—in spirit, it need hardly be said that Shakespeare's masterpiece stands poles asunder from the crudities of Kyd, Marston and the rest—seems to have been made by Chettle, whose *Tragedy of Hoffman* belongs to the same year as *Antonios Revenge*[2]. The change is twofold. The ghost disappears; and, what is far more significant, the avenger of blood is no longer the hero, but the villain, of the piece. Both changes are repeated—the latter, however, with sweeping modifications—in the next play of Marston, *The Malcontent* (1604, or earlier), to which, indeed, it is quite possible that the credit of innovation may belong rather than to *Hoffman*. The modifications are as follows. The murderer of the original version is replaced by a usurper who drives the rightful prince into exile. This, necessarily, involves the disappearance of the ghost. And revenge, though retained, is retained in a form so softened that the avenger contents himself with melting one of his enemies to at least outward repentance and dismissing the other with magnanimous contempt.

It was at this point that Tourneur—or the author of *The Revengers Tragoedie*, whoever he may have been—took up the tale. Reverting to murder as the starting-point of his action, he

---

[1] As to this play see *Ward*, vol. ii, p. 672.　[2] See Henslowe's diary, 7 July, 29 December 1602.

entirely dispenses with the ghost and, in the very moment of victory, the cup of triumph is dashed from the lips of his 'revenger.' It is clear that he felt the theme of vengeance to be an outworn convention. It is equally clear that he surrendered it with extreme reluctance. The whole fabric of the piece is based on the assumption that revenge is a binding duty. And, when the tables are turned, when the performance of the duty is visited at the last moment with condign punishment, it is inevitable that the reader should feel himself defrauded. Never had a play so lame and impotent a conclusion as this. And, for that reason, if for no other, it is a relief to turn from *The Revengers Tragoedie* to *The Atheist's Tragedie*. Here, at any rate, the central thought is consistently maintained from beginning to end. Here, at any rate, the dramatist flies without faltering to his mark. The innovation, which he had been blindly feeling after in *The Revengers Tragoedie*, is here boldly carried out. Vengeance is thrust down from the rank of duties; forgiveness is exalted in its stead. If the ghost of the murdered man is restored to something of his former rights, it is to cry not for revenge, but for mercy; to reiterate, with a fervour more moral than dramatic, that 'vengeance is the Lord's.' The dramatic weakness of the change is obvious enough. But it is significant as marking the final stage of the tragedies of revenge.

The White Divel, in all probability, was produced during the very year in which *The Atheist's Tragedie* was published. At first sight it might be taken for a reversion to the earlier type of this class of drama. Revenge for innocent blood is once more the main theme of the dramatist. It is presented, however, no longer as a duty, but as a passion; and with the cry of 'wild justice' is mingled the baser note of wounded pride. Our sympathies, again, so far from being with the avengers, are cast, rather, on the side of their victim. The result of such changes is to reduce the motive of vengeance to a secondary place. It supplies not the core of the building, but its scaffolding, or little more. The vital interest belongs not to the story—this, in truth, might have been told more clearly—but to the characters who sustain it, and the passions which are let loose in its course. One more proof is thus furnished, if proof were needed, that the theme of revenge was now losing its fascination; that the dramatist, even when he professed to work on it, was now driven by an overmastering instinct to degrade it from its original supremacy.

The same tendency appears still more clearly in *The Dutchesse Of Malfy*. Here, again, revenge is the nominal theme. It is not, however, revenge for murder, but for an outrage on the insensate pride of family; and it is reinforced by the yet more sordid motive of avarice—a motive which had been carefully excluded from the earlier play. The sympathies of the spectator, which, in *The White Divel*, are somewhat divided, are, here, solely and absolutely, with the victim. And, as if to mark the change in the most glaring manner possible, the whole of the last act is devoted to the nemesis which falls upon the avengers. The dramatic interest suffers; but the intention of the dramatist is proved beyond all possibility of mistake. The upshot of all this is that the motive of vengeance, already weakened in the earlier drama, fades almost out of recognition in the latter; and that, with *The Dutchesse Of Malfy*, revenge—except in survivals so obvious as the last act of *Women beware Women*—may be said to disappear from among the dominant themes of Elizabethan tragedy[1].

With all its great qualities, the first tragedy of Webster is not without traces of immaturity. The crudeness of incident which he had inherited from his forerunners, is not entirely purged away; the plot is wanting in clearness; even the portraiture of the heroine bears some marks of vacillation. Most, if not all, of these weaknesses are absent from *The Dutchesse Of Malfy*. The plot of this play is perfectly simple; the characters, if we except that of Bosola, are drawn with an unfaltering hand; in unity of tone, the play surpasses all others of the period, save those of Shakespeare. As to the sources of this tragedy, and its date, there is little room for discussion. The story is certainly taken, with many refinements, from Painter's *Palace of Pleasure*, as that, in its turn, drew upon the *Histoires Tragiques* of Belleforest, and this upon Bandello. Crawford has proved that Sidney's *Arcadia* not only exercised a deep influence upon the thought and language of the play, but that it also furnished the hint, and more than the hint, of its most highly wrought situation: that in which the duchess is persecuted with every variety of physical and mental torture. It is also more than probable that the echo song, which Webster had in mind (act v, sc. 3), and which he turns to purposes of the highest imaginative effect, is that of the *Arcadia* (book II) rather than any other. The play of Lope de Vega[2], which may have been written about the same time, has little in common with Webster's, and can hardly have been known to him. The date of *The Dutchesse Of Malfy*, again, can now be determined within very

---

[1] [See addenda.]   [2] *El Mayordomo de la Duquesa de Amalfi.*

narrow limits. It was not printed until 1623. But, as the part of Antonio is known to have been created by Ostler, the first performance cannot have been later than 1614, the year of that actor's death. It is true that the opening dialogue manifestly refers to the execution of Concini, maréchal d'Ancre, which took place in April 1617, and speedily became known, through translations of official documents, in this country. There is, however, no difficulty in supposing that this passage was added by Webster some time between that event and the date of publication. Indeed, if, as is practically certain, the play described by Busino, chaplain to the Venetian embassy, in February 1618, is *The Dutchesse Of Malfy* —the amours of a Cardinal, his solemn exchange of a churchman's for a soldier's garb and his 'poisoning' of his sister are specifically mentioned and, in spite of the slight inaccuracy, can hardly refer to any incidents except those of our play—it may well be that the addition was made for a revival of the play at the beginning of that year. In any case it is now certain that *The Dutchesse Of Malfy* was composed within two or three years of *The White Divel*[1].

The later play is a marked advance upon the earlier. The old motives, as we have seen, are retained, but represented in a softer, a more human, form ; and the effect on the imagination is entirely different. The interest is shifted from the avengers to the deed which provokes their malice. The real theme of the drama is not revenge, but the graciousness of a noble and loving woman, and the unflinching firmness with which, in the face of nameless tortures, she possesses her soul, undismayed by all until a brutal deception convinces her that the bodies of her murdered child and husband lie before her. The constancy of the victim, the remorse which it wakens even in the base nature of her tormentor, are painted with the fewest possible strokes, and each is charged to the utmost with imaginative effect. After this, it must be admitted, the interest flags ; the fate of Antonio, the miserable end of the persecutors and their accomplice, are in the nature of an anti-climax. Had the play ended with the fourth act, the tragic impression would have been yet deeper and more harmonious than it is. Yet it is easy to see how Webster was drawn into this by-path. During this period—in that which followed it is strangely different—he was filled with notions of nemesis and poetic justice. Hence, the necessity for bringing the two brothers and Bosola to condign punishment. He was also possessed with a gloomy con-

[1] See Wallace, C. W., letters to *The Times*, 2 and 4 October 1909.

viction, perhaps partly inherited from Marston, of the corruption of man, and particularly of such men as haunted courts. In the loves of Julia and the cardinal, he found a text for this sermon too tempting to be passed by. Finally, he was strangely attracted towards subtle intricacies of character ; and, in the portrait of Bosola, he strove to probe them to their depth. The general result of all this is to deepen the gloom of the atmosphere still further, but, at the same time, to blunt the edge of the tragic effect. The true tragedy is with the duchess. When she is gone, what are Bosola and Julia, what are Ferdinand and the cardinal, but hateful superfluities ? Even Antonio, beautiful as is the poetry which Webster weaves around him, suffers eclipse when the sun, which gave him light and warmth, is quenched.

From the tragedies we pass to the closing period of Webster's activity (1618 ? to his death). The plays which would seem to belong to this period are five : *The Guise* (mentioned in the dedication to *The Devils Law-case*), and *A Late Murther of the Sonne upon the Mother* (in partnership with Ford, 1624), both, unfortunately, lost; *The Devils Law-case*, published in 1623 ; *Appius and Virginia*, in 1654 ; and *A Cure for a Cuckold*, in 1661. None of the three which survive approaches the level of the two tragedies. All, however, contain occasional flashes of the genius which created *The White Divel* and *The Dutchesse Of Malfy*, though rather of its poetic, than its dramatic, quality. Save in *Appius*, which owes much to the Roman tragedies of Shakespeare, Webster is now working under quite other, and less inspiring, influences. With him, as with other dramatists of the period, the star of Fletcher is in the ascendant.

Appius and Virginia stands apart from the other plays, and may conveniently be taken first. Its date cannot be fixed by either external or internal evidence ; a play of the name, however, is mentioned in a list of dramas appropriated to the Lord Chamberlain's company (1639), and it may be Webster's[1]. For his materials, Webster seems to have used Painter's *Palace of Pleasure*, Livy and, possibly, Dionysius of Halicarnassus. Of his own invention, apparently, are the plot of Appius for reducing Virginius to poverty, the quarrel between Virginius and Icilius, the production of Virginia's body by the latter for the purpose of nerving Virginius to vengeance ; above all, the introduction of the clown Corbulo and the pretentious advocate, the latter being a familiar butt of the ridicule of Webster. The drama has a certain massive simplicity, which is probably due to the influence of Shakespeare ;

[1] [See addenda.]

and the humorous element has been thought, perhaps rightly, to point in the same direction. But the general effect is disappointing. The subject has always proved itself intractable upon the stage. And not even the pure poetry and pathos of the father's farewell to his daughter can avail to put our sympathies entirely on his side.

The two remaining plays have proved strangely baffling to the critics; and that, no less in regard to source and date than to intrinsic value. *The Devils Law-case*, as it stands, cannot have been written before the latter part of 1620; for there is a clear allusion[1] to an unhappy affray, in August 1619, with the Dutch in the East Indies (not Amboina), news of which can hardly have reached England till the autumn of the following year. There is a suspicious resemblance in the central incident, the lying self-slander of Leonora, to incidents in Fletcher's *Spanish Curate* and *The Faire Maide of the Inne*. The latter, however, was not licensed for acting until January 1626; and it contains an explicit reference to the massacre of Amboina, which did not become known in England till May 1624. It can hardly, therefore, have served as material for Webster in or before 1623. *The Spanish Curate*, licensed October 1622, is a more likely source, or *Gerardo*, itself the source of Fletcher's play, which was translated into English in that year[2]. It has been urged, though this seems less probable, that Webster may have taken the hint from a like incident in *Lust's Dominion*, which, probably, dates back to 1600. Other sources of Webster's incidents are Goulart's *Histoires Admirables* (2nd ed. 1606), which had already been used by him in *The Dutchesse Of Malfy*, and which suggested the cure by stabbing in this play; perhaps, also, the trials for sorcery conducted in France 1610—11. An account of these, by Michaelis, had been translated into English in 1613—the highly protestant introduction may well have appealed to Webster—and they seem to be alluded to more than once in this play (especially at the end of act IV, where the reference to France is quite irrelevant) and may even have suggested its title. It is not impossible that the very name of Romelio may be an adaptation of Romillon, who took a leading part in these grim investigations. But, whatever the exact sources of this puzzling drama, its whole spirit betrays the influence of Fletcher. This appears in the romantic cast of the incidents, in the irresponsibility of the characters, and in the nonchalant charity of the author towards the insufferable baseness of Romelio. Fletcher's influence, however, is conspicuously

---

[1] Act IV, sc. 2.   [2] Cf. *ante*, Appendix to chap. v.

absent from the rhythm, unless the marked increase of fluency, as compared with the two tragedies, may be attributed to this source. On the whole, however, there is more substance, and more elevation of spirit, in Webster's tragicomedy than in most of Fletcher's. As a drama, in spite of obvious blemishes, the former deserves more praise than it has commonly received. And there are touches of poetry, as well as of metrical effect, which worthily recall *The Dutchesse Of Malfy.*

A Cure for a Cuckold is assigned by its original editor to the joint workmanship of Webster and William Rowley. Webster's authorship, though it has sometimes been questioned, is attested by the style, as well as by not a few echoes of phrasing. If the underplot, which gives title to the play, is from his hand, we might be tempted to see in it a return to the inspiration of Dekker. Yet if any share belongs to Rowley, it can hardly be other than these scenes. And the question is too speculative to be profitably discussed. As to the influence of Fletcher on the main theme, there can be no manner of doubt; and it is yet more marked than in *The Devils Law-case.* The action is yet more full of startling and romantic incident; the shiftings of mood and purpose are still more sudden; the stress thrown on scenic effect, at the expense of character, is still stronger. That the plot is modelled on anything to be found in Fletcher, cannot be asserted. *The Little French Lawyer*[1] is the only play which, in this respect, offers any analogy; and the analogy is not very close. On the other hand, there is the strongest resemblance between the plot of Webster's play and that of Massinger's *The Parliament of Love* (licensed November 1624). The central incident of both is a duel imposed on a man, without reason, by his mistress—an incident, the germ of which is to be found in *The Dutch Courtezan* of Webster's early partner, Marston[2]. And, considering Webster's docility, it is hard to resist the conclusion that the debt, probably, was on his side. Nor is there anything against this supposition save the opinion, which, after all, has no evidence to support it, that Webster died in 1625 (August— September) and that he worked too slowly to have produced a play in the interval. The point, however, is not of first importance. For the influence of Massinger, at any rate in his earlier work, bore entirely in the same direction as that of Fletcher; and the younger poet may fairly be called the disciple of the elder. Thus, the last play of Webster carries on the tradition of that which had gone before it. Alike in plot and in general spirit, it belongs, directly

[1] Cf. *ante*, chap. v.   [2] Cf. *ante*, chap. ii.

or indirectly, to the school of Fletcher, and reflects his influence. The seriousness of the two tragedies has completely vanished; and it is ill replaced by the honest highwayman, the seafight, the groundless jealousies and the no less groundless returns to reason, which form the staple of *A Cure for a Cuckold*. In the graver part of the play, there is only one scene, that on the sands of Calais, where the genius of Webster can be said worthily to assert itself. And the comic scenes, which are more likely to be the work of Rowley, are far better sustained than the main plot with which they are interwoven. Fletcher, with all his brightness and poetic feeling, has much to answer for; and nowhere was his influence less happily put forth than upon the essentially serious genius of Webster.

Of *The Thracian Wonder*, published in 1661 by the same editor (Kirkman) as *A Cure for a Cuckold*, there is no need to speak. No one, except that editor, has ever supposed that Webster can have had a hand in it. A word will suffice as to *Monuments of Honor*, a city pageant, or *A Monumental Column*, an elegy on the death of prince Henry (1613), the only poem of length by Webster which has come down to us. It contains a few fine lines, more than one of which were subsequently transferred to his dramas—an apologue conceived in the same vein as that of *The Dutchesse Of Malfy*, and a few turns of thought and phrase which recall the author's spiritual affinity with Donne.

It remains only to ask: what is the secret of Webster's genius? What are the qualities which give the distinctive seal to his imaginative creations? For the answer to this question we need hardly go beyond the two tragedies. His later works offer reflections, more or less faint, more or less intermittent, of the qualities we associate with his genius. But the authentic image, the clear-cut features, the colour and the harmony, are here alone.

First, then, within somewhat narrow limits, Webster shows a profound knowledge of human character and a keen sense of the tragic issues of human life. Vittoria and the duchess are among the great creations of the Elizabethan drama. Setting Shakespeare aside, there is no character of that drama which surpasses them in vividness; only two or three which approach them. Nor, in the duchess, at any rate, is there any marked quality to lay hold of. It is by atmosphere and temperament, by her sweet womanliness and unstudied dignity, that she becomes known to us. And these are just the things which are most impalpable, which only the highest genius can bring home to the imagination. No less important, perhaps even more so, is the sense of tragic issues. And, here again, Webster comes nearer to Shakespeare than any other of the Elizabethans, with the possible exception of Ford. Shakespeare found the deepest tragedy in the resistance of inborn heroism to all assaults from without; in the triumph of the inner self, when all outward happiness is dashed in pieces. So it is in *Hamlet, King Lear* and *Othello*. And something of the same effect is attained in *The White Divel* and *The Dutchesse Of Malfy*. It is attained, also, in Ford's *The Broken Heart*.

Webster, however, is not only a great tragic dramatist. He is also a great poet. And the same sombre cast of thought which made him the one appears also in the other. His imagination loves to linger round thoughts and symbols of mortality, to take shape in 'strange images of death.' The grim horrors of *The Dutchesse Of Malfy* will at once recur to the memory; the yew tree of Vittoria spreads its gloom over the whole drama. Yet nothing is more remarkable than the thrift with which Webster uses this perilous material. His reserve presents the strongest contrast with the wild waste of the other dramatists of blood. Everything in the two tragedies is subordinated to imaginative ends; everything is presented with the self-restraint of the artist. Nowhere is the essentially poetic genius of the dramatist more manifest than here; nowhere does his kinship with all that is best in the other arts, particularly that of the painter, appear more plainly. The latter point has hardly received due attention. Yet no reader can fail to notice the eagerness with which this poet provides a pictorial setting for the action of his drama; the pains he takes to imprint upon the eye the countenance, gestures and bearing of the characters in his most significant scenes. The opening scene of *The Dutchesse Of Malfy* is devoted largely to this purpose. The same appears in the trial scene of *The White Divel*. And other instances, mainly from *The Dutchesse Of Malfy*, will readily suggest themselves. It is doubtful whether this quality is so persistently marked in any other dramatist, with the single exception of Marston. And no one will claim that the pictures of Marston approach those of Webster in imaginative genius. Allied with this, perhaps, is his love of connecting a whole train of thought with a tangible image, of embodying his reflections on life in symbols which, at the first moment, may seem insignificant or repulsive, but which acquire a curious fascination from the surroundings in which he places them. It was this that made him, like Donne or Sir Thomas Browne, a lover of strange learning or forgotten fragments of erudition, and led him, like Burton, to ransack the dustheaps of antiquarian research. The instinct is typical of his age; but no man put it to uses more imaginative. With this peculiar cast of imagination, the style of Webster is in marvellous accord: compressed and pregnant; full, at once, both of grace and of severity; capable of sudden flashes—'Cover her face; mine eyes dazzle; she died young'—capable, also, of a sustained musical cadence, as in Cornelia's dirge, or the wonderful lyric of Leonora.

CHAPTER VIII

FORD AND SHIRLEY

ONE of the most significant facts in connection with the two poets who close the list of the major dramatists of the great period is that their work was produced in the years following the publication of the first collected edition of the plays of Shakespeare. Previous playwrights had studied and imitated their predecessors; but, for the most part, such study had been carried on in the theatre. Gradually, the drama had been winning acknowledgment of its right to be regarded as literature, and the appearance of the first folio of Shakespeare, in 1623, may fairly be taken as marking the achievement of victory. The result of this new attitude was twofold : first, the works of the master and his contemporaries could now be brooded over and assimilated in the study, and, secondly, the younger playwrights wrote with a view to being read as well as heard and seen. Evidences of the coming of the change are, of course, to be found before this date, certainly as early as the Jonson folio of 1616 ; but Ford and Shirley stand out as belonging exclusively to this 'literary' stage. Ford is never tired of insisting that he was a gentleman of letters, not a theatrical hack ; and Shirley wrote at least one closet drama. In dealing with their works, then, we are discussing not merely the last phase of Elizabethan theatrical activity, but, also, the first chapter of what may be called, in a special sense, modern dramatic literature.

John Ford was a native of Ilsington in Devonshire, where he was baptised on 17 April 1586. On his father's side, he belonged to an old landed family, and, on his mother's, he was related to lord chief justice Popham. He may have studied at Oxford, since there is a record of the matriculation of a John Ford at Exeter college in 1601 ; but his university career must, in any case, have been short, as he became a member of the Middle Temple in the November of the following year. Further information about his career is confined to what can be gathered from the dedications of his works, and from the exchange of commendatory verses of the conventional sort. After the publication of his last play, in 1639, he disappears from view. He seems to have been a man of a somewhat melancholy temperament, independent in his attitude towards the public taste, and capable of espousing unpopular causes.

An instance of this last named quality appears in his first publication, *Fame's Memorial* (1606), an elegy on the death of Charles Blount, earl of Devonshire, second husband of the famous Penelope Devereux. No reason is known why Ford should have chosen to publish a eulogy of a man who had died out of favour at court ; but the fact is noteworthy as hinting an interest in a story which, as we shall see, may not improbably have suggested to him part of the plot of one of his most famous plays. The poem itself is long and tiresome, smooth in versification, abstract in diction, often obscure and affected in style.

His romantic tendencies were further displayed in the same year in his *Honor Triumphant; or the Peeres Challenge.* In the prose part of this pamphlet, Ford supplies a highflown defence of four 'positions' which four young nobles had undertaken to support in a tournament in honour of the visit to England of king Christian IV of Denmark. The positions were that knights in ladies' service have no free will ; that beauty is the maintainer of valour ; that fair lady was never false ; that perfect lovers are only wise. The triteness of the matter, the prevailing hyperbole and the lingering traces of Euphuism that mark the style, would hardly call for mention here, were it not that, in the very theses which Ford is half seriously upholding, we find a significant connection with the motives underlying some of his most important mature work. What we must note is that Ford, at the age of twenty, is writing prose and verse highly romantic in spirit, and involving a tolerant, if not an admiring, attitude towards conduct entirely at variance with conventional standards. *The Monarches Meeting*, appended to this pamphlet, is an early instance of the stanza of Gray's *Elegy*.

Ford's non-dramatic work closes with *A Line of Life* (1620), a didactic tract on conduct, apparently influenced by Bacon's *Essays*, but lacking their pithiness and epigrammatic vigour. It may be significant of Ford's personal attitude towards religion that this serious lay sermon is purely pagan in inspiration and in spirit.

Omitting consideration of works no longer extant, we find Ford's earliest attempts at dramatic writing made in collaboration with Dekker. *The Witch of Edmonton* is based on the story of Elizabeth Sawyer, who was executed for witchcraft in 1621, and it was probably written soon after that date. The respective shares of Dekker and Ford in this production are still unsettled, perhaps William Rowley, too, had a share in it[1]; but the directness of the moral lesson conveyed, the witch plot with its comedy and its realism in the treatment of humble life and the picture of the yeoman's household, are as characteristic of Dekker as they are unlike anything certainly Ford's. On the other hand, Frank, whose weakness and crime bring about the main tragedy, finds his defence in laying the blame on Fate in the fashion of Ford's other sinners; and in the scenes where this character is prominent, possibly the larger part of Ford's share is to be found. The play is a domestic tragedy of great impressiveness, its chief flaw being the failure of the attempt to join the two plots.

The Sun's-Darling: A Moral Masque (acted 1624, but not published till 1656) is generally believed to have been originally written by Dekker and revised, with additions, by Ford[2].

The first independent drama printed by Ford was *The Lover's Melancholy*, acted in 1628 and published in the following year. This somewhat slow-moving romance turns on the melancholy of a prince grieving over the disappearance of his sweetheart. The girl, whose loss has also deprived her father of his senses and delayed the marriage of her sister, is present throughout in the disguise of a man, and the love she inspires in the princess is, in turn, the obstacle that prevents her cousin from winning that lady. The discovery of the lost girl's identity, which might as well have occurred in the first act, solves all the entanglements and permits a happy ending; but this discovery is delayed in order to enable Ford to occupy his scenes with a psychological analysis of the 'lover's melancholy.' This analysis is strongly influenced by Burton's *Anatomy of Melancholy*, from which are directly taken the materials for the *Masque of Melancholy* in the third act. The account of the finding of the disguised girl is reminiscent of *Philaster*, and is made the occasion for the telling of the story of the nightingale's death from Strada's *Prolusiones*. The main plot has recently been traced by Stuart Pratt Sherman to Daniel's *Hymens' Triumph*, and reminiscences of *Hamlet, Lear* and other Shakespearean plays are obvious. In spite of all these borrowings,

---

[1] Cf. *ante*, chap. II.   [2] See *ibid.*

and of the fact that many of the characters belong to well recognised stage types, the play afforded the contemporary observer abundant evidence of the advent of a new dramatist. The delicacy shown in the treatment of emotion, the sweetness of the verse and the happiness of the phrasing pointed to a poet who only needed discipline in stagecraft to achieve distinction.

Ford acquired this technical skill with wonderful rapidity, if we are correct in supposing *The Broken Heart* (printed in 1633) to have been his next play. The plot of this tragedy shows much originality, and it is conducted through many intricacies to a highly effective catastrophe. The princess Calantha loves and is loved by Ithocles, a brilliant young warrior, who had forced his sister Penthea, in spite of her love for Orgilus, into a marriage with the jealous Bassanes. Penthea remains faithful to her husband to the despair of her lover, and Orgilus, repulsed, turns to seek revenge. Penthea goes mad and dies, and, beside her dead body, Orgilus causes to be placed a chair in which he induces Ithocles to sit, and which closes on him and holds him helpless while Orgilus stabs him to death. In the last act, news is brought to Calantha in the midst of revels at court of the death of her father, then of those of Penthea and of Ithocles ; but she dances on to the end. Orgilus is condemned, and, in the final scene, Calantha, before the altar, puts a wedding ring on the finger of the dead Ithocles, hands over her newly inherited crown to the prince of Argos and dies of a broken heart. The last two scenes, if somewhat deliberately theatrical, are among the most beautiful and memorable in the drama of the period. No source has been found for the story of Calantha, though suggestions from Sidney's *Arcadia* seem to have been used throughout. In the prologue, it is implied that the plot has a foundation in fact, and Sherman has ingeniously argued that, in the situation of Penthea, the dramatist consciously treated the story of that Stella whom Ford had long before sought to justify in *Fame's Memorial.* Burton's influence is again discernible in the treatment of the jealousy of Bassanes ; but, on the whole, this play is much less imitative than its predecessor. Since something will have to be said on the subject of Ford's dubious morality, it is only just to point out that, in this play, Penthea reaches a lofty standard in her perception of the essential unchastity of a loveless marriage. Yet, as we shall see, her conviction is not unconnected with the theory that undermines the morality of the later plays—the dogma of the supremacy and inevitableness of passion.

The influence of Sidney and Shakespeare persists in the next
tragedy, *Loves Sacrifice* (printed 1633). Illicit passion is here the
dominant theme. The duke of Pavy has married the beautiful
but humbly born Bianca, who is loved by his favourite Fernando.
The duchess's virtuous resistance to Fernando's suit leads him
to change his passion to friendship, and his strength is soon tested
by the weakening of Bianca, who comes at night to his chamber
and offers herself to him, purposing to kill herself afterwards.
They swear mutual but chaste love. Meantime, the duke's sister
Fiormonda, whose love Fernando has repulsed, and the villainous
secretary d'Avolos, excite the duke's jealousy, and arrange to
make him spectator of a love scene between Fernando and the
duchess in her bedchamber. The duke breaks in and accuses
Bianca. She acquits Fernando of guilt, confesses to having
tempted him and brazenly tells her husband that she preferred
Fernando as the better man. The duke, enraged, kills her, and
then seeks Fernando, who, in turn, acquits Bianca and blames
himself. The duke believes, and, at the funeral, eulogises Bianca
as a model of chastity, when, from the tomb, Fernando enters
defiant and drinks poison. The duke stabs himself; and Roseilli,
the now accepted suitor of Fiormonda, becomes duke, condemns
d'Avolos and divorces his own bride. The purely physical view of
chastity which is characteristic of much of the Jacobean drama is
nowhere exhibited so extravagantly as here. Ford clearly sym-
pathises with the lovers throughout, and, in the duke's admiring
attitude at the close, carries his theory to a climax that would be
revolting if it were not patently absurd. In the main plot, the chief
literary influences are from *Othello* and *Macbeth* and Middleton's
Women Beware Women, the story itself being derived, according
to Sherman, from Gascoigne's *Ferdinando Jeronimi*. The sub-
plot of Ferentes is based on the story of Pamphilus in Sidney's
Arcadia, the wretched farce being Ford's own.

Tis Pitty Shees a Whore (printed 1633) is the tragedy most
frequently cited in evidence of Ford's 'decadent' tendencies. The
main plot turns on the love of a sister and brother. The sister
accepts a husband to conceal her sin, and, when discovery is
inevitable, the brother kills her and rushes into the presence
of the father with his sister's heart on a dagger. In the general
catastrophe that follows, father, husband and brother all die.
This simple plot is combined with no fewer than three sub-plots,
two of which are woven into it with great skill. The third sub-
plot, that of Bergetto, is, in the beginning, farcical; but the

foolish hero of it meets his death through a mistake that gives a thrill of horrified pity. The dialogue is rich in passages of great beauty, and the characterisation, especially in the differentiation of the two lovers and their attitude towards the crime, is managed with subtlety. No objection lies against the introduction of the fact of incest, but the dramatist's attitude is sympathetic, and he apparently assents to the fatalism with which the brother excuses his passion. Both the strength and the defects of Ford are here fully revealed ; and nowhere else do the tenderness and poetry of his verse, the delicacy of his psychology and the impressiveness of his handling of a dramatic situation, lend their aid to an assault at once so insidious and so daring upon the foundations of accepted morality. The plot, so far as is known, is original, such parallels as have been noted being too remote to be regarded as direct sources.

The air clears in *Perkin Warbeck* (printed 1634), a notable return to the chronicle history, which had scarcely been cultivated for a generation. The play is based on Bacon's *History of Henry VII* and Thomas Gainsford's *True and Wonderful History of Perkin Warbeck* (1618), and, in his substantial adherence to history, the dramatist follows the tradition of this dramatic type. He obviously found his model in the histories of Shakespeare; and the slightly archaic flavour of the whole work is increased by the use of blank verse somewhat more formal and regular than Ford is accustomed to write. The plot, however, is simpler than in the Shakespearean histories, there is less richness of episode and the play falls short chiefly in a certain lack of intensity. The hero derives dignity from the carefully preserved assumption that he believed in his own claims, and Huntly and his daughter Katherine, whom Warbeck marries, are admirable figures. In Dalyell, Katherine's rejected suitor, Ford had the opportunity, of which he might have been expected to make more, of creating a telling romantic figure. The comedy is confined to the low-born followers of Warbeck, who are kept well in character, and who, if only mildly amusing, have none of the vulgarity of the comic figures in Ford's earlier plays. On the whole, it is unmistakably a workmanlike performance.

The comedy of *The Fancies, Chast and Noble* (printed 1638) is a somewhat careless performance. Octavio, marquis of Siena, through the instrumentality of his nephew and Livio, a courtier, induces Livio's sister Castamela to join 'the Fancies,' three young girls kept in seclusion by the supposedly impotent marquis. It appears later that the girls are Octavio's nieces, and that the marquis's relations and intentions are honourable. But the hoax, which is played not only on the court but also on the audience, prolongs a more than doubtful situation. So imperfectly are the motives of the action indicated that it almost seems as if the dramatist had clearly worked out neither his plot nor his conception of the main characters, until his play was half written. Livio, the most interesting man in the piece, is guilty of a puzzling change of attitude ; and Castamela's repulse of the suggestions, first of the marquis and, later, of her brother, which occasions the finest scenes in the drama, is weakened by the fundamental unreality of the situation. The underplot deals with the relations to her brother and husbands of Flavia, who has been bought by a great lord from her first husband. Out of this unpromising material, some effective situations are developed; but here, too, Ford seems to have been at the beginning uncertain as to the kind of character to give to the heroine. The prologue states that the plot is original, a claim that by no means disposes of Sherman's attempt to trace a strong line of influence from Jonson's *Volpone*.

The list of Ford's extant plays closes with the romantic comedy, *The Ladies Triall* (acted 1638). The main plot of this play is very simple. Auria, a noble Genoese driven by poverty to the wars, leaves his young wife under the eye of his friend Aurelio. Adurni, a gallant lord, attempts her virtue and is repulsed ; but Aurelio's suspicions are aroused, and, on Auria's return, Aurelio kindles the husband's jealousy. Through the frankness of Adurni, the heroine is cleared, and all ends well. Both husband and wife are nobly drawn, and the suspicious but faithful friend is clearly conceived. The scene in which the wife defends herself is full of dignity and beauty; and the discontented lover, Malfato, late in the play rises in language and conduct to heights that Ford seems not to have contemplated at the outset. This is another of the indications which occur, especially in the later plays, of a certain carelessness and languor in the management of both action and character. It is further exemplified in the sub-plot of Levidolche, where the absurdity of the stage convention of disguise is carried to a high pitch in the failure of Benatzi's nearest relatives to recognise him in ragged clothes. A second sub-plot, that of Amoretta and her mock-suitors, shows the influence of Jonson. The main plot seems to be original, and certainly calls for no great inventive power. Benatzi shows indebtedness to Ancient Pistol.

Several of Ford's productions have perished. Four of these, *An Ill Beginning has a Good End* (1613), *The London Merchant, The Royal Combat* and *Beauty in a Trance*, though entered in the Stationers' register, were not printed, and the manuscripts are said to have been among those destroyed by Warburton's cook. In the last of these, as in the masque entitled *The Fairy Knight* and in *The Bristowe Merchant* (both licensed 1624), Ford collaborated with Dekker, and, in *A Late Murther of the Sonne upon the Mother* (licensed 1624), with Webster. These bring the total of the plays in which Ford had a share to sixteen; and it must be remembered in summing up his achievement and his characteristics that we must base our judgment upon little more than half of his work.

It is customary to instance Ford as typical of the decadence of the Elizabethan drama, and it therefore becomes important for a view of that drama as a whole, as well as for an estimate of Ford individually, to enquire what the term means and whether it can be justified. Applied to Ford, it has reference both to his subjects and to his manner of treatment. Of his three tragedies, two are, almost in the modern sense, 'problem plays,' in which the chief characters are faced by the dilemma of having to choose between love and loyalty to legal ties; the third deals with incest. Here, already, we have themes all but unused by Shakespeare and his predecessors, and the mere fact of a dramatist's absorption in such subjects might be regarded as a symptom of change. But Beaumont and Fletcher, to name no others, many years before had touched these themes, and Ford is generally regarded as marking a more advanced stage than they. The difference becomes more striking when method of treatment is considered. Not only is the difficulty of the tempted soul treated sympathetically by Ford, but the question is almost left open and the burden of guilt is shifted to the shoulders of Fate. In this, there is a clear departure from the assumption by the earlier dramatists of the validity of accepted morality, and there is brought into these tragedies an atmosphere of moral instability. Another evidence of change may be found in the violence and sensationalism of Ford's catastrophes. Fernando, crawling from the tomb to drink his poison and die over the corpse of the woman his love had ruined; Giovanni, rushing into the presence of his father with the heart of his sister-mistress on a dagger; Calantha, with the theatrically contrived setting for her own death—all point to the exhaustion of more natural appeals to the emotions, to a desperate attempt to whip up excitement at all costs. Finally, in his attempts at comedy, Ford sinks to a lower level than any dramatist of his class, and his farce lacks the justification of much of the coarse buffoonery of his predecessors. It is not realistic; it is not the expression of high spirits; it is a perfunctory attempt to season tragedy and romance with an admixture of rubbish, without humour and without joy.

Of the first and most fundamental of these defects, some explanation may be found in Ford himself. We have noted his youthful defence of such romantic propositions as that 'knights in ladies' service have no free will.' This and similar ideas are frequent enough in the romantic pastoralism of Sidney, Spenser and their contemporaries. But in these writers such theories of the supremacy and divine origin of love were presented in an Arcadian setting, under purely ideal conditions, and, on the whole, were kept clear of practical life. The young Ford was steeped in this romantic idealism, and we have seen him applying it to actual persons in his apology for Stella and Charles Blount. But the mature Ford was a dramatist who had learned his craft from Shakespeare, Jonson, Middleton, Massinger and the rest; and, when we find this lawless idealism given form with all the skill in characterisation, dialogue and action inherited from the masters of realism, it ceases to be a harmless dream and becomes, instead, a fountain of anarchy. But it does not lose all its beauty. The depth of Ford's insight into the human heart torn by conflicting passions, the intensity of his sympathy, his mastery of a beautiful and tender diction and of a blank verse of great sweetness, along with such technical powers as have already been noted, suffice to give him a distinguished position among writers of tragedy.

James Shirley was born in London in September, 1596, and entered Merchant Taylors' school on 4 October 1608, where he seems to have shown himself an apt scholar. From school, he went, in 1612, to St John's college, Oxford, then under the presidency of Laud. It is recorded by Wood in *Athenae Oxonienses*, our chief source of information concerning Shirley's life, that Laud, who liked and appreciated Shirley, objected to his taking orders on account of his having a large mole on his left cheek. The length of Shirley's stay in Oxford is unknown; but it was probably short, for he is known to have transferred himself to Catharine hall, Cambridge, whence he took his degrees. Having taken orders, about 1619, he obtained a living at St Albans in Hertfordshire; but, as he was shortly afterwards converted to the church of

Rome, he resigned his charge and became a master in the grammar school of St Albans, in 1623. In February 1625, his first play was licensed, and it was probably soon after this that he gave up teaching for playwriting, coming to London and residing in Gray's inn. His dramatic labours brought him a considerable income, and drew the favourable notice of the court, especially of queen Henrietta Maria; but it does not appear that this resulted in any substantial advantage to the poet. His standing in the fashionable world may be inferred from the terms of the dedications of his plays to various noble personages, and, with more assurance, from the fact that he was chosen to write the great masque, *The Triumph of Peace*, which the four inns of court presented to the king and queen in 1634. In 1635, John Ogilby opened a theatre in Dublin, and it was probably he who induced Shirley to visit Ireland. The dates of this visit are a matter of inference; but it seems likely that Shirley first crossed in 1636, and returned to England for a short time in the next year, but did not permanently take up his residence in London again till 1640. While in Ireland, he produced *The Royall Master, The Doubtfull Heir, The Constant Maid* and *St Patrick for Ireland. The Gentleman of Venice* and *The Polititian* may, also, belong to this period. His dramatic activity continued uninterrupted until 1642, when the closing of the theatres left him with *The Court Secret* on his hands, finished, but not acted. On the outbreak of the civil war, Shirley left his wife and children in London and followed his patron, the earl (later marquis and duke) of Newcastle, to the field; 'for that count,' says Wood, 'had engaged him so much by his generous liberality towards him, that he thought he could not do a worthier act, than to serve him, and so consequently his prince.' Wood also reports that Shirley assisted the duke in the composition of certain plays, but this collaboration has not been held to have increased the reputation of Shirley. After the defeat at Marston moor in 1644, Newcastle fled to the continent, and, later, Shirley came back to London, where he attempted to earn money by the publication of earlier writings as well as by new compositions. He was helped by the patronage of the wealthy scholar, Thomas Stanley, but soon returned to his former profession of schoolmaster, which sustained him for the rest of his days. With the reopening of the theatres, he did not resume the writing of plays, though several of his earlier works were revived. He injured his reputation (more, probably, than he benefited his purse) by assisting Ogilby in his translations of Homer and Vergil, using a classical knowledge which he had put to better employment in the writing of Latin grammars. The end is best told in the words of Wood:

At length ... he with his second wife Frances were driven by the dismal conflagration that happened in London an. 1666, from their habitation near to Fleet Street, into the parish of S. Giles's in The Fields in Middlesex, where being in a manner overcome with affrightments, disconsolations, and other miseries, occasion'd by that fire and their losses, they both died within the compass of a natural day: whereupon their bodies were buried in one grave in the yard belonging to the said church of S. Giles's, on the 29th of Octob. in sixteen hundred sixty and six.

From the uniformly friendly tone of Shirley's references to his contemporaries and fellow dramatists, and of theirs to him, we infer that he was a man of amiable character; and his more personal writings indicate his modesty. But, beyond these characteristics, there is little in the record to help to a picture of the man.

In 1646, Shirley collected and published a number of his non-dramatic poems. A manuscript in the Bodleian library[1] supplies variant versions of a large number of these, and a few additional pieces. For the most part, these poems are amorous and personal, and show, to a much greater extent than his dramas, evidences of that discipleship to Ben Jonson which he was ever ready to acknowledge. Many of them appeared originally as songs in the dramas, or as prologues and epilogues; others are epithalamiums, epitaphs and elegies. Though conventional in manner and matter, they are often graceful and ingenious. One song rises far above the rest, and is one of the great lyrics not merely of Shirley's age, but of English literature. 'The glories of our blood and state,' the funeral chant which closes *The Contention of Ajax and Ulysses*, would have been sufficient to ensure a place for Shirley in our anthologies, even had all memory of his dramas been lost. *Narcissus, or The Self-lover* is almost certainly a republication of *Echo, or The Infortunate Lovers*, which Shirley had issued in 1618. This is an example, not without beauty, of the elaborate re-telling of Ovidian tales which many Elizabethan poets attempted. Shirley's immediate model seems to have been the *Venus and Adonis* of Shakespeare.

To the closing of the theatres, which checked the production of Shirley's dramas, we are indebted for the preservation of an exceptionally large proportion of them; for the enforced cessation

---

[1] Rawlinson, Poet. 88.

of acting during the puritan domination led to the printing of many plays that might otherwise have perished in manuscript. Out of some forty dramatic pieces recorded as Shirley's, not more than three have been lost. Of the remainder, seven are tragedies, twenty-four are comedies, three are masques and three belong to none of the recognised dramatic types of the time. The tragedies, though comparatively few, contain Shirley's most memorable work. They begin with *The Maides Revenge* (1626), based on a story of the jealousy of sisters from Reynolds's *God's Revenge against Murder*. The characters are mostly familiar types re-drawn with fair skill. The comic element reaches a climax in an amusing farcical scene in the study of a quack, who is seen treating a succession of patients. Five years passed before Shirley again attempted tragedy ; and, when *The Traytor* appeared, in 1631, he showed that he had mastered the technique of stagecraft. The plot of this really great drama is a free treatment of the story of Lorenzino de' Medici, who, as the Lorenzo of the play, is represented as a villain of consummate agility and daring ; prompted solely by unscrupulous ambition, he plays with amazing skill upon the licentious nature of his brother the duke and upon Sciarrha's fiery sense of family honour. Although the way in which Cosmo yields his betrothed to his friend Pisano fails to convince, the plot, as a whole, is admirably contrived and well knit, and, in general effectiveness, ranks with such a play as Beaumont and Fletcher's *Maides Tragedy*, to which, probably, it is indebted. Shirley's favourite device of concentrating the comic element in one elaborate scene is well exemplified here in the mock trial of Depazzi by his page. Few plays of the period convey so vivid a picture of the Italy of the renascence on the side of ambition and intrigue.

In the same year, Shirley produced *Loves Crueltie*, in which he achieves a rare intensity in the depicting of unlawful passion. The initial motive which launches the heroine on her downward career is as natural as it is original. Clarissa's husband has a friend, Hippolito, who refuses to meet her, lest her beauty should tempt him to disloyalty to his friend. Piqued by curiosity, she visits Hippolito at his dwelling, and, without disclosing her identity, involves him in the intrigue that finally brings disaster on the whole group. In spite of the disgusting talk of the old rake Bovaldo, the moral effect of the play is sound and impressive to a high degree. One leading situation is to be found in the *novelle* of Margaret of Navarre and of Cinthio ; the rest may be of Shirley's invention.

The Dukes Mistris (1636) would be better classified as a
tragicomedy, since the four main characters are happily reunited
at the close, and only the two villains die. But the tone of the
drama is serious throughout, except for the comic underplot, which
turns on the assumed preference of the hero's friend Horatio
for ugly women. The distinction of the play lies in the lofty
character of the two heroines, the neglected duchess, to whom the
wandering affections of the duke finally return, and Ardelia, who
resists successfully the solicitations of the duke and, finally, is
married to her betrothed. In the killing of the villain Valerio,
behind the arras, there is an evident reminiscence of the death of
Polonius.

The Polititian, also, might be called a tragicomedy, since
the plot ends happily for most of the persons who claim our
sympathy, and the tragic element is hardly greater than that in
Cymbeline, which, in the figure of the villainous step-mother, it
somewhat resembles. The story is said by Langbaine to resemble
one in the first book of the countess of Montgomery's *Urania* ; but
the question of priority needs further examination. Though not
printed till 1655, this play may have been produced in the Dublin
period (1636—40). Like *The Gentleman of Venice* (licensed 1639),
the date of the production of which is, also, subject to some
uncertainty, it has prefixed to it interesting 'small characters' of
the persons, summarising their chief qualities. The plot is laid in
Norway, and moves in an atmosphere which, at times, recalls *King
Lear* and *Hamlet.*

In *The Cardinall* (1641), Shirley believed that he reached his
highest achievement, and, but for *The Traytor,* which surpasses
it in construction, we should be obliged to agree. Its quality
is indicated when we say that, though strongly reminiscent of
Webster's *Dutchesse Of Malfy,* it is not altogether unworthy of its
great model. A peculiar change takes place in the fifth act, in
which the cardinal, hitherto somewhat in the background and
scheming on behalf of a favourite nephew, comes forward as a villain
of the deepest dye, seeking in rape and murder the satisfaction of
his own lust and revenge. Another unexpected turn is given at
the close by the discovery that the dying confession of the cardinal,
which the convention of the tragedy of blood leads us to accept
as genuine, is a mere trick contrived to poison the duchess with
a pretended antidote. But the excess of ingenuity, and the double
catastrophe, do not prevent us from understanding the claim that
we have here a tragedy greater than any produced in England

between its own date and the nineteenth century. In the intensity of its interest, the vitality of its characters, the splendour of its poetry and the impressive fusion of the great tragic motives of ambition, love and revenge, it brings to a fitting close the tremendous file of Elizabethan tragedy.

The comedy of Shirley falls into two main classes, the comedy of manners and romantic comedy, the latter sometimes described in the early editions as tragicomedy. The scenes of the comedies of manners are, with one exception and that only nominal, laid in London or its immediate neighbourhood, and the time is contemporary. One or two are satirical in purpose, others are dramas of situation or intrigue; but all serve to lay before us a lively picture of city life in the time of Charles I. Though noblemen appear occasionally among the *dramatis personae*, the scenes are not laid at court, and the society represented is that of the man about town and the well-to-do citizen. This group of plays, ten in all, begins with Shirley's first dramatic attempt, *Love Tricks: or, The Schoole of Complement* (1625). This somewhat dilettante and imitative production contains much topical satire, and it is redeemed from insignificance by the detached comedy scene which gives the play its sub-title, and which, in an amusing manner, parodies the affectations of polite address by the device of a school where they are taught for a fee to all comers. *The Wedding* (1626) shows a great advance in construction, and the serious plot is skilfully conducted to an effective *dénouement*. It turns upon the interruption of a wedding by a charge against the purity of the bride; and the interval before the lady's character is cleared serves to test the qualities of the chief persons more deeply than is usual in this kind of comedy. The farcical underplot, here again, provides a highly comic scene in the duel between a fat man and a lean one, both arrant cowards. *The Wittie Faire One* (1628) is bright in dialogue and ingenious in construction, with somewhat conventional characterisation. But the modern reader finds it hard to accept an ending as happy in which a girl of character and spirit accepts as husband a rake who has been frightened into respectability by the preposterous device of all his friends behaving as if he were dead. The principal comic scene is provided by a foolish knight receiving lessons in geography from his tutor. *Changes: Or, Love in a Maze* (1632) is admirably named, since the plot is so contrived that the three pairs of lovers attach and detach their affections as often as possible in the course of five acts. The farce consists in dressing up a page as a rich widow, who

is wooed by the foolish knight, Sir Gervase Simple. An amusing
piece of satirical literary criticism is introduced in the scene
where Caperwit, the poetaster, discusses the function of adjectives
in verse. The value of *Hide Parke* (1632) is almost altogether
in the minutely realistic study of fashionable life, especially of
horse racing in the park. The underplot lacks emphasis, the
interest is scattering and the characterisation is sketchy. *The
Ball* (1632), again, is highly topical, being evidently designed to
dissipate slanderous reports that had been circulated concerning
the newly originated subscription balls, and, perhaps, also to give
the actors opportunity for personating 'divers... lords and others
of the court,' as the master of the revels complained they did.
Romantic interest is entirely subordinated to the exposing of a
variety of typical humbugs and fraudulent adventurers. On the
title-page of the original edition, Chapman is named as Shirley's
collaborator ; but, in spite of a strong suggestion of the older
method of Jonson in the handling of the types, it is clear that, in
the play as we have it, Chapman's share is negligible[1]. Though in
execution a lively picture of contemporary manners, *The Gamester*
(1633), in its main intrigue, is strongly reminiscent of the *novella.*
It was made, says Sir Henry Herbert, 'out of a plot of the king's,
given him by mee,' but Langbaine found the story both in the
Ducento Novelle of Malespini[2] and in Margaret of Navarre's
Heptameron[3]. Though coarser in tone and incident than is usual
with Shirley, the comedy is worked out with great ability, and the
sordid improbability of the Hazard-Wilding plot is, in part, atoned
for by the fine romantic spirit of the underplot of Leonore and
Violante. The making and unmaking of the younger Barnacle as
a 'roarer' supplies some good farcical scenes. The conduct and
influence of the chaste wife, Bellamia, raise *The Example* (1634) to
a much loftier level than the preceding play. The difficult feat of
rendering a would-be adulterer's conversion plausible is skilfully
accomplished here, though why he should insist, later, on fighting
with the husband is not made very clear. Here, again, Shirley
shows himself critical of current literary style; and, in the character
of Sir Solitary Plot, returns again to the method of the comedy of
humours. *The Lady of Pleasure* (1635) is frequently regarded as
Shirley's best performance in its kind. The main plot, which turns
on the curing a wife of her desire for a life of fashionable folly, is
thoroughly sound and well carried out. The minor plot of the young
widow Celestina gives occasion for some fine speeches, but is less

---

[1] Cf. *ante*, chap. II.   [2] Part II, nov. 96.   [3] Day 1, nov. 8.

convincing in itself. The satire against rakish men about town is scathing enough ; but, like many satirists, Shirley proves unable to touch pitch without defiling himself. In *The Constant Maid* a play of the Dublin period, the author displays no new or striking characteristics. It is a conventional comedy of artificial misunderstandings, supported by an equally conventional underplot and a masque.

The most numerous group of Shirley's plays is that of romantic comedy. The scenes of these fourteen dramas are laid in the Mediterranean countries, usually Italy, and the action, in almost every case, takes place at court. The list of *dramatis personae* is headed by a king or duke, and most of the characters are courtiers. The nature of the incident is often appropriate to the nominal scene; but the kind of social intercourse pictured, to a large extent, is that of the court of Charles I. The main plot is usually serious, and, much oftener than in the comedy of manners, comes within sight of tragedy, thus accounting for the name 'tragicomedy,' by which they are sometimes described in early editions. There is more stress on character, too, than in the lighter comedies, and the plot is apt to work up to a more exciting climax and to make more use of suspense.

The distinction between these two types of comedy was much less clearly recognised by Shirley at the beginning of his career than later. Thus, the first two comedies of manners have several characteristics of the romantic comedy, and, on the other hand, *The Brothers* (1626), though laid in Madrid and touching depths of feeling not usually reached in light comedy, is not a court comedy, and, in the story of Jacinta and her lovers, deals with material quite appropriate to the group we have just been discussing. The main theme is the foiling of the tyrannical father who seeks a wealthy alliance for his daughter ; and this familiar type is nowhere more unmercifully ridiculed. But the more serious secondary theme which gives the name to the play, the enforced rivalry of two brothers for the approval and fortune of their father, is saved from tragedy only by the resuscitation of the parent who had pretended death in order to test his elder son. In *The Gratefull Servant* (1629), the type of romantic comedy is thoroughly established. The tone of the main plot is raised to an uncommon height by the disinterested Foscari, who is willing to be supposed dead rather than hinder the marriage of his betrothed lady to the duke. This kind of generosity, which occurs not unfrequently in Shirley, forms a link between him and Thomas

Heywood, and has the effect of giving the reader an amiable impression of the author rather than of convincing him of the probability of the story. In the disguised heroine Leonora, and, in the self-important steward Jacomo, one is forcibly reminded of *Twelfth Night.* The conversion of the unfaithful husband Lodwick, in the underplot, is very dubiously managed.

If, as seems probable, Fleay is right in identifying the next play, *The Bird in a Cage* (printed 1633) with *The Beauties,* licensed in 1633, the number of Shirley's lost plays is reduced to two. A sarcastic attack on Prynne, then in prison, forms the dedication, and may have suggested the re-naming of the play. The comedy contains some novel spectacular elements, such as the birdcage in which the hero gets himself smuggled into the castle where the princess is confined, and the play of Danaë, appropriately acted by the ladies-in-waiting to amuse their mistress. The scene at the close, where the lovers stand together against the wrath of the outwitted duke, is not without nobility. *The Young Admirall* (1633) won the special approbation of the master of the revels as being in the 'beneficial and cleanly way of poetry.' It is, indeed, exceptionally free from coarseness, and, in every respect, an excellent piece of stagecraft. The interest of plot is very high, the motives adequate and varied, the characters clearly conceived and originally presented and the speeches often highly poetical. It turns on a series of problems, such as love against patriotism, and conjugal love against filial love. Amusing farce is provided by a trick played on Pazzarello, a coward who is persuaded that a witch has made him invulnerable. The source of the play is stated by Stiefel to be Lope de Vega's *Don Lope de Cardona*; and the same scholar has found, in Tirso de Molina's *El Castigo del Pensèque* (printed in 1634), a Spanish original for *The Opportunitie* (licensed in the same year). This amusing play turns upon the matrimonial opportunities lost by a travelling adventurer who arrives in Urbino and is mistaken by everyone for the absent son of a prominent courtier. Shirley departs from his source in the last act by depriving the hero of both the ladies he had wooed, whereas the Spanish author makes him lose the duchess, but marries him to one of her ladies. The point of the plot of *The Coronation* (1635) lies in the successive discovery of two brothers of a reigning queen, whose crown thus shifts from head to head, producing a succession of effective situations, in which lies the chief merit of the play. It contains a masque, but no low comedy. This piece was included in the second folio of Beaumont and Fletcher's works, but no considerable part of the play is to be ascribed to any hand but Shirley's. The main interest of *The Royall Master*, performed first in Dublin and printed in 1638, lies not in a somewhat conventional, if skilful, central intrigue, but in the secondary figure of the young girl Domitilla, who imagines that the king is in love with her, and is cured of her infatuation by her royal master, who pretends to seek her love basely. This situation is taken from the *Decameron*[1]; the main plot is stated by Stiefel to be Spanish in origin[2]. Another Dublin play, licensed in 1640, is *The Doubtfull Heir*. The interest here, as in *The Coronation*, lies in the surprises of the action, the fortunes of Ferdinand, the lost heir of Murcia, undergoing a series of most violent changes; while the charm of the piece is in the constancy of the hero and his betrothed, which gave the play its original name *Rosania, or Love's Victory*. There are two plots of almost equal importance in *The Gentleman of Venice* (1639). In one, an interesting contrast of character is elaborated between the duke's son, supposed to be the gardener's, and the gardener's son, supposed to be the duke's. In the other, a plot of an uncommonly painful nature is handled with delicacy. *The Arcadia*, printed in 1640, but, perhaps, performed some years before, is a frank dramatisation of the main incidents of Sidney's romance, with much elaboration of the farcical elements. *The Humorous Courtier* (printed 1640), also of uncertain date of production, has an ingenious plot, but is spoiled by the gratuitous coarseness of the scenes dealing with Orseolo, the pretended misogynist but actual libertine, who gives the play its name. The main plot turns on the testing of her courtiers by the duchess of Mantua, who, secretly betrothed to the duke of Parma, gives out that she means to marry at home, and enjoys the spectacle of her lords covering themselves with ridicule in their efforts to gain her hand. *The Imposture* (1640) was considered by Shirley to be in the first rank of his compositions. It is, indeed, cleverly manipulated, and the interest is well maintained through a highly complicated plot. But the devices are lacking in both novelty and probability. An ambitious favourite, seeking to secure the daughter of the duke of Mantua for himself, substitutes for her his own discarded mistress when the son of the duke of Ferrara comes wooing. The low comedy is supplied by a young coward Bertholdi, who seeks to ingratiate himself with the gallants by offering to each in turn the

[1] Day x, nov. 7.   [2] For modern analogues, see *Ward*, vol. iii, p. 116, note 1.

hand of his widowed mother, a lady of wit and independence. *The Sisters* (1642) was the last play by Shirley performed before the theatres were closed. It is a lively and amusing treatment of the theme of the proud and the humble sister. After the former has been fooled by a captain of bandits masquerading first as a fortune teller and then as a prince, she is discovered to be the child of a peasant, and the estates and the real prince go to her modest rival. The farce is frankly absurd, but, on the stage, must have been highly amusing. The dedication has an interesting picture of the condition of poets in England just before the war began, and the prologue contains eulogies of Shakespeare, Fletcher and Jonson. *The Court Secret*, the latest of Shirley's regular dramas, was not acted till after the Restoration. It deals with the familiar theme, already several times employed by him, of the hidden heir, and surpasses other works on the subject only in the extreme intricacy of the plot. Mendoza, the father of the supposititious prince, is handled with some freshness and humour being rendered miserable by the possession of 'the court secret, but without the courage to reveal it. The real and the false princes are treated with a delicacy of comparison that distinguishes them clearly from the similarly situated but broadly contrasted pair in *The Gentleman of Venice*.

A number of miscellaneous pieces remain to be mentioned. The most curious of these is the extraordinary hodge-podge written for the Dublin theatre, and called *St Patrick for Ireland* (printed 1640). The main plot, derived from the life of the saint, may be regarded as something between a chronicle history and a miracle-play; the love story is tragicomedy; the figure of Rodamant is farcical. The device by which a lover gets access to a virtuous girl in the guise of a god is as old as Josephus and was already familiar on the English stage. A bracelet making the wearer invisible is used both in the serious and in the low comedy parts. Though the piece contains scenes and speeches that might find appropriate enough place in regular dramas, the effect of the whole is grotesque; and even the noble figure of St Patrick suffers in dignity from its patchwork background.

Interesting in a different way is the allegorical drama, *Honoria and Mammon* (pub. 1659), an elaboration of a morality, *A Contention for Honour and Riches*, which Shirley had printed in 1633. The purpose of the 'Moral,' as he calls it, is the exalting of the scholar as against the courtier and the soldier, and the exposing of the deceitfulness of riches. In its form, there is much conventional dramatic material; but, on the allegorical side, it is a more interesting production. The characters, which, in the earlier form, are largely abstractions, become, in the revision, types; and this change makes them much more effective for the pictures of contemporary life in which lies the main value of the piece.

The Tragedie of Chabot Admirall of France (licensed 1635) is ascribed on the title-page of the quarto to Chapman and Shirley. Chapman was dead before the play was acted, and Shirley may have given it some revision; but, in all essentials, it is evident that it is the work of the older poet[1]. Like most of Chapman's tragedies, it is founded on French history; it is full of his weighty diction and serious thought; and it is much less well adapted to the popular stage than we should expect had Shirley had any considerable share in it.

Besides the masques introduced into nine or ten of his plays, Shirley has left three separate productions of this class: *The Triumph of Peace* (1633), *The Triumph of Beauty* (printed 1646) and *Cupid and Death* (1653). The first of these has already been referred to as the great entertainment presented by the inns of court to the king and queen. Except in scale and splendour, it does not differ notably from most other productions of its kind, and today it is memorable chiefly as a document in social, rather than in literary, history. *The Triumph of Beauty* deals with the judgment of Paris, and it is introduced by an extensive and obvious imitation of the rehearsals of 'Pyramus and Thisbe' by Bottom and his friends in *A Midsummer Night's Dream*. *Cupid and Death*, on the familiar fable of the exchange of the weapons of the two deities and its disastrous results, was written for performance before the Portuguese ambassador.

The Contention of Ajax and Ulysses for the Armor of Achilles (printed 1659), though often described as a masque, is, in reality, nothing of the sort. It is a short dramatic piece, based on Ovid's *Metamorphoses*, intended for private production. It contains nothing spectacular and no dancing. Some of the speeches are eloquent, though both the main characters suffer from the obvious comparison with Shakespeare's *Troilus and Cressida*. The piece is now remembered for the great lyric already mentioned, with which it closes.

Of the originality of Shirley's plots, it is at present somewhat hazardous to speak. In the foregoing pages, we have been able to

---

[1] Cf. *ante*, chap. II.

indicate sources for only about one-fourth of his plays, and it has been customary to credit him with a greater share of inventiveness than most of his fellow dramatists. But Stiefel, who proved the Spanish origin of the plot of *The Opportunitie*, named another for *The Young Admirall*, and stated that *The Wedding, The Humorous Courtier, The Example* and *The Royall Master* are, also, from Spanish sources. If this can be made good, it is clear that it is too soon to pronounce on the question of invention in this sense. But, from those plays whose sources are known, we can draw inferences as to his skill in treating a source ; and our evidence is sufficient to justify us in crediting to him a high degree of ability in making over a story for stage purposes, in leading the interest up to a well prepared climax and in arranging effective situations. This last power had, indeed, distinguished most of his predecessors in the seventeenth century, but he does not so often as, say, Beaumont and Fletcher, sacrifice the unity of impression of the whole play, or the consistency of character, for the sake of single sensational scenes.

In characterisation as in theme, he had both the advantages and disadvantages of the situation described at the beginning of the present chapter. Fifty years of drama lay behind him of which to follow or avoid the example. Could we read half a dozen of the best plays of Shirley without any knowledge of his predecessors, we should, doubtless, rank him much higher in the literature of the world than we do ; but he is usually read, as he wrote, at the end of the series, and we are thus obliged to recognise constant echoes, reminiscences and imitations of the giants who went before. It was, perhaps, hardly possible for any writer of his date to avoid the familiar types and situations which had been often employed. A dramatist of the time of Charles I had to walk through a field honeycombed with pits, and it was futile to seek to follow a straight course and avoid them all. If frequent conventionality in these matters implies decadence, then Shirley was undoubtedly decadent.

The moral standards of Shirley were not those of Ford. Shirley has his share of grossness, both in incident and dialogue, but this grossness is neither more frequent than in his predecessors, nor is it by any means habitual. Of Ford's moral agnosticism there is no trace in Shirley. In some of his plays, the moral is almost obtrusive ; in none of them is the general drift immoral. Nor is he notable for the violence or sensationalism of his catastrophes. The slaughter which closes *The Traytor, Loves*

Crueltie and *The Cardinall* is no more wholesale than that at the end of *Hamlet* or *King Lear*, and, in intention at least, it is like Shakespeare's, the necessary outcome of character and previous action, not, like Ford's, an ingenious horror concocted for a final thrill. In comic power, he stands high above Ford. Without being primarily a comic artist, Shirley yet displays much genuine comic power, both in conceiving amusing situations, and in creating comic characters. In versification, too, Shirley seems to belong to an earlier and sounder school than Ford. His metre is singularly correct and easily read ; Ford uses much licence and not infrequently gives us lines hard to scan. Both men were capable of great sweetness of melody, and both adorned their finer speeches with a wealth of flowery imagery, not always dramatically appropriate, but frequently of great beauty and imaginative suggestiveness.

Yet, with all Shirley's greater soundness, greater versatility, surer versification and admirable craftsmanship, one feels that there are certain heights and depths achieved by Ford which the younger man never reached. When we turn to the most wonderful things in Ford, we find a tenderness, a poignancy and an insight that Shirley cannot match. Shirley is the more balanced mind, the better workman ; Ford, the rarer genius. The best things in both give them assurance of their place in the ranks of the greater dramatists of their age, and, if so, then of any age. And these facts must be carefully considered before, together or apart, they are set down as examples of their art's decline.

CHAPTER IX

LESSER JACOBEAN AND CAROLINE DRAMATISTS

THE Elizabethan drama, undoubtedly, followed a natural law of development. It culminated in tragedy in the first decade of the seventeenth century, because men and women reveal themselves most fully and finally in the furnace of affliction; and, therefore, the dramatist who desires to express the truth of human nature arrives, sooner or later, at tragedy as his most penetrating and powerful method. After the height has been reached, a necessary rest and suspension of effort ensue, and of such a nature was the Jacobean and Caroline age of the drama. But a second cause was at work to increase this exhaustion and to hasten the decadence of an art that had lost its freshness. The tension of feeling as to things political and religious, which led, at last, to the civil war, was unfavourable to all artistic effort, but was especially hurtful to the drama. It took possession of the minds of all but the most frivolous. Theatre-goers ceased to be drawn from all ranks, as they were in Elizabeth's days, and began to form a special class composed of careless courtiers and the dregs of the town populace. Such a class required only lesser dramatists to supply its wants; and, as we approach the date of the closing of the theatres (1642), the greater lights go out one by one till only a crowd of little men are left, writing a drama which has neither form nor spirit remaining in it.

The accident of the survival of Henslowe's diary helped us to group together in some kind of natural order the more active of the lesser Elizabethan dramatists. We have no document of this sort to aid us in the case of the Jacobean and Caroline writers; but we are confronted by a remarkable personality whose relations with the dramatists and poets of his age were as honourable and unselfish as Henslowe's were mercenary and mean. A young dramatist, writing to Henslowe for a loan, signs himself, in Elizabethan fashion, 'your loving son.' It was a slight extension of this usage which made Jonson the literary father of a large family of 'sons,' all proud to be sealed of the tribe of Ben. His position as the leader of literary and dramatic taste and the centre of literary society in London was a new thing in English life, and his influence was so commanding and complete that most of the lesser dramatists stood in some sort of relation to him, either of attraction or repulsion: they were either friends or foes. It may also be conjectured that Jonson's art lent itself to imitation by lesser men more readily than Shakespeare's. Shakespeare's apparent artlessness covered a far more subtle method and mystery than did Jonson's strict canons of conformity to definite theories of dramatic composition. Secondly, Jonson's theory of 'humours' simplified human nature and enabled the lesser dramatist, in setting about the composition of a comedy, to choose his basic humour, and get to work on inimitable humanity with some confidence. And, thirdly, while Jonson's massive common sense and satiric intensity are, in bulk, colossal, they can be readily imitated by lesser men who manufacture smaller pieces of the same stuff. Jonson's most remarkable plays were quarries from which contemporary writers chose what suited them, diligently working it into some sort of artistic shape. For these reasons, Jonson occupies an exceptional relation towards the literature of the Jacobean age, and may be regarded as a centre round which the lesser dramatists are grouped. He fails us only when we deal with romantic tragicomedy, in which species Fletcher and Massinger are the dominating influences. But the lesser writers of romantic drama are so weak that we shall have no space for detailed examination of their work.

We propose to begin our survey with John Day, adding a list of smaller men, whose comedy is either Elizabethan in general character, or Elizabethan with the additional influence of Middleton's hard, bright realism. We shall next consider the work of two men who came personally under Jonson's tuition and have a special right to be entitled his 'sons'—Nathaniel Field and Richard Brome. Field's work, like John Day's, has distinction and originality. Brome was a careful and strenuous craftsman, pursuing his vocation steadily till the stage was silenced. Field was the foremost actor of his day, and Brome was intimately acquainted with stage life. Together, they cover the Jacobean and Caroline age till 1642. Both of them continue the Elizabethan impulse, and Brome may justly claim to be noted, with Shirley, as having worthily maintained the Elizabethan tradition till the end. Brome has left fifteen plays, none of which is without its interest, and, on the whole, he is the most considerable writer who will come before us. Two other men, although they have no claim, like Field and Brome, to a place among those who continue the Elizabethan dramatic impulse, nevertheless are distinguished by a wit and genius raising them above the crowd of lesser men who show that the Elizabethan impulse is dead. These are Thomas Randolph and Sir John Suckling. When we have dealt with their work, there remain to us only dramatists whose plays are either meritorious and dull, or extravagant and dull. We shall make an effort to discover among these the precursors of the next age, and, accordingly, the last name on our list will be that of Sir William D'Avenant.

As a member of the group of robust collaborators who wrote assiduously for Henslowe during the last year of Elizabeth's reign, John Day failed to produce distinctive work. It was, perhaps, by writing for the children of the revels that he struck into his own vein and produced three plays, which, because they stand apart in style and manner from the main stream of dramatic work, attract an attention hardly due to their actual merits as literature. And they have a second claim upon the student. Day's pleasant little masterpiece, *The Parliament of Bees*, which is not a play, is directly related to his plays; and we can see in his plays those qualities at work which make *The Parliament of Bees* charming. *The Ile of Guls* was produced in the spring of 1605. The plot is taken from Sidney's *Arcadia*. Duke Basilius has left his kingdom under his brother and retired with his queen and two daughters to a 'desert isle,' sending a general challenge 'to all the youthful bloods of Africa' to

> Woo, win, entice, or any way defeat
> Me of my charge, my daughters of their hearts.

The successful suitors—both of them, apparently—

> Shall with their loves wear my imperial crown.

But, before the play begins, there is a prose induction containing the conversation of three gentlemen, who interrupt the prologue, supposing him to be the boy who should provide them with stools. They ask whether the play has any connection with the recent *West-Ward Hoe*[1] and suppose that there is some political libel in it, since the title, *Ile of Guls*, is obviously suggested by Nashe's *Isle of Dogs*[2]. To the disappointment of the first gentleman, the prologue protests fervently against these suppositions. He desires 'to

---

[1] Cf. *ante*, chap. VII. [2] Cf. *ante*, vol. V, chap. VI.

hear vice anatomized and abuse let blood in the master vein'; he asks of the play, 'Is there any great man's life charactered in't?... And there be not wormwood water and copperas in't, I'll not like it.' The second gentleman cares for none of these things; his tastes are simpler; 'Is there any good bawdry in't, jests of an ell deep and a fathom broad?' He wants scenes 'that will make a man's spirits stand on their tip toes and die his blood in a deep scarlet, like your Ovid's Ars Amandi.' When the prologue objects that chaste ears would never endure it, he retorts, 'What should chaste ears do at a play?' But the third gentleman cares for neither railing nor bawdry; he requires 'a stately penned history'... 'high-written'—'mere fustian,' his friend calls it, 'full of tear-cut thunderclaps.'

Upon these three kinds, says the dramatist, the popular audience insists—'all these we must have and all in one play or 'tis already condemned to the hell of eternal disgrace.' The induction shows that Day intended to produce a new style if he could; it shows, also, that he was very much afraid of failing; he has none of Ben Jonson's sturdy scorn of popular taste; when the prologue is finally allowed to speak, we get only a faint-hearted defiance of 'Opinion's voice,' whose tyranny is

> The misery that waits upon the pen
> Of the best writers.

It is not surprising, therefore, that Day fails to emancipate himself from the evils he deprecates. In the matter of bawdry especially, he yields to the base demands of 'opinion.' He is not more coarse than others and he makes no attempt to dye our blood in a deep scarlet; but he takes his story and his characters from Sir Philip Sidney's *Arcadia* and besmirches the sweet and noble romance of his original with the indecencies of the work-a-day Elizabethan drama. It may be urged that Shakespeare does the same thing, even in *As You Like It*. But Shakespeare creates such a soul of purity in his heroines that their most outrageous jests and words fail to hurt them. Day puts no soul at all into his women; his characters have almost no personality. Although he protests that he will not be a satirist, it is his railer, Dametas, who comes nearest in his play to being a live man, and the duke and his queen are vulgarised as well as the heroines. We are frequently reminded of Shakespeare's earlier comedies in reading Day. In *The Ile of Guls*, we catch echoes from *A Midsummer Night's Dream*. But this similarity almost forces us to compare Day's duke and duchess with Shakespeare's Theseus and Hippolyta.

What would have become of the romance and charm of Shakespeare's play if Theseus—and, with him, Hippolyta—had been
involved in a clumsy intrigue, depriving the king and hero of all
grace and dignity? The two pairs of lovers are equally uninteresting. It is enough to say that Day in no way differentiates them;
and we are unable to care much about what happens to either
couple. All these things interfere with our appreciation of Day's
art in providing us with a pretty tangle, neatly and deftly untied
at the end. Such an art there is in *The Ile of Guls,* and it is a
new thing in the Elizabethan drama as Day uses it. It points
forward to Restoration comedy, and has some kinship with the
comedy of Molière.

And it is not only in his plot that Day shows clear conception
of a comedy different from the Shakespearean romantic comedy
and from the Jonsonian comedy of humours—both of them full of
life and humanity; in his dialogue there is a new note—a new convention of epigram and repartee—which, together with neatness of
plot, marks the typical Restoration comedy. In *The Ile of Guls,*
the plot by which all the characters are collected together at
the end of the play blindfolded, as it were, to find themselves
plain gulls when the bandage is taken off, is cleverly and neatly
elaborated; but, in the course of the play, we also have a continued
effort to present a dialogue duly arranged and ordered, in which
the wit has a scheme and keeps the rules. The most notable
instance is the famous tennis match scene in the second act.
Bullen says truly: 'Outside of Shakespeare's early comedies it
would be difficult to find among the dramatists of the time such
another *tour de force* of sprightly repartee'; but, although
Shakespeare's early work, probably, was the chief influence in
producing Day's type of comedy, there is a noticeable contrast
between the two kinds. The copiousness and exuberance of all
the punning and repartee of *Love's Labour's Lost* produce an
effect the exact opposite of Day's balanced and considered epigrams. Shakespeare gives his characters full play in the scenes
of quip and repartee; Day holds his in. His art has not enough
vigour and flow in it; Shakespeare's has too much. Shakespeare,
again, is eager to break loose from the fetters of rime for the
larger scope and movement of blank verse; Day, on the contrary,
desires to get back to rime; he has not breath enough for Elizabethan blank verse. Shakespeare's fountain gushes and leaps, with
much danger to artificial restraints of all sorts; Day's rivulet, on
the contrary, flows obediently whither it is led, and often trickles

nearly dry. Elizabethan extravagance and overstrain are foreign to his art, which is Attic, or even Doric, in its simplicity and orderliness. It is not, therefore, to be wondered at that Day never does himself justice in his plays ; he is too much hampered and confused by the alien conditions in which his genius has to work. In *The Ile of Guls*, it is only the induction which is quite easy and lucid. The tennis scene, perhaps because the terms used are no longer familiar, is hard to follow, and the verse effects are too complicated. We see what the artist means, but his execution is not perfect. A scene in *Law-Trickes*, where the countess discourses to her maids as they sew, is his nearest approach to dramatic effectiveness in his own style. This play, probably, was written in 1606, and *Humour out of Breath* in 1607. The three plays present, quite recognisably, a new dramatic type, but they do not coherently and adequately realise it.

The title *Humour out of Breath* is actually quoted from *The Comedy of Errors*, and the influence of Shakespeare's early comedies is very evident in all three plays; but the neatness and compactness of Day's prose style in his dialogue is more akin to the manner of another master—John Lyly. Lyly does not exhibit in his comedies the copiousness and exuberance which characterise Shakespeare's first work. Lyly's plays, even more than Day's, lack flesh and blood, and belong to a world of moonshine and shadow. But, within their limits, they have a true charm of fancy, and their style escapes the pedantry and tediousness of the writer's prose work, and is as deft and crisp as Day at his best. To complete the parallel, we may note that Lyly (supposing him to be their author[1]) gives us a handful of beautiful lyrics, remarkable as belonging not to the true Elizabethan type, but, rather, to the later style of Herrick. Day's best lyric work in *The Parliament of Bees* is, in the same way, post-Elizabethan. It must be compared with Browne's *Pastorals* or Milton's *L'Allegro*.

Day describes *The Parliament of Bees* as 'an allegorical description of the actions of good and bad men in these our days.' But he composed it from scenes contributed to two plays which have reached us under the titles *The Noble Souldier* and *The Wonder of A Kingdome*. Dekker, in cooperation with Samuel Rowley, was mainly responsible for these plays. Between their style and Day's, there could be no real accord, and only enough of Day is left to make it clear that *The Parliament of Bees* was not, as we might suppose, completely fresh work

[1] On this question, cf. *ante*, vol. v, chap. vi, p. 125.

constituting a new departure in the art of the writer. Scenes contributed to more than one play were the groundwork upon which Day composed his dainty and graceful series of 'Colloquies' or 'Characters.' The fact throws a true light on Day's dramatic work; but the drama was not his natural vein. What would be interesting to know is how he came to write *The Parliament of Bees.* In the excellent prose tract, *Peregrinatio Scholastica,* written, apparently, before *The Parliament,* he speaks of himself as 'becalmed in a fog of necessity,' that is to say, he writes because he needs money, which he hopes to get not only from the printer, but, also, from the patron to whom he dedicates his book. He says, also, that he is lying at anchor 'before the Islands, Meliora Speramus.' Fleay's tempting suggestion is that Day means holy orders by this, and by the 'shrine of Latria,' towards which, in the allegory, the 'sometimes student of Gunvill and Caius Colledge in Cambridge' is travelling. If this were so, it would be necessary for the old playwright, until he was duly ordained, to make money by some more edifying form of literature than plays. He, therefore, wrote *Peregrinatio* and, after that, used certain scenes from old plays to make his unique *Parliament of Bees.* There is extant a manuscript copy of *The Bees* earlier than the quarto of 1641, and the changes are not all of them merely in style; the poem is made definitely graver in revision. The delightful first title disappears as too flippant—'An olde Manuscript conteyning the Parliament of Bees, found In a Hollow Tree In a garden at Hibla, in a strandge Languadge, And now faithfully Translated into Easie English Verse by John Daye, Cantabrig.' The poem, it should be noted, is not a masque in the ordinary and technical sense. It rather resembles a series of pastoral eclogues. The successive scenes have no continuity, except such as is supplied by the idea of making all the characters bees. Day conceives his poem as a series of satires; but he charges his bees to

> Carry an humble wing
> Buzz boldly what I bid, but do not sting
> Any particular.

It is only the usuring bee whom we can identify:

> Most of the timber that his state repairs
> He hews out o' the bones of foundred players:
> They feed on poets' brains, he eats their breath.

This can be none other than Philip Henslowe.

We gather, from both *Peregrinatio* and *The Parliament,* that Day was not seeking orders from any unworthy motives. The prose of the tract is more fluent than that of the plays. The style of the poem, too, has, more fully than that of the plays, Day's special gift—'a sense of delicate music in the fall and arrangement of quite common words[1].' In spite of the 'fog of necessity' around him, the writer is at peace with himself and the world. A note of peevishness and bitterness which occasionally obtruded itself in his earlier work has disappeared, and the poet's music in his last poem is serene, spontaneous and sweet. John Day died before the quarto of *The Parliament* was printed, probably in the autumn of 1640.

A belated Elizabethan of considerable interest whose extant work was printed in the early years of king James was Robert Armin, reported to have been trained by Tarlton and called his 'son.' He followed William Kemp as player of Dogberry about 1599, continued in Shakespeare's company for some years and has a place in the list of players in the 1623 folio. His single play, printed 1609, is entitled *The History of the two Maids of More-clacke; With the life and simple maner of John in the Hospitall.* On the title-page, there is a cut of Armin in the character of John in the hospital. In his words to the 'friendly peruser,' Armin calls the play 'a Historical discourse,' and says that he would have 'againe inacted' John, if he had been able. His age, presumably, prevented him, for he seems to have been born about 1564 and was dead by 1612. He adds, you shall find verse, as well blancke, as crancke, yet in the prose let it pass for currant.' The blank verse of the play is in so disordered a state that it has been compared with the mutilated 1603 quarto of *Hamlet*. The phenomena suggest the solution that Armin was not responsible for the verse, but supplied the prose of the old-fashioned fool's part of John, in which, earlier, he had made a hit. He was no more the author of the serious part of the play, than William Kemp was of the whole of *A Knack to Know a Knave*. But the play is interesting, in spite of its corrupt condition. There are in it indications that, in some form or other, it dates back to Elizabeth's reign; but, also, echoes from Shakespeare's tragedies—from *Macbeth*, for instance—which date, apparently, from about 1608. Humil's doubt of his mother's honour reminds us of Hamlet, and the play is worth careful study for its bearing on the *Hamlet* problem. The plot is absurdly complicated and full of incident, and, in this respect, we are reminded of Chettle's *Tragedy of Hoffman*. The play has genuine dramatic

---

[1] *Nero and other plays*, p. 208.

power, forcible eloquence and fine poetry, all of which we should
be inclined to ascribe to Dekker or Chettle, if another author than
Armin himself must be looked for. There are, however, some resemblances between Armin's other works and our play. In 1605,
he published *Foole upon Foole, or, Sixe Sortes of Sottes*, a prose
tract, amplified, in 1608, into *A nest of Ninnies*[1], in the dedication of which 'To the most true and rightly compleat in all good
gifts and graces, the generous Gentlemen of Oxenford, Cambridge,
and the Innes of Court' he declares 'I have seene the stars at midnight in your societies.' This, apparently, gave offence to some
of the graver spirits among the old player's hosts, and his next
and last tract, dated 1609, contains a kind of apology for it. This
tract, *The Italian Taylor and his Boy*, a verse translation from
the Italian, is written with considerable dexterity, and raises our
opinion of Armin's gifts and scholarship. It is curious that we
should have nothing from his pen earlier than 1605, although
Nashe and Harvey, in 1593, speak of him as a common pamphleteer and 'son' of Elderton.

Middleton's influence on comedy is apparent in the two surviving plays of the lawyer Edward Sharpham—*The Fleire*, acted
probably early in 1606, and *Cupid's Whirligig*, produced about a
year later. Both plays were frequently reprinted, from 1607
onwards. They owed their popularity to their wit and rapidity
of action, but can hardly claim to be more than farces; there
is in them the shadow of Middleton's art, and more than the
substance of his grossness. Much better than these is Lodowick
Barry's single play *Ram-Alley or Merrie-Trickes*, acted perhaps
as early as 1609 and extant in several quartos. Ram alley was
a particularly disreputable lane, leading from Fleet street to the
Temple, and of the coarseness promised by the title of the play we
find, as it proceeds, a full supply. But this realistic indecency
is relieved by some breath of life and character. Many echoes
from Shakespeare's plays are introduced, both by way of parody
and of imitation. There is much of the London of the period—
both of the place and its manners—in this comedy; and it not
only shows force in its presentation of life and character, but is
also marked by a vigour in its blank verse, which, in one or two
places, almost reaches distinction. The prologue says that, if the
play succeeds, the writer will attempt something more serious,
which even puritans will accept as satisfactory. Barry, no doubt,

[1] Cf. *ante*, vol. IV, p. 532.

overrated the complaisance of puritans; but he was right in feeling
that he had in him the power to produce work of a higher rank
altogether than his Ram alley obscenities. It is disappointing
that this one play and his name are all that we know of him.

Two other single plays, *Greene's Tu Quoque* and *The Hog hath
lost his Pearl*, we may mention at this point, because they belong
rather to the early comedy of Haughton than the later Jonsonian
comedy. They are less touched by Middleton's influence than
Ram-Alley. The clever acting of Thomas Greene made *Greene's
Tu Quoque or The Cittie Gallant* very popular about 1611. It was
printed in 1614 as 'written by Jo. Cooke, Gent.,' and Thomas
Heywood contributes a preface stating that both the author and
the actor Greene are dead. It is one of the pleasantest and live-
liest among the productions of the lesser dramatists. The blank
verse is not so good as Barry's; but Cooke's art and his capacity
for working out a comic idea are above the ordinary, and his prose
is excellent. The master, Staines, changes places with his man,
Bubble, and coaches him to take his place in the fashionable
world. There is an excellent scene in which the affectations of the
Italianate Englishman are taken off, probably aimed at Coryate.
The women in the play remind us of the girls of Porter and
Haughton; they are, perhaps, more refined—the sisters of
university students rather than of tradesmen—but they are very
naturally and pleasantly drawn. A scene in which Joyce, anxious
to hide the state of her heart, confounds and bewilders her lover,
first by her silence and then by her speech, recalls the vigorous
domestic comedy of Porter[1]. It is curious that we should know
nothing whatever of 'Jo. Cooke,' and that, like Barry, he
should have just one play to his credit. *The Hog hath lost his
Pearl* is, again, the single play of a writer whose name—Robert
Tailor—is all that is known about him. Tailor's literary capacity
is below that of either Barry or Cooke. To a play of low comedy,
he tacks on a romantic plot of a painful character[2] which only a
master of dramatic art could make endurable. Tailor manages the
prose of his comedy much better than the verse of his moral
romance; the main interest of the play, however, is not in its style
or story but in the circumstances of its production. Sir Henry
Wotton, in a letter dated 1612[3], tells us that 'some sixteen

---

[1] See *ante*, vol. v, chap. XIII.

[2] Otway's *Orphan* deals with the same plot.

[3] *The Life and Letters of Sir Henry Wotton*, ed. Smith, L. P., vol. II, p. 13.

apprentices,' having secretly learnt their parts, 'took up the White Fryers for their theatre,' and invited their friends to see them perform *The Hog hath lost his Pearl*. The sheriffs intervened before the end of the performance and carried off six or seven of the apprentices to prison. He adds that it was supposed that Sir John Swinnerton was meant by the hog, and the late lord treasurer by the pearl. The prologue of the printed play alludes to this incident, but says that

> our swine,
> Is not as divers critics did define,
> Grunting at state affairs or invecting
> Much at our city vices;

if the play pleases, 'we'll say 'tis fortunate, like Pericles.' Like the two plays mentioned before it, Tailor's is full of interest for the student of Jacobean London.

We come now to the main stream of Jacobean dramatic work, in which the influence of Jonson, both personal and by his art, is all-pervasive.

Among the extant plays of the reign of king James, two by Nathaniel Field are of such merit as to suggest that the writer, probably, would have risen above the ranks of the lesser dramatists, had he persevered in the prosecution of his art. He was born in 1587, a few months before his father's death. That father was the famous preacher John Field, whose rousing discourse upon the collapse of a gallery in Paris garden in 1583 has come down to us[1]. It contains interesting details about the catastrophe and a violent attack upon theatrical performances, with valuable information about London players and their theatres. Nat's elder brother, Theophilus, was educated at Cambridge and rose to be bishop of Hereford; and it is singular, therefore, that Nat Field's name should be found first among the six 'principal comedians' of the band of lads called the children of the queen's revels, who acted in Jonson's *Cynthia's Revels* in 1600. These boys were the 'young eyases' discussed by Hamlet. For a time, as has been seen[2], they rivalled men players in public favour; and Field, as he grew older, maintained his position and may claim to have succeeded Burbage as the leading actor on the English stage. Jonson, no doubt, owed a debt to Field for his clever acting in *Cynthia's Revels* and *Poetaster*, and the debt is repaid by the mention of Field, in 1614, in *Bartholomew Fayre*—'Which is your Burbadge now?...

---

[1] Cf., as to this incident, *post*, chap. xiv.
[2] Cf. *ante*, chap. ii, and *post*, chap. xi.

Your best actor, your Field?' Field joined the King's company
before he finally retired from the stage, and, in the 1623 folio of
Shakespeare's plays, he is seventeenth in the list there given of
twenty-six players. Jonson told Drummond[1] that 'Nat Field was
his scholar.' An interesting proof of Jonson's regard for Field is
afforded by the insertion of an extra sheet[2] of commendatory
verses addressed by Field to Jonson in some copies of the 1607
quarto of *Volpone*. Field's verses are amateurish—he speaks
justly of his 'weak flame'—but they show a great awe of Jonson,
whom 'to dare commend were damnable presumption.' The
lines should be compared with the much more mature address
'to his worthy and beloved friend Master Ben Jonson on his
Catiline[3].' Field had been educated by Mulcaster at the
Merchant Taylors' school, but 'taken' by N. Giles as one of the
company of the children of the revels. Giles was accused of
kidnapping boys against their parents' wishes, and we may conjecture that Field would not have been annexed, had his strenuous
father been alive to protect him.

Field's first play, *A Woman is a Weather-cocke*, was produced
in 1610. In the first scene, Scudmore is discovered reading a
vehement letter from Bellafront, the lady he loves. To him, thus
occupied, enters his friend Nevill on his way to a wedding. The
lover very prettily takes his friend into his confidence, enlarges
like a Romeo on his mistress,

> Whose face brought concord and an end of jars,

and passionately proclaims,

> She is the food, the sleep, the air I live by.

He ends with the lady's name; whereupon his friend blurts out in
amazement, 'But that's the wedding I was going to.' This dramatic
scene is put before us with a force and vividness remarkable in so
young a writer. In itself, it is an excellent beginning; but the
Jonsonian 'humours' of the next scene jar a little. They are not
in the same key as the romantic passionate opening of the play.
But Field's wit is considerable and is not a mere copy of
Jonson. His manner has a sprightliness and good-humour, and

---

[1] They read Horace and Martial together; see *Notes of Ben Jonson's Conversations
with Drummond*, ed. Laing, D., p. 11.

[2] It is contained in the British Museum copy, C 12, c. 17, which was presented by
Jonson to John Florio with an inscription in Ben's autograph to 'his loving father
and friend, the aid of his Muses.' See Percy Simpson in *Notes and Queries*, Ser. VIII,
vol. VIII, p. 301.

[3]
> But in this age where jigs and dances move
> How few there are that this pure work approve.

an occasional naturalness, which are his own, and differentiate his comic style quite definitely from Jonson's.

The second act is constructed on the same plan as the first. It begins with a semi-romantic scene and ends with 'humour.' When captain Pouts, who has been rejected by Katharine, publicly insults her at the door of the church in which she has just been married to Strange, she urges her new husband to vindicate her honour; and, perhaps, no better example could be given of Field's capacity as a writer of strong, direct, blank verse than her invective:

> Thou wert ordained,
> And in thy cradle marked to call me wife,
> And in that title made as my defence,
> Yet sufferedst him to go away with life,
> Wounding my honour dead before thy face!
> Redeem it on his head, and his own way,
> Even by the sword, his long profession,
> And set it clear amongst the tongues of men,
> That all eyes may discern it slandered,
> Or thou shalt ne'er enjoy me as a wife.

The verse is in the manner of Shakespeare in the *Henry V* period, although with less music and very little imaginative decoration, and the excellence of its directness and spontaneity is due, no doubt, to Field's training as an actor. His use of language, too, is free, like Shakespeare's—to be understood by the audience though not always approved by the grammarian. In the passage quoted, 'his long profession,' with the meaning, 'for so long a time his profession,' has a Shakespearean sound, as, also, has the rather enigmatic, but still forcible, 'made' of the third line. Strange's speech, a little later, about the law's inequalities, again, is forcible, eloquent blank verse. But the second part of the plot overloads the play as a whole. Field, as a scholar of Jonson, desires to show his dexterity as a plotter; but, like all young writers of promise, and like all immature dramatists, he gives his audience too much, and cannot endure to limit his own scope.

In this play, which is full both of matter and of varied promise of dramatic ability, Ben Jonson is obviously the master most consciously copied. The 'humours' are in Jonson's manner, as are the complicated plottings. The compression of the action into exactly one day is in accordance with Ben's teaching. It might be contended that a certain intensity in the serious scenes copies the splendid passion of Volpone, which is the high water mark of Jonson's art. This, however, would be a mistake. The serious scenes of the play are essentially romantic and idealistic, suggesting *Romeo and Juliet* rather than *The Alchemist*. But

Romeo has been brought up as a player and has appeared upon
the public stage from his childhood, and Ben Jonson has been his
schoolmaster. He has, therefore, lost all exterior softness and
sentiment, and, at first reading, a certain hardness and bravado
in his manner deceive the student. Field's second play, *Amends
for Ladies*, followed hard upon the first, and was intended to atone
for the many hard things said against women in the first play.
There are three heroines, the lady Honour, the lady Perfect and
the lady Bright, who, as maid, wife and widow, vindicate, respectively, the claims of their sex to constancy and virtue. It will be
seen, therefore, that, again, the scheme of the play is too full of
incident; there are three plays in one. The second play, on the
whole, is a more hasty piece of work than the first; it has the
drawbacks of an after-thought; but there is a distinct maturity
and strengthening to be noted in its style. Field's natural bent
is, more obviously than before, to draw ideal heroes, headstrong
and indomitable. He does not yet show much power of characterisation; his heroes and heroines are all repetitions of one type.
We remember that one of his great parts was Bussy D'Ambois,
and that Chapman addresses some lines 'to his loved son Nat
Field.' The comic scenes of the second play are less original and
less amusing than those of the first. There is something perfunctory about 'the merry prankes of Moll Cut-purse, Or, the humour
of roaring.' And, again, all that part of the play which uses the
plot of 'The Curious Impertinent' in *Don Quixote*, in which a
husband, in order to prove his wife's virtue, eggs on his friend to
tempt her, is intolerable to modern feeling. Field's audacity and
directness of treatment make him, when his subject is unpleasant,
unusually outrageous, even for the Jacobean stage. Yet he
cherishes an ideal of incorruptible and unassailable virtue which
was rare in the drama of the period.

Besides writing these two comedies, Field collaborated both
with Fletcher and Massinger. Of these collaborations, we need
mention only *The Fatall Dowry*, produced about 1619, shortly
before Field retired from the stage[1]. It has been common to
refer to Field the lighter parts of plays in which he collaborated;
but what we have noted in his work will make it highly probable
that Field, quite as much as Massinger, was responsible for the
romantic side of the play and especially for the uncompromising
honesty of Romont. In this respect, Chapman was his master;
and, from Chapman and Jonson equally, he learnt to remind his

[1] Cf. *ante*, chap. VI.

reader that 'a play is not so idle a thing as thou art, but a mirror of men's lives and actions.' And yet his profession irked him; 'thou know'st where to hear of me for a year or two and no more,' he says, in the address to the reader which we have quoted. He married about 1619 and became a publisher, dying in 1633. In 1616, he addressed a letter to Sutton, the preacher at St Mary Overy, who, like Field's own father, was a great denouncer of the stage. Field very loyally defends his profession; but his letter is very remarkable for its religious earnestness, which, in itself, is enough to explain his retirement.

Richard Brome[1], like Field, was in a special sense educated by Jonson, and it will be convenient to consider his work after Field's.

The stagekeeper who opens the induction to *Bartholomew Fayre*, having occasion to pronounce the play 'a very conceited, scurvy one,' looks behind the arras 'lest the poet hear me or his man, Master Brome.' This was in 1614. Prefixed to Brome's *Northern Lasse*, and dated, therefore, not later than 1632, we have Jonson's characteristic sonnet 'to my old faithful servant and by his continued virtue my loving friend... Mr Richard Brome.' In the first line, 'I had you for a servant, once, Dick Brome,' we almost hear Jonson speak. He goes on to say that Brome has sedulously worked at his profession :

> You learned it well, and for it served your time,
> A prenticeship.

Fleay regards this apprenticeship as extending over the whole of the seven years 1623 to 1629. In 1623, we first hear of Brome as an author. *A Fault in Friendship* was licensed in that year, 'written by Brome and young Jonson.' Unfortunately, the play has not survived ; but we may allow ourselves to suppose that the servant and the son pursued their dramatic studies together, under the father's august and austere supervision. We know nothing of Brome's parents; but a sonnet of some literary merit by a brother Stephen is printed among the poems prefixed to *The Northern Lasse*. We must beware, therefore, of assuming that Brome was of very lowly rank and uneducated till Jonson took him in hand. This notion is suggested by the low life in Brome's plays, as well as by a humility towards public and private patrons in Brome's prologues and epilogues, which, sometimes, is almost servile. But the sonnet must not be ignored ; and, when we find

---

[1] Pronounced 'Broom.'

Jonson, in a well known epigram[1], expecting his 'man' to read 'a piece of Virgil, Tacitus, Livy, or of some better book' to his guests at supper, we conjecture that the servant was not so much a valet as a secretary and amanuensis, whose duties, from the first, in connection with Jonson's dramatic and literary work, required a grammar school education. The same inference is suggested by the easy use of Latin in the sketch of the amusing pedant Sarpego in *The City Witt*. Jonson is copied unblushingly. Sarpego's speech, 'Diogenes Laertius on a certain time demanded of Cornelius Tacitus, an areopagite of Syracusa, what was the most commodious and expeditest method to kill the itch,' is modelled on Clove's in *Every Man out of His Humour*: 'Aristotle in his daemonologia approves Scaliger for the best navigator in his time, and in his hypercritics he reports him to be Heautontimorumenos![2]' But there is very little of this misuse of long words and classical names in the part; Sarpego redeems his promise, 'His grace will see that we can speak true Latin and construe *Ludovicus Vives*'; and his Latin has a sprightliness and comicality hardly to be attained by a writer whose studies began after his school days were over. But, if Brome's education was not much inferior to Field's, the contrast between the personal characters of Jonson's two 'sons' is all the more striking. Field has more than a touch of Jonson's arrogance, and inherits some of his strength of style. Brome's meekness verges on servility. The note of self-depreciation continually recurs:

> A little wit, less learning, no poetry
> This playmaker dares boast.

He is always reverent and loyal to Jonson; but his attitude of deference to his audience, and his modest estimate of his own powers as a writer, make quite clear his unlikeness to his master. For all his sedulous imitation of Jonson's style and methods, Brome has little of his master's soul in him. He can only be Jonson on a small scale; but Jonson on a small scale is not Jonson. Brome's sketches of London life are varied, minute, careful, spirited, and yet they displease; they cannot be read continuously without weariness, and are extremely coarse. Some critics have been pleased to decide that Brome describes life from the groom's point of view, and have ascribed his coarseness to his want of education and humble origin. The truer explanation is

---

[1] Epigram ci.

[2] This parallel is noted in Faust's dissertation, *Richard Brome*, Halle, 1887, p. 52.

that he uses Jonson's manner without Jonson's full-blooded, massive humanity, without his satiric intensity, without his intellectual power; so that the Jonsonian scenes in Brome, his numerous efforts to describe the humours of London life, repel or tire the reader.

Fifteen of Brome's plays have come down to us. Four of these were published in quarto in Brome's lifetime; five were printed together, in 1653, shortly after his death; five more in 1659; and one other, in quarto, in 1657. The plays have been conveniently classed under the headings of comedies of manners, romantic comedies and romantic dramas of intrigue. These divisions exhibit Brome's debt to Jonson, for the first class is much the largest, including nine plays[1]. But these nine plays are not purely Jonsonian. *The Northern Lasse* is the earliest of the extant plays. It was printed in 1632 and, again, in 1635 and in 1663. It was the most popular of Brome's plays and definitely made his reputation as a writer. It is full of humours, which fill up the scenes of an ingenious plot; but its popularity was mainly due to the romantic note struck in the character of the northern lass herself. The modern reader finds it hard to detect the charm of Constance; she is very thinly and imperfectly drawn, and her 'northern' speech is clumsy; but she pleased John Ford and Thomas Dekker. It would appear that the seventeenth century found in her some faint anticipation of the charm of the Scottish heroines of *The Waverley Novels*. Brome did not get this romantic note from Jonson, and the six romantic plays suggest to us that it was more natural to him than Jonson's hard, intellectual satire, and that he would have done better work if he had used it oftener. But the nine plays of Jonsonian humour and plot have certain merits. Brome always does his best. He works without enthusiasm, but steadily and conscientiously, and, as pieces of stagecraft, the plays are never contemptible. As a picture of the London of the period, they are full of interest and value. If their outlook were broader, if they depicted not only the vices and follies of life, but, also, its virtues and amenities, they would be read with eagerness, but it is not fair to blame Brome only for this defect. It is the weakness of the satiric method of Jonson that it tends continually to describe only what it can scourge, so that its world gets uglier and uglier. Brome's temperament fitted him for a kindlier type

---

[1] *The Northern Lasse, The Antipodes, The Sparagus Garden, Covent Garden Weeded, The New Academy or The New Exchange, The Damoiselle, The Court Beggar, The Madd Couple well matcht, The City Witt.*

of comedy, and there are many indications in his plays that he
would have produced better work under a gentler master than
Jonson. Jonson's satire is often mitigated by the introduction
of a purely comic idea, which is not vicious or even eccentric, but
merely whimsical, such as Morose's hatred of noise. Brome shows
a special aptitude in copying his master in this respect, and his
touch is lighter. Jonson is sometimes over-ingenious and his
workmanship heavy-handed. *The Antipodes* is Brome's best
effort in this kind.

Among the less interesting of the comedies of manners
which may be regarded as fairly representative of Brome's usual
work, *The Sparagus Garden*, acted 1635, takes its title from
the custom of going to eat asparagus in a garden where it
was grown. Such places were haunts of disreputable people of
both sexes, and the 'humours' of the garden are coarse though
sketched with much vivacity and some wit. They bulk so largely
in the play that it is justly classed as a comedy of manners.
The scenes in which Timothy Hoyden, a yeoman's son from the
country, is shown the way to become a fine gentleman, are excellent comedy ; they are whimsical as well as witty, and written
with a genuine gaiety. When Brome's humours have this gaiety
and lightness of touch, we are reminded of another master than
Jonson ; we are conscious of something of the spirit of Dekker.
Among the commendatory verses prefixed to *The Northern Lasse*
are some characteristic lines 'To my Sonne Broom and his Lasse,'
by Thomas Dekker. How much friendship these words imply we
have no means of discovering ; but Brome is more truly a 'son' of
Dekker than of Jonson. His best and happiest work is in the
vein of Dekker. But the scenes of our play are not all in the
asparagus garden. The first two suggest a quiet domestic drama
which might turn to tragedy or comedy, but would not harmonise
properly with the garden humours. Two young men decide to
attempt the reconcilement of two angry old men by proposing a
match between the son of one of them and the adopted daughter
of the other. The first scene describes the attempt and its failure.
In the second scene, the two friends try to console the son for
their failure and resolve to help him. Brome's verse rises to an
almost passionate height, as Gilbert insists that

> Love is wit itself,
> And through a thousand lets will find a way
> To his desired end.

Both these scenes describe common life simply and naturally, and with a touch of idealism not very common in Brome, who recants his usual creed when he confesses:

> Poets they are the life and death of things.

The play is a mine of allusions and references to the life of old London. From this point of view, Brome will always be worth reading.

The brightest and pleasantest of Brome's comedies of manners is *The City Witt, or The Woman wears the Breeches*. It is the best, just because it most successfully keeps in one key. Fleay contends that it is the earliest of the extant dramas, and says: 'Dekker's influence is more clearly visible in it than in the other plays.' He means that the gaiety and lightness of touch which we have noted as Dekker's rather than Jonson's are very noticeable in the play. But the prologue, composed by Brome for a revival of the play, states that it 'past with good applause in former times'; adding that

> It was written when
> It bore just judgment and the seal of Ben.

We must suppose, therefore, that Dekker's influence was subordinate to Jonson's, and that Brome himself was unconscious of the force of the former. Its strength was due to its suitability to Brome's temperament. The lines prefixed to *The Northern Lasse* were the last we have from Dekker's pen; he, probably, died before the end of 1632.

In his plots, Brome is apt to be over-ingenious, so that the action of his plays is either obscure or too episodical. It is the merit of *The City Witt* that its episodes are all held together by one central idea which is clear and simple, so that the play is well-knit and easily keeps the attention of the spectator to the end. A young citizen, Mr Crasy, by his kindness and easy-going disposition, has involved himself in many difficulties, and discovers that his fairweather friends all fall away when he asks for their help. He disappears, therefore, and returns disguised, with the object of bringing his false friends to book for their meanness. The play is a lively and laughable protest against worship of rank and money, and has in it a true breath of that unworldly spirit which is conspicuous in Dekker's best plays. The protest is all the more effective as coming from the tradesman's level. In that age, the development of trade brought with it new temptations. Dishonest speculation and the making of fortunes by all sorts of trickery were becoming common. At the same time, the new

devices by which bankruptcy was made profitable were scorned
by oldfashioned tradesmen. Crasy declares

> I must take nimble hold upon occasion
> Or lie for ever in the bankrupt ditch
> Where no man lends a hand to draw one out.
> I will leap over it or fall bravely in't,
> Scorning the bridge of baseness, composition,
> Which doth infect a city like the plague,
> And teach men knavery that were never born to't.

His troubles are largely due to the odious malice of his mother-
in-law, Mistress Pyannet Sneakup, who illustrates the evil effect
upon tradesmen's wives of the degenerate times. Her son-in-law
asks gently, 'May not an honest man—,' when he is taken up by
the irate lady—

> Honest man! Who the devil wished thee to be an honest man? Here's my
> worshipful husband, Mr Sneakup, that from a grasier is come to be a Justice of
> Peace: and, what, as an honest man? He grew to be able to give nine
> hundred pound with my daughter; and what, by honesty? Mr Sneakup and
> I are come up to live i' th City, and here we have lyen these three years;
> and, what? for honesty? Honesty! What should the City do with honesty,
> when 'tis enough to undoe a whole Corporation? Why are your wares
> gumm'd; your shops dark; your prices writ in strange characters? what, for
> honesty?

This 'woman of an eternal tongue, this creature of an ever-
lasting noise' is the most considerable character in the piece;
but Sarpego is equally good in another direction. We have already
touched upon him. His sudden scraps of Latin are very comical—
'*O Dii! Quem video? Nonne Mr Sneakup?*'—and one wonders
how far they were followed by the audience. Some of his para-
phrases are very happy—'*Tempora mutantur*; the town's ours
again'; '*Lupus in fabula*; the devil's in the woman's tongue';
'*Sic transit gloria mundi*; the learned is coney-caught.' The
briskness and bustle of the play are maintained to the end, and,
if it were not for the absence of Mrs Tryman from the list of
dramatis personae, the *dénouement* would be a complete surprise.
Crasy's honesty, his 'unsuspicious freeness' and 'most easy goodness' flavour the play and convince us that Brome, with all his
grossness, was unsophisticated.

By way of proving this point more fully and carrying further
the comparison of Brome with Dekker, we may next consider
Brome's masterpiece, *A Joviall Crew, Or, The Merry Beggars*.
It was the latest play written by Brome, being produced in 1641
and continuing on the stage till it came to be the very last play
acted before parliament closed the theatres in 1642—'it had the

luck to tumble last of all in the Epidemicall ruin of the Scene !'
In his prologue, Brome notes that his title promises mirth,

> Which were a new
> And forc'd thing in these sad and tragic days;

but, since he finds that plays are now liked which tediously and
tearfully relate lovers' distresses, up to the point at which

> some impossibility
> Concludes all strife and makes a comedy,

he, therefore, composes a kind of parody on this popular style, in
which he hopes the sadness will not make any woman weep.   This
interesting account of the genesis of the play would hardly have
been surmised by the critic without the author's help.   The finest
thing in the play, and, indeed, in all Brome's writings, is the
description of the steward Springlove's annual hunger for the
green grass and the careless content of the wandering beggar.

> You kept a swallow in a cage that while.
> I cannot, Sir, endure another summer
> In that restraint with life: 'twas then my torment
> But now my death.

We have to wait till the days of George Borrow and R. L. Stevenson for a repetition of Brome's conception of the joy and glory of
vagabondage.   The sketch of the beggars' content is combined
with a very natural picture of the kind and compassionate master
and squire.   There is a touch of religious feeling in the picture of
Oldrents's kindness of heart, and his compassion for the poor and
unfortunate ; the only drawback to the charm of the play is the
occasional coarseness of the realism in the description of the
jovial crew of beggars.   The first act of this play is work of high
and rare merit.   Brome's English is admirably plain, unaffected
and direct ; his blank verse is unadorned, but clear and natural,
and he reaps the reward of his simplicity.   To the student of
decadent romanticism, this play has the perfection of a cup of
cold water in a dry and thirsty land.

  A Joviall Crew is classed among Brome's romantic dramas
of intrigue[1]; and two plays, *The Queen and Concubine* and *The
Queenes Exchange*, have been reckoned as pure romantic dramas.
This division, of course, is merely intended to meet the require-
ment of convenience.   Of the six romantic plays, the last two
mentioned and *The Love-sick Court* best illustrate Brome's ideas
of romance and poetry, and thus call for some notice.   Brome's
modest conception of himself as a playwright and not an author

---

[1] With three others, *The Love-sick Court*, *The Novella* and *The English Moor*.

or poet—his disinclination to indulge in imaginative effort—stamps him as out of sympathy with the fashionable taste for lengthy imaginative sentiment. He had a real sense of artistic form, and recoiled not only from the sentimentality, but from the incoherence, both in plan and metre, of the later Caroline drama. We have already quoted his account of the composition of *A Joviall Crew*. In the prologue to *The Antipodes*, he complains that 'opinion' cares only for plays that

> carry state,
> In scene magnificent and language high,
> And cloathes worth all the rest, except the action.

The taste of the journeyman playwright, on this head, was certainly far sounder than that of the king and his court. Yet Brome did essay romantic drama, and with very interesting results. *The Love-sick Court* was, probably, the earliest of the batch; *The Queenes Exchange* dates from about 1632, and *The Queen and Concubine* from after 1635. In these plays we see Brome manfully striving to write as a poet and to achieve a good romantic play. In the first two, he is often at a loss; his art fails him, and only fumbling work is produced; but *The Queen and Concubine* marks a very definite advance, and shows that Brome might have produced excellent romantic work if his public had asked for it. Shakespeare, rather than Fletcher, is the master from whom Brome takes his suggestions, and the good queen Eulalia, whose trials and virtues are touchingly described, is a blend of the patient Grissill of Dekker and queen Katharine in *Henry VIII*. There are two fine songs in the play; one of them—'What if a day, or a month, or a year'—possessing the true Elizabethan charm of Campion or Dekker. The shining merit of Brome in these plays, for all their feeble workmanship, is his capacity for the unsophisticated and direct expression of emotion. We escape from inflated sentiment and return to a simplicity of moral feeling which belongs to the earlier days of the drama. Brome's humility was described above as almost servile; and the suggestion was made that his unaffected modesty is reflected in the restraint and the naturalness of his art. Like Day, Brome proves his manliness when he falls on evil days. He wrote his dedication of *A Joviall Crew*, when it was printed in 1652, a few months before his death, 'in these anti-ingenious Times,' when the theatres had been closed for ten years. 'Since the Times conspire to make us all Beggars,' he says, 'let us make ourselves merry.' That is what his 'play drives at.' He does not flinch in his extremity: 'I am poor and proud,' he tells us; 'you know, Sir, I am old and cannot cringe.' This is his last word.

Among Jonson's most eager admirers was Thomas Randolph; but he was not, like Field and Brome, a pupil of the old poet. He was a king's scholar of Westminster school, who became a fellow of Trinity college, Cambridge. At the end of 1629, a year of plague broke up the schools at Cambridge, and Randolph made Jonson's acquaintance during his stay in London; he was probably adopted as a 'son' before he returned to Cambridge. He had written by this time his two earliest 'shews'—*Aristippus* and *The Conceited Pedler*, which were printed in 1630. These lively sketches recall that early type of dramatic performance, the clown's jig, in which a famous comedian, such as Tarlton, poured forth an improvisation of his own, which was a mixture of prose, verse and antics. But it is Randolph's command of racy English, his high spirits and his exuberant wit that suggest this comparison. His pieces belong to that large body of 'college drama' which is described in another chapter[1]. *Aristippus, or, The Joviall Philosopher* is a dispute on the rival merits of ale and sack. All the technical terms of Aristotle's logic are crowded into a hilarious laudation of sack and a decrying of malt liquor, which never flags. Randolph's classical and scholastical learning supplies matter for a cataract of ingenious puns and word play, and, therefore, his transference of Aristotelian metaphysic into English farce is to be contrasted with, rather than compared to, Robert Browning's profuse employment of the details of Attic drama in his *Aristophanes' Apology*. Both poets, while crammed with learning, have no pedantry in their nature. The marvellous agility of some of the riming in *Aristippus* is another point of contact with Browning's poetry.

In March 1632, king Charles visited Cambridge, and the Trinity men acted before him *The Jealous Lovers*, written for the occasion. It is Randolph's only failure. Its dramatic character is so bad that the ability of the writing cannot redeem it. After the king's visit, Randolph left Cambridge for London, 'called thence to keep the flock of Corydon.' In *An Eglogue to Mr Johnson*[2], he describes how he had relished his Aristotelian studies—'those deep and learned layes' which 'the shepherd of Stagira used to sing'; but now he has to keep 'another's flock,' and not he but 'the Master shears the sheep.' Fleay's interpretation of this passage is that Randolph was manager of prince Charles's men acting at Salisbury

---

[1] See *post*, chap. XII, where more is said about *The Jealous Lovers*.
[2] *I.e.* Ben Jonson.

court in 1632 and 1633.   At Salisbury court theatre, Fleay thinks.
The Muses Looking-Glasse was presented towards the end of 1632.
(It was not printed till 1638, when the writer was dead.)   This
theory accords very well with the character of Randolph's masterpiece, and explains the genesis of this new and distinct type of
dramatic art.   It is just such a work as the writer of *Aristippus*
might be expected to produce if he were called upon to expand
his short 'shew' into something that could compete in length,
interest and dignity with the plays of a better class.   Randolph's
creative capacity had been stimulated to this effort by close contact with the drama of the London stage; but the Aristotelian
student is still in evidence.   The main part of the piece consists
of a series of fifteen scenes, in which the vices of Aristotle's *Ethics*
appear in couples or singly and, in accordance with the theory
of comedy put forward in the first act of the piece, hold up a
mirror in which spectators may note their own defects; this is
how comedies 'laugh' people 'into wit and virtue.'   These scenes,
therefore, are planned like the 'colloquies' of Day's *Parliament of
Bees*; but the contrast is great between Day's delicate rimes and
Randolph's masculine and emphatic blank verse, which only
occasionally uses the heroic couplet.   Kolax, the flatterer, remains
on all the time because 'Any vice yields work for flattery.'   In
these strongly written scenes, the influence of Jonson's satiric
plays is very obvious.   In act I, there is an excellent scene in
which Comedy, Tragedy, Mime and Satire dispute together and
expound their functions according to classic theory.   Before the
vices come in, we have a masque,

a rude dance,
Presented by the seven deadly sins.

In act V, after Mediocrity, the mother of virtues, has expounded
in a hundred lines Aristotle's doctrine of the mean, she presents a
masque of her daughters, 'wherein all the Vertues dance together.'
The invention of all this is both copious and happy.   The author
describes his work as containing

No plot at all, but a meer Olla Podrida,
A medley of ill plac'd and worse penned Humours,

borrowed from the man

to whom he owes
All the poor skill he has, great Aristotle.

Randolph is pleasantly unconscious that the creative and artistic
faculty is too often, as in Jonson's case, smothered, rather than
nourished, by theory, however sound.   But we have still to mention

the most delightful feature of the play. The 'moralising' scenes
are presented before Bird, a feather-man, and Mistress Flowerdew,
'wife to a Haberdasher of Small Wares.' These worthies bring
feathers and pins and looking glasses to sell to the players; but
they belong to 'the Sanctified Fraternity of Black-Fryers': that is
to say, they are puritans. This device is not new. Beaumont used
it admirably in *The Knight of the Burning Pestle*. But Randolph
employs it to lighten the didactic tendency of his main scenes;
moreover, his two puritans are to be converted to the theory of
comedy put forward in the play; they are, therefore, described
with more good humour, with more restraint and naturalness,
than is usual in Elizabethan comedy. When the virtues are to be
presented, Bird hopes there are no 'cardinal vertues'—

> I hate a vertue
> That will be made a Cardinal,

—he adds that even 'Bishop vertues are unwarrantable,' and,
generally,

> Vertues in Orders are unsanctified.

He is disturbed when the virtues dance:

> O vile, absurd, Maypole-Maid-Marian Vertue!

Yet, as the play goes on, Mistress Flowerdew begins to relent:

> I have picked
> Out of the garden of this play a good
> And wholesome salad of instruction.

And, finally, both are mollified. Bird says

> I'll teach devotion now a milder temper,

while Mistress Flowerdew admits,

> I might have gone to hell the narrow way.

We have called *The Muses Looking-Glasse* Randolph's masterpiece,
though this title might be claimed for his fine pastoral *Amyntas*.
But the later production has to compete with even finer work
by Jonson and Fletcher, while the former is unique of its kind.
Randolph died in 1635, at the age of twenty-nine; and he is to be
counted among those poets whose achievement, considerable as it is,
is an earnest only of what his matured powers might have given us.

It remains to attempt a hurried survey of the lesser dramatists
of the end of the age, who were writing from the later years of
James until the closing of the theatres. They exhibit very clearly
the exhaustion of the great dramatic impulse which begins with
Marlowe and ends with Shirley and Brome. A tasteless and
featureless mediocrity or a pretentious extravagance are the

characteristics of work which was ceasing to conform to type
and losing all sense of true dramatic form.   On a first casual
inspection, the more meritorious of these plays seem better written
and more judiciously planned than much of the Elizabethan work
which has survived; but a closer study reveals the essential
insipidity of the later work, due, in the first place, to exhaustion
of the dramatic impulse, and, in the second, to the deterioration
of the audiences and the practical cessation of a demand for good
plays.

Thomas May, the historian of the Long parliament, whose
character Clarendon and Marvell[1] unite in decrying, began his
literary career with two comedies, *The Heir* and *The Old Couple*,
written about 1620.   *The Heir* is a Fletcherian tragicomedy; *The
Old Couple*, which Fleay thinks the earlier of the pair, a play of
Jonsonian intrigue and manners.   After producing these plays, May
turned to the work by which he is best known—his translations of
the *Georgics* and of Lucan's *Pharsalia*.   Jonson wrote lines 'to my
chosen friend the learned translator of Lucan, Thomas May, Esq.,'
and May was a contributor to *Jonsonus Virbius*.   Jonson's influence
and that of the classics would seem to have turned May to classical
drama, and he produced three tragedies, of which the first, *Antigone,
the Theban Princess* is dedicated to Endymion Porter, and may
have been written before 1626.   Fleay has suggested that May
is the author of the anonymous *Nero*, printed 1624.   We are to
suppose that the fire and energy of this fine play were the result
of May's first study of Tacitus, perhaps before he had been too
much obsessed by Jonson's influence and method.   But May's
study of Tacitus would seem to have been later than 1624.   His
Cleopatra is dated 1626, and *Julia Agrippina* 1628.   May's
imagination is pedestrian; his style is regular and painstaking.
Nero is the work of a scholar whose imagination is fiery and
strong, and who contrives to crowd into his play a great deal
of the excitement, the incident and the underlying unity of the
Roman historian's picture of the tyrant.   May's first two plays
are meritorious; there is care and correctness in the blank verse,
and much careful invention in the plot and the conception of the
characters; but his classical plays are no better and no worse
than his continuation of *Pharsalia*.   They are pale reflections of
Jonson's work in *Sejanus* and *Catiline*.   May is nothing more than
a 'son' of Ben, who copied his adoptive father's least inspired work.

Meritorious, like May's, was the work of Robert Davenport,

[1] 'Most servile wit and mercenary pen.'

whose activity begins in 1623. Three of his plays survive, two comedies and a tragedy. The tragedy is a careful rewriting of Munday and Chettle's *Death of Robert, Earle of Huntington*[1]. Chettle's drama is stripped of its crudities and banalities; so far as may be, the horrible is replaced by the pathetic, and a considerable adornment of poetic diction and imagery is added. The versification, of course, is brought up to date and irregularities disappear. The old play has a deeper significance than that which it expresses: we read it with impatience; but we remember it with interest, because of its suggestion of horror and gloom. Davenport, on the other hand, we read with respect for his industry, and we forget him at once. It is a plausible conjecture that his comedies were remodellings of older material; so that all his work looks backward. But *The City-Night-Cap* and *A New Tricke to Cheat the Divell* are, both of them, interesting and able comedies, like the two plays of May which we have just considered. The former dates from 1624. As this play takes its main story from 'The Curious Impertinent' in *Don Quixote*, there can be nothing surprising in the fact that, in some respects, it is unpleasant; indeed, its comic part is intolerable; but, on the romantic side, it has merit. It contains echoes of *Measure for Measure*, of *Cymbeline* and of *The Winter's Tale*; it is highminded, with some grace of diction and force of eloquence, but dramatically unreasonable and wrong. The other play is slighter and more humorous, and, on the whole, more agreeable. Two of Davenport's friends were players; of his circumstances nothing is known.

Thomas Nabbes seems to have belonged to the same social level as Davenport, and, like him, to have produced his tragedy, *Hannibal and Scipio*, by revising an older play; he was a friend of Richard Brome. His *Microcosmus* is a morality play which he calls a masque. His best work is to be found in his three comedies, *Covent-Garden*, 1632, *Totenham-Court*, 1633, and *The Bride*, 1638. Nabbes breaks away from the prevailing coarse type of comedy, intended to hit the taste of the man about town, and takes pains and pleasure in representing people of virtuous life and conversation. With just a little more distinction and force, both in his writing and in his characterisation, Nabbes would have risen above the ranks of third-rate dramatists. *The Bride* is a comedy of considerable effectiveness, distinguished among the plays of its time by the goodness and purity to be found in its men and women. His heroes and heroines are amiable and sincere; somewhat colour-

---

[1] Cf. *ante*, vol. v, chap. XIII.

less when compared with stronger dramatic work; but without the
two diseases of the time, the convention of coarseness, and the
convention of fantastic sentiment.

Two writers who were among the 'sons' of Ben and of great
repute in their day need not detain us long.   William Cartwright
was the son of an innkeeper at Cirencester.   He was educated at
Westminster and Christ Church, Oxford, and rose to be the most
noted man in his university as a strenuous scholar, an admired
dramatist and a 'seraphical' preacher.   His first play, probably, was
his comedy *The Ordinary*, produced about 1635.   This was followed
by three tragicomedies, *The Lady Errant*, *The Royall Slave* and
The Siedge or Love's Convert.   After taking holy orders in 1638, he
did not write any more plays.   He died in 1643.   His plays, therefore,
were probably composed hurriedly.   They are essentially the work
of a man of parts, who writes for reputation without any true
respect either for his art or for himself.   His comedy is a flashy
and vulgar imitation of Jonsonian 'humours,' as tedious as it is
coarse.   His tragicomedies belong to the school of enervated
romance which pleased king Charles and was suited to the
French tastes of the queen.   *The Royall Slave* was presented
before the king and queen at Oxford on 30 August 1636, by
the students of Christ Church, and, again, six months later, at
Hampton court, by the king's players.   The students are said to
have acted best.   Very probably, professionals found it difficult
to adapt themselves to the extravagant sentiment and preciosity
of Cartwright's style.   Jonson's saying, 'my son Cartwright writes
all like a man,' suggests a directness of style and truth of inspiration which are not found in Cartwright's plays.

Jasper Mayne, dramatist, translator and archdeacon, was a
Devonshire man, educated at Westminster school and Christ
Church, Oxford.   Like his friend Cartwright, he was an admired
preacher.   He produced a tragicomedy, *The Amorous Warre*,
and a comedy, *The Citye Match*, which was acted at Whitehall by
the king's command in 1639.   It is a much better comedy than
Cartwright's, with plenty of life and movement in it, and, although
it has no moral elevation, it is without Cartwright's obscenity.
Mayne's[1] most useful contribution to the literature of his country
was his translation of Lucian.

The tragicomedies of Cartwright and Mayne belong to the
group of romantic plays specially characteristic of the closing
years of the drama, written to please the court and the current
liking for inflated sentiment and fantastic emotion.   But, before

[1] Both Cartwright and Mayne contributed to *Jonsonus Virbius*.

we deal summarily with these plays, a figure of some consequence calls for a less perfunctory consideration.

In 1642, the year of the closing of the theatres, Sir John Suckling poisoned himself in Paris. All his plays are not worth his handful of incomparable lyrics; but they have some salt of genius in them which entitles them to a place of their own among the work of lesser dramatists. *Aglaura*, a tragedy of court intrigue, of which the scene is supposed to be Persia, was acted in the winter of 1637, when its literary qualities received less attention than the novelty and magnificence of the scenery used and the dresses presented by the author to the actors. King Charles is said to have requested an alternative final act with a happy ending, which Suckling afterwards wrote. Flecknoe saw the play when it was revived at the Restoration, and his criticism, that it was 'full of flowers, but rather stuck than growing there,' applies to all Suckling's dramatic work. He has imagination, fancy and wit, but these faculties are not usually employed upon his plot and his characters. The famous lyric, 'Why so pale and wan, fond lover?' occurs in the fourth act of *Aglaura*. *The Goblins* was probably written next; it was acted in 1638, and is Suckling's best play. His goblins are thieves who masquerade as devils, and their pranks are mixed up with the feuds of two noble families and a double love story. The so-called goblins administer justice in the style of Robin Hood and his men in older plays. Suckling's restless temperament expresses itself in the impossible rapidity and abruptness of the action; but the sprightliness of the play is undeniable and its mixture of song and witty dialogues caught Sheridan's attention, and, undoubtedly, influenced his style. His lyric 'Here's to the maiden' is suggested by a catch in *The Goblins*. Although *The Goblins* is Suckling's most satisfactory performance, the tragedy *Brennoralt* is a work of more promise and a more striking evidence of his poetic capacity. It did not appear till 1646; but it had been printed in a shorter form in 1640 as *The Discontented Colonell*. The interest of *Brennoralt* lies mainly in our seeming to detect in the hero something of the inner self of the author, and to find that self better and sounder than the shallow prodigal who caught the public eye. The gloomy colonel, in spite of his strict loyalty, is clearly aware of defects in his king. The rebel Lithuanians are meant for Scots, of about the year 1639. The rebels having been informed that the king cannot be unjust to them 'where there's so little to be had,' their leader Almerine replies, 'Where there is least, there's liberty.' Suckling's style perceptibly strengthens in the play. The fine things are less obviously stuck in. Sententious force, by which his political experience receives apt expression, is added to genuine poetic vigour. Brennoralt is left alive, his rival and both the heroines being dead. The false Caroline ideal of tragicomedy prevents the solution of suicide demanded by the tone of the play. But the melancholy, disillusioned character of Brennoralt, who points forward to Byron, rather than backward to Marston, may help to explain Suckling's own suicide, which seems very inconsistent with the rest of his career. The versification is spasmodic and formless. A blank verse line, here and there, suggests to us what the metre is supposed to be, and, occasionally, such a line as 'Oh! it is wisdom and great thrift to die!' proves that Suckling had it in him to write blank verse. In all his plays, he has a trick of appropriating Shakespearean phrases and lines, and, in *The Goblins*, the courtship of Orsabrin and Reginella is copied unblushingly from the courtship scenes in *The Tempest*. Although Shakespeare's work is weakened, Suckling's courtship scenes are the prettiest scenes in his play, and his hero Orsabrin is a brave spirit of true heroic strain.

A friend and companion in arms of Suckling, who died before him in 1639, was Shackerley Marmion, author of the considerable poem *Cupid and Psyche*. He produced three comedies before his poem, not, as we should expect, in the romantic vein, but all of them rather thin imitations of Jonson. *The Antiquary* is the best of these. Veterano, from whose pursuits the play is named, is an original conception; but the author fails to give him life, lacking the capacity to use the opportunity with which he has provided himself.

In conclusion, we may rapidly enumerate among later writers of the Jacobean age those dramatists who are important only because they initiated the type of play which, in its full development in the Restoration period, came to be known as the 'heroic drama.' In this connection, the insipid and tedious tragicomedies of Lodowick Carlell have importance. Carlell is said to have come from the stock which afterwards produced Thomas Carlyle. He was a Scot, born in 1602, who came to court to make his fortune and rose to the position of keeper of the forest at Richmond. Of his plays, which began in 1629, four tragicomedies remain, two of which are in two parts. They are taken from contemporary romances, Spanish or French. French romance, as written by D'Urfé and Mlle de Scudéry, was characterised by a refinement of sentiment which cut it off from real life and made it vapid and extravagant. In our own drama, the romance of Fletcher shows a tendency to exaggeration; the dramatic thrill ceases to represent reality; it begins to have a note of hysteria, and to enjoy its own deliciousness; emotion is dwelt upon, sentiment is refined, till love, honour and friendship are taken altogether out of the world of reality. Queen Henrietta Maria's French tastes and upbringing added the example of French romance to tendencies already prevailing in England, and rendered the influence of the court upon the drama merely enervating. Fleay says that Carlell's plays 'show what rubbish was palatable to Charles and Henrietta.' The peculiar extravagance of romantic sentiment which these plays exhibit goes along with a looseness and incoherence of blank verse very accurately described by the same critic as 'a riot of hybrid iambic.' Dryden's use of rime was almost needed to bring back some form into this chaos. The plays of Henry Glapthorne are noticeable from this point of view. His three comedies, at their worst, sink as low as Cartwright and, at their best, touch the level of Mayne or Nabbes; but his more serious work, consisting of *The Ladies Priviledge, Argalus and Parthenia* and *Albertus Wallenstein,* approaches more nearly to literature than any of the parallel efforts of Carlell, Mayne, Cartwright, or Thomas Killigrew. The first of these plays, which ends as a comedy, belongs to the type of tragicomedy in which extravagant sentiment insists upon submitting itself to absurd tasks in the effort to prove its heroism. The second is a pastoral, also conforming to the tragicomedy type; and the third is history treated on the same lines. The plays, therefore, illustrate the enervating and disintegrating effect of heroic sentiment on all the chief forms of English drama. But it is William D'Avenant whose work best enables us to observe the transition to the heroic drama of Dryden. His first two plays were tragedies in Fletcher's grimmest style, dated 1626 and 1627, and these were followed by two able comedies which enjoyed considerable popularity. After 1630, illness incapacitated him for several years; and, when he resumes work as a dramatist, his style has altered, and four plays, *Love and Honour*, 1634, *The Platonick Lovers*, 1635, *The Fair Favourite*, 1638, and *The Unfortunate Lovers*, 1638, show him under French influences and as the leading exponent of the cult of platonic love, of which queen Henrietta herself was the patron. *The Platonick Lovers* is a budget of speeches and disputations on this unreal and undramatic theme; it is curious to the student of manners, but futile as literature. D'Avenant lived to revive the theatre shortly before the Restoration, and to contribute to its literature after that date. He will, therefore, receive some further notice in a later volume.

CHAPTER X

THE ELIZABETHAN THEATRE

WHEN Elizabeth came to the throne, she found attached to
the court not only musicians and minstrels, but eight players of
interludes. This body had been a permanent part of the court
establishment for some reigns ; and, in the new theatrical activity
of Elizabeth's reign, it was supplanted by other bodies, but
not dissolved. It accompanied her occasionally on her progresses, and only gradually died out. Companies of such players
had long been attached to the households of men of wealth and
position, whose 'livery' or badge they wore on their sleeves.
A statement in Heywood's *Apology for Actors* (1612) may be
taken to mean that some kind of royal licence was considered
necessary or advisable by these companies, so far back as the
reign of Henry VIII.

In many cases, these companies supported themselves by
playing before the public in various parts of the country. The
practice seems to have been for players, on coming to a town,
first to attend the mayor, to inform him whose servants they were
and to receive his licence for public playing. If the mayor liked
the company or wished to honour their master, he would pay them
a sum (which the entrance money charged to the public would
supplement[1]) to give a first performance before the corporation, to
which the public were admitted. Several cases are on record
where players received a fee, though they were forbidden by the
town's bylaws or otherwise to give a performance. Travelling
players appeared frequently, also, at private houses, at weddings
and on other festival occasions ; and, occasionally, even in
churches. At Exeter, Yarmouth and Worcester, there seem to
have been regular playhouses ; at other times, the actors played

---

[1] Murray, John Tucker, 'English Dramatic Companies in the towns outside of
London, 1550–1600,' *Modern Philology*, vol. II, p. 539.

at the guildhall, or in an innyard. Such incidents as the remonstrance issued by the privy council to the lord president of the north in 1556, touching the seditious plays acted by 'certain lewd persons naming themselves to be the servants of Sir Frances Lake,' suggest that some, at least, of the companies attached to great houses had received no recognition or licence from the crown; while 'common players of interludes,' orders for whose regulation or arrest were occasionally issued, did not belong, either in fact or in name, to any nobleman's establishment. In addition to companies bearing the names of patrons, there were still in existence a large number of wandering troupes of jugglers and players, descendants of the old minstrels, who owned no kind of patronage. Certain municipal corporations had their band of players; and, in Cornwall and elsewhere, local associations of amateurs still met to perform town or village plays and pageants which the reformation had shorn of their old glory. The competition of travelling companies was, perhaps, as important an element in the decadence of these local bodies as was the hostility of the puritans.

A few months after her accession, Elizabeth issued a proclamation providing that no interlude should be played without being notified beforehand and licensed by the mayor or chief officer of a town, or, in the country, by lieutenants or two local justices of the peace. And, in 1572, the question of these unattached companies was finally settled by a law providing that common players in interludes not belonging to a baron or honourable personage of greater degree, or not having a licence from two justices of the peace, should be deemed rogues and vagabonds. This, practically, is the close of the history—so far as their influence on the progress of the drama is concerned—of any theatrical bodies except those definitely under patronage. The early part of Elizabeth's reign saw not only the triumph of the professional actor over the amateur, but the supplanting of the old player of interludes by the better equipped companies then newly formed by nobles anxious to please their sovereign.

In the city of London, jurisdiction over public theatricals rested, under the proclamation of 1559, in the mayor and corporation, steady foes of the drama. The decay of the feudal system under the Tudors had increased the importance not only of the immediate neighbourhood of the court, but of the capital; and London was now the centre of theatrical activity. Elizabeth's own love of the play tended to the same result; and the privy council, on the whole, supported her in defending the acted drama against the attacks of the city government. The difference between court and city was the cause of many disputes and much uncertainty, as is shown at length in a later chapter[1] of this volume, where it is also related how an unforeseen result of the city's opposition was the enormous stimulus given to theatrical art by the building of playhouses outside the common council's jurisdiction but within easy reach of the citizens of London.

The quarrel[2] was due to other causes besides the religious difference, and the inevitable conflict between the feudal privilege from which companies drew their origin, on the one hand, and, on the other, the rights of the corporation, which meant the growing importance of the middle class. A very reasonable objection was advanced against the overcrowding of narrow streets by people riding or, later, driving to the playhouses, and by the concourse of loafers and beggars; furthermore, apprentices and others were tempted to play truant and occasional tumults or crimes resulted from the massing of numbers of people in holiday mood. A theatrical performance, like the performance of a miracle-play in earlier times, meant a procession through the streets with drums and trumpets. It would not be fair, however, to ascribe to plays alone all the disturbances which are on record. Such incidents as those which took place outside the Theater in 1584, when 'one Browne, a serving man in a blew coat, a shifting fellowe,' attacked an apprentice with a sword, were due rather to the fact that the neighbourhood of this house was the 'ordinary place for all maister-les men and vagabond persons... to meet together and to recreate themselfes[3].' The gravest cause for the corporation's objection to plays—a cause which the privy council readily supported them in avoiding—was, however, the recurrence of the plague, to the grievous and prolonged visitations of which full reference is made in the chapter discussing the conflicts between puritanism and the stage[4]. But, in the reigns of Elizabeth, James I and Charles I, every year was a plague year, and, besides 1582—3, 1558, 1586, 1593, 1603, 1613, 1625 and 1636 were very bad plague years. It was important to check the spread of infection by preventing the gathering of crowds, and plays were forbidden whenever it seemed desirable. Early in the reign of James I, all performances were prohibited

---

[1] See *post*, chap. xiv.

[2] For an interesting suggestion as to the influence of the Blackfriars playhouse in and after the year 1597, see Wallace, C. W., *Children of the Chapel*, chap. xii.

[3] *Remembrancia*, vol. ii, p. 103.   [4] See *post*, chap. xiv.

when the number of deaths a week reached 30 ; and, in or about 1619, 40 was fixed as the limiting number[1]. This frequently entailed the closing of places of public performance during the whole of the summer and autumn, when companies sometimes 'broke,' sometimes went on tour in England and sometimes travelled abroad. The history of these travels is well worth study, but lies outside the scope of this work[2].

In the conflict between the drama and the corporation, the weight of Elizabeth herself was thrown entirely on the side of the drama. The list of performances at court shows that, while masques were frequently performed by amateurs at the beginning of her reign, their place was almost entirely taken later by the performances of professional actors whom her patronage helped to bring to efficiency. The stock excuse offered by the privy council for contravention of the prohibitive regulations of the city authorities is that players must be allowed full opportunities of practising their art in order that they may exercise it fitly before the queen, during the Christmas holidays or at Shrovetide—the great seasons of performances at court. In 1583, the queen, at the suggestion of Walsingham, and probably as a countermove to a decision of the common council, had her own company selected from the best actors of the day ; and every attempt was made to regard public performances as mere rehearsals for those at court. It is easily possible to make too much of the pretext, which, doubtless, was convenient at the time. The chance of a play being awarded a place among the few to be performed at court would scarcely have sufficed to encourage playwrights to produce work of the quantity or the character left by Elizabethan dramatists. Occasional state performances, rewarded with a small fee, could not be prize enough to keep large numbers of men working hard at acting, and at nothing else, all the year round; and players grew well-to-do and respectable, not because they played now and then at court, but because court favour enabled them to meet the ardent desire for theatrical performances which had been largely thwarted in previous troubled reigns, but which, when it could be indulged, to a great extent supplanted the love of athletic or acrobatic exhibitions that had had to suffice for earlier times. Such exhibitions still survived ; but the drama either swept them into its own

[1] Greg's *Henslowe's Diary*, vol. ii, p. 145.
[2] See Cohn, A., *Shakespeare in Germany* and ' The English Comedians in Germany,' by Harris, C., in *Publications of the Modern Language Association of America*, N.S. Vol. xv, No. 3, and cf. the opening passages of chap. xii, vol. v, *ante*.

net, or tried to make their separate existence dependent on its pleasure as regards time and place of performance. The patronage of the queen and the eagerness of nobles to supply her with a favourite amusement provided the opportunity, rather than constituted the cause, of the people's new interest in the play. It is true that the royal favour first enabled the stage to stand alone, both as an art and as a business ; but, after 1591, the queen's own company having by that time lost its prestige, royal patronage as an active force dwindled until the accession of James I ; and, if the honour of playing at court was still eagerly sought, it was largely for the sake of the immunity from molestation by the city which the privy council usually extended to the companies selected. Nevertheless, the hope of playing before the queen seldom debarred a company from producing a satirical or seditious play which would attract the public.

The opposition between the city government and the privy council was, indirectly, a benefit to the art of the theatre, in that it led at once to control and to encouragement. The somewhat complicated history of the various moves on both sides shows the common council determined, with varying success, to keep players out of the city, the privy council determined to check sedition and, while fostering dramatic art, to limit the number of playhouses and companies, and each party inclined to oppose, or to neglect, the recommendations of the other. The position of players was uncertain and sometimes dangerous, as is proved by their petitions and remonstrances, and by the occasional imprisonment of offending companies. In such circumstances, only the strongest could survive with dignity or comfort. The tendency was always towards consolidation, though the experiment of the Queen's company, formed in 1583, was not to prove successful for long. The path of the Chamberlain's and the Admiral's companies was smooth and profitable on the whole, and the steady influence of royal favour supported them.

That influence became all important on the accession of James I. The position of the favoured companies, thenceforth, was assured by the issue of licences which brought them directly under royal patronage, and by the statute of March 1604, which abolished private patronage by forbidding nobles to license men to go wandering abroad. All public theatricals remained directly under royal patronage during the reigns of James I and Charles I, until the ordinance of the lords and commons of September 1642 brought them to an end.

Playwrights and players were further subject to the control of the master of the revels. Originally instituted, as it seems, by Henry VII, for the management of the finances and the material of performances at court, the office grew constantly in power. It became the duty of the master of the revels to summon the companies before him and, after seeing them perform, to select such actors and such plays as he approved and order such changes to be made in the plays as, in his opinion, should render them suitable for performance before the sovereign. At least so early as 1574, we find him empowered to examine every play that was to be played in any part of England. No play might be played or printed without his licence, and he had the power to alter, to forbid and even (as the action of Sir Henry Herbert, master of the revels under Charles I, would seem to show) to destroy, any play he found objectionable. He was entitled to charge a fee for every play he examined, and for every play which he licensed for printing, besides a fee which rose from 5s. a week in 1592 to £3 a month in 1602, for licensing each playhouse[1]; and, later in the period, we find the two leading companies paying him, first the results of two performances, and then a fixed sum in every year. Sedition, no doubt, was the offence he principally attempted to check; but profanity and immorality were also the objects of his attention.

Besides the companies of players under royal or noble patronage there were, on Elizabeth's accession, two other classes of dramatic company, both composed of boys or youths. These were the 'children' of St Paul's and of the chapel royal, and the boys of the public schools, Eton and Westminster and Merchant Taylors'[2].

The most important of the companies of men was that which was originally formed by Robert Dudley earl of Leicester, and which, in 1574, was the first to receive the royal licence. The numbers of the company mentioned in the document are five: James Burbage, John Perkyn, John Laneham, William Johnson and Robert Wilson; but two or more boys and some minor actors must, also, be supposed to have been attached to the company. When the first playhouse, the Theater, was built in 1576, it was occupied by Leicester's company, who remained there, probably, until in 1583, its place was taken by the new Queen's company, into which Burbage, Laneham and Wilson were drafted. In 1585, Leicester took his company

---

[1] Greg's *Henslowe's Diary*, vol. II, pp. 114–118.
[2] Of these boys' companies a separate account is given in the next chapter (XI) of the present volume.

abroad with him; in 1587, they were touring in England and acted at Stratford-on-Avon. Of those who believe that Shakespeare became a member of this company, some hold that he joined it during, or shortly after, this visit to his native town. In 1588, Leicester died, and, not long afterwards, the leading actors of the company that had gone abroad are found as members of the company of Ferdinando Stanley, lord Strange. The new company, which, through some kind of amalgamation with the remains of the Admiral's men, during these years included Edward Alleyn himself, played first at the Cross Keys inn in Gracechurch street, and later, in February 1592, at Philip Henslowe's playhouse, the Rose in Southwark[1]. On 3 March 1592, they produced a new play entered by Henslowe in his diary as 'harey the vj,' which is believed by many to have been Shakespeare's *King Henry VI, Part I*. If so, the conditions of the time imply that Shakespeare, by that date, was a member of the company. In April 1594, lord Strange, who had become earl of Derby in September 1593, died, and the company passed under the protection of Henry Carey, lord Hunsdon, then lord chamberlain, to be thenceforth known as the Chamberlain's servants. In the June of 1594, they played a short time with the Admiral's men at the playhouse at Newington Butts; but, in the same month, the Admiral's men, with Alleyn at their head, resumed an independent existence. In March 1595, we have the first documentary evidence that Shakespeare was a member of the company: the treasurer's accounts show that 'Wil. Kempe,' 'Wil. Shakespeare' and 'Rich. Burbage' received payment for two comedies played at court on 26 and 28 December, 1594. In 1595 or 1596, the company was at the Theater. The first lord Hunsdon died in July 1596, and the company descended to his son George Carey, second lord, who, in March 1597, himself became lord chamberlain. In July 1597, the Theater was shut up and the company possibly played at the Curtain, before moving, in 1599, into the most famous of all Elizabethan playhouses, the newly erected Globe on the Surrey bank. In this playhouse, Shakespeare was a shareholder, and at this playhouse and by this company all Shakespeare's plays written after that date were produced. In May 1603, the company received a patent, as the King's men, a title which they retained till the suppression in 1642. Thenceforward, they were members of the royal household, holding the rank, as the Queen's company had before them, of grooms of the chambers, and being entitled, every two years, to four yards of

---

[1] Greg's *Henslowe's Diary*, vol. II, pp. 45, 73.

scarlet cloth for a cloak, and a quarter of a yard of crimson velvet for a cape. Their licence permitted them to play at their usual house, the Globe, and within the liberties and freedom of any other city, university, town or borough whatsoever. In 1608[1], the Blackfriars playhouse was occupied by this company, who, thenceforth, continued to use both houses till all the playhouses were closed by the ordinance of 1642. The company's career was uneventful in the sense that it was seldom in trouble ; though, in 1601, it was under suspicion of implication in the Essex conspiracy ; in 1615, it was summoned before the privy council, in the persons of Burbage and Heminge, then its leaders, for playing in Lent ; and, in 1624, Middleton's *Game at Chesse*, which attacked the Spaniards, caused the players, at the instance of Gondomar, the Spanish ambassador, to be inhibited for a fortnight. Many lists of actors are extant to show the composition of the company, and among its principal members at various times were Shakespeare, Richard Burbage, Augustine Phillipps, John Heminge and Henry Condell (afterwards the editors of the first folio Shakespeare), Slye, Pope, William Kemp and John Lowin. Richard Burbage died in March 1619; Shakespeare retired in 1610; Condell in 1619; Pope died in 1604, and Slye in 1608. Concerning the parts played by the principal actors, information is scanty. Shakespeare is known to have acted in Ben Jonson's *Every Man in His Humour* (tradition assigns him the part of old Nowell) and *Sejanus*; Rowe, making enquiries about his acting early in the eighteenth century, 'could never meet with any further account of him this way than' (what he heard, possibly, from Betterton) 'that the top of his performance was the ghost in his own Hamlet'; Oldys records that 'one of Shakespeare's younger brothers' had seen him play Adam in *As You Like It*; and, in 1610, John Davies of Hereford states that Shakespeare 'plaid some kingly parts in sport,' which is open to the interpretation that he acted the parts of kings on the stage. Of Richard Burbage, as an actor, more is known. His name appears as early as 1592. There is good evidence that he was the original Richard III, Hamlet, Othello and Lear in Shakespeare's plays, and it is probable that he also played Romeo. It is supposed, with reason, that he was the creator of all the leading parts in the plays which Shakespeare wrote for the company; and there is evidence that he played, also, the leading parts in all the most successful of Beaumont and Fletcher's plays produced in his

[1] Wallace, *op. cit.* pp. 44–45.

lifetime, as well as in the plays of Ben Jonson produced by his company. In fact, he was the leading man, especially in tragedy, of the company—a position in which Taylor succeeded him. Malone had read in 'some tract, of which I have forgot to preserve the title' that Heminge was the original Falstaff, a part which is soon found in the hands of Lowin ; and Condell is supposed by Collier to have played Bobadill.

The Queen's company, as we have seen, was formed in 1583 at the suggestion of Sir Francis Walsingham. Its members were selected by the master of the revels, then Edmund Tilney, from the best companies of the day, including Leicester's and the earl of Warwick's, and it was licensed by the privy council. It played frequently at court between 1584 and 1591, and its public house was, probably, the Theater ; but in, or about the end of, 1592, it had left London, and it is not heard of after Easter 1594. The original members included James Burbage, John Laneham, Robert Wilson and Richard Tarlton from Leicester's company, and Laurence and John Dutton from Warwick's. James Burbage, originally a joiner by trade, had been the chief of Leicester's company. Of Laneham, as an actor, nothing is known, and Wilson is more famous as a playwright[1]. Tarlton is a famous figure in the theatrical history of the time. A clown, who took to the stage, as it appears, comparatively late in life, he achieved a popularity that long outlasted his death. His extemporal riming and his 'jiggs' were the delight of the groundlings, and he left some volumes of verse and jests, besides the play of *The Seven Deadly Sins*, the 'platt' or scheme of which survives in manuscript at Dulwich[2]. Among the authors whose plays this company acted were the university wits, Greene, Lodge and Peele; and, possibly, Marlowe's *Jew of Malta* was in their *répertoire*.

A company under the patronage of Charles second lord Howard of Effingham is found acting at court between 1576 and 1578, and probably continued to exist until 1585. Soon after Howard's appointment as lord high admiral, a company appears as the Admiral's, playing at court and evidently, also, at some innyard. The partial dispersal of this company and its loose combination with that of lord Strange have already been mentioned. In October 1592, Edward Alleyn, who is first heard of in January

---

[1] That is, supposing him to be the R. W. who wrote *The Three Ladies of London*, and *The Three Lords and Three Ladies of London*. On Wilson, see *Ward*, vol. I, p. 140, and *Fleay's English Drama*, vol. II, *s.v.* Wilson, Robert, senior.

[2] As to Tarlton, cf. *ante*, vol. V, chap. XIII, and vol. IV, p. 360 and bibl.

1583, as a member of the earl of Worcester's company, and joined, in or about 1589[1], that of the Admiral, married Joan Woodward, step-daughter of Philip Henslowe, who, in the previous spring, had put in order[2] his playhouse, the Rose in Southwark. By 1594, the Admiral's men had severed their connection with Strange's (then the Chamberlain's) company, and started independently at the Rose with Alleyn as their leading actor. Barabas, in Marlowe's *Jew of Malta*, Tamburlaine and Dr Faustus were among the parts he created, and it is probable, also, that Orlando Furioso in Greene's play of that name was in his *répertoire*. By 1592, Nashe is found comparing him with Roscius and Aesop to their disadvantage ; Ben Jonson has left a tribute to him as one 'who gave so many Poets life.' In 1597, he 'left playing': whether for good or only temporarily is not certain. There is no direct evidence that he ever acted again, and his only recorded public appearance in a similar capacity is his delivery of an address to James I at his reception by the city on 15 March 1604. In 1597, Howard was created earl of Nottingham, and his company is sometimes called by that name. Though deprived of its leading actor, it continued, with the usual interruptions, to perform at the Rose, until the building of the Fortune by Henslowe and Alleyn in 1600. This remained the company's house, except for a few years in its latest period. Early in the new reign, the company was transferred to the patronage of prince Henry, James's eldest son ; after prince Henry's death in 1612, it was taken up, for a time at any rate, by Frederick V, elector palatine, who married James's daughter Elizabeth in February 1613, and was known as the Palsgrave's company ; and, in 1632, prince Charles, afterwards Charles II, became its youthful patron. It was for this company that Marlowe wrote *The Jew of Malta* and *Dr Faustus*; and Lodge, Greene, Ben Jonson, Dekker, Chapman, Drayton and Middleton, were, at one time or another, in its employ as authors.

Besides the three of whose history a slight sketch is here given, there were, of course, many other companies of players. In spite of the privy council's restraining supervision and the enmity of the city, there were seldom less than four or five companies, besides usually two companies of boys, acting in and about London at the same time. The amount of competition, therefore, though not excessive as in the present day, was sufficient

---

[1] Greg's *Henslowe's Diary*, vol. II, p. 83.
[2] Greg, *op. cit.* vol. II, pp. 40–48.

to maintain a healthy rivalry, which may be contrasted in its results with the evils that followed upon the establishment of two, and only two, 'patent' houses after the Restoration.

When Elizabeth came to the throne, the usual places of public theatrical performance in London were certain innyards. An account written in 1628 enumerates five of these yards, where plays were publicly performed : one in Gracechurch street (the Bell), one in Bishopsgate street (the Bull), one on Ludgate Hill (the Bell Savage), one in Whitefriars and one 'nigh Paul's.' Plays were also performed at an inn in Blackfriars, and at the Cross Keys in Gracechurch street. The exact arrangement or appliances of a play in an innyard it is now impossible to establish. Whether the platform stage stood in the centre of the yard or against one end is not known ; or whether a price was charged for admission, or whether the performers depended for reward on the goodwill of the audience. The galleries which surrounded the yard on three sides were, obviously, good positions for spectators, and we may imagine a crowd standing round the stage, on three, or even on all four, sides of it, in the 'yard,' a name which was applied also to the ground level of the playhouses proper when these came to be built. A statement made by Flecknoe, in his *Short Discourse of the English Stage* (1664), that some remains of these theatres were, at that day, to be seen at the Cross Keys and the Bull, would imply, if it is to be trusted, that some kind of permanent structure was erected ; but the evidence is too slight and too late in date to be made a foundation for conjecture.

The opposition to playing in the city led to the erection, in 1576, of the first Elizabethan playhouse, the Theater. It was built by James Burbage, formerly a joiner by trade, and a member of the earl of Leicester's company. Just outside the city walls on the north lay Finsbury fields, an open holiday ground where archery, fencing, swordplay and other sports were practised, and where the trained bands drilled. At the edge of these fields, on land that had but recently belonged to the priory of Holywell, and close to the road leading from Bishopsgate to Shoreditch church (the site is now in the triangular patch between Curtain road, Holywell lane and Great Eastern street) James Burbage put up his playhouse. It was outside the city, but on the edge of a neighbourhood inhabited by noblemen and 'strangers born' (*i.e.* both foreigners and English people not of London birth and citizenship), and easily accessible from Bishopsgate, or through Cripplegate or Moorgate and across

the fields. Burbage acquired the land by lease from Giles Allen
for 21 years from 13 April 1576, and borrowed 1000 marks
(£666. 13s. 4d.) from his father-in-law, Brayne, with which to
build his playhouse.

The word 'theater' had been in use before for the platform on
which shows were given, and Burbage probably named his playhouse the Theater on that account. In shape, as we know from
several indications, as well as from the account left by de Witt,
a Dutchman who visited London, probably about two years before
its demolition, the Theater was an amphitheatre. Much has been
written on the various influences which may have combined to
cause the adoption of this shape. The Roman amphitheatres at
Dorchester, Banbury and Shrewsbury, which were still in use for
sports or dramatic exhibitions; the Cornish 'rounds,' where the
guirimir or miracle-plays were acted; the arrangement of stage and
scaffold at a London performance of miracle or morality; even the
disposition of the churches during a religious play—all these have
been called in ; while, for the internal arrangement of the building,
the innyard is supposed to be largely responsible. It seems hardly
necessary to go so far afield to account for what was the natural
and simple plan. It must be remembered that already, on the
south of the Thames, there were 'rings,' 'scaffolded about,' in
existence within which bears or bulls were baited, and fencing
or swordplay matches took place. For a spectacle which can be
watched equally well from any point, the circle is the formation
into which spectators naturally gather ; and, just as naturally,
there is one point of the circle that is left free for the convenience
of ingress and egress by the performers to and from the ring.
When James Burbage built his playhouse on the edge of Finsbury
fields, a common meeting ground for sports, the drama, though it
was rapidly absorbing these sports, had not taken their place, and
the Theater was not confined to dramatic performances. To make
his playhouse round, with the platform stage occupying a large
part of the groundspace, but touching at one point the edge of the
circle, was only to do what all constructors of amphitheatres had
done before—the easiest thing. The erection of a room or building
in which the actors could dress, and from which they could make
their entrances, would naturally follow. The stage was a movable
platform on trestles. When some sport for which it was not
wanted was to take place, it was taken to pieces and packed
away ; and Burbage's innovation, reduced to its fundamental
principle, was merely the building of a high wall all round his

ring, so that his spectators should be compelled to pay for admission. The innyard, doubtless, was responsible for the galleries round the inside of that wooden wall, which increased the housing accommodation and gave a measure of privacy to those who desired it. Neither to indoor performances at court, nor to those which may be supposed to have taken place in the courtyards of noblemen's houses, can any debt be traced in the plan of the Theater.

The lease from Giles Allen to Burbage contained a clause by which, if the lessee, within ten years of the date of the lease, spent £200 in buildings, he should be entitled to an extension of the term to 1607 and to take down the buildings he might erect. In 1585, a new lease was prepared, but not executed. Early in 1597, negotiations began again for an extension of the lease, and it appears that Allen consented to execute it, on condition that the yearly rent was raised by £10, and that the Theater should be used as a playhouse for five more years only. James Burbage died in 1597, and was succeeded in the property by his sons Richard and Cuthbert. The lease expired, and the Theater was closed. The company probably moved to the Curtain; and, in the winter of 1598—99, availing themselves of the clause in the lease, the Burbages forestalled Allen by pulling the Theater down, to erect it on the other side of the river as the Globe.

The history of the Curtain is obscure. There is evidence that the Theater was the first playhouse to be built; but the Curtain is mentioned very shortly afterwards, and its opening may be dated in 1577. It stood near Finsbury fields, not far to the south of the Theater, within the precinct of the same priory of Holywell, and took its name from Curtain close, a meadow once in the possession of the priory on which, later, was built a house called Curtain house. The name survives in Curtain road, Shoreditch. Who built it and what it cost are points yet to be discovered ; but that, like the Theater, it was round in shape and built of wood are suppositions that can hardly be controverted, even if reliance be not placed on the argument that Shakespeare's *King Henry V* (the prologue of which refers to 'this wooden O') was acted here in the summer of 1599. It would be unsafe to deduce from the word 'cockpit' in the same passage that the Curtain was unusually small. Its history was uneventful. On the closing of the Theater, the Chamberlain's company seems to have removed there, and they kept it open during the early days of the Globe. When leave was sought to open the Fortune in Cripplegate, it was granted by the privy council on the understanding that the Curtain was to be closed ; nevertheless, it remained open, and, after the accession of James I, became the home of queen Anne's (lately the earl of Worcester's) company. It is mentioned as in use in 1623, and as standing in 1627.

Little is known of the playhouse at Newington Butts. The direct evidence consists of, first, an entry in the privy council register for 1586, stating that the council had desired the lord mayor to prohibit plays in the city, and had taken the like order for the prohibiting of plays at the Theater 'and th' other places about Newington'; secondly, an undated warrant from the privy council, now referred to August 1592[1], rescinding an order which had restrained lord Strange's servants from playing at the Rose, and had enjoined them to play three days (? a week) at Newington Butts ; thirdly, an entry in the accounts of Philip Henslowe, the theatrical manager, at the head of a list of receipts from performances : 'In the name of God Amen begininge at Newington my Lord Admeralle men and my Lorde Chamberlen men, As ffolowethe 1594'; and, last, an enumeration by Howes, in his continuation of Stow's *Annals* (1631), of the London playhouses built within the last sixty years, which concludes with: 'besides one in former time at Newington Buts.' Indirect evidence has been drawn from analogy[2]. The warrant of the privy council above mentioned implies that the house had then been standing for some years. Nothing further is known of its history.

Philip Henslowe, by trade a dyer, and an acute man of business interested in undertakings of various kinds, leased an estate in the Clink liberty, Southwark, in 1585, and, in 1587, was contemplating the building upon it of a playhouse, of which, if it was built at all, we hear nothing till some years later. In his diary or book of accounts, which is one of the chief authorities for the dramatic history of the period, he is found in February 1592 sharing the receipts of lord Strange's men—nothing being said of the playhouse at which they were acting. Another entry (in a book which must be admitted to be one of the most confused accountbooks ever kept, besides having suffered from neglect and unscrupulous treatment) is a statement of the money he spent 'a bowte my playe howsse' (the Rose) 'in the yeare of oᵣ lord 1592.' Nothing is said in the account about repairs, and it bears

---

[1] Greg's *Henslowe's Diary*, vol. II, pp. 45 and 52—53. For the text, see *eund.*, *Henslowe Papers*, p. 43.

[2] By Ordish, p. 144.

all the marks of a building account; while Henslowe's want of regularity in following the Marian or the popular system of dating by the year—or, indeed, any system at all—makes the confusion still greater. It seems pretty certain, however, that 1592 here means 1592; that the account is not for building, but for extensive repairs amounting almost to rebuilding; and that the work was completed in the early part of the year, in time for lord Strange's men to occupy the house in February. This implies that the playhouse contemplated in 1587 had been built and, therefore, used[1]. In June 1594, the Rose on the Bankside in Southwark was the playhouse of the Admiral's company, with Edward Alleyn at its head. Alleyne 'left playing' in 1597; and, in 1598, the Chamberlain's company moved across the water from the Curtain, and built the Globe. The prosperity of the Rose began to decline, perhaps through unequal competition. By 1600, it had fallen into a bad state of repair, and its situation was considered inconvenient in winter. When the Admiral's company moved to the Fortune, in 1600, other companies occasionally occupied the Rose till 1603. After the accession of James I, it was used sometimes for sports. The Rose was built mainly of timber, lath and plaster, though entries in Henslowe's accounts for bricks and bricklaying seem to imply a brick foundation for the wooden walls. The stage was painted; there was a tirehouse, or actors' dressingroom, behind it, with a room over it, and a flagstaff.

Though the Blackfriars was the next playhouse to be built, it is more convenient to consider first the most important of Elizabethan playhouses, the Globe. The reason why the Chamberlain's men left the Curtain for the other side of the river is not clear. There may have been some decline in the attractiveness of Finsbury fields as a holiday ground; or the common council may have protested with effect against the usual procession through the city. Bankside was certainly a popular resort, and Southwark the district where pleasureseekers went to see bullbaiting and bearbaiting, to the public gardens and to the stews. Unable to come to terms with the landlord of the Theater, Richard and Cuthbert Burbage, as we have seen, pulled down their old playhouse and used the materials in building the Globe, which stood, as is commonly supposed, to the south-west of Paris garden and to the south of what was then Maiden lane and is now the east-to-west part

---

[1] The account of the Newington Butts house and the Rose given above follows that of Greg, *Henslowe's Diary*, vol. II, pp. 43—48 and 73. For another view, which must be held to be superseded, see Ordish, pp. 149—155.

of Park street, on ground at present occupied by a brewery[1]. This was the house, from its opening till 1642, of the Chamberlain's and King's company ; here Richard Burbage acted, and here Shakespeare's greatest plays were produced. Our knowledge of the appearance and construction of the Globe is chiefly derived from the contract for the building of the Fortune, which was to be made like it, specifically in certain details, as well as generally, with certain minor exceptions. The contract will be quoted in connection with the Fortune theatre. Shops, stews and playhouses all had signs at that time, and the earliest Globe was so called from its sign of Atlas bearing the globe on his shoulders. It appears in a drawing of 1610 as a round structure, rising above a larger round substructure of some considerable height, which, it has been suggested, enclosed a passage leading from the entrance door (or doors) to various entrances to the 'yard.' Structure and substructure were, almost certainly, of wood, resting on a foundation of bricks and cement. Its interior arrangements will be discussed later. On Tuesday 29 June 1613, a new play on the history of Henry VIII called *All is True* was being performed, and, when the king entered the masque at cardinal Wolsey's, certain 'chambers' were shot off. 'Some of the paper or other stuff,' is Sir Henry Wotton's account, 'wherewith one of them was stopped, did light on the thatch' (on the roof over the galleries). The house was burned to the ground within less than an hour. 'Yet nothing did perish but wood and straw, and a few forsaken cloaks.' Another contemporary statement says that the escape of the audience was marvellous, 'having but two narrow doors to get out.' Whether these two include the door by which the players entered the tiringhouse, or whether they were both for the use of the audience, cannot now be determined. The usual practice appears to have been to have one entrance door only to the body of the house. A contemporary ballad advises 'stage-strutters' to give up their dissipations and spend their money on tiles for the roof. This advice, or the latter part of it, seems to have been taken when the playhouse was rebuilt in the following year, more handsomely than before, its 'thatched hide' being then a thing of the past. The cost of the new playhouse was £1400, and it was the 'fayrest that was in England.' Its shape on rebuilding was octagonal outside, and, apparently, inside also.

[1] On the situation of the Globe, however, see Wallace, C. W., in *The Times* of 2 October 1909, p. 9, col. 4, and subsequent correspondence in *The Times* and *The Athenæum.*

It has been supposed that, after the King's company began to act at the Blackfriars, the Globe became their summer playhouse, the Blackfriars being used in winter. Further evidence is needed before this question can be determined, though we have seen that the situation of the Rose was considered inconvenient in winter; the Globe is found in use in February.

In February 1596, James Burbage, already in difficulties with the landlord of the Theater, bought of the executor of Sir Thomas Cawarden, late master of the revels, for £600, the freehold of a complicated collection of rooms, great and small, stairs, cellars and yards (including 'seven great upper rooms' all on one floor, formerly one great and entire room), which lay in Blackfriars, near the Pipe office, adjoining the house of Sir George Cary. The buildings, which had been in the occupation of Cawarden, were in the old precinct of the 'Blackfriars preachers,' or Dominican monks, and had formed part of their monastic dwelling. Blackfriars, in those days, was a popular resort, not, like Finsbury fields, for the people, but for nobles and gentry, who went there to play tennis; there were also a few aristocratic houses on a small portion of the site of the monastery. In making up his mind to establish a play-house, in defiance of the law, within the city walls, Burbage must have counted for support less on the people than on the nobility; and, to some extent, the proceeding is an argument in favour of the view that royal and aristocratic support was the chief encouragement of the drama. These seven rooms Burbage turned into an indoor or 'private' playhouse, spending on it a larger sum than had hitherto been spent on any playhouse in London, and constructing a building which recent discoveries have shown to be much larger than was commonly supposed[1]. The term 'private' does not imply that the public were excluded; the corporation, in an order for the suppression of the Blackfriars in 1619, refer to it explicitly as a 'publique playhowse.' Burbage's intention, however, was, doubtless, to construct a playhouse which should attract aristocratic patrons by greater seclusion and comfort, the auditorium being completely roofed over, and, perhaps (though this is thorny ground), by a stage which might reproduce to some extent the scenic completeness attained in the indoor performances at court. In November 1596, the inhabitants petitioned against the establishment of a playhouse in their midst, but ineffectually. In July 1597, letters patent were issued to Nathaniel Giles, master

[1] See, in *The Times*, 11 September 1906, p. 6, cols. 1 and 2, 'Old Blackfriars Theatre,' by Wallace, C. W., and *eund.*, *Children of the Chapel*, chap. I.

of the chapel children, to impress boys for the Queen's service; and, about this time, the chapel children are found occupying Burbage's new playhouse. In 1600, Richard Burbage leased the Blackfriars to one Henry Evans for 21 years at a yearly rent of £40, and Evans continued the children's performances. Later, came trouble over Evans's too drastic exercise of the powers granted to Giles under the patent; the playhouse ceased to pay; the lease was assigned; the chapel children, who, after James's accession, had been reconstituted as the children of queen Anne's revels, lost the royal patronage after their performance of *Eastward Hoe* in 1605, and were again obnoxious in their production of *Biron*. In August 1608, Richard Burbage took back the lease to Evans, and, a little later, the King's company began to use the house themselves. In January 1619, the corporation tried to close the Blackfriars, but the privy council stepped in and confirmed its use; and the King's company continued to play there without interruption till 1642.

The move of the Chamberlain's men to Bankside left the north bank of the Thames without any strong theatrical attraction, and Henslowe and Alleyn endeavoured (not without strenuous but ineffectual opposition from local and municipal authorities) to cater for the population of that part of the town by building the Fortune playhouse off Golding (now Golden) lane in the parish of St Giles without Cripplegate. The extant contract for the building, made by Henslowe and Alleyn with Peter Street, carpenter, is so interesting, in the light it throws on the material and structure of the Globe and the Fortune, and, indirectly, of Elizabethan playhouses in general, that part of it deserves quoting *verbatim*.

The frame of the saide howse to be sett square and to conteine ffowerscore foote of lawfull assize everye waie square wthoutt and fiftie five foote of like assize square everye waie wthin wth a good suer and stronge foundacōn of pyles brick lyme and sand bothe wthout & wthin to be wroughte one foote of assize att the leiste above the grounde And the saide fframe to conteine Three Stories in heighth The first or lower Storie to Conteine Twelve foote of lawfull assize in heighth The second Storie Eleaven foote of lawfull assize in heigth And the Third or upper Storie to conteine Nyne foote of lawfull assize in height all which Stories shall conteine Twelve foote and a halfe of lawfull assize in breadth througheoute besides a Juttey forwardes in either of the saide Twoe upper Stories of Tenne ynches of lawfull assize with ffower convenient divisions for gentlemens roomes and other sufficient and convenient divisions for Twoe pennie roomes wth necessarie Seates to be placed and sett Aswell in those roomes as througheoute all the rest of the galleries of the saide howse and wth suchelike steares Conveyances & divisions wthoute & wthin as are made & Contryved in and to the late erected Plaiehowse On the Banck in the saide pishe of Ste Savio^{r}s Called the Globe Wth a Stadge and Tyreinge howse to be made erected & settup wthin the saide fframe

wth a shadowe or cover over the saide Stadge. .... And wch Stadge shall conteine in length ffortie and Three foote of lawfull assize and in breadth to
extende to the middle of the yarde of the saide howse The same Stadge to be
paled in belowe wth good stronge and sufficyent newe oken bourdes And likewise the lower Storie of the saide fframe wthinside, and the same lower storie
to be alsoe laide over and fenced wth stronge yron pykes And the saide Stadge
to be in all other proporcōns Contryved and fashioned like unto the Stadge of
the saide Plaie howse Called the Globe Wth convenient windowes and lightes
glazed to the saide Tyreinge howse And the saide fframe Stadge and Steare-
cases to be covered wth Tyle and to have a sufficient gutter of lead to Carrie &
convey the water frome the Coveringe of the saide Stadge to fall backwardes
And also all the saide fframe and the Stairecases thereof to be sufficyently
enclosed wthoute wth lathe lyme & haire and the gentlemens roomes and Twoe
pennie roomes to be seeled wth lathe lyme & haire and all the fflowers of the
saide Galleries Stories and Stadge to be bourded wth good & sufficyent newe
deale bourdes of the whole thicknes wheare need shalbe and the saide howse
and other thinges beforemencōed to be made & doen To be in all other
Contrivitions Conveyances fashions thinge and thinges effected finished and
doen accordinge to the manner and fashion of the saide howse Called the
Globe Saveinge only that all the princypall and maine postes of the saide
fframe and Stadge forwarde shalbe square and wroughte palasterwise wth
carved proporcōns Called Satiers to be placed & sett on the Topp of every of
the same postes[1].

The contract is dated 8 January 1599/1600, and the work, which
was to cost £440, was to be finished by 25 July. The actual cost
worked out at £520, and the playhouse appears to have been
opened in November or December 1600, by the Admiral's men, who
occupied it throughout the remainder of the period. It is noticeable that the outside was square. The Fortune was burned down
in 1621, and all the wardrobe and playbooks were destroyed; it
was rebuilt, some two years later, round in shape and of brick.
It appears, in its later years, to have become a popular house,
rather despised by the more refined.

The Rose fell out of use in 1603, and the importance of the
Blackfriars and the Fortune robbed Bankside of much of the
patronage of playgoers. When the Globe was burned in 1613, it
seems to have been feared that the King's men would move back
to the north of the river; and a petition was addressed to the
king by the company of Watermen, praying that the players might
not be allowed to have a playhouse in London or Middlesex within
five miles of the city—which petition was not granted.

In 1589, Francis Langley, who held a small office at court,
purchased the manor of Paris garden. In November 1594, we
find the lord mayor protesting against his intention to build a
playhouse on his property. The project was not dismissed; but
it is not certain when the Swan playhouse was built. It may

---

[1] Transcribed from Greg, *Henslowe Papers*, pp. 5 and 6.

have been open in 1596. The Swan was used for plays, at any rate until 1620, and was still standing, though in a dilapidated state, in 1632. Dramatically, its history is unimportant; but the house has acquired notoriety from the fact that a contemporary drawing, or copy of a drawing, of its interior—the earliest view known of the interior of a playhouse—is in existence. Probably in or about the summer of 1596, John de Witt, a Dutchman, visited London. (It may be noted here that much of our information concerning the London playhouses of the day comes from foreigners, to whom they were objects of great interest and surprise.) The drawing in question was discovered in the library at Utrecht, in the commonplace book of another Dutchman, Arend von Buchell, accompanied by a descriptive passage headed *Ex observationibus Londinensibus Johannis De Witt.* The passage, with the drawing, may have been copied from a now lost letter or journal written by de Witt. The drawing, a rough sketch, must be used, therefore, with caution; but so many of its details correspond with the details of the Swan found in the contract for the building of the Hope, which was to be like it in many respects, that it may be taken as giving a rough idea of the general plan of an Elizabethan public playhouse[1]. The drawing is made from a point which, roughly speaking, would correspond to the position of a man sitting in the middle of the front row of the upper circle of a large modern theatre, or the gallery of a small one.

The main features of the playhouse are clear enough. It is a tall, round (or, possibly, oval)[2] structure some fifty feet high[3], with three roofed galleries, divided into 'rooms,' or boxes, running right round it and interrupted only by the tirehouse behind the stage. The yard is open to the sky; there are no seats in it, and the audience can stand close to the stage on three sides, finding it

[1] All reproductions of this drawing (*e.g.* in Ordish, *Early London Theatres*, p. 265) having beneath them the words *Ex observationibus Londinensibus Johannis De Witt*, taken from the manuscript, are made, not from the original, but from the engraving published by Gaedertz in his *Zur Kenntnis der altenglischen Bühne*, Bremen, 1888. For a full-sized reproduction direct from the original, see Wheatley, *On a contemporary drawing of the Interior of the Swan Theatre*, N. S. S. 1888; and for a reproduction on a reduced scale, *The Quarterly Review*, April 1908, facing p. 450. The engraving is fairly accurate; but the lines indicating the part of the circumference of the playhouse furthest from the tire-house have been omitted, to make room for the misplaced words mentioned above.

[2] That is, round, or oval, inside. In Vischer, *View of London*, 1610, it appears twelve-sided. See, also, the 1627 map of the manor of old Paris garden in Furnivall's *Harrison's England*, vol. II, facing p. i.

[3] For a calculation of the measurements, see Wheatley, *u.s.*

probably between waist-high and shoulder-high. The description accompanying the drawing states that the building would hold *tres mille homines in sedilibus*—three thousand persons in the *sedilia* or galleries. Calculations have been made[1] to prove that, if de Witt is rightly reported and meant what he said, and if the number of rows in the three galleries be taken to be eleven, a house two thirds of the size of the present Drury Lane theatre would be required to afford sitting accommodation for that number of spectators, if every seat in the entire circle was full; while the open yard would give standing room to a great many more. The number 3000, moreover, is not so surprising as appears at first sight; and that the Swan theatre should provide room for $1\frac{1}{2}$ per cent. of the total population of London and Westminster does not seem fantastic, when it is remembered that, according to John Taylor, three or four thousand persons daily crossed the river to Bankside in the days when the Globe, Rose and Swan were all open as playhouses, and bearbaiting, also, was in progress. A difficulty is caused by de Witt's statement that the Swan was built of flint-stones heaped together and supported by wooden columns, painted so like marble as to deceive the shrewdest eye. In no extant specification, not even that of the Hope, is there any mention of stone, and another foreigner, who visited London two years later, expressly states that all the playhouses on Bankside were of wood—sometimes, as we know from other sources[2], plastered over. Various suggestions have been made for getting round de Witt's statement. It is simpler to believe him correct and to suppose that, in this feature (as, perhaps, in another to be dealt with later) the Swan was exceptional.

The extant contract with the builder[3] shows that the Hope on Bankside, which had been a bear-house, was newly built as a playhouse by Henslowe and Jacob Meade in 1613. Possibly, the burning of the Globe in that year induced Henslowe to try for the Bankside public once more. The house was occupied by the lady Elizabeth's and the Prince's companies, and Ben Jonson's *Bartholomew Fayre*, which was acted there in 1614, informs us that it was a dirty and evil-smelling place. In 1616, apparently, it fell out of use as a playhouse. As the contract states, it was of the same size as the Swan, and the roof over the galleries was tiled, not thatched. Vischer's *View of London*

[1] In Wheatley, *u.s.* But see Greg, *Henslowe's Diary*, vol. II, p. 134, note 1.
[2] *E.g.*, the contract for the Fortune: *ante*, pp. 258—9.
[3] Printed in Greg, *Henslowe Papers*, pp. 19 f.

(1616) shows it octagonal outside ; but Hollar (1647) makes it round. It was of wood, with a brick foundation.

Three other playhouses belonging to this period must be mentioned. The Red Bull stood at the upper end of St John street, Clerkenwell, and seems to have been opened about 1599. In 1633, Prynne's *Histrio-Mastix* mentions it as recently rebuilt and enlarged. It was occupied early in James I's reign by the Queen's company, and remained in use, till 1642, by this and other companies. Between 1642 and 1660, several attempts were made to act there ; it was opened at the restoration by Rhodes, formerly prompter at the Blackfriars ; Samuel Pepys saw a play wretchedly performed to a poor house there, in 1661; and, by 1663, it was abandoned.

The Cockpit was a 'private' playhouse in Drury Lane, and seems to have been erected on the site of a cockpit in or about 1615. It was opened by the lady Elizabeth's company, which, in 1625, passed to queen Henrietta; and it remained in use till 1642. After 1660, it was occupied by the Duke's company under Sir William D'Avenant, till they moved to the new theatre in Portugal row, Lincoln's Inn fields in 1662. Its second name, the Phoenix, probably came into use when it had been restored after the sacking of it by the 'prentices in 1617.

The Salisbury court or Whitefriars playhouse was built in 1629 near the hall of the old Whitefriars monastery, which had previously, at any rate since 1610, been used for plays. It was occupied first by the children of the King's revels, and then by the Queen's. It was a 'private' playhouse, and was in use for a brief time after the restoration.

The capital difference between the pre-rebellion public stage and the modern stage lies in the fact that the former was a platform stage, while the latter is a picture stage. The modern audience sees the drama as a moving picture in a frame, or as in a room with one wall, and only one, knocked out. / The Elizabethan audience surrounded the stage on three sides, partly encroaching even on the fourth / they saw the drama as a scene enacted in their midst and—in the case of the groundlings, the spectators standing in the yard—very close to them. / It is practically impossible for performers on the stage to compose groups that shall show an equally artistic shape on three sides at once, and the use of daylight prevented many of the visual effects that have been practised since the time of Garrick. The eye was appealed to less forcibly than the ear. The drama was rhetorical, and the actor more of a rhetorician than he is today, since the audience looked to his enunciation of the poet's words for much of the pleasure that the picture stage supplies through the eye. 'Spectacular' plays, such as *England's Joy*, produced at the Swan in 1603, were not unknown; spectacle was aimed at and enjoyed; but word, voice and action were the chief elements in the drama. And authors, being free from the modern playwright's necessity to lead up to a 'situation,' a stage picture, on which the curtain may fall sharply at the close of each act, made the play, rather than each division of it, the artistic whole.

The stage begins with the bare platform on trestles, which could be taken away when the space was needed for sports that did not require it. Later, the space between the platform and the ground is found concealed with boarding, and a low rail runs round the edge of the stage. The rudest performance, whether in innyard or 'ring,' supposes some place where actors can dress and wait concealed, and whence they may have access to the platform when their turn comes. This gives opportunity for a background—a matter, however, of small importance in a stage open on three sides—and also develops into the tirehouse. Questions as to the nature and use of this background and as to the development of the tirehouse into a somewhat elaborate structure lie at the root of all the difficulties in the restoration of an idea of the Elizabethan stage.

It is impossible not to turn back with curiosity to the drawing of the Swan theatre, the earliest extant view of the stage of the period. The platform it shows is supported near the front on two rough, solid beams, concealed by no 'paling.' Halfway, or rather more than halfway, towards the back, two very solid turned pillars, resting on heavy square bases and with capitals above, stand on the stage, at a distance from each other of nearly its whole breadth, and support the front edge of a pentroof, which seems to project over the stage to a much smaller distance than the position of the pillars would indicate. This discrepancy is but one of many difficulties raised by the drawing. Behind the pillars, under the pentroof and right at the back of the stage, rises a wall with two large arched doors, each about halfway between the centre of the back wall and its outer extremity. On the wall, between the doors, the draughtsman has written *mimorum aedes*, indicating that this is the 'actors' house.' At some distance above the tops of the doors, the wall is broken by a gallery, in which sit what may be musicians, or actors taking part in the play, but what certainly seem to be spectators ; and, above the gallery again, the wall rises to the point where the upper edge of the pentroof starts.   Above the level of the pentroof, there appears another story, of equal or nearly equal width with the wall of the tirehouse.   There are two windows in it, facing the auditorium, and, in a little doorway open in the side, on the (spectator's) right, a man, either holding a flag or blowing a trumpet, stands on the upper edge of the pentroof (which must be supposed to turn the corner of the building on both sides). The roof of this upper story, apparently, is thatched, and from the summit on the (spectator's) right flies the flag bearing the sign of the house, a swan.   Near the front of the stage, an actor in woman's dress is sitting on a bench; behind the bench stands another, also in woman's dress; while, from the corner on the (spectator's) left, an actor, bearing a long spear or staff, is striding along the front of the stage towards the centre.   There are no hangings of any kind visible in any part of the drawing.

Some features in the drawing may be recognised from other descriptions as correct—the existence of the tirehouse, the turret, the waving flag showing that it is a play day, the blowing of the trumpet showing that the play is about to begin (though the draughtsman has shown the house as empty).   Further examination raises a number of difficulties.

In the first place, this stage is not movable; or, if it can be removed, those two heavy pillars supporting the small pentroof must rest, not on the visible bases on the stage, but on the ground below.   If the stage is moved, the pillars will be in the way of any exhibition that is taking place, and it is difficult to imagine that these pretentious bases are shams.   We are forced to conclude that the stage of the Swan was not movable.   Again, how far are these pillars intended to be from the back wall of the stage, the front wall of the tirehouse ?   The drawing shows them at the very least a third of the way down the stage; yet the perspective is so faulty that the pentroof seems to project at the most a few feet forward from the wall.   Granted that the pillars are right and the pentroof wrong, the latter still does not correspond at all closely with the 'heavens' or roof, which, in the Hope, as we know from the contract, was to extend all over the stage, and which is known to have existed in other playhouses of the period.   The matter is trifling at first sight, but is of importance because, mainly on the position of the pillars in this drawing, a whole theory of the production of plays has been formed[1]. To clear the ground, it may be said at once that there is no occurrence before 1640 of anything which can fairly be considered evidence of a front curtain on a public stage (though, doubtless, it was in use at court and university performances), and that the theory of the common use of a front curtain is no longer tenable. On the other hand, there is ample evidence that, somewhere on the stage, there were hangings of silk, or wool, or 'painted cloth,' sometimes, apparently, when tragedies were acted, of black. Of hangings painted in perspective to represent the scene of the play, there is no mention in a public or private playhouse, though they were in use at court and university performances. We hear of actors peeping through before the play begins, and of an impatient audience throwing things at the hangings. Stage directions printed in the playbooks, though rendered an untrustworthy guide by the impossibility of telling whether they were drawn up by the author or manager, or by the printer or some other unauthorised person, and whether they applied to performance at court, in a public playhouse, a private playhouse, or a provincial hall or innyard, seem to show that the public stage of the day required at least three divisions: namely, the front part of the stage; a back part, commonly used for interiors, which could be disclosed by the drawing of curtains, and which, when disclosed, could, of course, absorb the front part and occupy the entire stage; and, thirdly, a place above to serve for upper chambers, balconies like Juliet's, galleries, towers and so forth. Arguing from this and from the position of the pillars in the drawing of the stage of the Swan, the theory referred to supposes a regular course of 'alternation' throughout an entire play, much like that which was followed by each act of an old-fashioned melodrama, in which the front scene was used while the back scene was being 'set,' the author's duty, in the days of Elizabeth as in our own, being to contrive a scene of some sort, which the plot might or might not require, to fill up the time needed by the 'tire-men' or sceneshifters. Accordingly, the theory mentioned supposes a curtain or 'traverse' hung between the pillars shown in the drawing of the Swan, that is, at about one third, or half, of the depth[2] of the stage, which should conceal

---

[1] Chiefly by Brodmeier, C., *Die Shakespeare-Bühne nach den alten Bühnenanweisungen*, Weimar, 1904. It has been exhaustively criticised by Reynolds, G. F., *Some principles of Elizabethan staging*, Chicago, 1905.

[2] Some confusion might be avoided if the word 'depth' were consistently used for the measurement from the front of the stage to the back, and 'width' for that from side to side.

from spectators the preparations for the next scene going on behind it.

The attempt to work out this 'alternation' theory by dividing the extant plays of the period into front and back scenes has not been successful[1]. A further difficulty arises from the fact that not all the spectators were in front of the stage. A traverse between the pillars would not conceal what was going on behind it from people on either side of the stage. To block out their view, further traverses at right angles to that between the pillars would be necessary. The result, inevitably, would be to conceal not only the back scene from them, but a great deal of the front scene, too, on which action would be in progress. An even greater difficulty attends the suggestion that, since there are notable instances where it would be absurd for actors to enter the front scene by the only available entrance, that is, through the traverse, there must have been hangings all along both sides of the stage so that actors might enter from the sides. It is to be noted, too, that this theory supposes the upper stage or balcony to be concealed by the traverse. This would mean that all scenes in which the balcony was occupied must be back scenes, which is not easy to establish, and makes it impossible that the audience should ever have used the balcony; while three extant illustrations of the stage—the title-pages to Richards's *Messallina* (1640) and Alabaster's *Roxana* (1632), and the picture of a 'droll' on the stage of the Red Bull which forms the frontispiece to Kirkman's *The Wits* (1673)—distinctly show the traverse hanging from below the balcony, while the first and the last show a separate curtain for the balcony itself.

This theory seems to lose sight of the simple origin of the stage —a temporary platform erected in the midst of a crowd and surrounded by spectators regarding it from nearly all the four sides— and to err from over-anxiety to credit an Elizabethan audience with a susceptibility to the incongruous. The very naïve tradition of the miracles and early moralities, in which two or more scenes, sometimes representing localities hundreds of miles apart, were on the stage simultaneously, had not died out; and the audience may be fairly supposed to have been no more offended by the conventions of dramatic space than is a modern audience by those of dramatic

[1] See Reynolds, *op. cit.*, and Wegener, R., *Die Bühneneinrichtung des Shakespeareschen Theaters*, Halle, 1907. For the practical defects of Brodmeier's proposed reconstruction, see Archer, W., in *The Quarterly Review*, no. 415, April 1908. The 'Elizabethan' stage reconstructed at Harvard in 1904 was planned on the alternation theory. For an illustration and description, see 'Hamlet on an Elizabethan Stage,' by Baker, G. P., *Shakesp. Jahrbuch*, vol. XLI (1905), pp. 296 ff.

time, which allow an imaginary half-hour to pass in an actual five minutes. In his *Apologie for Poetrie* (written about 1580—1), Sidney writes:

> For where the stage should alwaies represent but one place,... there is ... many places, inartificially imagined. But if it be so in *Gorboduck*, how much more in al the rest, where you shal have *Asia* of the one side, and *Affrick* of the other, and so many other under-kingdoms, that the Player, when he commeth in, must ever begin with telling where he is, or els the tale wil not be conceived?

His words are borne out by numerous cases in extant plays, where two or more places are imagined to be on the stage at the same time; and it scarcely needs the evidence of ascertainable instances to prove that an Elizabethan audience would not have the least objection to seeing properties (such as the bench in the drawing of the Swan) brought on the stage without concealment and left there after they had served their turn, though it is extremely likely that susceptibility to the incongruous grew, as time went on, under the influence of Jonson and the classical playwrights. In spite of this, it is abundantly clear that there was a back stage, which could be revealed by drawing a curtain.

The fact is significant that, just as the Hope, though planned on the lines of the Swan, was to be built of wood, not flint, so, in the contract with the builder, it is directly stated that he 'shall also builde the Heavens *all over* the saide stage to be borne or carryed *without any postes or supporters to be fixed or sett uppon the saide stage.*' It is possible, therefore, that the pillars of the Swan were as the drawing shows them, and that the pentroof covered half or nearly half the stage; but that the plan was found inconvenient, was confined to the Swan and was discarded by Henslowe when he built the Hope. In that case, the Swan may have had the front and back scenes divided by the lofty traverse, and have used them as suggested by the theory summarised above; but it is at least unfortunate that the draughtsman should have hit on a playhouse the arrangement of which was unique and discredited.

The construction may well have been different in different houses; and there are several ways in which the necessary back stage may be reconstructed and the requirements of stage directions fulfilled, without imposing a strict 'alternation theory' or incurring the difficulties referred to above. According to one scheme[1], the pillars supporting the 'heavens' (if pillars there be) play no part in the division of the stage. The stage proper runs

---

[1] This account follows, in the main, that suggested by Chambers, E. K., 'The Stage of the Globe,' in the *Stratford-on-Avon Shakespeare*, vol. x, pp. 351 f.

right back to the wall of the tirehouse. The gallery either does not project, or projects only very slightly, in front of that wall. From the level of its floor, hangings fall to the stage, occupying, not the whole width of the stage, but most, or the whole, of that part of it which lies between the two doors, the doors being left uncovered. For this purpose, it is necessary to suppose the doors further apart than they are in the drawing of the Swan. These hangings, when drawn back, reveal the lower chamber of the tirehouse in use as part of the stage, possibly with a floor raised slightly above the stage level. Here, the strolling players in *Hamlet* would perform, and here, Henry VIII would sit in his closet. The room would be big enough to hold a fair number of people; in the Fortune, for instance, an inner chamber 20 feet wide would still leave 11½ feet on either side for the doors. And the scene could always overflow on the stage proper. And, since a third entrance is frequently mentioned and almost always necessary, a door in the back of this chamber must also be supposed, large enough to admit of 'properties' such as beds, banqueting tables and so forth being brought through it. The stage proper is thus entirely free of hangings, except those in front of the chamber under the tirehouse; and the fact that this chamber must have been low and dark seems of less importance when it is remembered that plays were acted in unencumbered daylight. There were hangings, also, in front of the balcony above. The theory is not without its difficulties, the chief of which are that many of the audience must have been unable, from their position in the house, to see into the inner chamber, and that, when there were actors or spectators in the balcony, they, too, would have been unable to see into it[1]. This view, to some extent, is borne out by the title-pages of *Messallina* and *Roxana* mentioned above; but, as neither of these shows the whole width of the stage, no certain conclusions can be drawn from them. Another scheme makes the gallery project some feet from the wall of the tirehouse, with the traverse hanging from its floor and concealing all the doors when it is drawn. There is, thus, a kind of corridor stage behind the stage proper ; but, once more, any actors or spectators there may be in the gallery will be unable to see what is taking place on the back stage, and it is also necessary to imagine that every scene in which doors are mentioned must have been a scene in which

---

[1] Wegener's suggestion (*op. cit.*), that there was a kind of *ekkyklema* on which deathbeds and the like could be wheeled over the back stage and brought forward, does not seem to be supported by sufficient evidence, though such a contrivance would certainly have been useful.

the back stage was used. To obviate these difficulties, a suggestion has recently been put forward[1] that the two side doors were not flat in the wall of the tirehouse but set in walls slanting towards it, while the traverse before the corridor hangs further up the stage (*i.e.* nearer the back wall) and, when drawn, conceals only the third, central door. The same suggestion curves the gallery forward at each side, at an angle corresponding with that of the walls containing the side doors, so that its occupants might see the back stage, and even provides semicircular projections, or bays, in order to make quite sure[2].

The space beneath the stage was sometimes 'paled in' by boarding, which, though not shown in the drawing of the Swan, must have been a common feature, because many instances occur of actors (especially when playing ghosts) appearing and disappearing through trapdoors, and of dead bodies being thrown down through them. We read of flames and even of a 'brave arbour' appearing from below. If the stage was strewn with rushes, as it seems to have been, the use of the trap must, sometimes, have been difficult; and, in any plays where the trapdoor was needed, the 'matting' on the stage, which Sir Henry Wotton mentions, apparently as an unusual thing, in his account of the burning of the Globe in 1613, must have been out of the question. There was also, in some playhouses at all events, an appliance by which players could be let down from above, as if descending from heaven, though it appears to have been more difficult to draw them up again. Whether the appliance worked from the balcony or the 'heavens' is not ascertained.

Painted scenery on the public stage there was none, though the mention in an inventory of the Admiral's men's properties, compiled by Henslowe in 1598, of 'the clothe of the Sone and Mone,' certainly seems to imply some attempt of this nature, and though the figures of men and animals frequently appeared in the woven or painted hangings. But there is abundant evidence that the properties were many and elaborate. Houses, beds, rocks, ramparts, wells, property horses, and even structures serving as shops, are mentioned as being brought on the stage, and there is strong evidence for the solid

---

[1] By Archer, *u.s.* See, in particular, the reproduction of a model by an architect, Walter H. Godfrey, of a stage according to the specification of the Fortune, illustrating Archer's article. The model itself was on view in the *Exposition théâtrale*, Paris, 1908.

[2] One objection to this arrangement is that it would make the drawing of the traverse (which we know the gallery to have had) a very complicated affair.

representation of woods and separate trees[1]. Though there was no attempt at creating a picture, considerable care and expense were incurred in the provision of properties. Yet these attempts at realism, for which an Elizabethan audience, according to its lights, had as keen a desire as a modern audience, long went hand in hand with the simplest devices. The names of the places were fastened over the doors, especially in cases where the stage represented two scenes at once; and where the presence of spectators on the stage reduced the space, the properties for which there was not room were sometimes indicated by nuncupative cards, a practice which prevailed, at this time, also in France. Such cards, however, must be distinguished from the 'title-boards,' which, in private theatres, were fastened up, or held up by the speaker of the prologue, to give the title of the play.

Performances at private playhouses[2] may be taken to have approximated to those at universities, inns of court and royal residences, in aiming at the taste of more refined audiences than did the public playhouse—though too much stress should not be laid on the supposition. Noblemen, ambassadors and other great people went to the public playhouses; but, while it is on record that Elizabeth went to the Blackfriars, she is not known to have ever visited the Globe. Private playhouses were completely roofed over, and, though performances took place there in the afternoons as in public playhouses, they were, occasionally at all events, performed in artificial light, the windows being covered over. Instead of the 'yard' filled with 'understanding' spectators or 'groundlings,' there was a pit, with seats.

The evidence shows that a performance at court was very different from a performance in a public or private playhouse. It was for this honour, ostensibly, that the company worked all the year, and, when the master of the revels had selected, after competition, the companies and the plays they should perform, the author was often called upon to revise his play; and the performance ended with prayers for the queen. Elizabeth's accounts show an annual outlay for airing and furbishing up the court stock of costumes and appliances, besides considerable expense for wires, lights, properties and mechanical contrivances[3]. The old *domus* of the miracles survive in the 'painted houses' of the players at

[1] On properties, see Reynolds, *op. cit.*, and his article, 'Trees on the stage of Shakespeare' in *Modern Philology*, vol. v, p. 153.

[2] On this question, see Wallace, *op. cit.*

[3] All the evidence has been collected by Feuillerat, A., *Documents relating to the Office of the Revels.*

court; and there can be little question that painted scenery was not unknown[1]. Under James I, great advances were achieved by the arts of stage decoration and production through the masques written by Ben Jonson and mounted by Inigo Jones; but the public stage was little affected, if at all. Not until the return of D'Avenant and other adherents of Charles I and II from France and Italy, to be followed by Betterton's mission to Paris—not until the drama became more nearly dependent on court favour than it had been made even by the exclusive royal patronage of companies on the accession of James I, did the public stage make a corresponding advance; and then it drew its inspiration from other sources. The main appeal to the eye in public playhouses before the rebellion was made by the costumes of actors. Now and then, as in miracles, a rudimentary attempt at dramatic propriety in costume was made. For the most part, players wore the ordinary dress of the day, some, even of the male characters, appearing in wigs, and some—especially, it would seem, in cases of disguise and of minor players acting more than one part—having their faces concealed by masks. Makeshift and errors of taste were not unknown even in London playhouses; but Henslowe's extant accounts show that the costumes were splendid and costly—velvet, gold lace, copper lace and other rich materials being freely used. The speaker of the prologue appeared in a black cloak.

The creation of an atmosphere for the play (which is the aim that modern stage production is endeavouring, often in strangely inartistic fashion, to achieve by scenery) was left to the descriptive words of the poet, the voice of the actor and the imagination of the audience. The audience of those days must certainly be supposed to have been more susceptible to the message to the ear, and less to deficiencies in the message to the eye, than that of our own time; but, while taking into account the larger part played by the Elizabethan drama in intellectual life, we must be careful not to credit the spectators with a much greater earnestness in the playhouse. Abundant evidence proves that—what with the throng of groundlings in the yard, intent mainly on the fighting and the broader humour; what with the gallants making their way through the tirehouse and lying or sitting on stools on the stage[2], smoking the pipes which their pages filled for them, and intent on displaying themselves rather than on listening to the play; what with the

---

[1] For distinct evidence of scene shifting in a university performance, see Nichols: *Progresses of King James I*, vol. I, p. 538.

[2] On this subject, see Wallace, *op. cit.* chap. XI.

women of the town and their admirers in the galleries ; what with here and there a Bobadill or Tucca ready to brawl at any moment —the Elizabethan audience, whether in a public or in a private playhouse, was not the rapt body of enthusiasts which later times have been tempted to imagine it. It included, however, Walsinghams and Southamptons, refined and intellectual admirers of the drama, and their numbers must have exceeded those of the Sidneys who scoffed and of the Northbrookes who railed. It is impossible to reconstruct past acting ; but it is safe to conclude that the players whose duty it was to embody the creations of Shakespeare, Marlowe, Beaumont and Fletcher, to the satisfaction of the best intellects of the reigns of Elizabeth and James, with practically no scenic illusion to aid them, must have cultivated to a high degree the arts both of declamation and of expressing character. The improvement in the drama consequent on the coming of university wits probably called forth a corresponding improvement in the actor's art, and there is some evidence that a decline in acting followed or accompanied the decline of the drama in the seventeenth century. That declamation was often attended by its besetting sin of rant is recorded in Hamlet's advice to the players (*Hamlet*, act III, sc. 2) as well as in various passages of other contemporary writers, which imply that the actors of the Fortune (in its later days), the Red Bull and the Cockpit were great offenders in this respect, and that the evil grew during the latter half of the period. The player's response, however : 'I hope we have reform'd that indifferently with us, Sir,' coupled with the admonition of Hamlet, is pretty good evidence that, at the Globe, declamation was not allowed to degenerate. As to the quality of the character acting, the elegy on Richard Burbage shows how vivid this was at its best; though, of course, it is impossible to tell how deeply, even under Shakespeare's guidance, Burbage penetrated into the significance of the characters he played. The evidence of Flecknoe, who, in his *Short Discourse of the English Stage* (1664) praises Burbage for a 'delightful Proteus' that maintained his character throughout, 'even in the tyring-house,' must represent a tradition and an ideal rather than the statement of an eyewitness. That the female characters were all played in the playhouses by boys, youths, or young men, generally implies, to modern minds, incongruity and poor acting ; but the popularity of boys' companies goes to show that boys, when thoroughly trained, can do better than we give them credit for today[1]. The spectacle,

---

[1] See Wallace, *op. cit.* chaps. IV and IX; and cf. Raleigh, W., *Shakespeare* (1907), pp. 119–120.

at any rate, must have been pleasanter than that of women playing male parts, and 'squeaking Cleopatra' may have boyed her greatness with better artistic effect than some actresses have achieved.

Much of the inequality in the plays of Shakespeare, as well as of their popularity during his lifetime, can be explained by the consideration that he wrote for a mixed audience, and succeeded in pleasing all[1]. The appeal of his plays to the best intellects of the time needs no showing. For the more intelligent of the common spectators, in whose lives the drama filled the place now occupied by the lending library, the press and, to some extent, the pulpit, there was not only the strong story but the expression of comment and criticism on many aspects of life and on facts of the varied world, some of them only remotely connected with the actual plot. For lovers of sport and action, there were exhibitions of swordplay, wrestling and so forth, which the drama had woven into its own texture, besides battles, murders and other incidents which, as St Évremond noticed a century later, the English public liked to see on the stage. For all amateurs of wit, there were exhibitions or contests in punning and jesting— another form of entertainment which the drama, to a great extent, absorbed into itself—ranging from the keen wordplay and literary parody to the gross joke or hint for the groundlings. That Shakespeare would willingly have dispensed with the latter, we know from the passage in *Hamlet* referred to above. The 'gag' of the clown must have been the more annoying because it was the common practice to conclude a performance, and sometimes to interrupt it, with a 'jig,' performed by Tarlton, Kemp, Armin, or some other 'fool'—an indispensable member of every company—answering to the 'laughable farce' which followed the tragedy until days within the memory of living men. To the possible attractions of the playhouse must be added music, played both during and between the acts. That at Blackfriars was especially esteemed, as was, naturally, that of the children's companies, and public theatres attempted to emulate their success in this matter. Where the 'noise,' or orchestra, sat is not certain; it was not till after the Restoration that it was placed between the stage and the audience, and, in the period under notice, it probably occupied in some playhouses the space marked *orchestra* in the drawing of the Swan, perhaps on both sides of the stage.

[1] On this question, see Bridges, R., in the *Stratford-on-Avon Shakespeare*, vol. x, and contrast Bradley, A. C., in *Oxford Lectures on Poetry*, pp. 361 ff.

The occurrence of songs in plays is well known; and we read that in the country, at any rate, the music was more popular than the play itself.

Another fact to be noticed is the intimate connection between author and company. It was not only actor-authors, like Shakespeare and Nathan Field, who attached themselves to one company and wrote their plays for it during life or a term of years. The tradition that Hamlet was made 'fat' because Burbage was fat, and the still less trustworthy tradition that Iago was written for a comedian, with opportunities introduced into the part for making the audience laugh, do not go so far to prove the effect of this practice on Shakespeare's work as does the consideration that any sensible playwright writing for a certain company will take care that the parts are adapted to its members. Authors often worked very fast, plays being written sometimes in the short space of a fortnight; and they looked for very little reward. The Admiral's company seems to have ordered and produced more new plays than the Chamberlain's and King's company[1], whose plays, possibly, could bear more frequent repetition; and they only paid sums varying from £5 to £8 for a play until 1602, though as much as £25 seems to have been obtainable later in the period under notice. The author seems to have received a fee for altering his play for production at court; but, though the company received a regular fee of £6. 13s. 4d., with a present of £3. 6s. 8d. for each play performed at court in London, and double those sums when the performance entailed a journey to Hampton court or Windsor, the author cannot be proved to have had a share of this reward. He was present, no doubt, when the company assembled at an inn to read and consider his new play over refreshments paid for by the company, and he had a right to free admission to the playhouse—a privilege which Ben Jonson used to abuse by sitting in the gallery and making wry faces at the actors' delivery of his lines. The author received a fee for altering his play for a revival, 5s. for a prologue and epilogue and, sometimes, a *bonus* at the first performance; and there is good evidence that, in certain cases, if not regularly, the author had a 'benefit,' as later times would have phrased it, on the second or third day of performance. If his play was published, he could gain 40s. by dedicating it to a patron.

---

[1] So Fleay, *Stage*, p. 117, says that he has 'not been able to trace...more than four new plays produced by them [the Chamberlain's company] in any one year.' Greg, *Henslowe's Diary*, vol. II, p. 112, n. 1, suggests that the preservation of Henslowe's and the loss of the King's company's papers may partly account for the disproportion.

The play was bought by the company, though there are scattered cases in which individual persons exercised the rights of ownership; the manuscripts formed part of the stock owned in shares by the company, who could sell the play, if they wished, to another company, but, naturally, disliked printing it, lest a rival company should produce it unlawfully. For the same reason, the author was not encouraged to print his play; the company purchased the copyright, and it was considered sharp practice for the author to sell it also to a bookseller. Many plays crept into print in a mangled form through some surreptitious sale by a member of the company, or through stenographers, who attended the playhouse to take down what they could of a successful play.

The bulk of the profits on a play went, not to the author or authors, but to the company. Finance was mainly conducted on the share system. One share or more might be purchased, or might be allotted instead of salary; and, in the second half of the period, shares were clearly regarded as property that could be sold or devised by will. The proceeds of each performance, after certain deductions had been made, were divided among the members of the company according to their holdings of shares. In the case of Henslowe's company, at the Hope, those deductions, at one time, in 1614, included the money received for admission to the galleries and through the tiringhouse, half of the sum going to Henslowe and Meade as owners of the theatre, and the other half to Henslowe on account of advances made by him for the stock of costumes, which was also the company's property. Henslowe has been generally accused of harshness and injustice in his dealings with the companies under his control. Pawnbroker and moneylender, he acted, doubtless, to some extent, on the principle put into his mouth by his players in their *Articles of Grievance and Oppression* of 1615: 'should these fellowes Come out of my debt, I should have noe rule with them.' Excessive value placed upon clothes and other property which he purchased for them, bonds for repayment and the not infrequent 'breaking,' or disbanding, of companies which protested, kept his actors in a state of subjection. The case may have been different with the Chamberlain's and King's company; but we are ignorant of its internal arrangements during nearly the whole period. The recent discovery[1] of documents setting forth the company's financial arrangements during the years 1598 to 1615

[1] Made by Wallace, C. W., and communicated by him to *The Times* of 2 and 4 October 1909, p. 9. This discovery, with others recently made by the same investigator, will be dealt with at length in *Shakespeare, The Globe and the Blackfriars*, a work now being prepared by him for publication.

is entitled to rank among the most important contributions to what is known in this field.   In 1599, a lease of the site of the Globe was granted for 31 years, one half of the interest in the property to the brothers Burbage, who paid one half the whole annual rent of £14. 10s. 0d., the other half to Shakespeare, Heminge, Phillipps, Pope and Kemp, who paid the other half of the rent in equal shares, *i.e.* £1. 9s. 0d. each.   In 1610, Shakespeare and the four other holders of tenths admitted Condell to an interest, their shares thus becoming twelfths ; and, in 1612, these twelfths were further divided into fourteenths by the admission of William Osteler.   This arrangement lasted till 1630, each share, it appears, being assigned on the death of its owner to the Burbages or the survivor of them, to be reassigned to some new actor.   In the Blackfriars, Richard Burbage held one seventh share, leaving one seventh each to Shakespeare, Heminge, Cuthbert Burbage, Condell, Slye and Thomas Evans, each of the seven paying an annual rental of £5. 14s. 4d.—a total of £40. 0s. 4d.   This arrangement also lasted till 1630.   In the documents in the suit brought by Thomasin Osteler against her father Heminge, the purchase value of one seventh of the Blackfriars is estimated at £300, and the purchase value of one-fourteenth of the Globe at the same sum ; and a year's profits on each are estimated—no doubt somewhat in excess, for purposes of the suit—at £300.   In return for this, each actor-sharer not only paid his share of the cost of building and keeping up the playhouse and of the incidental expenses—wardrobe, servants and so forth—but gave his services as actor ; and the later passing of the shares by sale or demise into the hands of persons other than actors led to dispute and litigation.   The almost equally important discovery by Halliwell-Phillipps of papers concerning a dispute of this nature among sharers in the Globe and Blackfriars playhouses in 1635 had thrown a light on the later finances of those houses.   The company was then divided into three classes : housekeepers, sharers and hired men and boys.   The housekeepers' shares in the Globe were sixteen in number, and, at the date of the dispute, they were held as follows : three and a half by Cuthbert Burbage, son of James and brother of Richard, three and a half by the widow of Richard Burbage, now Mrs Robinson, two by the widow of Henry Condell, three by the actor John Shankes and two each by the actors Taylor and Lowin. There were thus, among the housekeepers, three actors holding seven shares, all of which they had purchased, and the remaining nine shares were owned by 'neither actors, nor his Majesties servants,' but the heirs or legatees of actors.   The Blackfriars was divided into eight shares, three being in the hands of Cuthbert Burbage and the widows of Richard Burbage and Condell, the remaining five in the hands of Shankes, who held two, and Taylor, Lowin and Underwood (another actor), who had one each. The housekeepers had to pay the rent of the two houses (which they put down at £100 yearly, while their opponents reckon it as £65, less a sum of between £20 and £30 for a sub-let portion of the premises), and to keep them in repair ; they received one half of all the money taken except at the outer doors, that is to say, half of all the fees for galleries, 'rooms' and admission through the tirehouse, for which a fee was charged, and for stools on the stage, which had to be hired. The shareholders, *i.e.* actors who were not housekeepers, had, in earlier years, received money taken at the outer doors only; by 1635, they divide exactly with the house-keepers the fees for galleries, and so forth, and have to deduct out of their earnings about £3 a day for wages to hired men and boys, music, lights and the like, and also sums spent for costumes and for purchase of plays. Considerable though their profits seem to have been, certain shareholders felt that too much money went into the hands of the housekeepers and that the existing dis-tribution among the actor-housekeepers was unfair, and their petition to the lord chamberlain for a compulsory sale to them-selves of certain shares was, apparently, granted.

The price of shares, doubtless, varied with the company, the circumstances and the date. In 1593, Francis Henslowe appears to have paid only £15 for a share in the Queen's company on the eve of a provincial tour, and, two years later, the same actor paid £9 for a half share in another company. The values of shares in the Globe and the Blackfriars in 1615 have been mentioned above. In 1633, Shankes paid £350 for one housekeepers' share in the Blackfriars for a term of five years, and two housekeepers' shares in the Globe for a term of one year. The pleadings in the dispute referred to state that actors who were not housekeepers received £180 each in the year 1634, while the housekeepers' shares appear to have brought in something over £100 each share. A writer in 1643 speaks of housekeepers sharing as much as 30*s.* a performance. The sums are not surprising when we remember that, to the price of admission (which varied between one penny at a public playhouse to six at a private) paid to the single 'gatherer' at the entrance door, were added the extra fees, amount-ing sometimes to 2*s.* 6*d.*, demanded by the extra 'gatherers' within, for the use of the various parts of the galleries. Hired men were engaged by contract either by the company or the manager,

and received a weekly salary, varying from 5s. to 8s. Boys were
bought as apprentices by individual players, for sums varying
from £2 to something like £15, their masters, presumably, also
maintaining them ; and, in some cases, boys appear to have been
bought and maintained by the company. Strict regulations were
made for the behaviour of all members of the company, shareholders and hired men alike, and fines were exacted for lateness,
drunkenness, absence from rehearsal and other offences.

A man who was at once a sharing actor and a playwright, like
Shakespeare, clearly had it in his power to make fairly large sums
of money[1] ; and Alleyn, who had other sources of income, was in
an even more fortunate position. No surprise need be felt at
Shakespeare's purchase of New Place, nor at Alleyn's heavy outlay
on property at Dulwich and his renowned benevolence. The
fortunate and respectable actor—even though he held no office
under the crown like Alleyn's—was received into good society
and was befriended and admired by the best intellects of his
time ; he lived a comfortable and secure existence, and, perhaps, indulged in the purchase of a coat of arms. Henry Condell
was a sidesman of the parish of St Mary's, Aldermanbury, in
1606 : his respectability is unimpeachable. But the besetting sins
of the player—luxury, extravagance and intemperate living—for
which Hazlitt found generous excuses in later years, seem to
have existed then as ever. We read much of the player's love
of fine clothes and display. And there can be no doubt that the
frequent interruptions caused by the plague, the deterrent action
of such managers as Henslowe and the notorious uncertainty of
theatrical affairs, resulted in much poverty and distress among
lesser actors and lesser companies. Those on tour, especially,
suffered hardships, being forced to pawn their wardrobe, to 'pad
the hoof' instead of riding from town to town and to beg, instead
of play, for their keep. The extremes of the profession were as
far apart then as now ; but the age of Elizabeth and James undoubtedly raised it as a whole into respect as well as popularity ;
and the outspoken envy of those—by no means all of puritanical
bent—who railed at the pride and display of actors was the natural
result of the advance which the period witnessed. During the
reign of Charles, the greater prevalence of the plague, the shadow
of coming troubles and the deterioration of the drama itself caused
something of a decline, and the rebellion brought all to a close.

[1] Wallace, *u.s.*, calculates Shakespeare's yearly profits from the Globe as never
exceeding £300, and a similar amount from the Blackfriars.

CHAPTER XI

THE CHILDREN OF THE CHAPEL ROYAL
AND THEIR MASTERS

THE Chapel Royal and its relations to the history of drama
in England form an extremely puzzling and interesting subject
of enquiry. The origin of the chapel is lost in unrecorded
antiquity, the date of its earliest histrionic efforts is uncertain
and the records of its later activity are woefully incomplete. But
it entered the histrionic field early; it was, if we may trust the
extant records, a pioneer in the production of some important
kinds of plays; some of its authors seem to have set fashions
in dramatic composition; and Shakespeare himself honoured its
rivalry with one of the few clear notices of things contemporary
that we have from his pen.

Of the membership and organisation of the chapel in the
earliest times, we have not any systematic account; but, under
Edward IV, according to *Liber Niger Domus Regis*, it consisted
of a dean, twenty-four chaplains, two yeomen, eight children,
a master of song and a master of the grammar school. Later,
a sub-dean was added, the number of boys was increased to
twelve, and there were various increases in the number of chaplains,
or gentlemen of the chapel, to say nothing of the long list of
probationers awaiting vacancies among the gentlemen; but these
changes affected the size and not the functions of the institution.
It has always been an organisation primarily for the celebration
of divine service in the royal household, and its functions in its
earliest years, as during the last three centuries, were, perhaps,
limited strictly to this primary purpose.

But under the Tudor sovereigns, if not earlier, notable unofficial
additions were made to its functions. Both the gentlemen and
the children took part, frequently if not regularly, in the pageants,
masques and plays produced at Christmas and on other festal

occasions. During the reigns of Henry VII and Henry VIII, the gentlemen seem to have figured in pageants and plays nearly as often as the children; but their histrionic career seems to have ceased early, perhaps because even then such frivolous perform- ances seemed inappropriate to gentlemen 'endowed,' as *Liber Niger* specifies, 'with virtues morolle and specikative, as of the musicke, shewinge in descante, eloquent in readinge, suffytyente in organes playinge.' It is very probable, indeed, that the histrionic activity of the gentlemen began with morality plays and pageants presenting moral allegories, and ceased soon after the drama and other amusements of the court took a more secular turn. The histrionic career of the children—possibly because they were children—continued longer. In 1569, to be sure, they were attacked in a pamphlet entitled *The Children of the Chapel Stript and Whipt*:

Even in her majesties chappel do these pretty upstart youthes profane the Lordes Day by the lascivious writhing of their tender limbs, and gorgeous decking of their apparell, in feigning bawdie fables gathered from the idolatrous heathen poets;

but it was not until the following century that the children ceased to act. It is with the children, therefore, rather than the gentlemen, that we are here concerned.

The earliest record relating to the children and their master[1] that has been found is the commission (12 July 1440)

to the king's clerk, Master John Croucher, dean of the Chapel within the king's household, to take throughout England such and so many boys as he or his deputies shall see to be fit and able to serve God and the King in the said Royal Chapel.

We have here no mention of anyone specially delegated for the training and supervision of the boys, and it is possible, though

---

[1] In his introduction to *The Old Cheque Book of the Chapel Royal*, Rimbault says: 'The earliest facts on record relating to the "King's Chapel" are contained in the *Liber Niger Domus Regis*, a manuscript of the time of Edward IV'; and this statement has been taken by later writers to mean that we have no earlier notice of the organisation. There exists, however, in the Patent Rolls, a long series of earlier notices, beginning with the mention of 'Thomas de Lynton, Dean of the Chapel of the King's Household,' 20 August 1380. Among the most important of these are: the notice of John Boor as dean in 1389; the acquittance (10 March 1403) 'to Richard Kyngeston, late dean of the King's Chapel within the household, who received divers jewels, vestments, ..., for the same from John Boor, late Dean of the Chapel of Richard II by indenture, and has delivered them to Richard Prentys, now dean...'; various licences to Prentys in 1406 and 1412; and the commission, 20 November 1433, to distribute among the clerks who had been in the chapel of Henry V the sum of £200, bequeathed to them in his will.

unlikely, that there was no such officer, and that there had been no children in the chapel choir before this time, or, at least, no special official recognition of them. These suppositions, however, may be thought to derive a certain support from the next two entries : 4 November 1444, a

grant to John Plummer, one of the clerks of the King's Chapel, for the exhibition of eight boys of the Chapel and for his reward, of 40 marks yearly, from Michaelmas last, so long as he have the keeping of the said boys or others in their place, from the ulnage of woollen cloth for sale and from a moiety of the forfeiture thereof in the town and suburbs of Bristol ;

24 February 1445, a

grant, during good behaviour, to the king's serjeant John Plummer, one of the clerks of the Chapel, for his daily labours in the teaching and rule of the king's boys of the Chapel, of the said teaching, rule and governance.

This grant was surrendered 30 May 1446 for another of the same tenor. In any event, the first master of the children was not, as is commonly supposed, Henry Abyndon, for he was certainly preceded by John Plummer.

From 1465, the series of masters can be made out with tolerable completeness and certainty. On 2 July 1465, there was a

grant to the king's servitor Henry Abyndon of 40 marks yearly from Michaelmas last from the issues of the county of Wilts for the provision of clothing and other necessary apparel of the boys of the Chapel of the king's household and for their instruction and governance, so long as he shall have the said provision, instruction and governance ;

and this grant was renewed 14 February 1471. It is not yet ascertained when Henry Abyndon (or Abingdon) ceased to be master; but, on 6 February 1479, a

grant was made to Gilbert Banaster of 40 marks yearly from the petty custom in the port of London and ports and places adjacent for the maintenance, instruction and governance of the boys of the Chapel of the household from Michaelmas last, on which day he undertook these, so long as he shall have the same.

When Banaster's successor was appointed does not appear; but this successor was almost certainly not William Cornish, as is commonly supposed. Cornish, as we shall see, was the successor of William Newark[1]. Newark was granted a corrody from the priory of St Mary, Thetford, at some date prior to 23 November

[1] It is, of course, very unlikely that Cornish preceded Newark, was replaced by him and then succeeded him. That Cornish was master in 1493 seems to be one of Collier's unjustified inferences.

1480; nevertheless, in the document of this date he is not called master of the children but 'one of the gentlemen of the King's Chapel,' and in the grant (6 April 1485) of a yearly rent of £20 from the king's manor of Bletchingley, county Surrey, he is spoken of only as 'the King's servant.' It is, however, clear that he was the predecessor of Cornish as master of the children. On 23 May 1509, he was appointed 'gentleman of the Chapel in the royal household and master of the boys of the Chapel, during pleasure.' As this was scarcely more than a month after the king's accession, and as he was already a gentleman of the chapel in 1480, the appointment, doubtless, was only a renewal of one made in the preceding reign. On 12 November 1509, he is mentioned as lately deceased; but the appointment of his successor seems, for some reason, to have been delayed for several years, for among the 'Fees and Annuities Paid by the King in 1516' occurs a record of £26. 13s. 4d. to 'W. Cornyshe, Master of the Children of the Chapel, *Vice* W. Newark, during pleasure,' and it seems improbable that Newark would have been mentioned if any master had come between him and Cornish, or if Cornish had held the appointment since Newark's death[1]. Cornish is mentioned as late deceased on 7 November 1524, and he seems to have been succeeded, though not immediately, by William Crane, who had long been one of the gentlemen of the chapel. Crane's appointment as master of the children is dated 12 May 1526. His immediate successor was Richard Bower. The official appointment was made 31 October 1545, but it was to date from 30 June 1545, 'since which time he has by the king's command exercised the office.' Whether Crane was then dead or not, is not certain. In the 'Augmentations,' a William Crane, apparently the person here in question, is recorded as receiving his annuity on 8 May and 16 October 1545, and there is a later record of payment of an annuity out of St Edmondesburye to a William Crane in 1546. It seems, however, probable that there were two William Cranes, whose names appear in the records of these years, as there seems also to have been a Richard Bowyer (*alias* Styrley, or Strylly, or Strelley) who has sometimes been confused with Richard Bower, gentleman of the chapel and master of the children. According to the entry in *The Old Cheque Book of the Chapel Royal*, Bower died 26 July 1563; but Stow

[1] Of Clement Adams, who is said (*Babees Boke*, p. lxxvi) to have been master of the children in 1516, no such record can be found. John Melyonek and Philip Van Wilder are also sometimes given as masters, in 1484 and 1550 respectively; but they were merely commissioned to take up singers for the chapel.

gives 1561 as the year, and this seems supported by the fact that, on 4 December 1561, a commission to take up children for the chapel was issued to Richard Edwards, who is expressly called master of the children. Edwards, perhaps the most famous of the masters, did not long enjoy his office, as he died 31 October 1566. He was succeeded by William Hunnis (erroneously called Thomas and John in contemporary documents), who served until his death, 6 June 1597. With Nathaniel Giles, who was appointed master three days later, our interest in the masters of the children ceases, for he was the last under whom the boys were permitted to act. Not only did the boys who acted cease, at the accession of James, to be called children of the chapel and become children of the queen's revels; but, when in 1626, Giles was commissioned to take up boys for the king's chapel, it was expressly provided

that none of the said Choristers or Children of the Chappell, soe to be taken by force of this commission, shal be used or imployed as Comedians, or Stage Players, ... for that it is not fitt or desent that such as should sing the praises of God Almighty should be trained or imployed in such lascivious and prophane exercises.

The importance of the children of the chapel in dramatic history is due, in part, to their histrionic success and, in part, to the success of some of their masters, and other authors who wrote for them, in dramatic composition. Of the work of the earlier masters, we, of course, know very little. Gilbert Banaster is commonly credited with dramatic composition on the basis of Warton's remark that he 'wrote in English verse the *Miracle of saint Thomas*, in the year 1467'; but a *miracle* is not necessarily a miracle-play. William Cornish seems, however, from the entries in the 'Household Book of Henry VIII,' to have composed some of the plays produced by the boys under his direction. If the 'story of Troylous and Pandor,' performed by him and the children before the king at Eltham, Christmas 1515, was written by him, he may be regarded as the earliest known dramatiser of romantic fiction. Ward suggests that this may have been merely a pageant; but there is no evidence that it was customary to use similar stories as the subjects of pageants, though, undoubtedly, as the list of costumes and the number of actors—fifteen—indicate, this play was highly spectacular. But pageants usually bore such titles as 'the Golldyn Arber in the Arche yerd of Plesyer' (13 February 1511), 'Dangerus Fortrees' (9 March 1511), or 'the Pavyllyon un [on] the Plas Parlos' (6 January 1515), and the 'accounts' usually contain elaborate descriptions of the pageant features. Moreover, it should be remembered that, not long after this, plays on similar subjects were not uncommon, though, unfortunately, only one of them has been preserved to us. It seems, therefore, only fair to ascribe more importance to this record than has usually been done, and to regard Cornish as a pioneer in the production, if not in the composition, of romantic drama. The interlude called 'the triumpe of Love and Bewte,' 'wryten and presentyd by Mayster Cornyshe and oothers of the Chappell... and the chyldern of the sayd Chapell,' Christmas 1514, was of a more conventional character, and can hardly have been more than an allegorical pageant, with words and music. It should, perhaps, be mentioned that Cornish had the devising of the pageants on Sunday night at the Field of the Cloth of Gold.

Whether William Crane was an author is unknown. He was certainly a man of much business; in 1523, letters of protection were granted him as gentleman of the king's household, *alias* gentleman of the chapel, *alias* comptroller of the petty custom of the port of London, *alias*, of London, draper; and, at various times, he was granted permission to import woad and wine and to export double beer, and he was appointed to furnish five of the king's ships. He seems to have been a favourite of the king, and received many grants in addition to his salary and allowances.

Richard Bower's claim to rank as a dramatic author depends, so far as we know, upon his identification with the 'R. B.' who wrote *Apius and Virginia*[1]. This, though by no means certain, seems highly probable. We have no earlier copy of the play than that printed in 1575; but it was entered in the Stationers' register in 1567/8, and seems, from the allusion to the sweating sickness, to have been written not later than 1551, the last year, according to Creighton, of the occurrence of this epidemic in England. Whether written by Bower or not, the play obviously belongs to a group of plays which show certain similarities in motives and technique. The group includes, besides this play, Edwards's *Damon and Pithias* (and, probably, also his lost *Palamon and Arcyte*), Fulwell's *Like wil to like*, Pikeryng's *Horestes*, Wapull's *The Tyde taryeth no Man*, Preston's *Cambises*, the anonymous *Common Conditions*, and *Syr Clyomon and Syr Clamydes* and, perhaps, some others. One has only to read these plays in succession to be struck with their mutual resemblances. Most notable, perhaps, are the large amount of attention given in them to 'stage business' and the provision of action; the use, in several of them, of unrelated

[1] As to this play, cf. *ante*, vol. v, chap. IV, pp. 63—65.

comic scenes for the same purpose; the similarity of the rustic characters which appear in most of them; the use, in most of them, of a Vice who 'plays with both hands,' inciting to evil or folly and then aiding in its punishment; the curious warnings to the audience to beware of 'Cosin Cutpurse'; and the no less curious allusions to the 'trump of fame.' These characteristics are less marked in the work of Edwards than in the other plays; but this may be due to his greater independence and originality. The group would seem to have originated with *Apius and Virginia*. If this be the case, we may attribute the existence of the group to the prestige of the children of the chapel and their masters.

In regard to one of these plays, a word may be permitted, although it does not strictly belong to this chapter. We know from the title-page of *Cambises*[1], that it was written by Thomas Preston, and it is universally assumed that this was the Thomas Preston who gained the favour of Elizabeth on her visit to Cambridge in 1564. Commentators on *A Midsummer Night's Dream* have not only recognised that Shakespeare ridiculed this play, but have also seen in the lamentations of Flute over Bottom's loss of sixpence a day for life an allusion to the pension given by the queen to Preston on her memorable visit. The fact need not be insisted upon that sixpence a day is a different thing from the £20 a year granted to Preston[2], but it seems not amiss to point out that Preston's two Latin orations were the prime basis of the queen's pension and choice of him as her scholar. Nor does it seem very probable that the distinguished scholar, who was fellow of King's college in 1556, B.A. in 1557, M.A. in 1561 (and incorporated M.A. at Oxford in 1566) and proctor of his college in 1565, who was directed by the authorities in 1572 to study civil law and, four years later, to proceed to the degree of LL.D. and who became master of Trinity hall in 1584, should have published, in 1569 and 1570, *Cambises* and the two ballads entitled:

A geleflower gentle or swete mary golde
Where in the frutes of terannye you may beholde

and

A Lamentation from Rome how the Pope doth bewayle
The Rebelles in England cannot prevayle.

Surely the Preston of Cambridge would not have published these things; or, if he had, neither he nor his publishers would have failed to print his academic titles.

[1] As to *Cambises*, see *ante*, vol. v, chap. iv, pp. 63—65.
[2] It is, perhaps, more to the point to observe that 6*d*. a day was exactly the wages of the yeoman of the queen's revels, while the master received only £10 a year.

So much is known of Richard Edwards and William Hunnis that only the briefest notice of them can be given in the space available here[1]. It may suffice to say that Edwards was a university man (as Richard Bower may also have been) and Hunnis obtained, in some way, the equivalent of a university training. Both were celebrated by contemporary writers as authors of dramatic and of non-dramatic works, the fame of Edwards lasting till 1598, though his death occurred in 1566. Non-dramatic writings from the pens of both have been preserved; of their dramatic compositions, we have only Edwards's *Damon and Pithias*, though chance has preserved for us a very detailed account of his other known play, *Palamon and Arcyte*, produced at Oxford in 1566[2]. Mrs Stopes has suggested that Hunnis was the author of the *Tragedie of the King of Scots*, produced by the children in 1567, the first recorded performance after his succession to the mastership, and of several others of the plays produced under his supervision. Among these were *Narcissus*, 1571, the *History of Loyaltie and Bewtie*, 1579, the *History of Alucius*, 1579, and a satirical *Comedie or Morrall devised on A game of the Cardes*, 1582. Probable as the suggestion is, we have no means of verifying it. But the accounts of Edwards's *Palamon* and Hunnis's *Narcissus* indicate that, as stage managers, they carried on the traditions of the group of plays discussed above. The two passages are so interesting in themselves and so important in their bearing upon the history of the stage that they may be quoted briefly:

In the said play [*Palamon and Arcyte*] was acted a cry of hounds in the Quadrant, upon the train of a fox in the hunting of Theseus, with which the young scholars, who stood in the windows, were so much taken (supposing it was real), that they cried out, 'Now, now!—there, there!—he's caught, he's caught!' All which the Queen merrily beholding, said, 'O, excellent! these boys, in very troth, are ready to leap out of the windows, to follow the hounds.' This part, it seems, being repeated before certain courtiers, in the lodgings of Mr Robert Marbeck, one of the Canons of Christ Church, by the players in their gowns (for they were all Scholars that acted) before the Queen came to Oxford, was by them so well liked, that they said it far surpassed *Damon and Pithias*, than which they thought nothing could be better. Likewise some said, that if the author did any more before his death, he would run mad: but this comedy was the last he made; for he died a few months after. In the acting of the said play, there was a good part performed by the lady Amelia, who, for gathering her flowers prettily in a garden then represented, and singing sweetly in the time of March, received eight angels for a gracious

[1] Good accounts of Edwards have long been accessible, and Mrs C. C. Stopes has published two notable articles on Hunnis. (See bibliography.)

[2] As to *Damon and Pithias*, cf. *ante*, vol. v, chap. IV, and, as to this play and *Palamon and Arcyte*, chap. XII of the present volume. The university drama *Narcissus* mentioned in the same chapter is, of course, a different play from that mentioned in the text.

reward by her Majesty's command. By whom that part was acted I know not, unless by Peter Carew, the pretty boy before mentioned.

A scene in *Narcissus* may have been suggested by this play, as the *History of Loyaltie and Bewtie* may, possibly, have been suggested by Cornish's *Triumpe of Love and Bewte*, of 1515. The revels accounts for 1571—2 contain the following:

> John Tryce for mony to him due for Leashes, & Doghookes, with staves, & other necessaries: by him provyded for the hunters that made the crye after the fox (let loose in the Coorte) with theier howndes, hornes, and hallowing, in the playe of narcisses. which crye was made, of purpose even as the woordes then in utteraunce, & the parte then played, did Requier.... John Izarde for mony to him due for his device in counterfeting Thunder & Lightning in the playe of Narcisses.

For reasons which will soon appear, it seems improbable that Nathaniel Giles, the last of the masters with whom we are concerned, composed any plays for production by the children. But the *répertoire* of the boys was probably not confined, even in the early years of their histrionic career, to the plays written by their masters. Unfortunately, the early records are too scanty and too indefinite to permit of very positive statements on this point. As early, however, as 1584, two of the most distinguished authors of the time had written for them. John Lyly's *Campaspe* and *Sapho and Phao* were played before the queen by the children of the chapel in conjunction with the children of Paul's before this date, and another play by the same author, *Love's Metamorphosis*, originally written for the children of Paul's, was transferred to the chapel boys at some date before its publication in 1601. One of the most interesting of the plays of George Peele, and, in the opinion of some critics, his best play, *The Araygnement of Paris*, also bears upon the title-page of the first edition (1584) the statement that it had been 'presented before the Queenes Majestie by the Children of her Chappell.' Fleay, indeed, assigns the presentation of it to 5 February 1581, and the same writer gives 1581 as the date for *Campaspe* and 1582 as the date for *Sapho and Phao*. These dates seem probable; but we are not here concerned with their accuracy, as the essential fact is that both Lyly and Peele wrote for the children of the chapel. That Greene wrote anything for them is unlikely, but the *Tragedie of Dido Queene of Carthage*, by Marlowe and Nashe, is stated on the title-page to have been played by them, and it is highly probable that it was they who played Nashe's *Pleasant Comedie, called Summers last will and Testament* at Croydon in September 1592. The play alluded to here as having been presented by the same company in the preceding summer was, according to one of Fleay's conjectures, Marlowe and Nashe's *Dido*; according to another, the anonymous *Warres of Cyrus*, published in 1600; we have no means of knowing whether it was either.

To one unfamiliar with the stage history of the time these records might seem inadequate evidence for the brilliant and influential histrionic career ascribed to the children of the chapel. But those who know how scanty the records are will recognise that no other company in these early years presents greater claims to having exercised a real leadership in the drama. The children of Paul's were, indeed, at one time served by Lyly as dramatist[1]; but he began with the children of the chapel, who seem, in fact, to have been pioneers in many important features of both dramatic and histrionic development. That there were other companies of boys—notably those of Paul's and those of Windsor, those of Westminster school and those of Merchant Taylors'—and that many companies of men players performed at court and in public, does not detract from their primacy in these early years.

The opinion expressed above that Nathaniel Giles, who, as will be seen, became master in 1597, wrote nothing for the chapel boys is a mere conjecture, but is supported by two facts: first, that not long after he became master he seems to have allowed other men to use his commission to procure boys for the chapel to provide a company of professional child actors; and that, from this time onward, the actual choir boys of the chapel do not seem to have taken any part in the presentation of plays at court or in public. Since the professional company was supplied with plays by professional dramatists, and the boys under the immediate personal care of Giles did not produce plays, it is very improbable that he wrote any.

On 9 June 1597, Nathaniel Giles, bachelor of music and master of the children of St George's chapel, Windsor, became master of the children of the Chapel Royal, in succession to William Hunnis. By a privy seal of 3 July, he was authorised to take up boys for the service of the chapel. No essentially new provision appears in this commission. Giles is authorised to take up 'suche

---

[1] That Lyly ever occupied the official position of vice-master (*i.e.* assistant master) of Paul's, seems a solemn inference from a jesting satire. Harvey says he 'played the Vicemaster of Poules and the Foolemaster of the Theater.' Was there, then, a Foolemaster of the Theater? That neither epithet need be taken seriously is indicated by the additional 'sometime the fiddlesticke of Oxford, now the very bable of London.' So far as we know, there was no such officer as vice-master of Paul's. 'Vice,' in 'Vicemaster,' is, doubtless, the counterpart of 'Foole,' in 'Foolemaster.'

and so many children as he or his sufficient Deputie shall thinke meete,' and to provide 'sufficient lodging for him and the sayd Children, when they for our service shall remove to any place or places'; but the former clause is repeated from earlier commissions, and the latter would never have seemed anything more than a more explicit expression of a similar clause in previous commissions but for the events which ensued. At some unknown date after the issue of this commission, James Robinson and Henry Evans joined with Giles in exploiting the commission. They took up more boys than were needed for the chapel choir, lodged them in Blackfriars and established a regular theatrical company of the children of the chapel.

The highest interest attaches to this professional company of boy actors, but it is at present impossible to determine exactly when their career began. The Blackfriars property was purchased from Sir William More on 4 February 1596 by James Burbage, apparently because of its suitability for a playhouse. In November of the same year, the inhabitants of Blackfriars petitioned the privy council against Burbage, declaring that he 'is now altering it and meaneth very shortly to convert and turne the same into a common playhouse.' How effective this petition was in hindering or delaying the projected playhouse we have no means of knowing[1]. Burbage died early in the following year, and the next unmistakable evidence we have in regard to the Blackfriars playhouse is that, on 2 September 1600, Richard Burbage, son of James, leased it for twenty-one years to one Henry Evans; but it is certain that, before this date, it had been used as a playhouse by the children of the chapel, and that Evans was already interested in the company. In testimony given in a lawsuit in 1612, Richard Burbage says:

true yt is that this defendant, consideringe with himselfe that, except the said Evans could erect and keepe a companye of Playinge boyes and others to playe playes and interludes in the said Playhouse *in such sort as before tyme had bene there used*, etc.;

and Evans speaks of the playhouse as 'then or late in the tenure or occupacion of this defendant' (*i.e.* Evans himself). It is commonly held that the children of the chapel were playing there as early as the end of 1598, and this is probably true.

The evidence we have seems to indicate that Giles was only

---

[1] The order for the suppression of the Blackfriars playhouse, dated 21 January 1619, states, however, that 'their honors then (*i.e.* in 1596) forbad the use of the said house for playes.'

passively interested in the project, and that someone else—perhaps Henry Evans—first saw the great possibilities which lay in procuring, under the liberal terms of Giles's commission, a company of boy actors and exploiting them in the private playhouse of the Blackfriars. After about a year and a half of experience, we may suppose, Evans decided to take a long lease of the property, and this was effected on 2 September 1600. It was not very long, however, before he got into trouble about taking up boys. On an ill-fated Saturday, 13 December 1600, James Robinson, acting as deputy for Giles and as agent for Evans, seized Thomas Clifton, a thirteen-year-old boy, as he was on his way to school. Unfortunately, the boy's father, Henry Clifton, esquire, of Toft Trees, Norfolk, not only secured the aid of Sir John Fortescue, one of the privy council, to have his son released, but, about a year later, brought the matter before the court of Star chamber. A decree was rendered censuring Evans for taking up gentlemen's sons and ordering the severance of his connection with the company and playhouse. In anticipation, perhaps, of these proceedings, Evans, in October 1601, transferred all his property to his son-in-law, Alexander Hawkins. After the decree was rendered, Evans, acting through Hawkins, further entered into an agreement with Edward Kirkham, William Rastall and Thomas Kendall, allowing them to share in the management and profits of the playhouse. This is not the place to recite the quarrels between these shareholders; it may suffice to record that the success of the children was very great, that the profits of the undertaking are said to have been very large and that the company continued, with some vicissitudes, to act as the children of the chapel until, at the accession of James, they were re-named the children of the queen's revels, and, finally, were replaced by the company of men to which Shakespeare belonged.

During these years, this professional troupe of boys was served by some of the foremost dramatists of their time. Among the earliest was, doubtless, Chapman, who, perhaps, joined them in 1598, when he left the employ of Henslowe. He appears to have written for them his *May-Day*, his *Sir Gyles Goosecappe*, his *Gentleman Usher* and the extant version of *Al Fooles*. Another even more notable writer for their stage was Ben Jonson, from whom they received not only *The Case is Altered*, but, also, *Cynthia's Revels*, *Poetaster* and, perhaps, *A Tale of a Tub*. There is also some reason to believe that some of Marston's plays were written for them. Unfortunately, much of the stage history of the time is purely conjectural, but it seems practically certain that their vogue had become so great by 1601—2 as to draw from Shakespeare the airily satirical lines in *Hamlet* concerning the 'eyrie of children, little eyases, that cry out on the top of question and are most tyranically clapped for it.'

The names of some of these boy actors of this later period are known, some from Henry Clifton's bill of complaint and some from the lists in Ben Jonson's plays. One of them, Salathiel Pavy, as is well known, died early, and was celebrated by Jonson in a graceful, if somewhat 'conceited,' epitaph, full of the highest praise for his abilities as an actor. Others became renowned as members of the king's company in later years.

As to the ages of the boys, it is difficult to speak with certainty. Young Clifton was thirteen years old when 'taken up,' and William Hunnis found it necessary, in earlier times (1583), 'to kepe bothe a man servant to attend upon them and lykewyse a woman servant to wash and kepe them cleane.' In the case of the boys of the choir, it was customary, from early times, for the sovereign to provide for their education at one of the universities so soon as their 'breasts (*i.e.* voices) changed'; but, no doubt, when their principal function was acting they were held longer as children of the chapel, and Philip Gawdy writes in 1601: ''Tis sayde my Lady of Leoven hath marryed one of the playing boyes of the chappell.'

The success of the companies of choir boys in both early and later times was, doubtless, due, in no small degree, to the songs scattered through their plays and the instrumental music before the play began and between the acts. Other companies, of course, had incidental songs, but, apparently, not so many of them, and instrumental music seems not to have been given in the public theatres. That it was a prominent feature of the performances given by the boys, notwithstanding Clifton's declaration that his son and other boys taken up by Robinson, Evans and Giles were 'childeren noe way able or fitt for singing, nor by anie of the sayd confederates endevoured to be taught to sing,' we know from passages in several contemporary plays, as well as from the explicit statements of the duke of Stettin, who visited Blackfriars on 18 September 1602.

The special interest felt by queen Elizabeth in the chapel boys at Blackfriars may have been due, in part, at least, to their music. At any rate, there cannot be any doubt of her interest in them. According to a letter from Sir Dudley Carleton to John Chamberlain, she attended the play at Blackfriars on Tuesday,

29 December 1601.   The duke of Stettin speaks, indeed, as if the
queen had established the theatre and provided the rich costumes
of the plays, but the evidence in the suit of Kirkham *vs* Evans *et
als* (1612) indicates that the managers, Evans, Kirkham and their
fellows, bore all expenses and took all profits.   Kirkham was,
indeed, yeoman of the revels, and had charge of the costumes
and properties provided for the revels at court, but, though he
may have been able to borrow from the revels garments for the
use of his company, he could not have bought them without special
authorisation.   There is no evidence that the queen had any
active part in the establishment or maintenance of the children of
Blackfriars, though, of course, the company could not have been
established or maintained without her tacit consent.   She was
fond of the drama and of music.   On 8 April 1600, the privy
council addressed a letter to the Middlesex justices expressing
the queen's pleasure in the performances of Edward Alleyn and
his company, and her desire that he should be allowed to erect the
Fortune theatre.

Hasty as this survey of the long and brilliant career of the
children of the chapel has, necessarily, been, it can hardly fail to
have suggested their very great importance in the history of the
drama and the stage.   They were pioneers in more than one
interesting movement, they produced plays by some of the foremost dramatists of their time, they were prominent in the curious,
not to say ludicrous, 'war of the theatres,' and they were finally
put down because of the vigorous political satire spoken through
their mouths.

CHAPTER XII

UNIVERSITY PLAYS

TUDOR AND EARLY STEWART PERIODS

IT has been pointed out earlier in this work that, while the humanist movement at Oxford and Cambridge in the sixteenth century did not result in any important contributions to classical scholarship, it was remarkable for the production of a large number of Latin plays[1]. In the previous volume[2], the rise of the renascence academic drama on the continent was briefly traced, and its influence on early Tudor comedy, especially school plays, illustrated. But, in England, school plays had a comparatively limited vogue. It was at the universities that the humanist drama, written and acted by scholars, found its real home. Originating in didactic tendencies, and encouraged, as has been shown, by the framers of college statutes[3], its aims, at first, were educational rather than literary or recreative. But, amidst the medley of plastic influences in English university life, it was inevitable that drama at Oxford and Cambridge should not remain purely academic, in the narrower pedagogic sense. The gradually increasing proportion of plays in the vernacular produced on college stages, the ceremonial visits of kings and queens and other royal personages to 'shows' at the two seats of learning, the attractions, for the scholar playwrights and their audiences, of controversies, whether local and personal or of national significance—these were among the factors which speedily enlarged the bounds of university drama, and developed within it that variety of types which the following pages will attempt to sketch. But, to the last, it remained conscious, at least intermittently, of its distinctive origin and mission. Though influencing the popular stage, and being influenced by it in turn, yet, in the main, it followed an independent and diverging track, and it has both merits and limitations which are peculiarly its own.

[1] See vol. III, p. 424.   [2] See vol. v, chap. v, pp. 100 ff.   [3] See ibid. p. 103.

Mummery and impersonation in their more primitive forms can be traced back at the universities to the later fourteenth century. Though Warton's reference to 'the fragment of an ancient accompt-roll of the dissolved college of Michael-House in Cambridge' (it was merged in Trinity college) containing expenditure, under 1386, on a *comedia*, cannot now be verified, it may reasonably be taken as authentic. The statutes of New college, Oxford (1400) and of King's college, Cambridge (1443) expressly provide for the celebration of the favourite medieval ceremony of 'the boy bishop' on the feast of the Innocents and of St Nicholas's day respectively. In the King's college account-books there is an entry of expenses incurred *circa ludos* on Christmas day, 1582, and of a payment *lusoribus in aula collegii*, on the following day. Similar entries of expenditure on Christmas *ludi* or 'disgysynges' are found in 1489, 1496, and later[1]. The account-books of Magdalen college, Oxford, show that provision was made for 'the bishop' on St Nicholas's day frequently between 1482 and 1530, as well as for scriptural *ludi* on the chief church festivals, and miscellaneous interludes and entertainments. The register of Merton college, Oxford, records the election of another mock dignitary, *Rex Fabarum* or king of beans, who was chosen on or about the eve of St Edmund (19 November). In the first entry, in 1485, the election is said to be *per antiquam consuetudinem*, and the names of successive 'kings' are given annually till 1539, when the ceremony seems to have fallen into disuse[2].

It was while such medieval plays and ceremonies retained a flickering vitality that humanist drama at the universities began. At Oxford, the mention in the Magdalen accounts for the first time of a *comedia* in 1535, and, again, in 1539, and of a *tragedia* in 1540, probably indicates the transition to neo-classic types. According to Anthony à Wood, the Magdalen comedy of 1535 was *Piscator or The Fisher Caught*, by John Hoker, a fellow of the society. In 1536, the *Plutus* of Aristophanes was acted in Greek at St John's college, Cambridge. The production in 1546 of the Athenian playwright's Εἰρήνη or *Pax*, by John Dee the astrologer, at Trinity college, Cambridge, of which he was a fellow, seems, also, to have been in the original tongue. But these precedents were not

---

[1] See *Plays performed in Cambridge Colleges before 1585* by Smith, G. C. Moore in *Fasciculus Joanni Willis Clark dicatus*, p. 267.

[2] The register is in MS, but the present writer has been given facilities for consulting it.

Nicholas Grimald

295

followed, and there appears to be no record of a classical tragedy
being acted in Greek on the Tudor university stage[1].

Seneca, not Sophocles, was the pattern of the English humanist
when he essayed to write tragedy[2]. It is thus typical of the
blending of old and new influences that the earliest extant university plays should be on scriptural subjects, and should be cast
in approximately Senecan mould. Their author was Nicholas
Grimald, born in 1519, and a member, successively, of Christ's
college, Cambridge, and of Brasenose, Merton and Christ Church,
Oxford[3].

The first of these plays, *Christus Redivivus*, printed at Cologne
in 1543, was written and acted at Brasenose, as Grimald relates in
a dedicatory epistle, soon after his migration to Oxford in 1540.
It combines a Senecan treatment of the Gospel story of the
resurrection, in which Mary Magdalene plays the most effective
part, with a comic underplot centring in the four Roman
soldiers who guard the sepulchre, and who are cleverly discriminated types of the military braggart. Grimald's second
tragedy, *Archipropheta*, printed at Cologne in 1548, was written
in 1547, on his election to the newly constituted society of Christ
Church. It dealt with the career of John the Baptist, which
Buchanan had already dramatised in his *Baptistes*, acted at
Bordeaux a few years previously[4].

But, in spirit and in style, the two plays are remarkably
different from each other. The Scottish humanist follows the
strict Senecan model, and makes the Baptist the mouthpiece of
his own political and religious opinions. In Grimald's work, John
plays a comparatively passive part. The interest centres in the
voluptuous passion of Herod and his unlawful wife Herodias,
which is portrayed with a lyrical intensity and opulence of phrase
unmatched in Tudor drama till the time of Marlowe. Equally
foreign to the scriptural theme and to the Senecan convention is
the comic note struck by Herod's fool, Gelasimus.

These two Latin tragedies of Grimald, if they were known to
Roger Ascham, did not earn from him in *The Scholemaster* the

[1] John Christopherson, according to Warton, exhibited in 1546 at Trinity college,
of which he was afterwards master, a *Jephtha* of his own composition in Greek and in
Latin. The MS of the Greek play is in the library of Trinity college.
[2] Smith, G. C. Moore, *u.s.*, pp. 269—270, mentions performances at Cambridge
of *Troas*, 1551/2 and 1560/1, *Oedipus* and *Hecuba*, 1559/60, and *Medea*, 1560/1 and
1563. These were almost certainly Seneca's plays (*Troas* = *Troades*).
[3] On Grimald's English poems, see vol. III of the present work, pp. 179, 180.
[4] See vol. III of the present work, p. 161.

commendation of being 'able to abyde the free touch of Aristotles preceptes and Euripides examples' which he reserved for Buchanan's *Jephthes* and the *Absalom* of Thomas Watson of St John's, Cambridge. Watson, owing to scruples on a minor metrical point, never published the play; but it is probably that preserved in the Stowe MSS 957, which is a tragedy of the strict Senecan type. The story of the revolt in the royal house of Israel lent itself as naturally to Senecan machinery as did legendary dynastic feuds of early British kings, and Chusi's relation to David, in act IV, of the overthrow of Absalom's ill-armed troops and of his hapless end, is a vivid piece of narrative.

Religious drama of an entirely different type made its appearance on the Cambridge stage when, during the Lent of 1545, Kirchmayer's *Pammachius* was acted at Christ's college. Though it was condensed for the occasion, no excisions could disguise its savage anti-papal satire. It was inevitable that the orthodox chancellor of the university, Gardiner, bishop of Winchester, should write letters of remonstrance to the vice-chancellor, and order him to hold an enquiry concerning the performance. Dissatisfied with the report, Gardiner laid the matter before the privy council, which instructed the vice-chancellor to reprove the offenders, but took no further disciplinary measures. The members of Christ's college probably avoided controversial dramas in future; but entries in the college accounts testify to great dramatic activity in the immediately following years. The leading spirit in these entertainments was William Stevenson, who entered Christ's in 1546, graduated B.A. in 1550, M.A. in 1553 and B.D. in 1560, and was twice elected a fellow of the college. A play by him is mentioned in the accounts for 1550—1, and, again, in those for 1551—2; and, in the following year, he is reimbursed 18*d*. for expenses on his 'plaies.' There is another entry of a play by him in 1553—4, and a final one in 1559—60, during the second tenure of his fellowship. Hence, it has been conjectured that Stevenson is the author of *Gammer Gurtons Nedle*, 'played on stage, not longe ago in Christes Colledge in Cambridge. Made by Mr S. Mr of Art[1].'

The first edition of this comedy was not published till 1575, but its printer Colwell had obtained, in 1562/3, a licence to issue *Dyccon of Bedlam*. As 'Diccon the Bedlem' is the leading figure in

---

[1] The traditional ascription of the play to John Still rests merely upon a conjecture of Isaac Reed in 1782, and may be dismissed. But it is remarkable that John Bridges, dean of Salisbury, a member of Pembroke college, is spoken of in two of the Martin Marprelate tracts, 1588, as the reputed author of the comedy.

'Mr S.'s' play, the licence probably refers to it, and there are bibliographical grounds for the conjecture that the work was printed long before it was put on sale. A reference to arrest 'in the kings name' in act v suggests that the comedy was written before the death of Edward VI in July 1553. If Stevenson were its author, it would thus appear to have been composed between 1550 and 1553, and, if the title-page is to be trusted, revived later, probably in 1559—60. However this may be, *Gammer Gurtons Nedle* is of enduring interest as the earliest university play in English which has come down to us. At first sight, it shows little trace of scholarly influences. The 'fourteener' in which it is mainly written is a rough and tumble metre ; and the dialogue, often coarse in strain, is, as a rule, in that south-western dialect which became the conventional form of rustic speech on the Elizabethan stage. The plot turns on the complications produced in a small village society by the loss of the gammer's needle, and the characters are typically English, including Diccon, who combines the *rôles* of a Vice and a vagrant Tom of Bedlam. But, on closer examination, the effect of classical models is seen. The comedy is divided into acts and scenes, and the plot has a real organic unity. The parts played by the different personages in the village community, from 'Master Baily' and the curate downward, are neatly discriminated. The triumph of pastoral convention had not yet blurred for English humanists the outlines of genuine English country life.

The golden period of academic drama may be dated from the visits paid by queen Elizabeth to the two universities early in her reign. The visit to Cambridge began on 5 August 1564, and, in a letter from Grindal, bishop of London, written about three weeks before, the university authorities were admonished to

put themselves in all readinesse to please her Majestie, to welcome her with all manner of scholastical exercises, viz. with Sermons, both in English and Latin; Disputations in all Kinds of Faculties; and playing of Comedies and Tragedies; Oratios and Verses, both in Latin and Greek.

Under the direction of Roger Kelke, 'who was by the Vice-Chancellor and Heads of Colleges specially appointed to set forth and teach such plays as could be exhibited before her Grace,' a varied dramatic programme was provided. It began with a performance of the *Aulularia* of Plautus[1] on the evening of Sunday,

---

[1] Plautus appears to have been the favourite classical dramatist at Cambridge in the sixteenth century. Smith, G. C. Moore, *u.s.*, pp. 269—271, records sixteen performances of his plays between 1549 and 1583; four performances of comedies by Terence are noted during the same period.

6 August, in King's college chapel. A 'great stage containing the breadth of the Church from the one side to the other' was erected for the performance at the queen's own cost, and so keen was her interest that she remained till the final *plaudite*, without betraying the slightest weariness, though some of her suite grew impatient, owing to their ignorance of Latin or their desire for sleep.

On the following evening, a tragedy called *Dido*, written by Edward Halliwell, fellow of King's college, was performed. It was in hexameter verse, and drawn, for the most part, from the *Aeneid*. Like the earlier school drama on the same subject, acted before Wolsey in 1532[1], it is not extant; but the contemporary narrative of Nicholas Robinson describes it as *novum opus sed venustum et elegans*, though considered too long by some carping spectators.

A still more regrettable loss is that of the next evening's play, *Ezechias*, an English Biblical drama by Nicholas Udall[2]. As Udall was an Oxford man, and had been dead for about seven years, the production of a play by him on this occasion is somewhat remarkable, and was probably due to his long connection with court entertainments. Though the work is not extant, the accounts of the performance by Hartwell and Robinson show that it dealt with Hezekiah's destruction of the idols of the grove and the brazen serpent, the resentment of the populace, the mission of Rabshakeh at the head of the Assyrian host and the mysterious destruction of the invaders in a single night. As in the case of miracle-plays, lighter episodes were evidently mingled with Biblical incidents. *Mirum vero quantum hic facetiarum, quantum leporis in re tam seria ac sancta, et veritatis tamen certa serie nunquam interrupta.*

Great 'preparations and charges' had been 'employed and spent about' another play, *Ajax Flagellifer*, a Latin version of the Sophoclean tragedy, which was to be given on 9 August, the eve of the queen's departure. But she was so much wearied by her exertions that the performance had to be abandoned[3]. Before her departure on the following morning, Elizabeth gave a present in money and other marks of her favour to Thomas Preston, fellow of King's, afterwards author of *Cambises, king of Persia*, who had pleased her by his acting in *Dido* and his skill in disputation.

This visit of the queen to Cambridge had its counterpart two

---

[1] See *ante*, vol. v, chap. v, p. 102.

[2] On Udall's other plays, see *ante*, vol. v, chap. v, pp. 103—6.

[3] See *post*, p. 317, as to the performance of an *Ajax Flagellifer*, doubtless the same play, before James I.

years later in one to Oxford, which began on Saturday, 31 August 1566, and lasted till Friday, 6 September. She arrived from Woodstock, and had to undergo so formidable a succession of welcoming orations from the university and civic authorities on her way to Christ Church that she was unable to be present the following evening at the first play performed in her honour in the college hall. On a stage specially prepared at the queen's own cost, with 'stately lights of wax, variously wrought,' *Marcus Germinus*, a comedy in Latin prose, was performed. It was the joint composition of several Christ Church scholars, and was produced with the help of Richard Edwards. From the analysis of the plot given by Bereblock, it appears that it dealt with a conspiracy against Germinus, a native of Campania, in the reign of Alexander Severus, by jealous rivals who think that they have compassed his ruin, but whose designs are foiled by the evidence of honest freedmen.

On the following night, 2 September, the first part of *Palamon and Arcyte*, an English play by Richard Edwards, was acted in the queen's presence[1]. The report of the magnificence of the decorations, and the eagerness to see Elizabeth, drew such a vast crowd of spectators (*infinita ac innumerabilis hominum multitudo*) that part of the wall of the staircase leading to the hall collapsed, killing three persons and wounding others. The catastrophe, however, did not interfere with the performance or with the queen's enjoyment of it. From the analysis of the plot given by Bereblock, it is evident that it was exactly on the lines of Chaucer's *Knight's Tale*. The first part ended with Theseus's discovery of the two rivals for Emily's love fighting in the wood, and his determination that the matter should be decided by a tournament. The second part, acted on 4 September, dealt with the tournament, the victory of Arcite, his sudden death and the betrothal of Palamon and Emily. The loss of the play, which anticipated by about half a century the treatment of the same theme in *The Two Noble Kinsmen*, is a matter of great regret. Not only was the queen delighted with it, but a party of courtiers who had seen a rehearsal of it 'said it far surpassed *Damon and Pithias* than which they thought nothing could be better.'

The series of plays performed before the queen during this visit terminated with a Latin tragedy, *Progne*, by James Calfhill, canon of Christ Church. The plot was drawn from the sixth book of Ovid's *Metamorphoses*, and dealt, doubtless on Senecan lines, with the gruesome tale of the revenge of Progne, wife of king Tereus,

[1] On Edwards's previous career as a dramatist see *ante*, vol. v, chaps. iv and v.

upon her husband for the wrongs done to herself and her sister Philomela. It is not surprising that such a work 'did not take half so well as the much admired play of *Palamon and Arcyte.*'

But the relative merit of the pieces performed during these two royal visits to the universities is of less import than the remarkable variety of their subjects and their style. A play of Plautus, a tragedy on Dido in Vergilian hexameters, an English verse play on Hezekiah, a Latin version of the *Ajax* of Sophocles, a neo-Latin prose comedy, an adaptation of *The Knight's Tale,* a tragedy in the Senecan manner on an Ovidian theme—here is a microcosm of the motley literary elements which, combined with features of more popular origin, went to the shaping of the Elizabethan drama. It was into academic societies in which such varied stage productions formed part of the regular ritual of social and intellectual life that, within the next two decades, Marlowe, Peele, Greene and Nashe were to enter, and it was thence that they were to carry away lessons destined to exercise a momentous influence on the future of the London theatre.

To the immediately following years, no extant university play can be assigned with certainty. But, from the register of Merton college, Oxford, we learn that performances, both in English and in Latin, were given in the warden's house or in the college hall. On 3 January 1566/7, *Wylie Beguylie*[1], an English comedy, was performed by the scholars, *merito laudandi recte agendo*; and this was followed, about a month later, by the *Eunuchus* of Terence. In the January of the following year, the Merton scholars revived Edwards's *Damon and Pithias,* and, a few days later, acted the *Menaechmi* of Plautus.

Byrsa Basilica by J. Rickets, a play of unique character suggested by the foundation of the Royal Exchange in 1570, appears, from the epilogue, to be of university origin, though it deals in fantastic fashion with the career of Sir Thomas Gresham, and with various aspects of London commercial life, in bizarre combination with the figures and machinery of southern comedy[2]. The political

---

[1] The loss of this early Oxford play in the vernacular is particularly unfortunate, as we cannot tell whether it bore any relation to the later *Wily Beguiled* (printed 1606), which was almost certainly a Cambridge play (cf. *Ward,* vol. II, pp. 612—3). *Wily Beguiled,* however, was influenced so directly by *The Spanish Tragedie, The Merchant of Venice* and *Romeo and Juliet* that it is doubtful whether it can be connected with the Merton comedy of 1567.

[2] Gresham's civic career, with an admixture of episodes from the general history of the period, afterwards furnished materials for the popular stage in *Part II* of Thomas Heywood's *If You know not me, You know no bodie* (1606).

and dynastic, instead of the economic, aspect of the national
annals furnished material for another, and better-known, play, which
attained unusual popularity, and which is of special interest
as illustrating the Senecan treatment of a theme which afterwards
became the basis of a Shakespearean chronicle history play. This
work, preserved in a number of manuscripts, is *Richardus Tertius*,
by Thomas Legge, master of Caius college, Cambridge, and twice
vice-chancellor. It was acted at St John's college in the spring of
1580, and in two of the manuscripts the list of performers is given.
It ranges over the long period from the death of Edward IV
to the battle of Bosworth field, and, hence, is in tripartite form,
consisting of three *actiones* performed on successive evenings. It
thus departs from the strict Senecan model in its comprehensive
sweep and in its disregard of the unities of time and place. It also
dispenses with the moralising chorus. Otherwise, it is a typical
Senecan tragedy, in metre and language, in motives and situations
and in the general conception of a royal tyrant akin to Nero in
Octavia and to Atreus in *Thyestes*. It has the characteristic faults
of the school to which it belongs—monotony and an excess of wire-
drawn declamation—but Legge had genuine skill in technique and
expression, and taught the lesson that structural design and
rhetorical embellishment are essentials in a historical play.
Greene, who took his B.A. at St John's in 1578, was still in residence
at Cambridge when the play was produced, and Marlowe entered the
university in the following year. There can be little doubt that
Legge's drama was known to them, and that, at least indirectly,
it also influenced Shakespeare in *Richard III*. The Senecan
series of reverses of fortune in Shakespeare's play, the passages of
semi-lyrical declamation, the dialogues in στιχομυθία, the peculiarly
sombre colouring of the work and the two wooing scenes, which
have no source in Holinshed but are anticipated in Legge's tragedy,
all point strongly to this conclusion.

Not long after the production of *Richardus Tertius*, a number
of Senecan plays dealing with more remote and exotic historical
subjects were performed. *Solymannidae*, an anonymous tragedy,
was acted, at one of the universities, in March 1581/2. It treats
of the murder of Mustapha, son of Sultan Solyman II, at the instigation of his ambitious step-mother Rhode, who wishes the throne
for her own son Selymus. Another Senecan tragedy on an oriental
historical theme, *Tomumbeius*, by George Salterne of Bristol, deals
with the tragic fate of Tuman-bey, who became sultan of Egypt in
1516. Its dedication to Elizabeth proves that it was written during

her reign; but, otherwise, its date and place of performance are unknown. Even more uncertain is the *provenance* of the pseudo-historical Senecan tragedy *Perfidus Hetruscus,* the plot of which has points of contact with *Hamlet.* On the death of Sorastanus, duke of Tuscany, his brother Pandolphus seeks to gain the throne by conspiring against his nephews Columbus and Lampranus. His chief agent, at first, is a Jesuit Grimalfi (an indication that the author was a strong protestant), who, however, is slain by the ghost of Sorastanus. Through the further machinations of Pandolphus, Columbus is banished by Lampranus ; but the ghost of Sorastanus appears to him in exile, and bids him return to kill his uncle. He obeys the command and fights a duel with Pandolphus, who sends for a poisoned cup of wine. The traitor himself drinks by mistake from the poisoned cup, but recovers, and afterwards strangles Columbus, and poisons Lampranus during his sleep. He succeeds to the vacant dukedom, but dies after donning the crown which he himself had poisoned. Preserved in a single manuscript, and never printed, this play has not attracted the attention to which its plot entitles it. It is of greater interest than the much better known *Roxana,* by William Alabaster, of Trinity college, Cambridge, acted about 1592. This is a close version, with most of the names altered, and with no indication of its source, of an Italian play, *La Dalida,* by Luigi Groto, published in 1567. Alabaster lays the scene in Bactria; and the plot, which centres round Roxana, a princess of the imaginary royal house, exceeds even the usual measure of horrors in a Senecan tragedy. Doubtless, this characteristic (in consequence of which 'a gentlewoman fell distracted' at the performance), together with the elegant Latinity of the play, gained for it the popularity of which an echo remains in Dr Johnson's laudatory allusion to it in his *Life of Milton.*

The Senecan school of university dramatists produced its most important figure in William Gager, who is included in Meres's list (1598) of the chief dramatists of the day, though, strange to say, among writers of comedy. Born between 1555 and 1560, he entered Christ Church, Oxford, in 1574, graduated in 1577 and became a doctor of civil law in 1589. During his long residence, he took the lead in writing plays for performance by members of his college. With the exception of his single comedy, *Rivales,* no longer extant, they were Latin tragedies on classical subjects. The first of these, *Meleager,* was produced in 1581, and revived, three years later, in the presence of the earl of Leicester, chancellor of the university, and Sir Philip Sidney. The author of *An Apologie for Poetrie,* as he watched the performance, must have rejoiced that there had arisen a dramatist who carried out to the letter his critical precepts, preserving the unities in the strictest fashion, and taking care not to match 'hornpipes and funerals.'

In 1583, before another visitor of distinction, Albertus Lasco, prince palatine of Poland, two other plays by Gager were acted, the comedy *Rivales* already mentioned, and 'a verie statelie tragedie,' *Dido,* in the preparation of which George Peele took part. For this tragedy, which was ·produced with 'strange, marvellous, and abundant' scenic effects, Gager, like Halliwell at Cambridge twenty years before, drew the chief situations and much of the dialogue (though cast into Senecan form) from the *Aeneid.* Another of the Christ Church dramatist's tragedies, *Oedipus,* of uncertain date, is only partly extant in manuscript. But the last and finest of his classical plays, *Ulysses Redux,* was printed a few months after its production in February 1591/2, when *Rivales* also was revived. *Ulysses Redux,* though Senecan in form, is far from being a lifeless piece of classical imitation. Drawing its subject from the later books of the *Odyssey,* it is not unworthy of its source. The incidents are skilfully grouped, and many of the scenes, including the fight between Irus and Ulysses, and the efforts of the suitors to bend the bow, are full of dramatic vigour. The conjugal affection of Penelope for her lord is provided with an effective foil in the passion of the handmaid Melantho for Eurymachus—an un-Homeric episode which Gager develops in the spirit of romantic drama.

But of greater permanent value than Gager's tragedies is his masterly defence of academic plays and players contained in a letter to John Rainolds of Queen's college, afterwards president of Corpus, a puritan antagonist of the drama. Of both sides of the correspondence an account is given in a later chapter of this volume[1]. The arguments with which Gager meets Rainolds objections to the impersonation of women by men in feminine attire, and to Sunday performances, are full of interesting references to contemporary college life, and he sets forth eloquently the aims and ideals of academic playwrights and actors.

We doe it to recreate owre-selves, owre house, and the better parte of the Universitye, with some learned Poeme or other; to practyse owre owne style eyther in prose or verse; to be well acquantyed with Seneca or Plautus... to trye their voyces and confirme their memoryes, to frame their speeche; to

[1] See *post,* chap. XIV.

conforme them to convenient action; to trye what mettell is in everye one, and of what disposition they are[1].

But Seneca and Plautus were not the only exemplars with whom university dramatists were 'well acquainted.' From about 1580 onwards, their productions in the sphere of comedy, even when written in Latin, had, usually, an Italian, and not a classical, source. To this period belongs *Victoria*, by Abraham Fraunce of St John's, Cambridge, a metrical Latin version of Luigi Pasqualigo's prose comedy *Il Fedele*, published in 1575. This is a typical product of the southern stage, with a complicated intrigue between rivals for the favours of a married lady, with impersonations and disguisings and with the stock figures of a braggart and an enamoured pedant. Fraunce's version, except for the addition of an episode taken from *The Decameron*, and the revision of portions of the later acts, is very close. It thus contrasts with the free English adaptation of *Il Fedele* by Anthony Munday, *Fedele and Fortunio*, wherein the braggart, who is called captain Crackstone, becomes the chief figure in the comedy[2].

A more ingenious and skilful adaptation from the Italian than *Victoria*, though from *The Decameron* and not from a play, is the anonymous *Hymenaeus*, acted at St John's, Cambridge, probably in March 1578/9. The list of actors, which included Fraunce, is virtually identical with that which took part in *Richardus Tertius*, except that the latter has a considerably larger cast. Boccaccio tells of the remarkable experiences of a gallant called Ruggieri, who makes love to the beautiful young wife of an aged doctor of Salerno, and who swallows a sleeping draught by mistake. In *Hymenaeus*, the young wife is the daughter of an elderly father, with three suitors—a doctor, a drunken German and a young Venetian whom she favours. It is the Venetian who drinks the potion prepared by his rival, the doctor, for the heroine's father, and who, in consequence, goes through a series of adventures which nearly ends on the gallows, before he succeeds in winning his mistress's hand. To the same group of Latin comedies in Italian style, though no immediate source of them has been hitherto traced, belong several St John's college plays of somewhat later date. These include the pastoral *Silvanus* (January 1597), with resemblances of situation to the Silvius-Phoebe-Rosalind love-

---

[1] For a full account of Gager's letter, by the present writer, see *The Fortnightly Review*, August 1907.

[2] See *ante*, vol. v, chap. xiii, and bibl. vol. v, pp. 474—5, for an account of Munday's play.

complication in *As You Like It*, and with a Latinised echo, in the closing song, of the August roundelay in *The Shepheards Calender*; and *Machiavellus* (December 1597), in which the bearer of the title *rôle*, and a Jew, Jacuppus, carry on a contest with a remarkable series of disguises, plots and counterplots, for the hand of the heroine, till her betrothed, who is supposed to have been killed in the wars, returns just in time to claim her once more as his own. Two comedies which can be traced to their Italian sources are *Leander* (1598 and 1602) and *Labyrinthus* (1602), performed at Trinity college, Cambridge, and written by Walter Hawkesworth, fellow of the college, who acted the chief part in both plays. Their popularity is evidenced by the number of manuscripts in which they are still extant; but they were merely Latin adaptations of *La Fantesca* and *La Cintia* respectively, both by G. B. della Porta, the Neapolitan playwright. Of all these Cambridge versions of Italian comedies, the most important is the anonymous *Laelia*, acted at Queens' college in 1590, and revived in 1598. It is founded on *Gl' Ingannati* (1531), and its action is similar to that of the main plot of *Twelfth Night*. The source of Shakespeare's play has always been doubtful, though Rich's *Apolonius and Silla* and Emanuel Ford's *Parismus* have features in common with it. Nor is it safe, as has been attempted by W. H. Furness and F. E. Schelling, to identify *Laelia* as the direct original of *Twelfth Night*, though it is just possible that it may have been. In any case, the university play and the Shakespearean comedy present an instructive contrast of methods, the advantage not being all on one side. *Laelia* lacks the lyric beauty, the delicate, imaginative charm of *Twelfth Night*, without hint of its superbly humorous underplot; its characters are of the conventional southern type, including the stock figures of a pedant and a nurse. But the plot of *Laelia* is a very deft piece of stagecraft; and, by representing Flaminius (Orsino) as having loved Laelia (Viola), before he transferred his affections to Isabella (Olivia), it makes more plausible the final union of hearts between hero and heroine.

The plays dealt with hitherto in this chapter are academic in the sense that they were written and acted by university men within college walls, and that, whether English[1] or Latin, they were influenced, almost without exception, by the classical or

---

[1] It is curious that the Cambridge authorities, when asked to 'prepare A Comedie in Englishe' to be acted at court by students before the queen at Christmas, 1592, wrote to Burghley, 'Englishe Comedies, for that wee never used any, wee presentlie have none.' See 'Dram. Records from Lansdowne MSS' in *Malone Society Collections*, vol. I, part 2, p. 199.

Italian models which were of paramount authority in learned
societies of the renascence period. We now have to deal with
a group of comedies which are academic in a more special and
intimate sense ; which deal with the studies and the experiences of
scholars young and old, with the notable figures of contemporary
university life, with the immemorial feud of town and gown.

Of these plays, chiefly connected with Cambridge, probably the
earliest extant, as it is one of the most diverting, is *Pedantius*, a
Trinity college comedy. Though not published till 1631, it probably dates from the winter of 1580 or spring of 1581. Nashe, in
Strange Newes, ascribes it to 'M. Winkfield,' *i.e.* Anthony Wing-
field, fellow of Trinity, who, in March 1581, was a successful rival
of Gabriel Harvey for the office of public orator. Nashe, who
matriculated at St John's, in October 1582, cannot well have been
mistaken, though claims have been made[1] on behalf of Edward
Forcet or Forsett, fellow of Trinity, who is named as author in
a Caius college manuscript of the play.

Pedantius is an admirable combination of Plautine machinery
and types with the conditions of English university life in the later
sixteenth century. The lovesick pedant of southern comedy is here
transformed into a Cambridge humanist, who is the unsuccessful
rival of a freedman for the hand of a slave girl Lydia, and whose
rhetorical flights avail him nothing except to stave off payment of
his tailor's bills. But the pedant is not merely modernised, he is
individualised into a caricature of Gabriel Harvey. This is
vouched for by Nashe in *Have with you to Saffron Walden*, where
he declares that, in 'the concise and firking finicaldo fine schoolmaster,' Harvey 'was full drawen and delineated from the soule of
the foote to the crowne of his head.' Internal evidence confirms
the identification. Not only is Pedantius, as was Harvey, according
to the view of his enemies, a fop and a sycophant, but phrases from
the Cambridge rhetorician's works occur repeatedly in the play,
and his *Musarum Lachrymae* is directly named. As satellite
and contrast to the main figure appears another contemporary
academic type, the solemnly argumentative, logic-chopping philosopher Dromodotus.

The university stage, in this burlesque of Harvey, may claim
the dubious honour of having first made use of the drama in
England for purposes of personal attack. And, according to Nashe,
there were other plays, now lost, ridiculing members of the Harvey

---

[1] See G. C. Moore Smith's introduction to his edition of the play in Bang's
Materialien.

family. *Tarrarantantara turba tumultuosa Trigonum, Tri-Harveyorum, Tri-harmonia*, a show at Clare hall, was directed against the three brothers, Gabriel, Gilbert and Dick, while *Duns Furens : Dickey Harvey in a Frensie*, at Peterhouse, so exasperated its butt, 'the little minnow,' that he broke the college windows during the performance and was set in the stocks 'till the Shew was ended, and a great part of the night after.' Doubtless, personal satire, in some form, was a feature of *Terminus et non terminus*, acted at St John's in or soon after 1586, and written by Nashe and another member of the college. For, according to Harvey (*Trimming of Thomas Nashe*), the latter was expelled for his share in it ; why Nashe, who appears to have played the part of 'Varlet of Clubs' in the show, was more leniently dealt with, does not appear.

For attacks on academic personages like the Harveys, Latin was the suitable instrument ; but, when college playwrights took a hand in the chronic feud between university and town, as represented by the civic authorities, they naturally fell back upon the vernacular. A remarkable episode in this connection is chronicled by Fuller in his *History of the University of Cambridge*, under date 1597—8.

> The young scholars ... having gotten a discovery of some town privacies from Miles Goldsborough (one of their own corporation) composed a merry (but abusive) comedy (which they called *Club-Law*) in English, as calculated for the capacities of such whom they intended spectators thereof. Clare-Hall was the place wherein it was acted, and the mayor, with his brethren and their wives were invited to behold it, or rather themselves abused therein. A convenient place was assigned to the townsfolk (riveted in with scholars on all sides) where they might see and be seen. Here they did behold themselves in their own best clothes (which the scholars had borrowed) ... lively personated, their habits, gestures, language, lieger-jests, and expressions.

So incensed were the civic dignitaries at the insult, that they complained to the privy council, which, however, made little of the matter, merely sending some 'slight and private check to the principal actors.'

Fuller's narrative is scarcely to be accepted as authentic in all its details[1], and it is noticeable that no mention of the incident is found in the register of the privy council. But the play to which

---

[1] In his introduction to *Club Law*, Smith, G. C. Moore argued that the date of the production was 1599—1600, and that the mayor of Cambridge, satirised as Niphle, was John Yaxley. Since then, he has found confirmation of his conjecture in a Jesus college MS, ascribed to Fuller himself, which mentions the production in 1599—1600 at Clare hall of 'Club Law *fabula festivissima*.' See *The Modern Language Review*, vol. IV, no. 2, pp. 268—9.

he alludes, and which was thought to be no longer extant, has recently been rediscovered in manuscript in the library of St John's college, Cambridge, by G. C. Moore Smith. The manuscript is imperfect, lacking the title and the first three scenes of act I and scene 3 and parts of scenes 2 and 4 of act IV. But that the play is the *Club Law* acted at Clare is proved by the constant introduction of the phrase, and by the general character of the comedy.

In an unconventional dramatic framework, wherein 'Commike rules,' as confessed in the epilogue, are not observed, the playwright gives an animated though bitterly partisan picture of the relations between university and town in the closing years of the sixteenth century. The chronic hostility between them arose from the peculiar privileges granted to the university by a series of royal charters and by parliamentary enactment. These privileges included powers of interference with the trade of the town, of searching the houses of citizens and of punishing them in the university courts. Every mayor on his accession to office had to take an oath to preserve the privileges of the university—an obligation which aroused the keenest resentment.

Of all these circumstances, the Clare hall dramatist makes skilful use. Two graduates of Athens (Cambridge), Musonius and Philenius, egged on by a waggish younger scholar, Cricket, determine to make the 'muddy slaves,' the rebellious citizens, 'feele our stripes for their disobedience and renewe the ancient Club-lawe.' At the same time, the newly chosen burgomaster (mayor) Niphle announces to the electors that he 'will rout out the whole generation' of academicians, 'they shall not nestle with us in our streets, nor out brave us in our owne dunghills.' And he afterwards arranges a plan of campaign against them, including the retaliation of 'their owne Clublawe.' There are traitors, however, in the citizens' camp; Mrs Niphle and Mrs Colby, wife of a leading 'headsman,' to win the good graces of Musonius and Philenius, reveal the plot, and give the scholars directions for appropriating the clubs which were to be used against them. Meanwhile, the burgomaster has been caught out in a midnight visit to a courtesan at the house of his sergeant, the Welshman Tavie; and Colby has been detected in the act of carrying away corn in sacks supposed to contain coal. Both are sent to jail by virtue of the rector's (vice-chancellor's) authority, and bills of 'discommoning' are issued, prohibiting scholars from having any dealings with prominent members of the corporation. It is this measure, whereby their means of livelihood are cut off, that brings the citizens to their knees, even more than their rout in a street skirmish by the 'gentle Athenians' armed with the purloined clubs. A deputation headed by Niphle, who has been released from jail, comes to proffer submission to Musonius and Philenius.

Wee crave pardon, and craving pardon we tender our supplication, that it may please you to letts live by you, and recover our old estats, that is, to reape what benefits we may by you, which if it please you to grant, I being the mouth of the rest doe promise for the rest hereafter to be obedient to you in any reasonable demand.

But it is not till the promise is confirmed by an oath that the scholars hold out to the suppliants a prospect of the renewal of their former privileges. The play hangs loosely together, and the satire is so acid and unrelieved throughout that it goes beyond the limits of dramatic plausibility. The author's knock-down blows are themselves a species of 'club law.' But he has a remarkable command of idiomatic and racy vocabulary, which gives pungency to the dialogue. The broken English of Tavie, the Welshman, and of Mounsier Grand Combatant, a French braggadocio, and the north-country dialect of Rumford, one of the corporation, give further evidence of the writer's quick ear for characteristic modes of speech.

Broadly contemporary with *Club Law* is the *Parnassus* trilogy, which, in originality and breadth of execution, and in complex relationship to the academic, literary, theatrical and social life of the period, ranks supreme among the extant memorials of the university stage. Both the first and second parts of the trilogy remained in manuscript till 1886, when they were published by W. D. Macray. The third part had appeared in quarto in 1606, with the title *The Returne from Pernassus: Or the Scourge of Simony: Publiquely acted by the Students in Saint Johns Colledge in Cambridge*. Internal evidence proves that this third part must have been written before the death of Elizabeth, and indicates Christmas 1602 as the probable date of the performance. On similar evidence, *The Pilgrimage to Parnassus*, and *Part I* of *The Returne from Parnassus* (as the recovered plays have been named), may be assigned, respectively, to 1598 and 1601. The writer of the trilogy is unknown, for, though he throws out tantalising clues in the prologue to *Part I* of *The Returne*, they are not sufficient to identify him. The ingenious argument in support of the authorship of John Day is open to serious chronological and other objections. But, whoever he may have been, the St John's playwright was a man of singularly penetrating intelligence,

acute observation and wide reading. His mordant wit disdained to
flow in the conventional academic channel of Italianate comedy,
where a 'lisping gallant' and his 'wench,' or a 'sire' acknowledging
'his lost son,' were the stock figures. He struck out on a path of
his own, with increased vigour and boldness at each stage.

The Pilgrimage is an allegory, in dramatic framework, of the
difficulties and temptations that beset the scholar in his pursuit
of learning. Two cousins and fellow students, Philomusus and
Studiosus, are plodding to Parnassus by the well worn track of
the *trivium*. In Logic land, 'muche like Wales, full of craggie
mountains and thornie vallies,' they encounter Madido, a votary of
the winecup, who tells them that 'Parnassus and Hellicon are but
the fables of the poets: there is no true Parnassus but the third
lofte in a wine taverne, no true Hellicon but a cup of browne bastard.' Thence they pass to the 'pleasant land of Rhetorique,' where
'shrille Don Cicero' sings sweetly, and where they are overtaken by
Stupido. He is a type of the narrowest puritanism, who declaims
against the 'vaine arts of Rhetorique, Poetrie and Philosophie;
there is noe sounde edifying knowledg in them. Why they are
more vaine than a paire of organs or a morrice daunce.' But the
fiercest trial is in the land of Poetry, where Amoretto, a voluptuary, who perverts the muse into an agent of sensual passion,
bids them 'crop the joys of youth,' and allures them for a time
from their path. But, before it is too late, they realise that
wantonness is 'sourelie sweete,' and they press on to the land of
Philosophy. Here they meet an old schoolfellow, Ingenioso, who
is hurrying away 'in a chafe,' and who cries to the pilgrims 'What!
I travell to Parnassus? why I have burnt my bookes, splitted my
pen, rent my papers, and curst the cooseninge harts that brought
mee up to noe better fortune.' These words, and others that
follow, are taken, with some modification, from Nashe's pamphlet
Pierce Penilesse (1592), in which he bewailed the miseries of the
life of a man of letters. The bitter cry of so gifted a member of
the college must have come home to the St John's audience, some
of whom may have been present at the performance of *Terminus
et non terminus* in the previous decade. But the pilgrims turn a
deaf ear and fare blithely on to the 'laurell mounte,' where, for a
time, they lie with 'Phoebus by the muse's springes.'

In *Part I* of *The Returne*, the playwright is in more sombre
mood, and his satire is more incisive. He drops almost entirely
the allegorical scheme, and, in a series of realistic genre pictures,
portrays the miserable shifts to which scholars, when their course

is completed, are reduced to earn a living. Philomusus goes through pitiful experiences as a parish clerk and sexton till he is dismissed for incompetency. Studiosus, who tries to find consolation in the moral commonplaces of Senecan tragedy, leads a dog's life as tutor to an idle and unruly 'dandipratt' in a vulgar household. But he is sent packing, because he will not yield precedence to a servant at table, and the two friends, as a last hope, resolve to seek their fortunes under another sky, at 'Rome or Rheims.' Here, however, they fare as ill as at home and they hurry back, feeling

> That it's as good to starve mongst English swine
> As in a forraine land to beg and pine.

But the adventures of Philomusus and Studiosus furnish only one of the themes in this part of the trilogy. Another is found in the relations of Ingenioso to Gullio, a vainglorious pseudo-patron of letters, modelled in part on Nashe's portrait of 'an upstart' in his *Pierce Penilesse*. Gullio, who is 'maintaining' Ingenioso in most niggardly fashion, bids him personate his mistress, Lesbia, that he may rehearse amorous speeches afterwards to be addressed to her. These speeches are mainly variations on lines in Shakespeare's *Venus and Adonis* and *Romeo and Juliet*. Gullio afterwards commissions Ingenioso to write specimen verses for his lady 'in two or three divers vayns, in Chaucer's, Gower's, and Spenser's and Mr Shakspeare's.' He quotes the opening lines of *Venus and Adonis* as the preferable model, and cries sentimentally:

O sweet Mr Shakespeare! I'le have his picture in my study at the courte.

When Ingenioso submits his poetical exercises for approval, the lines in 'Mr Shakspeare's vayne' are instantly preferred:

Ey marry, sir, these have some life in them! Let this duncified worlde esteeme of Spencer and Chaucer, I'le worshipp sweet Mr Shakespeare and to honour him will lay his Venus and Adonis under my pillowe.

But the lines, accompanied by a Latin epistle of Gullio's own composition, fail to move Lesbia, and Ingenioso is dismissed by his indignant patron.

It is certainly not with complimentary intent that the author makes Shakespeare the favourite poet of the shallow and affected courtier. Further light is thrown on his attitude in act 1 sc. 2 of *Part II* of *The Returne*. In this famous scene, the Cambridge dramatist, under the thin disguise of Judicio, reviews the merits of a number of the contemporary poets from whom selections had been

included in Bodenham's *Belvedere,* an anthology issued in 1600.
Shakespeare is briefly dealt with:

> Who loves not Adons love, or Lucrece rape?
> His sweeter verse contaynes hart throbbing line,
> Could but a graver subject him content
> Without loves foolish lazy languishment.

The critic, while recognising the beauty of language and versification in Shakespeare's two early poems, evidently considered that
he was misusing his talents in producing luscious studies of amorous
passion, though they might move Gullio and his kind to sentimental raptures. His qualified tribute to the actor-poet contrasts
with his panegyric on Spenser and his generous praise of Drayton,
Nashe and other writers of the day.

In a later scene of *Part II* of *The Returne,* the St John's writer
again deals with Shakespeare, not as a poet, but as a dramatist
and an actor. The references, doubtless, are inspired by reminiscences of a recent visit of the lord chamberlain's company to
Cambridge. Owing to the competition of the boy actors at the
Blackfriars theatre, Shakespeare and his fellows had had to go on
tour, probably in 1601. That they visited Oxford and Cambridge,
we know from the title-page of the first quarto of *Hamlet* (1603),
where the play is said to have been acted 'in the two Universities.'
With its scholar-hero, and semi-academic atmosphere, the surmise
is plausible that it was adapted from Kyd's earlier play with a
special view to its being acted in the university towns. It was a
fresh mortification to the St John's dramatist, embittered by the
woes of scholars, to see low-born actors from the capital make
a triumphal entry into Cambridge.

> England affords those glorious vagabonds
> That carried earst their fardels on their backes,
> Coursers to ride on through the gazing streetes,
> Sooping it in their glaring Satten sutes,
> And Pages to attend their Maisterships:
> With mouthing words that better wits have framed,
> They purchase lands, and now Esquiers are namde.

It is thus in a spirit of fierce mockery that he represents Philomusus and Studiosus, by way of a last resource, becoming can-
didates for the professional stage, and being tested by Burbage and
Kemp, who make merry over the deficiencies of scholars both as
actors and as dramatists.

KEMPE. The slaves are somewhat proud, and besides it is a good sport
in a part to see them never speake in their walke, but at the end of the

stage, just as though in walking with a fellow we should never speake but at a stile, a gate, or a ditch, where a man can go no further. . . .

BUR. A little teaching will mend these faults, and it may bee besides they will be able to pen a part.

KEMPE. Few of the University[men] plaies well, they smell too much of that writer *Ovid*, and that writer *Metamorphosis*, and talke too much of *Proserpina* and *Juppiter*. Why heres our fellow Shakespeare puts them all downe, I and Ben Jonson too. O that Ben Jonson is a pestilent fellow, he brought up Horace giving the poets a pill, but our fellow Shakespeare hath given him a purge that made him bewray his credit.

The whole purport of this well known passage is misunderstood unless it be recognised that it is written in a vein of the bitterest irony. The gownsman is holding up to scorn before an academic audience the judgment of illiterate boors who think that *Metamorphosis* is a writer, and that their fellow Shakespeare puts to shame the university playwrights, and has had the upper hand in a duel with Ben Jonson, the protagonist of classical orthodoxy in dramatic art. With the relations of Shakespeare and Jonson in 'the war of the theatres' we are not here concerned; but it is profoundly significant that the anonymous author of the *Parnassus* trilogy, perhaps the ablest of all the academic dramatists, should have singled out Shakespeare in his mid-career for his satiric shafts. The foremost representatives of the academic and the professional stage stand revealed in this brief illuminating flash, sundered by an impassable gulf of class prejudice and divergent ideals of art. Nor could the scholar-playwright have been expected to see that the supreme master of irony, Time, would turn back his ridicule with crushing effect upon himself.

In other scenes of *Part II* of *The Returne*, which account for the sub-title, *The Scourge of Simony*, the feud between town and gown finds as bitter expression as in *Club Law*. But the satire is now particularly directed against Francis Brackyn, deputy recorder of Cambridge, who had taken a leading part in asserting the claims of the burgesses against the university. The feeling against Brackyn was intensified by the fact that he stood for common law, while the academic jurists, at this time, were striving to revive the influence and authority of civil law. Under the name of the Recorder, Brackyn figures in the play as one of a confederacy who out of greed and spite, bestow the cure of souls on moneyed blockheads instead of on poor but deserving scholars. The other members of the gang are Sir Frederick, a dissolute and rapacious patron of livings, and his son Amoretto, an affected braggart. Academico, who has been a college contemporary of Amoretto and used his talents on his behalf, asks him for his good offices with his father. But Immerito, the boorish son of a country bumpkin, is preferred to the benefice because his father can give one hundred 'thanks' in current coin. The Recorder approves the patron's choice, and seizes the occasion for a malignant outburst against the scholars and their colleges:

> But had the world no wiser men than I,
> Weede pen the prating parates in a cage;
> . . . .
> Knights, Lords, and lawyers should be log'd and dwel
> Within those over stately heapes of stone
> Which doting syres in old age did erect.

But, later, the scholars prove themselves the Recorder's match in vituperation, and we get a foretaste of the yet more overwhelming ridicule of Brackyn in *Ignoramus*.

To us, the *Parnassus* trilogy is without an equal among academic plays in the combined intimacy and breadth of its appeal. But contemporary taste seems to have been hit more successfully by another Cambridge drama, *Lingua, or The Combat of the Tongue and the five Senses for Superiority*. This comedy, first printed in 1607, went through six editions before the Restoration. Its date is uncertain, though it must be later than 1602, which is mentioned in one of the scenes. Its author, as we learn from a memorandum by Sir John Harington, a high authority on the university plays of his day, was Thomas Tomkis of Trinity college, who graduated in 1600—1, and whose name appears on the title-page of *Albumazar*, acted before James I at Trinity in 1615. *Lingua* falls in with the contemporary fashion of personifying or allegorising the parts and faculties of man, which finds its chief expression in Phineas Fletcher's *Purple Island*. The scene 'is Microcosmus in a Grove,' and the plot is concerned with the attempt of *Lingua*, the tongue, to vindicate her claim to be a sixth sense. To breed strife among the five recognised senses, she leaves in their path a crown and a royal robe with the inscription:

> He of the five that proves himself the best,
> Shall have his temples with this coronet blest.

Tactus first finds the royal emblems, and invests his 'brows and body' with them. Thereupon, the other senses dispute his sovereignty, and make preparation for deadly combat. But Communis Sensus, the vicegerent of queen Psyche, undertakes 'to umpire the contention' and orders them 'their arms dismissed to appear before him, charging everyone to bring, as it were in a shew, their proper

objects, that by them he may determine of their several excellencies.' Visus's show includes Lumen, Coelum, Terra and Colour, whom he 'marshaleth about the stage, and presents before the bench.' Auditus afterwards leads in Tragedus and Comedus, whose likeness and unlikeness are delineated in words of admirable critical insight. Olofactus presents 'the mighty emperor Tobacco, king of Trinidado, that, in being conquered, conquered all Europe, in making them pay tribute for their smoke.' Gustus has in his train Bacchus and Ceres; but Tactus has to appear alone, because his show was to have included 'a nice gentlewoman,' and in five hours a dozen maids have not had time to attire a boy for the part. Finally, Communis Sensus delivers judgment. On not very cogent grounds, he assigns the crown to Visus and the robe to Tactus, while the three other senses are consoled with appointments to high offices under queen Psyche. Lingua's claim to be a sense is rejected—with a significant reservation:

The number of the Senses in this little world is answerable to the first bodies in the great world: now, since there be but five in the universe, the four elements and the pure substance of the heavens, therefore there can be but five senses in our Microcosm correspondent to those ... wherefore we judge you to be no sense simply: only this much we from henceforth pronounce, that all women for your sake shall have six Senses, that is, seeing, hearing, tasting, smelling, touching, and the last and feminine sense, the sense of speaking.

Lingua, enraged at being proclaimed 'half a sense,' revenges herself by making the senses drink a drugged wine at a supper to which Gustus invites them. Their wits become deranged, and strife threatens to be renewed among them; but Somnus charms them, and the mischief-maker Lingua, into sleep. In her sleep, Lingua confesses her trickery[1], and is punished by being committed 'to close prisin, in Gustus's house ... under the custody of two strong dons, and ... well guarded with thirty tall watchmen, without whose licence she shall by no means wag abroad.'

It is not, however, in the plot, ingeniously worked out as it is, that the chief attraction of the play lies. Its distinguishing excellence is the style, or variety of styles, in which it is written. In the prose scenes, Tomkis proves himself a master of polished and flexible dialogue, which has often a curiously modern note. The wit is sparkling and unforced, but lacks the Aristophanic pungency of *Club Law* and the *Parnassus* plays. In the few

[1] In *The Modern Language Review*, vol. IV, no. 4, pp. 518—520, the present writer has suggested that this episode is probably a parody of the sleep-walking scene in *Macbeth*.

verse passages where the author aims at a serious effect, he writes with scholarly grace. But most of the metrical speeches are in a vein of burlesque, or are parodies of lines in plays of the day. Thus, there are intentionally ludicrous imitations of famous speeches in Kyd's *Spanish Tragedie*, besides what appear to be caricatures of phrases or situations in several Shakespearean dramas. A hundred and one incidental allusions show the width of the author's reading, and the remarkably detailed stage directions prove his interest in matters of costume and heraldry. The statement made in 1657, and elaborated by later tradition, that Oliver Cromwell acted in the play, is, probably, a bookseller's figment, but might, conceivably, be true if a revival took place about 1617, when the third edition of the work appeared.

The last decade of Elizabeth's reign, which was very fruitful in Cambridge plays, has left few memorials of dramatic activity at Oxford, which seems to have been more dependent on the external stimulus of royal visits. But, at St John's college, which, from the beginning of the seventeenth century, rivals Christ Church as a centre of academic stagecraft, there was produced in 1602/3 the 'twelfe night merriment,' *Narcissus*. The prologue declares that 'the play wee play is Ovid's own Narcissus,' and it is true that the plot is taken from book III of the *Metamorphoses*. But the story is considerably expanded and treated throughout in a burlesque vein. Thus, Tiresias, 'the not seeing prophet,' adorned 'in byshoppes rochett,' is introduced to tell the fortune of the beautiful youth from the 'table' of his hand; and the trickery of the mischievous nymph Echo leads to mock tragedy. Throughout, the author shows a remarkable command of out-of-the-way phrases and grotesque rimes, and, in its farcical treatment of a classical legend, *Narcissus* is curiously akin to the interlude of *Pyramus and Thisbe* in *A Midsummer Night's Dream*.

Two and a half years later, in the summer of 1605, St John's took part with Christ Church in the series of entertainments provided for king James on his first visit to Oxford. The king, accompanied by the queen and Henry, prince of Wales, made his entry on 27 August. Special preparations had been made for the festivities. In Christ Church, where the king and queen lodged, a stage had been

built close to the upper end of the Hall, as it seemed at the first sight. But indeed it was but a false wall fair painted, and adorned with stately pillars, which pillars would turn about, by reason whereof, with the help of other painted clothes, their stage did vary three times in the acting of one Tragedy.

That the actors in the various plays might be suitably apparelled, a number of costumes and properties were supplied by the office of the revels. Lists of these are preserved in the university archives.

The success of the performances seems, however, to have been scarcely on a level with the magnitude of the preparations. On the first evening, a pastoral play *Alba* was presented. 'In the acting thereof they brought in five or six men almost naked which were much disliked by the Queen and Ladies.' It needed the entreaties of the chancellors of both universities to prevent the king leaving 'before half the comedy had been ended.' On the following night, James saw *Ajax Flagellifer*. James would have done well to imitate his predecessor in countermanding[1], as he 'was very weary before he came thither, but much more wearied by it, and spoke many words of dislike.' Nor did matters fare much better on the third evening, when *Vertumnus sive Annus Recurrens*, by Matthew Gwinne of St John's, was performed on the Christ Church stage. Though it was well acted by a company consisting chiefly of St John's men, the king fell asleep in the middle. But the play produced on the following evening 'made amends for all.' It was *The Queenes Arcadia* of Samuel Daniel, memorable as the first English pastoral drama written for the academic stage[2]. Guarini's *Il Pastor Fido* had been acted a short time previously at King's college, Cambridge, in a Latin version, *Pastor Fidus*. *Parthenia*, a similar version of Luigi Groto's *Pentimento Amoroso*, preserved in manuscript at Emmanuel college, Cambridge, is of uncertain date. Daniel, as was natural, followed the general lines of Italian pastoral drama; but the statement of a contemporary Cambridge visitor to Oxford, that 'it was drawn out of *Pastor Fidus*,' is misleading. So far as Daniel's play owes a direct debt to a foreign original, it is to Tasso's *Aminta* rather than to Guarini's work, while the conception of the plot, though not of a number of episodes, must be put down to the English poet's own credit. It deals with the entanglements and evils produced in Arcadia by the machinations of sophisticated representatives of the outer world. Chief among these are Colax, 'a corrupted traveller,' and Techne, 'a subtle wench of Corinth,' who, by their nefarious schemes, delude the shepherd Amyntas into the belief that Cloris, whom he wooes in vain, is a wanton. In despair, he tries to take his own life, but, in an episode imitated

---

[1] Cf. *ante*, p. 298.

[2] For a brief sketch of the progress of the pastoral drama in England see the following chapter (XIII).

from *Aminta,* is rescued by Cloris, whose heart has, at last, been touched by love. The arch evildoers, after plotting not only against the hero and heroine but against other Arcadian lovers, are banished for ever. Subordinate, but more amusing, mischief-makers are Lincus, a pettifogging lawyer, and Alcon, a quack doctor, into whose mouth is put a description of tobacco as

> a certaine herbe wrapt up in rowles
> From th' Island of *Nicosia* where it growes:
>
> * * * * * * *
>
> And this he said a wondrous vertue had,
> To purge the head, and cure the great catarre.

This, of course, was intended to tickle the ears of the author of *A Counterblaste to Tobacco.* But the permanent attraction of Daniel's play lies not in its topical references or even in its plot and characterisation, but in the lyrical sweetness of its verse and the limpid grace of its diction and imagery. Its production at Christ Church is amongst the most memorable records of the Oxford stage. Probably, however, none of the Christ Church plays gratified the king so much as a more informal open-air interlude which took place in front of St John's college on the day of his entry into Oxford. Three young scholars, dressed as nymphs, suddenly appeared in his path. They announced that they were the sibyls who had formerly foretold to Banquo the rule of his descendants, and that they had come again to prophesy all happiness to James, and the perpetuity of Banquo's stock upon the British throne. They then saluted the king in turn with a triple *salve,* and greeted similarly the queen and prince Henry. James 'did very much applaude' the 'conceipt,' which was devised by Matthew Gwinne, and it is possible that some account of it reached the ears of Shakespeare and suggested the writing of *Macbeth* in the following year.

The stimulus of the royal visit to theatrical activity at Oxford, especially at St John's college, seems to have lasted for some time afterwards. To this, we have remarkable testimony in a unique memorial of the academic stage preserved in the St John's library. It is a manuscript written by Griffin Higgs, a member of the college, who successively became fellow of Merton and chaplain to Elizabeth of Bohemia, and entitled *A true and faithfull relation of the risinge and fall of Thomas Tucker, Prince of Alba Fortunata, Lord St Johns &c., with all the occurrents which happened throughout his whole domination.* No extant document, not even Gager's letter to Rainolds, lets us so completely behind the scenes of the collegiate theatre, or brings home to us so intimately the hopes and fears, the labours and difficulties, connected with the performances. The manuscript is an account of a series of festivities which lasted from All Saints' eve (31 October) 1607 till the first Sunday in the following Lent[1]. On All Saints' eve, Thomas Tucker, a bachelor of arts (later, a fellow of the college and canon of Bristol) was elected 'Christmas Lord or Prince of the Revells... to appoint & moderate all such games and pastimes as should come.' Two 'bills' were, therefore, sent out to the masters craving allegiance to his authority and 'money & maintenance.' Among those who contributed were Laud and Juxon, each assessed at ten shillings. But, in order to raise an adequate sum, Tucker (like a true Stewart ruler) had to levy a further requisition on ex-fellows and commoners and on college tenants. Sufficient provision thus made, he was publicly installed on St Andrew's day by means of a Latin 'devise,' *Ara Fortunae*. In this, the prince, with his leading councillors, visits the temple of Fortune and is assured by her priestess of the favour of the goddess. He accordingly announces that he no longer reigns by popular favour but by divine right, and that he is preparing 'pomps and triumphs' for the entertainment of his faithful subjects.

On Christmas day, the prince sat at high table in the vice-president's place, and a boar's head was carried in as 'the first messe' by the 'tallest and lustiest' of his guards, to the accompaniment of a brisk carol. In the evening, a short Latin interlude, *Saturnalia*, was performed, introducing a *Dominus* and a *Servus* in the inverted relation peculiar to the Roman festival, and afterwards Hercules, who, by interpreting aright an equivocal Delphic oracle, shows that waxen lights and not human sacrifices are the offerings enjoined at this anniversary. As the season of the Saturnalia coincided approximately with Christmastide, these waxen lights, it is hinted, are the source of Christmas candles; and, in a prose epilogue, an ingenious parallel and contrast are drawn between the pagan and the Christian festival.

The same sense of classical and Biblical analogies dictated the choice of a play for Innocents' day. A Senecan tragedy on the story of Philomela was written for the occasion, as it was thought that the

---

[1] The narrative part of the manuscript and one play *The Seven Dayes of the Weeke* were printed in 1816, with the title *The Christmas Prince*. The present writer has been given facilities for consulting the manuscript, and the account of the other plays is here printed for the first time.

subject 'well fitted the day, by reason of the murder of Innocent Itis.' But the performance had to be postponed for a day because the carpenters were 'no way ready wth the stage.' Then a further mishap occurred. 'The Prince himself who was to play Tereus had gott such an exceeding cold that it was impossible for him to speake, or speaking to be heard.' However, with the unnamed author of the tragedy in reserve as an understudy should he be 'constrained to leave,' the resourceful Tucker got through his part with credit. 'The whole play was wel acted and wel liked,' a more favourable verdict than had been pronounced on Calfhill's tragedy on the same story acted before Elizabeth at Christ Church in 1566.

It is characteristic of the academic taste of the time, that *Philomela* was much more appreciated than an English play *Time's Complaint*, acted on New Year's day as part of 'the princes triumphs.' The failure of this piece, which received only 'two or three cold plaudites,' was partly due to the blunders of amateur actors, of which Higgs gives amusing details, and to the overcrowding on the stage. But, doubtless, the fault also lay largely in the plot, which combines awkwardly a semi-allegorical tale of Time's attempt to recover his daughter Veritas, kept in thraldom by Opinion and Error, and a farcical series of mistakes and entanglements arising out of the theft of goodwife Spigott's goods by a drunken cobbler, Swallow. Yet, *Time's Complaint* is far from being without interest. It contains genre pictures of characteristic Elizabethan types, such as the dispossessed countryman, the cashiered soldier and the professional beggar. It introduces, also, in Studioso, the poor and embittered scholar, and in Philonices, the grasping, pompous lawyer and justice, two figures akin to those in the *Parnassus* plays.

The spirits of the St John's actors, which had been grievously depressed by the cold reception of *Time's Complaint*, were revived by the success of an amusing show, *The Seven Dayes of the Weeke*, acted at the president's lodging on Sunday, 10 January, and repeated by special request before the vice-chancellor and other dignitaries a week later. Equally successful was a Latin comedy *Philomathes*, mingling abstractions with Plautine characters. After its performance 'the stage & scaffold were pul'd downe wch had stood from Cristmas'; but they were set up again on Shrove Tuesday for the prince's resignation. This, like his public installation, was solemnised in the form of a play, *Ira seu Tumulus Fortunae*. The goddess has now grown angry with the prince because he has not paid her sufficiently constant homage. His ministers resign their symbols of office and desert him. In vain he visits again the altar of Fortune, and seeks to placate her wrath. He, therefore, strips himself of the emblems of sovereignty, and lays them in a sepulchre in her temple, dedicating himself henceforth to the service of Minerva.

Thus ended the memorable reign of Thomas Tucker; but, as the stage and scaffolds had been re-erected, and, as an English tragedy on the story of Periander, tyrant of Corinth, had been prepared, it was decided to perform this on the following Saturday. It attracted such a concourse that hundreds could not find room in the hall. They 'made such an hideous noice, and raised such a tumult wth breaking of windows all about the colledge, throwinge of stones into the hall, and such like ryott' that the officers of the college had to rush forth, 'wth about a dozen whifflers well armed and swords drawne.' The rioters then ran away, but some of the ringleaders were arrested, and imprisoned in the porter's lodge till the play was over.

Curiously enough, about a week later, on 20 February, there was a similar riot at Cambridge, when there was 'foul & great disorder committed at the time of a comedy in King's College,' probably a lost play by Phineas Fletcher. In the same month, four years later, there was a yet more serious disturbance at Cambridge, when the St John's men, angry at being excluded from a comedy acted at Trinity college, began an affray outside the Great Gate, which led to proceedings in the vice-chancellor's court. In sharp contrast to these tumultuous proceedings was the scene in the hall of Trinity on 2 March 1613, when prince Charles and Frederick, the elector palatine, saw Samuel Brooke's comedy called *Adelphe*, and when the elector slept during the greater part of the performance, which lasted from seven in the evening till one. On the following evening, the princes were again provided with solid entertainment by the performance of *Scyros*, a Latin version by Brooke of Bonarelli's pastoral drama, *Filli di Sciro*.

On 7 March 1615, James himself, with prince Charles, came to Cambridge, and stayed at Trinity for four nights. As the sovereign had not visited the university since Elizabeth's 'progress' in 1564, elaborate preparations were made to celebrate the event. The days were devoted to learned disputations and the evenings to plays. The first piece, *Aemilia*, a Latin comedy written by Edward Cecil of St John's, was not very successful; but ample amends were made on the following evening when, in the hall of Trinity, *Ignoramus* was launched on its triumphant career. Its author was George Ruggle, fellow of Clare hall, who had formerly been a scholar of Trinity, and the actors were chosen from various colleges, difficulty being found in filling suitably the female parts. On one side, *Ignoramus* is linked with the group of Latin adaptations of Italian comedies mentioned above, for it is founded on G. della Porta's *Trappolaria.* But Ruggle transformed his original by extensive additions, and by a fundamental change in the central character, converting him out of a soldier into the lawyer who gives his name to the play. Thus metamorphosed, the typically southern comedy became the climax of Aristophanic attacks by gownsmen upon the town and its officials. The title part is a merciless caricature of the detested recorder, Brackyn, who had already been ridiculed in *The Returne from Pernassus, Part II.* The animus against him as a common lawyer had been intensified by public events. The law dictionary *The Interpreter*, published in 1607 by John Cowell, regius professor of civil law, had been suppressed on the demand of the House of Commons, because its tendency was to exalt the royal prerogative at the expense of common law. The civilians of the university and the king himself were, therefore, delighted when Ruggle brought upon the stage a burlesque figure talking a barbarous jargon of bastard Latin and the technical terms of common law. It is the novelty of this conception and the gusto with which it is developed that give the play its unique character. In the course of its intricate plot, Ignoramus goes through a variety of humiliating and painful experiences. On a visit to Bordeaux, he falls in love with the heroine, Rosabella, and engages to pay 600 pieces of gold for her hand. But, through the stratagems of Antonius, the favoured suitor of the girl, Ignoramus obtains possession instead of the heavy-handed virago, Polla, who belabours him soundly. Amazed at his incomprehensible outcries, she thinks he is bewitched and goes to fetch her husband and a monk, who, in a scene of richly farcical humour, exorcise the evil spirits out of him and carry him off, shrieking, to a monastery for his final cure. Rosabella, of course, is finally united to Antonius, and a mystery attaching to her birth is cleared up.

Ignoramus, with its mixture of learning and horseplay, was exactly suited for captivating James. The play presented on the following night, *Albumazar*, though adapted by Tomkis, author of *Lingua*, from another comedy of della Porta, *L'Astrologo*, was less successful. But it contains two amusing characters in

Albumazar, the rascally astronomer, and Trincalo, the rustic whom Albumazar 'transforms' into his absent master, Antonio, with ludicrous consequences when the latter unexpectedly returns home. In its printed form, the play was fortunate enough to attract both Dryden and Garrick, both of whom revived it on the London stage. But, on its production, it seems, from a contemporary account, to have been less appreciated not only than its predecessor, *Ignoramus*, but than its successor on the following evening, *Melanthe*, a Latin pastoral drama from the pen of Samuel Brooke, whose *Adelphe* and *Scyros* have been mentioned above. The king could not stay to see the last play prepared for his entertainment, *Sicelides*, by Phineas Fletcher; but it was acted a few days later. He thus missed seeing the first English 'piscatory' on the stage, as he had already seen at Oxford, in 1605, the first English pastoral drama. The main plot of *Sicelides*, dealing with the romantic love stories of Perindus and Glaucilla and Thalander and Olinda, is, apparently, original, though episodes and motives are derived from classical and Italian sources. One underplot centres round Cosma, the typical 'light nymph' of 'Messena,' and the other round Cancrone and Scrocca, low-comedy fishermen whose talk is largely a farrago of 'malapropisms' and topical allusions. The machinery of the play is unduly intricate and perplexing, and the characterisation is not vivid. But the work has real charm in its delicate delineation of emotions, in the graceful imagery of its descriptive passages and in the lyric sweetness of its choruses.

James was so delighted with *Ignoramus* that he revisited Cambridge in May to see it a second time. Its triumph marks the close of the most vital period of the university drama. Henceforward, no new type was evolved, and the distinctively academic element dwindles. Allegorical plays became increasingly popular with college dramatists, though *Lingua* remained unrivalled for wit and *verve*. Thus, in February 1618, *Technogamia or The Marriage of the Arts*, by Barten Holiday, was acted at Christ Church 'with no great applause'; but it was repeated before the king at Woodstock in August 1621. Though James seems to have found the piece very dull, it is not without merit. The action shows how some of the arts and sciences endeavour to enter into unnatural unions. Thus, Poeta seeks to win the hand of Astronomia, but is finally allied to Historia and promises that his love shall follow her 'more inseparably than the Hexameter the Pentameter.' Closely related to *Lingua*, to which it contains direct references, is *Pathomachia or The Battell of Affections*, published by 'a Friend of the deceassed Author,' in 1630, and 'written some years since.'

It deals with the revolt of the Affections against Love and Hatred, 'whom heretofore they counted their King and Queene.' Love and Hatred are aided by the Virtues, headed by Justice, while the rebels have the support of the Vices disguised as Affections or Virtues, and commanded by Pride. Justice, however, unmasks them, and sends them to confinement, whereupon the Affections tender their submission and are pardoned. The work is in prose throughout, and contains interesting passages and many allusions to recent events, but lacks dramatic movement and vivacity.

Religious satire is another predominant element in the later university plays—a foretaste of the dread conflict that was fast approaching. *Loiola*, by John Hacket, acted at Trinity before the university on 28 February and before James on a third visit to Cambridge on 12 March 1623, is an entertaining Latin comedy, which attacks impartially Roman Catholics and Calvinists, the former in the person of Loiola, 'an unscrupulous Jesuit,' the latter in that of Martinus, a canting elder of Amsterdam, where the scene is laid. To the same year belongs the semi-allegorical *Fucus Histriomastix*, wherein the title *rôle*, that of a hypocritical puritan minister, was played by Robert Ward of Queens' college, who was probably the author of the piece. Fucus, who hates all plays and amusements, seeks to prevent the marriage of Philomathes and Comoedia, otherwise, the production of an academic comedy. The arguments he uses are the same as those of Rainolds in his controversy with Gager, and seem derived from his book. But his intrigues are foiled, and he also comes off badly in a feud with the merry-making countryman, Villanus, who is in love with Ballada, an illegitimate sister of Comoedia[1].

Another actor in *Fucus* was Peter Hausted, afterwards fellow of Queens', who, when Charles and Henrietta Maria visited Cambridge in March 1632, wrote in their honour the singular play *The Rival Friends*. This is linked to the comedies satirising religious hypocrisy by its caustic portraiture of the wooers of the deformed and foolish Mistress Ursely, whose hand carries with it an 'impropriate parsonage.' More realistically humorous personages are Stipes, the shepherd of the simoniacal patron, and his wife and daughter, all genuinely rustic figures without the customary pastoral veneer. From Hausted's preface to the play when it was published, it is evident that his low-life portraiture had been adversely criticised as unbefitting the royal presence. But to

---

[1] See *Fucus Histriomastix*, edited by Smith, G. C. Moore (1909), introduction and notes, pp. 98—9. The editor suggests that the play may have been partly inspired by an attempt, recorded by Chamberlain, to suppress the performance of *Loiola*.

modern taste this appeals much more strongly than does the pseudo-romantic main plot. The two friends, Lucius and Neander, rivals for the love of Pandora, vie in their readiness to abdicate in each other's favour, and carry their altruism so far that the lady gives her affections, at first in pretence, afterwards in reality, to a third wooer. The popularity, however, of such fantastic themes was evidenced by the successful production at Trinity, during the same royal visit, of Thomas Randolph's *The Jealous Lovers.* Randolph, a distinguished *alumnus* of Westminster and Trinity, had already written two short academic 'shows,' *Aristippus or The Joviall Philosopher* and *The Conceited Pedler. The Jealous Lovers* was his first complete play, and the rapturous welcome accorded to it does little credit to either the university or the court. Randolph's inventiveness and rhetorical fluency cannot redeem the essential falsity of the main plot. Tyndarus is insanely suspicious of the faithfulness of his beloved Evadne, and Techmessa similarly mistrusts her devoted Pamphilus. The two 'jealous lovers' go through a mock funeral (which gives occasion for an imitation of the gravedigger's scene in *Hamlet*) as a final test of the constancy of the seemingly bereft pair. But, after this ordeal has proved their loyalty unswerving, Hymen forbids the proposed unions, and it transpires that Tyndarus is the brother of Evadne, and Techmessa the sister of Pamphilus. Interwoven with these pseudo-romantic episodes is an underplot of gross humour.

The royal pair, accompanied by their nephews, the palatine princes, paid a second visit to Oxford in August 1636, when the last important series of academic plays was produced in their honour. William Strode, public orator, welcomed the king to Christ Church with a speech, and with an allegorical drama, *The Floating Island,* which was staged with great elaboration, and furnished with music by Henry Lawes. The title and general conception of the work, in which the island represents the human mind afloat on the sea of the passions, was, doubtless, suggested by Phineas Fletcher's *The Purple Island or The Isle of Man,* published at Cambridge in 1633. But Strode develops the theme on lines of his own, and with the added spice of political and religious satire. A conspiracy is formed by Audax, Irato and others against the rule of king Prudentius and his counsellor, Intellectus Agens. Prudentius resigns his crown, and Fancy is proclaimed queen, her only law being 'that each man use his proper humour, be it vice or virtue.' Discord and tumult are the result, and Prudentius is finally implored to resume the crown, after each of the plotters has declined it in turn. The implied lesson on the evil results of rebellion, and the castigation of Prynne, in the person of Melancholico, a play-hating puritan, helped to recommend the play to the royal favour. Equally successful were the two dramas produced on the following day. One of these, *Love's Hospitall*, by George Wilde, fellow of St John's, was performed in the afternoon at that college at the expense of Laud, who, as chancellor of the university, was present to welcome the king and queen. The piece is an entertaining comedy of humours, in almost farcical vein, and is in no way characteristically academic. This is also true of William Cartwright's *The Royall Slave*[1], acted in the evening at Christ Church. An Ephesian captive, Cratander, in accordance with an old custom among the Persians, is granted for three days before his execution the full insignia and privileges of kingship. During this period, he displays such nobility of soul that heaven intervenes in his favour, and he is spared to become the wearer of a real crown. This theme is handled by Cartwright with genuine rhetorical effectiveness, and his drama was furnished with special scenic effects by Inigo Jones and incidental music by Lawes. So delighted was the queen with the performance that she afterwards borrowed the costumes and scenery for a repetition of the play by her own company at Hampton court.

The academic stage was to number yet one more illustrious recruit in Cowley, whose *Naufragium Joculare*, based on classical sources, was acted at Trinity college, Cambridge, in 1638, and was followed in 1642 by his satirical comedy *The Guardian*, remodelled after the Restoration into *Cutter of Coleman Street*. But the royal visit to Oxford in 1636 marks the close of these elaborate university displays, which had begun with Elizabeth's coming to Cambridge in 1564. Even in the traditionally loyal community on the banks of the Isis, there were ominous symptoms of the rapidly growing resentment against the autocratic rule of Charles and Laud. As the king and queen rode away from Christ Church, the streets, according to custom, were lined with 'Scholers of all degrees,' but 'neither they nor the citizens made any expression of joy, nor uttered, as the manner is, *Vivat Rex*.' When Oxford, some seven years later, again opened its gates to Charles, it was not to entertain him with 'masques and triumphs,' but to afford him shelter in his stern conflict with his parliamentary foes.

The civil war and the commonwealth mark a period of deep cleavage in English stage history. With the Restoration, came new men and new methods, and a forgetfulness of all but the greatest dramatists of 'the former age.' It was virtually

[1] See, as to Cartwright's plays, *ante*, chap. IX.

the work of the nineteenth century to rediscover the lesser Elizabethan writers for the popular stage. The university drama, bilingual in utterance, and with its memorials not easy of access, has had to wait for yet tardier recognition. It had, of course, patent faults. It produced much that was artificial, amateurish and unduly imitative, and its moral standard was as unexacting as that of the London theatre of the day. But it had behind it truly formative influences, in the renascence ardour for classical lore and delight in pageantry, in the gownsmen's haughty resentment of the buffets of fortune to which they were exposed, and in the traditional hostility between scholars and townsmen by Isis and by Cam. Hence sprang that special type of Aristophanic comedy, unique in this period of the drama, represented by *Pedantius* and *Ignoramus*, *Club Law* and the *Parnassus* trilogy. And, in addition to these distinctively topical university plays, we owe to the academic stage a number of dramas moulded and coloured by the peculiar conditions of their origin. Such are the semi-Senecan plays on religious, historical and mythological subjects, like *Archipropheta*, *Richardus Tertius* and *Ulysses Redux*; comedies like *Laelia* and *Hymenaeus*; allegorical pieces like *Lingua*, *Fucus* and *The Floating Island*; pastorals like *The Queenes Arcadia* and *Sicelides*. In these and kindred productions, noted in this chapter or merely recorded as 'comedy' or 'tragedy' in college account-books, the university humanists preserved elements of classic and neo-classic culture which would otherwise have been almost entirely lost to the stage. From Oxford and Cambridge, these influences permeated to the capital. For, sharp as in general was the division, social and intellectual, between academic and professional playwrights, the latter and larger class was constantly being recruited from graduates who had gained their earliest dramatic experience as spectators, actors, or, in some cases, authors, of college 'shows.' The royal visits to the universities helped further to extend the range of influence of the amateur stage. And they did something more. Under the personal rule of the Tudors and Stewarts, the centre of national life was not fixed in Westminster, as at present; it moved with the movements of the sovereign. And thus, the university plays, as the principal magnet which drew Elizabeth, James and Charles with their courts to Oxford and Cambridge, performed a more important function than has been usually recognised. They helped materially for nearly a hundred years to keep the two seats of learning in contact with the throne, from which radiated, for good and for ill, the dominating forces of the age.

CHAPTER XIII

MASQUE AND PASTORAL

THE Elizabethan drama, being without scenery and elaborate stage apparatus, made its appeal to the mind rather than to the eye, and used language as the main instrument by which the imagination of its audience was aroused and satisfied. This familiar fact goes far to explain the essentially intellectual character of the Elizabethan drama, and the wonderful literary power of the great dramatists. But we should misinterpret the facts very seriously if we allowed ourselves to suppose that the Elizabethan age was indifferent to the appeal of the eye, or to imagine that, because the Elizabethan playgoer was without the elaborate scenery and staging of the modern theatre, he was disdainful of spectacle, and unwilling to spend time and money on gorgeous shows in which the master art of pageantry combined music, singing, painting, dancing and architecture in united effort to charm and delight his senses.

The Elizabethan, for all his intellectual energy, was intensely sensuous. In this respect, he represents the end of the Middle Ages rather than the beginning of modern times. We cannot here consider the meaning of that reaction against pageantry which was an important part of puritanism, but we may note that the modern student does not see the Elizabethan age as it saw itself; for he overlooks as childish those things which it most cared for. The drama meant, broadly, the introduction into popular entertainment of a new intellectual element, which gradually discredited pageantry, so that it ceased to be the art of the educated and refined. But, all through the Elizabethan age and until the closing of the theatres in 1642, masque and pageantry held their place in the public eye, and in the public interest, as the most important and honourable and magnificent of the arts. The masque at court and among the nobility, and the pageant among the citizens, were practised with an energy that, for the

time being, made them the most obvious, if not the most characteristic, of the national activities, the means by which corporate
and national feeling most readily expressed itself.   This old world
splendour of masque and pageant has, for the most part, perished.
Neither antiquarian researches nor modern adaptations can make
it live again, but, before it died, the intellectual power of the new
dramatic art came to the rescue and infused into the Elizabethan
masque a literary element, which has been a preservative against
decay.   The leading dramatists were pressed into the service of
masque and pageant, and contributed an element to the spectacle
which, in many cases, has survived.   The words supplied to pageants
and masques by Munday and Middleton, by Campion, Chapman,
Beaumont and Browne and, above all, by Jonson, form a small, but
very interesting, appendix to the many volumes of the drama.
The extant masques have considerable literary merits, and they
lead on to Milton's *Comus*, in which masque expands into pastoral:
with pastoral, generally, they have an important connection.   But,
in studying masques as a literary form, we have to bear in mind
that we are not dealing with essential masque.   Even Ben Jonson's
words are not much more than the stick of the rocket after the
firework has flamed and faded.   Essential masque was the appeal
of the moment to the eye and the ear, the blaze of colour and
light, the mist of perfume, the succession of rapidly changing
scenes and tableaux, crowded with wonderful and beautiful figures.
All the gods of Olympus, all the monsters of Tartarus, all the
heroes of history, all the ladies of romance, the fauns, the satyrs,
the fairies, the witches—all these were presented to the eye, while
every kind of musical instrument charmed the ear, and eye and
ear together were delighted by an elaboration of dance and
measured motion which has never been known since.   We have
put away these childish things : but our maturity has elaborated
no art equally joyous and whole-hearted.   The actual remains
of the masque with the careful description of the scenes, written,
afterwards, in cold blood by the deviser, even though that deviser
were Jonson himself, are but broken meats of a banquet that
is over.

The curious modern reaches a direct and adequate conception
of the vanished splendour and joy, and is enabled to comprehend
clearly the medieval instinct, only when the medieval passion for
masque and pageant receives imaginative expression in the work
of a great descriptive poet.   Such a poet there was, but he was
not a dramatist.   Spenser came before the drama.   The masque

was not drama ; in many respects, it was the antithesis of drama.
Dramatists who wrote while the masque was still alive often,
in some metaphor or description, thrill us with a touch of its
glamour.   Shakespeare, for instance, regards the masque as a
symbol of the evanescent.   This world and all its inhabitants

> shall dissolve
> And, like this insubstantial pageant faded,
> Leave not a rack behind.

The words express negatively the delight of the spectator in the
show by exhibiting his dismay that it must stop—'Our revels now
are ended.'   But we require a positive description, in which the
masque is not what it must be to the dramatist, unreal and un-
satisfying ; rather, on the contrary, the expression of life's wonder
and joy.   This positive description is given us with extraordinary
power and fulness in Spenser's *Faerie Queene*, especially in the
first three books, which were published in 1590, before English
drama had developed its strength.

But, before we touch upon the relation of Spenser's art to the
masque, we must attempt to summarise the history of masque and
pageant before his time.   The masque, like the drama, runs back
into remote antiquity, and we must make an effort to conceive
of masque as it was practised in England during the fifteenth and
sixteenth centuries, if we are to understand clearly what a masque
was, and what modifications it underwent while, in Ben Jonson's
hands, it was the main amusement of the English court and
nobility.   Out of numerous accounts of masques that have come
down to us, we may take two as typical of the kind of entertainments which, by their combination, finally produced the true
masque.   For the first, we will go back to the fourteenth century.

Edward III died on 2 January 1377.   On the second of February
following, being Candlemas day, 'the Commons of London made
great sporte and solemnity' in honour of his successor, prince
Richard, who was lodged with his mother and the leading nobles
of the realm at the palace in the royal manor of Kennington,
which had been a favourite residence of the Black prince.   'At
night and in the night,' a cavalcade of 130 men, 'disguizedly
aparailed and well mounted on horsebacke to goe on mumming,'
rode 'from Newgate through Cheape' over London Bridge to
Kennington. They went 'with great noyse of minstralsye, trumpets,
cornets and shawmes, and great plenty of waxe torches lighted.'
First came 48 esquires, two and two, 'in cotes and clokes of red
say or sendall, and their faces covered with vizards well and

handsomely made'; next followed 48 knights, 'well arayed after
the same maner'; then a single figure, 'as he had bene an
emperor'; then another single figure, 'as a pope'; after him,
24 'arayed like Cardinals'; and, last, 8 or 10 'with black vizardes
like devils, nothing amiable, seeming like legates.' On reaching
the palace, all alighted and entered the hall, into which presently
came the prince, his mother and the leading nobles, whom 'the
said mummers saluted'; the mummers then proceeded to play
with a pair of prepared dice with the prince and other gentry for
valuable gifts. When the gifts had all been won, 'the prince and
the lordes danced on the one side and the mummers on the other
a great while,' and then they drank and took their leave and
departed to London.

In this account, we have what is probably the oldest and
simplest form of what is afterwards the masque[1]. It is called
'a mumming,' and the performers are 'mummers.' The word
means that the disguised performers say nothing that would
betray their identity. They dice in silence, using only dumb show
where they wish to signify their meaning. But they are all
disguised with vizards, the old word for mask ; they are accompanied by musicians ; they dance together among themselves when
their 'mumming' business is over and torchbearers conduct them
on their way. Simple as their scheme was, the entry of masked
mummers with blare of trumpets and blaze of torches into the
great banqueting hall must have been highly picturesque. The
impressiveness of the moment is splendidly given by the dramatist :

> Night, like a masque, is entered heaven's great hall,
> With thousand torches ushering the way[2]!

In this particular 'mumming,' the vizarded procession represented the emperor and pope as coming with attendant knights
and cardinals to greet the uncrowned king. When a 'mumming'
was regarded from the point of view of the dress assumed by the
'mummers,' it was called a 'disguising'; and, by the sixteenth
century, this name quite superseded the other, as, in the seventeenth century, it was itself superseded by 'masque'; so that Ben
Jonson, in 1622, makes Notch aver, 'Disguise was the old English
word for a masque, Sir'; to which the groom of the revels answers,
'There is no such word in the office now, I assure you, Sir ;

---

[1] We shall use this spelling for the spectacle, and ' mask ' for a vizard.
[2] *The Insatiate Countesse*, at end.

I have served here, man and boy, a prenticeship or twain, and I should know[1].'

'Mumming' came to be applied particularly to the custom, practised usually at Christmas time, of going round in masking habit from house to house and gaming with dice ; the game itself was called 'mumchance.' There are many allusions to it in the Elizabethan dramatists. Finally, we may notice in this example of a disguising, the '8 or 10 with black vizardes, like devils, nothing amiable' ; these are the germ of the Jonsonian antimasque.

For our second typical instance, let us go to the reign of Henry VII in the year 1501. The marriage of prince Arthur to Katharine of Arragon was celebrated in London with great magnificence. The walls of Westminster hall were 'richly hanged with pleasant clothes of arras,' and, in the upper end, had 'a Royall and great Cupboard' erected, upon which was displayed a 'goodly and rich treasure of plate.' The king and queen took their seats 'under their Clothes of Estate,' and all the nobility 'were ordered in their Roomes.' To this great assembly entered a 'most goodly and pleasant disguising, convayed and shewed in pageantes proper and subtile': of which 'the first was a Castle right cunningly devised sett uppon certaine wheeles and drawne into the said great hall of fower great beastes with chaines of gold.' The beasts were two lions, a hart and an ibex, personated, each one of them, by two men. In the castle were 'disguised VIII goodly and fresh ladyes looking out of the windowes of the same,' and, in the turrets, 'fowre children singing most sweetly and harmoniously.' The castle was drawn into the hall and up to the king's state[2], and then set on one side to allow of the entry of a second car, this time 'a shippe,' having 'her mastes toppes sayles her tackling and all other apperteynances necessary unto a seemely vessel as though it had been sayling.' The ship cast anchor in front of the king, next the castle. On board the ship was a lady, in apparel like to the princess of Spain. Hope and Desire go from the ship to the castle as ambassadors from the knights of the mount of Love ; but the ladies in the castle will have nothing to say to the knights. 'Incontinent came in the third Pageant,' a mountain, with eight knights upon it, to whom the ambassadors recounted their ill-success with the ladies. Thereupon, the knights make a great show of assaulting the castle, and the ladies surrender. The cars are wheeled back, and the knights and ladies 'daunced together divers and many goodly

---

[1] *The Masque of Augures.*   [2] The royal seat.

dances.' The cars then came back for the masquers and took them away; after which, prince Arthur and his bride and other distinguished people in the audience danced, including young prince Henry and his sister Margaret. This 'disguising' was succeeded on the following evenings by three others, nearly as elaborate as the first. The whole display makes it quite clear that the early sixteenth century had not much to learn from the early seventeenth. The splendour of these shows reached a high water mark in the reign of Henry VIII, and then, again, in the reign of James I, when the mechanical and artistic genius of Inigo Jones introduced new contrivances and a more elaborate arrangement of scenery, suppressing almost entirely the processional character of the masque and the early car.

Our second example of a masque has added to the first the important item of the pageant or car. This, of course, suggests a connection between the 'disguising' and the medieval miracle-plays, which were performed on the movable waggon called a pageant. It is easy to see how the grandeur of the cavalcade would be increased if the emperor and pope were put in cars. In the British Museum, there is a design by Albert Dürer, dated 1522, of a triumphal car for Maximilian, which may serve as an illustration of the way in which a car would become a 'pageant'—an elaborate structure to hold masquers. This pageant, as the above example shows, is capable of very varied developments. But, as the car becomes more elaborate, it cannot easily form part of a long procession; to draw it the length of the hall taxes the ingenuity of the carpenters; and, finally, it becomes stationary, suggesting something approximating to the modern stage at one end of the hall. The car, moreover, when it is a ship or a lanthorn or a 'herbour,' requires some explanation; and an exposition of the device of the car is added to the original dance of the masquers. This is the masque in its simplest outline—certain men or women disguised, who arrive in some setting which corresponds to their dress, and which has to be explained before they dance their measures; they retire as they came.

The disguisings had an extraordinary vogue under Henry VIII, and they found a historian whose prose descriptions have hardly received the attention which their great merit deserves. Edward Hall was a lawyer and a politician. His parents were in sympathy with advanced reformers. He affords, therefore, a remarkable instance of the passion for pageant displaying itself in a hard-headed political trimmer, bred up in a sober and serious middle-class family. Pageant was Hall's one passion. His English style takes on a new distinction when he begins to describe the splendid succession of festivities which distinguished the reign of Henry VIII. His masterpiece is, perhaps, his account of the Field of the Cloth of Gold ; but, everywhere, thanks to his enthusiasm, his accounts of masques and entertainments are gorgeously coloured and wonderfully full of movement.

He is the writer who notes the coming of the word 'masque.' On the evening of Epiphany, 1512,

the kyng with a XI other wer disguised, after the maner of Italie, called a maske, a thyng not seen afore in Englande; thei were appareled in garmentes long and brode, wrought all with gold, with visers and cappes of gold, *and* after the banket doen, these Maskers came in, with six gentlemen disguised in silke, bearing staffe torches, and desired the ladies to daunce, some were content, and some that knewe the fashion of it refused, because it was not a thyng commonly seen. And after thei daunced, and commoned together as the fashion of the Maske[1] is, thei toke their leave and departed, and so did the Quene and all the ladies[2].

This passage raises problems which are still under discussion. What was the 'thyng not seen afore in Englande?' What was the 'thyng not commonly seen,' which made some of the ladies refuse to dance? In short, what was the difference between the 'disguising,' familiar in England for centuries, and this innovation 'after the maner of Italie, called a maske'? The probable answer is that there was a difference in dress which was connected with a difference in procedure. The masquers not only danced with one another, but, after their own dance, they chose partners among the spectators. This introduced into the masque a new element of courtship and intrigue. For this device to maintain its proper piquancy, the disguise of the masquer must be complete ; his costume must, like a domino, conceal any peculiarities of mien and shape which might betray him if he wore a more closely-fitting disguise. Whether this sufficiently explains Hall's language must be considered a question still under discussion ; but two points are clear. There is a common conviction, both in France and England, that, in some of its characteristic aspects, the masque was Italian. Ronsard says that 'masquerade' came from the Italians, and mentions '*ses vestemens, ses mœurs et ses façons,*' as the things which were copied. Reyher, after quoting Ronsard,

---

[1] The edition of 1550 reads ' Masques.'

[2] Hall (1548), f. 16r°. For the views that have been expressed on the passage, consult Reyher's first appendix, in *Les Masques Anglais*.

suggests that this borrowing from Italy took place *au moment des expéditions françaises de la fin du XVe et du début du XVIe siècle*. In our own literature, Marlowe's ' I'll have Italian maskes by night[1]' is familiar. But, secondly, the motive of intrigue, whatever its derivation, was a most important addition to the masque's attractiveness. Clearly, it was much appreciated by Henry VIII. It is a breath of natural drama introduced into what is essentially undramatic. Because it is natural drama, it is often the means by which the masque gets a place in dramatic literature. The masque in *Love's Labour's Lost*[2] is delightfully dramatic, and it is an excellent comment, so far as it applies, on the passage in Hall. It is in a masque that Romeo loses his heart to Juliet[3]; and, more interesting still, Henry VIII conceives his passion for Anne Boleyn, in the same way, in the masque of the first act of the play. Many other instances[4] occur in the dramatists, where this dramatic moment in the masque is utilised. But, in the masque itself, this item remains an episode upon which the deviser of the masque never lays his hands; in Henry VIII's reign, the undramatic character of the masque shows no sign of changing.

When we reach the reign of Elizabeth, Spenser's poetry, even more adequately than Hall's prose, reflects and revives the glory of the medieval masque and pageant. His genius, in some of its most characteristic aspects, was exactly fitted to describe and appreciate the world just beyond the real world with which the masque dealt. The masque of the Seven Deadly Sins[5] and the masque of Cupid[6] are magnificent examples of the processional masque. The former shows that the antimasque is implicit in the masque from the beginning. The house of Temperance and the attack upon it[7] recall the knights' onslaught on the castle of the ladies described above. Such famous descriptions as the cave of Mammon[8] and the bower of Bliss[9] are like the set pieces which Inigo Jones tried to make real to the eye when the masque became a fixture at the end of the great hall. There are cantos in *The Faerie Queene* in which we seem in spirit to follow the procession until it reaches the hall, where the full device is displayed before us in all its intricacy. Spenser's abstractions, Coelia, Fidelia, Speranza, Charissa, the porter Humiltá of the

---

[1] *Edward II*, act I, sc. 1. [2] Act v, sc. 2. [3] Act I, sc. 5.
[4] Reyher gives a list of plays with masques inserted; *Les Masques Anglais*, p. 497.
[5] Bk. I, canto iv. [6] Bk. III, canto xii. [7] Bk. II, cantos ix and xi.
[8] Bk. II, canto vii. [9] Bk. II, canto xii.

house of Holiness[1] and scores of others, are just such as meet us in masques; but a line of description like 'bitter Penaunce with an yron whip,' calls up the figure before us more effectually than Jonson's most exact prose; and Spenser's poem abounds in similar vivid lines and stanzas. The poem, again, like almost every masque, is an elaborate compliment. Its relation to Elizabeth is precisely that of Jonson's masques to James or Charles. Spenser's poem, it should be remembered, greatly influenced Ben Jonson and other writers of masque—Ben Jonson in especial.

Elizabeth's frugality prevented the masque from developing in her reign. It was in frequent use, but the queen had not the special taste for it which made it prominent as an amusement of the aristocracy in the courts of Henry VIII and James I. But 'entertainments,' during the queen's numerous progresses, were plentifully produced. The entertainment was the masque out-of-doors, and consisted of some kind of welcoming device or function arranged for greeting the queen on her arrival, or 'discovered' afterwards, as she was conducted round gardens and park. The entertainment had more dramatic possibilities in it than the masque, because it depended less upon scenery, but the English climate kept it always short and slight. One, by Sir Philip Sidney, of considerable merit, has survived—*The May Lady*[2], presented in May 1578, when the queen visited his uncle, the earl of Leicester, at Wanstead. Jonson's reverence for Sidney makes it likely that he did not overlook Sidney's work when he composed the entertainments which were the beginning of his masque work. But it seems more probable that *The May Lady* guided Jonson's views on pastoral than that it influenced his conception of masque, and it remains by itself as a short out-of-doors scene of pastoral comedy, not without influence upon Shakespeare's early comedy. The schoolmaster, master Rombus, is, obviously, an ancestor of Holofernes, and the play's likeness to masque lies in its complimentary character. Some of Lyly's plays, also, have affinities with the masque. They are elaborate compliments; their ideas are not concerned with the real world of men and women; their characters are mythological[3]. But perhaps their most important connection with the masque is their influence upon Jonson's *Cynthia's Revels*[4]. This play magnifies at all points Lyly's limited strength to such a degree that the reader may easily fail to notice its debt to Lyly. But its connection with Jonson's masques is

---

[1] Bk. i, canto x.   [2] Called, also, *The Lady of the May*.
[3] See vol. v, chap. vi.   [4] Cf. *ante*, chap. v, p. 18.

obvious. In *Cynthia's Revels*, a great realist, the author of *Bartholomew Fayre*, succeeds in making us understand how he came to write masques. We see his mind becoming absorbed in the particular art and method of which the masque was an expression.

But, before we pass to Jonson's masques, one Elizabethan play must be mentioned which was neither a masque, nor a pastoral, nor a drama, but partook of the character of all three. It is, perhaps, the most elaborate and beautiful entertainment extant, and the brilliance of its total effect makes us regret that such a delightful type of renascence art did not receive fuller development. Peele's *Araygnement of Paris* comes before the development of the masque, as Milton's *Comus* comes after it, to suggest to us that in the method of the out-of-door entertainment or pastoral there is inherent a truer breath of poetry than is to be found in that of the indoor masque, in which scenery and carpentry and music and dance were always tending to smother and suppress the poetical soul[1].

The first court masque after king James's accession was produced on 8 January 1604 at Hampton court, because plague was prevalent in London. It was *The Vision of the Twelve Goddesses*, in which the masquers were queen Anne herself and eleven of her ladies. By the recommendation of Lucy countess of Bedford, Daniel was chosen to design and write the masque. An indiscreet printer presumptuously brought out an unauthorised account, and this obliged Daniel in self-defence to print a description 'of the whole form thereof in all points as it was then performed by a most magnificent Queen, whose heroical spirit and bounty only gave it so fair an execution as it had.' Daniel thinks that 'these ornaments and delights of peace' deserve to be remembered; and, therefore, he relates how he devised his twelve goddesses to represent the blessings enjoyed by the realm under king James. Night ascends from below and awakes Somnus, who is sleeping in his cave, that he may conjure up the visions which are to delight and entertain the spectators. By the waving of the white horny wand of Somnus, the spectators are enabled to see the temple of Peace, elaborately constructed, where a sibyl stands as priestess,

> Preparing reverent rites with holy hand.

To her, comes Iris from a mountain raised at the lower end of

---

[1] As to *The Araygnement of Paris*, see vol. v, chap. vi, and cf. chap. xi of the present volume.

the hall, to announce the coming of a 'celestial presence of Goddesses,' who are leaving their ancient haunts to visit Britain, 'the land of civil music and of rest.' Iris hands Sybilla a 'prospective' through which to view the goddesses : and Sybilla proceeds to describe all the twelve, one after the other, in four-lined stanzas. Of these, that descriptive of Flora is the best :

> Then cheerful Flora all adorned with flowers,
> Who clothes the earth with beauty and delight
> In thousand Sunday suits, whilst shining hours
> Will scarce afford a darkness to the night.

The stanzas read like faint echoes of Tennyson's descriptions in his *Dream of fair Women*, except that the last line is not shortened. After being thus described, the goddesses descend from the mountain, in threes, ushered by the three graces, with their torchbearers, also in threes, separating them. As they come down, 'the cornets sitting in the concaves of the Mountain, and seen but to their breasts ; in the habit of Satyrs, sound a stately march.' This is the entry of the masquers. The company halt before the temple, and 'the consort music begins'—the musicians being concealed in the cupola of the temple. Meanwhile, the goddesses, one after another, ascended to the temple and delivered their presents to Sybilla, while the graces sang. Then came the dance of the masquers, to the music of viols and lutes placed on one side of the hall. It was performed 'with great majesty and art, consisting of divers strains framed into motions circular, square, triangular, with other proportions exceeding rare and full of variety.' This ended, the graces sang again, in order to rest the ladies; after which, the masquing ladies 'prepared to take out the Lords to dance ; with whom they performed certain measures, galliards and corantos.' Iris then came to say that the deities must return, and, after her speech,

they fell to a short departing dance and so ascended the Mountain, whilst the cornets taking their notes from the ceasing of the music below, sounded another delightful march.

From this description, we can gather what the masque was in its outward features. A band of masquers assume an impressive and magnificent disguise. Some sort of explanation must be given of the nature and meaning of the disguise culminating in the entry of the masquers, which should be as sudden and impressive as possible. After the entry, the main or chief dance is performed by the masquers alone. Then, the masquers 'take out' partners from among the spectators—lords if the masquers are ladies, but, more usually, ladies, the masquers being lords. With these partners, slow dances, called by Daniel 'certain measures,' are performed; and then quick dances— 'galliards and corantos.' It is to these quick dances that the title 'the revels' is properly and strictly given[1]. After the revels, the masquers make their exit, usually with some preliminary dance by themselves. In Daniel's account of his masque, we see clearly how large a part of the interest was absorbed by spectacle, music and dance. The poet has his opportunity only when Sybilla pretends that she can see through her prospective or spy glass the masquers who are presently to march in, and describes them that they may be understood when they appear. The poetry for which occasion is thus found has some touch of the quiet grace of Daniel's best work, and the pure English of his prose and poetry alike is delightful to read. But this masque would seem to have survived in order to mark Ben Jonson's superiority. Daniel's contemplative temperament is contented to keep the masque undramatic, without either briskness or fire, and undifferentiated, without any contrast of its parts. In other words, he does not in the least realise the possibilities of the art he is practising. By his own rashness in the publication of *Philotas*[2], he lost favour at court, and the queen's next masque was written by Jonson.

But, before we consider this, we must examine some slighter pieces by Jonson, which preceded his first court masque[3]. In June 1603, the queen and prince Henry, when they first came into the kingdom, were received by Sir Robert Spencer at Althorp, and Jonson composed the entertainment[4] which welcomed them. As the queen came through the park, certain cornets sounded, whereupon a satyr 'advanced his head above the top of the wood,' wondering at the solemnities and, after a short strain on his pipe, jumped down to look close at the queen and prince, declaring,

> That is Cyparissus' face!
> And the dame hath Syrinx' grace!
> O that Pan were now in place—
> Sure they are of heavenly race.

---

[1] The derivation of the word, according to Skeat, is neither from *réveiller*, to awaken, nor from *rêver*, to dream, but from O. F. *revel*, meaning rebellion, disorder, sport, and coming from Latin *rebellare*, to rebel.

[2] As to the supposed reference in *Philotas* to Essex's plot, cf. vol. v, chap. xiv, p. 371, and see *Ward*, vol. ii, p. 619.

[3] For some general observations on Jonson's masques, cf. *ante*, chap. i, p. 12.

[4] Gifford calls it *The Satyr*.

He runs off in a fit of shyness and, 'to the sound of excellent soft music,' a bevy of fairies come tripping up the lawn attending on Mab their queen. The fairies dance in a ring, and queen Mab begins to welcome queen Anne, when the satyr peeps out of the bush again and interrupts :

> Trust her not, you bonnibell,
> She will forty leasings tell;
> I do know her pranks right well.

The fairies try to catch the satyr, while he runs about singing in riming eight-syllabled couplets a graphic account of Mab's traditional pranks. Finally, he is caught and well pinched, but escapes again into his bush. Then the style changes from gay to stately, while a song of welcome is sung to Oriana—*quasi Oriens Anna,* Jonson explains in a note ; this song is not quite the poet's best. But it is in such a setting as this that Jonson produces exquisite lyrics. Suddenly, he heightens his style, while the movement and merriment cease, and, for a moment, all ears listen. After the song, Mab presents the queen with a jewel, the fairies 'hop away in a fantastic dance,' and the satyr runs out again with his saucy octosyllables. After some references to Sir Robert Spencer, he fetches out the eldest son, attired and appointed like a huntsman, who is presented to the service of the prince along with some more gifts :

> The bow was Phoebe's, and the horn
> By Orion often worn ;
> The dog of Sparta breed, and good,
> As can RING within a WOOD ;
> Thence his name is : you shall try
> How he hunteth instantly.

At this, the whole wood resounded with the noise of cornets, horns and other hunting music, and a brace of choice deer were driven up and 'fortunately killed, as they were meant to be, even in the sight of her majesty.'

Nothing could be better in its kind than this vivacious entertainment. It is not too long ; it is full of movement, being broken up into dialogue, song and speeches, all written in easy rimes. The satyr is own brother to Fletcher's satyr in *The Faithfull Shepheardesse.* Jonson expands him into a charming antimasque in *Oberon the Faery Prince.*

It is surprising to find Jonson, who often gives us too much, and sows with the whole sack, restraining his hand thus artfully. It would seem as if he were able to put off his satiric and moralising instincts only when he conceives himself to be called upon for mere amusement. Perhaps, the awe of royalty natural to an Elizabethan held him in. Next year, on 1 May 1604, he composed a second entertainment[1], when the king and queen visited Sir William Cornwallis at Highgate. It is not so happy as the first; but it is quite new in its invention. The Penates or household gods, correctly attired, receive the king at the porch, addressing him in eight five-lined stanzas. The Penates lead the royal party into the house, where Mercury receives them in a prose speech which has more breath of poetry in it than the stanzas. Mercury takes them through the house into the garden, where are various goddesses—Maia, Aurora, Flora and others. Three of the goddesses, when Mercury's speech is ended, sing a three-part song, beginning, 'See, see, O see, who here is come a maying.' Maia then recites some graceful octosyllabic verses of welcome. This is the morning's entertainment. After dinner, the king and queen are, once more, taken into the garden, when Mercury again accosts them. He explains that 'a certain son of mine, whom the Arcadians call a god, howsoever the rest of the world receive him,' is at hand: 'yonder he keeps, and with him the wood nymphs.' This is Pan. Mercury apologises for Pan's uncouth appearance and behaviour, but asks the royal guests to accept from him a cup of 'a lusty liquor, that hath a present virtue to expel sadness,' and is flowing from the fountain of Bacchus in the middle of the lawn. Pan then accosts the king, and, in rollicking verses, hopes he will let a god be his skinker[2]. When the king has drunk, the lords and ladies are served. A last word of apology for Pan's familiarities follows from Mercury, 'and thus it ended.' The fancy of all this is sprightly and the execution adequate. What is especially to be noticed is Jonson's effort to get some contrast into his show, first, by means of the satyr, and, secondly, of Pan. The entertainment is not to be mere spectacle; the tableaux are not to be merely explained; they explain themselves. A breath of the drama gives them life. The entertainment lent itself to this semi-dramatic treatment more readily than the masque, which was a lengthy evening function in a large hall.

But Ben Jonson, having written these two entertainments, was less likely to let his masque be mere spectacle enlivened only by tedious description. He was commanded to supply queen Anne's second masque, *The Masque of Blacknesse,* 'personated at

[1] Called, by Gifford, *The Penates.*
[2] Drawer of wine or ale.

the Court at Whitehall on the Twelfth-Night, 1605,' in which, again, the queen and her ladies were the masquers. It lacks the light touch of the two entertainments; it is a first attempt, and, evidently, the effort to devise an ingenious, splendid and impressive spectacle has made too absorbing a demand on Jonson's attention. How ingenious this spectacle was may appear from a short summary of Jonson's graphic description. Oceanus, presented in human form, the colour of his flesh blue, and Niger, in form and colour of an Aethiop, riding on two great sea-horses, with attendant tritons and sea-maidens, seem to advance out of the sea, which is artfully made to shoot forth as if it flowed to the land. This cavalcade 'induces' the masquers, who are twelve nymphs, negroes and daughters of Niger, attended by twelve Oceaniae, who are their lightbearers. The masquers are all placed in 'a great concave Shell, like mother of pearl, curiously made to move on those waters and rise with the billow'; the torch-bearing Oceaniae are on the backs of 'six huge sea-monsters,' disposed round the great shell. Cunningly placed lights raise the whole elaborate show to the highest point of brilliance. The 'lines of prospective' of this show were planned with exact reference to the state at the upper end of the hall. 'So much for the bodily part, which was of master Inigo Jones's design and act.' When the shell came to a standstill, a triton and two sea-maidens sang a song—a tenor and two trebles. Then, Oceanus enquires of Niger why he is far out of his course here in the west. Niger explains that his daughters, having heard the fable of Phaëton, are discontented with their blackness, and have seen a vision which ordered them to seek a land whose name ends in the syllables 'tania.' They have tried Mauritania and Lusitania and Aquitania; can Oceanus help them to any other? Oceanus answers that they have arrived at Albion, named after his own son ; but, at this point, a vision of the moon, 'discovered in the upper part of the house,' as a beautiful queen on a throne, makes Niger 'interrupt Oceanus with this present passion': 'O see, our silver star,' he begins. The Aethiopians, of course, worshipped the moon as Aethiopia ; and this is Aethiopia herself come to tell them that this is the land they are seeking. It is ruled by a sun

> Whose beams shine day and night and are of force,
> To blanch an Æthiop and revive a corse.

King James is the sun :

> His light sciential is, and, past mere nature,
> Can salve the rude defects of every creature.

Then comes the main dance of the masquers. When it is
finished, and the masquers are about 'to make choice of their
men, one from the sea was heard to call them with this Charm,
sung by a tenor voice.' The song very aptly bids the sirens of the
sea beware of the sirens of the land. After the measures and
corantos with the men, which are 'the revels,' the ladies 'were
again accited to sea with a song of two trebles whose cadences
were iterated by a double echo from several parts of the land.'
The echo song over, Aethiopia gives a receipt for removing 'this
veil the sun has cast Above your blood'; and the masquers 'in a
dance returned to sea where they took their Shell, and with this
full song went out.'

We have said that this is not one of the best of Jonson's
masques. The general conception is richly poetical; but he
writes the heroic couplet awkwardly, the rimes are very harsh
and the addresses of Oceanus and Niger are stiff. The arrangement of the songs is admirable; but their effect must have depended more upon the music and singing than the words. There
is a lack of charm in the workmanship when we compare it with
later work, or even with the earlier entertainments; but this makes
only more apparent the contrast in method between this masque
and Daniel's. The latter, in the main, is a description of the
masquers; Jonson perceives the absurdity of describing to the
audience what they can see for themselves. Since he has no
elaborate description, he must invent some incident, and, accordingly, we have Niger's journey, his colloquy with Oceanus and the
appearance of Aethiopia—all ingeniously contrived to compliment
king James. For the use of those who did not see the masque,
a prose description of the '*landtschape*,' the dresses of the masquers
and the scenic arrangements—a fine piece of terse English—is
prefixed to the actual words; and we are told in a short foreword
that 'it was her majesty's will to have the masquers blackmoors
at first[1].' This curious desire of the queen and her ladies is the
starting-point of Jonson's scheme of Niger, whose people 'are the
blackest nation of the world[2].'

There were no court masques in the beginning of 1606 and
1607; but Jonson was a second time requisitioned for the masque
of 10 January 1608. The queen wanted the daughters of Niger

[1] 'At first' must not be taken to mean 'in the first part of the masque.' This
would introduce an antimasque too soon; we must paraphrase, 'it was originally her
majesty's will.'
[2] For other sources of Jonson's ideas, see Reyher, p. 161.

344   *Masque and Pastoral*

again, with 'their beauties varied according to promise,' and four
ladies added to their number.   *The Masque of Beauty*, therefore, is
a continuation of *The Masque of Blacknesse*.   Master Thomas Giles
'made the dances,' which were exceptionally elaborate, and personated the river Thamesis.   The six steps before the throne were
occupied by the torchbearers—'a multitude of Cupids, chosen
out of the best and most ingenious youth of the Kingdom, noble
and others.'   Here, unconsciously, the device of the antimasque is
anticipated.   As in some other masques, the torchbearers wear a
distinctive dress, which makes them at once a kind of antimasque.
Moreover, *The Masque of Beauty*, in itself, is a contrast to *The
Masque of Blacknesse*, and their relation must have helped Jonson
to reach that theory of the antimasque which is fully developed
in his third court masque, *The Masque of Queens*.   But, before
going on to this, we have to consider two masques written for
weddings.

Jonson's share in the solemnities which celebrated the marriage[1]
of the earl of Essex, Robert Devereux, and Frances Howard[2], on
5 January 1606, was the masque *Hymenaei*, printed with a careful
account of the whole arrangement of the dresses and spectacle in
the same year.   This, therefore, is the first full-grown masque as
distinguished from an entertainment which he published.   The
introductory note shows the high ideals with which Jonson took up
the composition of masques.   It braced and encouraged his genius
to feel that he was producing work to be presented by the highest
notabilities of the realm, the queen herself taking the lead.

'It is a noble and just advantage,' he says, 'that the things subjected to
understanding have of those which are objected to sense; that the one sort
are but momentary and merely taking; the other, impressing and lasting:
else the glory of all these solemnies had perished like a blaze, and gone out,
in the beholders' eyes: so short-lived are the bodies of all things in comparison of their souls.'

This consideration has made 'royal princes and greatest persons,
who are commonly the personators of these actions,' not only
'studious of riches and magnificence in the outward celebration
or shew,' but, also,

curious after the most high and hearty inventions to furnish the inward
parts, and those grounded upon antiquity and solid learning; which though
their voice be taught to sound to present occasions, their sense or doth or
should always lay hold on more removed mysteries.

---

[1] It was dissolved on the ground of nullity, and the lady was married again to the
favourite of James, Robert Carr, earl of Somerset.

[2] The earl of Suffolk's second daughter.

This is an admirable statement of what we find in Jonson's earlier masques. The splendour and ingenuity of the spectacle set forth some central idea, the characters are taken mainly from classical literature, and the details of their dress and equipment are all minutely accurate—that is to say, Jonson is ready to quote the passage which sanctions his choice. Six masques—the three already named, the second wedding masque, *The Masque of Queens* and *The Masque of Augures*—are elaborately annotated by him[1]. In the dedication of *The Masque of Queens* to prince Henry, we are told that the prince[2] asked for this annotating and, accordingly, it is in this instance that Jonson is most copious. It has, he says, proved 'a work of some difficulty to me to retrieve the particular authorities to those things, which I writ out of fulness and memory of my former readings.' We can hardly believe, though Jonson would seem to hint as much, that he composed these masques without a most diligent ransacking of all the classical authors within his reach ; but, after making this deduction from his claim, his annotations remain astonishing, and of special and unique interest as an exhibition of the scholarship of an Elizabethan man of letters. Jonson did nothing carelessly ; and these notes set a standard of style and establish annotation as a branch of English literature. It is hardly necessary to add that they throw a flood of light upon the culture of the time. The introduction to *Hymenaei* denounces the folly of those 'who squeamishly cry out that all endeavour of learning and sharpness in these transitory devices, is superfluous.' This, doubtless, is a gird at Daniel, who, in his *Twelve Goddesses*, had spoken slightingly of 'whosoever strives to shew most wit about these punctilios of dreams and shews.' Jonson insists that the masque is to draw its types and personages from classical mythology, and considers 'a few Italian herbs, picked up and made into a sallad' a meal much too light for a scholar. *Hymenaei* begins with a bridal procession, very carefully arranged according to ancient Roman ritual, and conceived as a sacrifice of the bride and bridegroom to the goddess Juno or Unio. It is ushered in by Hymen, who is said to have been personated by Jonson himself[3]. Hymen, having addressed

---

[1] He supplied notes, first of all, to his account of the coronation entertainment in London, which he and Dekker devised.

[2] Jonson also mentions the fact in his autograph address to the queen, written in the copy presented to her, now in the British Museum library.

[3] Fleay's conjecture ; because Pory, describing the masque, says that 'Ben Jonson burned the globe of earth standing behind the altar.'

the royalties seated in the state, 'the first masque of eight men'
appears out of a microcosm or globe marvellously planned in
its movement and adornment. These nobles personate the four
Humours, and the four Affections, who propose to disturb the
marriage ceremonial; whereupon, Hymen invokes Reason's aid to
curb the rudeness of the masquers. They are, therefore, a kind
of antimasque. Reason descends from the summit of the globe,
and, at his admonition, the Humours and Affections sheathe their
swords. Then, the upper part of the scene, 'which was all of
clouds and made artificially to swell and ride like the rack,' began
to open. Juno is discovered with eight of her nuptial powers,
each bearing one of her surnames, as used by classical writers.
The eight nymphs dance out in pairs led by Order, who is Reason's
servant. These ladies form the second masque. After dancing
alone, they pair with the men masquers, and the whole sixteen
dance, 'with this song provoked':

> Now, now begin to set
> Your spirits in active heat,
> And since your hands are met,
> Instruct your nimble feet,
> In motions swift and sweet,
> The happy ground to beat.

Jonson had prepared an epithalamion of fifteen eight-lined stanzas,
admirably translated from Catullus; but 'only one staff was
sung,' the company being exhausted by the length and elaboration
of the performance. The poet, however, 'sets it down whole'
when he prints—'and I do heartily forgive their ignorance whom
it chanceth not to please.'

While this masque does not reach the highest level of Jonson's
achievement, it is yet a beautiful and dignified composition, only
less charming than his next marriage masque, produced for the
marriage of lord Haddington[1] on 9 February 1608, at which Venus,
instead of Juno, is the presiding goddess. She appears in her
chariot at the top of the scene, and, descending on foot with the
three graces, declares that Cupid has disappeared and that she
must have him cried, 'and all his virtues told.' The verses in
which the three graces 'cry' Cupid, 'Venus' runaway,' are the perfection of grace and lightness : a sprightlier opening to a masque
could hardly be imagined. As the verses end, Cupid discovers
himself, 'attended with twelve boys, most antickly attired, that
represented the Sports and pretty Lightnesses, that accompany

---

[1] Called, by Gifford, *The Hue and Cry after Cupid*.

Love.' Cupid gives the order to his 'little jocund Sports'—'with your revel fill the room'; whereupon

they fell into a subtle capricious dance to as odd a music, each of them bearing two torches, and nodding with their antic faces, with other variety of ridiculous gesture which gave much occasion of mirth and delight to the spectators.

But these boys are not the masquers. In the forewords of his next masque—*The Masque of Queens*—Jonson calls them 'an anti-masque of boys'; but his first conception of them made them a dance of antics, who perform no true measures but a 'revel' of 'ridiculous gesture.' A dance of antics, in which the performers wore absurd or monstrous masks, was not unknown in Elizabeth's time[1]. This, however, means only that Jonson does not reach a full realisation of the antimasque until *The Masque of Queens*. The torch-bearing Cupids of *The Masque of Beauty*, the contrast between this and *The Masque of Blacknesse*, the contrast of the two sets of masquers in the masque *Hymenaei*, and, finally, the twelve boys in antic attire of *The Hue and Cry after Cupid*, are the gradual steps by which the idea of the antimasque was reached in Jonson's mind. After the dance of the twelve boys, Cupid is about to explain what he has been doing when Hymen intervenes and introduces the king to Venus as the modern *pius Aeneas*, relating how the bridegroom of this great wedding has saved his monarch's life[2], and expatiating upon the virtues of the bride. Venus is further overwhelmed by the appearance of Vulcan, at whose command, the red cliff[3] at the end of the hall is cloven apart, revealing the wonderful globe in which are the masquers as the twelve signs of the zodiac. All the twelve are ingeniously explained as

> Sacred powers
> That are presiding at all nuptial hours.

Inasmuch as in the 18th book of the *Iliad*, Vulcan's gifts for Thetis were 'twenty tripods or stools with golden wheels to move of themselves miraculously,' Jonson, regarding this passage 'a most elegant place and worthy the tenth reading,' makes the dances of the masquers signify the magic stools of Vulcan. Two Cyclopes, as the masquers danced, 'beat a time to them with their hammers.' An epithalamion of seven verses comes at the end; and, this time, the poet insured the recitation of the whole

---

[1] In Munday's *John a Kent and John a Cumber* there is 'a merry antique showe, in which four antics dance (Collier's edition, pp. 31—34).

[2] At the time of the Gowrie conspiracy.

[3] The bride was lady Elizabeth Radcliffe, daughter of the earl of Sussex.

of it by the device of putting four dances by his masquers
'full of elegancy and curious device' between the verses. 'The
two latter dances were made by Master Thomas Giles, the two
first by Master Hier. Herne,' who were the Cyclopes. 'The tunes
were Master Alphonso Ferrabosco's. The device and act of the
scene Master Inigo Jones's.' The epithalamion is a noble lyric,
which prepares our ears for the more wonderful music of Milton.
Again and again, in the verse of Jonson's masques, we find workmanship afterwards elaborated and improved upon by Milton,
between whom and the Elizabethans Jonson is the true link.
His ardour and idealism prepare us for the deeper spiritual
sublimity of the puritan poet. These two wedding masques have
a special charm of their own, and the second of them is the finest
of its kind in the language.

We come now to *The Masque of Queens*—the third masque
written for queen Anne—in which, as we have said, the idea of the
antimasque is fully reached by Jonson and definitely stated by
him in his commentary. It was presented at Whitehall on
2 February 1609, and immediately printed by prince Henry's command. The dedication to the prince is worthy of comparison with
the dedication, two years earlier, of *Volpone* to the universities.
The same lofty note is struck; 'poetry, my lord, is not born with
every man, nor every day'; and the poet goes on to explain that
because 'the nobility of the invention should be answerable to
the dignity' of the persons taking part in the masque, he

chose the argument to be *A celebration of honourable and true Fame, bred
out of Virtue*, observing that rule of the best artist[1], to suffer no object of
delight to pass without his mixture of profit and example.

This combination of the moralist and idealist is characteristic of
Jonson in all his art, but it forms the very soul of his masques
and gives meaning and dignity to all their glitter and mechanism.
He now gives us his definition of the antimasque.

And because her majesty (best knowing that a principle part of life in
these spectacles lay in their variety) had commanded me to think on some
dance or shew that might precede hers and have the place of a foil or false
masque, I was careful[2] to decline, not only from others, but mine own
steps in that kind, since the last year I had an anti-masque of boys; and
therefore now devised that twelve women in the habit of hags or witches,...
the opposites to good Fame, should fill that part; not as a masque but as a
spectacle of strangeness.

[1] Horace's maxim is meant, *Omne tulit punctum qui miscuit utile dulci, Ars Poet.*
343.
[2] Fleay is certainly right in explaining 'Careful to decline' as='afraid of declining' (*English Drama*, vol. II, p. 4). See 'Careful, 5,' in Oxford Dictionary.

To make a band of witches the foil or opposite of a band of heroines is a striking thought, and interesting from the light it throws upon the general conception of the witch in Jacobean times. The idea took a strong hold of Jonson's mind and, in his masque, he worked it out with energy. The witches of the masque hold their own beside even the weird sisters of *Macbeth*. They are the witches of popular superstition, and Jonson's exceptionally elaborate annotations show the close agreement between these superstitions in ancient and modern times. Jonson's witches 'with a kind of hollow and infernal music came forth' from 'an ugly Hell.' There were eleven, with their dame. After a dance, each one relates her misdeeds to the dame, who proposes that they shall try to blast with their wicked incantations the glory of the masque that is beginning:

> Darken all this roof
> With present fogs: exhale Earth's rot'nest vapours,
> And strike a blindness through these blazing tapers.

They fall into 'a magical dance, full of preposterous change and gesticulation[1].' The loud music of the real masque interrupts them, driving the witches back into hell and disclosing the magnificent house of Fame in which the twelve true masquers are seated. Heroic Virtue, 'in the furniture of Perseus,' explains the heroines, who are twelve great queens, beginning with Penthesilea and ending with Bel-Anna. The lyric at the close, 'Who Virtue can thy power forget,' influenced the ending of *Comus*. In the witch scene, Jonson's wonderful power of specialising as a dramatist—of 'getting up' a particular trade, or profession—is shown to perfection. Elsewhere, we occasionally miss in him the fire of imagination required for blending the accumulations and observation of his intellect into a vitally artistic product; but, in the present instance, his imagination is at its height, and he puts out his full strength. The third charm conveys powerfully the horrid thrill that was the soul of the witch superstitions, and that depended for its force upon all things ugly and foul in nature.

> The owl is abroad, the bat, and the toad,
> And so is the cat-a-mountain,
> The ant and the mole sit both in a hole,
> And the frog peeps out o' the fountain;

[1] It must have been impressive. The witches do all things at their meetings 'contrary to the custom of men, dancing back to back, and hip to hip, their hands joined and making their circles backward, to the left hand, with strange fantastic motions of their heads and bodies. All which were excellently imitated by the maker of the dance, Master Hierome Herne.'

The dogs they do bay and the timbrels play,
 The spindle is now a turning;
The moon it is red, and the stars are fled,
 But all the sky is a burning:
The ditch is made and our nails the spade,
 With pictures full, of wax and of wool;
 Their livers I stick with needles quick;
 There lacks but the blood, to make up the flood,
Quickly, Dame, then bring your part in,
Spur, spur, upon little Martin[1].

Jonson, having reached a clear idea of the antimasque, did not go back upon it. But this antimasque quite eclipses its masque. The queens are mere wax-works after the witches. Jonson's imagination concentrated itself upon the first half of his work. Perhaps he left it to Inigo Jones to supply, by the magic of his scenery, the necessary contrast; in Jonson's own work, certainly, this is not done. If the second part had been carried out with the imaginative intensity of the first, this masque would have formed the prototype of an artistic species of great and enduring significance.

In 1610, Daniel supplied the masque for the court, and his *Tethys' Festival* shows no advance upon *The Vision of the Twelve Goddesses*. In 1611, Jonson is again at work: on 1 January 1611, he produced *Oberon* at Whitehall for prince Henry, and, in the beginning of February, *Love freed from Ignorance and Folly* for queen Anne. *Oberon* is a most delightful masque. The opening is written in dainty octosyllabic verse and elaborates into a charming antimasque the part of the satyr in the entertainment already described. This antimasque made a distinct impression upon the literature of the day[2]. *Oberon* may be taken as an almost perfect example of the first kind of Jonsonian masque, in which the antimasque is not so much 'a foil or false masque' as an antic-masque, something lighter and less dignified than the main masque, but in keeping with it rather than in contrast, and not yet, in any true sense, dramatic. The grace, balance and finish of the whole composition are beyond praise. Unfortunately, this is the last masque annotated by Jonson for the 1616 folio ; his notes stop in it halfway, before he reaches prince Oberon. The only later masque which he annotated was *The Masque of Augures*, specially printed as the first masque presented in the new banqueting hall

---

[1] 'Their little Martin is he that calls them to their conventicles. They find him in the shape of a great buck goat upon whom they ride to their meetings.'

[2] See Reyher, *Les Masques Anglais*, p. 324. It is conjectured that the three dancers of *The Winter's Tale*, act IV, sc. 4, 329, had been among Jonson's satyrs.

at Whitehall. *Love Freed* is a companion piece to *Oberon*, but inferior to it in conception and workmanship.

If January 1612 be the date of *Love Restored*, it is important for the student of the masque. Jonson innovated again on previous practice. The masque proper is preceded, not by an antimasque, but by a scene of excellent comedy. The scene is the development in a new style of the part of the presenter, and still gives to that character the larger part of the dialogue, which is in prose. Just as the satyr of the first entertainment was the germ of the antimasque of *Oberon*, so the prose of Pan and his dialogue with Mercury in the second entertainment may have prompted this scene. The king and court being ready, Masquerado enters to declare that there can be no masque, 'the rogue play-boy, that acts Cupid, is got so hoarse, your majesty cannot hear him half the breadth of your chair.' But Plutus, 'as Cupid,' here interrupts, ordering Masquerado off. 'What makes this light, feathered vanity here? Away, impertinent folly! Infect not this assembly.' Plutus objects to the expense of the masque: 'I tell thee, I will have no more masquing; I will not buy a false and fleeting delight so dear: the merry madness of one hour shall not cost me the repentance of an age.' But, here, Plutus is interrupted in his turn by Robin Goodfellow, who is aghast at the news of there not being any masque. He declares,

I am the honest plain country spirit, and harmless; Robin Goodfellow, he that sweeps the hearth and the house clean, riddles for the country maids, and does all their other drudgery, while they are at hot-cockles: one that has discoursed with your court spirits ere now; but was fain to-night to run a thousand hazards to arrive at this place: never poor goblin was so put to his shifts to get in to see nothing.

Plutus will not listen: 'Your rude good-fellowship must seek some other sphere for your admitty.' Robin's answer is a triumph of comic description. It puts before us all the crush and crowding, all the tricks and pretences, which were a part of the fierce competition to get a place at these great court masques. Robin has been hit over the head by the porter, and shoved off a ladder by one of the guards; then he tried 'the carpenters' way,' but 'the wooden rogues let a huge trap-door fall on my head.' He thought of getting in in a trunk, 'but that I would not imitate so catholic a coxcomb as Coryat.' So he tried disguises. 'I was an engineer and belonged to the motions'; then, 'an old tire-woman'; then, 'a musician—marry, I could not shew mine instrument and that bred a discord': then, a feather-maker of Blackfriars,... but they all made as light of me, as of my feathers; and wondered how I could be a Puritan, being of so vain a vocation; I answered, We are all masquers sometimes.

At last, 'with my broom and my candles,' he was himself, 'and came on confidently, giving out I was a part of the Device.' This admirable speech exhibits Jonson's comic power in its most genial and, therefore, most delightful vein. When Plutus goes on protesting against the expense of masques as 'superfluous excesses,' Masquerado and Robin detect him for an impostor—'Plutus, the god of money, who has stolen Love's ensigns.' At this point, the real Cupid enters in his chariot 'guarded with the Masquers, in number ten,' who, says Cupid, were 'the spirits of courts and flower of men.' But, here again, the masque, as it has come down to us, is quenched by its antimasque. That antimasque, quite frankly, is a dramatic scene, although the long harangue of Robin Goodfellow may be called only a modification of the presenter's oration, and the colloquy is suggested rather by what was customary at an entertainment than by the new idea of the antimasque.

In Jonson's remaining masques, there are many similar scenes, and they are all admirable. But their right to a place in the masque may be called in question. They represent the intrusion of drama into masque, and it may be contended that Jonson never succeeds in evolving a type of masque which really absorbs them. The plays of Aristophanes afford an example on the grandest scale of the kind of artistic product that is aimed at, and Jonson, in the scene we have just criticised and in other places in his masques, is Aristophanic in his combination of robust naturalism with imaginative fancy. Another consideration must be kept in mind. The masquers themselves were always the highest notables of the land, and, therefore, of course, amateurs in everything but dancing. The nobleman could dance exquisitely, but he might not act. This fact, of itself, prevented the development in a dramatic direction of the real masque. But the presenters and the allegoric personages who explained the masque were, usually, professionals, and the antimasque, when it came, was performed very largely by professionals. This is why the development of the antimasque in a dramatic direction was easy, and why the real coherence of masque and antimasque when the dramatic element intruded was impossible.

The development of the Jonsonian masque is now complete, although we have not yet considered half his work. Broadly speaking, there are two types of Jonsonian masque : the masque proper, in which the antimasque is a foil to the masque ; and the masque improper, in which the antimasque is a dramatic scene. But the masque proper may be said to include two species ; that in which the antimasque is an antic-masque, and that in which it is a true foil or opposite of the masque.

The date 1612, which we have now reached, offers a suitable occasion for considering shortly the work of certain other masque writers, since Jonson wrote no masque for the January and February of 1613.

The death of prince Henry in November 1612 plunged the nation into great grief. Nevertheless, in three months' time, it welcomed, as an excuse for throwing off its gloom, the marriage of the princess Elizabeth to the elector Palatine. The festivities on this occasion were of an unparalleled magnificence and cost. It was arranged that, on the evening of the wedding, being Sunday 14 February, the courtiers should present the first masque, known since as *The Lords' Masque*, and written by Thomas Campion, and that, on the two following evenings, the inns of court should present masques. So exhausted were the king and court generally by the elaborate proceedings, that the third masque had to be put off till the 20th of the month. The second masque—*The Masque of the Middle Temple and Lyncolnes Inn*—was written by George Chapman, and the third—*The Masque of Grayes-Inne and the Inner-Temple*—by Francis Beaumont. Jonson said to Drummond that 'next himself only Fletcher and Chapman could make a masque[1].' Probably, he had Beaumont's masque in his mind, as we have no record of a masque by Fletcher. But Campion, rather than either Chapman or Beaumont, deserves the next place— *longo intervallo*—to Jonson[2]. *The Lords' Masque* has an anti-masque of 'Frantics.' These are such characters as the lover, the self-lover, the melancholic man, the schoolman overcome with fantasy, the over-watched usurer, with others that made an absolute medley of madness. These 'Lunatics' danced 'a mad measure fitted to a loud fantastic tune,' after which the music changed to a solemn air, which drove out the 'Frantics.' Prometheus displays eight stars shining and dancing—a kind of second anti-masque of stars. 'The stars moved in an exceeding strange and delightful manner, and I suppose few have ever seen more neat artifice than Master Inigo Jones shewed in contriving their motion.'

---

[1] *Jonson's Conversations with Drummond* (ed. Laing, D.), p. 4. It is curious that Jonson gives *The Faithfull Shepheardesse* to Fletcher *and* Beaumont.
[2] For a general account of Campion's life and work, see *ante*, vol. IV, chap. VIII.

Campion's own songs, which accompany the scenic effects, have that special charm of melody and natural grace which make his lyrics more than any other man's typically Elizabethan. The stars, vanishing, become the eight masquers, 'in their habits, which were infinitely rich, befitting states[1].' To accompany these knights, sixteen pages, 'like fiery spirits,' break from the earth with torches, and 'The Torchbearers' Dance' follows, making the second antimasque. When the time came for the masquers to take partners from the audience, 'first of all the princely bridegroom and bride were drawn into these solemn revels.' The revels are interrupted by a second 'set-piece' of elaborate splendour, from which a 'high vast obelisk dedicate to Fame' is drawn out by Sybilla, who, in choice Latin verse, prophesies prosperity to the wedded pair[2].

It will be seen, from this imperfect summary of a masque remarkable for its elaboration, that Campion depends more upon Inigo Jones than does Jonson. Jonson instinctively feels for some situation which he must explain and which has in it a logical development involving some slight dramatic interest; Campion merely adorns the stage carpenter's ingenuities with beautiful songs and poetic recitative. Nevertheless, Campion's songs are very charming, and his masque has a poetic beauty in its conceptions as sweet and splendid as any of Jonson's. But it does not join to poetic beauty his moral impressiveness; melody and beauty are the ingredients of Campion's magic. We may add that Campion's account of his work is written in prose of which the ease and charm are not less remarkable than are the vigour and exactitude of that of Jonson's notes; while, in his references to his fellow workers, Campion reveals himself as a man of a generous personality, eager to praise his friends. His three masques and single entertainment survive, as they deserve; they are all of them remarkable for the melody of their lyrics and the beauty of their conception. He would stand beside Jonson as a masque writer if he had written as many masques.

Chapman's masque is in pleasant contrast to Campion's. It is full of semi-dramatic matter and of quaint, picturesque, fantastic detail quite different from the purely beautiful detail of the first masque. It is interesting, also, because the cavalcade or procession from the rendezvous in Chancery lane to Whitehall was a special

---

[1] *i.e.* noblemen, as these all were.
[2] The gist is :

> *Additur Germaniae*
> *Robur Britannicum : ecquid esse par potest ?*

attraction of the show, and is carefully described by Chapman.
The masque is very topical. It is founded, mainly, upon the
current interest in the attempt to colonise Virginia[1], the chief
masquers being Indian princes, while their attendant Phoebades,
or Virginian priests of the sun, form a second antimasque.
The first antimasque satirises the globe-trotting propensities of
Englishmen. The main items of the cavalcade were, first, 'a mock
masque of Baboons horsed with asses and dwarf palfreys, with
yellow foot cloths, casting cockle-de-moys about in courtesy by
way of largesse'; then, in a car, the twelve Phoebades, 'chief
musicians of our kingdom'; then, the twelve chief masquers riding
in Indian habits, as Virginian princes; and, finally, another car
driven by Capriccio with Honor and Plutus on the top, and their
attendants Eunomia and Phemis beneath them. Capriccio, who
has a pair of bellows on his head, describes himself as a 'man of
wit'; he is a parallel figure to Jonson's Fencer in *Pan's Anniversarie* or to his Christmas in *The Masque of Christmas*, where
a single character takes the part of a presenter. When the hall
is finally reached, he has a lively opening dialogue with Plutus[2],
who replies to his contemptuous invective:

Sinful? and damnable? What, a Puritan? Those bellows you wear on
your head shew with what matter your brain is puffed up, Sir; a religion-
forger I see you are and presume of inspiration from these bellows; with
which ye study to blow up the settled government of kingdoms.

Chapman spells 'antemasque' with an *e* and speaks of his prose
dialogue as a 'low induction'; his baboons' dance, he tells us, was
'anticke and delightful.' His conception of the antimasque, therefore, makes it rather like the farce in a modern theatre. It is
to be noted, also, that his torchbearers have a dance—they descended and 'performed another antemasque dancing with torches
lighted at both ends.' Chapman's work, obviously, is influenced
by Jonson; but he has not grasped the principles of balance and
composition which his master employs[3]. It is delightful, however,
to find him in his explanatory narrative echoing exactly Jonson's
arrogant note. He inserts a page 'to answer certain insolent
objections made against the length of my speeches and narrations,'
in which he shews himself the true mate of Ben, the only other
Elizabethan who matches his pride in his poetic craft.

---

[1] Already, in *Eastward Hoe* (act III, sc. 2), Chapman puts into the mouth of captain
Seagull a graphic account of Virginia's wonders.

[2] There seems here a clear reference to the Plutus of Jonson's *Love Restored* (*ante*,
p. 351).

[3] Cf. *ante*, chap. II.

Beaumont's masque is a worthy third to the first two. The Inner Temple and Gray's inn made Winchester house, on the south bank of the river, their rendezvous, and their procession was by water. Unfortunately, Beaumont does not describe this with the fulness with which Chapman describes the cavalcade by land of the previous night; but we know, from other sources, that it was very elaborate. The gentleman-masquers 'were placed by themselves in the King's royal barge, with the rich furniture of state, and adorned with a great number of lights, placed in such order as might make the best show.' They were 'led by two Admirals,' and a multitude of barges and galleys attended upon them, 'with all variety of land music and several peals of ordnance.' The king and the prince and the newly married couple watched the landing at Whitehall; but the hall of the palace was found to be too small for the performance. This is the reason Beaumont gives for the postponement till Saturday. We learn, however, from a private letter, that the king's fatigue was the real cause of the delay:

Sir Francis Bacon ventured to entreat his Majesty that by this disgrace (*i.e.* the postponement) he would, as it were, bury them quick: and I hear the king should answer, that they must bury him quick, for he could last no longer.

But the masquers were reconciled to the delay by getting permission to use the banqueting house instead of the hall on Saturday.

Beaumont's masque is remarkable for the high quality of its blank verse, which has in it a hint of Miltonic music, and for the beauty of the lyrics, which, however, are few and short. The words of the masque are quite subordinate to the elaborate music, dances and scenic effects. Beaumont is at pains to point out that his antimasque is 'not of one kind or livery (because that had been so much in use heretofore) but as it were in consort like to broken music.' This innovation tended further to disintegrate the masque and break it up into a variety entertainment. For the second antimasque, Iris, 'in token that the match shall likewise be blessed with the love of the common people,' calls to Flora to bring in 'a May dance or rural dance, consisting likewise not of any suited[1] persons,' but of a pedant, May lord, May lady; servingman, chambermaid; a country clown, country wench; a he-baboon, she-baboon; a he-fool, she-fool; these rush in, dance their measure and as rudely depart. 'The music was extremely well fitted,' says Beaumont; 'but the perpetual laughter and

[1] Persons dressed alike.

applause was above the music.' The king was so pleased that he called for the second antimasque again at the end, and, also, for the first, 'but one of the statues by that time was undressed.'

We have now to notice in Jonson's work the rapid growth of dramatic interest. Passing over the graceful and original *A Challenge at Tilt* and the realistic *The Irish Masque*, both produced in December 1613, we find that, for four successive years, Jonson wrote the Twelfthnight masque at court and, in 1617, added a second, produced in February, as well as *The Masque of Christmas*, of the previous 25 December. *Mercury Vindicated from the Alchemists*, 1615, is the first of these. The antimasque, broadly, is in the style of *Love Restored*. Mercury delivers two admirable addresses in prose, worthy of a place beside the harangues of Robin Goodfellow. The scene is 'a laboratory or alchemists' work-house, Vulcan looking to the registers,' with a Cyclope tending the fires. The Cyclope begins with a beautiful song, 'Soft, subtile fire, thou soul of art.' Mercury then peeps out 'at the tunnel of the middle furnace,' whereupon Vulcan cries to hold him— 'Dear Mercury ! Help. He flies. He is scaped. Precious golden Mercury, be fixt : be not so volatile !' Mercury, after running 'once or twice about the room, takes breath,' and begins a long relation of his troubles—

> Now the place and goodness of it protect me.... I will stand close up anywhere, to escape this poult-footed philosopher, old Smug here of Lemnos, and his smoky family.... The whole household of them are become Alchemists.

The comic invention of this opening is in Jonson's happiest vein ; and Mercury's speech worthily maintains it. In his masques, Jonson's prose is more uniformly strong and distinguished than his verse, and has not received the attention it merits. Mercury recounts all he has suffered :

> It is I, that am corroded, and exalted, and sublimed, and reduced, and fetched over, and filtered, and washed, and wiped ; what between their salts and their sulphurs, their oils and their tartars, their brines and their vinegars, you might take me out now a soused Mercury, now a salted Mercury, now a smoaked and dried Mercury, now a powdered and pickled Mercury : never herring, oyster, or cucumber past so many vexations.

And his account of what the alchemists claim to perform comes to an excellent climax :

> They will lay you an old courtier on the coals like a sausage, or a bloat herring, and after they have broiled him enough, blow a soul into him with a pair of bellows, till he start up into his galliard, that was made when Monsieur was here.

There are two antimasques : one, 'a troop of threadbare Alchemists'; and the second, a troop 'of imperfect creatures with helms of limbecks on their heads,' which Vulcan and his alchemists by their art have created. These 'ridiculous monsters' vanish at Mercury's command, and a glorious bower appears in which are Nature, Prometheus and the twelve masquers. The lyrics are melodious, but short, and their effect in the reading is insignificant, after the vigorous life of the first scene.

The Golden Age Restored, of 1 and 6 January 1616, goes back to the lyrical style. It is a graceful and beautiful conception, but not very fully reported. For next Christmas, Jonson wrote *The Masque of Christmas,* which Fleay says was 'not a mask proper.' By the allusions to Burbage and Heminge, we gather that it was acted by the king's players, and, consequently, there is no real masque—it is all antimasque, and, in style and form, very like the opening of *Love Restored.* Christmas takes the place of Robin Goodfellow as presenter, but is not allowed speeches of such length. Nowhere in our literature is the old merry Christmas more graphically put before us : 'I am old Gregory Christmas still, and though I come out of Pope's-head alley, as good a Protestant as any in my parish.' He has brought a masque of his own making, 'and do present it by a set of my sons, that come out of the lanes of London, good dancing boys all.'... 'Bones o bread, the King!' (seeing James). His sons and daughters enter, ten in number, 'led in, in a string, by Cupid, who is attired in a flat cap and a prentice's coat, with wings at his shoulders.' The family are, Misrule, Carol, Minced-Pie, Gambol, Post and Pair, New-Year's-Gift, Mumming, Wassel, Offering and Baby-Cake. Each has his torchbearer, and Jonson's magnificent knowledge of English ways and manners finds delightful scope in their attire, which is succinctly described. In place of the usual elegant lyrics, we have a rollicking song, sung by Christmas to drum and fife ; but, before this can be delivered, there is a short scene of comedy. 'Venus, a deaf tire-woman' presents herself ; she is Cupid's mother ; she dwells in Pudding lane ; 'yes, I can sit anywhere, so I may see Cupid act ; I had him by my first husband, he was a smith, forsooth, we dwelt in Do-little-Lane then.' 'Will you depart,' says Christmas, impatiently ;

Ay, forsooth he'll say his part, I warrant him, as well as e'er a play-boy of e'm all. I could have had money enough for him, an I would have been tempted, and have let him out by the week to the King's players. Master Burbage has been about and about with me, and so has old Master Hemings too.

The old dame has to be silenced by the drum, but a slight delay occurs because some of the properties are forgotten—'Mumming has not his vizard neither.' 'No matter! his own face shall serve for a punishment, and 'tis bad enough.' Misrule's suit is too small! 'The players have lent him one too little, on purpose to disgrace him.' The song has eighteen verses, which give the names and addresses of the masquers :

> Next in the trace, comes Gambol in place;
> And to make my tale the shorter,
> My son Hercules, tane out of Distaff-lane;
> But an active man and a porter.

It is the first purely humorous lyric with which we have met in a masque, and it smacks of the soil, or, to speak more exactly, of the street. It is banged out on the drum with glorious energy, and, when we are breathless with the speed of it, Cupid is called upon to say his piece; but his mother interrupts and puts him out, so poor Cupid breaks down ignominiously and has to be taken away, Venus exclaiming, 'You wrong the child, you do wrong the infant, I 'peal to his Majesty.' It was, perhaps, the knowledge that his work was to be acted by skilled professionals that inspired Jonson in this fascinating little sketch. It has to be confessed that, when the dramatist in Jonson gets to work in his masques, we obtain results worth more as literature than all the non-dramatic lyrics and descriptive verse. And Jonson's humour in his masques is without the acrid, scornful element which, in his great plays, too often obtrudes itself. In this little show, he is with Shakespeare and Dickens in the hearty kindliness of his comic observation. On the Twelfthnight after this Christmas day, *The Vision of Delight* was presented. It is a notable masque, containing the beautiful lyric, 'Break, Phant'sie, from thy cave of cloud,' and, in remarkable contrast, the long speech of Phant'sie in doggerel lines of four beats. There is no prose. But we must pass it over, as, also, the interesting *Lovers Made Men*[1], in order to mention *Pleasure Reconciled to Vertue*, presented Twelfthnight, 6 January 1618, because this masque supplied Milton with the main idea of *Comus*.

It was prince Charles's first masque. The scene is the mountain Atlas, 'who had his top ending in the figure of an old man.' From a grove at his feet, comes 'Comus, the god of cheer or the Belly, riding in triumph,' with one in front bearing

---

[1] Called, by Gifford, *The Masque of Lethe.*

the bowl of Hercules. The companions of Comus begin with a
'Hymn ; full chorus':

> Room! room! make room for the Bouncing Belly
> First father of sauce and deviser of jelly,
> Prime master of arts, and the giver of wit,
> That found out the excellent engine, the spit.

After nearly thirty lines in this style, the bowl-bearer speaks
a prose oration on the Belly, which introduces the first antimasque of 'men in the shape of bottles, tuns, etc.' Hercules,
the 'active friend of virtue,' enters, to reclaim his bowl and
denounce Comus and his crew ; 'Help, virtue ! These are sponges
and not men.' He drives them off, asking, 'Can this be pleasure,
to extinguish man ?' Then he lies down at the foot of Atlas, and
the pigmies forming the second antimasque steal in and try to steal
his club. At his rising, they run into holes, and Mercury descends
to crown Hercules with poplar, because he has 'the voluptuous
Comus, God of cheer, Beat from his grove, and that defaced.' So
far, the idea is clear and well-balanced, and the moral that
pleasure must be the servant of virtue is expressed with an intensity that, obviously, influenced Milton in his *Comus*. But it is
interesting to contrast the gross homely Comus of Jonson, the
Belly god, with Milton's dignified abstraction, and to note, that to
match his Comus, Jonson's dramatic instinct supplies, not Virtue,
but Hercules. There is fine poetry in the conception and workmanship of Jonson's masque; but it loses coherence after the crowning
of Hercules. Hercules is told that, in James's court, the 'cessation
of all jars' between pleasure and virtue is to be found ; and, as
a proof, twelve princes are brought forth, bred upon Atlas, 'the
hill of knowledge.' These, led by prince Charles, are the true
masquers. The chaplain of the Venetian ambassador[1] has described
the masque.

He says that, after many dances, the dancers began to flag, ' whereupon
the King who is naturally choleric got impatient, and shouted aloud, " Why
don't they dance ? What did you make me come here for ? Devil take you
all ; dance !" On hearing this, the marquis of Buckingham, his majesty's
most favoured minion, immediately sprang forward, cutting a score of lofty
and very minute capers with so much grace and agility, that he not only
appeased the ire of his angry sovereign, but, moreover, rendered himself the
admiration and delight of everybody. The other masquers, being thus
encouraged, continued successively exhibiting their prowess with various
ladies; finishing in like manner with capers and by lifting their goddesses
from the ground.'

[1] Rawdon Brown's translation, quoted in Harrison's *England*, Part II, Forewords,
p. 58. (New Shakspere Society)

Finally, James, delighted at the grace of the prince's dancing, kisses him affectionately, and pats the marquis on the cheek. The king caused the masque to be repeated, but with 'additions.' This, apparently, meant that his majesty did not appreciate the opening part of the masque. Contemporary critics asserted that Inigo Jones had lost his charm, and that Ben Jonson 'should return to his old trade of brickmaking[1].' Jonson, therefore, rewrote it for its second performance on 17 February, making it elaborately complimentary to Wales[2]. Mount Atlas now becomes Craig-Ereri, and we have a dialogue between three Welshmen, which, like the dialogue in *The Irish Masque*, is inferior in wit and vigour, but curious for the Welsh-English. The Welshmen criticise the first device of Hercules and the Comus rout—'there was a tale of a tub'—and the pigmies, and we have, instead, a dance of men and a dance of goats—'the Welsh goat is an excellent dancer by birth'—as antimasques, with songs in Welsh-English; and then, apparently, the real masquers with their dances and songs followed. Though the first part of *Pleasure Reconciled to Vertue* seems to have been too serious for the taste of king James, it was able to stir Milton to the composition of *Comus*.

A break now occurs in Jonson's masque writing. His journey to Scotland took place in 1618, and Jonson was not in London again till about May 1619. The new banqueting house at Whitehall was burnt down on 12 January 1619. Queen Anne died in March. Jonson's quarrel with Inigo Jones was in progress. He produced no more masques till 6 January 1621, when the court called upon him again, and the admirable *Newes from the New World discovered in the Moone* was the first of a series of eight masques, containing some of his best work and ending in 1625 before his paralytic stroke. Every one of these, except the imperfectly reported *Masque of Owls*, contains dramatic work that brings before us contemporary London life and manners, with a lighter and easier touch than Jonson uses in his plays. In *Newes from the New World*, the printer, the chronicler and the factor allow us a glance, tantalisingly brief, at the lower walks of literature in London and the beginnings of the London press; *Neptune's Triumph*, in a witty dialogue between a cook and a poet, magnifies the art of Jacobean cookery; the Fencer, in *Pan's Anniversarie*, is an amalgamation of all the old gamesters who swaggered in the Elizabethan fencing ring; *A Masque of the Metamorphos'd*

---

[1] Brent to Carlton, *Cal. State Papers, Dom.* vol. xcv, p. 12.
[2] Called, by Gifford, *For the Honour of Wales*.

Gypsies, Jonson's longest masque, 'thrice presented to King James,' is an exhaustive study of gipsy manners and gipsy language, wonderful for scope and minuteness. It contains the ribald song of Cocklorrel, another song of the street, almost Aristophanic in lusty vigour. The ballad of the bearward, John Urson, in the excellent *Masque of Augures*, is another lyric of the same quality. This lyric of the gutter is found cheek by jowl with the solemn Latin notes about augurs as if to reveal to us the two sides of Jonson— the schoolmaster and the street arab. Both characters in Eliza- bethan London were endowed with a fuller humanity than their modern representatives. There is no failure of poetical power in these later masques. *Pan's Anniversarie* and *The Fortunate Isles* contain exquisite lyrical work, and there is hardly anywhere in the masques a finer song than the last 'hunting chorus' of *Time Vindicated*, with its characteristic ending

> Man should not hunt mankind to death,
>   But strike the enemies of man;
>   Kill vices if you can:
>   They are your wildest beasts,
> And when they thickest fall, you make the gods true feasts,

Two masques, in 1631, conclude his series. It would seem as if Jonson's experience in 1618 convinced him that he could not rely upon the contrast between the fantastic and poetic to hold the attention of his audiences. Popular taste began to ask for sen- sational antimasque, and the multiplication of these threatened to reduce the masque to chaos. Jonson fell back upon the dramatic scene as a means of compelling the interest of his audiences, and, either by the wit of his comic invention or the truth of his comic characterisation, succeeded nearly always in rising above mere farce.

Jonson has been called a prose Aristophanes[1]. In his masques, taken as a whole, he may be recognised as more truly Aristophanic than any other English writer. His serious lyrics are Horatian in their restraint and classic dignity and have none of the splendour of the imaginative choruses of Aristophanes. Nevertheless, in the lyrical and descriptive parts of the masques, Jonson's fancy, elevated as it is by his moral intensity and his sense of the poet's dignity, continually produces a total result which is more than fanciful—which, in a high sense, is imaginative. But, on the side of full-blooded humanity, of intense appreciation of the joy of life in

---

[1] *Jonson n'est pas seulement un Labiche ou un Scribe qui aurait du style; c'est pour ainsi parler, un Aristophane en prose*, Castelain, *Ben Jonson*, p. 353.

the coarsest and commonest types, of wonderful knowledge of contemporary men and manners, Jonson matches even Aristophanes. Moreover, in the rollicking energy of his lyrics of the gutter and his long prose harangues, the challenging insolence and swagger of the Aristophanic *parabasis* is more than suggested. Jonson's gusto, his vigour and virility, are the most natural and unforced part of his genius. They were cramped in the masque. They were cramped even on the Elizabethan stage. An Athenian Dionysiac festival might have given them scope. Jonson, therefore, expresses this side of himself in his masques only in fragments, and cannot be called Aristophanic unless his masques are taken as a whole.

Jonson, as a masque writer, had no successor. The two great sensations of Charles's reign, Shirley's *Triumph of Peace* and Carew's *Coelum Britannicum*, both produced in 1634, are aptly characterised by Schelling : 'as to form, Shirley's masque is chaos in activity, Carew's chaos inert.' D'Avenant's *Salmacida Spolia*, in which the king and queen took part in 1640, has so large a number of successive 'entries' in the antimasque as to make it very like modern pantomime.

But, in 1634, *Comus* was produced at Ludlow castle. We have pointed out that Milton took suggestions from Peele's *Araygnement of Paris* and from Jonson's *Pleasure Reconciled to Virtue*, but his main inspiration came from Fletcher's *Faithfull Shepheardesse*. *Comus* must not be classed as a masque because there is no disguising and no dancing. It is a species of outdoor entertainment, and, therefore, akin to pastoral. There is a natural tendency for the outdoor entertainment, if it be lengthy, to approximate to the pastoral ; and pastoral resembles the masque, because, by its conventions, it is undramatic.

It may, therefore, not seem inappropriate to consider the pastoral drama along with the masque. The one is an offshoot of the legitimate drama for indoor use, the other for outdoor. Both, in the main, may be described as efforts made by amateurs to bring the theatre into their own halls or parks. But it is not until the professed poet and dramatist come to the help of the amateur that any great art results. Jonson and Milton, so far, have been examples of this fact, which becomes even more apparent when we turn to pastoral drama in its fullest manifestation.

Pastoral poetry is without a place among the greater forms of literary art, because it is essentially a reaction. Its two motives are a longing for simplicity of thought and feeling and a longing for country as opposed to town. This latter longing is innate in man, because his original home was the field or the forest, and is the soundest and best part of pastoral art. The desire for simplicity, on the other hand, has in it an element of weakness and disillusionment. The pastoral poet is not strong enough to confront and master his own age and find in it the materials for his poem; his own age is too complicated and sophisticated. He, therefore, takes refuge in Arcadia—in an Arcadia of feeling and thought, which has the defect of being visionary and unreal. It is not the life the poet knows, but his refuge from that life. The Elizabethan drama was so firmly rooted in present realities of passion and thought that it swept pastoral poetry, for a time, out of sight. The prose of Sidney and the verse of Spenser, noble as they were, were superseded by the new art of drama, and it was only after the dramatic impulse had spent itself that the exhausted dramatists accepted pastoral as a sufficient exercise for their energies.

Theocritus and Vergil are the two fathers of pastoral poetry. Of the two, Theocritus is commonly preferred as less artificial than Vergil. The clear, bright naturalism of Theocritus, which, in fact, is the perfection of art, makes Vergil's *Eclogues* seem artificial; but these must not be considered apart from his *Georgics*. The Italian farmer was very real in Vergil. He was less of an artist but more of a man than the Greek, and, spiritually, he is far above Theocritus. All his work is touched and glorified by his natural piety, the wistful sincerity of his religious feeling and his contemplative intensity. On its dramatic and realistic side, pastoral poetry owes most to Theocritus; on its contemplative and visionary, to Vergil. Usually, both influences cooperated.

When the renascence begins in the fourteenth century, pastoral composition follows three main lines of development. First, there is the eclogue proper, beginning with the Latin eclogues of Petrarch and the Italian eclogues of Boccaccio and producing, in 1498, the extraordinarily popular twelve eclogues of Mantuan. In English literature, this type is represented by *The Shepheards Calender* of Spenser[1]. Secondly, there is the mixture of prose pastoral story and poetical interlude of which Boccaccio's *Admeto*[2] is the prototype. Boccaccio developed from it his own *Decameron*, and Sanazzaro's less potent genius, regularising the prose and verse sections, produced, in 1481, his *Arcadia*, which, in Spain,

---

[1] *Ante*, vol. III, p. 221.

[2] In 1341. Boccaccio calls it *Commedia della ninfe fiorentine*.

prompted the *Diana*[1] of George of Montemayor, printed about
1560   The Spanish romance added to the pastoral and classical
elements of the Italian writers a new chivalrous element.   In
English literature, these works inspired Sidney's *Arcadia*[2].   The
third type is the pastoral play, of which two famous examples
were published in Italy about the same time—Tasso's *Aminta*,
in 1581, and Guarini's *Il Pastor Fido*, in 1590. *Aminta* is
distinguished by its sensuous charm, its poetic grace and its
emotional sweetness : *Il Pastor Fido* by its intricate and ingenious plot.   Both works were printed in London in 1591, in
which year Fraunce translated *Aminta* into English verse.   But
the direct influence of this third kind of pastoral on English
dramatic literature is not apparent till the beginning of the seventeenth century.   The second kind reaches English writers earlier.
It has a great influence through the prose romances of Sidney[3],
Lodge and Greene, but, before this begins, Peele's *Araynement
of Paris* and Lyly's dramas—especially his *Gallathea* and *Love's
Metamorphosis*—exhibit an English type of pastoral so original
in its mixture of pastoral, mythology, allegory and satire, that
some critics have denied that it is pastoral at all.   And when
Shakespeare, in *As You Like It*, uses Lodge's romance, *Rosalynde*,
his play is closer to English traditions[4] of Robin Hood and
Sherwood forest than to anything Italian.   Among the lesser
dramatists of the end of Elizabeth's reign, Munday, in his use
of the Robin Hood stories, offers, on his own low level, an English
kind of pastoral similar to Shakespeare's.   The feature of this
dubious pastoral of Peele, of Lyly[5], of Shakespeare and of Munday
is that it is joyful, fresh and irresponsible.   It comes at the
beginning of a literary epoch instead of at the end, and the exhausted passion and elaborate artificiality of the court of Ferrara
are replaced by the heedless gaiety and robust life of Elizabethan
England. *The Shepheards Calender* and *The Faerie Queene*, as
well as *The Countess of Pembroke's Arcadia*, are examples of an
appropriation of influences from Italy, France and Spain, which
resulted in distinctive types of art.   The new romance type was
produced by the noble-minded idealism which characterised the

---

[1] *Los siete libros de la Diana de Jorge de Montemayor.* Bartholomew Young
translated it into English in 1583, but his translation was not printed till 1598.

[2] For Sidney's *Arcadia*, cf. *ante*, vol. III, p. 351.

[3] For plays founded on Sidney's *Arcadia*, see *ante*, vol. III.

[4] For the formation of pastoral traditions in England, consult chap. II of Greg's
Pastoral Poetry and Pastoral Drama.

[5] *The Maydes Metamorphosis*, a good play, of doubtful authorship, should be
included in this group.

genius of both Spenser and Sidney. In the plays, a parallel manifestation of the free and careless Elizabethan spirit produces again
a new type of art.

It is curious that Daniel should have been the writer who
attempted to reproduce in English the Italian pastoral play of
Tasso and Guarini, as he had tried to reproduce the Senecan
drama of Garnier. In 1602, he prefixed a sonnet to a translation
of *Il Pastor Fido* in which he claimed acquaintance with Guarini,
and, in 1605, he wrote for queen Anne at Oxford *The Queenes
Arcadia*, which he calls 'a Pastorall Trage-comedie.' In 1614, his
second pastoral tragicomedy for the queen, *Hymen's Triumph*,
was performed at Somerset house at the marriage of lord
Roxborough. These plays are not without interest and charm.
The satirical element in the first and the scholarly workmanship
of the second are worthy of attention. But they have neither the
freshness of Peele nor the passionate sentiment of Tasso. Daniel
is the schoolmaster in drama; his plays are never more than
praiseworthy exercises in composition. The effort of copying
Garnier or Guarini was sufficient to extinguish his small
dramatic gift, and his dramatic experiments did not produce any
results of importance. As the virile Elizabethan drama softened
and degenerated, pastoral revived, and meritorious plays were
produced, such as *The Careless Shepherdess* of Thomas Goffe
and *The Shepherd's Holiday* of Joseph Rutter.

But, before this decline came about, pastoral drama was three
times essayed by men of genius, with the consequence that the
Elizabethan and Jacobean period has left three plays which are
the best that the language has produced in the pastoral kind, and
are almost masterpieces. These are *The Faithfull Shepheardesse*
of Fletcher, *The Sad Shepherd* of Jonson and Thomas Randolph's
Amyntas. These three plays stand out conspicuously from the
generally feeble and formless work of the pastoral drama; and,
therefore, we shall leave on one side many works of minor importance, and endeavour shortly to indicate the interest, and estimate
the value, of these three best specimens of their kind.

These three plays are alike attempts by dramatists to put
pastoral poetry upon the boards. They are not, like Milton's
Comus, written for outdoor presentation. In all three cases, the
dramatist is consciously original. He is trying to see whether
the conventions of the pastoral drama can be used with advantage
on the London stage and be made to satisfy a London audience.

Fletcher, unmistakably basing his effort on Guarini's *Pastor*

Fido, was the first to try, and his attempt failed. He tells us
that the public, 'missing Whitsun-ales, cream, wassel, and morris-
dances, began to be angry.' They did not understand that pastoral
deals with shepherds who own their flocks, and not with 'hirelings,'
who would be reasonably expected to behave as rude rustics.
Such 'owners of flocks,' says Fletcher,

are not to be adorned with any art but such improper[1] ones as nature is said
to bestow, as singing and poetry; or such as Experience may teach them, as
the virtues of herbs and fountains, the ordinary course of the sun, moon and
stars, and such like.

His characters were to be unsophisticated, but not vulgar, country
people; and his play was to be a tragicomedy; there were to be
no deaths, but 'some were to come near it.' It is impossible to
read this note 'To the reader' without feeling that Fletcher, as
yet, has no practical experience as a dramatist. His effort is not
to create men and women but to observe certain rules of pastoral
tragicomedy. As a drama, the play fails; the plot is crude, and
the characters are without life. But Fletcher has taken it for
granted that his play must take us out of doors, and he has put so
much exquisite description of nature into it that his dramatic
failure hardly matters. Swinburne claims justly that *The Faithfull
Shepheardesse* 'is simply a lyric poem in semi-dramatic shape, to be
judged only as such, and as such almost faultless.' The liquid
melody of the verse, too, has the natural sweetness of the songs of
birds, and the rustle of leaves, and the flow of waters[2]. There is
no laboured description of nature; but green grass and cool
waters are everywhere in the play; the poet has the spring in his
heart, and his poetry blossoms like the flowers of April and
bubbles like the brook; there is no natural magic to compare
with it until we come to Keats; and, even in *Endymion,* there is
something hectic, something strained, when it is read along with
Fletcher's play. In *A Midsummer's Night's Dream* and *As You
Like It,* we get descriptions of nature which, in our literature,
are the nearest in their quality to Fletcher's work in *The Faithfull
Shepheardesse;* but Fletcher is both more copious and more concentrated than Shakespeare just because his art fails on the
dramatic side; whereas Shakespeare succeeds, and nature, in his
dramas, is duly subordinated to human character. As a work of
art, therefore, *The Faithfull Shepheardesse* is like *Comus.* Neither
is dramatic; although it is probable that, in both cases, the

[1] Not proper, not peculiar, general.
[2] As to the verse of *The Faithfull Shepheardesse,* cf. *ante,* chap. v, p. 117.

writers aimed at a kind of drama. But, in both poems, we find, instead of drama, descriptive poetry of extraordinary richness and beauty, the first full expression of the young writer's genius. But, here, a contrast begins. Fletcher is Elizabethan ; his self-consciousness is unruffled and unaware of the spiritual emotion stirring vehemently in Milton ; while, on the other hand, this self-consciousness of Milton puts him out of touch with nature—which, for two centuries, was to recede into the background in English poetry. In *Comus*, the beautiful descriptions of nature are incidental ; in no sense are they the reason or aim of the poem. And Milton's spiritual imagination is everywhere, ousting Pan and installing Apollo. But Fletcher's unembarrassed, happy enjoyment of Pan's Arcadia, in its natural greenness and freshness, is the abiding merit of his poem.

But a word must be said on the dramatic question. Fletcher has some plan of describing various types of love—for there is a 'modest shepherd,' a 'wanton shepherd,' a 'holy shepherdess' and a 'wanton shepherdess.' Having his mind fixed on some special grade of propriety or impropriety in love, he does not give us men and women. If we do not ask for men and women, there is much in his work that is beautiful. The conception of Clorin, who has 'buried her love in an arbour,' and has her mind fixed on holy things, except in so far as she pursues 'the dark hidden virtuous use of herbs' for the relief of the sick—that being an 'art' with which a shepherdess may be adorned—has much imaginative beauty and charm. The satyr, again, the wild creature tamed by a dim perception of spiritual beauty, and stedfastly loyal to that perception, is exquisite in its simplicity. But what can we say of Cloe, 'a wanton shepherdess'? If she were a woman, she would be endurable, however wanton ; but an abstraction illustrating wantonness in shepherdesses is unendurable, except when Fletcher forgets about the wantonness, and makes her talk pure poetry, as when she says to Thenot :

> Tales of love,
> How the pale Phoebe, hunting in a grove,
> First saw the boy Endymion, from whose eyes
> She took eternal fire that never dies;
> How she conveyed him, softly in a sleep,
> His temples bound with poppy, to the steep
> Head of old Latmus, where she stoops each night,
> Gilding the mountain with her brother's light,
> To kiss her sweetest.

This particular problem, as to how a young girl thinks of love, is particularly delicate and difficult for a young poet, whether the girl be good or bad. He reads his own mind into the woman's, and the result has an unnaturalness something like that which must have been the drawback of the acting of women's parts by men on the Elizabethan stage. This unnaturalness passes over from Fletcher's pastoral into Milton's *Comus*. There, it is the young Milton, disguised as a maiden, who utters, with some self-consciousness and bashfulness, the famous encomium on chastity. The speech is essentially undramatic—what neither the man nor the maiden would have said in their own persons.

Our second pastoral is Jonson's *Sad Shepherd*, which is almost as fine an achievement as Fletcher's *Faithfull Shepheardesse*. Of Jonson's work, something has already been said in an earlier chapter[1]. The work suggests a most perplexing problem of literary criticism. It was published after Jonson's death, and thus purports to be a work of his last years left unfinished because of his death. But this last effort of the partially paralysed poet is distinguished by a vigour of style and freshness of imagination that seem to mark it as a work of his prime. After reading Jonson's last masques and plays, in which a certain stiffening and flagging of his powers are clearly to be discerned, it seems impossible to ascribe *The Sad Shepherd* to the same date. Moreover, we hear of a work by Jonson called *The May Lord*, composed before his visit to Edinburgh, which has disappeared. The title may have been suggested by Sidney's *The May Lady*, in which case, Jonson's poem, probably, was some kind of pastoral play. Was *The May Lord* the first title of *The Sad Shepherd*, when Robin Hood was intended to be the central figure of the play? In that case, Æglamour's part would be a later addition. But Æglamour, in some respects, is the most remarkable of all the characters. He strikes the true romantic note, which is conspicuously absent in Jonson's main work. What could be finer in cadence and romantic suggestion than the first lines of the play, when Æglamour appears for a moment?

> Here she was wont to go! and here! and here!
> Just where those daisies, pinks, and violets grow:
> The world may find the spring by following her.

Even if we suppose that Jonson borrowed this opening from Goffe, we have not got over the difficulty, because Æglamour's speeches are consistently and strongly romantic in tone. It is easier to connect them in style and spirit with the additions to

---

[1] *Ante*, chap. i, p. 11.

The Spanish Tragedie than with anything else written by Jonson.
The man who wrote those additions and *The Sad Shepherd* might
have been a great romantic. Castelain[1] has pointed out that the
prologue divides itself into two parts. The first thirty lines are
the real prologue to *The Sad Shepherd.* They are beautiful in
feeling, and the silent passing of the Sad Shepherd over the stage
in the middle of them seems absolutely right in imagination, if we
omit the second thirty-six lines about the heresy 'that mirth by no
means fits a pastoral.' These last lines might have been a prologue
for *The May Lord,* but our problem is to decide when the first
lines were written which form an admirable prologue to *The Sad
Shepherd.* As to this, we must note that, in spite of the 'forty
years' of the first line, the succeeding statement, that the public
have 'at length grown up to him,' must refer to the vogue enjoyed
by Jonson from 1605 to 1615, and cannot mean that he has forgiven the rejection of *The New Inne.* Another fine romantic motive
in the play is Karolin's kissing of Amie under the mad Æglamour's
compulsion. It compels us to revise all our conceptions of Jonson.
He treats it with a sureness and delicacy of touch that Shakespeare
could hardly have bettered ; while, at the same time, he proves
his authorship of the episode by the absurd list of 'lovers'
scriptures' and by putting into innocent Amie's lips the reference to

> the dear good angel of the spring,
> The nightingale.

But, so far, we have only touched upon one side or aspect of
the play. We must add that the part of the witch is realised with
great power. Alken's speech beginning ' Within a gloomy dimble
she doth dwell,' and his later speech which describes the

> spanlong elves that dance about a pool,
> With each a little changeling in their arms,

are both in blank verse, marked by a freer movement than Jonson
usually permits himself, and they also convey the old world idea
of the witch with a force to be paralleled only in Jonson's own
Masque of Queens, presented in 1609. One would wish to place
these speeches of Alken within measurable distance of that date.
Finally, the presentment of Robin Hood and Marian, while not so
fully romantic as Æglamour's part, is such sunny sweet realism as
touches upon romance ; and may have led Jonson to add a fully
romantic note to a play originally intended to prove that mirth
befitted pastoral. Puck-Hairy or Robin Goodfellow appeared in the

[1] See the note in his *Ben Jonson,* p. 459.

masque *Love Restored,* which we have dated 1612; again, we desire
to put the Puck-Hairy of the play and all its Robin Hood scenes
not too far from the splendid Robin Goodfellow of the masque.
But the Scottish dialect, which is the only serious drawback to
the artistic effect of the play, must, surely, have been introduced
after the poet's visit to Scotland in 1618[1]. That visit may have
stimulated Jonson to compose *The Sad Shepherd* as we have it;
our fragment began, perhaps, as *The May Lord,* for which the
last thirty-six lines were originally intended as prologue. Its
composition should be placed both before and after the visit.

The doubtful question of the date must not divert our attention
from the merits of Jonson's play. *The Sad Shepherd* reads as if
the poet had forborne to write out his play in prose, as he tells us
was his custom, and had set down his first sketch in verse, rapidly,
with his impulse fresh upon him. Perhaps, he found he could not
finish it by his usual methods. Perhaps, he was disconcerted by the
unfamiliar features of this surprising child of his imagination and
was half-ashamed of it. It is strongly dramatic, and the breath of
Jonson's realism gives it substance, but it is touched by a romantic
grace which is almost romantic passion ; and, therefore, it stands
alone among Jonson's dramas and will always have a special
fascination for his readers.

The third and last pastoral on our list does not require so full
a consideration as the first two. It is not a poem like Fletcher's,
nor unfinished like Jonson's ; but it belongs to a new order of
art, which has not the full humanity or high imagination of the
Elizabethan era. Randolph does not attempt, like Fletcher and
Jonson, to cast the pastoral into a new mould. His *Amyntas or
the Impossible Dowry* follows the conventions of Tasso and
Guarini, and its plot is deliberately artificial, removed from any
contact with life's realities. His style recalls the work of John
Day, and has a scholarly finish and point that raise the play above
the other pastorals of Jacobean times[2]. It is in curious contrast
to *The Muses Looking-Glasse.* In that play, the force of the
writing, and a touch of dramatic reality in the sketch of the
puritan onlookers, are remarkable. In *Amyntas,* Randolph's muse
is strangely subdued and gentle. He develops a very individual
type of pathetic and ironical fantasy in his delineation of the mad
Amyntas, which seems very far removed from the boisterous fun

---

[1] Compare the Irish of *The Irish Masque,* December 1613, and the Welsh of
For the Honour of Wales, February 1618.

[2] As to Randolph's university plays, see *ante,* chap. XII.

and rollicking rimes of *Aristippus*. This mellowing and softening
of Randolph's spirit extends to the comic scenes of the play, and
gives us the Latin rimes of the orchard-robbing elves—the

> *beata Fauni proles*
> *Quibus non est magna moles.*

Few such Latin rimes have been written since the Middle Ages.
There are sweet and tender passages of poetry continually occurring in the careful blank verse in which most of the pastoral is
composed, but they are so unemphatic and quiet in tone that some
familiarity with the poem is necessary before the reader becomes
aware of them. Fletcher impetuously injects into his artificial
plot and characters the fire of his poetic genius; Randolph, with
wonderful art and restraint, keeps his true vein of poetry always
in the right key—his play is a more complete and coherent production than either Fletcher's or Jonson's, but it is essentially
artificial; its excellence is all in the handling and embroidery.
It was, presumably, the last work of Randolph, and it raises our
opinion both of his art and of his genius.

CHAPTER XIV

THE PURITAN ATTACK UPON THE STAGE

SEEING that the stage has always been intimately associated
with religion, we can scarcely be surprised to find it the subject of
vehement controversy at the two most important periods of religious revolution known to history—the rise of Christianity and
the dissolution of the medieval ecclesiastical system. The latter
event, being less fundamental and less universal than its predecessor, was, also, less disastrous to the stage, and in England alone,
where the forces for and against the drama were most evenly
matched, was there any real struggle. This struggle possessed
many of the characteristics of that which had gone before; and
indeed, at first sight, the puritan attack upon the Elizabethan
theatre seems little more than a distant echo of the great battle
which had raged around the Roman *spectacula*. Yet the stage
was hated as sincerely and as bitterly in the sixteenth and
seventeenth centuries as it was in the third and fourth, and for
reasons strikingly similar. These reasons were both theological
and ethical; and it will be instructive to consider them separately
by way of introduction.

The Roman stage was essentially a pagan institution and remained such, in spirit, long after the triumph of Christianity. The
early church hated it, therefore, first and foremost for its idolatry.
It represented the old religion in a peculiarly alluring and in-
eradicable form, and it was the most dangerous of those 'pomps'
which every Christian renounced at baptism[1]. So long as the
Roman theatre existed, it was felt to be a rival of the church, and
not until the dramatic elements inherent in the catholic ritual had
given birth to the religious drama of the Middle Ages was a
temporary reconciliation between church and stage brought about.
From that time forward, the stage was included in the ecclesiastical
machinery and was freed from the attacks of all save heretics

---

[1] Tertullian, *De Spectaculis*, § 4.   See also, bibliography *s.v.* Prynne.

and reformers[1]. In the fourteenth century, for example, there was produced in England *A tretise of miraclis pleyinge*[2], in all probability by one of Wyclif's followers, which condemns the miracle on the score of its profanity. The reformation itself, however, was at first not at all, and never completely, hostile to the stage. Fired by the renewed interest in the classical drama and conscious of the convenience of the religious play as a controversial weapon[3], reformers, among whom Melanchthon stands conspicuous, were, in the first half of the sixteenth century, setting themselves, all over Europe, to bring the stage into the service of the reformation. England, like Germany, had her protestant dramatists, chief of whom were John Bale and, strange as it may sound, John Foxe, both working under the direct influence of the Lutheran drama; while, at Cambridge, the movement found its theoretical exponent in Melanchthon's disciple, Martin Bucer, whose *De honestis ludis*[4], was published about 1551. Precept and example, however, were alike soon forgotten in England, and this for two reasons. First, the English stage was destined by force of circumstances to become secular. The frequent religious changes in the middle years of the sixteenth century made it dangerous for the government to allow the theatre to be used for partisan purposes, and, accordingly, one regulation after another was passed to prevent the handling of matters of religion or state upon the stage, culminating in the proclamation of 16 May 1559, whereby Elizabeth provided for the strict licensing of the drama. Secondly, the reformation was itself rapidly changing its character; and, as Geneva became its centre of authority instead of Wittenberg, the realm of anti-Christ was mapped out with greater precision and was found to embrace many spheres of activity which had hitherto been considered honest[5]. When protestants became puritans, they were not long in discovering that the drama, which they had been forbidden to utilise for their own purposes, was without authority in holy writ, and before long, that it might not be suffered in any Christian commonwealth. It was natural, also,

[1] The most important of these, before Lollard days, were Gerhoh of Reichersberg and Robert Grosseteste. See *Chambers*, vol. II. pp. 98—100.

[2] *Hazlitt's English Drama and Stage*, p. 73.

[3] Chambers, *op. cit.* vol. II, pp. 216 ff.; for the part played by the drama in the Scots reformation, see *ante*, vol. III, pp. 122, 141, 161, and, for the whole topic of the Protestant and humanistic drama, see *Creizenach*, vols. II and III.

[4] *Scripta Anglicana*, 1577, pp. 141—6; Symmes, *Débuts de la critique dramatique*, app. A.

[5] Calvin himself was reluctantly brought into conflict with the stage by the zeal of his disciples. See Stähelin, *Calvin* (1863), vol. I, pp. 392—4.

that they should hark back to the early fathers for their arguments : for the puritans had the same *casus belli* as the fathers, though in a stronger form. The Elizabethan drama was, in a measure, the direct heir of the medieval miracle-play : probably, the contemporaries of the later growth scarcely realised the fundamental differences between the two. And the medieval miracle-play was, in origin, half liturgy and half folk-play : in other words, it was twice damned, since, like the maypole, it was heathen, and, like the mass, popish. 'Idolatry,' Cyprian had declared, 'is the mother of all public amusements'; the puritan could add a second parent—popery. As William Crashawe, father of the poet, put the case in a sermon at Paul's cross :

> The ungodly Playes and Enterludes so rife in this nation, what are they but a bastard of Babylon, a daughter of error and confusion, a hellish device (the devils own recreation to mock at holy things) by him delivered to the Heathen, from them to the Papists and from them to us[1].

As a 'bastard of Babylon,' the stage which Shakespeare trod was, in the eyes of his puritan contemporaries, more than immoral : it was unholy. When this is realised, we catch and understand the note of passion in tracts which at first sight seem academic essays in polemic borrowed from early Christian divines.

In other and more obvious ways, also, dramatic performances conflicted with the religious prejudices of puritans. For example, there was a conscious rivalry, frequently referred to in the literature of the subject, between the pulpit and the stage. The function of the latter, until quite recently, had been almost entirely didactic ; and, as we shall see, its defenders maintained that it was so still. But the protestant preacher, with the newly-opened Bible in his hand, would brook no competition. At the mere thought of comparing a play with a sermon, he raised the cry of 'blasphemy intolerable'; or he admitted the comparison, only to declare that 'enterludes weare the divells sarmons[2].' Again, the actor's practice, also derived from medieval tradition, of performing on Sundays[3] and holy days did not tend to soften the exasperation of the godly, who listened with indignant horror to the sound of the player's trumpet passing the open door of the church and

---

[1] *Sermon*, 14 February 1607. See, also, Selden, *Table Talk* (1892), p. 134.

[2] Harington, *Nugae Antiquae*, vol. I, p. 191, quoting a puritan objector. Osmund Lake, *A Probe Theologicall*, 1612, declares that God's blessing cannot rest upon the Scriptural play 'because he hath ordained the Preaching, and not the Playing of his word,' pp. 267—272.

[3] Furnivall (*Stubbes's Anatomy*, part I, pp. 296—301) brings together many interesting passages in reference to Sunday sports and Sabbath-breaking.

mingling defiantly with the peal of the bells. Finally, the actor, as
the early fathers had discovered and every puritan was careful to
point out, was bound by the very necessities of his craft to infringe
the divine law which forbade one sex to wear the costume of the
other ; and the point was a particularly telling one in an age when
it was customary for boys to act female parts[1]. All things considered, it was natural that the stage should appear to rest under
the peculiar displeasure of God. Lists of divine judgments meted
out to sinful players or those who visited the theatre are a common
feature in the tracts of the period. An earthquake, the fall of a
scaffold or, indeed, a public disaster of any kind, also, seemed to
the devout primitive intelligence of the time to indicate the
Almighty's wrath at the continued existence of playhouses. Few
things of this kind made a greater impression than London's
grim annual guest—the plague. As one of the earliest writers
against the stage unanswerably put the matter : 'the cause of
plagues is sinne, if you look to it well : and the cause of sinne
are playes : therefore the cause of plagues are playes[2].'

Turning from the theological to the moral aspect of the matter,
we may notice that here, too, puritans were walking in the
steps of the early fathers. Roman shows and Elizabethan stage
plays were both denounced as sinks of iniquity. Led into many
absurdities by his theological prejudices, the puritan reformer,
nevertheless, was at one with the best tendencies of his age
in his attack upon 'abuses.' A considerable literature upon
this subject has come down to us from the sixteenth century,
the most famous example being Stubbes's *Anatomie of Abuses*.
A perusal of this and similar productions shows us that puritanism was largely a revolt against medievalism; for a great
number of the evils denounced were medieval practices and
observances, folk festivals and such like, often innocent enough
in themselves but commonly tending to rioting and wantonness.
And, in singling out the theatre from among these as the special
object of his abhorrence and invective, the puritan was not
actuated by theological reasons alone. Undoubtedly, the stage
was the main channel through which what may be called the

[1] *Deuteronomy* xxii, 5. Ben Jonson thought the matter so important that he asked
Selden's advice upon it. The antiquary's letter in reply, dated 28 February 1615, is
interesting as an early example of biblical criticism. See *Opera Omnia* (1726), vol. II,
pp. 1690—6 ; also, *De Venere Syriacâ (Opera*, vol. II, p. 365) and *Table Talk, u.s.*

[2] Thomas White, *Sermon*, 1576, p. 47 ; and the lord mayor remarks, in 1584,
that to play in plague time increases the plague by infection, to play out of plague time
calls down the plague from God. See *Malone Society Collections*, part I, p. 173.

saturnalian elements of medieval life emptied themselves into the broad stream of the renascence. Furthermore, the rise of a secular theatre was one of the many problems created by the break-up of the medieval world which were engaging the attention of popular writers all over Europe in the sixteenth century. It is remarkable that, with hardly an exception, they condemned it as a sinister development, and gave moral reasons for excluding the player from the commonwealth. When a man like Montaigne, in one essay, classes 'enterlude-players' with 'harlots and curtizans[1],' and, in another, describes them as 'vagabond objects,' we are not surprised to find Jean Bodin expressing the strongest disapprobation of plays in his *Six livres de la République*[2], and the well known Jesuit publicist Mariana, in a chapter on 'Spectacles' in his *De Rege et Regis Institutione* (1599), denouncing the evils of the theatre and recommending its strict regulation[3]. Not a few of these continental writers were translated into English and so came to influence the development of puritan opinion. It is interesting, for example, to notice that two of the most popular translations of the Tudor period, North's version of the Spaniard Guevara's *El Relox de Principes* (1557) and Sandford's rendering of the German Cornelius Agrippa's *De incertitudine et vanitate scientiarum* (1569), contain unfavourable references to the stage. Puritans, however, did not have it all their own way. In 1559, William Bavand produced a translation of a Latin treatise, this time, appropriately enough, from Italy, under the title : *A Woorke of Joannes Ferrarius Montanus touchynge the good orderynge of a common weale*, which is important as being the first book in English to offer a defence of the secular drama, assigning it a place in a well ordered state on the ground that it 'doth minister unto us good ensamples[4].' This was exactly the line of argument that all subsequent English defenders of the drama adopted. Equally important on the other side is Sir Geffraie Fenton's *Forme of Christian pollicie gathered out of French*[5]. In his treatment of stage plays and enterludes, the unknown French writer anticipates in a few pages all the principal arguments of the puritans, and his book, translated in 1574 just

[1] See *Essays* (Florio's translation), bk. I, chaps. XLII and XLIII.
[2] English edition, 1606, bk. VI, chap. I, pp. 645, 646.
[3] Bk. III, chap. XV. Cf., also, his *Contra los Juegos Publicos* (*Obras*, vol. II, pp. 413—462).
[4] Bk. V, chap. VIII.
[5] Yet Fenton, in his *Tragicall Discourses* (1567), employs the same arguments in support of the novel as were used later by apologists for the drama.

before the attack began in England, exercised an appreciable influence upon Northbrooke and was read and quoted by the author of the *Third Blast*. Other examples, also, might be added to our list, such as a translation from Petrarch by Francis Twynne[1], who introduces into his original an unfavourable comment upon the newly erected Theater and Curtain.

The puritan opposition to the English stage did not burst forth in any violence until about 1576 ; but there are indications of its existence, apart from the translations just noticed, long before this date. English humanism, for example, though, for reasons already given, inclined to look favourably upon the drama, was in this as in many other respects laying down the lines upon which puritanism developed later. Roger Ascham was no puritan; yet his famous outburst against the popular romances of the day is remarkably similar in tone and feeling to the invectives launched by subsequent writers against plays which, to a large extent, were nothing but dramatised versions of these very romances. The connection between the humanistic attack upon the Italian novel and the puritan attack upon the romantic drama comes out most clearly in the case of William Alley, bishop of Exeter, whose condemnation of 'Wanton Bookes' in *The Poore Man's Librarie* (1565) expressly embraces plays. Alley appears to have been the first in England, since Lollard days, to take up the pen against the stage; he was the first Englishman, also, to cite with approbation the example of the ancient city of Marseilles, which 'kept so greate gravitie' that it would never allow a player within its walls. A classical precedent of this kind was so well adapted to the case of the city of London that it was eagerly seized upon by later writers and reappears in almost every pamphlet written against the stage. Another remarkable indication of the prevalence of the anti-dramatic spirit at this comparatively early period is to be found in the prologue of Lewis Wager's *Life and Repentance of Marie Magdalene*, first printed in 1566 but probably acted considerably earlier, which shows us a dramatist not only already on the defensive but employing the same arguments as were used, afterwards, by Lodge, Gager and Heywood. But perhaps the most tangible proof of the rising puritan flood was the quiet but persistent suppression by bishop, preacher and zealous mayor of local plays and pageants throughout England during the middle years of the sixteenth century, as no longer seemly in 'this happie

[1] *Phisicke against Fortune* (v. bibliography).

time of the gospell[1].' London, almost the only city in the kingdom with its own stage when the cleansing process was completed, was to be the scene of the great struggle between puritan and player.

The puritan forces advanced against the London stage in three lines : preachers, pamphleteers and civic authorities. In the nature of the case, it is impossible to do more than indicate here the incessant denunciation of the stage from the pulpits, and especially from the famous rostrum at Paul's cross. The work of the preachers was to sound the note for battle and to urge the godly forward in the war ; but, save for one or two sermons which have found their way into print, few traces of their contribution to the controversy have come down to our day. With the pamphleteer it was different ; his weapon was the book, and the book has a tendency to endure. It will be well, however, to defer our consideration of this aspect of the campaign until we have examined the efforts of the corporation of London to drive players out of the city ; for, in its opening phases at any rate, the literary attack was of secondary importance as compared with the administrative. Indeed, to some extent, it seems to have been prompted and controlled by the lord mayor himself.

The city merchant had reasons, other than those already mentioned, for hating the player. The customary processions through the streets, before playing, interfered with traffic. Public performances were a possible source of disturbance. As for the actor himself, he and his like, as the lord mayor informed the privy council upon one occasion, were 'a very superfluous sort of men[2].' He was either the retainer of some nobleman, in which case he was supported by his master, instead of being left to make his living at the public expense[3], or he was by law a rogue and a vagabond and ought to be dealt with accordingly. He lived for and by pleasure alone, grew rich by beguiling the simple poor of their money and, hereupon, aped the manners and habits of gentlefolk, swaggering about the city in dress so extravagant and costly as to be positively offensive to the eye[4]. In short, his profession, as it seemed to the civic mind, represented a definite and constant drain on the national resources. In the language of the day, he was a 'caterpillar of the commonwealth.'

The player, therefore, could expect no mercy from the city authorities ; but, fortunately for the development of the English

---

[1] Chambers, *op. cit.* vol. II, pp. 110—113 ; *Laneham's letter*, Furnivall, pp. 26—28.
[2] *Malone Society Collections*, part I, p. 46.
[3] *A Second and Third Blast*, Hazlitt, *op. cit.* p. 133.
[4] *Schoole of Abuse*, Arber, p. 39. *Anatomy of Abuses*, Furnivall, p. 146.

romantic drama, he found a rock of defence in the queen and her courtiers. Elizabeth liked to be provided every Christmas with theatrical amusements, but refused to be responsible for the entire maintenance of a special company. The privy council, accordingly, was instructed to satisfy both her love of pleasure and her passion for economy by seeing that the 'common players' were allowed full opportunity, not merely of practising for Christmas festivities, but of earning sufficient to maintain themselves at other seasons. The privy council was not sorry to have an excuse for interfering with the city's internal policy; but there was no reason why without special royal injunctions, it should have lifted a finger to succour the stage. Throughout its whole career, the Elizabethan theatre, though essentially popular in origin and character, depended for its very existence upon the patronage of the court, and the quarrel which we are now to consider was an early trial of strength between the same forces which, later, broke up England into two hostile camps. Apart from other considerations, the legal status of the actor would have been sufficient of itself to produce a conflict. It was defined by two regulations: the proclamation of 16 May 1559, issued to prevent the handling of religious and political questions upon the stage, which forbade performances in any town without a licence from the mayor; and the statute of 1572, which imposed the penalties of vagrancy upon any player not in the service of some nobleman[1]. In other words, acting companies, while placed under the direct protection of great lords at court, were not allowed to produce plays without the express permission of the lord mayor. Thus, the stage was subject to two authorities, not only different in character but rivals in policy and interest. The lord mayor was perpetually trying to put his legal powers into force and so to clear the city of actors; the court party, on the other hand, as perpetually intervened through the privy council, or overrode the mayor's authority by royal patents and other expedients of a similar nature. In the end, the stage succeeded in freeing itself from the grip of the city, but found itself, *ipso facto*, more than ever dependent upon the court, and under the particular sway of the master of the revels.

A detailed account of the struggle would be scarcely possible in the present state of our knowledge—so meagre, fragmentary and tantalising is the evidence hitherto brought to light upon the subject. The normal course of the controversy may, however, be followed in the correspondence between the privy council and

---

[1] Cf. as to these regulations, *ante*, chap. x; and see Hazlitt, *op. cit.* pp. 19, 21.

the lord mayor, to be found in the council's register and in the city archives known as *Remembrancia*[1]. The letters are amusing enough. The city's trump card, played with wearisome monotony, was the plague, almost as inevitable in Shakespeare's London as smoke is in ours. While the sickness raged, the privy council was as ready to close the playhouses as was the corporation[2]. But, ordinarily, the plague was only a summer visitor. In the autumn, therefore, the lord mayor would receive a letter from the council reminding him that the queen must have her Christmas amusements, and requiring him to allow the actors an opportunity of practising their art. The city usually resisted these recommendations with all the power and ingenuity at its command.

Matters remaining in this constant state of tension, an occasional crisis was inevitable; especially when an unusually severe epidemic gave the lord mayor an excuse for attempting to suppress the stage altogether. The documents at our disposal give us the particulars of three such crises, two of which had an appreciable influence upon the character and number of the tracts we are to examine later. We even catch a glimpse of a possible fourth at the time of the great plague in 1563, when Grindal, then bishop of London, is found writing to Cecil to advise a year's inhibition of all plays in the city and for three miles round, adding, significantly, 'and if it were for ever it were not amiss[3].' Our records, however, do not begin till 1572 when, as Harrison tells us, with approval, in his *Chronologie*[4], players were expelled because of the plague; and it seems that the lord mayor refused to re-admit them, if we may judge from the letters of the privy council on their behalf in 1573 and, again, in the spring of 1574[5]. These letters, evidently, were of no avail; for, on 7 May 1574, the court party found it necessary to take out a royal patent in favour of the earl of Leicester's company, giving it express permission to play within the city notwithstanding any orders to the contrary, and eluding the consequences of the proclamation of 1559 by stipulating that its performances should be licensed by the master of the revels[6]. This is the beginning of the policy of subordinating the

---

[1] See *Acts of the Privy Council*, ed. Dasent, T. R., and *Malone Society Collections*, part I, the latter of which gives all the letters from the *Remembrancia* and the *Burghley Papers*, dealing with the stage. Unfortunately, there is a gap in the register from June 1581 to Feb. 1586, and in the *Remembrancia*, from March 1584 to Jan. 1587.

[2] Cf. *ante*, chap. x.

[3] *Remains of Grindal*, Parker Soc. Publications, pp. 268, 269, *Malone Society Collections*, part I, p. 148.

[4] Furnivall, *Harrison's Description of England*, New Shaksp. Soc. part I. p. liv.

[5] *Acts, op. cit.* vol. VIII, pp. 131, 132, 215.   [6] Hazlitt, *op. cit.* p. 25.

stage to the revels' office. Its immediate effect was to force the city to open its gates; but, later in the same year, the lord mayor retaliated by procuring an order of the common council requiring that all playhouses, companies and plays should be licensed by the corporation, and enumerating in a preamble all the 'great disorders and inconvenyances' occasioned by the drama; which proves beyond doubt that the city's attitude was largely influenced by puritanical convictions[1]. At this juncture, our information becomes insufficient to follow the sequence of events. But the upshot of the conflict is clear. Certain players, finding the city obdurate and unwilling to submit to its severe regulations, began to look about them for some means of carrying on their business out of reach of the mayor's authority. Thus, while the innyards of the city continued to be used for dramatic purposes, in 1575, the foundations of the first permanent playhouse in London were laid 'in the fields to the North of the City,' and, in 1576, or the following year, the buildings were completed[2]. The puritan watched with horror the rise of these 'houses of purpose, built with great charges for the maintenance of them and that without the liberties, as who shall say: there, let them say what they will, we will play[3]'; but he could not do anything save vent his rage in sermons and tracts.

The second crisis appears to have centred round the great plague of 1582—3, though there are signs of its approach several years earlier. In 1578, we find Fleetwood, the city recorder, referring to certain standing orders by Burghley for dealing with plays[4]; and, in the correspondence of 1580, it is evident that a campaign is on foot for the abolition of the stage not only in the city but also in the fields[5]. An earthquake in April that year, celebrated in a contemporary ballad beginning:

Comme from the plaie, comme from the playe:
the house will fall so people saye:
the earth quakes lett us hast awaye[6],

probably did much to strengthen the city's cause, and the plague came to its assistance in 1581, so that the playhouses were shut all through the summer. Then began the customary struggle over the

---

[1] Hazlitt, *op. cit.* p. 27; *Malone Society Collections*, part I, p. 175.
[2] Cf. *ante*, chap. x.   [3] Stockwood, *Sermon*, 1578, p. 134.
[4] Wright, *Elizabeth*, vol. II, p. 88; *Malone Society Collections*, part I, p. 157.
[5] *Malone Society Collections*, part I, pp. 46—49.
[6] Arber, *Stationers' Register*, vol. II, p. 167 b. Cf. passage from Gardniers' *Doomesday Booke*, 1606, quoted in Halliwell-Phillipps, J. O., *Outlines*, vol. I, p. 343, and Stubbes's *Anatomie*, part I, p. 180.

players' re-admission. In December, we find the privy council, in answer to a pitiful petition from the acting companies, obliged to renew in a stronger form its usual reminder to the lord mayor that the Christmas festivities were approaching[1]. And, on 24 December, the master of the revels was granted by royal patent certain wide, if vague, powers over the whole stage which seem to have been intended to counterbalance, if not to override, the powers of the lord mayor[2]. It was probably this patent which called forth, as an answer from the city, the famous undated act of common council for the permanent prohibition of plays in the city which has been usually, but, as has now been proved, erroneously, ascribed to the year 1575[3]. London had followed in the wake of Marseilles; the filthy player had been expelled. At the beginning of 1582, the privy council pleaded with the mayor to invoke his late 'inhibityon[4],' but in vain, and further discussion was stopped for that year by the plague.

It was not until the autumn of 1583 that the plague abated sufficiently to allow of a renewal of the dispute. But, in the meantime, two events of great importance had taken place; the first probably doing more than a thousand learned treatises to stamp the stage as an unholy institution. On Sunday 13 January 1583, great crowds were gathered to watch the bearbaiting at Paris garden, a pleasure resort outside the jurisdiction of the city, when a wooden scaffold on which many were seated collapsed, killing a few and injuring many more[5]. It seemed a direct fulfilment of the prophecies of puritans, a 'judgment' which not even the most abandoned playgoer could disregard. Yet the court hardened its heart like Pharaoh, for, on 10 March, it once more stepped in on the players' behalf. At Walsingham's suggestion and under the direction of the master of the revels, 'a companie of players for her Majestie' was formed[6]. This, obviously, was intended as a move against the lord mayor, though it led, also, to important consequences for the stage. As in the case of the Leicester

---

[1] *Acts*, vol. XIII, p. 269.   [2] Chambers, *Tudor Revels*, pp. 62, 72, 75.

[3] *Orders appointed to be executed* (Singleton), Art. 62. For the question of date, v. Chambers, *The Academy*, 24 August 1895, and *Malone Society Collections*, part I, pp. 168—9.

[4] *Malone Society Collections*, part I, pp. 52—54; *Acts*, vol. XIII, p. 404. There is evidently some confusion of dates here. The letter of the privy council is given 11 April in the *Remembrancia* and 25 April or May in *Acts*. These are not different letters, as is stated in *Malone Society Collections*, part I, p. 54.

[5] *Malone Society Collections*, part I, pp. 59, 61, 65, 159, 161, 171 for references to this incident.

[6] *Tudor Revels*, p. 62.

company ten years before, the city was forced to yield for the moment, and, by arrangement with the privy council, the royal company was admitted into the city from the autumn of 1583 till the following Shrovetide[1]. When, however, her majesty's players sought re-admission in the autumn of 1584, they were met with the absolute refusal of the lord mayor. He had been tricked the season before, for all the playhouses had been filled with men calling themselves the queen's players. The company could do nothing beyond appealing to the privy council. The text of this appeal, together with a detailed answer from the city and certain other documents connected with it, has been preserved for us among the Burghley papers[2]; but we are completely ignorant of the events that followed. In much the same tantalising fashion, we catch a glimpse of an attempt upon the Theater and the Curtain in the same year. The lord mayor's letters of 1580 tell us that he was then already preparing to stretch forth his hand against the impudent Jerichoes in the fields; and, in 1583, we find him pleading with Walsingham that they should be closed. In June 1584, he actually seems to have accomplished his purpose; for, apparently, by reason of a brawl outside the Theater entirely unconnected with actors or their craft, he managed to procure an order from the privy council for the destruction of the houses[3]. Again the curtain falls at the most exciting point. We do not even know whether the order was ever carried out.

The year 1584, evidently, was a very critical one in the history of the English stage; yet we cannot doubt that the players successfully weathered the storm. Certainly, plays did not cease to be acted in London; nor do the houses in the fields appear to have suffered any material damage. Meanwhile, the stage drifted more and more under the control of the revels' office, until, in 1592, we find the lord mayor, apparently on the advice of archbishop Whitgift, proposing that the master, Edmund Tilney, should be bought over to the city's point of view by an annuity[4].

The third, and, so far as we know, the last, serious crisis in the relations between the city and the stage occurred in 1597. Thomas Nashe, writing to a friend in 1596, complains that

---

[1] *Malone Society Collections*, part I, pp. 66, 67.   [2] *Ibid.* p. 168.
[3] *Ibid.* pp. 164—6. Cf. as to this brawl, *ante*, chap. x.
[4] *Ibid.* pp. 68—70; *Tudor Revels*, p. 78, for the skirmish between the authorities and the stage, in 1589, which arose out of the Marprelate controversy, was nothing to do with the matter in hand. See above, vol. III, of the present work, p. 392; *Malone Society Collections*, part II, p. 180; *Acts*, vol. XVIII, pp. 214—5; Collier, vol. I, pp. 275—7.

the players ... are piteously persecuted by the Lord Mayor and the Aldermen; and however in their old Lord's time they thought their estate settled, it is now so uncertain they cannot build upon it[1].

The 'old Lord' here referred to was lord Hunsdon, lord chamberlain, a staunch supporter of the players' interests in the privy council. He died on 22 July 1596 and was succeeded in office by the puritanically minded lord Cobham[2]. We do not know to what measure of persecution in 1596 Nashe is here referring; but, on 28 July 1597, we find the lord mayor addressing an interesting letter to the council and enclosing a statement of 'the inconveniences that grow by stage playes,' which we recognise as the basis of many earlier letters. The council was desired to take measures 'for the present staie and fynall suppressinge' of plays both within and without the liberties[3], and it immediately complied by sending an order to the justices of Middlesex for the dismantling of the Theater and Curtain 'so as they maie not be ymploied agayne to suche use[4].' Once again, however, we are left in the dark as to the fate of the houses in the fields. As a matter of fact, the Theater was closed this very month and year, but the cause appears to have been nothing more serious than a difficulty in renewing the lease. Perhaps, the death of lord Cobham and the influence of the new lord chamberlain, another lord Hunsdon, may have weakened the force of the order. In any case, the civic authorities do not seem to have gained much from a fight of over a quarter of a century. Sunday performances were abolished, at least in theory; playing was forbidden in Lent; and certain other restrictions were placed upon the freedom of the actor. But the enemies of the stage had aimed at abolition, not regulation[5].

It is now time to turn to the literary side of the puritan campaign and to speak of the bombardment which the pamphleteers kept up, while the city fathers made their repeated assaults upon the stage. It will be remembered how the players had nonplussed the corporation by setting up their houses outside the walls of the city. The question was now as to what could be

---

[1] *Fleay's Chronicle of Stage*, p. 157; Collier, vol. I, pp. 292—4.

[2] *Malone Society Collections*, part I, p. 39.　　　[3] *Ibid.* pp. 78—80.

[4] Halliwell-Phillipps, J. O., *Outlines* (7th ed.), vol. I, p. 356; *Acts*, vol. XXVII, p. 313.

[5] For the order against the theatres in 1600, which, curiously enough, the city did not carry out, perhaps because it had some reference to the Essex rising, perhaps because the lord mayor of the year seems to have been himself in favour of plays, see Simpson, *New Shaksp. Soc. Trans.*, 1874, vol. II, pp. 386—9; Lee, *Life of Shakespeare*, pp. 174—6, 212—3; *Fleay's Chronicle of Stage*, p. 161; Halliwell-Phillipps, J. O., *Outlines*, vol. I, pp. 307—9.

accomplished by the voice of the preacher and the pen of the pamphleteer. The erection of the Theater and the Curtain in 1576 and 1577 acted at once upon the already highly charged atmosphere and called down a veritable hail of sermons and tracts. Of the former, only one or two, which are preserved for our edification in book form, need here be noticed. There is, for example, the sermon of one Thomas White, delivered at Paul's cross on 9 December 1576 and, apparently, repeated on 3 November in the following year, to which we are indebted for the syllogistic statement of the plague argument already quoted, and which, by its reference to 'the sumptuous Theatre houses, a continuall monument of London's prodigalitie and folly' helps us to determine the date of their establishment. Another divine who, by publication, sought a larger congregation than had assembled to hear him at Paul's cross was John Stockwood; his sermon, dated 24 August 1578, laments the immorality of playhouses and the immense gains of players, and gives a very forcible expression to that feeling of rivalry between stage and pulpit to which we have referred.

From the printed sermon to the godly treatise is no great step. The honour of taking it belongs to John Northbrooke, a puritan clergyman residing near Bristol, who had suffered imprisonment at the hands of his bishop, apparently for some act of nonconformity. As his *Treatise, wherein Dicing, Dauncing, vain Playes or Enterludes with other idle Pastimes etc. commonly used on the Sabbath day, are reproved by the Authoritie of the Word of God and auntient Writers*, was entered for publication in the year 1577, it is natural to suppose that the erection of the playhouses was the immediate occasion of its appearance. Yet the book was rather a general arraignment of the 'abuses' of the age than a special treatise on the subject of stage plays, to which scarcely more than a sixth of its space was given. Indeed, while its debt to Fenton's *Forme of Christian pollicie* is considerable, it became, in its turn, as regards both contents and dialogue-form, the model for Stubbes's *Anatomie of Abuses*. When he addresses himself to the subject of plays, it is the moral aspect of the question upon which Northbrooke lays especial stress, providing his readers with an appalling list of the vices which might be learnt at the theatre; while his remark that 'it is better to be subject to a magistrate under whom nothing is lawful than under him to whom all things are lawful[1]' indicates the remedy which commended itself to him and to most of his fellow puritans.

[1 Cf. Bacon, *Apophthegms.* 'Galba succeeded Nero....']

Quaint, simple-minded and long-winded Northbrooke remained a solitary pioneer. He has his special niche, of course, in Prynne's pantheon of stage haters, and Stubbes, as we have said, evidently read him and learnt from him; but his immediate successors either did not know of him or deliberately ignored his existence[1]. In 1579, the very year when a second edition of his book was appearing, a new writer was, with considerable ostentation, 'setting up the Flagge of Defiance' to the prevailing abuses of the day, and claiming to be the one to 'found the schoole and reade the first lecture of all'[2]. This fresh arrival in the lists was Stephen Gosson, one of the most interesting and important of those who took up arms against the stage. Though not more than twenty-four years of age when he published *The Schoole of Abuse*, he had already, if Meres is to be believed, written pastorals which ranked among the best of his age, though none of the specimens of his poetry that have come down to us soars above the commonplace. In addition to this, the style of his *Schoole* suggests that he deserves almost as much credit as Lyly for giving to Euphuism its final and complete form; both having been bitten with the craze at Oxford, very possibly in company. Like Lyly, also, Gosson left Oxford for London, and took to the stage as both actor and playwright. At least three dramas were produced by him, as he tells us himself: *Catalines Conspiracy*, which appeared at the Theater, 'a cast of Italian devices called *The comedie of Captaine Mario*' and 'a moral' entitled *Praise at Parting*[3]. From certain hints he gives us, we are led to suppose that his theatrical career was neither prosperous nor successful. Whether for this reason or, as he would rather have us think, because the nonconformist conscience was already beginning to make the playwright discontented with his surroundings, about the end of 1578 he left London and became a private tutor in the country, where he prepared his *Pleasaunt invective against Poets, Pipers, Plaiers, Jesters and such like Caterpillers of a commonwelth*, which was entered at Stationers' Hall on 22 July of the year following.

If *The Schoole of Abuse* was intended as a puritan palinode, it

---

[1] That he was not forgotten altogether is clear from a reference to his book in *A true reporte of the death...of M. Campion* (1582) which, incidentally, affords a proof that this topic was interesting to Catholics as well as to puritans. See *The Modern Language Review*, vol. IV, p. 485.

[2] In the same year there appeared a pamphlet by 'T. F.', entitled *Newes from the North*, which complains of playhouses, and especially the Theater and Curtain. Ed. 1585 sig. F 4.

[3] See *The Schoole oj Abuse*, ed. Arber, p. 40, and *Plays Confuted*, Hazlitt, *u.s.* p. 165.

certainly does not read like one. Its worldly, flippant air, very different from the sober dulness of Northbrooke, suggests that this assault upon Parnassus was little more than a trick to catch the public ear and to win something of the success of *Euphues*, which had appeared a few months earlier. Doubtless, its author also hoped that his remarks upon the drama would attract the favourable notice of London puritans. Among the letters at the end of the book is one addressed to the lord mayor and aldermen, applauding their policy with regard to the players, and touching the root of the matter in the remark that, 'if their letters of commendation were once stayed, it were easie for you to overthrow them.' As Gosson was one of the few anti-dramatic writers who possessed a first-hand acquaintance of the theatre, it is interesting to observe that there is very little he can find to advance against it. He is careful to point out that nothing of an unseemly nature ever went on within the precincts of the playhouse itself; that actors might even be 'sober, discreete, properly learned honest householders'; and that there were several 'good playes and sweete playes' to be seen in London, among which, of course, are those by Stephen Gosson himself.

The patron at whose feet Gosson laid this work was none other than that 'right noble gentleman, Master Philip Sidney Esquier,' who, as we learn on the authority of Spenser, was anything but flattered at the tribute[1]. Indeed, there can be little doubt that the famous *Apologie for Poetrie*, written in the autumn of 1581 though not published before 1595, was undertaken, in the first place, as a reply to Gosson ; the disdainful reference to 'that kinde of people, who seek a prayse by dispraysing others, that they doe prodigally spend a great many wandering wordes, in quips and scoffes[2]' being a palpable hit at him and his pamphlet.

Despite its affectation and folly, *The Schoole of Abuse* gained its immediate object. It was widely read, and met with a storm of opposition. Gosson refers to this in the introduction to his second book, *The Ephemerides of Phialo*, published in the autumn of 1579, making special mention of a tract, no longer extant, which assumed the curious title of *Straunge Newes out of Affrick*. Possibly this name, very similar to that of hundreds of news-pamphlets of the time, was intended to cloak the real nature of the publication from the eyes of the authorities. The author,

---

[1] *Three proper and wittie familiar Letters*, by Immerito and G. H., 1580, p. 54.
[2] *Apologie*, Arber's reprint, pp. 48, 49. See *ante*, vol. III, p 299, for the place of the controversy in the history of literary criticism.

whose name Gosson knew but did not disclose, has been conjectured to be Lyly, but without sufficient foundation[1]. At the conclusion of *The Ephemerides* appears *An Apologie for the Schoole of Abuse.* Much of a piece with the work it sets out to defend—being, indeed, little more than a disquisition on the immorality of the pagan deities—this fresh contribution was undertaken in answer to a second champion who had come forward in defence of the arts. Gosson asserts that, after offering rewards at both universities to anyone who would write for them, the players had found a writer in London to comply with their needs. He had put forth a book, of which, at the time of writing, Gosson knew nothing save its title, *Honest Excuses.* This, there seems no reason to doubt, was the pamphlet by Thomas Lodge which has come down to us without a title-page[2].

This tract, the earliest publication of the future author of *Rosalynde,* and usually described as *A Defence of Poetry, Music and Stage-Playes,* must have been written immediately after Gosson's *Schoole* appeared, and printed in the late summer of 1579. It appeared surreptitiously, however ; for it was refused a licence—a very striking indication of the power and determination of the puritan opposition. In other respects, there is nothing in any way remarkable about the book. A piece of very ordinary Elizabethan prose, full of classical allusions and, every now and then, attempting the euphuistic manner, it is yet in no way inferior to the work it attacks. After the controversial fashion of the age, it contains a considerable amount of personal insinuation, which, probably, bore some relation to the truth, since Lodge and Gosson, apparently, had been contemporaries at Oxford and, undoubtedly, were acquaintances later in London. It is worth noticing, in view of Gosson's accusation that Lodge had been hired by the players, that the defence of poetry and music is quite as lengthy and serious as that of plays. The last topic is treated in a remarkably moderate tone. After a discussion of the antiquity and origin of play making, which anticipates the line of defence taken up later by Heywood, Lodge proceeds to consider the condition of the contemporary theatre. Here, he is ready to own, there is much room for improvement, and he admits that he wishes ' as zealously as the best that all abuse of playinge were abolished'; but this, he

[1] Indeed, a favourable reference to *The Ephemerides* in *Euphues and his England* would seem to preclude the possibility altogether. See Bond, R. W., *Lyly,* 1902, vol. II, p. 99.

[2] See *The Modern Language Review,* vol. III, pp. 166—8.

adds, is no reason for abolishing the stage itself. Such frank recognition of the claims of reform makes the refusal to license his book all the more remarkable.

We must turn aside from Gosson and Lodge for the moment, to notice the entrance of another combatant. The year 1580, which, as we have seen, was the beginning of the second great struggle between the city and the court, also marks a new development in the tactics of the pamphleteer. Up to this point, the stage had been attacked in company with other 'abuses'; but, late in 1580, there appeared for the first time a book which devoted itself exclusively to the subject of stage plays. It was entitled *A Second and third Blast of retrait from plaies and Theatres,* and, lest there should be any mistake as to the source of its inspiration, it bore the arms of the corporation of London upon the reverse of its title-page. No clearer proof than this can be needed of the close connection between the administrative and literary attacks. The lord mayor had evidently discovered the usefulness of the pamphlet agitation, and the sudden increase in the output of tracts during the next two or three years points unmistakably to encouragement by the authorities. In addition to all this, the book is instructive as affording a fresh illustration of the fact that the puritan attack was largely an echo of the old conflict between the pagan theatre and the primitive church; for the *Second Blast* (the first, of course, had been sounded by Gosson) was a translation of Salvian's attack on the iniquities of the Roman stage, which forms a section of his *De Gubernatione Dei*[1]. But a greater interest attaches itself to the work of the other devout trumpeter whom the title proclaims, 'a worshipful and zealous Gentleman now alive.' Like every other writer in the controversy, he borrows largely from his predecessors, especially from Twynne and Fenton. Being under the patronage of the city, he is naturally chiefly concerned with the administrative side of the problem. The root of the evil, he declares, as Gosson had done, is the support that players receive from the nobility; and he even goes on to say that, unable or unwilling to maintain their servants at their own cost, noblemen allowed them to live at the expense or charity of the general public. These bold words could scarcely have been uttered a year or two later when the queen herself had her company of actors. Yet, curiously enough, violent as the language of the tract is, it proposes no drastic measures of reform.

---

[1] The *editio princeps* of his works was published this same year at Paris.

The magistrate is advised to go slowly, and to begin by stopping all Sunday playing.

This tame conclusion, in all probability, may be put down to half-heartedness, or even insincerity, on the part of the author. Gosson, two years later, in his *Playes Confuted*, asserted that, beside himself, no playwright had written against plays 'but one who hath changed his coppy and turned himself like ye dog to his vomit to plays againe[1].' As the author of the *Third Blast* himself informs us that he had previously 'bene a great affector of that vaine art of Plaie-making,' it is natural to suppose that it is he to whom Gosson refers. The present writer is of opinion that the apostate playwright in question was that Elizabethan Jack-of-all-trades, Anthony Munday, who had been deliberately hired for the purpose by the opponents of the stage[2]. If this theory, which is supported by a good deal of circumstantial evidence, be true, it throws a somewhat sinister light upon the tactics of the puritan party, as having taken out a year's lease of a scapegrace actor's pen and paraded his sham conversion as a triumph for the cause of public morality[3].

Meanwhile, the players had been seeking to discredit puritans in general and Gosson in particular. They had revived two of his plays, which, as he tells us, they 'impudently affirmed' to have been written since the publication of *The Schoole of Abuse*. Moreover, on 23 February 1582[4], a drama in the manner of the old moralities was produced at the Theater, under the title: *The Playe of Playes and Pastimes*, which Prynne, probably erroneously, ascribed to Lodge[5]. The play is not extant, and was probably never even printed; but we learn a great deal about it from Gosson who is ever very liberal in his accounts of his antagonists' movements. Its object was to show how dangerous Zeal, or puritanism, might become as the sole guide to Life. Only when 'somewhat pinchte

[1] Hazlitt, *op. cit.* p. 212.

[2] See *Fleay's Chronicle of Stage*, pp. 51, 52 ; *The Modern Language Review*, vol. IV, pp. 484—7. Cf. however, *ante*, vol. v, p. 313, note.

[3] *A Treatise of Daunses* (1581), usually quoted as one of the pamphlets in the controversy, contains no reference whatever to the stage, the word 'playes' on the title-page, which has misled the unwary, meaning games of chance.

[4] This date is given us by Gosson, *Plays Confuted*, Hazlitt, p. 189. Halliwell-Phillipps (*Tarlton's Jests*, Old Shakesp. Soc., 1844, p. xx) prints from 'a manuscript in the possession of Mr Collier' Tarlton's *Jigge oj a horse loade oj Fooles*, cf. *ante*, vol. IV, p. 531, which brings in Gosson as a Puritan-fool, 'for sure a hypocrite.' If genuine (which, however, is a very doubtful assumption) the 'jigge' was probably written about this time.

[5] *Histriomastix*, p. 700. Prynne was evidently confusing *The Playe of Playes* with Lodge's *Defence*. The controversial 'morality' was also employed against the Martinists. See *ante*, vol. III, pp. 393—4.

in the wast' and in company with Delight and Recreation was she tolerable, being then ready to allow the use of comedies, provided, of course, 'that the matter be purged, deformities blazed, sinne rebuked, honest mirth intermingled and fit time for the hearing of the same appointed[1].'

For a long time, Gosson had been unable to procure a copy of Lodge's suppressed pamphlet. His rejoinder, therefore, promised in *An Apologie for the Schoole of Abuse,* did not make its appearance until 1582, and included an answer to the players also. *Playes confuted in five Actions,* as he calls his book, is unlike *The Schoole of Abuse* in every respect, and the complete change of tone, in all probability, may be attributed to the influence of the lord mayor, for we have little confidence in the sincerity of Gosson's sentiments[2]. Like the author of the *Second* and the *Third Blast,* he is now concerned with the stage alone, which has overshadowed all other 'abuses' in his eyes. Plays 'are not to be suffered in a Christian commonweale,' for are they not 'the doctrine and invention of the Devill'? Even Lodge cannot deny that they were originally dedicated to idols, or that the first theatre was erected to facilitate the rape of the Sabine women. And the style has changed with the matter. Euphuism and the classics are laid aside, and, in their stead, we are treated to divinity and the early fathers; there is no longer even a pretence at pleasantry in Gosson's invective. The book, probably, was written in haste, for, despite its division into 'five actions,' which anticipates the acts and scenes of *Histriomastix,* it has no intelligible arrangement of topics. Revenge is taken for Lodge's personalities in the dedication, which, this time, is addressed to Sir Francis Walsingham[3], a scarcely more fortunate choice than Sir Philip Sidney. Gosson declares that his antagonist had been 'hunted by the heavy hand of God and become little better than a vagrant.' Whether these words are merely an outburst of spleen or actually referred to a discreditable passage in the doctor-novelist's life, is not known. Lodge, at least, did not consider them worthy of any immediate reply, and, when, two years later, he recalled the controversy in the dedication of his *Alarum against Usurers* (1584), he charitably excused Gosson for his spiteful

---

[1] Hazlitt, pp. 201—3.

[2] The coarse *Pleasant Quippes for Upstart Gentlewomen* (1596), almost certainly by Gosson, could hardly have been written by a genuine puritan.

[3] Cf. the lord mayor's letter of 1583 (*Malone Society Collections,* part i, p. 63). It seems that, in spite of his action on 10 March 1583, puritans had some reason for regarding Walsingham, in Gosson's words, as 'a Hercules in the Court' to cleanse the Augean stables.

remarks, declaring that he bore him no grudge for them. Thus closed the earliest and most important of those hand to hand encounters which occasionally enlivened the course of the struggle.

The next tract we have to notice deals with the Paris garden disaster of January 1583, which was too striking not to evoke something more permanent than the inevitable broadside ballad. Within a week of its occurrence, a small octavo of forty pages appeared from the press of the puritan printer, Robert Waldegrave[1]. It was the work of John Field, part author of the first *Admonition to Parliament* and posthumous contributor to the Marprelate controversy. He had long been known as an opponent of the stage, and, in a letter, dated 25 November 1581, thanking Leicester for procuring his release from prison, into which he had been thrown for nonconformity, he actually takes occasion to chide his benefactor for his love of 'these impure interludes and playes[2].' His *Godly Exhortation*, as he styled it, deals with the drama chiefly from the Sabbatarian point of view and contains the usual list of terrible judgments, among which the late disaster at Paris garden, naturally, took a prominent place. This interesting little tract is far better written than the majority of the series.

In the same year, 1583, a book was published which has an importance far beyond that belonging to it as a contribution to the controversy under discussion. This was *The Anatomie of Abuses*, by the foremost of puritan social reformers, Philip Stubbes. Practically, nothing is known of his life, and it is unfortunate that the only contemporary testimony extant concerning his character is a ribald story in the anti-Martinist tract, *An Almond for a Parrat*. His literary activity, which covered a period of some thirteen years, seems to have begun about 1581, when he published a broadside ballad setting forth the fearful fate that had befallen 'a lewde fellow usually accostomed to sweare by Gods Blood.' A second edition of this, containing another ballad of similar nature, appeared shortly afterwards. Stubbes continued this practice of turning the public taste for horror to godly purposes in his fourth and most important work, by bringing together a formidable array of examples of divine judgments suddenly executed upon sinners of various kinds. This book, the famous *Anatomie of Abuses*, the title of which, perhaps, was intended to suggest

---

[1] Dated on the last page 17 Jan. Fleetwood notes its appearance in an entry in his diary under 19 Jan. (*Malone Society Collections*, part I, p. 161).

[2] Collier, J. P., vol. I, pp. 243—6. Another pamphlet on the same topic, Henry Cave's *Narration of the Fall of Paris Garden* (1588?), seems to have disappeared.

comparison with the fashionable *Anatomy of Wit*, was printed on 1 May 1583 and, immediately becoming popular, passed through four editions in three years. It was followed, a few months later, by a second part no less interesting, if less well known, than its predecessor. Both were 'made dialogue-wise' and consist of descriptions and condemnations, backed by scriptural texts and the aforesaid terrible examples, of those evils in the commonwealth which needed abolition or reformation. In all this there was nothing original. The records of the time are full of references to tracts against dicing, gaming, sabbath-breaking, usury and so forth. Excellent as his intentions were, Stubbes's title to fame rests rather on the vigour and picturesqueness of his style, the shrewdness of his observations and, above all, the surprising knowledge he displays as to the manners and customs of his age. *The Anatomie of Abuses* and Harrison's *Description of England*, which is dealt with elsewhere, are our two chief contemporary sources of information upon the social and economic conditions of the Shakespearean period. The lengthy description which Stubbes gives of the extravagances of Elizabethan fashion is a unique storehouse of facts relating to late sixteenth century costume. But this famous passage has tended unduly to obscure the merits of the rest. The opening words of *The Anatomie* give us to understand that the author had been travelling up and down the country for 'seven winters and more,' collecting material for his book. Certainly, nothing but the greatest patience and industry could have brought together all these details upon a great variety of subjects. The flippant Nashe, attacking Stubbes and his like in *The Anatomie of Absurditie*, declared that they 'extend their invectives so farre against the abuse, that almost the things remaines not whereof they admitte anie lawfull use[1].' There is some truth in this; but, had Stubbes been less earnest and less sweeping, we should have had none of those interesting and curious allusions to church-ales, barbers, football, astrologers and a hundred other seemingly trivial matters. Moreover, there is much sound commonsense behind most that he writes. While pleading on almost every page for the rights of the poor, he has no sentimental pity for the idle vagrant. Rackrenting, prison reform and many other problems that still press for solution, are touched upon in a manner that would do credit to a modern socialist. *The Anatomie of Abuses* is a very remarkable book. It is essentially the work of an original thinker, and, in fact, is an early attempt to

[1] McKerrow's *Nashe*, vol. I, p. 20, l. 7.

sum up the moral and economic forces of a nation in a fashion far removed, but not radically different, from that employed by the sociologists or political economists of the twentieth century.

Though confined to a short section of some five or six pages, entitled 'Of Stage-Playes and Enterludes, with their wickedness[1],' Stubbes's condemnation of the theatre is far the most uncompromising and intolerant that had yet appeared in England. Also, he was unmistakably sincere, which is more than can be said of any of his predecessors except Northbrooke and the preachers. The devilish origin of plays and their ghastly moral results are sharply and effectively driven home in Stubbes's hammerlike style, weighted by the authority of Scripture and the early fathers. There is no mincing matters; to patronise the theatre is 'to worship devils and betray Christ Jesus,' and, as for players themselves, they can only be earnestly exhorted to repent and so flee from the wrath to come, which, as Stubbes thought, was to come speedily. These trenchant observations, in a book which at once became popular, must have gone to swell the rising puritan opposition. Stubbes himself, it may be noted, rose with the tide; for a conciliatory preface, admitting that some plays were 'honest and chaste' and, as such, 'very tollerable exercyses,' was omitted after the first edition, thus proving that his final opinion on the matter was one of unqualified condemnation[2].

In William Rankins, who, in 1587, published his pretentious *Mirrour of Monsters*, we seem to have a case somewhat similar to that of Munday. The *Third Blast* rings weak and hollow beside Rankins's strident denunciations of the 'spotted enormities that are caused by the infectious sight of Playes'; yet, in 1598, Henslowe lent his company £3 in order to purchase one of Rankins's plays[3]. So rapid a fall from the heights of virtue creates suspicion. Despite the violence of its language, the *Mirrour* does not quite succeed in striking the note of sincerity. The voice is the voice of the godly; but the euphuistic style and the elaborate pageant 'Of the marriage of Pride and Luxury' with which the book closes suggest the flesh pots of Egypt[4].

---

[1] Furnivall's edition, part I, pp. 140—6.

[2] George Whetstone's *Touchstone for the Time*, published with his *Mirour for Magestrates* (1584), and Thomas Newton's *Treatise, touching Dyce-play and prophane Gaming* (1586), are two books, belonging to this period, which express a desire to see the stage reformed but not abolished.

[3] *Henslowe's Diary*, part I, p. 96; part II, p. 198.

[4] For a curious letter, on the subject of stage plays, of the same date as Rankins's *Mirrour*, see Halliwell-Phillipps's *Illustrations*, part I, app. XVII.

The pamphlets we have hitherto considered cover a period of about ten years, the agitation to which we owe them being directly traceable to the erection of the playhouses in 1576. But these houses, in spite of all the efforts of the city authorities, were now firmly established, and, though puritan feeling against them did not in any way decrease, the general public, we may suppose, began to take considerably less interest in the discussion. The failure, too, of the city's determined attack of 1583—4 probably took the heart out of the pamphleteers. Moreover, in 1588, a fresh topic of public interest arose in the famous attack upon the bishops by Martin Marprelate, which, indeed, made so large a stir as to throw into the shade for some time to come all other aspects of puritanism. Nor is it fanciful to suppose that the great struggle with Spain, which belongs to the same period, diminished the demand for pamphlets of this nature. Preachers, we cannot doubt, continued to denounce the stage with unabated vigour. Theologians, we know, did not cease in the course of their treatises to warn their readers against it[1]. But such contributions to the controversy as possess any importance, in the last fifteen years of Elizabeth's reign, are almost entirely on the side of the players. It was, for example, doubtless by way of apology that Robert Greene penned the "large digression" on "Playes, Play-makers, and Players" in his *Francesco's Fortunes* (1590)[2]. Again, his friend, Thomas Nashe, whose satirical pen was the most powerful that had yet been wielded against the puritans, in his earliest work *The Anatomie of Absurditie*, the title of which, probably, was intended to recall that of Stubbes's[3], who, indeed, is attacked by name, devotes considerable attention to the writers upon 'abuses,' 'who make the Presse the dunghill whither they carry all the muck of their melancholicke imaginations[4].' And, in his *Pierce Penilesse*, published in 1592, during which year, be it noted, the theatres had been closed because of a riot[5], he advances still further into the enemy's quarters. After 'a bout' with those who presumed to attack poetry, he here embarks upon a lengthy defence of plays. He declares that they are the salvation of idle men about town, keeping them from worse occupations and giving them something upon which to sharpen their wits. The playgoer has

---

[1] Among these may be mentioned bishop Babington's *Very Fruitful Exposition of the Commandments* (1583) which drew largely upon Stubbes. See Furnivall, *Anatomy of Abuses*, pp. 75*—93* for copious extracts.

[2] Grosart's *Greene*, vol. VIII, pp. 129—133.

[3] But see McKerrow, *Nashe*, vol. IV, p. 3.

[4] *Ibid.* vol. I, p. 20.   [5] *Acts*, vol. XXII, p. 550.

not only an opportunity of learning the history of his country, but the examples of the great and good of the past are set before his eyes, while vice, in all its forms, is 'most lively anatomized.' As for the attacks of the city, he asserts that they were made solely in the interest of the

Vintners, Alewives and Victuallers, who surmise, that if there were no Playes, they would have all the companie that resort to them, lye bowzing and beere-bathing in their houses every afternoone[1].

So telling an argument was not likely to be allowed to rust for want of use. A few months later, it did service in an enlarged form as Tarlton's defence of 'the profession' in Chettle's *Kinde Hart's Dreame*[2]. For any reply to these, however, or, indeed, for anything in the nature of a definite attack upon the stage, we may look in vain among the pamphlets published in London at this period[3]. One more passage at arms took place before the end of the century; for this, however, we must turn from the capital to the universities.

As puritanism, in its origin, was intimately connected with humanism, it was only natural that the anti-dramatic spirit should have early penetrated to Oxford and Cambridge. Gosson asserted that 'many famous men in both Universities have made open out-cries of the inconveniences bredde by playes.' It is probable, however, that the number of these was never very large at a time. In 1565, we hear of 'two or three in Trinity College,' Cambridge, who did not think that Christians ought to countenance plays[4]; and, in 1579, there broke out a 'controversy between Mr Drywood of Trinity, and one Punter a student of St John's, Cambridge' on the same subject[5]. Four years previously, at the same university, the privy council had forbidden all 'common plays,' with a view to keeping the youth of the nation undefiled[6]. This and a similar order, in 1593[7], seem to indicate that the

[1] McKerrow, *Nashe*, vol. I, pp. 211—215.

[2] *Shakespeare Allusion Books*, part I, pp. 62—66 (New Shaksp. Soc.); McKerrow, *op. cit.* vol. IV, pp. 133—5.

[3] Sir John Harington's amusing *Treatise of Playe* (*Nugae Antiquae*, 1804, vol. I, p. 186), written about 1597, seems to show that the city's third attack revived a certain amount of public interest in the question.

[4] *Correspondence of Bp. Parker*, Parker Soc., p. 226. This appears to be the earliest indication we have of the anti-dramatic spirit at the universities. The case of *Pammachius*, in 1545, sometimes cited, is that of a protestant controversial morality condemned by Gardiner, and, therefore, not to the point.

[5] *State Papers, Domestic*, 1547—80, p. 638.

[6] Collier, *op. cit.* vol. I, p. 223, quoting Lansdowne MSS, 71.

[7] For the order of 1575, and the long correspondence preceding the order of 1593, see *Malone Society Collections*, part I, pp. 190—202.

council's real convictions, on these occasions, at any rate, inclined towards puritanism, and that its support of the stage in London was largely actuated by the wishes of the queen and, perhaps, by a desire to interfere with the city's authority. Such orders, of course, did not touch academic or private plays, which, naturally, flourished at the seats of classical learning. Most puritans, indeed, allowed them to be harmless. At Oxford, for example, a certain John Case, in his *Speculum Moralium Quaestionum*, published in 1585, while utterly condemning the public or 'common' play, not only allows, but goes out of his way to defend, the academic play. Yet Case's defence in itself shows that the matter was already under discussion in university circles; while his pointed reference to the Mosaic text, forbidding persons of one sex to wear the dress of the other, proves that the lines of the later controversy had been thus early laid down.

When, therefore, William Gager of Christ Church, a well known Latin dramatist, and John Rainolds, an eminent theologian, afterwards president of Corpus Christi, crossed swords, in 1592, on the subject of the propriety of the academic play, they were fighting over old ground. The duel, however, attracted considerable attention at the time owing to the reputation of the combatants. Never before had the drama a more learned opponent than Rainolds or a more accomplished defender than Gager. The dispute broke out over the performance of Gager's *Ulysses Redux*, a Latin tragedy, to which Rainolds had been invited by a friend. By way of covering them with ridicule, Gager, following a common practice among Latin dramatists of this age, had placed some of the puritan objections to the drama in the mouth of one of his characters. Unknown to Gager, Rainolds had used many of these very arguments in the letter in which he had refused the invitation, and he naturally supposed that their reproduction was intended as a personal insult to himself. A correspondence followed, in the course of which Gager sent his opponent a printed copy of his *Ulysses Redux* by way of self-justification. Rainolds's reply, which forms the first section of a volume entitled *Th'Overthrow of Stage-Playes* printed at Middleburg in 1599[1], attacks both this and a comedy by Gager known as *Rivales*, at the same time setting forth at full length his objections to all forms of dramatic representation. Gager, like other stage apologists, had appealed to antiquity; Rainolds refers

[1] Collier, *Bibliographical Catalogue*, p. 246, suggests that it was printed in view of the projected erection of the Fortune theatre.

him to a Roman praetor's decree against actors. Gager's performers, moreover, had twice broken the divine law, first in
playing on the Sabbath and, secondly, by donning women's clothes.
The latter point, a stock argument in the puritan portfolio, is
treated with overwhelming fulness. Gager's elaborate reply,
dated 31 July, has never yet been printed and was, indeed,
practically unknown, until attention was called to it two years
ago[1]. It is claimed as one of the most graceful and convincing
of the treatises in answer to the puritan attack. Every argument
of Rainolds is courteously but firmly met, while, at times,
the learned dramatist waxes eloquent in defence of his art.
Despite this urbanity and the request with which the letter closes,
that the dispute should be dropped, Rainolds was in no mind
to allow his adversary the last word. After a delay occasioned
by sickness, he produced, on 30 May 1593, a very lengthy reply
in which, however, he did little more than recapitulate and
enlarge his previous arguments[2]. Gager received this fresh outburst in contemptuous silence, but his friend Alberico Gentili
entered the lists on his behalf and a discussion in Latin followed,
chiefly dealing with the legal aspects of the dispute.

This Oxford controversy, it should be borne in mind, was of
a different nature from the discussion upon the merits of the
public stage which had been proceeding in London. Indeed, one
of the most interesting points about it is Gager's manifest contempt for the professional side of his craft. While valiantly
defending himself and his young actors from the aspersions of
Rainolds, he admits the worst his opponent has to say about
'common playes.' As an occasional recreation for learned gentlemen, acting received his highest praise ; as a regular means of
livelihood, it was regarded with scorn. This contempt of the
gentleman for the rising class of actors, which had only a
remote connection with the loathing and abhorrence of the puritan,
was, undoubtedly, a factor in determining the social status of
Shakespeare and his fellows. The latter were often, it is true, on
terms of familiarity with the noblemen of the day ; but, however
great a favourite he might be, and however respectable and
wealthy he might become, the Elizabethan common player was a
'servant' in the eyes both of the nobleman to whose company
he belonged and of everyone else. Even Shakespeare's main

[1] By Boas, F. S., in *The Fortnightly Review* for August 1907. The letter itself is
preserved among the manuscripts of Corpus Christi college, Oxford.

[2] This is also to be found in *Th'Overthrow of Stage-Playes*.

ambition, apparently, was to become a 'gentleman.' It is not difficult to understand the disgust of those who amused themselves with the time-honoured academic play, at this intrusion into their sphere of persons whom they would deem base-born hirelings.

After Elizabeth's death, and under a new dynasty, a change came over the character and position of the stage. In 1604, the right of noblemen to patronise players was virtually withdrawn by the repeal of the previous statutes exempting the members of their companies from the penalties of vagrancy[1]. This gave a formidable weapon into the hands of any provincial corporation and magistrates that wished to rid their community of the presence of travelling actors, as Sir Edward Coke carefully explained to the good people of Norwich on his circuit of 1606[2]. On the other hand, by extending the policy introduced by Walsingham in 1583 and placing the great companies, one after the other, under the direct patronage of the crown, the position of the London stage was rendered practically impregnable. Yet the theatre lost more than it gained. It ceased to be a national institution and became a department of the revels' office ; while its direct subordination to the court made it more unpopular than ever with the puritans, who were rapidly becoming the anti-court party. The actor could scarcely be anything but royalist. The dramatist could see but one side to those great questions which were sweeping England on to civil war. But there was another side to this matter, which should not be overlooked. While there can be no doubt whatever that, among the generality of puritans, the detestation of the stage was steadily on the increase at this period, wealthier citizens now began to look with more favourable eye upon theatrical performances. The playhouses, in short, or, at least, the best known among them, by entering into close relations with the court added the finishing touches to the reputation for respectability which they had been slowly acquiring during Elizabeth's last years. They lost, to a large extent, their popular character and became fashionable resorts which citizens and, more especially, citizens' wives found it both pleasant and socially advantageous to attend. This fact helps to explain the almost complete cessation of the city's attacks and later pamphleteers, such as Rawlidge, do not hesitate to compare the more complacent citizens of Stewart London with 'the religious senators' of a previous day.

Puritan anti-dramatic literature, with the exception of the

---

[1] Prothero, G. W., *Select Statutes*, p. 253.
[2] *The Lord Coke his speech and charge*, Nath. Butter, 1607.

sermon and the theological treatise[1], was almost as scanty under James I as it had been during the last decade of Elizabeth's reign. The first to revive the old controversy was a writer of the theatrical party. In 1612, Thomas Heywood took upon him to defend his calling, apparently from some attack on the part of the authorities of which we have no knowledge[2]. His tract was entitled *An Apology for Actors*. The poems by various of the author's friends with which it opens are not its least interesting feature. John Webster's name figures among them; but his contribution is scarcely so entertaining as that by Richard Perkins, which makes some amusing hits at the hypocritical aspect of puritanism. Heywood divides his book into three parts, which set out to display the 'antiquity,' the 'ancient dignity' and the 'true use' of his profession. Much of his argument recalls that of Lodge, whose 'patchte pamphlet,' *A Defence of Stage-Playes*, doubtless, he had studied. Among new lines of defence may be noticed the observation that, though the classical stage was at its height at the time when Christ and His apostles were on earth, yet there is not a single text in the whole New Testament condemning it. Great stress is laid upon the value of the drama as a moral tonic, and the puritan method of backing an argument with lists of divine judgments is cleverly adapted to the actors' purposes by a series of stories illustrating the strange and wonderful workings of a powerful play upon a guilty conscience. The inevitable puritan reply appeared three years later and is conjectured to have been the work of one John Greene. In *A Refutation of the Apology for Actors*, as it is called, Heywood is laboriously answered point by point. The author borrows largely, and, at times, almost verbally, from Stubbes, while, in the methodical arrangement of his argument and in his tedious list of quotations from the fathers, he anticipates the work of Prynne[3].

In 1614, a new literary fashion was started by the publication of Sir Thomas Overbury's *Characters*, and it was but natural that the controversy concerning the stage should be reflected in this and many similar publications. In 1616, for example, the author of *The Rich Cabnit furnished with a Varietie of exquisite*

[1] See above, p. 375.
[2] *Apology*, ed. Collier, p. 14.
[3] A year after Heywood's *Apology*, appeared George Wither's *Abuses Stript and Whipt*; but, notwithstanding the familiar ring of its title and the unfavourable references to the stage which it contains, this slashing satire in verse is of a quite different order from the ordinary puritan 'abuse' pamphlet.

Discriptions devoted a chapter of his book to the character of
a player. He is ready to admit that the actor possesses certain
excellent accomplishments such as 'dancing, song, ellocution, skill
of weapon, pregnancy of wit'—a suggestive list of what was required of those who trod the Jacobean stage—but he can find
no epithets strong enough to describe the immoral results of
frequenting the theatre.

These character writers, however, hardly belong to the ranks of
the regular combatants. We catch a better glimpse of the real
strength of the feeling against the stage at this period, and of what
the actor frequently had to suffer on its account, from an interesting letter, preserved among the *State Papers* for 1616, by Nathaniel
Field, actor and playwright, to a certain 'Mr Sutton, Preacher att
St Mary Overs.' Stung to the quick by the railings, frequently, it
appears, spiced with personal allusions, which the worthy minister
hurled at the heads of the members of the 'Hope' company who
formed part of his congregation, Field, at length, felt forced to take
up the pen in self-defence. His letter, manly and independent in
tone, protested in almost impassioned language against the puritan
conception of an actor's mode of life, and appealed in pathetic
terms to Heaven in self-justification. As the son of that doughty
opponent of both bishop and stage, whose pamphlet in reference
to the Paris garden disaster we have already noticed, Field was,
doubtless, in a delicate position[1]. But, having been left an orphan a
year after his birth, he had been brought up as one of the children
of the Chapel Royal, and, if he had ever been troubled by any
scruples about the profession for which fortune had fashioned him,
a diligent study of the Bible, in which he found no 'trade of life
except conjurers, sorcerers and witches, *ipso facto*, damned' had
long removed them. However, it was a case of mutual irritation ;
for if, as Field's letter shows, the pulpits resounded with invectives
against that monster of vice and minister of sensuality, the actor,
the audience at the theatre daily shook its sides over the antics of
that ludicrous compound of nasal piety and furtive hypocrisy, the
puritan. Lucy Hutchinson, writing of the treatment which puritans
suffered at this period, declares that

every stage, every table and every puppet play belched forth profane scoffs
upon them, the drunkards made them their songs and all fiddlers and mimics
learned to abuse them, as finding it the most graceful way of fooling[2].

---

[1] John Field's other son Theophilus, it is interesting to notice, became a
bishop.

[2] *Memoirs of Colonel John Hutchinson*, ed. 1885, vol. I, p. 115.

The drama of the age is full of references to puritans, and, as time went on, these became more and more contemptuous and insulting. Lucy Hutchinson's words and Nathaniel Field's letter, both brimming over with passionate resentment, give us more insight into the real exasperation of the two parties than treatises stuffed with patristic and classical lore.

The foolish and short sighted policy of the first two Stewarts was not likely to diminish, in any way, this bitter feeling against the unholy amusement which they favoured and protected. Instead, it raised up a fresh engine of reform before which both court and stage, eventually, went down. In 1625, the year of Charles's accession, an anonymous puritan opened a new, and, in the light of subsequent events, an ominous, line of attack. It was hopeless to ask the crown to cleanse the Augean stables, and the city had long since given up the task in despair ; he, therefore, addressed himself to parliament, round which the hopes of all reformers were beginning to cluster. His petition, calling itself *A Short Treatise against Stage-Playes*, is a brief and exceedingly businesslike enumeration of the chief arguments against the drama. In these twenty-eight pages may be found the whole gist of *Histriomastix*; indeed, the tract reads so much like a first draft of its unwieldy successor that the suspicion is forced upon us that it was either written by Prynne himself, who as we know, began to collect his materials in 1624, or taken by him from another writer to be made the basis of his book[1].

When we of the twentieth century hold in our hands the cube of printed matter known as *Histriomastix*, and turn over its eleven hundred pages, in which marginal notes and references to authorities, for the most part, long since forgotten, often take up more room than the text itself, we find it very difficult to realise just what the book meant in its own day. To us, it seems half pathetic and half ridiculous, a gigantic monument of misplaced energy and zeal, a pyramid left gaunt and useless on the sands of time. To a great extent, the work was the outcome of a peculiar personality. Prynne was a fanatic of that indomitable and most intolerant kind—the moral enthusiast. Apparently

---

[1] The Brit. Mus. Cat., on what grounds is not apparent, attributes it to Alexander Leighton, whose cause and character were very similar to those of Prynne. In 1628, Richard Rawlidge, in *A Monster lately found out and discovered or the Scourging of Tipplers*, wrote unfavourably of the theatre. His bitter language is rendered all the more remarkable by his obvious commonsense in other matters. His book, which refers to Whetstone's *Mirour*, must rank with that as one of the secondary contributions to the controversy.

with very little of the milk of human kindness in his composition, he burned with an internal flame of righteous conviction, and this alone could have sustained him, not merely in his
sufferings, but, also, in those untiring labours which his pen produced, over and above the immense *Histriomastix*. Yet, at the
same time, he was thoroughly representative, his idiosyncrasies
being extreme developments of, rather than departures from, the
normal characteristics of his fellow reformers. If it be ever
possible for one man to sum up a movement in his own person,
Prynne summed up puritanism. And, since his book epitomises,
likewise, the whole puritan attack upon the stage, a consideration
of author and book together form a suitable close to the present
study.

The story of its publication and of his cruel punishment is too
well known to require lengthy treatment here. Nor is this the
place to go into the vexed question as to whether he was techni-
cally guilty of seditious libel. After more than seven years' labour,
and after several fruitless attempts to procure a licence, he managed
at last, in 1632, to get his great work through the press. About
the time when the last sheets were being worked off, queen
Henrietta Maria and her women were engaged in rehearsing a
pastoral play for a performance at Whitehall, which, apparently,
did not actually take place until the book was in circulation.
The idea of women appearing on the stage was new and shocking
to English spectators. In 1629, a company of French actresses, at
the invitation of the queen, had attempted to give a performance
at Blackfriars and had been 'hissed, hooted and pippen-pelted from
the stage.' Prynne referred to this incident in great glee and,
whether in ignorance of the impending pastoral or of set purpose,
inserted in the table of contents at the end of his book an expression stigmatising women actors as 'notorious whores.' He
was immediately summoned before the Star chamber; and,
though it is not clear what was the exact charge, there can be
no doubt that his chief offence was the accidental or intentional
application of these words to the queen's person. The upshot
was that he was condemned to stand in the pillory, a penalty he
underwent on two separate occasions, to lose both his ears, to be
branded as a seditious libeller on both cheeks, to pay a fine of
£5000 and to be perpetually imprisoned. Perhaps, the loss of
his Oxford degree and his expulsion from Lincoln's inn were
not the lightest part of the punishment to a man of Prynne's
habits and temperament. His life sentence was afterwards can-

celled by parliament; but he suffered the remainder of the sentence in patience and serenity. Prynne was a narrow-minded, dry-hearted, fierce fanatic; but, could he stand before us now, with his cropped ears and the letters S.L. burnt into his cheeks (*Stigmata Laudis* he interpreted them, in a rare burst of humour), we should acknowledge that the narrow-mindedness and fanaticism were not all on one side.

Despite its enormous length, there is nothing new in *Histriomastix, The Player's Scourge or Actors Tragedie*[1], except, perhaps, the extraordinary fierceness of its denunciation. Prynne's knowledge of the stage was of the scantiest description. He owns, indeed, with shame, that, when a 'novice,' he had been enticed by evil companions to attend 'foure severall Playes'; but, with these exceptions, he seems to be completely ignorant of the dramatic literature of the age, his only reference to our greatest dramatist being the indignant observation that 'Shackpeers Plaies are printed in the best Crowne paper, far better than most Bibles.' But, if Prynne knew little of contemporary drama, his seeming knowledge of anti-dramatic literature was astounding. Laud asserted that, merely to read the works cited by Prynne would take sixty years of an ordinary man's life. The truth was that Prynne could not have read a tithe of his authorities; and he quotes, for the most part, not from the authors themselves, but from the quotations of previous puritan writers. During a campaign of over sixty years, carried on by a large number of eager seekers for chapter and verse, half the accessible writers of antiquity, and most of those since the beginning of the Christian era, had been ransacked for even the slightest hint of anti-dramatic feeling, which, when discovered, was pounced upon and pigeonholed under its special argument. The same points, too, were made by puritan after puritan with scarcely a change of word, and in sublime innocence of the sin of plagiarism. Thus, the stream of argument and quotation went on swelling from year to year, until, at last, it emptied itself into Prynne's great reservoir[2]. In his case, such a method was extremely dangerous; for his was the pursuit of proof, not of truth. A single statement from an author in dispraise, or apparent dispraise, of plays is allowed to outweigh the testimony of the writer's whole life and character. Thus,

[1] For the full title, which, if given above, would occupy a whole page, see bibliography. A very useful analysis of the contents of the book is to be found in *Ward*, vol. III, pp. 241—3.

[2] Thus the Table (40 pp.), at the end of *Histriomastix*, forms, perhaps, the best index to the whole controversy.

Plutarch, Horace and Cicero are found in company with the early fathers as abhorrers of stage plays. This must not be taken as an impeachment of Prynne's honesty. He was honest enough; but he often quotes at second hand, and, even when he had the original before him, he was blinded by the force of zeal to anything that conflicted with his argument — as what controversialist is not?

Perhaps the most original thing about the book is its arrangement. It is divided into two parts, and these, in turn, are subdivided into acts and scenes with an occasional chorus. This dramatic setting, curious in a book written against the stage, was intended to carry out the idea of *The Actors Tragedie* suggested on the title-page; but, also, it was an extremely convenient form for the purposes of the argument. The first act, for example, naturally deals with the satanic origin of the theatre, while, in the seventh, Prynne triumphantly marshals his mass of authorities in seven different squadrons or scenes, according to period or character, the whole being crowned with a chorus in which he announces that none can withstand his 'all-conquering troopes.' This plan of arrangement may owe something to Gosson's *Playes confuted in five Actions*; but the execution and the details were all Prynne's.

His book is the last of the series which we have to note. Its size and elaboration, the supposed insult to the queen, the celebrated trial and the sufferings of the author, must have brought the topic of stage morality very much to the fore and have greatly increased the bitterness of the puritan party. But *Histriomastix* had no imitators. It had completely exhausted the subject. Besides, it was now dangerous to write against the theatre, since this involved the risk of offending royalty and of thus falling into the inexorable hands of the high commission. Further than this, events were fast drifting towards revolution, and the minds of men were filled with other and greater matters than the stage[1]. Whether, as has been suggested, Prynne's attack did anything to reform the stage, it would be extremely difficult to determine; and, in any case, the question is a somewhat idle one. Of greater importance is the fact that the theatre was in a far from prosperous condition immediately before its suppression, as is clear from a curious little tract printed, in 1641, under the title *The Stage-Players Complaint.*

[1] This, probably, also accounts for the fact that Prynne's book, apparently, remained unanswered until 1662, when Sir Richard Baker published his *Theatrum Redivivum.*

Monopolers are down, Projectors are down, the High Commission Court is downe, the Starre Chamber is downe, and (some think) Bishops will be downe and why should we then that are farre inferior to any of these not justely feare that we should be downe too?

Such is the burden of the author's tale, and the atmosphere of impending disaster which pervades the tract appropriately culminates in the concluding words: 'From Plague, Pestilence and Famine from Battel, Murder and Suddaine Death—Good Lord deliver us.' Few contemporary documents give a better picture of the gloom and sense of coming catastrophe that had come over a large part of the nation at this juncture in our history. But the words of the Litany were applicable to present needs and sorrows as well as to future fears. The plague had been more than usually violent since 1630, and, in consequence, the playhouses had been shut for the greater part of each year. The net result of these various factors in the situation was that the ordinance of 2 September 1642 for the total suppression of stage plays was received, not only without surprise, but almost without attention. In estimating parliament's reasons for this step, political considerations should not be left out of account. The actor was now hated, not only on account of his profession, but, also, as the minion of the despot, and the passage just quoted shows that he realised the fact well enough. Moreover, the stage, obviously, was too dangerous an institution to be tolerated by any anti-royalist government. Players were 'malignants' almost to a man, and, however efficient the censorship might be, the performance of an apparently harmless play might easily develop into a demonstration in favour of the king. Yet, for all this, we cannot doubt that the main intentions of the act were moral. The stage was swept away by the tide of puritan indignation and hatred, of which we have been watching the rise.

It was not to be expected, however, that so drastic a measure could be carried out without difficulty. Parliament found it necessary in 1647 and, again, in 1648 to pass further and more stringent ordinances against the stage, ordering all players to be apprehended and publicly whipped, all playhouses to be pulled down and any one present at a play to pay a fine of five shillings. Protests were not wanting against this policy. In 1643, two tracts appeared: one, *The Actors Remonstrance*, a humble request for the restoration of acting rights in return for sweeping reforms, which, incidentally, gives an interesting glimpse of what went on behind the scenes of theatrical life; the other, *The Players*

Petition to the Parliament, a piece of satirical verse, which mocked at the Rump under pretence of appealing to it. The sauciness of the latter, however, was nothing to that of an unknown person who, at the beginning of 1649, actually published a book called *Mr William Prynne, his defence of Stage-Playes or a Retraction of his former book.* Needless to say, the indignant victim of this effrontery at once issued a denial of the charge[1].

We have now enumerated and described the chief documents and events relating to the puritan campaign against the stage, culminating in the victory of 1642. The controversy has never really died out. It burst forth again in all its old vigour and with all its characteristic pedantry at the end of the seventeenth century. Curiously enough it was a high Anglican non-juror, Jeremy Collier, upon whose shoulders the puritan mantle fell; and his example was followed, thirty years later, by yet another Jacobite, William Law, the author of *A Serious Call.* Even modern writers have found it difficult to discuss the Elizabethan stage without ardently defending the puritans who attacked it. Yet the influence which the early fathers, like distant planets, seemed to exert upon every puritan in turn, the wholesale manner in which each borrows the arguments and expressions of his predecessor and, above all, the almost complete ignorance displayed by a large proportion of the assailants as to the real character of the institution they were attacking, combine to give the whole discussion an air of academic unreality. This impression, perhaps, is partly due to controversial methods which appealed forcibly to the Elizabethan intelligence, but which, by exasperating the modern reader, blind him to the genuine feeling that lies under their antiquated and absurd forms. For there can be no doubt whatever that puritan antipathy amounted to a fierce loathing, of whose strength a generation living in blander times cannot have any conception. In a word, the whole movement, from the outset, was not one for reforming the theatre but for abolishing it. Proposals for reform came rather from those who wrote in defence of the theatre, and whose attitude, it may be observed, was, in one sense, singularly in accord with that of their opponents. In

---

[1] The fortunes of the players under the Commonwealth may be followed in some detail in James Wright's *Historia Histrionica* 1699 (reprinted in *Hazlitt's Dodsley* (vol. xv), and in Whitelocke's *Memorials.* It is, perhaps, worth noticing here that, in 1658, William Cartwright found courage to reprint Heywood's *Apology,* under the title *The Actor's Vindication.*

the modern sense of the word, at least, they were puritans to a man. The stage-hater stoutly maintained that the drama did not and could not fulfil any ethical function. On the other hand, Bavande, Wager, Lodge, Gager, Nashe and Heywood, one and all, regarded the drama, first and foremost, as an engine for moral instruction. That such a man as Heywood should express himself thus, proves that he had scarcely more understanding than Stubbes and Prynne of the real nature of the drama which he represented. No one can pretend that Shakespeare and his fellow playwrights troubled themselves about theories of conduct. The defenders of the stage made pitiful attempts to justify their craft upon moral principles ; but, in admitting the subordination of art to ethics, they had yielded their whole position. Had puritans only studied the theatre more and the early fathers less, they might, starting with the premisses which their antagonists gave them, have made out a much better case for prosecution. They had all the logic on their side. On the side of the apologists, was all the commonsense—if they could only have seen it !

THE CAMBRIDGE HISTORY OF
ENGLISH LITERATURE

The Library,
Worcester College of Higher Education,
Henwick Grove, WORCESTER.

VOLUME VI

THE DRAMA TO 1642

PART TWO